PRIVACY IMPACT ASS

CW00544242

Law, Governance and Technology Series

VOLUME 6

Series Editors:

POMPEU CASANOVAS, *UAB Institute of Law and Technology, Bellaterra, Barcelona, Spain*

GIOVANNI SARTOR, *University of Bologna (Faculty of Law-CIRSFID) and European University Institute of Florence, Italy*

Scientific Advisory Board:

For further volumes:
http://www.springer.com/series/8808

PRIVACY IMPACT ASSESSMENT

Edited by

David Wright
Trilateral Research & Consulting, London, UK

Paul De Hert
Vrije Universiteit Brussel, Belgium

 Springer

Editors
David Wright
Trilateral Research & Consulting
Lexham Gardens 82 - 84
W8 5JB London
United Kingdom
david.wright@trilateralresearch.com

Paul De Hert
Vrije Universiteit Brussel (LSTS)
Avenue de la Plaine 2
1050 Brussels
Belgium
paul.de.hert@vub.ac.be

ISBN 978-94-007-2542-3 (hardcover)   ISBN 978-94-007-2543-0 (eBook)
ISBN 978-94-007-5402-7 (softcover)
DOI 10.1007/978-94-007-2543-0
Springer Dordrecht Heidelberg London New York

Library of Congress Control Number: 2011943107

Printed on acid-free paper

Springer is part of Springer Science+Business Media (www.springer.com)

Foreword by Gary T. Marx: Privacy Is Not Quite Like the Weather

Privacy, like the weather, is something everyone talks about.[1] But unlike the weather, there is much that should, and can, be done about it. This welcome volume documents and explains an important tool for doing that. It should be in the library of any professional concerned with collecting, processing, using or determining the fate of personal data (whether as policy-setter, administrator or researcher). This state-of-the-art book describes the most comprehensive tool yet available for policy-makers to evaluate new personal data information technologies before they are introduced.[2]

Privacy impact assessment aims to contribute to organisational practice, as well as culture. It recognises that machine-processed data on persons requires special protections, particularly when new tools are involved. It anticipates problems, seeking to prevent, rather than to put out fires. The PIA model is based on avoiding future problems by learning from the past and imagining how new technologies might bring new problems – including that intriguing class of the "unknown unknowns".

PIA is very much a work in development and offers a general model whose content needs to be adjusted depending on the specifics of the case. One size does not fit all. The variation these chapters consider precludes a standard form, at least with respect to substance and the range and degree of attention to potential problems.

Details of the assessment and expectations of what is appropriate will vary depending on the institution/organisation and goals – private vs. government (and within government national security and crime control as against education or welfare); the role played; location (as in geographical co-ordinates or in public or private places, as in visible and/or accessible); whether data is immediately available or requires technical enhancements or otherwise pried out or constructed, the kind of data – sensitive vs. non-sensitive and intimate vs. non-intimate personal information; the tool and fullness of the form of data it offers (audio and video documenting

---

[1] These observations draw from various articles at www.garymarx.net and Marx, Gary T., *Windows into the Soul: Surveillance and Society in an Age of High Technology*, University of Chicago Press [forthcoming].

[2] Of course, as several of the chapters note, a perennial problem and trade-off is intervening too early or too late. Runaway trains can't very well be called back, even as those who build fast trains need the freedom to experiment.

behaviour vs. merely noting location); identification – unique, masked, fully anonymous or group identification; and the fate of the data – is it shared with the subjects, is it sealed, destroyed or available to the public; and the costs of trying to prevent a risk relative to its seriousness and the likelihood of its occurring. It will also vary at different stages of data collection, analysis and use, and for local, historical, cultural and social factors.

What is being assessed? Most of the chapters in the volume use privacy broadly to refer to information pertaining to an individual, particularly as it is machine-processed. It begins when the borders of the person are crossed to either take information from or impose it upon a person. Privacy is a general term and there are endless arguments about what it applies to and if it is the best term to capture contemporary concerns.

Most of the authors in this book are implicitly using the form of information privacy identified by Westin[3] – this emphasises control by the subject. This implies an individual right and the actors' ability to make choices. The assumption is that individuals will be well served by a policy when they decide for themselves what personal information to release. What matters is choice and treating the data in accord with Fair Information Practices. That is admirable, but it leaves untouched other important issues.

Applying the conventional principles for the machine processing of information just to information privacy will seem too narrow for many observers. Other issues of great salience for citizens and society are slighted such as the implications for social stratification; for fairness (when the choices are specious or not equally available); for human rights and for silently creating creeping precedents that might lead to unwanted results. Other forms of privacy may also be ignored.

Noting this limitation, Paul De Hert (Chapter 2) considers the need for assessments concerned with human rights more broadly than privacy may (or may not directly) connect with. Raab and Wright (Chapter 17) discuss extending assessments to take more explicit account of various surveillance activities that may touch privacy but are not synonymous with it in its narrow sense.

Whether privacy is the best term to apply to current personal data and new surveillance issues is subject to debate. In an informative exchange in *Surveillance & Society*,[4] Colin Bennett acknowledges the limitations of the concept but makes a strong case for using privacy as a catch-all term for a variety of relevant information issues beyond itself. In popular culture and for interest groups, the term is becoming inclusive of an array of data issues that may connect to privacy, but go far beyond it.

---

[3] Westin, Alan, *Privacy and Freedom*, Atheneum, New York, 1967.

[4] The debate on the value of privacy in surveillance studies was initiated by Colin Bennett's essay "In Defence of Privacy", *Surveillance & Society*, Vol. 8, No. 4, 2011, pp. 485–496. Respondents, in the same issue, were Priscilla M. Regan ("A Response to Bennett's 'In Defence of Privacy'", pp. 497–499), John Gilliom ("A Response to Bennett's 'In Defence of Privacy'", pp. 500–504), danah boyd ("Dear Voyeur, Meet Flâneur… Sincerely, Social Media", pp. 505–507) and Felix Stalder ("Autonomy beyond Privacy? A Rejoinder to Colin Bennett", pp. 508–512). The debate can be downloaded as a single file: http://www.surveillance-and-society.org/ojs/index.php/journal/article/downloadSuppFile/privacy_defence/privacy_debate

This discussion leads us to ask: what is the PIA tool intended to prevent or, alternatively, what goals to drive forward? What does (and should) the assessment assess and why? This is forejudged to a degree by using the term privacy. But that choice can be problematic since the latter is such a general concept and can refer to such varied phenomena. Some clarification of the terms *private* and *public* and *surveillance* may be helpful.

Untangling Terms

> *If this [dissemination of FBI criminal history records] is done properly, it's not a breach of privacy.*
>
> Clarence Kelley, FBI Director[5]

Privacy is related to a broader family of terms such as publicity, surveillance, anonymity and secrecy. If PIA is to be an effective tool, there is need for a broad and systematic view of the setting and for conceptual differentiation in terminology.

How do surveillance and privacy relate? Surveillance is often wrongly seen to be the opposite of privacy. Kelvin emphasised this role of privacy as a nullification mechanism for surveillance.[6] But at the most basic level, surveillance is simply a way of discovering and noting data that may be converted to information. This obviously can involve invasions of privacy as with the employee in a lab testing for AIDS who sold information on positive results to a mortuary.

Yet surveillance can also be a means of protecting privacy. Consider biometric identification and audit trails required to use some databases, or defensive measures such as a home security video camera. Privacy for whom and surveillance of whom and by whom and for what reasons need to be specified in any assessment.

Depending on how it is used, active surveillance can affect the presence of privacy and/or publicity. As nouns, the latter can be seen as polar ends of a continuum involving rules about withholding and disclosing, and seeking or not seeking, information. Depending on the context, social roles and culture, individuals or groups may be required, find it optional, or be prohibited from engaging in these activities, whether as subjects or agents of surveillance and communication.

The right to privacy can be matched by a right to publicity. There might even be a need for *Publicity Impact Assessments* to be sure that personal information is collected and, when appropriate, given access to a wider public.

Such assessments would be sure that surveillance and/or communication of results are *mandated* rather than prohibited! One form involves a right to know as with freedom of information rules. Another form can be seen in the right to be acknowledged and noted, implied in the idea of citizenship, for example, in being entitled to have a driver's licence, register to vote or obtain a passport or a national

---

[5] *U.S. News and World Report*, 15 October 1973, p. 59.

[6] Kelvin, P., "A Social-Psychological Examination of Privacy", *British Journal of Social and Clinical Psychology*, Vol. 12, 1973, pp. 248–261.

identity card.[7] In some ways, this is the reverse of an expectation not to be defamed or lied about.

When the rules specify that a surveillance agent is not to ask certain questions of (or about) a person and the subject has discretion about what to reveal, we can speak of *privacy norms*. When the rules specify that information must be revealed by the subject or sought by the agent, we can speak of *publicity norms* (or better perhaps *disclosure norms*). The subject has an obligation to reveal and/or the agent has an obligation to discover. With publicity norms, there is no right to personal privacy that tells the agent not to seek information, nor that gives the subject discretion regarding revelation. Rather there is the reverse – the subject has an obligation to reveal and/or the agent to discover. This also suggests a way of broadening assessments regarding personal data. Here the goal is visibility rather than data protection.[8] A source of confusion in discussions of both privacy and publicity involves the failure to differentiate these as adjectives from nouns.

Private and Public as Adjectives

Information as a normative phenomenon involving moral expectations (whether for protection or revelation and whether based on law, policy or custom) can be differentiated from the actual empirical status of the information as known or unknown. For this, we need the related terms *private* and *public* – adjectives that can tell us about the status of information. Whether information is known or unknown has an objective quality and can be relatively easily measured. For example, in face-to-face encounters, the gender and face of a stranger are generally known, regardless of place in the street, an office or a home.[9] The information is "public", as in readily accessible.[10] In contrast, their political or religious beliefs are generally invisible and unknown.[11]

Of course, normative expectations of privacy and publicity do not always correspond to how the adjectives *public* and *private* are applied to empirical facts. Thus,

---

[7] The Spanish Data Protection Agency in its justifying Spain's new mandatory national identity card claims that the card goes along with the citizen's right to a national identity. Ouzeil, Pablo, *The Spanish Identity Card: Historical Legacies and Contemporary Surveillance*, Unpublished Master's thesis, University of British Columbia, Victoria, 2010.

[8] Marx, Gary T., "Turtles, Firewalls, Scarlet Letters and Vacuum Cleaners: Rules About Personal Information", in W. Aspray and P. Doty (eds.), *Making Privacy*, Scarecrow Press, Lanham, MD, 2011.

[9] There may, however, be rules about the subsequent recording, communication and use of such information.

[10] Identification may be controlled through anti-mask laws or conversely through requiring veils for females or the display of religious or other symbols (tattoos, brands, badges) or clothing indicating status.

[11] Revelation, of course, may be mandated by rules requiring the wearing of symbols indicating these. This paragraph also assumes that in most cases people "are" what they appear to be, i.e., no cross-dressing.

the cell phone conversations of politicians and celebrities that have privacy protections may become public. Information subjected to publicity requirements such as government and corporate reports and disclosure statements may be withheld, destroyed or falsified. Information not entitled to privacy protections, such as child or spouse abuse, may be unknown because of the inaccessibility of the home to broader visibility. The distinction here calls for empirical analysis of the variation in the fit between the rules about information and what actually happens to it.

Privacy and publicity can be thought of in literal and metaphorical spatial terms involving invisibility-visibility and inaccessibility-accessibility. The privacy offered by a closed door and walls and an encrypted e-mail message share information restriction, even as they differ in many other ways. Internet forums are not geographically localised, but in their accessibility can be usefully thought of as public places, not unlike the traditional public square where exchanges with others are possible.

There would be more agreement, or at least greater clarity, if assessments of privacy were clearer about whether they are talking about respect for the rules protecting privacy or the empirical status of information as known or not known. When the laws are followed, former FBI director Clarence Kelley (in the quote that begins this section) can correctly claim that they haven't been breached with respect to privacy. But he could not claim that, as an empirical matter, privacy is not altered when such records are created and circulated.[12]

Types of Privacy

Privacy is a multi-dimensional concept with fluid and often ill-defined, contested and negotiated contours, depending on the context and culture. PIAs should be clear about what privacy means for the context with which they are concerned (and often more than one meaning will apply).

Within informational privacy with which the chapters here are largely concerned, we find the conditions of anonymity and pseudo-anonymity, often referred to as being necessary for another type of privacy involving seclusion and being left alone. Personal borders are obviously more difficult to cross if an individual cannot be

---

[12] There can, of course, be verbal prestidigitation, not to mention bad faith, in simply defining away invasions of privacy as non-existent because the law or rules are followed. The deeper issue is what degrees of control does the individual have over personal and private information and are the lines appropriately drawn given a society's values and broader transcendent values of human dignity and life.

There are also other sources of confusion such as the legal definition of geographical places and information as public or private, custom and manners (e.g., averting the eyes) and roles which offer varying degrees of access to information. See Marx, Gary T., "Identity and Anonymity: Some Conceptual Distinctions and Issues for Research", in J. Caplan and J. Torpey (eds.), *Documenting Individual Identity*, Princeton University Press, 2001.

reached via name or location. The conditions around revelation or protection of various aspects of identity are central to the topic.

Informational privacy encompasses physical privacy. The latter can refer to insulation resulting from natural conditions such as walls, darkness, distance, skin, clothes and facial expression. These can block or limit outputs and inputs. Bodily privacy is one form of this. This is seen in crossing the borders of the body to implant something such as a chip or birth control device or to take something from it such as tissue, fluid or a bullet.[13]

A related, taken-for-granted form is aesthetic privacy[14] which refers to the separation, usually by a physical barrier of bedroom or bathroom, of activities involving one's "private parts" (a curious term given public knowledge of the limited variation of the parts) and unguarded moments. Alderman and Kennedy discuss a number of such cases in which the shock of discovering a violation surfaces norms of which we are hardly aware because they are so rarely violated.[15] Clothes and manners also sustain this. The concern over full body airport scans is also illustrative.

Informational privacy can be further descriptively considered as it ties to institutional setting (e.g., financial, educational, health, welfare, employment, criminal justice, national security, voting, census); places and times; the kind of data involved such as about religion or health, apart from the setting; participant roles (communications privacy as involving two-party, one-party or no-party consent); and aspects of the technology such as wire or wireless, phone, computer, radio or TV. PIAs need to consider setting, data type and means – factors that are central to legislation and regulation and rich in anomalies.[16]

In emphasising informational privacy, several other commonly considered forms such as decisional[17] or proprietary[18] privacy are slighted. These primarily involve application or use, rather than information discovery.

Defining cases in the US such as *Griswold* v. *Connecticut* 381 U.S. 479 (1965) and *Roe* v. *Wade*, 410 U.S. 11 (1973) involve decisional privacy with respect to personal and intimate matters such as family planning, birth control, same sex

---

[13] The physical border perspective has limits too, thus taking/giving a urine, breath sample or photo involves using things that have already left the body and are different and beyond the literal physical protective border. The situation is the same for garbage. The borders in such cases are cultural – note the tacit assumption that one's garbage isn't to be examined – at least in a personally identifiable way.

[14] Rule, James, Doug McAdam, Linda Stearns and David Uglow, *The Politics of Privacy*, New American Library, New York, 1980.

[15] Alderman, Ellen, and Caroline Kennedy, *The Right to Privacy*, Alfred A. Knopf, New York, 1996.

[16] Thus, in the US, the Federal Communications Commission has jurisdiction over content delivered over a wire but not that by satellite. In countries such as Germany and France, privacy rights are defined in reference to broad constitutional principles such as the dignity of the person, while in the US, the particular technology or institution plays a much larger defining role.

[17] DeCew, Judith, *In Pursuit of Privacy: Law, Ethics, and the Rise of Technology*, Cornell University Press, Ithaca, NY, 1997.

[18] Allen, Anita L, *Why Privacy Isn't Everything: Feminist Reflections on Personal Accountability*, Rowman & Littlefield, Lanham, MA, 2003.

marriages or physician-assisted suicide. Proprietary privacy – use of a person's information without consent for commercial and other purposes also involves control and liberty questions and the extension of market principles to symbolic material that is often immaterial (at least physically).

While distinct, informational privacy shares with the other forms inclusion in the broader category of privacy as control over access to the person or at least the person's data, these may be connected. Thus, if individuals can control their personal information – whether not having to reveal their purchase of birth control pills (when this was illegal) or keeping paparazzi from taking pictures, then they need not worry about that information being used.

In addition to conceptual elaboration and reflection on the broader consequences of data collection, privacy assessment needs can be analysed in more detail when protective activities and problem avoidance are connected to a series of sequential stages that can be observed in the process (and processes) of data generation and use. Various types of privacy problem do not occur randomly, but tend to cluster at particular social locations.

Data Stages

Privacy protection is not like a vaccination that occurs once and is over. Rather it is part of an enduring process involving a series of separate actions.

Table 1 lists seven kinds of activity called *surveillance strips* that follow each other in logical order. The strips are temporally, conceptually, empirically and often spatially distinct.

Over time, the distinct action fragments of these stages combine into stories about personal data and illustrate the emergent character of surveillance and privacy as multi-faceted abstractions made up of many smaller actions. These are not unlike the frames in comic books (although not intended to be entertaining and the patterns are more like the fluid, jumpy sequences of cyberspace explorations than the rigid frame ordering of the comic book).

When viewed sequentially and in their totality, these elements constitute *surveillance occasions.*[19] A surveillance occasion begins when an agent is charged with

Table 1 Seven surveillance strips	(1) tool selection (2) subject selection (3) data collection (4) data processing/analysis [raw data] numerical/narrative (5) data interpretation (6) uses/action – primary, secondary uses/users and beyond (7) data fate (restricted, sealed, destroyed, made public – conditions and time periods for such actions)

[19] Goffman discusses strips (1964) and occasions (1974) in referring to face-to-face interaction. See Goffman, Erving, *Behavior in Public Places: Notes on the Social Organization of Gatherings,*

the task of gathering information. Following that, the seven phases in Table 1 can be considered.[20] Studying the behavioural sequences of tool selection, subject selection, data collection, data processing, interpretation, resulting action (or inaction) and fate of the data offers a way to order the basic behaviours occurring within the family of direct surveillance actions.[21] The stages are the direct pressure points where most problems will be found.

Sometimes these occur almost simultaneously as when a motion sensor is triggered, a message is sent to a central computer, an alarm sounds and a door is locked or a retinal pattern is matched to a given identity and a computer unlocks or when a video camera does not save what unproblematic passes before it. But for a goodly proportion of applications, as with drug testing or data mining, these consist of different activities and stages and involve a division of labour with agent roles played by various actors.

In a given story, the stages may develop in a serial fashion as one stage logically leads to the next (e.g., from data collection to analysis) or it may stop early on (a tool and subject are identified but no data is collected, or the data is not analysed or applied). Looking across many cases suggests a variety of ideal-type career patterns (with different stopping and turning points). However, once data has been gathered, questions regarding the data's fate (the last item in the chain) can always be asked. Apart from any policies regarding destruction, sealed, limited or open access, in practical terms, the data's fate is affected by the form the data takes and how it is communicated. A paper record that exists in only one copy in a locked filing cabinet obviously differs greatly from a postable computer record that can endlessly recirculate, whatever the policies on access.

Most of the privacy and related problems with which PIAs are concerned occur (when present) at one of the stages in Table 1. The kind of problem may differ by stage – thus violations of consent are likely at data collection, of fairness and validity at processing and interpretation, of discrimination at use and of confidentiality at data fate.

It would be useful to have a checklist of problems that can occur and (when possible) of ways of avoiding them, or ameliorating them when they can't be prevented. The list would include various kinds of physical, psychological and social harm and unfairness in application and use; minimising invalid or unreliable results; not crossing a personal boundary without notice or permission (whether involving

---

The Free Press, 1963, and *Frame Analysis: An Essay on the Organization of Experience*, Harper and Row, London, 1974. However, as used here, they refer to bundles of discrete activity from the point of view of the observer and most do not involve face-to-face interaction of agents and subjects.

[20] Decisions about *who* is responsible for doing the surveillance and the design of the technology could be treated as the initial strips as well. However, attention here is on the next stage directly associated with doing the surveillance.

[21] This is said mindful of the fact that it is always possible to make ever greater differentiations within the categories identified and to push the causal chain back farther. For example, with respect to the data collection phase, contrasts can be made based on the tool, the sense involved, the kind of activity or the goal. The Table 1 conceptualisation captures the major natural breaks in activity once a problem in need of personal information has been defined and an agent designated.

coercion or deception or a body, relational, spatial or symbolic border). Other problems to be avoided involve violating trust and assumptions that are made about how personal information will be treated (e.g., no secret recordings, respect for confidentiality, promises for anonymity, for the compartmentalisation of kinds of data, and for their protection or destruction).

What are the trade-offs, advantages, disadvantages and conflicts in the various policy options for dealing with these problems (including doing nothing because of the rarity of some or because costs of prevention are deemed too great)? When do solutions bring new problems? How clear are the means and quality of evidence for assessing these issues?

Lists are one thing and can be a bit like waving the flag. Who, after all, would favour invalid results or violating trust? There is a strong need for research on the frequency and social locations of such problems. When are they common, patterned and systemic as against being infrequent, random and idiosyncratic?

Knowledge and policy are better served when these elements are differentiated. The stages in Table 1 can direct research on the correlates and location of particular kinds of problems. Awareness of the stages of the process can help in assessing the seriousness and likelihood that a risk will occur and the costs of prevention (whether by not using, regulating or amelioration after the fact).

The likelihood of prevention is also greatly affected by the stage. Just saying "no" to a data collection request (if honoured) is the ultimate prevention. But as the process moves from collection to the final fate, controls become more challenging. In the initial stages, the relevant actors and locations for accountability are known – but over time, if the information spreads out in wider circles and is combined with other data, as often happens, control weakens. The form of the data matters as well – the type of format, encryption, self-destroying, identity-masking, in a single highly secure file or in a more open system, The ointment-out-of-the-tube metaphor for digitised data speaks volumes.

Slices, Not Loaves

If the wise suggestions this specialised volume recommends were implemented, there would be far fewer problems associated with the collection and processing of personal data. However, the authors are hardly naïve reformers promising salvation if only their preferred solutions are followed. Limits are identified, as are ways of working within or around many of them.

Sceptical pundits removed from any responsibility for action can, of course, snipe from the sidelines about PIAs and their limits. PIAs are generally not mandated, requiring voluntary introspection and self-restraint on the part of goal-focused (often bottom line) organisations.[22] Businesses are not democracies and government's national security and crime functions require levels of secrecy. When a PIA

---

[22] There are a few exceptions as several chapters here note such as in Europe for RFID and in the US for e-government.

is carried out, results may not become public. Will a PIA's requirements be implemented? Or will PIAs serve as window dressing disingenuously prohibiting, while hiding behaviour that would be unacceptable if made public? Will they become another ritualised hurdle to jump over (or under) for busy practitioners with more important goals?

In an effort to learn and to legitimate, the ideal PIA involves relevant "stakeholders". This democratic impulse is admirable, but who decides who is a legitimate stakeholder? – e.g., do those arrested, but not charged or found guilty, have a seat at the table when decisions are made about preserving DNA? Do free speech as well as privacy advocates serve on a telecommunications committee charged with assessing a new technology?[23]

PIA faces the challenge of preventing a particular kind of future which involves new elements. It goes beyond routine audits of compliance with established rules and policies. Since the future hasn't yet happened, its assessment is forever vulnerable to challenges and doubts.

Given still other challenges – from political pressures to lack of resources, it is noteworthy that the stellar policy analysts in this book have not given up. They are thoughtful realists – dealing humbly, yet hopefully, with terribly complicated contemporary questions. In situations drenched in trade-offs, legitimate conflicts of interest and uncertainty, the lack of a full loaf should not be bemoaned, rather one should be grateful for slices of insight and the amelioration that PIAs can bring through transparency and a commitment to democratic values.

Cambridge, Massachusetts   Gary T. Marx

---

[23] The failure to not include types of consumers in the decision to roll out caller-ID created problems for US telephone companies in the 1980s. Those with unlisted numbers and shelters for abused women lost control over their phone numbers by technological fiat and there was much public outcry which led to revised policies.

Contents

Contributors

Kenneth A. Bamberger University of California, Berkeley, CA 94720-7200, USA, kbamberger@law.berkeley.edu

Emilie Barrau Commission Nationale de l'Informatique et des Libertés (CNIL), Paris, France, emilie.barrau@notaires.fr

Robin M. Bayley Linden Consulting, Inc., Victoria, BC, Canada, rmbayley@shaw.ca

Colin J. Bennett University of Victoria, Victoria, BC, Canada, cjb@uvic.ca

Laurent Beslay European Data Protection Supervisor (EDPS), Brussels, Belgium, laurent.beslay@jrc.ec.europa.eu

Tobias Bräutigam Nokia Corporation, Espoo, Finland, tobias.brautigam@nokia.com

Amanda Chandler Vodafone Group, London, UK, amanda.chandler@vodafone.com

Andrew Charlesworth Department of Computer Science, School of Law, Bristol University, Bristol, UK, A.J.Charlesworth@bristol.ac.uk

Roger Clarke Xamax Consultancy Pty Ltd, Canberra, Australia, Roger.Clarke@xamax.com.au

Stephen Deadman Vodafone Group, London, UK, stephen.deadman@vodafone.com

Paul De Hert Vrije Universiteit Brussels (LSTS), Brussels, Belgium; Tilburg University (TILT), Tilburg, The Netherlands, paul.de.hert@vub.ac.be

John Edwards Barrister and Solicitor, Wellington, NZ, jedwards@actrix.gen.nz

John Martin Ferris Ferris & Associates, Inc., Washington, DC, jmferris@erols.com

Anne-Christine Lacoste European Data Protection Supervisor (EDPS), Brussels, Belgium, Anne-Christine.Lacoste@edps.europa.eu

Gwendal Le Grand Commission Nationale de l'Informatique et des Libertés (CNIL), Paris, France, glegrand@cnil.fr

Emilio Mordini Centre for Science, Society and Citizenship (CSSC), Rome, Italy, emilio.mordini@cssc.eu

Deirdre K. Mulligan School of Information, UC Berkeley, Berkeley, CA 94720-4600, USA, dkm@ischool.berkeley.edu

David Parker Cranfield School of Management, Cranfield University, Cranfield, UK, david.parker@cranfield.ac.uk

Charles Raab University of Edinburgh, Edinburgh, Scotland, c.d.raab@ed.ac.uk

Artemi Rallo Lombarte Former Director of the Spanish Data Protection Agency (2007–2011) and Constitutional Law Professor at Universitat Jaume I, 12071 Castelló de la Plana, Spain, rallo@dpu.uji.es

Sarah Spiekermann Vienna University of Economics and Business (WU Wien), Vienna, Austria, sspieker@wu.ac.at

Blair Stewart Office of the Privacy Commissioner, Wellington, New Zealand, Blair.Stewart@privacy.org.nz

Jennifer Stoddart Privacy Commissioner of Canada, Ottawa, ON, Canada, Lindsay.Scotton@priv.gc.ca

Florian Thoma Siemens AG, Munich, Germany, Florian.Thoma@siemens.com

Adam Warren Department of Geography, Loughborough University, Leicestershire, UK, A.P.Warren@lboro.ac.uk

Nigel Waters Pacific Privacy Consulting, Nelson Bay, NSW, Australia, nigelwaters@pacificprivacy.com.au

David Wright Trilateral Research & Consulting, London, UK, david.wright@trilateralresearch.com

Part I
Setting the Scene

Chapter 1
Introduction to Privacy Impact Assessment

David Wright and Paul De Hert

1.1 Growing Interest

If privacy is a cornerstone of democracy,[1] then democracy is in trouble. Especially since the advent of the computer, the encroachments on privacy have proliferated. Terrorist attacks in the early 21st century have given governments all the justifications they need to bolster national security by forcing telecom companies to retain telephone records, to justify warrantless eavesdropping on our phone calls, to examine our bank records, to fuse personally identifiable information from multiple sources, to profile citizens to determine who presents a risk to the established order. Many companies have either aided and abetted governmental efforts or engaged in their own surreptitious amassing of the details of our lives. Personal data in real time has become the fuel of today's economy. The development of new technologies, while indisputably offering many benefits, is the proverbial two-edged sword: it cuts both ways, and if the wielder is not careful, he may suffer more than superficial lacerations. Technologies can be and are employed to discover more about where we are, where we go, what we are doing, what are our interests and proclivities, to manipulate our behaviour and choices in ways of which most people are not aware and, if they are, are powerless against the inexorable lust for personal data. It comes as no surprise that many would-be jeremiahs have already pronounced privacy is dead. Indeed, many of those who would like to preside over the last rites are the very people who stand to profit most from the burial of this fundamental right.

---

[1] The Supreme Court of Canada has stated that "society has come to realize that privacy is at the heart of liberty in a modern state … Grounded in man's physical and moral autonomy, privacy is essential for the well-being of the individual". R. v. Dyment (188), 55 D.L.R. (4th) 503 at 513 (S.C.C.). Also: "Without privacy, it is much harder for dissent to flourish or for democracy to remain healthy and robust. Equally, without privacy the individual is always at the mercy of the state, forced to explain why the government should not know something rather than being in the position to demand why questions are being asked in the first place." Goold, Benjamin J., "Surveillance and the Political Value of Privacy", *Amsterdam Law Forum*, Vol. 1, No. 4, 2009.

D. Wright (✉)
Trilateral Research & Consulting, London, W8 5JB, UK
e-mail: david.wright@trilateralresearch.com

D. Wright, P. De Hert (eds.), *Privacy Impact Assessment*, Law, Governance and Technology Series 6, DOI 10.1007/978-94-007-2543-0_1,
© Springer Science+Business Media B.V. 2012

But privacy is not dead. Opinion polls consistently show unease and distrust of our political leaders and the corporate warlords on matters of privacy. Citizens may choose to forego personal details, at the relentless urging of big business, but they still value what they have left.

One of the instruments for safeguarding privacy is privacy impact assessment (PIA). There is growing interest in PIA and, consequently, it seems timely to publish what we believe is the first book on the subject.

In Europe, the interest in PIA has been sparked by two main events. First was development and publication of a PIA handbook in the UK, the first in Europe, in December 2007.[2] Second was the European Commission's Recommendation on RFID in May 2009 in which the Commission called upon the Member States to provide inputs to the Article 29 Data Protection Working Party for development of a privacy impact assessment framework for the deployment of radio frequency identification (RFID) tags.

Article 4 of the European Commission's Recommendation on RFID said, "Member States should ensure that industry, in collaboration with relevant civil society stakeholders, develops a framework for privacy and data protection impact assessments. This framework should be submitted for endorsement to the Article 29 Data Protection Working Party within 12 months from the publication of this Recommendation in the Official Journal of the European Union."[3] The RFID PIA Framework, developed by industry, was endorsed by the Art. 29 Working Party in February 2011.

Since these two milestones, there have been frequent calls for PIA in Europe. The European Parliament, in its 5 May 2010 resolution on passenger name records (PNR), said that "any new legislative instrument must be preceded by a Privacy Impact Assessment and a proportionality test".[4]

European Commission Vice-President Viviane Reding said in July 2010 that "Businesses and public authorities... will need to better assume their responsibilities by putting in place certain mechanisms such as the appointment of Data Protection Officers, the carrying out of Privacy Impact Assessments and applying a 'Privacy by Design' approach."[5]

---

[2] Information Commissioner's Office (ICO), *Privacy Impact Assessment Handbook*, Wilmslow, Cheshire, December 2007, Version 2.0, June 2009.

[3] European Commission, Recommendation on the implementation of privacy and data protection principles in applications supported by radio-frequency identification, C (2009) 3200 final, Brussels, 12 May 2009. http://ec.europa.eu/information_society/policy/rfid/documents/recommendationonrfid2009.pdf

[4] European Parliament, Resolution of 5 May 2010 on the launch of negotiations for Passenger Name Record (PNR) agreements with the United States, Australia and Canada. http://www.europarl.europa.eu/sides/getDoc.do?pubRef=-//EP//TEXT+TA+P7-TA-2010-0144+0+DOC+XML+V0//EN

[5] Reding, Viviane, Vice-President of the European Commission responsible for Justice, Fundamental Rights and Citizenship, "Towards a true Single Market of data protection", SPEECH/10/386, Meeting of the Article 29 Working Party re "Review of the Data protection legal

In its Communication of 4 November 2010, the European Commission said it will examine the possibility of including in its proposed new legal framework on data protection "an obligation for data controllers to carry out a data protection impact assessment in specific cases, for instance, when sensitive data are being processed, or when the type of processing otherwise involves specific risks, in particular when using specific technologies, mechanisms or procedures, including profiling or video surveillance".[6]

The exact wording of the new data protection legislation in Europe remains to be seen, but the Commission's Communication seems to indicate that PIAs would be required of all data controllers, not just those from public institutions, but also from the private sector. Neelie Kroes, Vice-President of the European Commission for the Digital Agenda, pointed in this direction in April 2011 when she said the RFID PIA Framework "constitutes an interesting model that could be used for other similar situations or areas, such as smart metering and online behavioural advertising". She also said that the PIA Framework was "potentially also the start of a new policy approach, in fact a new commitment to involving all stakeholders in the process of solving privacy problems".[7]

In any event, although PIAs have been used mainly by governments, the private sector is also taking an interest in PIAs, as the chapters on Nokia, Siemens and Vodafone in this book make clear.

1.2 A Few Key Definitions

As the term suggests, a *privacy impact assessment* is a methodology for assessing the impacts on privacy of a project, policy, programme, service, product or other initiative which involves the processing of personal information and, in consultation with stakeholders, for taking remedial actions as necessary in order to avoid or minimise negative impacts.

A PIA is more than a tool: it is a *process* which should begin at the earliest possible stages, when there are still opportunities to influence the outcome of a project. It is a process that should continue until and even after the project has been

framework", Brussels, 14 July 2010. http://europa.eu/rapid/pressReleasesAction.do?reference=SPEECH/10/386

[6] European Commission, A comprehensive approach on personal data protection in the European Union, Communication from the Commission to the European Parliament, the Council, the Economic and Social Committee and the Committee of the Regions, COM (2010) 609 final, Brussels, 4 Nov 2010, p. 12. http://ec.europa.eu/justice/news/intro/news_intro_en.htm#20101104

[7] She also said that "the European Commission has issued a mandate to the European Standards organisations CEN and ETSI to assess if a translation of the PIA Framework into a standard is feasible." Kroes, Neelie, "Smart tags – working together to protect privacy", SPEECH/11/236, at the Privacy and Data Protection Impact Assessment Framework Signing Ceremony, Brussels, 6 April 2011. http://europa.eu/rapid/pressReleasesAction.do?reference=SPEECH/11/236&format=HTML&aged=0&language=en&guiLanguage=en

deployed. A good PIA will engage stakeholders from the outset as a way of gathering their views and ideas about how any intrusive privacy impacts can be avoided or mitigated.

Although PIAs are not used in many countries, the term has been defined in various ways[8] and the methodology employed, as this book makes clear, differs from one regime to another, from one company to another. Here are some examples:

Roger Clarke, one of the earliest proponents of PIAs and author of the chapter on Australia in this book, has defined a privacy impact assessment as "a systematic process that identifies and evaluates, from the perspectives of all stakeholders, the potential effects on privacy of a project, initiative or proposed system or scheme, and includes a search for ways to avoid or mitigate negative privacy impacts".[9]

The Australian PIA Guide says a privacy impact assessment is more than a compliance check. In addition to checking a project's compliance with legislation, regulations, codes of practice, etc., a PIA investigates how information flows affect individuals' choices, the degree of intrusiveness into individuals' lives, how the project fits into community expectations.[10]

Deloitte and Touche defined a PIA as "a process to help determine whether technologies, information systems and proposed programs or policies meet privacy requirements. It measures both technical compliance with privacy legislation and the broader privacy implications of a given proposal, project or product."[11]

The Hong Kong Office of the Privacy Commissioner for Personal Data defined PIA as "a systematic process that evaluates proposed initiatives or strategic options in terms of their impact upon privacy. To be effective a PIA needs to be an integral part of the project planning process rather than an afterthought. The purpose of this assessment is twofold:

• To identify the potential effects that a project or proposal may have upon personal data privacy e.g., the introduction of a multi-purpose smart card.
• Secondly, to examine how any detrimental effects upon privacy might be mitigated."[12]

---

[8] Clarke, Roger, "Privacy Impact Assessment: Its Origins and Development", *Computer Law & Security Review*, Vol. 25, No. 2, April 2009, pp. 123–135. PrePrint at http://www.rogerclarke.com/DV/PIAHist-08.html

[9] Clarke, Roger, "An Evaluation of Privacy Impact Assessment Guidance Documents", *International Data Privacy Law*, 2011. http://idpl.oxfordjournals.org/content/early/2011/02/15/idpl.ipr002.full or http://www.rogerclarke.com/DV/PIAG-Eval.html

[10] Office of the Privacy Commissioner, *Privacy Impact Assessment Guide*, Sydney, NSW, August 2006, revised May 2010, p. xxxvii. http://www.privacy.gov.au. On 1 November 2010, the Office of the Privacy Commissioner was integrated into the Office of the Australian Information Commissioner (OAIC).

[11] Karol, Thomas J., "Cross-Border Privacy Impact Assessments: An Introduction", *ISACA Journal*, Vol. 3, 2001. http://www.isaca.org/Journal/Past-Issues/2001/Volume-3/Pages/Cross-Border-Privacy-Impact-Assessments.aspx.

[12] See point 8.3 on this web page: http://www.pcpd.org.hk/english/publications/eprivacy_9.html

The New Zealand PIA Handbook defines a PIA similarly, as "a systematic process for evaluating a proposal in terms of its impact upon privacy," the purpose of which is to:

- identify the potential effects that the proposal may have upon personal privacy
- examine how any detrimental effects on privacy might be lessened.

A PIA can be used "to inform decision-makers about whether a project should proceed and, if so, in what form".[13]

Canada's PIA Guidelines define a PIA as "a process to determine the impacts of a proposal on an individual's privacy and ways to mitigate or avoid any adverse effects".[14]

The Alberta Office of the Information and Privacy Commissioner describes a PIA as "a due diligence exercise, in which the organization identifies and addresses potential privacy risks that may occur in the course of its operations".[15]

The US Office of Management and Budget (OMB) defines PIA as "an analysis of how information is handled: (i) to ensure handling conforms to applicable legal, regulatory, and policy requirements regarding privacy, (ii) to determine the risks and effects of collecting, maintaining and disseminating information in identifiable form in an electronic information system, and (iii) to examine and evaluate protections and alternative processes for handling information to mitigate potential privacy risks."[16]

The US Department of Homeland Security (DHS) defines PIA as "a vital tool that evaluates possible privacy risks and the mitigation of those risks at the beginning of and throughout the development life cycle of a program or system".[17]

Thus, although the wording of the definitions differs, there is considerable similarity in the principal ideas conveyed, i.e., that PIA is a process for identifying and evaluating risks to privacy, checking for compliance with privacy legislation and considering ways in which those risks can be avoided or mitigated.

Here, more briefly, are a few other key definitions:

> *Data protection impact assessment* – The European Commission has been using this term. It appears in its RFID Recommendation and, later, in its 4 November 2010 Communication on revision of the Data Protection

---

[13] Stewart, Blair, *Privacy Impact Assessment Handbook*, Office of the Privacy Commissioner, Auckland, March 2002, revised June 2007, pp. 5, 9. The similarity is not coincidental. Blair Stewart drafted both the Hong Kong and New Zealand handbooks.

[14] Treasury Board of Canada Secretariat, *Privacy Impact Assessment Guidelines: A Framework to Manage Privacy Risks*, Ottawa, 31 August 2002. http://www.tbs-sct.gc.ca/pubs_pol/ciopubs/pia-pefr/paipg-pefrld1-eng.asp

[15] http://www.oipc.ab.ca/pages/PIAs/Description.aspx

[16] http://www.whitehouse.gov/omb/memoranda_m03-22

[17] Department of Homeland Security, *Privacy Impact Assessments: The Privacy Office Official Guidance*, Washington, DC, June 2010. http://www.dhs.gov/files/publications/gc_1209396374339.shtm

Directive. Paul De Hert in Chapter 2 of this book equates "data protection impact assessments with simply checking the legal requirements spelled out in the European data protection framework", i.e., a data protection impact assessment is primarily a compliance check and, therefore, somewhat restricted in scope compared to a PIA.

Compliance check – A compliance check is to determine whether a project complies with relevant legislative and/or regulatory requirements. It might also check with relevant codes of practice, industry and/or community standards or ethical guidelines. A compliance check may be carried out at the beginning or during or following completion of a project.

Privacy audit – A privacy audit checks to see that PIA recommendations have been implemented and/or how effective privacy safeguards are. "An audit is undertaken on a project that has already been implemented. An audit is valuable in that it either confirms that privacy undertakings and/or privacy law are being complied with, or highlights problems that need to be addressed."[18]

Prior checking – This term has its origins in article 20 of the EU Data Protection Directive (95/46/EC) which says that "Member States shall determine the processing operations likely to present specific risks to the rights and freedoms of data subjects and shall check that these processing operations are examined prior to the start thereof." See Chapter 4 by Gwendal Le Grand and Emilie Barrau for more on prior checking.

Project – Here we use the term "project" as short-hand for any project, policy, program, service, system, technology or other initiative involving the processing of personal information or impacting privacy. A project can refer to a new initiative or changes to an existing project.[19]

1.3 A PIA Timeline

Privacy impact assessment may seem to be a new instrument in Europe, but, in fact, PIAs have been used for quite some time in other parts of the world. David Flaherty, former Information and Privacy Commissioner of British Columbia, said he could document use of the term "privacy impact statement" as early as the 1970s.[20] The Treasury Board of Canada Secretariat also claims that PIAs have been used as far back as the 1970s.[21]

---

[18] ICO, *PIA Handbook*, op. cit., p. 3.

[19] ICO also uses the term "project" in a wide sense: "The term 'project'….. could equally refer to a system, database, program, application, service or a scheme, or an enhancement to any of the above, or an initiative, proposal or a review, or even draft legislation." UK, *PIA Handbook*, op. cit., p. 2.

[20] See endnote 3 in Flaherty, David, "Privacy Impact Assessments: An Essential Tool for Data Protection", *Privacy Law and Policy Reporter*, Vol. 7, No. 5, November 2000. http://www.austlii.edu.au/au/journals/PLPR/2000/

[21] http://www.tbs-sct.gc.ca/pgol-pged/piatp-pfefvp/course1/mod1/mod1-3-eng.asp

Table 1.1 provides a timeline of key PIA guidance documents.

Table 1.1   Milestones in the development of PIA methodologies

Year	Milestones
1996	The **US** Internal Revenue Service issues its IRS Privacy Impact Assessment.[22] The Federal Chief Information Officers Council endorses it as a "best practice" in 2000.
1999	**Ontario**'s Management Board Secretariat (MBS), now part of the Ministry of Government Services, releases PIA Guidelines requiring provincial government ministries to accompany proposals for new Information and IT projects with PIAs.[23]
2001	**Hong Kong**'s Office of the Privacy Commissioner for Personal Data publishes an Information Book, a chapter of which is devoted to "E-Privacy Strategic Planning and privacy Impact Assessment".
	Deloitte and Touche publishes *A Guide To Cross-Border Privacy Impact Assessments*.
	Ontario's Management Board Secretariat (MBS), Information and Privacy Office, publishes *Privacy Impact Assessment: a User's Guide*. The Ministry of Government Services issues a *PIA Screening Tool* (undated).
	Alberta requires PIAs under its Health Information Act which comes into effect in April.[24]
2002	The **New Zealand** Office of the Privacy Commissioner publishes its *Privacy Impact Assessment Handbook* in March 2002, which is later revised in 2007.
	The Treasury Board of **Canada** Secretariat publishes its *Privacy Impact Assessment Policy* and *PIA Guidelines: A Framework to Manage Privacy Risks*.
	The **US** signs into law the E-Government Act, section 208 of which calls for PIA.
2003	The US Office of Management and Budget (OMB) issues "E-Government Act Section 208 Implementation Guidance".
	The Treasury Board of **Canada** Secretariat publishes a *Report on PIA Best Practices* and its *PIA e-learning tool*.
2004	The Treasury Board of **Canada** Secretariat publishes a Privacy Impact Assessment Audit Guide.
	The Victorian Privacy Commissioner in Australia publishes a PIA guide, which is significantly amended in 2009, such that Roger Clarke describes it as one of the three most useful in the world.[25]
	The **US DHS** issues its PIA guidance document *Privacy Impact Assessments Made Simple*. It issues a revised *Privacy Impact Assessment Guidance* in 2006, 2007 and 2010.[26]

---

[22] Internal Revenue Service, *IRS Privacy Impact Assessment, Version 1.3*, Washington, DC, 17 December 1996. www.cio.gov/documents/pia_for_it_irs_model.pdf

[23] Memo dated 16 December 1999 from D. Scott Campbell, MBS Corporate Chief Information Officer, to government Chief Information Officers, Chief Administrative Officers, IT Directors.

[24] Waters, Nigel, "'Surveillance-Off': Beyond Privacy Impact Assessment – Design Principles to Minimize Privacy Intrusion", Paper for the 16th Annual Privacy Laws and Business International Conference: *Transforming Risk Assessment into Everyday Compliance with Data Protection Law*, St John's College, Cambridge, England, 7–9 July 2003.

[25] See Chapter 5. The other two appreciated by Clarke are the UK ICO PIA Handbook and Ontario's PIA User's Guide.

[26] DHS, *PIAs: The Privacy Office Official Guidance*, op. cit.

Table 1.1 (continued)

Year	Milestones
2006	**Australia**'s Office of the Privacy Commissioner publishes its *Privacy Impact Assessment Guide.* A revised version is published in 2010. The **British Columbia** Ministry of Labour and Citizens' Services issues its *Privacy Impact Assessment Process.*
2007	The **UK** Information Commissioner's Office publishes its *Privacy Impact Assessment Handbook*, in December. A revised version is published in June 2009.
2008	The **International Organization for Standardization** (ISO) publishes its PIA standard 22307:2008 Financial services – Privacy impact assessment.
2009	On 12 May, the **European Commission** releases its Recommendation on RFID in which advocates a "privacy and data protection impact assessment".
2010	In July, the Treasury Board of **Canada** Secretariat issues its Directive on Privacy Impact Assessment, which supersedes its PIA Policy from 2002.
2011	In February, the **Art. 29 Working Party** approves an RFID PIA Framework developed by an industry group.

1.4 Why Carry Out a PIA?

Why carry out a PIA? There are various reasons why organisations, both governmental and business, carry out a PIA. In some cases, as in Canada, the US and perhaps the UK, they are mandatory for government departments and agencies. In other cases, organisations carry out a PIA because they want to avoid or manage risks and gain certain benefits.

1.4.1 To Manage Risks

A PIA should be methodologically based on a risk assessment and management process.[27] If a government agency or company or any entity dealing with personal data can avoid implementing a privacy-intrusive scheme, it will minimise downstream risks. PIA proponents have identified various risks to an organisation that collects or processes personally identifiable information and various benefits flowing from the conduct of a PIA to identify, avoid or mitigate those risks. Indeed, many of them see PIA as fitting into the organisation's overall risk management strategy. For example, Australia's Guide says: "PIA information feeds into broader project risk management processes."[28] Privacy risks may flow from any number of sources. Risks may arise from vulnerabilities within the organisation or the design and implementation

---

[27] The authors would like to thank Barbara Daskala of ENISA for her useful comments and suggestions on section 1.4 of this chapter.

[28] OPC, *PIA Guide*, op. cit., p. vii. The ICO PIA Handbook (p. 5) makes the same point: "Risk management has considerably broader scope than privacy alone, so organisations may find it appropriate to plan a PIA within the context of risk management."

of a project. They may also arise from external threats, e.g., from evil-doers who engage in social engineering to con personnel into giving them the information they want or who exploit weaknesses in the organisation's access control procedures. Virtually all PIA guides used in Australia, Canada, New Zealand, the UK and the US identify risks facing an organisation associated with the collection and processing of personal identifiable information.

We need to be a bit more precise about these "risks". It is useful to distinguish between vulnerabilities of assets, threats and risks, as the European Network and Information Security Agency (ENISA) does in its risk assessments of new information and communications technologies. ENISA defines a risk as "the potential that a given threat will exploit vulnerabilities of an asset or group of assets and thereby cause harm to the organization",[29] which is virtually identical to that used in the ISO 27005 standard upon which ENISA draws. If we accept the ISO's terminology, many of the "risks" in the PIA literature are actually threats or vulnerabilities.

1.4.1.1 Assets

According to the ISO/IEC 27005:2008 standard, an asset is anything that has value to an organisation and which therefore requires protection. The identification of the assets is a complex and challenging exercise but very important, since this will provide the basis on which assessment of the impacts and risks will be performed. The asset identification should be ideally performed at a suitable level of detail and according to the needs and the scope of the risk assessment.

Assets can be business processes and activities, information or hardware and software components, network, personnel, etc.

The asset is also valuated, since its value is a determinant in the estimation of the impact of a security incident. There are many different approaches that can be followed in order to do that; a very common basis for assets valuation is to consider the costs incurred due to the breach of confidentiality, integrity and availability as the result of an incident.

1.4.1.2 Vulnerabilities

A "vulnerability" refers to an aspect of a system or process (the assets) that can be exploited for purposes other than those originally intended, to weaknesses, security holes or implementation flaws within a system that are likely to be threatened. A

---

[29] http://www.enisa.europa.eu/act/rm/cr/risk-management-inventory/glossary. ENISA's definition of a risk is virtually identical to that in the ISO 27005 standard which defines an "information security risk as the potential that a given threat will exploit vulnerabilities of an asset or group of assets and thereby cause harm to the organization. It is measured in terms of a combination of the likelihood of an event and its consequence." International Organization for Standardization (ISO), *Information Technology – Security Techniques – Information Security Risk Management*, International Standard, ISO/IEC 27005:2008(E), First edition, 15 June 2008, p. 1.

vulnerability does not cause harm in itself[30]: to be considered a risk, a vulnerability needs to be exploited by a threat. In addition, vulnerabilities are independent of any particular threat. Understanding vulnerabilities is an important part of estimating risk. Vulnerabilities can increase risk, either by influencing the likelihood of some event or the severity of the consequences, should it occur, or both. Decisions about how to manage risks must also include consideration of ways to reduce vulnerabilities.[31]

Here are some examples of different types of vulnerabilities:

- Hardware – unprotected storage of personal data
- Software – insufficient testing of software or inadequate user authentication mechanism
- Network – unprotected communication lines
- Personnel – inadequate screening of new recruits or insufficient training
- Site – inadequate physical security (doors, windows)
- Organisation – lack of regular, third-party audits, lack of procedures for introducing software into operational systems, lack of records in administrator and operator logs.[32]

1.4.1.3 Threats

A threat has the potential to harm or compromise assets such as information, processes and systems and therefore organisations. Threats may be of natural or human origin, and could be accidental or deliberate. A threat may arise from within or from outside the organisation.[33] Physical or environmental threats such as a fire, an earthquake, a flood or a failure in the power supply or in telecommunications equipment may result in damage to computers, servers and networks used by an organisation to store or process personal data.

Personal data may also be *compromised* by other threats such as the following:

- Interception of communications
- Spying
- Theft of equipment, such as mobile phones, laptops, memory sticks, documents or data (identity theft)

---

[30] International Organization for Standardization (ISO), *Information Technology – Security Techniques – Information Security Risk Management*, International Standard, ISO/IEC 27005:2008(E), First edition, 15 June 2008, p. 13.

[31] Renn, Ortwin, *Risk Governance*, Earthscan, London, 2008, p. 69.

[32] For a much longer list of examples of vulnerabilities, see ISO/IEC 27005:2008(E), op. cit., pp. 42–45.

[33] For example, an employee of phone operator T-Mobile sold thousands of customer records to rivals. See Wray, Richard, "T-Mobile Confirms Biggest Phone Customer Data Breach", *The Guardian*, 17 November 2009. http://www.guardian.co.uk/uk/2009/nov/17/t-mobile-phone-data-privacy

- Retrieval of recycled or discarded media ("dumpster diving")
- Disclosure – such as AOL's disclosure of what it thought was anonymised data[34]
- Data from untrustworthy sources
- Tampering with hardware or software, including viruses and other malware[35]
- Position detection – Mobile phone companies are able to detect where we are more or less continuously[36]
- Unauthorised use of equipment or illegal processing of data
- Loss of data, e.g., through network failure or human error[37]
- Powerful new Internet technologies[38]
- Function creep, where data collected for one purpose is used for another purpose not previously specified.

Based on the above, the difference between a vulnerability, threat and risk can be illustrated thusly: An unprotected communications line is a vulnerability. Someone eavesdropping on that line is a threat. The risk is the probability that someone will actually do so and the consequence, the harm that will result. The risk may be minor – two teenagers discussing their homework assignment for tomorrow – or major, for example, a prime minister is recorded discussing his frolics with his teenage mistress. Here's another example: An organisation may not encourage employees to use strong passwords (a vulnerability). A hacker who can easily guess a simple password is a threat. The risk is the probability that he will do so and the consequence that may have for the organisation if he does so. Determining the risk(s) resulting from various vulnerabilities and threats requires some analysis and assessment, which is what a PIA can and should do.

---

[34] Barbaro, Michael, and Tom Zeller Jr, "A Face Is Exposed for AOL Searcher No. 4417749", *The New York Times*, 9 August 2006. http://query.nytimes.com/gst/fullpage.html?res=9E0CE3DD1F3FF93AA3575BC0A9609C8B63

[35] See, for example, BBC News, "Sites Hit in Massive Web Attack", 2 April 2011. http://www.bbc.co.uk/news/world-us-canada-12944626

[36] "Cellphone companies do not typically divulge how much information they collect, so Mr. Spitz went to court to find out exactly what his cellphone company, Deutsche Telekom, knew about his whereabouts. The results were astounding. In a 6-month period – from August 31, 2009, to February 28, 2010, Deutsche Telekom had recorded and saved his longitude and latitude coordinates more than 35,000 times." Cohen, Noam, "It's Tracking Your Every Move and You May Not Even Know", *The New York Times*, 26 March 2011. http://www.nytimes.com/2011/03/26/business/media/26privacy.html

[37] For example, British tax authorities lost two computer disks with the personal data of 25 million people in October 2007. See Pfanner, Eric, "Data Leak in Britain Affects 25 Million", *The New York Times*, 22 November 2007. http://www.nytimes.com/2007/11/22/world/europe/22data.html?hp

[38] "Worries over Internet privacy have spurred lawsuits, conspiracy theories and consumer anxiety as marketers and others invent new ways to track computer users on the Internet. But the alarmists have not seen anything yet. In the next few years, a powerful new suite of capabilities [referring to HTML 5] will become available to Web developers that could give marketers and advertisers access to many more details about computer users' online activities." Vega, Tanzina, "Web Code Offers New Ways To See What Users Do Online", *The New York Times*, 10 October 2010. http://www.nytimes.com/2010/10/11/business/media/11privacy.html?src=busln

1.4.1.4 Impact Assessment

A PIA should not only consider the impacts on privacy, but also the impacts on an organisation flowing from the compromise of privacy. Many organisations have scant regard for privacy, so convincing them of the merits of PIA may require a focus on the impacts of comprised privacy on the organisation itself. Impacts may be either direct or indirect. An organisation risks suffering various consequences from not taking adequate care of the personal data in its possession, including the following direct impacts:

- Negative media attention
- Loss of customer confidence, loss of credibility, damage to trust and reputation leading to a loss of electoral support or a loss of customers and/or suppliers[39]
- Infringement of laws and/or regulations leading to judicial proceedings and penalties or the imposition of new regulatory controls in response to public concerns about the project, which could result in unforeseen or unexpected costs to the organisation.
- Direct financial loss from fines or penalties[40]
- Dismissal or resignations of senior personnel[41]

---

[39] See, for example, Schich, Kathrin, "Axel Springer hit by New German Data Leak Scandal", *Reuters*, 19 October 2008. http://uk.reuters.com/article/internetNews/idUKTRE49H1GN20081019

[40] Culnan and Williams provide two examples:

- After ChoicePoint failed in its credentialing procedures enabling criminals masquerading as small business to gain access to customer accounts, the company had to send letters to 145,000 individuals notifying them that their personal information had been fraudulently accessed and used to commit identity theft. ChoicePoint costs have been estimated at $30 million including fines of $10 million plus $5 million to create a fund for consumer redress. In addition, ChoicePoint was required to undergo biennial independent assessments for 20 years and provide copies to the Federal Trade Commission upon request.
- US retailer TJX was faulted for storing unencrypted sensitive information, failing to limit unauthorised wireless access to its networks, and failing to employ appropriate security measures on its networks, which enabled criminals to access 45 million records. Costs to TJX have been estimated at $156 million including $40.9 million to Visa and $24 million to MasterCard to cover fraud losses.

Culnan, Mary J., and Cynthia Clark Williams, "How Ethics Can Enhance Organizational Privacy: Lessons from the Choicepoint and TJX Data Breaches", *MIS Quarterly*, Vol. 33 No. 4, December 2009, pp. 673–687. Re the cost of a data breach, see also Espiner, Tom, "Data Breaches Cost an Average Business £1.4m", ZDNet.co.uk, 25 February 2008. http://news.zdnet.co.uk/security/0,1000000189,39341215,00.htm

[41] See, for example, *The Inquirer*, "Head taxman quits after 25 million peoples' data lost", 20 November 2007. http://www.theinquirer.net/gb/inquirer/news/2007/11/20/head-taxman-quits-million. See also Richards, Jonathan, "Top Officials to be Held to Account for Data Losses", *The Times*, 22 April 2008. http://technology.timesonline.co.uk/tol/news/tech_and_web/article3797278.ece

- Retrofits or redesigns of projects[42] or outright cancellation of a project[43]
- Unexpected or untoward consequences as a result of erroneous personal data, for example, some people may be prosecuted or falsely accused or under suspicion or may suffer unduly (e.g., they are on a "no-fly list" or cannot enter a country or are turned down for a job) because the personal data held by the organisation is incorrect.

Examples of indirect impacts include

- Opportunity costs – The time an organisation spends in fixing a compromise of personal data is time that could have been spent on growing the business
- Loss of a competitive advantage
- Dilution of brand, reputation and image.

In addition to the consequences to an organisation, others also suffer. Individuals whose data has been compromised may spend a lot of time, money and stress in recovering from identity theft or the correction of erroneous data – if they can discover which organisation(s) hold personal data about them. Some people may be put at risk if their privacy or personal data is compromised (e.g., undercover agents, celebrities, vulnerable populations, such as children and victims of domestic violence) or, for example, may face higher insurance premiums or difficulties in getting or retaining a job.

Even other companies who were not involved in an incident may suffer spillover effects, as Culnan and Williams point out in the ChoicePoint and TJX cases:

> Incidents experienced by a single firm can cause spillover effects with repercussions affecting an entire industry.... For example, the ChoicePoint breach motivated Congress to hold hearings to investigate information practices in the data broker industry. Following the TJX breach, Massachusetts issued its 2008 security rule, which imposes stringent organizational and technical requirements on anyone who maintains personal information on Massachusetts residents, with other states expected to follow (Smedinghoff and Hamady 2008). Legislation was also introduced in several states to hold all retailers responsible for the costs incurred by banks in reissuing new credit cards to individuals whose credit card numbers had been stolen in a breach (Bureau of National Affairs 2007b). Spillover effects such as new regulations can also threaten an organization's legitimacy because they can cause other firms in the same industry to incur substantial new costs even though they were uninvolved in the original crisis.[44]

The risk assessment and management process in many of its phases is a qualitative process, meaning that it involves a lot of subjective estimations; it is also flexible and provides many levels of granularity, in accordance with the assessment needs. It provides a solid methodological structure upon which a PIA can be based.

---

[42] Lipton, Eric, "Bowing to Critics, U.S. to Alter Design of Electronic Passports", *The New York Times*, 27 April 2005. http://www.nytimes.com/2005/04/27/politics/27passport.html?scp=11&sq=biometric+passport&st=nyt

[43] Peev, Gerri, "Labour in Retreat as ID Card Plan is Axed", *The Scotsman*, 1 July 2009. http://thescotsman.scotsman.com/uk/Labour-in-retreat-as-.5415982.jp

[44] Culnan and Williams, op. cit., p. 683.

1.4.2 To Derive Benefits

A company or government department that undertakes a PIA with good intent, with a genuine interest in engaging stakeholders, including the public, has an opportunity of earning trust and goodwill from citizen-consumers. The extent to which it earns trust and goodwill will be a function of how open and transparent the organisation makes the PIA process. The more open and transparent the process is, the more likely the organisation is to overcome apprehensions, suspicions and mistrust in the development of a new service, product, policy, programme or project.[45] Even if a new service does not engender public concerns (or those of privacy advocates), and there appears to be no mistrust to overcome, the organisation can earn goodwill for being open and transparent about what it is planning to do. Businesses able to sustain a high level of trust and confidence can differentiate themselves from their rivals and thereby gain a competitive advantage.[46]

By engaging stakeholders in the PIA process, an organisation can benefit from ideas it may not have previously considered or it may find that stakeholders place much greater weight on some issues that the organisation had regarded as relatively minor. If the project does raise difficult issues with regard to privacy, ideas from stakeholders may be particularly welcome. Even if stakeholders don't manage to generate some new considerations, the organisation at least has an opportunity of gaining stakeholders' understanding and respect.

Transparency in the process may also be a way of avoiding liabilities downstream. If the organisation is able to demonstrate that it did engage and consult with a wide range of stakeholders, was forthcoming with information, considered different points of view, it will be more difficult for some stakeholders to claim subsequently that the organisation was negligent in its undertaking.[47] By being open and transparent from the outset, the organisation can minimise the risk of negative media attention.

The New Zealand PIA Handbook describes a privacy impact assessment as an "early warning system". The PIA radar screen will enable an organisation to spot a privacy problem and take effective counter-measures before that problem strikes the business as a privacy crisis. It goes on to say that the PIA process can help the organisation by providing credible information upon which business decisions can

---

[45] A PIA "enables an organisation to understand the perspectives of other stakeholders and make the aims of the project better understood." ICO, *PIA Handbook*, op. cit., p. 6. The Handbook seems to adopt the position of the project manager, rather than the privacy advocates, when it adds: "By actively seeking out and engaging the concerns of stakeholders, even those who are expected to oppose a particular project, you can discover the reasoning behind their position and identify where further information needs to be provided and pre-empt any possible misinformation campaigns by opponents of the project."

[46] Stewart, *PIA Handbook*, op. cit., p. 29.

[47] "A PIA provides an organisation with an opportunity to obtain a commitment from stakeholder representatives and advocates to support the project from an early stage, in order to avoid the emergence of opposition at a late and expensive stage in the design process." ICO, *PIA Handbook*, op. cit., p. 6.

be based and by enabling organisations to identify and deal with their own problems internally and proactively rather than awaiting customer complaints, external intervention or a bad press.[48]

As mentioned above, PIA is a form of risk assessment, an integral part of risk management. It encourages cost-effective solutions, since it is more cost-effective and efficient to build "privacy by design" into projects, policies, technologies and other such initiatives at the design phase than attempt a more costly retrofit after a technology is deployed or a policy promulgated. Some simple adjustments may be all it takes to make the difference between a project that is privacy intrusive and one that has built in necessary safeguards. Thus, a PIA creates an opportunity for organisations to anticipate and address the likely impacts of new initiatives, to foresee problems and identify what needs to be done to design in features that minimise any impact on privacy and/or to find less privacy-intrusive alternatives.

A PIA should also be regarded as a learning experience, for both the organisation that undertakes the PIA as well as the stakeholders who are engaged in the process. An open PIA process helps the public understand what information the organisation is collecting, why the information is being collected, how the information will be used and shared, how the information may be accessed, and how it will be securely stored.[49] The PIA's educational role is a way of demonstrating that the organisation has critically analysed how the project will deal with personal data. It might be the case that certain identified risks on privacy cannot be mitigated and/or have to be accepted (residual risks); even so, the PIA report, as the result of a clear and systematic process, is something to which interested parties can refer and be informed of the reasons why some assumptions were made decisions and decisions taken. Thus, a PIA promotes a more fully informed decision-making process.[50]

PIA can be used to enforce or encourage accountability. A PIA should make clear who intends to do what and who will be responsible for what. It should make clear that, as a minimum, the project is fully compliant with privacy laws, regulations and relevant codes of conduct. If an executive knows she will be held accountable for a privacy-intrusive action, she may be less inclined to proceed with an action that seems likely to anger the public or, if not the general public, at least privacy advocates or other stakeholders likely to contest the action in the media.

1.5 Variations in PIA Approaches

Just as the definitions of a privacy impact assessment vary, so too do the PIA methodologies. While there are similarities in approach, there are also differences, as indicated by Table 1.2, which is based on a comparison of the principal PIA

---

[48] Stewart, *PIA Handbook*, op. cit., pp. 6, 11.

[49] DHS, *PIAs: The Privacy Office Official Guidance*, op. cit., p. 4.

[50] Karol, Thomas J., *A Guide To Cross-Border Privacy Impact Assessments*, Deloitte & Touche, 2001. http://www.isaca.org/Knowledge-Center/Research/ResearchDeliverables/Pages/A-Guide-To-Cross-Border-Privacy-Impact-Assessments.aspx

Table 1.2 Similarities and differences in national PIA methodologies

PIA features	Australia	Canada	NZ	UK	US
PIA is mandated by law or must accompany budget submissions.		✓	V	✓	✓

In this table, V = variations. Principally these variations refer to differences in approaches to PIA among different Executive branch agencies in the US government

guidance documents at national level in Australia, Canada, New Zealand, the United Kingdom and the United States.

Of the five countries, the US is virtually unique in having legislation that mandates PIA. Section 208 of the E-Government Act of 2002 requires all Executive branch departments and agencies to conduct a PIA for all new or substantially changed systems that collect, maintain or disseminate personally identifiable information (PII). New Zealand's Immigration Act 2009 makes PIAs mandatory for systems collecting and "handling" biometric data (see Chapter 8). The Treasury Board of Canada requires federal departments and agencies to submit a PIA with funding submissions.[51] The UK government has made PIAs obligatory for government agencies,[52] but as there is no reporting requirement, or enforcement mechanism, it is impossible to know whether government departments and agencies are, in fact, carrying out PIAs.

PIA features	Australia	Canada	NZ	UK	US
PIA guidance is targeted at government departments and agencies only.		✓			✓

The US OMB guidance, while focused on Executive departments and agencies, does say that government contractors are also obliged to perform a PIA for IT projects that process PII.

---

[51] "Federal organizations seeking preliminary project approval (PPA) from the Treasury Board pursuant to the Project Management Policy must include the results of the Privacy Impact Assessment (PIA) in the body of the submission or project brief, where applicable." Treasury Board of Canada Secretariat, "A Guide to Preparing Treasury Board Submissions", Annex D, section 4. http://www.tbs-sct.gc.ca/pubs_pol/opepubs/TBM_162/gptbs-gppct09-eng.asp#d4. See also the TBS Privacy Impact Assessment Policy, section on accountability, 2 May 2002. http://www.tbs-sct.gc.ca/pol/doc-eng.aspx?id=12450&section=text

[52] The Cabinet Office has stated that the government has accepted the value of PIAs and that they will be used in all departments. UK Cabinet Office, Data Handling Procedures in Government: Final Report, London, June 2008, para 2.11. http://www.cabinetoffice.gov.uk/reports/data_handling.aspx

PIA features	Australia	Canada	NZ	UK	US
PIA guidance is targeted at government departments *and* the private sector.	✓	V	✓	✓	

In Canada, while the Treasury Board PIA guidelines have been prepared for government departments and agencies, PIA guidance at the provincial level is targeted at the private sector as well.

PIA features	Australia	Canada	NZ	UK	US
PIA guidance has been prepared by the funding agency.		✓			✓

The key PIA guidance document in Canada is that prepared by the Treasury Board Secretariat. In the US, it is that by the Office of Management and Budget. However, various US departments and agencies have prepared PIA guidance documents. The DHS guide is particularly good and somewhat more detailed than that of the OMB.

PIA features	Australia	Canada	NZ	UK	US
PIA guidance has been prepared by the privacy commissioner.	✓		✓	✓	
PIA should be initiated at early stage of project development, before decisions are taken.	✓	✓	✓	✓	✓
PIA guidance identifies benefits of undertaking a PIA.	✓	✓	✓	✓	✓
A PIA is regarded as a form of risk management.	✓	✓	✓	✓	✓
PIA guidance focuses on privacy risks involving personally identifiable information (aka informational privacy).	✓	✓	✓	✓	✓

PIAs are generally concerned with informational privacy. However, they could also address other types of privacy, something explicitly not ruled out by the Australian Guide[53] or the UK PIA Handbook.[54] The DHS Guidance seems to agree, at least implicitly, when it says, "A body screening device may capture the full

---

[53] "Information privacy is only one aspect of privacy. Other types of privacy include bodily privacy, territorial privacy, and communications privacy. These can be considered in the PIA process, particularly where they may pose risks to the overall success of the project." [Australia] OPC, *PIA Guide*, op. cit., p. iii.

[54] ICO, *PIA Handbook*, op. cit., pp. 6, 14, 85.

scan of an individual. While the information may not be maintained for later use, the initial scan may raise privacy concerns and a PIA could be required. Examples of technology with privacy implications could include: systems utilising radio frequency identification devices (RFID), biometric scans, data mining, or geospatial tracking."[55]

PIA features	Australia	Canada	NZ	UK	US
PIA guidance envisages a PIA as a multi-disciplinary exercise.	✓	✓			✓

The OMB guidance sees collaboration by different stakeholders, although it does not specifically say stakeholders external to the agency: "To be comprehensive and meaningful, privacy impact assessments require collaboration by program experts as well as experts in the areas of information technology, IT security, records management and privacy." The Treasury Board of Canada Secretariat's PIA policy says PIAs "are co-operative endeavours requiring a variety of skill sets, including those of program managers, technical specialists and privacy and legal advisors." The Australian PIA Guide similarly says: "a PIA generally means a team approach. It makes use of the various 'in-house experts'. . . and outside expertise as necessary."

PIA features	Australia	Canada	NZ	UK	US
PIA guidance puts emphasis on PIA as a process and not just preparation of the PIA report.	✓	✓		✓	

But reports are important too, as the DHS has said: "By documenting the procedures and measures through which the Department protects the privacy of individuals, the Department is more transparent and can better carry out its mission." Even the UK's ICO, which places heavy emphasis on PIA as a process, does not dismiss the importance of a PIA report:

The reasons for preparation of a PIA report are:

- as an element of accountability, in order to demonstrate that the PIA process was performed appropriately;
- to provide a basis for post-implementation review;
- to provide a basis for audit;
- to provide corporate memory, ensuring that the experience gained during the project is available to those completing new PIAs if original staff have left; and
- to enable the experience gained during the project to be shared with future PIA teams and others outside the organisation.[56]

---

[55] DHS, *PIAs: The Privacy Office Official Guidance*, op. cit., p. 5.

[56] ICO, *PIA Handbook*, op. cit., p. 39.

PIA features	Australia	Canada	NZ	UK	US
PIA guidance explicitly encourages engaging external stakeholders in the PIA process.	✓	V	✓	✓	

Canadian PIA policy does not explicitly say that stakeholders should be engaged in undertaking a PIA, but the PIA Guidelines say that a PIA can be "the basis for consultations with stakeholders", and in its checklist of questions, there are two that ask if key stakeholders have been provided with an opportunity to comment on the privacy protection implications of the proposal and whether public consultation will take place on the privacy implications of the proposal.

Generally, with the notable exception of the Canadian PIA Guidelines and the UK Handbook, PIA guidance documents do not describe in any detail PIA processes and, especially, stakeholder consultation mechanisms and participatory deliberation. Ortwin Renn has observed that "the European Union has highlighted the need for more stakeholder involvement and participation in risk management. However, how to implement this in day-to-day risk management is still under dispute."[57] His comment applies equally to PIA.

PIA features	Australia	Canada	NZ	UK	US
The PIA guidance contains a set of privacy principles.	✓	✓	✓	✓	V

The DHS PIA Guidance contains the Fair Information Practice Principles (FIPPs). The OMB Guidance does not. The Canadian PIA guidelines are based on privacy principles in the Code of Fair Information Practices in the federal Privacy Act as well as the 10 privacy principles attached to the Personal Information Protection and Electronic Documents Act (PIPEDA).

PIA features	Australia	Canada	NZ	UK	US
The PIA guidance puts primary emphasis on compliance.					V

All PIA guidance documents mention the importance of compliance with laws, regulations and/or codes of practice, but while compliance is important, it is not necessarily the primary purpose of the PIA. (The primary purpose is to identify risks to privacy and ways of dealing with those risks.)

---

[57] Renn, op. cit., p. 81. He cites European Commission, European Governance: A White Paper, COM (2001) 428 final, Brussels, 2001.

PIA features	Australia	Canada	NZ	UK	US
The PIA guidance provides questions for consideration during the PIA process or in preparing a PIA report.	✓	✓	✓	✓	V

The DHS Guidance contains a set of questions (unlike the OMB Guidance). While checklists can be criticised as mere box-ticking exercises, the questions usually require more than a straight yes or no response, i.e., the assessor or project manager is expected to describe the "how" or "what". In any event, the long lists of questions are actually valuable in prompting consideration of issues that might otherwise be neglected.

PIA features	Australia	Canada	NZ	UK	US
The PIA guidance contains a template for preparation of the PIA report.	✓	✓	✓	✓	V
PIAs are scalable, i.e., no one size fits all.	✓			✓	✓

"Because organisations vary greatly in size, the extent to which their activities intrude on privacy, and their experience in dealing with privacy issues makes it difficult to write a 'one size fits all' guide", says the UK Information Commissioner's Office.[58] "The depth and content of the PIA should be appropriate for the nature of the information to be collected and the size and complexity of the IT system", as the OMB guidance puts it. The UK Handbook offers templates for a "small-scale" PIA and a "full-scale" PIA. The Canadian PIA policy distinguishes between a "preliminary" and a "comprehensive" assessment.

PIA features	Australia	Canada	NZ	UK	US
The PIA policy provides for third-party, independent review or audit of the completed PIA document.		✓			V

According to the Canadian Directive on PIA,[59] government institutions must ensure "the approved core PIA provided to TBS is simultaneously provided to the Office of the Privacy Commissioner". Further, "heads of government institutions are required to notify the Privacy Commissioner of any planned initiatives (legislation, regulations, policies, programs) that could relate to the Privacy Act or to any of its

---

[58] ICO, *PIA Handbook*, op. cit., p. 2.

[59] Treasury Board of Canada Secretariat, Directive on Privacy Impact Assessment, Ottawa, 1 April 2010. This directive replaces the Privacy Impact Assessment Policy of 2002. http://www.tbs-sct.gc.ca/pol/doc-eng.aspx?id=18308&section=text

provisions or that could have an impact on the privacy of Canadians. This notification is to take place at a sufficiently early stage to permit the Commissioner to review and discuss the issues involved." The US Government Accountability Office (GAO), which bills itself as "the investigative arm of Congress", reviews PIAs prepared by Executive branch departments and agencies.

PIA features	Australia	Canada	NZ	UK	US
The PIA report and/or summary is to be published on the agency's website.		✓	V		✓

The Australian PIA Guide advocates (p. x) publishing the contents and findings of a PIA, but does not require it. The New Zealand PIA Handbook also advocates (p. 19) publishing the PIA findings, but does not require it. However, the NZ Immigration Act 2009 does require that PIAs regarding the collection and processing of biometric data be published on the department's website (see again Chapter 8 of this book). When the author asked for a PIA from a UK government department, he was told it would require a Freedom of Information request.

PIA features	Australia	Canada	NZ	UK	US
The PIA guidance says the PIA report may need to be revised and updated or a new PIA process undertaken.	✓	✓	✓	✓	✓

The DHS PIA guidance says, "The PIA is a living document that needs to be updated regularly as the program and system are changed and updated, not just when the program or system is deployed."[60] The New Zealand PIA Handbook also regards a PIA as a kind of "living" document.[61] And the Canadian PIA guidelines say, "A PIA is a dynamic process and as design changes occur in the business processes, the PIA should also be reviewed and updated."

1.6 Open Issues

As shown above, there are differences in the national approaches to PIA. Each has some good points as well as some shortcomings. Some of these shortcomings concern "open issues" discussed in this section as well as in subsequent chapters in this

---

[60] DHS, *PIAs: The Privacy Office Official Guidance*, op. cit., p. 2.

[61] "The privacy impact report can be an evolving document which will become more detailed over time." Stewart, *PIA Handbook*, op. cit., p. 17.

book. By "open issues", we mean issues that have been or are subject to debate, but on which as yet there has been no consensus, no general agreement on a common approach.

1.6.1 Scale and Scope of the PIA

The Australian guide says the first question to ask when assessing whether a PIA is needed is: "Will any personal information be collected, used or disclosed in the project?"[62] This is known as a threshold assessment. If the answer is yes, then a PIA is needed.

The scale and scope of a PIA depend on the significance of the project, the extent to which it collects, uses or discloses personal information, the PIA budget, the time it takes to conduct the PIA and the PIA's terms of reference. The Australia guide comments (p. xxv), "The more significant the scope, the more comprehensive the PIA should be." Conversely, if a project is relatively limited in scope, only a short PIA may be needed. Nevertheless, the guide advises (p. xxvi) that even a shorter PIA should address all of the key stages. Other PIAs may also be necessarily short, for example, "projects at the conceptual stages of development may only be able to address the PIA key stages in a less-detailed way" (p. xxvi). As the project develops and the issues become clearer, the PIA can be updated and supplemented, becoming more comprehensive. Others, such as the UK Handbook, have adopted a similar approach. The UK distinguishes between small-scale and full-scale PIAs.

Although the Australian PIA Guide deals with informational privacy, it notes (p. xx) that the PIA methodology could also be used for other types of privacy, such as bodily, territorial or communications privacy. The UK PIA Handbook similarly, but perhaps more explicitly, says (p. 14) a PIA could consider privacy of personal information, of the person, of personal behaviour and of personal communications. They are among the few PIA guides that make this distinction.

Most guidance documents give considerable discretion to organisations to determine (a) whether a PIA is needed and (b) the scale and scope of the PIA. Even in the US where the OMB obliges Executive branch departments and agencies and their contractors to undertake a PIA if they process personal data, and where they are obliged to report annually on their use of PIA, some PIAs can only be described as perfunctory at best, as short as two pages (see Chapter 10 by Kenneth Bamberger and Deirdre Mulligan).

There is little information available about the cost of a PIA. The cost will, of course, depend on the scale of the PIA, including the extent to which the project manager consults and engages with stakeholders, on the budget allocated for undertaking a PIA. To ask how much an "average" PIA costs is like asking "How long is a piece of string?". An equally critical consideration is how long it might take to perform the PIA. There may be considerable pressure, especially in the private

---

[62] OPC, *PIA Guide*, op. cit., p. xi.

sector, to complete a project, to develop and commercialise a service or to get a new technology or product into the market, with corresponding pressure to complete a PIA quickly so as not to delay the project.

Another related issue of importance is the terms of reference of the PIA team. The UK PIA Handbook, uniquely among the PIA guidance documents, discusses the terms of reference of the PIA team:

It is generally advisable for terms of reference for the PIA to be prepared and agreed. Important elements of the terms of reference include:

- the functions to be performed;
- the deliverables;
- the desired outcomes;
- the scope of the assessment; and
- the roles and responsibilities of various parties involved in the PIA.

The terms of reference should document the governance structure and processes, including the nature of the delegation of responsibility and authority provided to the person(s) or team(s) who are involved in the PIA.[63]

1.6.2 Who Should Perform the PIA?

In the first instance, the project manager (or policy-maker or technology developer) should be responsible (and accountable) for deciding whether a PIA should be carried out, the scale and scope of the PIA, and who to involve in undertaking the PIA. The Australian Guide says (p. ix), "Generally, whoever is handling the project is responsible for deciding if a PIA is necessary or desirable and ensuring it is carried out." Some projects will have markedly more privacy impact than others, in which case a "robust and independent PIA conducted by external assessors may be preferable". An "independent assessment may also help the organisation to develop community trust in the PIA findings and the project's intent" (Australian Guide, p. x).

PIAs may be prepared "in-house" or by consultants. Each has advantages. The New Zealand PIA Handbook says (p. 5) that "There are distinct advantages in outsourcing the preparation of a privacy impact report to lend impartiality to the process. That may be critical in influencing consumer or public opinion. Nonetheless, it is feasible to undertake PIA in-house, using the skills and experience of the project team and the wider organisation." Elsewhere, it says (p. 13), "Sometimes most of the necessary skills will reside in the team assembled to develop the project itself. Experts with particular skills may be brought in to assist with certain aspects. An agency's Privacy Officer may undertake a coordinating or checking role."

The PIA may also be undertaken by a mix of people, some in-house personnel, some external to the organisation. The NZ PIA Handbook says (p. 14), "Competent

---

[63] ICO, *PIA Handbook*, op. cit., p. 10.

privacy expertise... may be brought in even when most of the work will be done by the project team.... Where the PIA is solely undertaken internally, thought should be given to incorporating some external or independent oversight. One possibility is to use a privacy or data protection consultant to carry out such a check."

1.6.3 Should Engaging External Stakeholders Be Part of the PIA Process?

Some organisations may not want to engage external stakeholders in the performance of a PIA. They may feel the complexity of the project is such that it would take a big effort to "educate" or bring up to speed the external stakeholders to the point where they may be able to provide meaningful insights. They may not want to engage external stakeholders because they assume consensus would be too difficult to achieve given the diversity of opinion about the project. Or they may not want to deal with the criticism they may get. Or they may feel the project is too commercially sensitive or involves national security. Such considerations will usually be short-sighted. There are ways of responding to such objections, as Raab and Wright point out in Chapter 17.

The value of engaging with stakeholders is worth the effort. Australia's PIA Guide says (p. x), "Consultation with key stakeholders is basic to the PIA process." It adds that

> A PIA should always consider community privacy attitudes and expectations. Affected individuals are likely to be key stakeholders, so wider public consultation is important, particularly where a lot of personal information is being handled or where sensitive information is involved. Public consultation also adds to community awareness about the project and can increase confidence in the way the project (and the organisation) is handling personal information.

Engaging stakeholders in the PIA process has many benefits to the organisation. The benefits identified by the ISO in its standard on information security risk management are equally applicable to a PIA. Engaging stakeholders can help an organisation to

- Identify risks that might not otherwise be considered[64];
- Communicate the results of the organisation's risk assessment and how it intends to deal with those risks;

---

[64] ICO is of the view that if a PIA is undertaken solely from the viewpoint of the organisation itself, it is likely that risks will be overlooked. It therefore recommends that stakeholder perspectives are considered. See ICO, *PIA Handbook*, op. cit., p. 56. At p. 58, it makes the precision that risks may be overlooked unless they are considered from the various perspectives of each of the stakeholder groups, rather than just from the viewpoint of the organisation that is conducting the project. "There are often different impacts and implications for different sections of the population, especially disadvantaged groups."

- Avoid or reduce both occurrence and consequence of information security breaches due to the lack of mutual understanding among decision-makers and stakeholders;
- Support decision-making;
- Co-ordinate with other parties and plan responses to reduce the consequences of any incident;
- Give decision makers and stakeholders a sense of responsibility about risks;
- Improve awareness.[65]

1.6.4 Should PIAs Be Published?

The US E-Government Act of 2002 obliges the publication of PIAs. The US Department of Homeland Security publishes "approved PIAs" on its Privacy Impact Assessment web page[66] unless they are classified.

The Treasury Board Secretariat of Canada says only summaries of PIAs need publication on a government department or agency's website.

While others don't require publication, they advocate it. For example, the Australian PIA Guide (p. x) advocates publishing the contents and findings of a PIA because it "adds value; demonstrates to stakeholders and the community that the project has undergone critical privacy analysis; contributes to the transparency of the project's development and intent". However, the Australian Privacy Commissioner has acknowledged (p. xviii) that "there may be circumstances where the full or part release of a PIA may not be appropriate. For example . . . there may also be security, commercial-in-confidence or, for private sector organisations, other competitive reasons for not making a PIA public in full or in part." Where there are difficulties in making the full PIA available, the Commissioner encourages release of a summary version.

The New Zealand PIA Handbook advocates (p. 19) publishing the PIA findings: "Usually, there is merit in making completed privacy impact reports publicly available and organisations should consider posting the privacy impact report or a summary on their website. Openness about the findings can contribute to the maintenance of public trust and confidence in the organisation and can ensure that its practices and policies in relation to the handling of personal information are fair and freely available."

The ICO seems to favour publication as well,[67] but it is not mandatory, nor is there any reporting mechanism in the UK, so it is virtually impossible to know whether a PIA has been performed unless an organisation chooses to say so, and it would appear that few do so.

---

[65] ISO/IEC 27005:2008(E), op. cit., p. 22.

[66] http://www.dhs.gov/files/publications/editorial_0511.shtm

[67] ICO, *PIA Handbook*, op. cit., pp. 39, 40.

While some organisations, for competitive or security reasons, may not want to publish a PIA, the sensitive information can be redacted or separated into an appendix, which can be distributed less widely and/ or subject to confidentiality constraints.

1.6.5 Should PIAs Be Mandatory?

It could be argued that in view of the many instances when personal data has been compromised, PIAs should be mandatory.[68] The European Commission, in its Communication of 4 November 2010, seems to suggest that, in its envisaged revision of the Data Protection Directive, any data controller processing sensitive personal information would be obliged to conduct a PIA.

Not all PIA advocates favour making PIAs mandatory. For example, some argue that making PIAs mandatory reinforces "a 'compliance mentality' view of the PIA as yet another hurdle to be overcome in the already cumbersome project and funding process".[69]

There are practical difficulties in making PIAs mandatory. One difficulty is in determining when a PIA should be conducted. As the Australian PIA Guide (p. xx) says, "There is no hard-and-fast rule about when to do a PIA, and each project must be considered individually." A second difficulty is in determining the scale and scope of a PIA. If there were a directive or regulation that made PIAs mandatory, how would the parameters be drawn as to what constituted a PIA? Making PIAs mandatory might lead to some companies conducting the most cursory of PIA, a simple, one-page box-ticking exercise. It would be difficult to enforce a mandatory requirement. Would we need a PIA police force?

While there are difficulties, it is also possible to envisage solutions to some of these difficulties. For example, for government agencies, PIAs could be tied to funding submissions. If the funding agency (e.g., the Treasury Board of Canada) did not find the PIA of acceptable quality, it could withhold funding until the PIA was deemed acceptable. Requiring the deputy minister to sign off the PIA would bring accountability to bear. In the case of a company in the private sector, PIAs could be deemed to be part of good risk management practice. The company would be obliged to state how it is managing risks, including risks to privacy, in its annual report. PIAs could be made subject to independent, third-party review or audit.

---

[68] Wright, David, "Should Privacy Impact Assessment Be Mandatory?", *Communications of the ACM*, Vol. 54, No. 8, August 2011, pp. 121–131.

[69] Hope-Tindall, Peter, "Privacy Impact Assessment – Obligation or Opportunity: The Choice is Ours!", *Prepared for CSE ITS Conference*, Ottawa, ON, 16 May 2002. http://www.home.inter.net/gt/grabbag/Tindall_PIA_Material.pdf

1.6.6 Should the DPA or Privacy Commissioner "Approve" a PIA?

The Alberta Office of the Information and Privacy Commissioner will not "approve" a PIA submitted to them by an organisation. Once satisfied that the organisation has addressed the relevant considerations and is committed to the provision of the necessary level of privacy protection, the Commissioner will "accept" the PIA. Acceptance is not approval; it merely reflects the Commissioner's acceptance that the organisation has made reasonable efforts to protect privacy.[70]

In the instance of the Canadian federal government, departments and agencies are required to copy the Office of the Privacy Commissioner on the PIAs sent to the Treasury Board for funding submission.[71] In the UK, while PIAs are supposedly obligatory for government departments, there is no obligation for the Information Commissioner's Office to be sent a copy of the PIA,[72] nor are PIAs tied to funding submissions, so it would appear impossible to know whether government departments are, in fact, producing PIAs or how rigorous those PIAs might be.

The difficulty facing many data protection authorities and privacy commissioners is that they do not have the resource to review, let alone approve PIAs. Their review and approval of PIAs produced in the private sector would be an even more remote possibility.

Nevertheless, one could envisage solutions to this problem. One is to make PIAs subject to independent, third-party audit, much like financial accounts of companies listed on the stock exchange. Another is to require publication of the PIA (with legitimate exceptions or redacted as necessary in cases involving crime prevention or national security). Yet another is to create a national registry of PIAs, at least of those performed by government departments and agencies, which would make it easier for researchers, privacy advocates and others to find those relevant to their interest. Copying PIAs to the privacy commissioner seems like a good idea; even if the privacy commissioner is not able to review each one, it could review or carry out a random audit of at least some of them. Unless a PIA policy has some teeth, PIAs are unlikely to live up to expectations, as Nigel Waters (see Chapter 6) and others in this book have observed.

---

[70] http://www.oipc.ab.ca/pages/PIAs/Description.aspx

[71] "Government institutions must provide a copy of the final Privacy Impact Assessment to the Privacy Commissioner. This notification must occur at a reasonably early stage prior to implementing the initiative, program or service. Advance notification is intended to permit the Commissioner to review the issues and, if appropriate, to provide advice to the head of the institution." TBS, "Privacy Impact Assessment Policy", op. cit.

[72] In fact, the ICO PIA Handbook explicitly says (p. 11): "PIAs have been designed as a self-assessment tool for organisations and the ICO does not have a formal role in conducting them, approving or signing off any final report which is produced."

1.6.7 Should a PIA Apply to the Development of New Policy?

Canada's Directive on PIA says it "does not apply to the development of new legislation".[73] Although the policy says a PIA is to be applied for new programs or services, the PIA Guidelines say "A PIA is a process that helps departments and agencies determine whether new technologies, information systems and initiatives or proposed programs *and policies* meet basic privacy requirements." [Italics added.]

The ICO PIA Handbook says that a PIA could apply to "a system, database, program, application, service or a scheme, or an enhancement to any of the above, or an initiative, proposal or a review, *or even draft legislation*."[74] [Italics added.]

1.6.8 Two or More Organisations Collaborating on a PIA

Although Canada's PIA policy applies to both intra- and inter-departmental initiatives,[75] generally PIA policy and practice have focused on the individual organisation conducting a PIA, so there is the distinct possibility that projects, policies, systems, programs or technologies involving the collection and processing of personally identifiable information by two or more organisations escape the attention of a PIA. The audit undertaken by the Office of the Privacy Commissioner (see Chapter 20 by Jennifer Stoddart) has drawn attention to this fact. Hence, there would appear to be a requirement that PIA policy should cast its net more widely to ensure that projects involving two or more organisations are caught within its purview. There may be some logistical hurdles to be overcome in undertaking such PIAs, such as who would be responsible for leading the PIA and who would be held accountable for its adequacy, but these need not be insurmountable. If the organisations could not come to some agreement on such issues, the privacy commissioner could arbitrate or, if not the privacy commissioner, then the funding agency (e.g., the OMB in the US or the Treasury Board in Canada or the Cabinet Office in the UK). An alternative to a single PIA involving two or more organisations is two or more PIAs, each carried out by each organisation involved in the project.[76] A potential downside for such an approach is that the different PIAs come to different conclusions with regard to the privacy risks and how they should be mitigated. It would be desirable for government departments and agencies to come to some arrangement in such cases, so they could be cited as good practice to companies who similarly collaborate on projects. The European Commission and government procurement

---

[73] TBS, Directive on Privacy Impact Assessment, op. cit., section 2.4.

[74] ICO, *PIA Handbook*, op. cit., p. 2.

[75] And the Canadian PIA Guidelines contain a questionnaire designed for cross-jurisdictional initiatives.

[76] This is the approach recommended in the Canadian TBS PIA Guidelines: "An operating assumption for the development of the cross-jurisdictional PIA is that individual jurisdictions should complete their own PIA based on their specific statutory and policy provisions."

agencies could play a helpful role here too, e.g., when they elicit proposals from consortia for projects involving the collection and processing of personal data, they could specify a requirement for a PIA and it would be up to the consortium to decide on the practical procedures for its conduct (i.e., who would be responsible and accountable).

1.6.9 Are Trans-national PIAs Feasible?

So far, there have been almost no instances of a trans-national PIA, yet there are many projects or programmes that involve the participation of two or more countries, notably in regard to law enforcement and financial transactions in pursuit of criminals and terrorists. Such international projects or programmes often involve personal data and, with minimal oversight, the risk of unwarranted or disproportionate privacy intrusion appears to be particularly high. The hurdles mentioned above would appear to be even higher where national sovereignty is involved.

While there have been almost no instances of a trans-national PIA, some groundbreaking has taken place. Charles Raab and David Wright mention in Chapter 17 the case of a trans-national PIA involving medical data as well as the PIA guide prepared in 2001 by Deloitte and Touche specifically devoted to cross-border privacy impact assessment. Raab and Wright also suggest ways forward for the conduct of trans-national PIAs. Artemi Rallo, Director of Spain's Data Protection Agency, discusses the prospects for trans-national PIAs in Chapter 18.

1.7 Objectives and Scope of This Book

This book has three main objectives. First is to provide a reasonably comprehensive overview of PIA activity around the world. Second is to identify open issues, where there are differences of views or where no common approach has yet been achieved with regard to PIA policy and practice. Third is to identify some of the best elements of existing PIA policy and practice in order to make recommendations to policymakers, industry and other stakeholders on how PIA practice can be improved.

The book is divided into several parts. Following the Foreword by Gary Marx, the first part includes this Introduction, Chapter 2 on a human rights perspective on privacy and data protection impact assessments, Chapter 3 on regulatory impact assessment and what lessons can be learned for PIA, and Chapter 4 on prior checking, a forerunner to privacy impact assessments.

The second part covers PIA practice in Australia, Canada, New Zealand, the United Kingdom and the United States, the five countries with the most experience of PIA.

The third part includes chapters from Nokia, Siemens and Vodafone, three global companies, representatives from which describe their use of PIAs and how they assess privacy impacts in their organisations.

The fourth part covers two specialised PIAs, including that developed by and for the financial services industry under the auspices of the International Organization for Standardization, as well as two chapters devoted to the RFID PIA framework developed by industry and approved by the Art. 29 Data Protection Working Party in the European Union.

The fifth part addresses some specific issues – surveillance, the Madrid Resolution and the prospects for transnational PIAs, privacy and ethical impact assessments, the Canadian experience in auditing PIAs, optimising the regulator's role and, finally, the concluding chapter where we highlight some of the key findings from the contributions to this book and where we make recommendations for improving PIA policy and practice.

We are fortunate in having so many distinguished experts represented in this book. They are among the leaders in the field and include some of the earliest proponents of PIA. The authors include privacy commissioners, representatives from industry, academics and consultants. They have a wealth of experience with privacy impact assessment, which they kindly share with readers of this book. We, the editors, are grateful indeed that they have been willing to contribute to our project.

As stated at the outset of this Introduction, there is growing interest in PIAs. We hope that the experience evidenced in this book will help shape PIA policy and practice among those countries and companies contemplating the use of PIA to protect privacy against an increasing number of incursions.

Chapter 2
A Human Rights Perspective on Privacy and Data Protection Impact Assessments

Paul De Hert

This contribution looks at the concept of privacy impact assessments (PIA) from a human rights viewpoint within the European context. It explores the possibilities and limits of PIA by identifying the useful elements in the case law of the European Court on Human Rights with regard to the right to privacy as contained in Art. 8 of the European Convention on Human Rights (ECHR).

I address both the academic eager to understand the phenomenon of impact assessments in a wider context as well as the field-worker in need of criteria to start an impact assessment. My examples are mainly taken from the case law of the European Court of Human Rights (ECtHR) with regard to security and environmental related technologies that impact the right to privacy and the right to protection of personal data. After a terminological clarification, I briefly discuss the nature of data protection impact assessments. Then I turn to privacy impact assessments consisting of a bundle of at least seven tests to be carried out by private and public actors planning to develop and implement privacy-relevant technologies or to process personal data. Each test will be discussed in detail.

2.1 Terminology

A first question that arises is whether we need to talk about privacy impact assessments or data protection impact assessments. The question is more than formal. Following the example of some European Member States' constitutions, the Charter of Fundamental Rights of the European Union 2000 (CFR EU) differentiates between the two as separate rights:

P. De Hert (✉)
Vrije Universiteit Brussels (LSTS), Avenue de la Plaine 2, Brussels 1050, Belgium

Tilburg University (TILT), Tilburg, The Netherlands
e-mail: paul.de.hert@vub.ac.be

D. Wright, P. De Hert (eds.), *Privacy Impact Assessment*, Law, Governance
and Technology Series 6, DOI 10.1007/978-94-007-2543-0_2,
© Springer Science+Business Media B.V. 2012

Art. 7 – Respect for private and family life
Everyone has the right to respect for his or her private and family life, home and communications.
Art. 8 – Protection of personal data
1. Everyone has the right to the protection of personal data concerning him or her.
2. Such data must be processed fairly for specified purposes and on the basis of the consent of the person concerned or some other legitimate basis laid down by law. Everyone has the right of access to data which has been collected concerning him or her, and the right to have it rectified.
3. Compliance with these rules shall be subject to control by an independent authority.

The recognition of separate privacy and data protection rights should alert us when choosing terminology. In previous publications, my colleagues and I have shown that both rights can and should have separate and complementary meanings,[1] but that the Strasbourg-based European Court on Human Rights and the Luxembourg-based Court of Justice (ECJ) of the EU (and the General Court, formerly the Court of First Instance) superimpose criteria derived from both rights. Our courts operate both a privacy test and a data protection test when confronted with issues that have a personal data related dimension and a privacy dimension. Both tests are explained below, but it is important to underline here that, in most cases, both need to be applied together. The reason for insisting on their different nature is strategic. Ignoring one or privileging one to the detriment of the other – a situation that often arises in case law – necessarily results in a loss of concerns that are checked upon and never contribute to a comprehensive assessment paying due attention to their respective natures as fundamental rights. Hence, we opt to use both terms, "data protection impact assessment" and "privacy impact assessments", but never in an identical vein. In this contribution, the emphasis is on the privacy test that proves to be more complex, but again this does not imply that one test is more important than the other.

2.2 Data Protection Impact Assessments

To keep terminology and argumentation simple, I equate data protection impact assessments with simply checking the legal requirements spelled out in the European data protection framework, in particular, those contained in regulations

---

[1] De Hert, Paul, and Serge Gutwirth, "Privacy, Data Protection and Law Enforcement: Opacity of the Individual and Transparency of Power", in Erik Claes, Anthony Duff and Serge Gutwirth (eds.), *Privacy and the Criminal Law*, Intersentia, Antwerp, 2006, pp. 61–104.

created by the EU, especially the Data Protection Directive (95/46/EC),[2] the e-Privacy Directive (2002/58/EC),[3] as amended by Directives 2006/24/EC and 2009/136/EC,[4] the Data Retention Directive (2006/24/EC),[5] the Council Framework Decision 2008/977/JHA[6] (dealing with data protection with regard to criminal matters, i.e., former third pillar issues) and Regulation 45/2001[7] (laying down data protection rules for the institutions and bodies).

Depending on the nature of the data used, personal data and/or location data and/or traffic data, and depending on the nature of the processing involved (private, public, law enforcement), one can establish a checklist based on these regulations that when carried out properly will make up the data protection impact assessments. No more and no less. The nature of these regulations is well-known. After defining the terms and the scope of the respective regulations, they contain duties for those processing data and rights for those whose data is processed. The rights of the data subjects correspond to the duties of the data processors and controllers. In addition, these have duties to inform national data protection authorities and have to accept supervision by these authorities. Finally, the regulations contain provisions with regard to remedies and liabilities. The content of the regulations is very detailed and the checklist is both technical and exhaustive. This list – based on the Data Protection Directive – goes as follows:

1. **Personal data must be fairly and lawfully processed** – Art. 6(1)(a)
2. **Data minimisation**

   - collected for specific, explicitly defined and legitimate purposes and not further processed in a way incompatible with those purposes – Art. 6(1)(b)
   - retained only for as long as is necessary to fulfil that purpose – Art. 6(1)(c) (implicitly)

---

[2] European Parliament and Council, Directive 95/46/EC of 24 October 1995 on the protection of individuals with regard to the processing of personal data and on the free movement of such data.

[3] European Parliament and Council, Directive 2002/58/EC of 12 July 2002 concerning the processing of personal data and the protection of privacy in the electronic communications sector (Directive on privacy and electronic communications).

[4] European Parliament and Council, Directive 2009/136/EC of 25 November 2009 amending Directive 2002/22/EC on universal service and users' rights relating to electronic communications networks and services; Directive 2002/58/EC concerning the processing of personal data and the protection of privacy in the electronic communications sector and Regulation (EC) No 2006/2004 on cooperation between national authorities responsible for the enforcement of consumer protection laws.

[5] European Parliament and Council, Directive 2006/24/EC of 15 March 2006 on the retention of data generated or processed in connection with the provision of publicly available electronic communications services or of public communications networks and amending Directive 2002/58/EC.

[6] Council Framework Decision 2008/977/JHA of 27 November 2008 on the protection of personal data processed in the framework of police and judicial cooperation in criminal matters.

[7] European Parliament and Council, Regulation (EC) No 45/2001 of 18 December 2000 on the protection of individuals with regard to the processing of personal data by the Community institutions and bodies and on the free movement of such data.

3. **Data quality**

  - adequate, relevant and not excessive in relation to the purposes for which they are collected and/or further processed – Art. 6(1)(c)
  - accurate and, where necessary, kept up to date – Art. 6(1)(d)

4. **Legitimate basis** for processing – Art. 7

  - unambiguous consent of the data subject
  - performance of a contract to which the data subject is a party
  - compliance with a legal obligation of the data controller
  - protection of the vital interest of the data subject
  - performance of the task carried out in the public interest or exercise of official authority
  - legitimate interest pursued by the controller

5. **Data anonymisation** – Art. 6(1)(e)

  - kept in a form which permits identification of data subjects for no longer than is necessary for the purposes for which the data were collected or for which they are further processed

6. **Data security**

  - **confidentiality of processing** – Art. 16
  - **security of processing** – i.e., appropriate technical and organisational measures to protect personal data against accidental or unlawful destruction or accidental loss, alteration, unauthorised disclosure or access, in particular, where the processing involves the transmission of data over a network, and against all other unlawful forms of processing – Art. 17
  - **notification of processing data** – i.e., the data controller must notify the supervisory authority before carrying out any wholly or partly automatic processing operation – Art. 18(1) – and powers of supervisory bodies must be respected – Art. 28
  - **data breach notification** – in case of a breach of security leading to the accidental or unlawful destruction, loss, alteration, unauthorised disclosure of or access to personal data, the data controller shall notify the competent national authority – Art. 4(3) e-Privacy Directive

7. **Data subject rights**

  - the right to be informed about processing his/her personal data in a clear and understandable language – Art. 12(a),
  - the right to access his/her own personal data – Art. 12(a),
  - the right to rectify any wrong or incomplete information – Art. 12(b),
  - the right, in some cases, to object to the processing on legitimate grounds – Art. 14,

- the right not to be subject to an automated decision intended to evaluate certain personal aspects relating to the data subject such as his performance at work, creditworthiness, reliability, conduct – Art. 15,
- the right to judicial remedy and to receive compensation from the data controller for any damage suffered (short of *vis maior*) – Art. 22 and Art. 23, respectively.

8. **These data subject's rights correspond to the data controller's obligations to:**

- ensure the data subject's rights are duly observed,
- ensure observance of the data minimisation principle,
- ensure observance of the criteria for making the data-processing legitimate (e.g., consent or performance of the contract),
- safeguard confidentiality of processing,
- safeguard security of processing,
- notify processing of personal data to the national data protection authority (DPA),
- in case of the transfer to the third countries, ensure that these countries provide an adequate level of protection (in general).

Moreover, there must be special care when use is made of certain "sensitive" categories of data (Art. 8(1)) and when personal data is transferred outside the EU/EEA (Arts. 25-26). Next, rules on remedies and liability must be observed (Arts. 22-23) and powers of supervisory bodies must be respected (Art. 28). A rudimentary overview of a basic assessment, based on the provisions of Directive 95/46/EC, will imply carrying out the following checks or tests.[8]

Legitimacy test	Art. 7: Are the criteria for legitimate personal data processing respected?
Purpose restriction test	Art. 6: Are there restrictions to the purpose and use? This includes requirements with respect to data quality, accuracy, purpose specification and proportionality.
Security and confidentiality test	Arts. 16-17: Are measures taken to ensure the confidentiality and security of data processing? Article 8: Are the additional rules that exist for special categories of processing (health, religion, race, . . .) respected in cases where these data are processed?

---

[8] I am grateful to Hans Graux from time.lex, the Brussels-based law firm, for this systematisation of the basic provisions of the Directive.

Transparency test	Arts. 10-11: Is the right to information regarding essential aspects of the data processing guaranteed?
Data subject participation test	Art. 12: Is the right to access, correct or delete the data guaranteed?
Accountability test	Arts. 22-23: Have provisions been made for the rules on remedies and liability? Art. 28: Are the supervisory bodies properly informed about the processing operation?

To repeat: this is just a rough basic sketch. When, for instance, assessing technology based on the processing of geo-localisation data, more detailed checklists have to be generated, also based on the provisions of the e-Privacy Directive governing the processing of such data.

Whatever the length may be, these tests are fundamental to the idea of good processing of data in our information society. Every test within the bundle of tests has its merits. The answer whether a technology that processes data is "good" or "bad" should never be answered with one sweeping statement, but should always be based on carefully assessing all the different obligations taken from the relevant data protection regulations. So every specific test counts and one negative result jeopardises the legitimacy of the technology or processing operation.

There is, however, some ground not to consider these tests as building up to true impact assessments. Carrying them out amounts to a mere compliance exercise imposed by data protection law. There is, properly speaking, no duty to carry out data protection assessments in EU regulation (yet), but there is, of course, the general obligation to respect legal obligations. Checking on the data protection principles derived from EU law is just doing that.[9]

2.3 Privacy Impact Assessment: What Is Privacy?

Beyond compliance checks with legal regulations, one must consider more qualitative requirements that have to do with legality, legitimacy, participation and, especially, proportionality. References to these requirements are included in data protection regulations, but they share their place with more technical or formal requirements such as the requirement to secure data and have data closed off to third parties. These qualitative principles – accounting for the difference between a compliance check and a true impact assessment – are key considerations in determining whether privacy is respected in the context of the ECHR and the relevant case law of the ECtHR. The Convention confers the right to respect for

---

[9] Section 2.11 below notes that the Court of Human Rights integrates the data protection check in the broader framework of proportionality requirements.

private life, family life, home, correspondence and communications (Art. 8(1)). Using innovative interpretational approaches such as the "living instrument" doctrine and the "practical and effective" doctrine,[10] the Court has given the rights in the Convention, including those in Art. 8 ECHR, a generous interpretation. Especially the privacy right has served as a catch-all tool, covering a sophisticated collection of interests, ranging from intimacy, sexual choice, personal identity, moral and physical well-being, reputation, formation of human relationships, health and environmental protection, collection of and access to personal information. (This chapter also discusses cases concerning the right to a healthy environment and the protection against noise as well as the famous *Marper* judgment (see below) where the Court found body samples and materials such as DNA and fingerprint samples to be privacy relevant.)

The combined use of "the right to protection of private life" and "the right to protection of correspondence" allows the Court to provide legal protection for almost any attribute or behaviour that defines the individual's identity as a human being, including personal data.[11] In *Copeland* v. *The United Kingdom* (2007), the ECtHR found that the UK had violated Ms Copeland's right to respect for her private life and correspondence under Art. 8 by monitoring her telephone calls, e-mail correspondence and Internet use.[12] All of these media are protected by the rights in Art. 8 ECHR. In *Uzun* v. *Germany* (2010), a first case concerning GPS surveillance before the ECtHR, the Court again contended that the right to privacy applied, even though the surveillance receiver was attached to a car and not to a person. The authorities had systematically collected and stored data determining Mr Uzun's

---

[10] On numerous occasions, the Court emphasised that the Convention is "a living instrument which should be interpreted according to present-day conditions". See, e.g., ECtHR, *Tyrer* v. *United Kingdom*, Judgment of 25 April 1978 Series A-26, § 31, ECtHR, *Marckx* v. *Belgium*, Judgment of 13 June 1979, Series A-31, § 41, ECtHR, *Dudgeon* v. *United Kingdom*, Judgment of 22 October 1981, Series A-45, § 60, ECtHR, *Soering* v. *United Kingdom*, Judgment of 7 July 1989, Series A, § 102. In 1995, the Court held "It follows that these provisions cannot be interpreted solely in accordance with the intentions of their authors as expressed more than forty years ago. Accordingly, even if it had been established, which is not the case, that restrictions, other than those ratione temporis, were considered permissible under Articles 25 and 46 (art. 25, art. 46) at a time when a minority of the present Contracting Parties adopted the Convention, such evidence could not be decisive" (ECtHR, *Loizidou* v. *Turkey (prel. obj.)*, Judgment of 23 March 1995 Series A-310, § 71). In a similar vein, the Court has repeatedly stressed that the Convention is intended to guarantee "not rights that are theoretical or illusory but practical and effective"; see, e.g., ECtHR, *Airey v. Ireland*, Judgment of 9 October 1979, Series A-32, § 24 and ECtHR, *Soering v. United Kingdom*, Judgment of 7 July 1989, Series A-161, § 87. For more on this, see Mowbray, Alastair, "The Creativity of the European Court of Human Rights", *Human Rights Law Review*, Vol. 5, No. 1, 2005, pp. 57–79.

[11] Harris, David, Michael O'Boyle, Edward Bates and Carla Buckley, *Law of the European Convention on Human Rights*, second edition, Oxford University Press, Oxford, 2009, pp. 385–392; Nardell, Gordon, "Levelling Up: Data Privacy and the European Court of Human Rights", in Serge Gutwirth, Yves Poullet and Paul De Hert (eds.), *Data Protection in a Profiled World*, Springer, Dordrecht, 2010, pp. 43–52.

[12] ECtHR, *Copland* v. *United Kingdom*, Judgment of 3 April 2007, Application no. 62617/00.

whereabouts and movements in the public sphere. They had further used it in order to draw up a pattern of his movements, to conduct additional investigations and to collect additional evidence regarding the places to which he had travelled, which was later used at the criminal trial. The Court found those factors sufficient to conclude that the GPS tracking of Mr Uzun had interfered with his right to respect for his private life under Art. 8.[13]

2.4 Privacy Impact Assessments: Privacy and Permissible Limitations

A point of interest about the ECHR is the detailed way in which the founding fathers have described the limitations to the right to privacy. Contrary to the First Amendment in the US Constitution, the privacy right as codified in the ECHR is far from absolute. On the contrary, after the enumeration of the right in the first paragraph, a second, much longer paragraph follows, which spells out the requirements to be respected by governments when limiting the privacy right. Art. 8(2) allows a public authority to interfere so long as the measures taken are "in accordance with the law" and "necessary in a democratic society" in pursuance of a wide range of "legitimate aims", including prevention of crime and disorder and protection of the rights of others. Similar provisions are included in Arts. 9 (freedom of thought, conscience and religion), 10 (freedom of expression) and 11 (freedom of assembly and association) of the Convention.

Based on the wording of the text of Art. 8 et seq., we are able to identify three generic requirements that have to be met for privacy limitations that respect the Convention: legality (Is there a legal basis in law for a technology that processes data?), legitimacy (Is the processing pursuing legitimate aims?) and necessity (Is the processing necessary in a democratic society?).

To understand what these requirements imply is far from easy. Nardell correctly notes that the general principles applied by the Court when interpreting have been around for some years and are well known to most lawyers and many policy-makers, but in the same paragraph, he acknowledges that we are faced with open-textured concepts and that, therefore, we have to turn to the case law of the Court to understand requirements such as legality and necessity.[14]

We tend to disagree with Nardell about the familiarity of the principles. Not only has the interpretation of these requirements by the Court evolved over the years making the outcome of cases often unpredictable, but also there is an under-theorised political filter imposed by the judges on some cases allowing Member States broader discretion when deciding on privacy limitations and functionalities

---

[13] ECtHR, *Uzun* v. *Germany*, Judgment of 2 September 2010, Application no. 35623/05, §§ 49–53.

[14] Nardell, op. cit., p. 46. The third requirement – limitations of the right to privacy should serve certain "legitimate purposes" listed in Article 8(2) – has not attracted a lot of attention by the Court yet. Due to the very general listing of purposes that are considered legitimate, almost all governmental initiatives qualify under this requirement.

of technologies.[15] Depending on this, political filter requirements may not mean the same thing in two cases or, rather, may not have the same weight. This political filter consists of two elements. First, there is the complex margin of appreciation. The Court refuses to clarify this doctrine to an objective extent. The main idea – at least, this is known about this doctrine – is that States enjoy a certain margin of appreciation in determining the steps to be taken to ensure compliance with the Convention.[16] This margin *and* the standard of scrutiny will vary according to the context of the case. While there is enough written on this subject,[17] no one can predict how the Court will apply this doctrine in practice. Second, and on top of the margin filter, there is the presence of at least two standards of review by the Court. In some cases, there will be a stricter review, in others, a more ordinary review. The criteria are again unknown but as is the case for the margin theory, the nature of the right at stake is one criterion. Shocking as this may sound, not all rights are alike and some get more weight than others. Likewise, not all privacy interests will receive the same benevolent treatment by the Court.

Based on careful scrutiny of the Court, I have argued previously that for many reasons, an ordinary test only looking for manifest disproportionality will be applied in cases concerning Art. 8 (right to privacy), whereas the strict test is more likely to appear in the context of Art. 10 (freedom of expression).[18] Within the context of Art. 8, a strict test is more likely to be applied to matters touching people's identity (sex life, family ties, etc.)[19] than to matters touching people confronted with security policies.

The key to identifying these differences, amounting either to restrained review or to assertive scrutiny, is the way the margin doctrine and the proportionality test is

---

[15] De Hert, Paul, "Balancing Security and Liberty Within the European Human Rights Framework: A Critical Reading of the Court's Case Law in the Light of Surveillance and Criminal Law Enforcement Strategies After 9/11", *Utrecht Law Review*, Vol. 1, No. 1, 2005, pp. 68–96. http://www.utrechtlawreview.org/index.php/ulr/issue/view/1

[16] ECtHR, *Hatton* v. *The United Kingdom*, Judgment of 2 October 2001, Application no. 36 022/97, § 96.

[17] On the nature of the Court's review, see, e.g., ECtHR, *Handyside* v. *United Kingdom*, Judgment of 7 December 1976, Series A, Vol. 24, §§ 49–50 and ECtHR, Olsson, Series A, Vol. 30, §§ 67–69. Relevant factors include the nature of the Convention right at issue, its importance for the individual and the nature of the activities concerned. If the Court finds that one or more of these factors are present, e.g., the right at stake is crucial to the individual's effective enjoyment of intimate or key rights, then the State has a narrow margin of action. If they are not, the State's action will be assessed against a wider margin of appreciation. See Harris, O'Boyle, Bates and Buckley, op. cit., pp. 349–353; Guild, Elspeth, "Global Data Transfers: The Human Rights Implications", INEX Policy Brief, No. 9, May 2009. http://www.ceps.eu/ceps/download/3400.

[18] De Hert, Paul, "Balancing Security and Liberty Within the European Human Rights Framework: A Critical Reading of the Court's Case Law in the Light of Surveillance and Criminal Law Enforcement Strategies After 9/11", *Utrecht Law Review*, Vol. 1, No. 1, 2005, pp. 68–96.

[19] A very strict test is applied in ECtHR, *AD and OD v United Kingdom*. Judgment of 2 April 2010, Application no. 28680/06 (removal of a child from his parents in the context of child care). See my discussion below.

handled.[20] The Court serves us well by announcing as a rule what kind of margin it is going to recognise, but its use of the proportionality test is far less clear and never clarified by the Court. Interpretative guesswork is then the only solution. When the Court uses phrases such as that "any interference must be proportionate to the legitimate aim pursued", i.e., must "correspond to a pressing social need",[21] then there is a strong indication that a strict test will follow. Also indicative is the search for the existence of an alternative and less intrusive solution, the so-called subsidiarity test (whether the limitation can be obtained by less permissive means).[22] Until 2001, the Court never used that test explicitly in the context of Art. 8 cases.[23] This highly political test (which judges prefer to avoid) appeared more regularly in the context of Art. 10 cases. Lately, there seems to be a rhetorical inflation in references to the strict test. Its most visible features, such as the subsidiarity test, now also appear in the context of Art. 8, although one feels that the difference between cases in which judges confront governments and cases in which judges do not confront governments is still there.[24]

Contrary to Nardell, this chapter contends that a lot of mist remains to cloud our understanding of the Court's approach to legitimate limitations of privacy. Most commentators were and are unaware of the nature of the different tests applied by the ECtHR.[25] Very often, these commentators derive from case law (often cases in the context of Art. 10) a set of requirements, suggesting frequent use of a strict test that the Court in practice is not likely to follow in all cases.

Fundamentally, I have no objection to the presence of different tests in human rights law. One cannot lose sight of the essential contestable and political nature of human rights in general, including the right to privacy.[26] There are, contrary to

---

[20] Arai-Takahashi, Yutaka, *The Margin of Appreciation Doctrine and the Principle of Proportionality in the Jurisprudence of the ECHR*, Intersentia, Antwerp, 2001, p. 2.

[21] Cf., e.g., ECtHR, *Olsson v Sweden*, Judgment of 24 March 1988, Application no. 10465/83, Series A, Vol. 130.

[22] De Hert, "Balancing Security and Liberty Within the European Human Rights Framework", op. cit., p. 90.

[23] Rare examples of implicit use are given in Harris, O'Boyle, Bates and Buckley, op. cit., p. 359.

[24] In *Hatton v. The United Kingdom* (2001), concerning noise caused by night flying at Heathrow, the Court found that States are required to minimise, as far as possible, the interference with these rights, "by trying to find alternative solutions and by generally seeking to achieve their aims in the least onerous way as regards human rights. In order to do that, a proper and complete investigation and study with the aim of finding the best possible solution which will, in reality, strike the right balance should precede the relevant project." ECtHR, *Hatton v. The United Kingdom*, Judgment of 2 October 2001, Appl. no. 36 022/97, § 97.

[25] Arai-Takahashi, op. cit. In the same vein, see also van Drooghenbroeck, Sébastien, *La proportionalité dans de le droit de la convention européenne des droits de l'homme*, Bruylant, Brussels, 2001.

[26] "A major difficulty facing the evaluation of human rights performance is that human rights are contestable. Questions about human rights give rise to pervasive disagreement, even among people who agree that human rights exist and are valuable and who share whatever cultural context is necessary to make discussion of rights meaningful. As Jeremy Waldron argues, disagreement arises in relation to 'what it means to call something a right', 'what rights we have, what they are rights to and what they are based on'. In particular, even if there is a rough or overlapping

Dworkin's notion of human rights as "trumps", not many absolutes in the European human rights framework and there is definitely not a consensus about giving the right to privacy an absolute character. Judges will therefore reserve themselves some leeway while considering privacy conflicts. In many instances, there is no external or objective standard to which the evaluator can appeal to predict the outcome of court cases. Academics cannot be assumed to be better situated through detachment to assess initiatives in comparison to the assessment made by the members of national parliaments and members of the European Parliament or other evaluators, nor can they pretend to be capable of deriving final human rights standards from case law.[27]

In the following, I discuss the requirements of a strict human rights test with regard to initiatives and technologies that limit people's exercise of the right to privacy, and this regardless of the fact whether this test would be actually chosen by the Court. It is an ideal test, consisting of a bundle of more specific tests or criteria. Together, they are suited for an honest privacy impact assessment carried out by a government or a private actor undertaking an initiative or designing the functionalities of a technology and open to critical self-assessment. It is a more or less systematic list of criteria applied and identified by the ECtHR when assessing strictly combined with the second criterion taken from the German Constitution for reasons that will be explained below. The permissible limitation test can be described as:

1. In accordance and provided by the law,
2. Serving a legitimate aim (which is not enough, it must be *necessary*),
3. Respecting the inviolability of the essence of any human right,
4. Necessary in a democratic society,

---

consensus on a set of basic rights or civil liberties such as those secured by the amendments to the US Constitution or those enshrined in the European Convention on Human Rights (ECHR), there is ferocious disagreement about what this consensus entails so far as detailed applications are concerned. Debates about rights are an inescapable part of politics. What one group may regard as a step forward for rights, another (using the same rights framework) may regard as a violation, or even an abuse, of rights". Evans, Carolyn, and Simon Evans, "Evaluating the Human Rights Performance of Legislatures", *Human Rights Law Review*, Vol. 6, No. 3, 2006, pp. 545–569 [p. 551] with reference to Waldron, Jeremy, *Law and Disagreement*, Oxford University Press, Oxford, 1999, p. 11.

[27] See Evans and Evans, op. cit., p. 551: "The contestability of human rights means that in many instances there is no external standard to which the evaluator can appeal. The evaluator cannot assume that it is possible to adopt an Olympian detachment that gives their assessment of the legislation and its compliance with human rights some objective quality superior to the assessment made by the parliament. Nor can they simply adopt the rulings of judges or tribunals on human rights as a standard. While judges and tribunals can articulate and apply legal standards derived from human rights instruments, their rulings cannot resolve the moral, political and philosophical disagreements at the heart of many rights issues. (This is not to deny the concept of disciplinary expertise in human rights. Lawyers, philosophers, historians, political scientists and others have constructed their own frameworks for analysing and understanding rights. But even among such experts there will be disagreements, different perspectives and disciplinary biases.)"

5. Providing no unfettered discretion,
6. Proportionate, appropriate, least intrusive means,
7. Consistent with other human rights.

Some of these elements are enumerated in Article 51(1) of the 2000 EU Charter on the "Scope and interpretation of rights and principles" contained in the Charter: "Any limitation on the exercise of the rights and freedoms recognised by this Charter must be provided for by law and respect the essence of those rights and freedoms. Subject to the principle of proportionality, limitations may be made only if they are necessary and genuinely meet objectives of general interest recognised by the Union or the need to protect the rights and freedoms of others."

The permissible limitation test was recently carried out by Martin Scheinin with regard to full body scanners.[28] The test turned out to be negative for the scanners based on some of the requirements taken from the list. We will come back to this later on, but it is amusing to note that Scheinin's presentation was followed by Claudia Fusco from the European Commission (Directorate General for Mobility and Transport) who presented the first results of the Commission's assessment and seemingly heading towards a more positive outcome for scanners.[29]

The seven requirements or "PIA elements" are discussed one by one below. Even if they are general knowledge to some lawyers, it is interesting to make the analysis in the light of what has been said about the data protection assessment test above. When done properly, a true qualitative assessment is within reach.

The analysis is pertinent for public *and* private actors designing technologies or implementing procedures for processing personal data. Of course, only countries and, in the future, the EU can be sued before the ECtHR. When conflicts result from initiatives taken by private actors harming citizens, Member States can be held responsible in Strasbourg for not having prevented harm to citizens' rights caused by private actors.[30] A nice illustration is offered by *Oluić* v. *Croatia* (2010) about a person living in a house confronted with the opening of a noisy bar in another part of the house. The Croatian government was sued in Strasbourg and argued that the

---

[28] Presentation at the INEX Roundtable on Body Scanners, Brussels, 27 January 2011. http://www. ceps.eu/event/roundtable-body-scanners. Professor Scheinin is UN Special Rapporteur on the promotion and protection of human rights and fundamental freedoms while countering terrorism and involved in the DETECTER (FP7) research project.

[29] Fusco, Claudia, Presentation at the INEX Roundtable on Body Scanners, Brussels, 27 January 2011. http://www.ceps.eu/event/roundtable-body-scanners

[30] Cf. ECtHR, *Hatton* v. *The United Kingdom*, Judgment of 2 October 2001, Application no. 36 022/97, § 95: "The Court notes that Heathrow airport and the aircraft which use it are not owned, controlled or operated by the Government or by any agency of the Government. The Court considers that, accordingly, the United Kingdom cannot be said to have 'interfered' with the applicants' private or family life. Instead, the applicants' complaints are to be analysed in terms of a positive duty on the State to take reasonable and appropriate measures to secure the applicants' rights under Article 8 § 1 of the Convention (see the *Powell and Rayner* v. *The United Kingdom,* Judgment of 21 February 1990, Series A, Vol. 172, § 41, and the *Guerra* v. *Italy*, Judgment of 19 February 1998, Reports 1998-I, § 58)."

case concerned a dispute between two private parties and was not an interference by the State authorities with any of the applicant's rights protected under Art. 8 of the Convention. Moreover, the government added, the applicant herself had agreed to conversion of a part of the house to a bar and therefore must have known that she would have to suffer a certain level of noise, even at night since it was common knowledge that bars were generally open at night.[31] The Court admits that human rights, including Art. 8, essentially protect against arbitrary interference by public authorities, but the same rights also create a duty for governments to take measures designed to secure respect for private life even in the sphere of relations between individuals.[32] When governments fail to do so and leave citizens unprotected or not sufficiently protected in their relationships with others, the Court finds a breach of the Convention.

2.5 The Technology Should Be Used in Accordance with and as Provided by the Law (First PIA Element)

The additional value of the privacy test in addition to the data protection test immediately surfaces when discussing this first requirement of legality. Properly speaking, there is no requirement in data protection law to have a legal basis for the processing of personal data. The requirement surfaces in Art. 7 of the Directive but is only one of the many grounds for processing, consent being the other big one. A closer look reveals that data protection laws and regulations serve themselves as the legal basis for many of the processing operations they were formulated to regulate. If you want to process data, as a private or public actor, you need to respect the data protection requirements.

The least one can say is that the legality requirement in some aspects has a more fundamental role to play within the framework of the ECHR. The legality principle is expressly laid down in Arts. 2, 5, 6 and in the second paragraphs of Arts. 8 to 11. Interferences by the executive with the rights and freedoms of the individual should not be permitted unless there is a clear legal basis to do so. By the same token, individuals should be able to predict with reasonable certainty when and under what conditions such interferences may occur. Hence. the need for a legal basis to be

---

[31] ECtHR, *Oluić* v. *Croatia*, Judgment of 20 May 2010, Application no. 61260/08, § 43.

[32] ECtHR, *Oluić* v. *Croatia*, Judgment of 20 May 2010, § 46: "Although the object of Article 8 is essentially that of protecting the individual against arbitrary interference by the public authorities, it may involve the authorities' adopting measures designed to secure respect for private life even in the sphere of relations between individuals (see, among other authorities, *Stubbings and Others* v. *The United Kingdom*, Judgment of 22 October 1996, Reports 1996-IV, pp. 1505, § 62, and *Surugiu* v. *Romania*, Judgment of 20 April 2004, Application no. 48995/99, § 59). Whether the case is analysed in terms of a positive duty on the State to take reasonable and appropriate measures to secure the applicants' rights under paragraph 1 of Article 8 or in terms of an interference by a public authority to be justified in accordance with paragraph 2, the applicable principles are broadly similar."

accessible and foreseeable featured in the first requirement of the privacy check. In the wording of the Court, the phrase "in accordance with the law" in Art. 8(2) requires "the impugned measure both to have some basis in domestic law and to be compatible with the rule of law, which is expressly mentioned in the preamble to the Convention and inherent in the object and purpose of Article 8. The law must thus be adequately accessible and foreseeable, that is, formulated with sufficient precision to enable the individual – if need be with appropriate advice – to regulate conduct. For domestic law to meet these requirements, it must afford adequate legal protection against arbitrariness and accordingly indicate with sufficient clarity the scope of discretion conferred on the competent authorities and the manner of its exercise."[33]

In previous articles, I have commented extensively on the thick legality test done by the Court.[34] Concentrating on the requirement that privacy limitations should have a legal basis allows the judges to avoid the more political proportionality test that the Court usually postpones till the end of its analysis *if* it gets that far.[35] The golden trick for Strasbourg is to see almost every privacy relevant element as one that has to do with the required legal basis. Hence, the tendency of the European Court to see minimum safeguards with regard to data (e.g., safeguards on duration, storage conditions, usage, access by third parties and preserving the integrity of data) as being part of the first requirement (legality requirement),[36] whereas the

---

[33] ECtHR, *Case of S. and Marper v. the United Kingdom*, Judgment of 4 December 2008, Application nos. 30562/04 and 30566/04, § 95 with ref. to ECtHR, *Malone v. The United Kingdom*, 2 August 1984, Series A, Vol. 82, §§ 66–68; ECtHR, *Rotaru v. Romania* [GC], no. 28341/95, *ECHR* 2000-V, § 55; and ECtHR, *Amann v. Switzerland* [GC], no. 27798/95, *ECHR* 2000-II, § 56. On *Marper*, see De Beer De Laer, Daniel, Paul De Hert, Gloria González Fuster and Serge Gutwirth, "Nouveaux éclairages de la notion de 'donnée personnelle' et application audacieuse du critère de proportionnalité. Cour européenne des droits de l'homme Grande Chambre S et Marper c. Royaume Uni, 4 décembre 2008", *Revue Trimestrielle des Droits de l'Homme*, No. 81, January 2009, pp. 141–161; De Hert, Paul, and K. Weis, "La Conservation pour une durée indéterminée d'empreintes digitales, d'échantillons cellulaires et profils A.N.D. de personnes acquittées porte atteinte au respect de leur vie privée", Comment on Marper, *Vigiles. Revue du droit de police*, Vol. 15, No. 2, 2009, pp. 79–83; González Fuster, Gloria, "TJCE – Sentencia de 04.12.2008, S. y Marper c. Reino Unido", *Revista de Derecho Comunitario Europeo*, Vol. 33, 2009, pp. 619–633.

[34] De Hert, Paul, "Balancing Security and Liberty Within the European Human Rights Framework: A Critical Reading of the Court's Case Law in the Light of Surveillance and Criminal Law Enforcement Strategies After 9/11", *Utrecht Law Review*, Vol. 1, No. 1, 2005, pp. 68–96.

[35] The Convention organs treat the requirements as successive hurdles. This means that where they find that a measure complained of is not "in accordance with the law", then they do not proceed to examine whether the measure satisfies the requirement of "necessity in a democratic society". For instance, in *P.G. and J.H. v. The United Kingdom*, § 38: "As there was no domestic law regulating the use of covert listening devices at the relevant time ..., the interference in this case was not 'in accordance with the law' as required by Article 8 § 2 of the Convention, and there has therefore been a violation of Article 8 in this regard. In the light of this conclusion, the Court is not required to determine whether the interference was, at the same time, 'necessary in a democratic society' for one of the aims enumerated in paragraph 2 of Article 8." See also Cameron, Iain, *National Security and the European Convention on Human Rights*, Kluwer Law, The Hague, 2000, p. 36.

[36] ECtHR, *S. and Marper v. The United Kingdom*, § 95 with ref. to older case law.

German Constitutional Court in its data retention judgment of 2 March 2010 treats these safeguards as elements of the third requirement (proportionality).[37]

There might be good reasons for both approaches. Politically speaking, it is less painful to tell a Member State that it has violated the Convention because of a problem with its legal basis than to pass the message that an initiative favoured by a Member State or accepted by a Member State is, in fact, "not necessary in a democratic society" and, hence, violates the Convention. There are, however, limits to this strategy. The fact that a necessary safeguard was omitted when designing a technology often qualifies better as a problem of necessity and proportionality. Like the German Court, van Drooghenbroeck seems to consider that safeguards against abuse are part of the proportionality requirement, but they are, and this deserves some emphasis, to be considered as the more formal aspects of this requirement. The other half of the requirement of proportionality, the substantive part, consists of balancing the interests at stake.[38] A fixation on the formal requirements of proportionality would not bring us any further. It would again allow our judges to avoid the more sensitive, but necessary, substantive proportionality test.

Let us return to the legality requirement. Although I am not so fond of the thick Strasbourg approach to the legality requirement, its handling by the ECtHR is not without intelligence and wit. I have already observed that this Court has gradually developed the view that a legal basis for privacy infringements should not only exist, but that it should also meet some qualitative requirements, namely, accessibility and foreseeability. In its telephone tapping case law, the Court has set minimum requirements in this respect, which must be incorporated in national legislation. Secret monitoring is nearly always rejected by the Court, unless performed by the government which will have to provide extra guarantees in doing so. Of special interest in this sense is the judgment delivered in *Liberty* v. *the United Kingdom*.[39] In the UK, all outgoing communication is subject to mass recording, filtering and profiling on the basis of key words; the legal basis for these actions is unclear.

The Court was not impressed by all the complicated terminology and *security* arguments advanced by the British government in favour of its profiling practices. Profiling or not, the subject has a right to some sort of transparency as required by the legality requirement. The Court concluded that the legality principle contained in the Convention was violated because groups of person were listened to, and monitored on the basis of undisclosed key words and on the basis of legislation

---

[37] The EU Data Retention Directive 2006/24/EC requires telecommunications companies to store data about all of their customers' communications in order to facilitate "the investigation, detection and prosecution of serious crime, as defined by each Member State in its national law". Germany implemented the Directive in 2008. Law enforcement authorities were permitted to access retained data for the investigation of serious crime. They could also request Internet users to be identified for the investigation of any type of crime. In 2010, the German Constitutional Court annulled the German data retention law for interfering disproportionately with fundamental rights (see below for more information).

[38] van Drooghenbroeck, op. cit., p. 302 et seq. See also p. 728.

[39] ECtHR, *Liberty and Others* v. *The United Kingdom*, Judgment of 1 July 2008, Application no. 58243/00.

that does not clearly indicate when their communication is intercepted and what is subsequently done with their communication. In other words, the judges evaluate the transparency problems with certain new technologies,[40] and curb them by means of a classic element from the Strasbourg case law. A new technology, but no new problem, since the old criteria apply. Profiling and mass registration are not prohibited, but based on the legality requirement, the Court forces them to come out of the shadows of secrecy. When the legal basis of proposed governmental measures is not adequate, the "provided by law" test fails.[41]

2.5.1 Open Questions About the Transparency and Legality Requirement

To implement the legality requirement in practice does not seem easy. Several factors contribute to a lot of secrecy towards citizens. The problem of non-transparency by private actors can in theory be resolved by insisting on informed consent and using consumer pressure. The WikiLeaks turmoil of December 2009 shows that many in government still believe in secrecy. Amusing too is the debate about the article by Lichtblau and Risen in *The New York Times* revealing the Bush administration's secret SWIFT operation,[42] followed by a *mea culpa* by the newspaper's public editor sometime later.[43] Even in the body scanners debate, there remains much secrecy, such as data on the costs of these machines and their health implications, bringing Martin Scheinin to the legitimate conclusion that no proper assessment is possible if all the cards are not on the table.[44]

A problem of another order has to do with the question about when to regulate. Normally, technology needs to be tested out in practice. How can one regulate something that is not yet fully operational? Can governments and industry be innovative if everything they do has to be preceded by proper, rational and public decision-making? The question is a hard one. Advocating *privacy by design* and moulding technology in a human, friendly way, on the one hand, and not allowing trial and error, on the other hand, seem difficult to combine. Keeping body scanners for years in the labs without deploying them until the privacy-friendly version is developed

---

[40] Transparency is often one of the weakest facets of emerging technologies, especially in the security area. See, for example, González Fuster, Gloria, Serge Gutwirth and Erika Ellyne, "Profiling in the European Union: A High-Risk Practice", *INEX Policy Brief*, No. 10, 2010, p. 5.

[41] ECtHR, *Liberty and Others* v. *The United Kingdom*, § 69.

[42] Lichtblau, Eric, and James Risen, "Bank Data Is Sifted by U.S. in Secret to Block Terrorism", *The New York Times*, 23 June 2006.

[43] Calame, Byron, "Banking Data: A Mea Culpa", *The New York Times*, 22 October 2006. http://www.nytimes.com/2006/10/22/opinion/22pubed.html?pagewanted=2. Calame is the public editor at *The Times*. Bill Keller, the executive editor, disagreed with the mea culpa, as apparently did the publisher. See Brisbane, Arthur S., "Bill Keller Responds to Column on Swift Mea Culpa", *The New York Times*, 6 November 2006. http://publiceditor.blogs.nytimes.com/2006/11/06/bill-keller-responds-to-column-on-swift-mea-culpa/

[44] Scheinin, Martin, Presentation at the INEX Roundtable on Body Scanners, Brussels, 27 January 2011.

and all possible tests are effectuated does not look realistic. The EU 2008 Civil Aviation Security Regulation seems to be driven by the need to create some room for local experiments.[45] The Preamble states that the Regulation seeks to revise a former EU law [Regulation (EC) No 2320/2002] "in the light of the experience gained" (Recital 4), by responding to the need "for more flexibility in adopting security measures and procedures in order to meet evolving risk assessments and to allow new technologies to be introduced" (Recital 5). As a result, Art. 6 of the Regulation allows more stringent measures to be applied by Member States when acting "on the basis of a risk assessment and in compliance with Community law". "Those measures shall be relevant, objective, non-discriminatory and proportional to the risk that is being addressed. Member States shall inform the Commission of such measures as soon as possible after their application. Upon reception of such information, the Commission shall transmit this information to the other Member States" [Art. 6(2)]. Some room for experimentation is thus created. However, there is still the requirement to comply with Community law and the Regulation does not detail how the Member States need to guarantee the transparency required by the human rights framework. It is not my purpose to solve this matter here, if ever the matter can be settled, but the problem of regulating technology while in the meantime developing it further seems to be a very hard one for law to tackle, but if we do not consider it, Europe will outsource innovation to other continents and will never take the lead in technology development.

Another issue which needs discussion is the matter of publishing privacy impact assessments. There are a lot of good reasons to make privacy impact assessments publicly available (see Chapter 1 and section 2.10.3 below), but then what? As long as the quality of the assessments is not fully guaranteed, this may create some distortion in public perception. Munday seems to assume that impact assessments will never be undisputed, because they always fit a certain agenda, and deplores their use by Courts as sources of understanding legislation.[46] Requiring a legal basis for mandatory impact assessments is one thing, but then using impact assessment as a legal source in disputes or legal interpretation is another thing.

2.6 The Technology or Processing Should Serve a Legitimate Aim (Second PIA Element)

Art. 8(2) requires that any interference with the right to privacy must be: (1) prescribed by law (i.e., legality), (2) necessary in democratic society (i.e., necessity) and (3) serve the certain public interest (i.e., legitimacy). The second paragraph enumerates the following list of legitimate purposes: "There shall be no interference

---

[45] European Parliament and Council, Regulation (EC) No 300/2008 of 11 March 2008 on common rules in the field of civil aviation security, *Official Journal*, L 97, 9 April 2008, pp. 72–84.

[46] Munday, Roderick, "In the Wake of 'Good Governance': Impact Assessments and the Politicisation of Statutory Interpretation", *The Modern Law Review*, Vol. 71, No. 3, 2008, pp. 385–412.

by a public authority with the exercise of this right except such as is in accordance with the law and is necessary in a democratic society *in the interests of national security, public safety or the economic well-being of the country, for the prevention of disorder or crime, for the protection of health or morals, or for the protection of the rights and freedoms of others*" [italics added]. This long, broad list of legitimate purposes is very government and industry friendly. Frankly speaking, the Court does very little with the legitimacy requirement, in particular, when compared to the attention that goes to the purpose limitation principle within data protection regulations. If the Court has an approach to the legitimacy requirement, it is mainly a negative one and consists of saying that serving a legitimate aim is not enough and that more is needed in terms of the other requirements, in particular, the necessity requirement. A paragraph taken from *Hatton* (2001) allows us to illustrate this point: "States have a positive duty to take reasonable and appropriate measures to secure the applicants' rights under Article 8 and to strike a fair balance between the competing interests of the individual and of the community as a whole. *In the particularly sensitive field of environmental protection, mere reference to the economic well-being of the country was not sufficient to outweigh the rights of others.* States were required to minimise, as far as possible, the interference with these rights, by trying to find alternative solutions and by generally seeking to achieve their aims in the least onerous way as regards human rights" [italics added].[47]

It might well be that more contact with data protection sensibilities, in particular, with the complex and rich principle of use limitation, creates a new understanding in Strasbourg of the legitimacy test within the context of Art. 8 of the Convention. The way ahead is given to us by the 16 December 2008 judgment of that other European Court, the ECJ based in Luxembourg, in *Heinz Huber* v. *Germany*.[48] The proceedings dealt with the existence in Germany of a centralised, nation-wide database containing information on non-German EU citizens for the sake of applying the law relating to the right of residence, and its use by German authorities for crime-fighting. The register was in place even though no similar register had ever been created to store equivalent information on German citizens, so no equivalent processing of German citizens' personal data ever took place. The European Court of Justice was required to examine different questions[49] in relation to the existence of such a database and the secondary use of its content. It soon appeared that the

---

[47] ECtHR, *Hatton* v. *The United Kingdom*, Judgment of 2 October 2001, Application No. 36 022/97, § 97.

[48] European Court of Justice, *Huber* v. *Germany,* Case C-524/06, Judgment of 16 December 2008, following a request for a preliminary ruling made by the Higher Administrative Court of the federal state of North-Rhine Westphalia, in proceedings between an Austrian national resident in Germany (Mr. Huber) and the Federal Republic of Germany (hereafter, *Huber*). This part of my analysis borrows from González Fuster, Gloria, Paul De Hert, E. Ellyne and Serge Gutwirth, "Huber, Marper and Others: Throwing New Light on the Shadows of Suspicion", *INEX Policy Brief*, No. 11, June 2010. http://www.ceps.eu/book/huber-marper-and-others-throwing-new-light-shadows-suspicion

[49] Concretely, whether the storage of personal data of foreign citizens of the EU in a central register, when no equivalent storage applies for nationals, is compatible with the prohibition of discrimination of nationality against EU citizens who exercise their right to move and reside freely within the EU territory, with the prohibition of restrictions on the freedom of establishment of

issue of discrimination was at the very core of the case. Indeed, the European Court of Justice concluded that the discussed database was not contrary to Community law insofar as it contained only the data necessary for the application of the residence legislation, and insofar as its centralised nature enabled such legislation to be more effectively applied.[50] However, it established that its use for crime-fighting purposes had to be interpreted as putting in place a system for processing personal data precluded by the principle of non-discrimination of EU citizens.[51] In its assessment, the Court took the view that, as the fight against crime necessarily involves the prosecution of crimes and offences committed irrespective of the nationality of their perpetrators, it follows that, as regards a Member State, the situation of its nationals cannot be different in relation to this objective from that of non-national EU citizens who are resident in its territory.[52] The importance of the *Huber* judgment lies in the emphasis put on the effects of foreseeing secondary uses of information originally stored for other purposes. It warns against the temptation, apparently regularly experienced by policy-makers, to allow for the use of any existing database or available data for the purpose of crime-fighting.[53]

The duty to specify purposes will remain an important yardstick to assess future technologies. It obliges the responsible person to put his or her cards on the table, to say what he or she has in mind and to allow others to judge on the basis of that. *Huber* teaches us that a database set up for a legitimate purpose cannot be used in all cases to serve other interests even when they are legitimate too. The concern for discrimination does not allow any possible secondary use even for legitimate purposes.

2.7 The Technology Should Not Violate the Core Aspects of the Privacy Right (Third PIA Element)

One of the interesting features of the German Constitution – a constitution particularly apt to frame technologies[54] – is enshrined in Art. 19(2): "In no case may the essence of a basic right be affected." There is a need to refer to these kinds

---

nationals of a Member State in the territory of another Member State and with the requirement of necessity under Article 7(e) of the Data Protection Directive (94/46/EC).

[50] The ECJ expressly stated that the storage and processing of personal data in such a register for statistical purposes could not, in any case, be considered necessary in that sense.

[51] As established by Article 12(1) of the Treaty the European Community (TEC), now Article 18(1) of the Treaty on the Functioning of the European Union (TFEU): "Within the scope of application of the Treaties, and without prejudice to any special provisions contained therein, any discrimination on grounds of nationality shall be prohibited."

[52] European Court of Justice, *Huber*, §§ 78–79.

[53] See, for instance: European Commission, *Proposal for a Council Framework Decision on the exchange of information under the principle of availability,* COM(2005) 490 final, Brussels, 12 October 2005, p. 10.

[54] See the conclusions in Leenes, Ronald, Bert-Jaap Koops and Paul De Hert (eds.), *Constitutional Rights and New Technologies: A Comparative Study*, T.M.C. Asser Press (Information Technology & Law Series, Vol. 15), The Hague, 2008.

of warnings when testing new technologies that allow for total tracking and surveillance of individuals. In its famous judgment on digital identity of 15 December 1983 (the *Volkszählungsurteil*), the German Constitutional Court recognised a right to self-determination with regard to personal data.[55] The Court stated that the individual needs to "be protected from unlimited collection, storage, use, and transmission of personal data as a condition of the development of his or her free personality under the modern conditions of data processing". With unequalled precision, the Court of Karlsruhe explained in detail the shift of power that takes place whenever the state or private actors interact with an individual through ICT. The Constitutional Court reasoned that a person's knowledge that his or her actions are being watched inevitably curtails his or her freedom to act.

Twenty-five years later, on 27 February 2008, the German Constitutional Court gave a ruling about the constitutionality of secret online searches of computers by government agencies and added a new right, namely "the right to confidentiality and integrity of information systems".[56] It considered those searches to be contrary to this newly recognised basic right.[57] The court pondered that informational-technical systems, including laptops, PDAs and mobile phones, "alone or in their technical interconnectness … makes it possible to get insight into relevant parts of the conduct of the life of a person or even gather a meaningful picture of the personality". This affects the right to self-determination of the individual who might refrain, for instance, from opening a web-blog or disseminating e-mails. Hence, the need to recognise a right to confidentiality and integrity of information systems. The Court limits exceptions to this right to specific cases where exist "factual indications for a concrete danger" for the life, body and freedom of persons or for the foundations of the state or the existence of human beings, and declares that state spying measures can only be implemented after approval by a judge. Moreover, secret online searches must in any case be constrained by ad hoc technical measures not to interfere with "the core area of the conduct of private life".

As mentioned above, there is no similar provision in the ECHR prohibiting the emptying out of existing rights completely, but in *Uzun* (2010), there is a reference to "total and comprehensive surveillance" as a frontier not to be trespassed within the context of European human rights law.[58] The "German" requirement is explicitly taken on board of Art. 51(1) of the 2000 EU Charter containing the general

---

[55] *BVerfGE* 65 E 40. The new right was based on the *allgemeines Persönlichkeitsrecht*, as protected by Article 1 (human dignity) in conjunction with Article 2 (right of liberty) of the German Constitution.

[56] Published on 27 February 2008 (*OnlineDurchsuchung*, 1 BvR 370/07; 1 BvR 595/07).

[57] This right should be seen as a complement to the 1983 "fundamental right to informational self-determination" (see above).

[58] ECtHR, *Uzun* v. *Germany*, § 80: "The Court considers that in these circumstances, the applicant's surveillance via GPS had led to a quite extensive observation of his conduct by two different State authorities. In particular, the fact that the applicant had been subjected to the same surveillance measures by different authorities had led to a more serious interference with his private life, in that the number of persons to whom information on his conduct had become known had been increased. Against this background, the interference by the applicant's additional surveillance via

principles for understanding EU rights: "Any limitation on the exercise of the rights and freedoms recognised by this Charter must be provided for by law and *respect the essence of those rights and freedoms.*" [Italics added.]

The requirement that technologies and processing may never violate the essence of any human right reminds us that there is, properly speaking, no choice between restrained review or assertive scrutiny. Only assertive scrutiny based on a strict proportionality test will give real answers needed from a human rights perspective.[59] A weak proportionality test, consisting of a mere balancing of a fundamental right and another interest – for example, privacy and crime control – does not, in fact, offer any guarantee for the preservation of that fundamental right, since the approach itself assumes that preserving the one by definition implies the weakening of the other. It excludes the possibility that both interests can be fostered and protected together. Such a proportionality test is doomed to weigh one interest *against* the other, and makes impossible the search for a *reconciliation* in which the different interests at stake are all preserved in an optimal way.[60]

GPS thus necessitated more compelling reasons if it was to be justified. However, the GPS surveillance was carried out for a relatively short period of time (some three months), and, as with his visual surveillance by State agents, affected him essentially only at weekends and when he was travelling in S.'s car. *Therefore, he cannot be said to have been subjected to total and comprehensive surveillance*" [italics added]. See also ECtHR, *von Hannover* v. *Germany,* Judgment of 24 June 2004, Application no. 59320/00. In this judgment, the Court recognised that "the protection of private life has to be balanced against the freedom of expression guaranteed by Article 10 of the Convention", but it found that the German courts did not strike a fair balance between the competing rights and that there was a violation of Article 8 of the Convention. Partly this reasoning can be brought back to the idea that States should never give one right or interest total priority over others, unless the case concerns absolute rights such as those incorporated in Articles 2-4 of the Convention. See Harris, O'Boyle, Bates and Buckley, op. cit., p. 355.

[59] The following borrows from de Vries, Katya, Rocco Bellanova, Paul De Hert and Serge Gutwirth, op. cit. A shorter version of this article is published as de Vries, Katya, Rocco Bellanova and Paul De Hert, "Proportionality overrides Unlimited Surveillance: The German Constitutional Court Judgment on Data Retention", in CEPS Liberty and Security in Europe publication series, CEPS, Brussels, 2010. http://www.ceps.eu/book/proportionality-overrides-unlimited-surveillance

[60] "The balancing metaphor is dangerous because it suggests no principled basis for deciding how much torture we should facilitate, or for how many years we should jail people without trial. It leaves that decision up to politicians who are anxious to pander to the tabloids. The metaphor is deeply misleading because it assumes that we should decide which human rights to recognise through a kind of cost-benefit analysis, the way we might decide what speed limits to adopt. It suggests that the test should be the benefit to the British public, as Blair declared in his 'Let's talk' speech, when he said that 'the demands of the majority of the law-abiding community have to take precedence'. This amazing statement undermines the whole point of recognising human rights; it is tantamount to declaring that there are no such things. Most political decisions require a cost-benefit balancing in which disadvantages to some are outweighed by the overall benefit to the community. Building a new airport is bound to disadvantage some people, but the damage is justified if it is the best choice for the nation. However, some injuries to individuals are so grave that they cannot be justified by declaring that that is what the public wants. A civilised society recognises rights precisely to protect individuals from these grave harms." Dworkin, Ronald, "It Is Absurd to Calculate Human Rights According to a Cost-Benefit Analysis", *The Guardian*, 24 May 2006. http://www.guardian.co.uk/commentisfree/2006/may/24/comment.politics

Such criticism, however, does not apply to stronger proportionality tests that include the possibility to decide that some measures are unacceptable from a constitutional point of view – an exercise known to the Strasbourg court as the "necessary in a democratic state" test – since they encompass the possibility to refuse a measure because it harms the essence of a fundamental right or of the constitutional order, even if it can be shown that this measure can effectively realise another legitimate interest. The issue at stake then is not a "balancing" between two values, but an answer to the questions: "How much erosion of a fundamental right is compatible with the democratic constitutional State in which fundamental rights are a constitutive element?" or "In which society, do we want to live?". Another aspect of a stronger proportionality test is, indeed, the obligation to explore if there are alternative measures that allow for the realisation of the legitimate interest in a way that does not affect the fundamental rights in the same way as the proposed measure. That is, in other words, answering the question: "Is there a way to protect and enforce both values without loss of the fundamental rights?"

2.8 The Technology Should Be Necessary in a Democratic Society (Fourth PIA Element)

The next element in a privacy impact assessment concerns the question of whether a technology and the processing of data it allows can be deemed "necessary in a democratic society". I introduced this requirement in the preceding paragraph and above (see section 2.4) where I discussed the Court's tendency to substitute a test of strict scrutiny by a weaker version in some cases.

In the context of Art. 10 ECHR (freedom of expression), the Court has observed that "necessary ... is not synonymous with *indispensable*, neither has it the flexibility of such expressions as *admissible, ordinary, useful, reasonable* or *desirable,* but that it implies a *pressing social need".*[61] Not many cases with regard to Art. 8 echo this insistence on "necessity being something more than useful". Almost always, the necessity requirement is brought back to the question of proportionality, in some cases, supplemented by the requirement that the reasons for the interference are relevant and sufficient.[62] As observed above, there is some recent change, at least in the rhetoric. In *Peck* (2003), one can find a reference to the idea of "a

---

[61] ECtHR, *Handyside* v. *The United Kingdom*, Judgment of 7 December 1976, § 48.

[62] Compare with §76 of the *Peck* judgment: "In determining whether the disclosure was 'necessary in a democratic society', the Court will consider whether, in the light of the case as a whole, the reasons adduced to justify the disclosure were 'relevant and sufficient' and whether the measures were proportionate to the legitimate aims pursued" (ECtHR, *Peck* v. *The United Kingdom,* Judgment of 28 January 2003, Application no. 44647/98). We will come back to the proportionality test below, but we observe here that true impact assessments should go beyond the proportionality principle for reasons advanced above in section 2.7. It is therefore to be regretted that the Court often limits itself to the legality test and, whenever it goes beyond, seldom refers to the idea of a pressing social need.

pressing need".[63] Similarly, one reads in *Uzun* (2010) that in "determining whether the applicant's surveillance via GPS as carried out in the present case was 'necessary in a democratic society', the Court reiterates that the notion of necessity implies that the interference corresponds to a pressing social need and, in particular, that it is proportionate to the legitimate aim pursued."[64]

My view on this should be clear by now: it is indisputable that, in the area of technologies and processing operations, the question of necessity needs to be thoroughly assessed. It is simply not acceptable to assume that the government, consisting of political representatives with certain interests, and industry with its proper interest is always acting in good faith with regard to this requirement. Consider, for instance, the hypothesis where governments are reacting to public opinion, not to real security threats. In such a situation, the assessment will be that the necessity test probably fails. Equally, there is a failure where there is doubt about the effectiveness of certain measures or when there is a possibility of avoidance behaviour.[65] Of course, one cannot help but think about recent debates on biometrics and data retention. Avoidance behaviour seems to be at the heart of the discussion with regard to data retention. A January 2011 study by the civil liberties organisation *AK Vorrat*, itself based on an analysis by the German Federal Crime Agency (BKA), reveals that data retention, while in force, did not make the prosecution of serious crime any more effective.[66] According to *AK Vorrat*, user avoidance behaviour could account for the counter-productive effects of blanket data retention on the investigation of crime.[67]

---

[63] Note the use of the term "pressing social need" in the following quote: "In such circumstances, the Court considered it clear that, even assuming that the essential complaints of *Smith and Grady* before this Court were before and considered by the domestic courts, the threshold at which those domestic courts could find the impugned policy to be irrational had been placed so high that it effectively excluded any consideration by the domestic courts of the question of whether the interference with the applicants' rights answered a pressing social need or was proportionate to the national security and public order aims pursued, principles which lay at the heart of the Court's analysis of complaints under Article 8 of the Convention." ECtHR, *Peck* v. *The United Kingdom*, Judgment of 28 January 2003, Application no. 44647/98, § 100.

[64] ECtIIR, *Uzun* v. *Germany*, § 78 with ref. to *Leander* v. *Sweden*, 26 March 1987, § 58, Series A, Vol. 116; and *Messina* v. *Italy (no. 2)*, no. 25498/94, § 65, ECHR 2000-X.

[65] Scheinin, op. cit.

[66] For a study on data retention effectiveness, see Arbeitskreis Vorratsdatenspeicherung [Working Group on Data Retention], "Serious criminal offences, as defined in sect. 100a StPO, in Germany according to police crime statistics", [German] Federal Crime Agency (BKA), 19 February 2011. http://www.vorratsdatenspeicherung.de/images/data_retention_effectiveness_report_2011-01-26.pdf. With data retention in effect, more serious criminal acts (1,422,968 in 2009) were registered by police than before (1,359,102 in 2007), and a smaller proportion were cleared up (76.3% in 2009) than before the introduction of blanket retention of communications data (77.6% in 2007). Likewise, after the additional retention of Internet data began in 2009, the number of registered Internet offences surged from 167,451 in 2008 to 206,909 in 2009, while the clear-up rate for Internet crime fell (from 79.8% in 2008 to 75.7% in 2009).

[67] "In order to avoid the recording of sensitive information under a blanket data retention scheme, users begin to employ Internet cafés, wireless Internet access points, anonymization services, public telephones, unregistered mobile telephone cards, non-electronic communications channels and such like. This avoidance behaviour can not only render retained data meaningless but also

The alternative is to return to good old-fashioned, targeted collection of traffic data and even the German Minister of Justice Sabine Leutheusser-Schnarrenberger is now advocating shifting the Directive to a targeted investigative approach, involving the collection of data on suspect communications only.[68]

2.8.1 Necessity, Evidence and Politics

Evidence is crucial in the debate on necessity. Gathering evidence before launching an initiative is a prerequisite and the idea for impact assessments naturally fits this. In *Hatton*, the understandable need for studies is underlined together with the very amusing notion of "measures necessary for protecting the applicant's rights".[69]

> The Court would... underline that in striking the required balance, States must have regard to the whole range of material considerations. Further, in the particularly sensitive field of environmental protection, mere reference to the economic well-being of the country is not sufficient to outweigh the rights of others. The Court recalls that in the... *Lopez Ostra* v. *Spain* case, and notwithstanding the undoubted economic interest for the national economy of the tanneries concerned, the Court looked in considerable detail at 'whether the national authorities took the measures necessary for protecting the applicant's right to respect for her home and for her private and family life ...' (judgment of 9 December 1994, p. 55, § 55). It considers that States are required to minimise, as far as possible, the interference with these rights, by trying to find alternative solutions and by generally seeking to achieve their aims in the least onerous way as regards human rights. In order to do that, a proper and complete investigation and study with the aim of finding the best possible solution which will, in reality, strike the right balance should precede the relevant project.[70]

When discussing the proportionality test (understood as the fair balance requirement) below, I will come back to this duty to study the impacts of initiatives that limit human rights.

Evidence gathered through studies is crucial in the debate on necessity, but so is politics. To draw the line between illegitimate and legitimate (or necessary) is essentially a political decision. Constitutional courts in Member States take up this responsibility. It is an open question whether the ECtHR is well positioned to do that

---

frustrate more targeted investigation techniques that would otherwise have been available to law enforcement. Overall, blanket data retention can thus be counterproductive to criminal investigations, facilitating some, but rendering many more futile." See German Working Group on Data Retention (AK Vorrat), "Study Finds Telecommunications Data Retention Ineffective", 27 January 2011. http://www.vorratsdatenspeicherung.de/content/view/426/79/lang,en/

[68] Statement by the German Secretary of Justice: http://www.eu2011.hu/de/video/Doorstep_von_Deutscher_Justiz-Staatssekret%C3%A4r_Max_Stadler

[69] The notion is amusing: to pass the necessity test, States often have to take certain necessary measures to limit the limitation of the right in question.

[70] EHRM, *Hatton v. The United Kingdom*, Judgment of 2 October 2001, Application no. 36 022/97, § 97 with ref. to ECtHR, *Lopez Ostra v. Spain*, Judgment of 9 December 1994, Series A, Vol. 303-C, p. 55, § 55.

too, but the Convention in principle obliges the Court to do it.[71] A bit of it is present in the 2008 *S. and Marper* v. *UK* judgment,[72] provoked by two non-convicted individuals who wanted to have their records removed from the DNA database used for criminal identification in the United Kingdom.[73] They built their case on Art. 8 (right to privacy) and Art. 14 (non-discrimination).[74] The Court approached the case with assertive scrutiny in the light of the sensibility of the technologies and their privacy impact,[75] and the end result of the analysis sounds bluntly political:

> In conclusion, the Court finds that the blanket and indiscriminate nature of the powers of retention of the fingerprints, cellular samples and DNA profiles of persons suspected but not convicted of offences, as applied in the case of the present applicants, fails to strike a fair balance between the competing public and private interests and that the respondent State has overstepped any acceptable margin of appreciation in this regard. Accordingly, the retention at issue constitutes a disproportionate interference with the applicants' right to respect for private life and cannot be regarded as necessary in a democratic society. *This conclusion obviates the need for the Court to consider the applicants' criticism regarding the adequacy of certain particular safeguards, such as too broad an access to the personal data concerned and insufficient protection against the misuse or abuse of such data* [italics added].[76]

Certain of my colleagues and I have called for this political approach to privacy in our earlier writings.[77] Checking on data protection requirements is important but drawing a line between illegitimate and legitimate use of power in a democratic State by answering the question "What kind of processing do we really *not* want?" sometimes comes first.[78] Innocent people should not be included in databases dedicated to criminal identification and mainly destined to the storage of data of convicted

---

[71] Cf. section 2.10.1 below. When discussing *Hatton*, we will see that the Court retracts when the United Kingdom attacks the Court on this political role.

[72] ECtHR, *S. and Marper* v. *The United Kingdom*, Judgment of 4 December 2008, Applications nos. 30562/04 and 30566/04.

[73] More concretely, they asked for their fingerprints, cellular samples and DNA profiles, which had been obtained by police, to be destroyed as criminal proceedings against them had ended with an acquittal or had been discontinued (*Marper*, § 3).

[74] Article 6(2) (right to be presumed innocent until proven guilty according to law) was not referred to, but references to the values underlying this civil right were integrated into the Court's arguments.

[75] ECtHR, *S. and Marper* v. *The United Kingdom*, Judgment of 4 December 2008, Applications nos. 30562/04 and 30566/04, § 104: "The interests of the data subjects and the community as a whole in protecting the personal data, including fingerprint and DNA information, may be outweighed by the legitimate interest in the prevention of crime (see Article 9 of the Data Protection Convention). However, the intrinsically private character of this information calls for the Court to exercise careful scrutiny of any State measure authorising its retention and use by the authorities without the consent of the person concerned."

[76] ECtHR, *S. and Marper* v. *The United Kingdom*, Judgment of 4 December 2008, Applications nos. 30562/04 and 30566/04, § 125.

[77] De Hert, Paul, and Serge Gutwirth, op. cit., p. 104.

[78] Compare the use of the term "obviates" by the Court in § 125.

people. The mere storage of such information conveys by itself a risk of stigmatisation;[79] shadows of suspicion are projected upon those whose data is stored. Therefore, the storage of such data, when related to non-convicted individuals, has to be limited and stopped.

The *Marper* dictum is political in the sense that the Court draws a clear line between legitimate and illegitimate power based on a principled view. It does so in an explicit way. After having looked at the statistics and the numbers advanced by the UK government in defence of the broad sampling of people that the police encounter, the Court – unconvinced by these numbers – shrugged its shoulders and turned to the real stuff, namely, principles such as privacy and other rights and the need to curb excessive power.[80]

Often, the Court will argue for disproportionality on a less principled basis. It will find "arbitrariness" when a system is put in place that does not afford adequate legal protection against power, where the legal basis does not indicate with sufficient clarity the scope of discretion conferred on the competent authorities and the manner of its exercise.[81]

Only when illegitimate power is blocked and legitimate use of power is properly limited can the use of technologies and processing of data be considered in accordance with the requirements of the ECHR.[82] The argument that one is only showing the way to others and that others will follow when the benefits of new technologies are more clearly understood does not help. On the contrary, "having a pioneer role in the development of new technologies bears special responsibility for striking the right balance".[83]

---

[79] ECtHR, *S. and Marper* v. *The United Kingdom*, § 122. Moreover, the Court highlighted that the stigmatisation can be especially harmful when minors are concerned (Ibid., § 124). For a discussion of the significance of the judgment in terms of warning against risks of stigmatisation, see Bellanova, Rocco, and Paul De Hert, "Le cas S. et Marper et les données personnelles: l'horloge de la stigmatisation stoppée par un arrêt européen", *Cultures & Conflits*, No. 76, 2010, pp. 15–27.

[80] Cf. ECtHR, *S. and Marper* v. *The United Kingdom*, §§ 117–118: "While neither the statistics nor the examples provided by the Government in themselves establish that the successful identification and prosecution of offenders could not have been achieved without the permanent and indiscriminate retention of the fingerprint and DNA records of all persons in the applicants' position, the Court accepts that the extension of the database has nonetheless contributed to the detection and prevention of crime. The question, *however*, remains whether such retention is proportionate and strikes a fair balance between the competing public and private interests" [italics added].

[81] ECtHR, *Case of S. and Marper* v. *The United Kingdom*, Application nos. 30562/04 and 30566/04, Strasbourg, 4 December 2008, § 95 with ref. to ECtHR, *Malone* v. *The United Kingdom*, 2 August 1984, Series A, Vol. 82, §§ 66–68; ECtHR, *Rotaru* v. *Romania* [GC], no. 28341/95, *ECHR* 2000-V, § 55; and ECtHR, *Amann* v. *Switzerland* [GC], no. 27798/95, *ECHR* 2000-II, § 56.

[82] The judgment reviews different national approaches in Europe to collection and retention of DNA information in the context of criminal proceedings, and notes that the UK is the only Council of Europe Member State expressly to permit the systematic and indefinite retention of DNA profiles and cellular samples of persons who have been acquitted or in respect of whom criminal proceedings have been discontinued.

[83] ECtHR, *S. and Marper* v. *The United Kingdom*, §§ 111–112: "The Government lay emphasis on the fact that the United Kingdom is in the vanguard of the development of the use of DNA

2.9 The Technology Should Not Have or Give Unfettered Discretion (Fifth PIA Element)

The question "How should the applicable limits for legitimate uses of power be determined?" brings us to the requirement of legal safeguards against abuse and the requirement of proportionality. Both are strongly linked, but the Court's approach is particular. In the *Marper* judgment, the ECtHR underlined that the core principles of data protection require the retention of data to be proportionate in relation to the purpose of collection and insist on the importance of foreseeing limited periods of storage.[84] The Court's approach is particular in the sense that it tends to see the requirement of legal safeguards against abuse as part of the legality requirement as discussed above (section 2.5),[85] but even when a case passes the legality check, the test on legal safeguards will resurface when assessing proportionality and necessity. In other words, even if safeguards *are* provided (i.e., legality check), they must be *then* (subsequently) assessed if they safeguard *sufficiently* (proportionality check).

In section 2.5 above, I observed that secret surveillance is nearly always rejected by the Court, unless performed by the government which will have to provide extra guarantees in doing so.[86] When these guarantees are absent, the "provided by law" test fails. In *Uzun*, the Court recalled case law that goes back to older cases concerning telephone tapping and said that in view of the risk of abuse intrinsic to any

---

samples in the detection of crime and that other States have not yet achieved the same maturity in terms of the size and resources of DNA databases. It is argued that the comparative analysis of the law and practice in other States with less advanced systems is accordingly of limited importance. The Court cannot, however, disregard the fact that, notwithstanding the advantages provided by comprehensive extension of the DNA database, other Contracting States have chosen to set limits on the retention and use of such data with a view to achieving a proper balance with the competing interests of preserving respect for private life. The Court observes that the protection afforded by Article 8 of the Convention would be unacceptably weakened if the use of modern scientific techniques in the criminal justice system were allowed at any cost and without carefully balancing the potential benefits of the extensive use of such techniques against important private-life interests. In the Court's view, the strong consensus existing among the Contracting States in this respect is of considerable importance and narrows the margin of appreciation left to the respondent State in the assessment of the permissible limits of the interference with private life in this sphere. The Court considers that any State claiming a pioneer role in the development of new technologies bears special responsibility for striking the right balance in this regard."

[84] ECtHR, *S. and Marper* v. *The United Kingdom*, § 107.

[85] Cf. "Under the Court's case-law, the expression 'in accordance with the law' within the meaning of Article 8 § 2 requires, firstly, that the measure should have some basis in domestic law; it also refers to the quality of the law in question, requiring it to be accessible to the person concerned, who must, moreover, be able to foresee its consequences for him, and compatible with the rule of law" (ECtHR, *Uzun* v. *Germany*, § 60 with ref. to ECtHR, *Kruslin* v. *France*, Judgment of 24 April 1990, § 27, Series A, Vol. 176-A; ECtHR, *Lambert* v. *France*, 24 August 1998, *Reports of Judgments and Decisions* 1998-V, § 23; and ECtHR, *Perry* v. *The United Kingdom*, no. 63737/00, *ECHR* 2003-IX, § 45). In section 2.5 above, I quoted paragraph 95 of *Marper* where the Court clarifies that the requirement to be compatible with the rule of law "is expressly mentioned in the preamble to the Convention and inherent in the object and purpose of Article 8".

[86] See also Harris, O'Boyle, Bates and Buckley, op. cit., pp. 402–403.

system of secret surveillance – lack of public scrutiny and risk of misuse of power – such measures must be based on a law that is particularly precise, especially as the technology available for use is continually becoming more sophisticated.[87] Needed are "adequate and effective guarantees against abuse" and the assessment depends on all the circumstances of the case, such as the nature, scope and duration of the possible measures, the grounds required for ordering them, the authorities competent to permit, carry out and supervise them, and the kind of remedy provided by national law.[88]

Since the famous *Klass* judgment, we know through the findings of the Court that these guarantees can take different forms depending on whether they are carried out by criminal law magistrates or by secret services.[89] *Uzun* teaches us that the nature of the technology and the way people are surveilled is a second important factor. The Court underlines that surveillance via GPS of movements in public places is to be distinguished from other methods of visual or acoustical surveillance in that it discloses less information on a person's conduct, opinions or feelings and thus interferes less with his or her private life. The Court, therefore, does not see the need to apply the same strict safeguards against abuse that it had developed in its case law on the interception of telecommunications, such as the need to precisely define the limit on the duration of such monitoring or the procedure for using and storing the data obtained.

I do not know on what basis or authority the Court reaches this particular finding and I see reasons to disagree. But that is not how constitutional law-making by Courts works. Again politics, again different tests, etc., even with regard to the choice of adequate and effective guarantees against abuse. In *Uzun*, the Court states

§ 65. As to the law's foreseeability and its compliance with the rule of law, the Court notes at the outset that in his submissions, the applicant strongly relied on the minimum safeguards which are to be set out in statute law in order to avoid abuses as developed by the Court in the context of applications concerning the interception of telecommunications. According to these principles, the nature of the offences which may give rise to an interception order; a definition of the categories of people liable to have their communications monitored; a limit on the duration of such monitoring; the procedure to be followed for examining, using and storing the data obtained; the precautions to be taken when communicating the data to other parties; and the circumstances in which data obtained may or must be erased or the records destroyed, have to be defined in statute law.[90]

---

[87] ECtHR, *Uzun* v. *Germany*, § 62 with ref. to ECtHR, *Weber and Saravia* v. *Germany*, Admissibility decision of 29 June 2006, Application no. 54934/00, § 93, *ECHR* 2006-XI; ECtHR, *Association for European Integration and Human Rights and Ekimdzhiev* v. *Bulgaria*, Judgment of 28 June 2007, Application no. 62540/00, § 75; ECtHR, *Liberty and Others* v. *The United Kingdom*, Judgment of 1 July 2008, Application no. 58243/00, § 62 and ECtHR, *Iordachi and Others* v. *Moldova*, Judgment of 10 February 2009, Application no. 25198/02, § 39.

[88] ECtHR, *Uzun* v. *Germany*, § 63 with ref. to ECtHR, *Association for European Integration and Human Rights and Ekimdzhiev*, § 77.

[89] ECtHR, *Klass and Others* v. *Germany*, Judgment of 6 September 1978, Series A, Vol. 28, § 50.

[90] The Court refers to ECtHR, *Weber and Saravia*, § 95, with further references.

§ 66. *While the Court is not barred from gaining inspiration from these principles, it finds that these rather strict standards, set up and applied in the specific context of surveillance of telecommunications* (see also *Association for European Integration and Human Rights and Ekimdzhiev*, cited above, § 76; *Liberty and Others*, cited above, § 62; and *Iordachi and Others*, cited above, § 39), *are not applicable as such to cases such as the present one*, concerning surveillance via GPS of movements in public places and thus a measure which must be considered to interfere less with the private life of the person concerned than the interception of his or her telephone conversations (see paragraph 52 above). It will therefore apply the more general principles on adequate protection against arbitrary interference with Article 8 rights as summarised above (see para 63) [italics added].

So in § 66 of *Uzun*, the Court refers us back to the "general principles on adequate protection" as laid down in § 63 of *Uzun*. There, one finds nothing more than the message that this assessment "depends on all the circumstances of the case, such as the nature, scope and duration of the possible measures, the grounds required for ordering them, the authorities competent to permit, carry out and supervise them, and the kind of remedy provided by the national law". When this is too vague, one simply has to take the strict requirements spelled out in § 65 and "find inspiration in them".

2.10 The Technology Should Be Appropriate, Least Intrusive and Proportionate (Sixth PIA Element)

Having been a cold lover of the ECtHR since my formative years, it is with some tongue in cheek that I now introduce the next privacy requirement, namely, "proportionality". Literally, this term is not in the text of the Convention – Art. 8(2) speaks about "necessity in a democratic society" – but everybody refers to the term. Proportionality today is clearly one famous requirement that all judges and lawyers like. This success is puzzling. Thirty years ago, "proportionality" was denied any legal or added value in most legal systems.[91] The last 20 years have witnessed the constant and gradual recognition of "proportionality" or "fair balance" as an instrument to interpret and apply law, and to assess conflicting interests and the goals of an action against the damage generated by the action.[92]

There is a lot to say in *favour* and *against* the use of proportionality. Critics put forward the proposition that recognising proportionality's legal value hampers the normative, prescriptive dimension of law. Also, fair balance as a principle has been criticised by voluntarist scholars for reflecting the realist legal approach.[93]

Our main problem here has to do with the lack of transparency that enfolds the Court's approach to the proportionality requirement. It is almost always the main

---

[91] van Drooghenbroeck, op. cit., p. 9.

[92] van Drooghenbroeck, op. cit., p. 10.

[93] van Drooghenbroeck, op. cit., pp. 12 and 71.

yardstick when addressing necessity,[94] but sadly enough in some judgments, it becomes the only one, reducing judicial review to a mere State-friendly, balancing act. Moreover, its elaboration is complex and the complexity is never sustained. So one has to trust the academic authors and their account of the Court's approach to understand its use by the European Court. Most will simply single out that what is "proportionate" will depend on the circumstances. According to Delmas-Marty, in determining proportionality, the Court takes particularly into account the nature of the measure taken (its breadth, whether it is general or absolute, its adverse consequences, the scope for abuse of the measure), whether the State concerned could have taken other measures or implemented them in a less drastic way, the status of the persons involved whose rights can legitimately be subject to greater limitation (e.g., prisoners) and, finally, whether there are any safeguards which can compensate for the infringement of rights which a measure can create.[95] Others, such as Scheinin, see proportionality *sensu lato* as a denominator for three components or requirements.[96] First, the national interference with a right guaranteed by the Convention must be appropriate to attain the legitimate goal pursued by the interference (requirement of appropriateness). Second, the interference must be necessary. What will be at stake here is the whole spectrum of means that would have enabled the legitimate goal to be attained (requirement of the least intrusive method). Third, the proportionality requirement *sensu stricto* refers to the balancing of the interests actually at stake on a case-by-case basis (the fair balance requirement).

In section 2.5 above, I referred to van Drooghenbroeck, who distinguished between the more formal aspects of the proportionality requirement and the substantive part in which the balancing of the interests at stake is done. The data protection requirements discussed at the beginning of this chapter are playing an increasingly important role when checking on the formal requirements of proportionality. The Court might conclude that a Member State violates the ECHR when it sets up processing operations without due respect to data protection regulations or when allowing private actors to process data without proper respect for these regulations. In *I* v. *Finland*, the Court held that security measures taken by a Finnish hospital, which were intended to guarantee observance of the privacy of an HIV patient working as a nurse in that same hospital, were inadequate and constituted

---

[94] Compare ECtHR, *Uzun* v. *Germany*, § 78: "In determining whether the applicant's surveillance via GPS as carried out in the present case was 'necessary in a democratic society', the Court reiterates that the notion of necessity implies that the interference corresponds to a pressing social need and, in particular, that it is proportionate to the legitimate aim pursued." See also Harris, O'Boyle, Bates and Buckley, op. cit., p. 349.

[95] Delmas-Marty, Mireille, *The European Convention for the Protection of Human Rights: International Protection Versus National Restrictions*, Martinus Nijhoff, Dordrecht, 1992, p. 26.

[96] Presentation at the INEX Roundtable on Body Scanners, Brussels, 27 January 2011. Cf. Harris, O'Boyle, Bates and Buckley, op. cit., p. 359.

a violation of Art. 8 of the ECHR.[97] To reach this finding, the Court first considered Finnish legislation regarding the use of personal data, the Personal Files Act of 1987. Article 26 of that Act requires the processing party to take security measures to ensure that only attending medical staff have access to the file. For the Court, the decisive point was that the records system in place in the hospital was clearly not in accordance with the legal requirements contained in section 26 of the Personal Files Act, a fact that was not given due weight by the domestic courts of Finland. Strict application of this provision, the ECtHR held, would have constituted effective protection within the meaning of Article 8 ECHR and would have allowed the hospital to monitor access to the data and prevent any disclosure of health records.[98]

The decision of the ECtHR is a clear demonstration of the importance of data protection requirements such as information security as part of the more formal proportionality test. The right to information security is a right that all citizens enjoy when data concerning them – and not only sensitive data – are being processed. Given that the right to privacy is a fundamental right, information security can be seen as a right safeguarding a fundamental right.[99]

2.10.1 Appropriateness and the Least Intrusive Method

As mentioned above, Scheinin and others see proportionality *sensu lato* as a denominator for three components or requirements: the requirement of appropriateness, the requirement for the least intrusive method and the fair balance requirement.

The first two requirements have been touched upon above, enabling us to be sparse with our comments. Whenever there is doubt about the efficiency of a technology, the proportionality test may fail.[100] Similarly, the test may fail when one has not chosen the least intrusive method or when no evidence is provided to show

---

[97] ECtHR, *I* v. *Finland*, Judgment of 17 July 2008, Application no. 20511/03. See also Råman, Jari, "European Court of Human Rights: Failure to Take Effective Information Security Measures to Protect Sensitive Personal Data Violates Right to Privacy – *I* v. *Finland*, no. 20511/03, 17 July 2008", *Computer Law & Security Report*, Vol. 24, No. 6, 2008, pp. 562–564.

[98] ECtHR, *I* v. *Finland*, § 40. Also §§ 47–49: "What is required in this connection is practical and effective protection to exclude any possibility of unauthorised access occurring in the first place. Such protection was not given here. The Court cannot but conclude that at the relevant time the State failed in its positive obligation under Article 8 § 1 of the Convention to ensure respect for the applicant's private life. There has therefore been a violation of Article 8 of the Convention."

[99] "Information security has changed – or at least is in the process of changing – *from a technical aid to a legal value.*" Saarenpää, Ahti, "The Importance of Information Security In Safeguarding Human and Fundamental Rights", Stockholm, 18 November 2008. http://www.juridicum.su.se/Iri/e08/documentation/ahti_saarenpaa-information_security_and_human_rights-paper.pdf

[100] Scheinin challenges on these grounds the need to install body scanners. The purpose and security principles are easy to avoid, since terrorists can adjust their tactics, and this is even more so when choice is introduced, and some passengers are allowed for reasons, such as health and religion, not to go through the scanner.

that the claim of necessity was made out.[101] *Craxi* (2003) and, in particular, *Peck* (2003) offer nice illustrations of these two tests.[102] In both cases, the Court looked at the intrusiveness of the action, the identity of the applicant and the availability of other means of achieving the purpose. In *Peck*, a judgment about a case in which a local council gave CCTV images showing a particular citizen to the media only to promote its security policies, the Court announced its check on appropriateness and the least intrusive method in the following terms: "In determining whether the disclosure was 'necessary in a democratic society', the Court will consider whether, in the light of the case as a whole, the reasons adduced to justify the disclosure were 'relevant and sufficient' and whether the measures were proportionate to the legitimate aims pursued."[103] By announcing these checks, one immediately feels that this time the European judges will really look at the case as a whole. That also happens. The Court did not dispute that CCTV systems are important for detecting and preventing crime and that the release of CCTV material with the aim of promoting their effectiveness in the prevention and detection of crime could render their role more successful. However, at least three alternatives are available for the local Council to allow it to achieve the same objectives: obtaining consent of the person filmed prior to disclosure; masking the relevant images or obliging the media to mask those images. The Council did not explore the first and second options. The Court also considered that the steps taken by the Council in respect of the third were inadequate. Accordingly, the disclosures by the Council of the CCTV material to media such as the BBC were not accompanied by sufficient safeguards to prevent disclosure inconsistent with the guarantees of respect for the applicant's private life contained in Art. 8 of the Convention. "As such, the disclosure constituted a disproportionate and therefore unjustified interference with his private life and a violation of Article 8 of the Convention."[104]

In section 2.7 above, I said that, properly speaking, there is no impact assessment possible without assertive scrutiny and this will often be accompanied by checks on appropriateness and the least intrusive method. A lot of security technology is used to "reassure" people.[105] Logical as this seems from a political perspective, it may not pass the proportionality check. Evidence in this regard is fundamental

---

[101] Harris, O'Boyle, Bates and Buckley, op. cit., p. 359.

[102] ECtHR, *Peck* v. *The United Kingdom,* Judgment of 28 January 2003 (to hand over CCTV images to the media violates Art. 8 ECHR and in particular the requirement of proportionality and subsidiarity, since other alternatives to make publicity for the CCTV initiative exist) and *Craxi (no. 2)* v. *Italy*, Judgment of 17 July 2003, § 124 (violation of Art. 8 ECHR since there is no "pressing social need, no proportionality and no necessity for handling private material about an ongoing trial to a newspaper").

[103] ECtHR, *Peck* v. *The United Kingdom,* Judgment of 28 January 2003, § 76.

[104] ECtHR, *Peck* v. *The United Kingdom,* Judgment of 28 January 2003, § 87. On *Peck*, see also Harris, O'Boyle, Bates and Buckley, op. cit., p. 413.

[105] Easton, Marleen, Lodewijk Moor, Bob Hoogenboom, Paul Ponsaers and Bas van Stokkom (eds.), *Reflections on Reassurance Policing in the Low Countries*, Boom Juridische Uitgevers, The Hague, 2008.

and evidence-gathering is therefore required. This closes the circle. To check on legitimate limitations of rights, one needs evidence and to obtain the green light from a human rights perspective, evidence-gathering is a prerequisite.[106]

The existence of such circle, which I would label the circle of assessment, is, however, an object of contestation. *Hatton* – a case on deprivation of sleep by exposure to noise from airplanes – was dealt differently by the Court Chamber (2001) and by the Grand Chamber (2003).[107] Before the Grand Chamber, the UK government simply challenged in the name of politics the use by the Court Chamber of the least intrusive method test,[108] *and* challenged the capacity of the Court to look at the evidence-gathering done by the British government.[109] This frontal attack worked reasonably well[110] – the UK won its case – and forced the Court to adapt its strategy. In cases "with conflicting views as to the margin of appreciation",[111] an assessment of the substantive merits will be complemented (i.e., will be replaced

---

[106] The need for evidence and procedures to build up evidence also surfaces in the third proportionality test, the fair balance requirement. See below.

[107] The case of *Hatton* concerns state responsibility for pollution generated by Heathrow airport. A strict assertive test by the Court Chamber finding the United Kingdom in breach of its obligation to protect people's right to privacy was replaced by a simple balancing test by the Grand Chamber finding no such breach in 2003. See ECtHR, *Hatton* v. *The United Kingdom*, Judgment of 2 October 2001, Application no. 36 022/97 and ECtHR (Grand Chamber), *Hatton* v. *United Kingdom*, Judgment of 8 July 2003. See also Harris, O'Boyle, Bates and Buckley, op. cit., p. 391.

[108] In its letter requesting that the case be referred to the Grand Chamber, and in its written and oral observations to the Grand Chamber, the government strongly objected to the "minimum interference" approach outlined by the Chamber in paragraph 97 of its judgment. The government argued that this test in the context of this type of case was at odds with a consistent line of Convention jurisprudence and was unwarranted in principle. They submitted that "the test reduced to the vanishing point the margin of appreciation afforded to States in an area involving difficult and complex balancing of a variety of competing interests and factors" [ECtHR (Grand Chamber), *Hatton* v. *The United Kingdom*, Judgment of 8 July 2003, § 87].

[109] "They accepted that inherent in the striking of a fair balance was a need to be sufficiently informed in relation to the relevant issues, in order to avoid making or appearing to make an arbitrary decision. However, the decision-making process was primarily for the national authorities, in this case, the government, subject to judicial review by the domestic courts. The European Court's powers in this context were supervisory: in the absence of any indication of an arbitrary or clearly inadequate investigation, a detailed and minute critique of the information which the government should take into account was neither necessary nor appropriate" (ECtHR (Grand Chamber), *Hatton* v. *The United Kingdom*, Judgment of 8 July 2003, § 89).

[110] "The Court reiterates the fundamentally subsidiary role of the Convention. The national authorities have direct democratic legitimation and are, as the Court has held on many occasions, in principle better placed than an international court to evaluate local needs and conditions (see, for example, *Handyside* v. *The United Kingdom*, Judgment of 7 December 1976, Series A, Vol. 24, p. 22, § 48). In matters of general policy, on which opinions within a democratic society may reasonably differ widely, the role of the domestic policy-maker should be given special weight (see *James and Others* v. *The United Kingdom*, Judgment of 21 February 1986, Series A, Vol. 98, p. 32, § 46, where the Court found it natural that the margin of appreciation 'available to the legislature in implementing social and economic policies should be a wide one')." ECtHR (Grand Chamber), *Hatton* v. *The United Kingdom*, Judgment of 8 July 2003, § 97.

[111] ECtHR (Grand Chamber), *Hatton* v. *The United Kingdom*, Judgment of 8 July 2003, § 103.

almost entirely) by an assessment of the decision-making process.[112] Hence, there is a need for a double fair balance or proportionality test: one of the rights at stake and one of the procedures implemented by Member States when starting up a technology or a processing operation.

This "new" fair balance requirement is the subject of the next section.

2.10.2 The Fair Balance Requirement, Evidence and Precaution

The fair balance seems to be the one golden trick that allows lawyers to come up with whatever answer.[113] If taken seriously, it is a requirement that allows the inclusion of a broad range of interests. In human rights law, it aims to assess whether or not a national interference with a right guaranteed, taking the form of a national authority's measure or the lack of such measure, even though interfering with the rights guaranteed by the Convention, does nevertheless respect the Convention's requirements. By requiring that all interests present, for instance, in environmental affairs, be duly identified and taken into account, the fair balance technique is meant to operate a balance between diverging and conflicting interests: on the one hand, the interests of the community as a whole being achieved through the measure having a legitimate goal and, on the other hand, the specific interests of the applicant.

What matters from our perspective in the two *Hatton* judgments is not the practical outcome of the case but the insistence in both judgments by both Courts on evidence-gathering and the decision-making process when operating the fair balance test. In the 2001 judgment, the Court held that:

> Whatever analytical approach was adopted, regard must be had to the fair balance that had to be struck between the competing interests of the individual and the community as a whole. In both contexts, the State enjoyed a certain margin of appreciation in determining the steps to be taken to ensure compliance with the Convention. The Chamber underlined that in striking the required balance States must have regard to the whole range of material considerations. Further, in the particularly sensitive field of environmental protection, mere reference to the economic well-being of the country was not sufficient to outweigh the rights of others. The Chamber considered that States were required to minimise, as far as possible, interference with Art. 8 rights, by trying to find alternative solutions and by generally seeking to achieve their aims in the least onerous way as regards human rights. In order to do that, a proper and complete investigation and study, with the aim of finding the best possible solution which would, in reality, strike the right balance, should precede the relevant project.[114]

---

[112] "The Court considers that in a case such as the present one, involving State decisions affecting environmental issues, there are two aspects to the inquiry which may be carried out by the Court. First, the Court may assess the substantive merits of the government's decision, to ensure that it is compatible with Article 8. Secondly, it may scrutinise the decision-making process to ensure that due weight has been accorded to the interests of the individual." ECtHR (Grand Chamber), *Hatton* v. *The United Kingdom*, Judgment of 8 July 2003, § 99.

[113] See *Hatton*, discussed in the preceding paragraph.

[114] ECtHR, *Hatton* v. *The United Kingdom*, Judgment of 2 October 2001, § 96–97.

This is not the first time the duty to study in advance, to gather evidence, is introduced as a human rights prerequisite.[115] In environmental cases, it is now accepted that authorities have a duty to assess satisfactorily in advance what risks an activity could create and that they have to take the appropriate measures to protect the rights of those concerned.[116] But the duty to collect evidence also works the other way around. In *Oluić v. Croatia* (2010), a case dealing with a noisy bar, the Court looked back at its former case law concerning the State's duty to protect citizens from excessive noise in several cases. It identified seven noise-related cases in which it did not find a breach of the Convention,[117] and advanced one simple explanation: lack of evidence from the applicants.[118] Both sides before the Court have to adduce evidence: the applicants that they suffer specific adverse effects or that States have not taken relevant measurements and the authorities that they have respected the requirements taken from the Convention and have set up and followed acceptable decision-making procedures.[119] In *Fägerskiöld v. Sweden*, a case concerning noise

---

[115] The Grand Chamber in its 2003 judgment on the same case picks up this more procedural part of the fair balance test and makes it a decisive element in its approach. See ECtHR (Grand Chamber), *Hatton v. United Kingdom*, Judgment of 8 July 2003, § 104. We recall that even the UK government did not dispute the relevance of a good decision procedure, although it challenged the ability of the European Court to do more than a marginal checking. See the discussion of § 89 of *Hatton* (2003) above.

[116] ECtHR, *Tatar v. Romania*, Judgment of 27 January 2009, Application no. 67021/01, § 112.

[117] "Thus it found that no disturbance incompatible with the requirements of Article 8 of the Convention had been suffered by the applicants as regards aircraft noise (see *Hatton and Others*, §§ 11–27 and 116–118; and *Ashworth and Others* v. *The United Kingdom*, Admissibility decision of 20 January 2004, Application no. 39561/98); noise from an electric transformer (see *Ruano Morcuende* v. *Spain*, Admissibility Decision of 6 September 2005, Application no. 75287/01); noise from a wind turbine (see *Fägerskiöld* v. *Sweden*, Admissibility Decision of 26 February 2008, Application no. 37664/04); noise from a tailoring workshop (see *Borysiewicz* v. *Poland*, Judgment of 1 July 2008, Application no. 71146/01, §§ 5 and 52–55); noise from a lorry maintenance and metal-cutting and grinding workshop (see *Leon and Agnieszka Kania* v. *Poland*, Judgment of 21 July 2009, Application no. 12605/03, §§ 5 and 101–103,); or noise emanating from a dentist's surgery (see *Galev* v. *Bulgaria* (dec.), Judgment of 29 September 2009, Application no. 18324/04)." ECtHR, *Oluić* v. *Croatia*, Judgment of 20 May 2010, Application no. 61260/08, § 50.

[118] ECtHR, *Oluić* v. *Croatia*, Judgment of 20 May 2010, § 51: "In reaching its conclusions in the above-mentioned cases the Court relied on findings such as that the level of noise had not exceeded acceptable levels; that the applicants had failed to show that they had suffered specific adverse effects; or that no relevant measurements had been carried out."

[119] This State responsibility extends to rights-limiting initiatives set up by private parties. ECtHR, *Oluić* v. *Croatia*, Judgment of 20 May 2010, § 46: "Although the object of Article 8 is essentially that of protecting the individual against arbitrary interference by the public authorities, it may involve the authorities' adopting measures designed to secure respect for private life even in the sphere of relations between individuals (see, among other authorities, *Stubbings and Others* v. *The United Kingdom*, Judgment of 22 October 1996, *Reports* 1996-IV, pp. 1505, § 62, and *Surugiu* v. *Romania*, no. 48995/99, § 59, 20 April 2004). Whether the case is analysed in terms of a positive duty on the State to take reasonable and appropriate measures to secure the applicants' rights under paragraph 1 of Article 8 or in terms of an interference by a public authority to be justified in accordance with paragraph 2, the applicable principles are broadly similar. In both contexts

by wind turbines erected not far from the applicants' house, the applicants submitted that the wind turbines' operation allowed by national authorities constituted an infringement with their right to property and their right to family and private life.[120] The Court found the applicants' submissions to be ill-founded and their case was found not admissible.[121] The main problem was evidence: insufficient evidence was brought to establish that the applicants had been physically affected by the nuisance and the applicants had also failed to provide evidence of housing prices to establish that the wind turbines had decreased the value of their house. In its fair balance test the Court started from a very favourable view on wind turbines.[122] The Court then recalled that States enjoy a wide margin of appreciation in matters raising environmental issues, and then underlined that "the nuisance caused to the applicants by the wind turbine cannot be considered so severe as to affect them seriously or impinge on their enjoyment of their property."[123]

It is interesting to note that in *Fägerskiöld* the Court refused to qualify the noise at stake as environmental pollution, relying explicitly on international standards such as those defined by the World Health Organisation to assess whether or not the noise could qualify as a pollution. Equally interesting is the Court's sensibility to constant review of the evidence. The Court took note of the diverse remedies available to the applicants while "a constant review of the measures already taken and the opportunity to request further measures are available to the applicants through the Environmental Code."[124]

Where there is a lack of evidence, precaution steps in. It is not required, the Court holds, that decisions can only be taken if comprehensive and measurable data are available in relation to each and every aspect of the matter to be decided.[125] However, this does not mean that when measuring is impossible, everything becomes possible. In *Tatar* (2009), the Court turned to the precautionary principle. After having underlined the progressive recognition of the precautionary principle in EU texts, the Court reported on the European Court of Justice case law establishing that States can adopt measures when there remain uncertainties concerning the existence or extent of risks for human health.[126] Applying

---

regard must be had to the fair balance that has to be struck between the competing interests of the individual and of the community as a whole."

[120] ECtHR, *Fägerskiöld* v. *Sweden,* Admissibility Decision of 26 February 2008.

[121] Ibid.

[122] "The Court must have regard to the positive environmental consequences of wind power for the community as a whole while also considering its negative impact on the applicants." Note that the precise paragraph from which this quote is taken cannot be identified in the decision since this admissibility decision, contrary to judgments, has no internal structure.

[123] Ibid.

[124] Ibid.

[125] ECtHR, *Taskın and Others* v. *Turkey,* Judgment of 10 November 2004, Application no. 46117/99, § 118.

[126] ECtHR, *Tatar* v. *Romania,* Judgment of 27 January 2009, Application no. 67021/01, § 69. This paragraph is followed by several pages on the relevant international legal sources, including

the idea of precaution, the Court calls upon States not to delay the adoption of effective and proportionate measures aimed at preventing the risk of serious and irreversible damages to the environment when scientific or technical certainties are lacking.[127]

In *AD and OD* v.*United Kingdom* [128] concerning a child with several fractures to his ribs being placed with foster parents, uncertainty, duty of care and need for evidence through risk assessments are nicely woven into a conceptual whole.[129] The Court first reiterated that mistaken assessments by professionals do not automatically render governmental measures incompatible with the requirements of Art. 8. Later on, it was proven that the child suffered a disease, a brittle bone disease that is difficult to diagnose in small children. The Court stated that although experts later found that the child indeed had suffered from the disease from birth, it did not follow that the medical evidence relied on at an earlier stage had been inadequate, confused or inconclusive. The Court therefore considered that the authorities could not be blamed for not reaching an earlier diagnosis of the disease or, in the absence of such a diagnosis, acting on the assumption that the injury could have been caused by the parents. The Court was not satisfied, however, that it had been necessary to relocate the family far from their home for the purpose of conducting a risk assessment. As a matter of fact, two flaws with the risk assessment were found. First, it was done too late in the process. The child might never have been placed in foster care. Second, the assessment itself did not satisfy the requirement of less intrusive measures (see below). Less intrusive measures would have been available for conducting a risk assessment, such as placement with relatives. The Court found that the local authority had dismissed those possibilities too quickly.

---

a discussion of the precautionary principle and of the cases ECJ, 5 May 1998, *United Kingdom* v. *Commission,* C-180/96, and ECJ, 5 May 1998, *National Farmer's Union*, C-157/96.

[127] ECtHR, *Tatar* v. *Romania*, Judgment of 27 January 2009, Application no. 67021/01, § 109.

[128] ECtHR, *AD and OD v United Kingdom*, Judgment of 2 April 2010, Application no. 28680/06.

[129] The case leading to the judgment is a very sad one. During medical examinations a few months after O.D.'s birth, physicians noticed several fractures to his ribs. Given the nature of the fractures and the lack of any clear explanation for them, a paediatrician concluded that they were sustained "non-accidentally". The paediatrician dismissed the possibility, raised by the mother A.D., that O.D. might have brittle bone disease (*Osteogenesis Imperfecta*). The local authority applied for an interim care order, which was granted by the county court. The family was required to relocate to a family resource centre so that a risk assessment could be made. The instructions given to the centre were ambiguous, and during the family's 12-week stay a parenting assessment was conducted instead of a risk assessment. In the absence of a risk assessment, the local authority believed that O.D. could not safely remain with the parents and decided to place the child with foster parents. As stated above, it was subsequently found that the child did suffer from brittle bone disease. The mother (and the child) turned to Strasbourg on the basis of Articles 8 and 13 (lack of effective remedy) ECHR.

2.10.3 The Fair Balance Requirement, Stakeholder Participation and Impact Assessments

Of interest to us is the Court's insistence on stakeholder participation. The fair balance requirement calls for the applicant's interests to be duly considered and licences given after a fair procedure allowing all stakeholders to be heard. In *Hatton* (2003), it said that

> In connection with the procedural element of the Court's review of cases involving environmental issues, the court is required to consider all the procedural aspects, including the type of policy or decision involved, the extent to which the views of individuals (including the applicants) were taken into account throughout the decision-making procedure, and the procedural safeguards available.[130]

In *Giacomelli* (2006)[131] – a judgment in a case of a citizen living close to a plant that obtained a permit to treat toxic waste – the Court recalled the *Hatton* finding that initiatives with an environmental impact on human rights require appropriate studies and investigations to be conducted. The public must have access to the studies and investigations' conclusions, and the possibility to appeal to Courts to challenge a refusal to provide access to these conclusions or the refusal to conduct studies or investigations. In the case at hand, the Court found the environmental impact assessment not to have been conducted before the operation of the company's activities, but seven years after the company began its activities.[132] The Italian Ministry of the Environment found twice that the plant's operation did not meet environmental regulations.[133] Nevertheless, the administrative authorities had not ordered the closure of the facility.[134] Consequently, the Court found that

> the procedural machinery provided for in domestic law for the protection of individual rights, in particular the obligation to conduct an environmental impact assessment prior to any project with potentially harmful environmental consequences and the possibility for any citizens concerned to participate in the licensing procedure and to submit their own observations to the judicial authorities and, where appropriate, obtain an order for the suspension of a dangerous activity, were deprived of useful effect in the instant case for a very long period.[135]

---

[130] ECtHR (Grand Chamber), *Hatton* v. *United Kingdom*, Judgment of 8 July 2003, § 104. Even the UK government did not dispute the relevance of a good decision procedure, although it challenged the ability of the European Court to do more than a marginal checking. See our discussion of § 89 of *Hatton* (2003) above.

[131] ECtHR, *Giacomelli* v. *Italy*, Judgment of 2 November 2006, Application no. 59909/00, §§ 82–83.

[132] Ibid. §§ 86–88.

[133] Ibid. § 89.

[134] Ibid. §§ 92–93.

[135] Ibid. § 94.

Accordingly, the Court concluded that the fair balance requirement was not met since the applicant's interest not to suffer from the effects of pollution caused by a plant could not have been properly acknowledged by national authorities.[136]

Evidence needs not only to be obtained but also to be shared. In *Tatar*, concerning the operation of dangerous mines, impact assessments had been carried out in time, but not made public. The Court reiterates that authorities had to ensure public access to the conclusions of investigations and studies and that the State had a duty to guarantee the right of members of the public to participate in the decision-making process concerning environmental issues. It stressed that the failure of the Romanian government to inform the public, in particular, by not making public the 1993 impact assessment on the basis of which the operating licence had been granted, had made it impossible for members of the public to challenge the results of that assessment.[137] The importance of access to studies is double: it enables members of the public to assess the danger or risks to which they are exposed and it enables them to appeal to the courts against any decision, act or omission where they consider that their interests or their comments have not been given sufficient weight in the decision-making process.[138]

The decision-making process needs to be open for all stakeholders involved.[139] Judgments like *Giacomelli* and *Tatar* build further on the principles developed in *Hatton* and seemingly go one step further in the direction of requiring true impact assessments. In *Giacomelli*, the Italian government was blamed for not conducting an impact assessment which is necessary for every project with potentially harmful environmental consequences as prescribed also by national law.[140]

A document drafted by the European Working Group on the Environment[141] rightly observed that even though the Court has not yet used the term "environmental impact assessment" to describe the procedural aspect of Art. 8,[142] the Court appears

---

[136] "The Court considers that the State did not succeed in striking a fair balance between the interest of the community in having a plant for the treatment of toxic industrial waste and the applicant's effective enjoyment of her right to respect for her home and her private and family life." Ibid. § 97.

[137] ECtHR, *Tatar v. Romania*, Judgment of 27 January 2009, Application no. 67021/01. The Court further noted that this lack of information had continued after an accident in January 2000, despite the probable anxiety of the local people.

[138] ECtHR, *Taskın and Others v. Turkey*, Judgment of 10 November 2004, § 119.

[139] However, an *actio popularis* to protect the environment is not envisaged by the Court and therefore only those specifically affected have a right to participate in the decision-making. See Steering Committee for Human Rights (Cddh), Committee of Experts for the Development of Human Rights (DH-DEV), Working Group on the Environment (GT-DEV-ENV), *Decision-making process in environmental matters and public participation in them*, Draft nr. GT-DEV-ENV(2011)_Draft_11_PII-SecA-ChV, Strasbourg, 21 December 2010, p. 3. http://www.coe.int/t/e/human_rights/cddh/3._Committees/

[140] See ECtHR, *Giacomelli v. Italy*, Judgment of 2 November 2006, Application no. 59909/00, § 94.

[141] Steering Committee for Human Rights, op. cit., p. 4.

[142] It has only found that States neglected to conduct environmental impact assessment studies that were prescribed by national law (see *Giacomelli v. Italy* above).

to require more and more impact assessments to fulfil the evaluation requirements set out by it.[143]

Further case law is required to clarify the scope of the duty to study the impact of certain technologies and initiatives, also outside the context of environmental health. Regardless of the terms used, one can safely adduce that the current human rights framework requires States to organise solid decision-making procedures that involve the persons affected by technologies. No fair balancing is possible without proper and transparent impact assessment. Art. 8 does not contain an explicit procedural requirement, but the decision-making process leading to measures of interference must be fair and such as to afford due respect to the interests of the individual as safeguarded by the article.[144] This requirement of fairness implies at least that evidence is gathered and that the impact of technologies are studied in advance, that the public has access to this evidence and that individuals can come up in court against decisions that, they feel, do not take their viewpoint into consideration.[145]

2.11 The Technology Should Not Only Respect Privacy Requirements But Also Be Consistent with Other Human Rights (Seventh PIA Element)

Let us return to Scheinin's negative assessment of body scanner technology. Our feeling is that the outcome of his analysis is partly due to a larger assessment exercise, going beyond privacy and data protection. Body scanners, Scheinin holds, affect primarily the right to privacy, but also the rights to non-discrimination, movement, bodily integrity and religion. The discriminatory dimension resides in the fact that many women experience greater intrusion when going through a body scanner, that some religious groups consider the scan to be of an intolerable level of intrusion and that the technology targets persons with disabilities and transgender persons.[146]

---

[143] "This is supported by the Court's finding against Romania in *Tatar* which was based partially on the conclusion that the national authorities had failed in their duty to assess in advance possible risks of their activities in a satisfactory manner and take adequate measures capable of protecting specifically the right to private and family life and, more generally, the right to the enjoyment of a healthy and protected environment." Steering Committee for Human Rights, op. cit., p. 4.

[144] ECtHR, *Taskın and Others* v. *Turkey,* Judgment of 10 November 2004, Application no. 46117/99, § 118.

[145] ECtHR, *Tatar* v. *Romania*, Judgment of 27 January 2009, § 88.

[146] Presentation at the INEX Roundtable on Body Scanners, Brussels, 27 January 2011. For a similar finding, see the Opinion of 16 February 2011 by the European Economic and Social Committee (EESC) on the use of body scanners in EU airports. The Opinion points at several omissions in the Commission Communication on the use of security scanners and urges the Commission to produce a thorough proportionality test in order to determine the necessity of their implementation versus alternative measures. The EESC suggests that the Commission seriously consider alternatives and that it might be better to wait for more precise and less intrusive technology which can recognise security hazards. As there exists no conclusive proof that these scanners

The more positive assessment of the body scanners presented at the same occasion by Claudia Fusco from the European Commission (Directorate General for Mobility and Transport) largely depended on the omission of these gender and religious elements. In this context, one can note that the European Parliament demanded a human rights impact assessment, which is wider in scope than a privacy impact assessment.[147]

From a human rights perspective, it makes sense to go to a full assessment of risks and threats. The notion of "fairness" discussed in the preceding paragraph leaves no room for selective assessments. The impact of technology affecting the environment goes well beyond the right to privacy.[148] The same is true for other technologies. In *Huber* (2008),[149] already discussed, the Advocate General appointed to the case, Poiares Maduro, insisted on the discriminatory nature of the processing of the registered personal data for the sake of crime fighting.[150] The importance of the *Huber* judgment lies in the emphasis put on the issue of discrimination and in particular on the indirect effects of foreseeing secondary uses of information originally stored for other purposes. Not the privacy-related nature of the data, but its potential discriminatory use is the problem.

A second reason for testing technologies and processing operations in the light of human rights has to do with the absolute nature of certain rights, such as the right

---

do not pose health risks to individuals, the EESC requests that the Commission provide a thorough scientific examination proving that passengers and personnel who fly frequently will not be exposed to any health risks. The Committee also reminded the Commission that its Communication did not include guarantees of effective recourse for passengers and personnel undergoing the scans, and failed to include guarantees that passengers will not be obliged to undergo body scanning, ensuring individuals reserve the right to "opt out" while not suffering longer wait times, more intrusive pat-downs, or be prevented from flying. See European Economic and Social Committee (EESC), Opinion on Use of Security Scanners at EU airports, 16–17 February 2011. http://eescopinions.eesc.europa.eu/viewdoc.aspx?doc=//esppub1/esp_public/ces/ten/ten429/en/ces361-2011_ac_en.doc. See also MacDonald, Reagan, "EESC Condemns Body Scanners as a Breach of Fundamental Rights", *EDRi-gram*, Number 9.4, 23 February 2011. http://www.edri.org/edrigram/number9.4/body-scanners-breach-privacy.

[147] See the European Parliament resolution of 23 October 2008 on the impact of aviation security measures and body scanners on human rights, privacy, personal dignity and data protection. http://www.europarl.europa.eu/sides/getDoc.do?pubRef=-//EP//TEXT+TA+P6-TA-2008-0521+0+DOC+XML+V0//EN

[148] See the discussion of all relevant rights, other than privacy, in Chope, Charles, "Preparation of an additional protocol to the European Convention on Human Rights, on the right to a healthy Environment", Rapporteur, Opinion presented to the Committee on Legal Affairs and Human Rights, Council of Europe, Doc. 1204329, September 2009. http://assembly.coe.int/Documents/WorkingDocs/Doc09/EDOC12043.pdf

[149] European Court of Justice, *Huber* v. *Germany*, Case C-524/06, Judgment of 16 December 2008, following a request for a preliminary ruling made by the Higher Administrative Court of the federal state of North-Rhine Westphalia, in proceedings between an Austrian national resident in Germany (Mr. Huber) and the Federal Republic of Germany.

[150] *Opinion of Advocate General Poiares Maduro in Case C-524/06 (Heinz Huber v Bundesrepublik Deutschland)*, delivered on 3 April 2008.

to life and the prohibition of slavery.[151] Interference with these rights is almost never allowed. The mere interference with these absolute rights will constitute an infringement of the Convention. The proportionality requirement does not come into play.

2.12 Conclusion

In this contribution, we have looked at privacy and data protection assessments from a European human rights perspective. With the recognition of data protection as a fundamental and autonomous right within the EU legal order, we see no obstacle against the idea to impose by law a duty for all to assess in advance the impact of a technology or a processing operation against the light of the provisions of the EU regulations on data protection. This paper first proposed a rough basic sketch of the data protection impact assessment to be carried out and pondered whether we need to label this exercise "impact assessment". With the detailed rules spelled out in the respective regulations, one could defend the view that there is no more at stake than a compliance check. Whatever the term used, such a check is imposed on us by legal text and there is no objection against better enforcement of these tests and a future clarification of the binding nature of this check.

The bulk of this chapter has been devoted to the concept of impact assessments of privacy, a test that I differentiate from the data protection test by requiring much more qualitative assessments. A true privacy impact assessment departs from the "permissible limitation test" consisting of the seven following elements identified by the ECtHR in the context of Art. 8 ECHR: (1) in accordance and provided by the law; (2) serving a legitimate aim is not enough; must be necessary for reaching it; (3) inviolability of the essence of any human right; (4) necessary in a democratic society; (5) no unfettered discretion; (6) proportionality: appropriateness, least intrusive means, proportionate to the interest, and (7) consistent with other human rights.

Private actors, public authorities taking new initiatives or checking on new initiatives undertaken by private actors, and (national) constitutional courts can find inspiration in these criteria. We have discussed the tendency of the ECtHR to refrain from political assessments by avoiding the check on the least intrusive method and by granting a margin of appreciation when needed (restrained review). Whatever the reasons the Court may have for this approach, only assertive scrutiny of the seven elements identified above can inform the debate and the assessment of new technologies and processing operations. Leaving out tests on appropriateness and least intrusive methods is an open invitation to remain in the abstract

---

[151] Art. 4(1). This is also the case for the rights guaranteed by Articles 2 (right to life), 3 (prohibition of torture), 7 (no punishment without laws), 1 and 2 of the sixth additional Protocol (abolition of the death penalty and death penalty in time of war), and 4 of the seventh additional Protocol (right not be tried or punished twice).

and to simple balancing of interests that are loosely circumscribed ("security" or "economic interests").

Principled, political decisions of what a democratic state respecting the rule of law does and will not tolerate are an integral part of this exercise. The bulk of the assessments will not only require principled decisions, but also evidence-based argumentation and regulation. Art. 8 of the Convention does not contain explicit procedural requirements, but the Court has, through its case law, developed a set of criteria to assess permissible limitations of privacy, with a preference for procedural guarantees against arbitrary use of data and technology. Translated to services offered by industry (think about social network sites and search engines), these guarantees need to realise values such as transparency and control by the user. The idea of a fair decision-making procedure providing stakeholders with evidence and facts, involvement and an opportunity to contest the choices made is developed in the context of the case law on a healthy environment, but should inspire all decision-making procedures.[152] It is clear that a right to have technologies assessed before their launch is emerging as a human right. Particularly valuable is the contention of the Court that involvement and opposition to given facts and choices need to be possible at the beginning, but also later on throughout the process (e.g., when new facts emerge).

Even more valuable is the requirement that citizens concerned by new technologies and processing operations are heard and given the necessary facts and data coming from impact assessments. Contrary to many impact assessments today, especially in Europe, there is a need to involve not only experts and industry, but also individuals.[153] These assessments need to be made public in order to allow individuals to go to court. A decision-making process should be based on facts and needs to be fair. Elements such as the cost of technology and health implications need to be made public. No proper assessment is possible if not all the cards are on the table. A principled distrust of impact assessments needs to be the default position; they are always fitting a certain agenda and therefore they will never be undisputed. That is, however, precisely the reason why these documents need to be made public: they allow contestation and public debate. Ideally, there is public consultation when technology is designed (technology can still be redesigned) or planned. A true assessment can only be made when all the details are known. The first concept of the assessment document should subsequently be made public in order to gather reactions. After conclusion, there is no reason to stop the assessment. A new assessment

---

[152] I have insisted on the need to create a possibility within the legal framework for local experiments. I have already mentioned above the problem of regulating technology, while in the meantime developing it further, the difficulty it presents to law and the risk of outsourcing innovation.

[153] This coincides well with the essential contestable and political nature of human rights in general and the lack of external or objective standard to which the evaluators can appeal. Standards in human rights assessments cannot be imposed but need to be found and developed through consultation and co-creation.

is required to check on implementation, but also to check on assumed efficiency and added value.

In an ideal world, assessing is done permanently and in a spirit of openness, probing and learning.

Acknowledgement   The author wishes to thank Dariusz Kloza for comments.

Chapter 3
(Regulatory) Impact Assessment and Better Regulation

David Parker

Regulatory impact assessment (RIA) shares many features in common with privacy impact assessment (PIA). This chapter provides an overview of RIA and its current status and concludes with some remarks about lessons that can be learned from experience with RIA in the further development of PIA policy and practice.

Regulatory impact assessment as a policy tool has its roots in the "smaller government" agendas of the 1980s and 1990s under President Reagan in the USA and Margaret Thatcher in the UK. Since 1995, the US Office of Management and Budget has published reports on the costs and benefits of government regulations and, in 2000, it published guidance on how to conduct RIAs. This widened the scope of their use to include non-quantifiable costs and benefits. There was also increased emphasis on risk assessment and the quality of information collection.[1] Since the mid-1990s, the Organization for Economic Co-operation and Development (OECD) has promoted the use of RIA to improve policy-making across the developed economies and today the World Bank is promoting its use in developing economies, although adoption remains particularly patchy and incomplete.[2] The OECD along with the European Commission has been championing the use of RIA in the transition economies of Central and Eastern Europe.[3] As a result, a growing number of countries have adopted the concept and it has been widened to include social,

---

[1] Office of Management and Budget, *Making Sense of Regulation: 2001 Report to Congress on the Costs and Benefits of Regulations and Unfunded Mandates on State, Local and Tribe Entities*, OMB, Washington, DC, 2001.

[2] Kirkpatrick, Colin, David Parker and Yin-Fang Zhang, "Regulatory Impact Assessment and Regulatory Governance in Developing Countries", *Public Administration and* Development, Vol. 24, pp. 333–344; Kirkpatrick, Colin, David Parker and Yin-Fang Zhang, "Regulatory Impact Assessment in Developing and Transition Economies: A Survey of Current Practice", *Public Money and Management*, Vol. 24, No.5, pp. 291–296.

[3] The OECD has a new Regulatory Policy Committee working with the EU to promote improved practices across Europe.

D. Parker (✉)
Cranfield School of Management, Cranfield University, Cranfield, UK
e-mail: david.parker@cranfield.ac.uk

D. Wright, P. De Hert (eds.), *Privacy Impact Assessment*, Law, Governance
and Technology Series 6, DOI 10.1007/978-94-007-2543-0_3,
© Springer Science+Business Media B.V. 2012

environmental, competition, ethnic, gender and other policy issues, in addition to state regulation. Hence, the concept is now commonly referred to as simply impact assessment (IA).

There are various definitions of RIA/IA, but all have in common the principle of evaluating government policy options to decide whether proposed new legislation, legislative changes or regulations are likely to produce the desired policy outcome. The UK Cabinet Office has defined IA as "a tool which informs policy decisions. It is an assessment of the impact of policy options in terms of the costs, benefits and risks of a proposal."[4] The successful use of IA is expected to contribute to both the *outcome* and *process* dimensions of policy-making, although like all initiatives to improve public administration, the precise result will depend upon the form the IA takes and the enthusiasm by politicians and civil servants to make the method work. This varies across the OECD countries at present, and seemingly between government departments and agencies even within the same country.[5]

In modern societies, the public has a tendency to turn to government when problems or risks occur and politicians are prone to be seen to be "doing something", and quickly, even when more considered policy-making would confirm that state intervention is not necessarily the optimal solution.[6] Sometimes self-regulation by professional and business bodies may produce outcomes which are superior both in terms of costs and benefits to state regulation. At other times, there may be no clear answer to a problem, or the answer may impose costs that outweigh any conceivable benefits. In other words, government policy-making is too often "knee jerk" in response to "crises", leading to hasty and ill-thought out policies with perverse consequences. The result is sometimes referred to as the "regulatory state".[7] RIA/IA is a tool intended to act as a check on poor policy-making by enforcing a process within government to ask the right questions, evaluate all options, thoroughly analyse their likely impacts and explore the underlying assumptions.

The objective is to achieve a situation where government intervenes only where necessary and with the maximum net benefit or at minimum net cost. The costs are both those to government of administering the policy and to business and other organisations in terms of complying with it. Wherever possible, the costs and benefits should be evaluated quantitatively, but in a number of cases this will not be possible and therefore qualitative evaluation will be used. The process of policy-making and implementation should be improved because integral to good RIA/IA is proper prior consultation with those likely to be affected by a policy change and

---

[4] Cabinet Office, *Better Policy Making: A Guide to Regulatory Impact Assessment*, Regulatory Impact Unit, London, 2003.

[5] Kirkpatrick, Colin, and David Parker (eds.), *Regulatory Impact Assessment: Towards Better Regulation?*, Edward Elgar, Cheltenham, 2007.

[6] OECD, *Risk and Regulatory Policy: Improving the Governance of Risk*, OECD Directorate for Public Governance and Territorial Development, Paris, April 2010.

[7] Majone, Giandomenico, "From the Positive to the Regulatory State", *Journal of Public Policy*, Vol.17, No. 2, May 1997, pp. 139–167.

re-evaluation of options in terms of the results of the consultation, sometimes leading to policy revision or even policy abandonment. Amongst the options that should be considered at all times is that of "do nothing" or leave policy unchanged from that which currently exists. The existence of a problem does not in itself justify government intervention.

This chapter discusses the development of RIA/IA in the context of better policy-making. Particular attention is paid to the use of the tool in the UK and EU. In the UK, RIA/IA has been given a new lease of life by the coalition government elected in May 2010. The changes introduced include an enhanced role for a body known as the Regulatory Policy Committee, which are described.[8]

3.1 The Development of (Regulatory) Impact Assessment

RIA/IA is a tool to help policy-makers make improved decisions and is designed to improve transparency in policy-making by promoting consultation and accountability. RIA/IA is intended to be both a continuous *process*, to help policy-makers think through and understand the consequences of government intervention, and a *methodology*, to enable an objective assessment of the positive and negative effects of contemplated intervention. As already mentioned, the use of RIA/IA is now encouraged throughout the OECD countries and is being promoted more widely to improve policy-making in developing countries and the transition economies of Central and Eastern Europe. In March 1995, the Council of the OECD adopted a Recommendation on *Improving the Quality of Government Regulation*, which made reference to the use of RIA.[9] In 1997, ministers of the member countries endorsed the OECD *Report on Regulatory Reform,* which recommended that governments "integrate regulatory impact assessment into the development, review, and reform of regulations".[10] Specifically within Europe, the European Commission has been active in establishing a modus operandi for RIA/IAs, both for use within the Commission and more widely, including in those countries that have become new EU Member States or have applications lodged for membership.

In all cases, RIA/IA needs to be championed across government if it is to become a really effective, comprehensive and consistent feature of policy-making and implementation. While the precise form of RIA/IA operated within government varies across countries, including within the EU, reflecting the distinctive political context

---

[8] The author is a Member of the Regulatory Policy Committee but this chapter has been written in a personal capacity and no comments made should be attributed to the Committee or any of its Members.

[9] OECD, *Recommendation on Improving the Quality of Government Regulation*, OECD, Paris, 1995.

[10] OECD, *The OECD Report on Regulatory Reform: Synthesis*, OECD, Paris, 1997.

Table 3.1   Common characteristics of IAs

1. *Statement of problem.* Is government intervention both necessary and desirable?
2. *Definition of alternative remedies.* These include different approaches, such as the use of economic incentives or voluntary approaches.
3. *Determination of physical effects of each alternative, including potential unintended consequences.* The net should be cast wide. Generally speaking, regulations or investments in many areas of public policy can have social, environmental and other implications that must be kept in mind.
4. *Estimation of benefits and costs of each alternative.* Benefits should be quantified and where possible monetised. Costs should be true opportunity costs not simply expenditures.
5. *Assessment of other economic impacts,* including effects on competition, effects on small firms, international trade implications.
6. *Identification of winners and losers,* those in the community who stand to gain and lose from each alternative and, if possible, the extent of their gains and losses.
7. *Communication with the interested public,* including the following activities: notification of intent to regulate, request for compliance costs and other data, public disclosure of regulatory proposals and supporting analysis, and consideration of and response to public comments.
8. *A clear choice of the preferred alternative,* plus a statement defending that choice.
9. *Provision of a plan for ex post analysis of regulatory outcomes.* It is important to establish a benchmark against which to measure performance. Planning is needed to ensure that procedures are in place for the collection of date to permit such benchmarking.

Source: OECD, "Regulatory Performance: Ex Post Evaluation of Regulatory Tools and Institutions", *Working Party on Regulatory Management and Reform*, Draft Report by the Secretariat, OECD, Paris, 2004, p. 7; Kirkpatrick and Parker, op. cit., p. 11

and administrative arrangements,[11] there are some common characteristics. These are summarised in Table 3.1. Typically, an RIA/IA involves a number of tasks to be carried out at each stage of the policy-making process within government departments and regulatory agencies. These include:

- a description of the problem identified and the objective of the new legislative or regulatory proposal,
- a description of the options (state regulatory and non-state regulatory) for achieving the objective,
- an assessment of the significant positive and negative impacts, including an assessment of the incidence of the quantitative and qualitative benefits and costs on consumers, business and other specified groups, including the public at large,
- a consultation process with stakeholders and other interested parties,
- a recommended policy option, with an explanation of why it has been selected as against the other options identified, including "do nothing".

---

[11] Radaelli, Claudio M., "Diffusion Without Convergence: How Political Context Shapes the Adoption of Regulatory Impact Assessment", *Journal of European Public Policy*, Vol. 12, No. 5, 2005, pp. 924–943.

When undertaking an impact assessment, evaluation can be conducted at several different levels, each using its own set of performance indicators. In particular:

- *Content evaluation* is input-based and checks the content of the RIA/IA report for compliance with the RIA/IA procedures and process.
- *Output evaluation* goes beyond the question of formal compliance with procedural requirements and measures the quality of the analysis undertaken.
- *Outcome evaluation* assesses the actual effect of the RIA/IA in terms of the quality of the regulatory outcomes.
- *Impact evaluation* assesses the impact of the change in regulation quality on the broader economic, social, environmental or other specified goals.

The expansion of the scope of RIA/IAs beyond simply economic regulation to the social, environmental, competition, ethnic, gender and other implications of policy initiatives has made the monitoring and evaluation of their use more complex. This is because more issues are embraced and the goals may not be readily compatible. This in turn raises the burden of data collection and analysis and the prospect of comparing incommensurate costs and benefits.

Nevertheless, where RIA/IAs continue to prove disappointing in terms of improvements to the outcomes and processes of regulation, this is more attributable to a lack of championing across government, and a failure to achieve the necessary "culture change" in terms of policy-making and evaluation, rather than the expansion in the scope of their use over the last decade. Politicians and civil servants are usually keen to get on and legislate, and legislating is already a complex, time-consuming and resource-heavy business. The introduction of RIA/IA procedures may be treated by politicians and officials as an unwelcome or even "pointless" extra burden on their time and resources. The proper adoption of IA is undoubtedly reliant upon unequivocal and continuing high-level political support within government.

Experience shows that the prospects for achieving the necessary "buy in" are significantly improved if there is a dedicated body within government responsible for ensuring that all departments operate RIA/IAs and on a more or less consistent basis. This body can publish guidance on the concept and its implementation, provide necessary training for officials, monitor the results and adapt the process over time. In some cases, this body has been placed in the President's or Prime Minister's office to provide the necessary authority or gravitas. In the UK, the use of IA was championed by a dedicated unit in the Cabinet Office, before it moved to the Department of Trade and Industry, since replaced by the Department of Business Innovation and Skills.

3.2 Use of RIA/IA in the UK

The systematic use of what was called RIA and now IA in the UK began after the election of the new Labour Government in May 1997. However, the origins can be clearly traced back to Margaret Thatcher's initiatives to reduce state regulatory burdens in the 1980s. These were only partially successful at best, not least because the privatisations of the 1980s and early 1990s led to the creation of a new raft of state regulatory bodies, to oversee the activities of the privatised utility businesses – telecommunications, gas, airports, electricity and the railways. Indeed, it can be argued that Thatcherism did not so much "roll back the frontiers of the state" but redefined the content, in favour of privatised, state-regulated businesses over nationalised industries.

In 1997, the Better Regulation Task Force (BRTF) was established, explicitly to improve regulation within the UK. In addition a Regulatory Impact Unit was set up in the Cabinet Office, with the support of the Prime Minister, Tony Blair. In 1998, the PM announced that no proposal for regulation should be considered by Ministers without an RIA being carried out and, in particular, all proposed new legislation should be accompanied by an RIA. Subsequently, improved guidelines for carrying them out were published and there was a concerted attempt to embody the use of RIA within all government departments and agencies, for example, through sharing good practice and training workshops. Departments were encouraged to establish their own regulatory impact units to promote and monitor the use of RIAs. An impact assessment toolkit was put together to assist departments and help ensure standard practice across departments. RIA templates (forms) were developed for use by departments accompanied by guidance on their completion. In the 2004 budget, there was an announcement that any future regulatory proposal that was likely to impose a major new burden on business would require a RIA agreed by the Cabinet Office Regulatory Impact Unit and clearance from a Panel for Regulatory Accountability, chaired by the PM.[12]

As more RIAs were published and subjected to public scrutiny, it became clear that while there had been progress, there remained weaknesses. This was confirmed by the examination of finalised RIAs in the UK undertaken by the National Audit Office (NAO) in 2001.[13] In April 2002, the House of Commons Public Accounts Committee recommended that the NAO should evaluate a sample of RIAs each year, and since 2004 the NAO has published a series of reports. These have established that the use of RIA/IA is increasingly well embedded within government, but problems continue in terms of quality and content and there remains unevenness in use across departments.[14] The first of the NAO reports, published in 2004, was based on a study of 10 completed RIAs. It concluded that there was a wide range of practices and approaches adopted in government, and within the sample, there was insufficient attention paid to quantifying costs and benefits and considering alternative

---

[12] Jacobs, Colin, "The Evolution and Development of Regulatory Impact Assessment in the UK", in Kirkpatrick and Parker, op. cit., pp.106–131 [pp.114–115].

[13] National Audit Office, *Better Regulation: Making Good Use of Regulatory Impact Assessments*, HC 329 2001-2, NAO, London, 2001–2.

[14] Humpherson, Ed, "Auditing Regulatory Impact Assessment: UK Experience", in Kirkpatrick and Parker op. cit., pp.132–144.

options, including alternatives to state regulation.[15] The next report, in 2005, again looked at a sample of 10 RIAs and, again, found deficiencies in practice, while the following report, in 2006, concentrated to a greater extent on departmental culture than the earlier reports. The conclusions, however, were similar in highlighting a lack of clarity in the presentation of analysis and weaknesses in assessment. RIAs were too often seen as a paper output rather than a truly integral part of the policy-making process.[16] Other research has endorsed such findings. For example, in a study published in 2003, Ambler, Chittenden and Shamutkova looked at 200 RIAs conducted by UK government departments between mid-1998 and mid-2002. They found little evidence that legislation had been aborted and only 11 cases of final RIAs where this possibility was identified.[17]

In recognition that improvements were needed, in March 2005, the Government accepted the recommendations of two important reports. The first was the Hampton Report on inspection and enforcement which, amongst other things, established key principles for good regulation, namely *transparency, accountability, consistency, targeting* and *proportionality*. The Committee also encouraged the adoption of a more risk-based approach to regulation. The second was a report from the BRTF called *Less is More*.[18] This report endorsed simplification and consolidation of regulations and the adoption of the Standard Cost Model (SCM) as the basis for quantification of costs. SCM is a method designed to reduce the administrative burdens imposed by regulation by providing a framework for measuring administrative costs consistently across government. This allows measurements to be more readily compared and areas for burden reduction identified.[19]

Around the same time, in May 2005, the Better Regulation Executive (BRE) replaced the BRTF within the Cabinet Office. In effect, this confirmed the importance of the better regulation agenda within government. The Cabinet tasked the BRE with taking forward the work of the BRTF and the Cabinet Office Regulatory Impact Unit. In January 2006, the Cabinet complemented the BRE by the creation of the Better Regulation Commission (BRC), with representation from business and other bodies outside government. The objective of the BRC was to provide independent advice to government about new regulatory proposals and to review the

---

[15] National Audit Office, *Evaluation of Regulatory Impact Assessments Compendium Report 2003-04*, HC 358 2003-4, NAO, London, 2004.

[16] National Audit Office, *Evaluation of Regulatory Impact Assessments Compendium Report 2004-05*, HC 341 2004-5, NAO, London, 2005; National Audit Office, *Evaluation of Regulatory Impact Assessments Compendium Report 2005-06*, HC 1305 2005-6, NAO, London, 2006. For a fuller discussion of the content of these reports, see Humpherson, op. cit., pp.132–144.

[17] Ambler, Tim, Francis Chittenden and Monika Shamutkova, *Do Regulators Play by the Rules? An Audit of Regulatory Impact Assessments*, British Chambers of Commerce, London, January 2003.

[18] Better Regulation Task Force, *Less is More*, BRTF, London, March 2005. http://www.bis.gov.uk/files/file22967.pdf

[19] Better Regulation Executive, *Measuring Administrative Costs: UK Standard Cost Model Manual*, BRE/Cabinet Office, London, September 2005. http://www.berr.gov.uk/files/file44503.pdf. Other countries in Europe have also adopted SCM.

government's overall regulatory performance. One important output of the BRC was a proposal, taken up by government, that the treatment of risk in regulation policy needed further investigation. This led to the announcement in January 2008 of the creation of the Risk Advisory Council, which concluded its work the following year. Its report revealed deep concerns about ill-thought out state intervention to counter risks that ought to be borne elsewhere. State intervention often occurs because there are perceived risks that need to be tackled. The risks may arise at work, at home, on the roads or public transport or elsewhere. An example is health and safety at work legislation; another is the mandatory use of seatbelts in cars to help reduce deaths and serious injuries in motor accidents. But a serious question arises about the extent to which government should intervene in an attempt to reduce life's risks, especially towards the level of zero. Doing so may be extremely costly; arguably, risk-taking is part of the human condition and human evolution has been all about taking and managing risks.

The treatment of risk becomes a particularly acute debate when regulation intrudes into what are referred to as lifestyle decisions. Recent examples in the UK relate to the regulation of alcohol labelling and smoking in public places. Such regulation often results from pressure from lobbying groups to tackle health and other social problems. While the resulting regulation can help protect public welfare, some may object that it reduces "freedom of choice" and that individuals should be allowed to make their own "lifestyle" choices.

Today in the UK, IAs are used to evaluate the consequences of possible and actual government interventions in the public, private and third sectors in the UK. They are required for any proposal that imposes or reduces costs on businesses or the third sector and for proposals affecting costs in the public sector, unless the costs fall beneath a given threshold (generally £5 million). IAs need to be produced for all forms of government intervention, including primary or secondary legislation, as well as codes of practice or guidance. All new legislation is accompanied by a final IA signed off by the relevant government minister before introduction to Parliament. The result is around 250 to 300 IAs published by government departments and agencies each year.

Usually a number of drafts of an IA are prepared and published during the policy-making process, with public consultation taking place (normally a minimum of 12 weeks are allowed for consultation).[20] In the UK, IAs are created over a normal policy development time period of six months to two years and are referred to at the first stage of the process as "preliminary", "partial" or "consultation" stage IAs, and at the second stage as "final" IAs. The process is summarised in Fig. 3.1. In terms of content, IAs are expected to cover the problem, the rationale for intervention, the policy objective, a description of the options considered (including "do nothing"), the costs and benefits of each option, the risks and assumptions underpinning the analysis, a statement on the administrative burden and policy-saving calculations, an assessment of wider impacts, and a summary and preferred option with description

---

[20] The government has published a code of practice on consultation since 2000. The latest version was released in 2008.

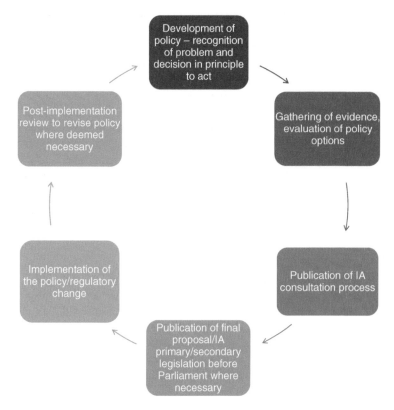

Fig. 3.1 The policy/regulatory process in the UK

of the implementation plan. With only certain exceptions, in the UK, IAs should be published:

- when a policy proposal is put out to public consultation;
- when a government bill, or private member's bill enjoying Government support, is introduced in either House of Parliament;
- when a draft statutory instrument is laid in Parliament;
- immediately prior to implementation of an act or statutory instrument or other regulatory measure; and
- at the review stage after the regulatory measure has been implemented.[21]

The general format for an IA is established by a template issued to departments by the BRE and includes:

---

[21] Better Regulation Executive (BRE) and Department for Business, Innovation and Skills (BIS), *Impact Assessment Guidance*, BRE, London, April 2010. http://www.bis.gov.uk/assets/biscore/better-regulation/docs/10-898-impact-assessment-guidance.pdf

- *Summary: Interventions and Options* – setting out the problem under consideration, why government intervention is deemed necessary, the policy objectives and intended effects, and policy options considered, with a justification of any preferred option – in summary form. This part of the IA includes the ministerial sign-off, confirming that the minister has read the IA and is "satisfied that, given the available evidence, it represents a reasonable view of the likely costs, benefits and impact of the leading options".
- *Summary: Analysis and Evidence* – providing details of the relevant annual costs and annual benefits with the totals appropriately discounted. There is also space to summarise other key "non-monetised" costs and benefits. This is followed by space for details of "Key assumptions/Sensitivities/Risks".

The IA template also contains questions on the geographical coverage of the policy, when the policy will be implemented, which organisation(s) will enforce the policy, the total annual costs of enforcement, whether the enforcement will comply with the Hampton principles for better regulation, whether the implementation will go beyond minimum EU requirements (where relevant), the value of any proposed offsetting measure, the value of changes in greenhouse emissions (if any) and whether the proposal has a significant impact on statutory equality duties, competition, small firms, health and well-being, human rights, justice, the rural sector and sustainability.[22] There is then space for the "Evidence Base", for departments to set out in more detail the basis for the figures, conclusions and assumptions included in the earlier summary pages. Relevant research that has been undertaken or accessed should be referenced and issues of risk addressed. Finally, the IA should include a "Post Implementation Review Plan".

In October 2009, the Department for Business, Innovation and Skills (BIS) reported that the estimated annual costs and benefits for new legislation enacted in 2008 and 2009 was £13 billion and £24 billion, respectively, implying that the IA process was working.[23] Nevertheless, despite the expanded and improved use of IAs in the UK, stimulated by the work of the BRE and departmental regulation units, poor IAs are still produced and some changes to regulation avoid the process altogether. Generally, business groups remain sceptical of the benefits claimed by government for IAs in terms of actually reducing the burden of regulation on business. Some have suggested that the IA process has insufficient independence from government and is subject to "manipulation" to produce the result desired by ministers. Business contends that the regulatory burden often results from small but cumulative changes made under enabling legislation and with insufficient consultation with those likely to be affected.

---

[22] Race, disability and gender IAs are statutory requirements for relevant policies. The equality statutory requirements will be expanded in 2011 when the Equality Bill comes into force.

[23] HM Government, *Summary of Simplification Plans*, London, 2009.

The British Chambers of Commerce has been a particularly vocal critic. In a recent report, it estimated that the cumulative net cost to business of new regulation since 1998 was over £88 billion, and while there had been advancements in regulatory processes and in the use of IAs, much more improvement was needed.[24] Similarly, the business organisation EEF found from a recent survey of UK manufacturers that 52 per cent believed that regulation was still an obstacle to growing their business. Respondents considered regulation to be the second worst aspect of the UK business environment, after taxation. The EEF study singled out employment and pensions regulations at the domestic level and employment and environmental regulations at the European levels as key culprits. It also criticised IAs for being "based on estimates developed by policy-makers rather than the costs actually imposed by the regulations. . . . Experience suggests that estimates are more likely to underestimate rather than overestimate the cost of a regulation."[25]

The latest NAO report, published in July 2010, was concerned specifically with assessing the quality of analysis in IAs, the capability of departments to produce robust analysis and the internal processes for assuring the quality of IAs. The conclusion was depressingly consistent with earlier findings, that the quality of analysis still varied and IAs continue to omit significant information. While option development was the strongest area of performance identified, this too was often limited. The NAO also found that IAs for proposals originating from the EU were often not prepared early enough to be effective. When IAs are produced later in the process, after an EU rule change, the scope for discretionary action within the UK is greatly constrained. On the departmental processes for producing IAs, the NAO confirmed an improvement in resourcing and guidance, but some continuing weaknesses in the consultation process. But perhaps the most disturbing finding was that the NAO reported that only a half of policy staff seemed to believe that IA was a useful part of the policy process. This NAO study was based on reviewing a randomly selected sample of 50 of the 196 IAs for new legislation in 2008/2009.[26] Clearly, while there has been a considerable progress in the use of RIA/IA within UK government, there still remains much scope for improvement.

In January 2008, the government decided to wind up the work of the BRC, but then quickly recognised that this created a vacuum in terms of both regulatory scrutiny and strategic thinking on regulatory policy. Therefore, in the budget of 2009, the Chancellor of the Exchequer announced that a new body would be established, which became the Regulatory Policy Committee (RPC). In addition, the Cabinet set up a new sub-committee on regulatory policy and decided to publish

---

[24] Ambler, Tim, Francis Chittenden and Andrea Miccini, *Is Regulation Really Good for Us?*, British Chambers of Commerce, London, April 2010, p.11.

[25] EEF (The Manufacturers' Organisation), *Reforming Regulation: Improving Competitiveness, Creating Jobs. Report by the EEF Regulation Task Group*, EEF, London, September 2010, especially pp. 7, 9.

[26] National Audit Office, *Assessing the Impact of Proposed New Policies*, Report by the Comptroller and Auditor General, HC 185 Session 1010-11, NAO, London, 1 July 2010.

a Forward Regulatory Programme for the next two years, setting out expected regulatory changes. The objective was to help business prepare better for proposed new regulations. It also requested departments and regulatory agencies to produce plans simplifying regulation.

The RPC came into being in November 2009 and is the first independent body in the UK to provide external scrutiny of the policy-making process. It comments on the quality of analysis supporting new proposed regulations (the NAO's reports are ex post assessments of IAs, i.e., for regulatory changes that have already been introduced). The RPC is composed of a chairman and five members drawn from business and professional backgrounds to act as independent reviewers of all new regulatory measures coming out of government departments and agencies. The committee is serviced by a small staff of civil servants. Its terms of reference in November 2009 were "to comment on the quality of analysis supporting policy decisions on new regulations and on whether the policy design will ensure the benefits justify the costs". Specifically included were assessments of the accuracy and robustness of the claimed costs and benefits, a review of the policy options considered and ensuring that "issues of public risk and the practicalities of ensuring compliance are taken into account". The committee was also requested to advise on the performance of regulators against the Hampton principles, although to date little work has been undertaken under this heading. This arises from the resource pressure of monitoring and assessing the tide of regulatory proposals from government departments with a small staff. Specifically outside its terms of reference were commenting on the government's policy objectives, financial services regulation (on the grounds of the current financial crisis and uncertainty about future financial regulation) and budget and taxation measures.[27]

Since late 2009, the RPC has reviewed a number of regulatory proposals at the consultation stage and published on its website an opinion on each IA where it considered there were grounds for concern. The RPC has liaised with departmental better regulation units and has made regular contact with trade bodies and other interest groups, to seek their views on particular regulatory proposals. In its first report, published in July 2010, the RPC revealed that it had undertaken a detailed review of 107 new regulatory proposals between December 2009 and May 2010, reviewing the quality of evidence and analysis contained in the IA and the supporting documentation. As a result, the committee published 22 opinions on its website of cases where it had found weaknesses, such as a lack of analytical rigour.[28] In other words, the RPC identified deficiencies in just over one in five IAs with a number failing to make the case adequately for the proposed policy change. For example, a new regulatory proposal on reservoir flood plains, requiring reservoir undertakers to have on-site flood plans, was found to lack a risk-based approach to the problem.

---

[27] http://regulatorypolicycommittee.independent.gov.uk/rpc/

[28] Regulatory Policy Committee, *Reviewing Regulation: An independent report on the analysis supporting regulatory proposals, December 2009 – May 2010*, RPC, London, July 2010, pp. 13–14. http://regulatorypolicycommittee.independent.gov.uk/rpc/wp-content/uploads/2010/08/RPC-Report-Final-Version-August-2010.pdf

The benefits the department claimed for the regulatory change were based on numbers of lives saved in the event of reservoir failure – even though there had been no fatalities since reservoir safety legislation was introduced in the 1930s. In the case of a proposed regulatory change to information that must be provided on alcoholic drink labels, the committee concluded that insufficient evidence had been provided that new labelling measures would successfully reduce alcohol consumption and therefore deliver the claimed benefits.

More generally, the RPC's conclusions complemented those of the earlier NAO and other studies that had concluded that a significant proportion of IAs published are still not up to the mark. The report commented that "there are a number of IAs that lack significant analytical rigour, are poorly presented, or appear to be produced as an afterthought, seemingly as a means of 'ticking the right boxes' to obtain the necessary approval for a proposed course of action."[29] The RPC made six recommendations for improvement: that policy-makers should not presume that regulation is the answer to the problem they are trying to solve; that more effort should be made to explore options other than the department's preferred option; that more substantive evidence of the need for the regulatory change should be gathered and published; that more reliable estimates of costs and benefits should be produced; that non-monetary impacts should be assessed more thoroughly; and that explanations and results should be presented more clearly.

The coalition government elected in May 2010 has acted quickly to signal its intention to continue and enhance the better regulation agenda of its predecessor. Under changes introduced during the summer of 2010, the RPC has been given a more prominent role and more responsibilities. It will now scrutinise all IAs produced within the UK government and advise a new Cabinet sub-committee on their quality and content, the Reducing Regulation Committee (RRC), chaired by the Secretary of State for Business, Innovation and Skills. The intention is that the RPC will provide independent scrutiny before new regulatory proposals are approved by government, including those intended for consultation. The RPC will therefore assist the RRC to reach a decision as to whether a regulatory proposal should proceed, be referred for further work or rejected. Although these are early days and we wait to see how the RPC, departments and the RRC will interact, in principle the RPC now provides independent scrutiny before new regulatory proposals are approved within government.

Also, the new government has introduced a "one in, one out" policy from 1 September 2010 for all new regulatory proposals that impose net costs on business (the policy may be rolled out to cover net costs imposed on other sections of society at a later date). While the full details are still to be published, in essence this means that departments requesting new regulatory powers that impose net costs on business are expected to propose a compensating regulatory reduction elsewhere. Any net regulatory cost will have to be compensated for by cuts to the cost of other

---

[29] Ibid., p. 5.

regulation, so that there is no net increase in the regulatory burden on business.[30] However, "one in, one out" will not apply to regulatory changes emanating from the EU. This is because finding compensating regulations to rein back would have imposed a huge challenge to departments given the volume of EU regulation. But as about half of all new regulations in the UK start in Brussels, this is a clear limitation of the new policy. Departments are expected to issue IAs relating to the regulations to be removed or reduced, and the RPC will also review these IAs and report the findings to the RRC.

In addition to these changes, a Regulatory Challenge Unit has been set up in the Cabinet Office to look at encouraging alternative approaches to regulation. Meanwhile, the BRE, located in the Department for Business, Innovation and Skills, was to undertake a "pipeline review" of all expected regulatory proposals from departments. The explicit aim of all of these changes is to stem the tide of regulation and to introduce a change of culture in government away from a rules-based approach to achieving policy outcomes. However, it remains to be seen whether this new set of initiatives will be more successful than earlier ones in limiting regulation to where there are real market failures and where it can be reasonably demonstrated that state intervention will lead to net benefits.

The position of the RPC in the regulatory process before the changes introduced by the coalition government is illustrated in Fig. 3.2, taken from the Committee's July 2010 report. The new, enhanced role of the RPC moves the Committee's intervention earlier into the policy-making process, at the pre-consultation stage when policy is being formulated, as well as afterwards when a revised IA is produced. The Committee is also expected to monitor the "one in, one out" policy. But one unfortunate result may be that in moving the RPC from reporting publicly on the quality of published IAs into working with departments and advising the RRC on a confidential basis, there will in future be less transparency in the way that the RPC operates. This in turn could prove to be a threat to its independence. There is particular uncertainty about what information the RPC will be able to publish in the future.

Many of the new regulations introduced in EU Member States result from decisions made at the EU level or in Brussels. Between 50 and 70 per cent of regulatory costs on business in the UK occur due to implementing EU rules. In December 2009, the think tank Open Europe estimated that the 100 most costly EU regulations introduced since 1998 would cost the UK economy £184 billion by the year 2020. While Open Europe concluded that some regulations were clearly beneficial, many regulations originating in the European Commission were judged to be overly

---

[30] The idea is being tried elsewhere. Australia has introduced "one in, one out" and France has been looking at the adoption of "one in, two out" to reduce regulatory burdens. Earlier, the UK had considered the introduction of regulatory budgets, by developing a system which sets a constraint on the costs of regulation introduced in any specified period. A regulatory budget would generally be set at a departmental level, covering the costs of all new regulation with an impact on business. See HM Government/BERR, *Regulatory Budgets: A Consultation Document*, London, August 2008. http://www.berr.gov.uk/files/file47129.pdf

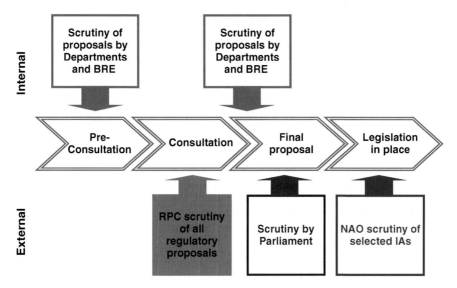

Fig. 3.2 Scrutiny of regulatory proposals in the UK, May 2010
Source: Regulatory Policy Committee, *Reviewing Regulation: An Independent Report on the Analysis Supporting Regulatory Proposals, December 2009 – May 2010*, RPC, London, July 2010

prescriptive and burdensome. The most costly new regulations were identified as the climate change act, energy performance certificates for buildings and the temporary agency workers directive.[31]

An IA should be prepared when seeking collective agreement for the UK's negotiating position on EU proposals. However, it appears that too often IAs are published in the UK "after the horse has bolted". Moreover, there are accusations that when EU rules are implemented in the UK, they are often "gold plated", adding unnecessarily to regulatory costs. Arguably, there is a need to ensure the preparation and publication of IAs *ahead* of the publication of an EU directive, so that proper consultation on options can still be undertaken and UK representatives in Brussels are better informed to influence the content of new directives. BIS stated in August 2010 that as part of the changes to the management of regulation in the UK, the Department would take a more rigorous approach to EU regulations, including engaging earlier in the Brussels policy-making process.[32]

---

[31] Monaghan, Angela, "EU Laws to Cost UK £184bn by 2010, Think Tank Says", *The Telegraph*, 21 Dec 2009. http://www.telegraph.co.uk/news/worldnews/europe/6859987/EU-laws-to-cost-UK-184bn-by-2010-think-tank-says.html

[32] Department for Business, Innovation and Skills (BIS), "New Rules to Hand Over Powers to Individuals and Companies by Cutting Red Tape and Bureaucracy", Press Release, London, 5 August 2010. http://nds.coi.gov.uk/content/detail.aspx?NewsAreaId=2&ReleaseID=414871&SubjectId=15&DepartmentMode=true

3.3 RIA/IAs and the European Commission

In addition to the UK, three EU Member States have established bodies to scrutinise the use of RIA/IAs: the Netherlands (ACTAL, Adviescollege Toetsing Administatieve Lasten),[33] Germany (the NKR, Nationaler Normenkontrollrat) and Sweden (the Better Regulation Council, Regelrådat).[34] But other Member States have no comparable institutions. At the EU level, there is the European Commission's Impact Assessment Board.

The Treaty of Rome in 1957 was about the creation of a common market, but the emphasis has changed over the decades, especially since the Treaty of Maastricht in February 1992, towards establishing more political and regulatory power in Brussels. The result has been more regulations emanating from the European Commission than from national governments, an increasingly voluminous and complex amount of EU legislation and growing complaints about regulatory burdens. Since the mid-1990s, EU institutions have been required to carry out RIAs, including environmental impact assessments. However, it was not until 2000 that a reasonably comprehensive agenda for better regulation surfaced at the EU level, following the resignation of the Santer Commission amid allegations of serious maladministration.

In November 2000, the European Commission established an expert group, the Mandelkern Group, to identify ways to improve the quality of EU legislation and to promote collaboration between Member States. Its report included an endorsement of the use of RIAs. Following its advice, the Commission established an ad hoc group of Directors and Experts on Better Regulation to promote and monitor better regulation. In June 2001, the European Council meeting in Gothenburg agreed that "sustainable development should become the central objective of all sectors and policies.... careful assessment of the full effects of a policy proposal must include estimates of its economic, environmental and social impacts inside and outside the EU."[35] The Commission established procedures with the objective of ensuring that each major legislative proposal was informed by an assessment of the potential impacts of the measure, both inside and outside the EU. The following March, the European Council launched the "Lisbon Strategy", including developing a programme to co-ordinate action to simplify the regulatory environment and rationalise the transposition of Community laws. Improved regulation was an integral part of the Lisbon objectives, to ensure that Europe achieved more dynamic, competitive and knowledge-based economies. A Communication of the European Commission on RIA/IA committed the Commission to undertake an impact assessment of all major policy proposals in order "to improve the quality and coherence

---

[33] ACTAL was something of a model for the UK's RPC. The Dutch were the first in Europe to introduce targets for reducing the regulatory burden.

[34] Such bodies have also been established in a few other countries, such as Australia and Canada.

[35] European Commission, Communication: A Sustainable Europe for a Better World: A European Strategy for Sustainable Development, COM (2001) 264, Brussels, 15 May 2001.

of the policy development process'", and to "contribute to an effective and efficient regulatory environment and further, to a more coherent implementation of the European strategy for Sustainable Development".[36]

From 2002 onwards, the EU has implemented and repeatedly endorsed the better regulation agenda.[37] As in the UK, RIA/IAs at the EU level are expected to cover problem identification, define objectives, develop, analyse and compare options and their impacts, and include procedures for monitoring and evaluation. They are expected to be used, for example, where there is "substantive" amendment to policy, although the definition of substantive has been open to interpretation and offers a convenient escape route for officials. At the same time, however, there has been a lack of clarity on definitions, roles and responsibilities and continuing concerns in Member States about the tide of new EU policy initiatives, many still lacking robust RIA/IAs.[38] Over the years, there have been a number of initiatives and papers on better regulation within the EU, both to achieve improved governance and greater competitiveness in Europe, and each has been warmly received. But effective action has somewhat lagged behind. Experience of the use of RIA/IAs within the European Commission, as in the UK, reveals equivocal results, with realistic quantification of costs and benefits a particular problem. For example, Vibert evaluated the first year of extended impact assessments undertaken by the European Commission, and found that "there is not a single case where EU action has been assessed to have negative net benefits or where the inability to quantify the net benefits has led to the conclusion that the measure should be withdrawn or that no policy would be the best policy".[39] Later, Lee and Kirkpatrick carried out a performance evaluation of a sample of "extended impact assessments" undertaken by the Commission and confirmed a number of weaknesses. These included poor identification of the problem to be tackled, unbalanced coverage of the different types of impacts of the policy change and a lack of clarity in the explanation of the analysis conducted. They also identified weaknesses in the presentation of the IA findings.[40]

In June 2005, the European Commission issued revised RIA/IA guidelines, involving an integrated approach to ensure that all benefits and costs were described

---

[36] European Commission, Communication from the Commission on Impact Assessment, Brussels, COM (2002) 276 final, Brussels, 5 June 2002.

[37] E.g., European Commission, Communication on European Governance: Better Law-making, COM (2002) 275 final, Brussels, 5 June 2002; European Commission, Communication from the Commission on Impact Assessment, COM (2002) 276 final, Brussels, 5 June 2002; European Commission, Better Regulation for Growth and Jobs in the European Union, COM (2005) 97 final, 16 March 2005; European Commission, Impact Assessment Guidelines, SEC (2009) 92, Brussels, 15 January 2009. http://ec.europa.eu/enterprise/policies/sme/files/docs/sba/iag_2009_en.pdf

[38] Allio, Lorenzo, "Better Regulation and Impact Assessment in the European Commission", in Colin Kirkpatrick and David Parker (eds.), *Regulatory Impact Assessment: Towards Better Regulation?*, Edward Elgar, Cheltenham, 2007, pp.72–105 [pp. 78–80].

[39] Vibert, Frank, *The EU's New System of Regulatory Impact Assessment – A Scorecard*, European Policy Forum, London, 2004, p. 9.

[40] Lee, Norman, and Colin Kirkpatrick, "Evidence-Based Policy-Making in Europe: An Evaluation of European Commission Integrated Impact Assessments", *Impact Assessment and Project Appraisal*, Vol. 24, No. 1, 2006, pp. 22–33.

and analysed.[41] These began to be implemented in August 2005 and were further revised in 2006 and 2009.[42] The new guidelines were to be applied to all items on the Commission's Work Programme, covering regulatory proposals, White Papers, expenditure programmes and negotiation of international agreements with economic, social or environmental consequences. In addition, the Commission would decide on a case-by-case basis to carry out an IA for a proposal which did not appear on the Work Programme. In other words, from 2005, there has been an expectation in Brussels that all major policy-defining and pre-legislative documents, along with all major legislative proposals, should include an RIA/IA. There has also been a move towards adopting a common inter-institutional approach to their use by EU institutions.

Therefore, since 2005, the Commission's IAs have improved, in both adoption and quality of analysis. Today, the use of RIA/IA is officially an important part of the better governance agenda in Europe with the stated objective of improving the quality of legislation and making European-level governance more transparent, responsive and accountable. But at the same time, there are still Commission policies that are not accompanied by an IA. Moreover, where IAs are produced they are still sometimes weak in content and analysis and sometimes produced by external consultants seemingly distant from the actual policy-making process. This is not assisted by the lack of independent scrutiny of RIA/IAs at the EU level.

In April 2006, Commission President Barroso made clear his support for the establishment of an impartial and independent mechanism to support and control the quality of IAs.[43] The outcome was the establishment of the Impact Assessment Board (IAB). The stated purpose of the IAB is to improve the quality of RIA/IAs at the EU level. The IAB "examines and issues opinions on the quality of Impact Assessment before the proposal reaches the Inter-Service Consultation". In 2008, the IAB considered 135 RIA/IAs and in 32 per cent of cases requested revisions. Consistent with findings in the UK, RIA/IAs were criticised for weaknesses in problem definition and objectives, impact analysis, the need for improved quantification and the comparison of options. However, while the creation of the IAB has been a welcome step to improving EU regulation, its opinions are non-binding. Also, they are not published until the Commission has already adopted the related policy proposal. This effectively diminishes the benefits of the independent scrutiny. It seems that, as in the UK, some officials still see IAs as an impediment to action. As the British Chambers of Commerce has commented: "The level of quality is not yet satisfactory for EU businesses and especially SMEs who are the primary reasons for an objective IA process. For others (non-EU business and consumers) it is also poor."[44]

---

[41] European Commission, Impact Assessment Guidelines, SEC (2005) 791, Brussels, June 2005.

[42] SEC (2009) 92. http://ec.europa.eu/enterprise/policies/sme/files/docs/sba/iag_2009_en.pdf

[43] Allio, op cit., p.97.

[44] Ambler, Chittenden and Miccini, op. cit., p.11.

The European Commission has recently continued and expanded the better regulation agenda of the previous Commission by launching a "Programme on Smart Regulation". As in the individual Member States, low economic growth is providing an incentive to reduce the regulatory burden, while arguably environmental concerns and the world financial crisis are pushing the other way. A High Level Group of Independent Stakeholders on Administrative Burdens at the European level, to which the RPC, ACTAL, the NKR and the Swedish Better Regulation Council contribute, is providing advice on burden reduction. The Commission has presented initiatives to reduce administrative costs, for example, proposals on e-invoicing and on the option to exempt micro enterprises from company law directives. However, the *acquis communautaire* remains a complex body of legislation. Concern continues to be expressed about the tide of new regulations coming out of Brussels and impacting business adversely.

The significant proportion of new regulation adopted in Member States originates in Brussels, as mentioned above, hence the need for improvements in policy-making within European institutions.[45] While Brussels has officially endorsed the use of RIA/IA, more needs to be done to improve both processes and outcomes.[46] The prize is worthwhile. The use of RIA/IA can strengthen both the legitimacy of European institutions in terms of democratic policy-making and better ensure that the regulatory outputs achieve their stated objectives, with minimal damage to economic competitiveness in Europe.

3.4   Conclusions

The better regulation agenda internationally has been driven by mounting evidence that state regulation does not necessarily achieve the desired goals, or at least without unexpected costs and economic distortions. Central to better regulation at governmental level has been the use of RIA/IAs as an integral part of the policy-making process. Governments should intervene in markets only where there is clear market failure and where state intervention is the least costly solution. The purpose of RIA/IA is to assess and measure the costs and benefits for a range of options so as to ensure that market failure is addressed at least net cost or with the largest net benefit. The use of RIA/IA is intended to contribute to good governance and in turn improved economic performance. Sometimes this may mean that, after careful analysis, the imperfect market outcome remains superior to any alternative that state regulation can reasonably be expected to deliver.

---

[45] This section of the chapter on early initiatives in the EU draws from Allio, Lorenzo, "Better Regulation and Impact Assessment in the European Commission", in Kirkpatrick and Parker, op. cit., 2007. Another useful study is Renda, Andrea, *Impact Assessment in the EU: The State of the Art and the Art of the State*, CEPS, Brussels, 1 Jan 2006.

[46] For example, the minimum consultation period is only eight weeks and needs to be extended to give more time for stakeholders across Europe to respond.

There is an inherent tendency in modern society for the public to look to government to minimise risks and provide "solutions", often oblivious of economic costs or distortions that might result. In response, politicians are prone to adopting "knee jerk" reactions, so as to be seen "to be doing something" in response to public pressure, even though in at least some (many?) cases, the optimal solution economically and socially might be to leave the risk to individuals and businesses to resolve. The use of RIA/IAs is intended to better identify when state intervention should or should not occur and the best form the intervention might take in terms of minimising net costs or maximising net benefits.

The use of RIA/IAs has been championed across the developed economies and now in developing and transition economies, as part of a wider better regulation agenda. But at the same time, the experience of the UK and EU in using the tool confirms that it faces a number of challenges and problems. In particular, there will always be an incentive for officials with their future careers in mind not to ask awkward questions or delay or block policy decisions that ministers and more senior officials clearly champion. There is the prospect that policy decisions are made within departments and that IAs are then written to endorse the policy decision already favoured, that is to say, providing an ex post justification for a prior preferred option or a "box ticking" exercise. In such cases, the use of IA becomes ritualistic within the government machinery and of questionable value.

The difficulties of operating an effective and efficient RIA/IA scrutiny regime within government and government agencies should not be under-estimated. The experience of the adoption of RIA/IAs in the UK and at the EU level confirms that while their use can improve policy-making and reduce unnecessary regulatory costs, challenges exist to embed the process consistently across the administrative machinery. Nevertheless, the effective and efficient use of RIA/IA can undoubtedly contribute to more informed policy choices and better policy outcomes.

From the experience of IAs at the UK and EU levels, we can note some key points that may be helpful in ensuring the development of a robust PIA methodology:

- There should be an independent agency able to provide guidance and comment on the use of (privacy) impact assessments.
- PIAs should be both a process and a methodology.
- Training in the proper application of the methodology will help overcoming using PIAs as a mere box-ticking exercise.
- PIAs should be initiated very early in the planning cycle and options or alternatives should be genuine rather than obviously inadequate so that planners do not or cannot manipulate the outcome to that which they desire.
- Production of PIAs should be transparent; the results should be published on a website unless there are good excuses (e.g., national security, commercial sensitivities). Excuses should be reviewed by the independent agency and if the agency disagrees, the originator should be obliged to justify his decision publicly.
- IAs and, presumably, PIAs need adequate resources and high level (e.g., ministerial) support. They should be signed off by the minister.
- They should be subject to independent, third-party audit.

Chapter 4
Prior Checking, a Forerunner to Privacy Impact Assessments

Gwendal Le Grand and Emilie Barrau

4.1 Introduction

Article 20 of the EU Data Protection Directive 95/46/EC addresses "prior checking". It provides that Member States shall determine processing operations likely to present specific risks to the rights and freedoms of data subjects and shall check that these processing operations are examined before they start.

This chapter makes a comparative study of the implementation of prior checking in Europe. It examines how prior checking has been implemented, how it works in practice and what can be learned from it as a regulatory instrument in the development and use of privacy impact assessments in Europe.

In order to acquire a broad understanding of how Article 20 of Directive 95/46/EC has been implemented in Europe, we sent a questionnaire to 30 national Data Protection Authorities.[1] This comparative study is based on the analysis of the 23 responses received.

This chapter is organised as follows: in the first main section, we describe how prior checking has been transposed in the various Member States. In the second section, we address and analyse the practical implementation of prior checking by the national Data Protection Authorities. Finally, in the third section, we assess the current prior checking systems and evaluate how they may evolve in the future, with a particular emphasis on the role privacy impact assessments (PIAs) may play.

---

[1] This includes the 27 authorities of the European Union Member States as well as Liechtenstein, Norway and Macedonia.

G. Le Grand (✉)
Commission Nationale de l'Informatique et des Libertés (CNIL), Paris, France
e-mail: glegrand@cnil.fr

D. Wright, P. De Hert (eds.), *Privacy Impact Assessment*, Law, Governance
and Technology Series 6, DOI 10.1007/978-94-007-2543-0_4,
© Springer Science+Business Media B.V. 2012

4.2 How Prior Checking Has Been Implemented

This section identifies the key similarities and differences in the transposition of prior checking (Article 20) in Europe, based on the answers national Data Protection Authorities provided to the questionnaire.

Data Protection Authorities were asked five questions:

1. Is prior checking provided for in your national legislation and is it used in practice?
2. Is prior checking only limited to operations likely to present specific risks?
3. What are the categories of processing operations concerned?
4. Are exemptions foreseen (e.g., appointment of a data protection official)?
5. Do you carry out prior checking in the context of preparation either of a measure of the national parliament or a measure based on such a legislative measure?

The responses to the questionnaire are summarised below.

4.2.1 Prior Checking Has Been Transposed in the National Legislation of Most Member States and Is Used by Most Member States

Almost all Member States have transposed Art. 20 of the Data Protection Directive or use prior checking procedures. Twenty-one countries responded positively to the question "Is prior checking provided for in your national legislation?", even though some Member States only use it in a limited number of cases or areas.

The scope of prior checking may sometimes be limited (e.g., to sensitive data or State databases).[2]

In two countries (Ireland and the United Kingdom), while prior checking is foreseen in the law, it is not in force[3] or has not been used in practice. In the UK, the Secretary of State has to make an Order specifying processing that is "particularly likely to cause substantial damage or substantial distress to data subjects, or otherwise significantly to prejudice the rights and freedoms of data subjects". This is then called "assessable processing" and there are provisions for the Data Protection Authority to assess this processing. However, the Secretary of State has never made such an Order.

---

[2] The authors therefore considered that the answer to this question should be classified as "rather yes" in the pie chart.

[3] In which case, the authors considered (in the pie chart below) that prior checking had "rather not" been implemented in national legislation.

Finally, Art. 20 of the Directive has not been implemented so far into the national Data Protection Act of Liechtenstein.

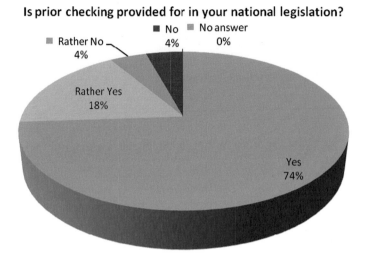

4.2.2 Prior Checking Is Limited to Operations Likely to Present Specific Risks in Most Countries

In 21 countries, prior checking is limited to operations likely to present specific risks. In three countries, however, it appears that prior checking is a more general obligation.

In particular, prior checking is limited either to sensitive data (Estonia, Greece, Norway), to certain risks (the Czech Republic, Ireland, Italy, Macedonia, the United Kingdom, Malta) or to certain cases (Lithuania). The legislation may also give discretion to the Data Protection Authority to prescribe what operations present risks.

Specific processing operations may also trigger prior checking by Data Protection Authorities. For example:

- the interconnection of databases is identified as being a sensitive issue which is specifically subject to prior checking in Cyprus,
- other countries (Estonia, France) conduct prior checking when scientific research is performed without the permission of the data subject.

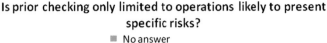

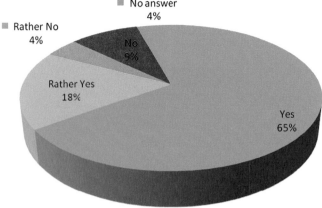

Is prior checking only limited to operations likely to present specific risks?

In some Member States (e.g., Greece), although prior checking is limited by law only to sensitive data, notification to the Data Protection Authority may in some cases lead to the issuance of a formal decision. In practice, notification of processing involving biometrics, genetic data, CCTV or other new technologies would be subject to control and lead to a formal decision by the Hellenic Data Protection Authority.

In Bulgaria, France and Hungary, prior checking is interpreted rather broadly since it is not limited to operations presenting specific risks and in Estonia, prior checking concerns all State databases.

4.2.3 Categories of Processing Operations, When They Are Defined, Are Not Homogeneous

Sixteen countries have defined the "categories of processing operations concerned" by prior checking, and five have not (Bulgaria, the Czech Republic, Cyprus, Norway, the United Kingdom).

When categories are defined, they may be related to different issues: i.e., the specific nature of the data (e.g., personal identification, racial or ethnic origin, genetic or biometric data as in Macedonia), specific usage (e.g., use of a social security number other than for its intended purpose, registration of personal data without informing the data subject, or sharing of criminal data with third parties without a permit as in the Netherlands), specific sectors (e.g., telecommunications or financial organisations in Hungary), or other specific cases.

The French Data Protection Act requires that an authorisation is delivered by the Data Protection Authority mainly in the following cases: (i) statistical processing by INSEE (the national statistics agency) and Ministries, or processing of sensitive data justified by public interest, (ii) processing of genetic data, (iii) processing of data relating to offences, convictions or security measures, (iv) blacklists (in the absence of any legislative or regulatory provision), (v) combination of files, (vi) processing of data which contain the social security number, (vii) data comprising assessments of the social difficulties of natural persons, and (viii) processing of biometric data.

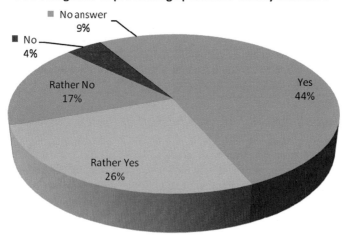

Are categories of processing operations clearly defined ?

- No answer 9%
- No 4%
- Rather No 17%
- Rather Yes 26%
- Yes 44%

In Norway, a licence from the Data Inspectorate (DPA) is required for the processing of sensitive data and for processing that will clearly violate weighty interests relating to protection of privacy – taking into account the nature and quantity of personal data collected and the purpose of the processing. This licensing system does not apply, however, to the processing of sensitive data which have been voluntarily provided by the data subject.

In Sweden, screening for hereditary disposition for disease as well as some cases of processing by the tax authority, the police and the coast guard are subject to prior checking.

In Slovenia, prior checking is limited to the introduction of biometrics and to the interconnection of data filing systems from official records and public books.

In Malta, examples of prior checking include the use of biometric systems, installation of CCTV systems especially those in the employment context or in sensitive locations. The competent Minister may define by regulation the processing operations involving particular risks and may prescribe rules in relation thereto.

In Ireland, to date, the Commissioner has only prescribed processing of genetic data in connection with employment.

In Italy, the categories of processing operations concerned encompass any operation concerning data – other than sensitive or judicial data – that entails specific risks to fundamental rights and freedoms as well as to human dignity. Specific technologies fall within this category, such as the use of biometrics in an employment context, the use of RFID technology, etc.

In Germany, automated data processing operations involving risks for the rights and freedoms of data subjects are concerned, in particular, if special categories of personal data are to be processed, or if the processing of personal data is intended to assess the data subject's personality, his or her abilities, performance or behaviour.

Austria considers that processing operations containing sensitive data, data about criminal offences, databases on creditworthiness, and databases in the form of a joint information system fed with data by multiple controllers require prior checking.

Finally, the transposition of prior checking in Belgian law covers different e-government processing operations that concern social security, national ID numbers, cross-point bank enterprises, automated data streams at federal level, justice department and statistics, and data streams at the level of the Flemish region.

4.2.4 Exemptions Are Foreseen in Half of the Countries

Eleven countries responded more or less positively to the question "Are exemptions foreseen (e.g., appointment of a data protection official[4])?" and 10 countries answered that they do not foresee any exemptions (Belgium, the Czech Republic, Cyprus, Hungary, Ireland, Italy, Malta, the Netherlands, Slovenia and the United Kingdom).

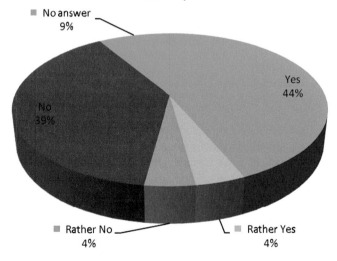

Are exemptions foreseen (e.g. existence of data protection official)?

No answer 9%

Yes 44%

No 39%

Rather No 4%

Rather Yes 4%

---

[4] Article 18 of Directive 95/46/CE allows Member States to provide for the simplification of or exemption from notification under certain circumstances. This includes cases where data controllers have appointed a data protection official in compliance with the national law.

Those exemptions concern either specific cases (e.g., data relating directly to an employment, medical data managed by doctors or judicial operational needs in Greece) or the appointment of data protection officials (which can simplify the process or even allow a circumvention of prior checking, depending on the country).

In Austria, model applications[5] ("Musteranwendungen") are generally subject to a simplified notification process. Model applications are designated by the federal chancellor in the form of an ordinance. Exceptions were defined for recognised religious groups and in cases of natural disasters, when databases of missing people must be created very quickly (such as for the 2004 and 2011 tsunami disasters).

In Germany, prior checking is not necessary when data processing is compulsory by law or the data subject has agreed to the data processing. Moreover, another exemption is foreseen when the processing or use of data is needed to create, carry out or terminate a legal or quasi-legal obligation with the data subject.

In Estonia, the approval procedure is not mandatory for State databases which are used internally or for document exchanges only.

In Greece, the law provides for several exceptions to notification of processing, including the case of sensitive data where an authorisation from the Data Protection Authority is usually required. Exceptions cover a wide variety of processing operations ranging from legal professions bound by an obligation of confidentiality to the operations of certain companies that process clients' or suppliers' data without disclosing them to third parties.

The Lithuanian law provides exemptions in the case of processing of sensitive data for purposes of internal administration, when data are necessary for a court hearing or in order to prevent and investigate criminal or other illegal activities.

In Sweden, exemptions concern special investigations by the police.

4.2.5 Prior Checking in the Context of National Legislative Measures and Regulations is Carried Out in Half of the Countries

Twelve countries responded positively to the question "Do you carry out prior checking in the context of preparation either of a measure of the national parliament or a measure based on such a legislative measure?" and 10 said they did not (Belgium, the Czech Republic, Cyprus, Germany, Greece, Ireland, Italy, the Netherlands, Sweden and the United Kingdom).

---

[5] If a large number of controllers carry out data processing in similar fashion and the prerequisites for a Standard Application ("Standardanwendung") do not apply, the Federal Chancellor can designate Model Applications by ordinance, i.e., a simplified notification form. Notifications of data processing the content of which corresponds to a model application contain limited information ((i) the designation of the model processing, (ii) the designation and address of the data controller as well as proof of statutory competencies or of legitimate authority, as far as this is required, and (iii) the registration number of the data controller, insofar as one has been already assigned to him.)

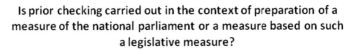

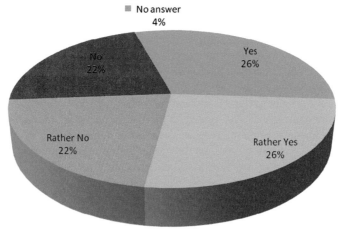

Prior checking in the context of preparation either of a measure of the national parliament or a measure based on such a legislative measure is mandatory and systematically required in some countries (Austria, France), and in some others, it is not (Bulgaria, Slovenian Republic). However, in countries where prior checking of legislative measures takes place (Belgium, France, Macedonia...), it appears that Data Protection Authorities only adopt an opinion which is not binding.

For instance, in France, an order of the competent Minister or a decree authorises, after a reasoned and published opinion of the Data Protection Authority, the processing of personal data carried out on behalf of the State for purposes such as:

- state security or public safety,
- prevention, investigation of proof of criminal offences,
- biometric data processed by the State.

In those countries where prior checking of national legislative measures and regulations is not foreseen as such (e.g., Germany), preparation and adoption of a legislative measure by the national parliament may include a comprehensive assessment of its impacts on various stakeholders which can refer – amongst others – to data protection and privacy issues. Moreover, procedural rules foresee that federal bodies, including the Data Protection Authority, are to be included at an early stage in any projects concerning their areas of responsibility.

Similarly, although prior checking is not formally used in Greece in this context, any check may be performed within the general competencies of the Data Protection Authority.

Finally, in some cases, prior checking of such measures is not systematic and the law may provide some flexibility. For instance, the Italian Data Protection

Authority is empowered to draw the Parliament's attention to specific issues related to bills and/or legislative measures, whilst its prior opinion is only mandatory for any item of secondary legislation (e.g., ministerial regulations) that impacts on data protection matters.

4.3 How Prior Checking Has Worked in Practice

In this section, we analyse how prior checking, when implemented into national legislation, has developed and is used in practice. In order to better understand national specificities, we asked national Data Protection Authorities the following questions:

1. What tools are available to the Data Protection Authority to carry out the prior checking (e.g., prior audit. . .)?
2. What is the format of the Data Protection Authority decision (e.g., prior authorisation, opinion, etc.), and how are the decisions of the Data Protection Authority publicised (e.g., letter, website, official journal. . .)?
3. Does the Data Protection Authority have a time limit to complete prior checking? If so, what are the consequences if the deadline is not met (e.g., tacit acceptance or refusal)?
4. In the context of prior checking, do notifications by the controller include more information than notifications for other types of processing mentioned in Article 18?
5. Has the Data Protection Authority developed specific instruments or procedures (e.g., templates, application forms, recommendations, PIA models in a specific sector) for any type of processing operation subject to prior checking or for pilot or experimental operations?
6. Can the processing operation start before receiving the decision of the Data Protection Authority?
7. If an authorisation by the Data Protection Authority is needed before the data controller sets up the processing operations, what are the means for him/her to appeal a (negative) decision by the Data Protection Authority?
8. What sanctions or consequences are faced by data controllers who set up processing operations without notifying the Data Protection Authority?

Based on the answers provided in the questionnaire, the following observations can be made.

4.3.1 Prior Checking Takes Different Forms at National Level; Data Protection Authorities Use Several Tools

In practice, prior checking can take different forms and may be seen as covering a variety of aspects ranging from checklists, to help data controllers upstream, to preliminary hearings. Prior checking has not been interpreted evenly in all countries: some have a wider vision of what it may encompass whereas others only see it in the context of formal procedures.

In most cases, prior checking is part of a formal procedural step – be it notification or authorisation. Mostly, the data controllers are asked to submit information and/or application forms and the Data Protection Authority checks this information and assesses the controller's situation in light of the national legislation.

Several tools have developed over time and can be used by Data Protection Authorities: on-site inspections (Bulgaria, Hungary, Estonia, Lithuania, Malta, Slovenia and Greece); hearings (Cyprus) or consultations (Hungary, Greece). Some Data Protection Authorities require further information when deemed necessary – as in Denmark, Ireland and Norway – and/or foresee a prior audit (Greece, Macedonia, Norway). While the Belgian authority has developed a model of security policy to help data controllers protect the personal data they process, the Slovenian authority performs an audit to control data security.

Germany, where data protection officers (DPOs) are compulsory, has a different approach. Prior checking is carried out by DPOs within companies who need to assess specific risks of the data processing and are in charge of checking the legality of automated data processing. In case of doubt, the DPO can consult the Data Protection Authority or, in case of postal and telecommunications companies, the Federal Commissioner for Data Protection and Freedom of Information.

4.3.2 The Format and Publicity of the Data Protection Authorities' Decisions Are Not Harmonised Across Europe

The format of Data Protection Authorities' decisions runs from simple registration or notification to prior authorisation. Several Data Protection Authorities issue opinions to approve or not a processing operation or grant authorisations. It very often depends on the nature of the data concerned and the type of data controller. For instance, in Germany, DPOs voluntarily provide written reports on processing activities.

When it comes to the publicity of their decisions, Data Protection Authorities also have their own specificities and usages.

Thirteen authorities publish their decisions on their websites; however, Macedonia only publishes decisions that have been anonymised and some authorities (Norway, Estonia) only publish some of the decisions. On the other hand, the Data Protection Authority of Malta does not publish its decisions and in Slovakia, all notified information systems are available in a register on their website.

While some authorities notify data controllers by mail (including Lithuania, Sweden and Norway), in the Netherlands, both the draft decision – sent to the data controller – and the final decision are published in the official State Gazette, which allows interested parties to comment on the draft decision or appeal the final decision. In Norway, decisions are also published in the official journal. In Cyprus, the Data Protection Authority's decisions are published in its annual report. Depending on the type of decision and on the nature of the data controller, the French Data Protection Authority either publishes its decisions in the Official Journal or notifies data controllers by mail.

How are the decisions of the DPA publicised ?

In Germany, there are no requirements on how to make decisions or reports of prior checking public. DPOs usually disclose their decisions or reports via the intranet of their agency/company or, at least, on request.

Decisions are also often available in a public registry, available online on the Data Protection Authority website but also at its premises. In the Czech Republic, for instance, records concerning notification are publicly accessible as part of the register of permitted data processing operations; nevertheless, other decisions and non-binding opinions could be made available to the public only on the ground of the Freedom of Information Act.

4.3.3 Data Protection Authorities Usually Set a Time Limit to Complete Prior Checking

The majority of Data Protection Authorities have a limited time to give their decision which ranges from 28 days to six months. Some only foresee a time limit in specific cases, for instance, for biometric measures in Slovenia. The average time limit is about two months.

Seven countries do not have a specified time limit in their legislation; in Macedonia, the time limit is not set in the data protection law but by general administrative rules (30 days). Similarly, while there is no absolute time limit in Norway, the Data Protection Authority has to notify the applicant if the time frame exceeds one month before it starts reviewing the application.

Two countries (Belgium, Ireland) indicate that the consequence of failure to meet the deadline is tacit acceptance, and one (Bulgaria) indicates that it amounts to a tacit refusal. France makes the distinction between the types of decision: tacit acceptance when the authority has to adopt a prior opinion – in the case of processing operations in the public sector – and tacit refusal when the authority has to authorise the processing operation in the private sector.

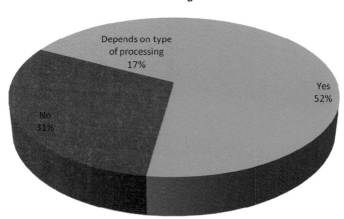

Have you specified a time limit for the DPA to complete prior checking?

In Italy, if the authority does not reply within the deadline (180 days), the applicant can challenge the Data Protection Authority's inaction.

4.3.4 In the Context of Prior Checking, Notifications by the Controller Usually Do Not Include More Information than Notifications for Other Types of Processing

Countries seem to be divided on whether notification of operations subject to prior checking should include more information than other "regular" processing operations mentioned in Article 18 of Directive 95/46/EC. A small majority of countries do not require more information (e.g., Germany, the Netherlands). However, in some countries Data Protection Authorities request more information if it is deemed appropriate, once they have received the original application (e.g., Ireland, Slovakia, France).

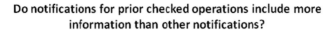

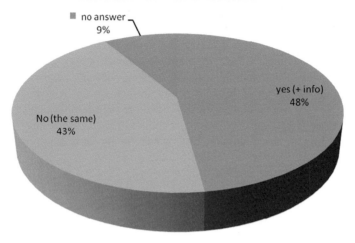

Do notifications for prior checked operations include more information than other notifications?

4.3.5 Data Protection Authorities Have Developed Specific Instruments or Procedures for Processing Operations Subject to Prior Checking

While eight authorities have not developed specific instruments or procedures, in general, Data Protection Authorities have developed such tools to help data controllers — and to facilitate their own assessment of operations subject to prior checking.

The Bulgarian authority has developed minimum standards for technical and organisational measures to help data controllers set up the appropriate level of security. The authority has also developed a questionnaire to be completed by the data controllers during an inspection. For cases involving sensitive data, the Estonian authority has put in place a self-assessment test and guidelines on its webpage.

In Germany, it is assumed that DPOs have developed models and privacy impact assessment (PIA), at least in larger institutions and companies.

The Dutch and French authorities have published general checklists, best practices or recommendations. Similarly, several Data Protection Authorities have issued recommendations for specific processing operations (for instance, on processing of political information, recruitment or geolocation purposes in France, on CCTV systems and advertising platforms in Greece, on the processing for historical scientific research purposes in Lithuania). In addition, the Greek authority has issued general recommendations for any type of processing (e.g., on the destruction of personal data).

4.3.6 Decisions of the Data Protection Authorities Can Generally Be Appealed Before an Administrative Court

In the vast majority of countries, Data Protection Authorities' decisions can be appealed before a court – be it a supreme administrative court (e.g., Belgium, Bulgaria, Cyprus, France, Greece) or a simple administrative court (e.g., Austria, the Czech Republic, Lithuania, Macedonia, Sweden, Slovenia, the Netherlands). In Norway, an appeal has to be brought before an independent administrative body subordinated to the King and the Ministry called the Board. In Greece and Estonia, the decisions should be appealed before the authority itself. While no rules regarding appeal are foreseen in Hungary, it seems that no appeal is possible against the Data Protection Authority decision in Slovakia.

4.3.7 Data Controllers Who Start Processing Operations Without Notifying the Data Protection Authority Most Likely Get Fined

The vast majority of Data Protection Authorities fine data controllers when they proceed with processing operations without notifying them.

The fines range from 900 euros (Macedonia) to 300,000 euros (France). In Slovenia, the penalty amount depends on the offence or type of processing at stake, from 830 to 12,510 euros (for biometric processing). Many Data Protection Authorities also have other sanctions they can use such as temporary or permanent revocation of a licence (Cyprus) or injunction to stop the processing (Estonia, France).

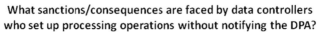

What sanctions/consequences are faced by data controllers who set up processing operations without notifying the DPA?

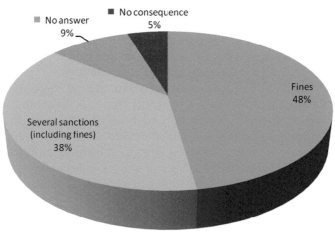

4.4 Lessons Learned from Prior Checking

In this section, we discuss the lessons learned from prior checking and analyse how prior checking can foster or limit the development of privacy impact assessments in Europe.

4.4.1 Assessment of the Current Prior Checking System and Potential Evolutions

Although most Data Protection Authorities are satisfied with the current prior checking system and wish to keep this control mechanism, some authorities have pointed out that prior checking imposes an administrative burden on data controllers and does not allow quality checking, due to their lack of resources.

This process is sometimes considered to be burdensome and time-consuming for both data controllers and Data Protection Authorities alike. It is also said to prevent Data Protection Authorities from focusing on ex post investigative actions. On the other hand, some authorities also consider that prior checking, amongst other things, helps them detect upstream problematic processing and control large data collection and processing by government bodies.

Therefore, some authorities envisage lightening or simplifying prior checking to focus only on data processing that presents specific risks (e.g., processing of sensitive data) and on processing that has not been examined before, either by the authority itself or by another body. In particular, some mentioned that prior checking should be compulsory for large data processing systems operated by public administrations that have been established by law and are not subject to notification obligation.

Data Protection Authorities have mentioned other possible solutions: one proposed to set up a "precedent clause", i.e., if the case submitted by the data controller is the same as one already handled and authorised by the Data Protection Authority, no prior checking should be necessary provided that the conditions and requirements laid down in respect of the earlier case are complied with in full. Electronic registration systems, appointment of DPOs and reinforcing the role of privacy impact assessments (PIAs) have also been highlighted as potential ways forward.

To remedy the burdensome aspect of prior checking, some Data Protection Authorities have already adopted simplified processes to make prior checking more efficient. For instance, the French authority has defined "unique authorisations" in various domains such as biometrics, human resources, etc. The latter allows a data controller that processes data according to the rules laid out in a "unique authorisation" to simply notify the French authority of his commitment to comply with the unique authorisation – and not to wait for a specific authorisation as normally required.

4.4.2 Data Protection Authorities Use Tools to Complement Prior Checking

Data Protection Authorities have developed or are currently developing tools that are designed to complement, or even replace in the long run, prior checking. Some Data Protection Authorities carry out audits to assess a data controller's compliance with the legislation. Others use risk assessment techniques and have developed their own tools to define and assess risks and to determine enforcement priorities. Other authorities perform security evaluation of data processing systems during inspections in specific cases (e.g., police). Similarly, some authorities are considering the possibility to develop privacy seals.

Moreover, a new tool is being increasingly mentioned by Data Protection Authorities and data controllers alike in the privacy landscape, i.e., privacy impact assessments (PIAs).

4.4.3 What Role for Privacy Impact Assessments?

4.4.3.1 PIA by Data Protection Authorities

Privacy impact assessment is a relatively new tool in the privacy world. Even though some Data Protection Authorities are involved in defining or even carrying out PIAs, the majority of Data Protection Authorities do not currently use this tool as such.

However, many authorities use "PIA-like activities" such as audit or assessment activities in specific cases such as the development of new legislation. A couple of authorities mentioned that they do not have the resources to regularly carry out PIAs or that they do not have a model to use PIA.

In contrast, some authorities have been much more proactive in promoting PIA, as a self-assessment tool, amongst companies who are designing new policies or systems. Two authorities have developed handbooks (United Kingdom, Denmark) that guide data controllers through the process of conducting a PIA. However, while these authorities give advice on how PIAs should be conducted, they do not approve or sign off an organisation's PIA.

In order to mitigate the potential burden of doing a PIA, an authority (United Kingdom) has promoted a methodology which assists organisations with integrating PIAs into their standard project management process. It also helps ensure that privacy risks are considered by project leaders instead of leaving them to, for example, privacy officers who may be less involved in the project.

4.4.3.2 PIA by Private Organisations and Governments

In the vast majority of countries, PIAs are not compulsory.[6] Some Data Protection Authorities encourage private entities to carry out PIAs – especially if they have

---

[6] In the future, PIA may develop at the European level in specific sectors. For instance, the European Commission has adopted a Recommendation on RFID in 2009, which asks Member

data protection officers – but this tool is very much seen as a voluntary internal self-assessment instrument. To date, this practice is not yet widespread amongst companies; when used, it would be by multinational or at least larger companies. It seems that only two countries impose PIA on all data processors (Macedonia, Norway) but the experience of one Data Protection Authority is that many entities do not comply with this obligation.

In addition, one country (United Kingdom) obliges just public entities to develop privacy impact assessment for all new central government projects involving significant amounts of personal data. PIAs may also be used by local government, policing and healthcare providers.

Finally, it is worth noting that in its strategic communication on a comprehensive approach on personal data protection in the European Union,[7] the European Commission stated that it will consider whether the future EU legal privacy framework should include "an obligation for data controllers to carry out a data protection impact assessment in specific cases, for instance, when sensitive data are being processed, or when the type of processing otherwise involves specific risks, in particular when using specific technologies, mechanisms or procedures, including profiling or video surveillance". Also, the European Parliament, in a recent resolution on Passenger Name Records[8] has considered that "any new legislative instrument must be preceded by a Privacy Impact Assessment and a proportionality test".

4.4.3.3 Nature of PIAs

Questioned on whether PIAs should become compulsory, Data Protection Authorities' answers are split.

On the one hand, some authorities believe that making PIA compulsory will increase administrative and financial burdens. As a consequence, it could lead to a "ticking the box" exercise, instead of being a process with which entities can properly engage, and it would thus be less effective than current audit practices carried out voluntarily. Some authorities also argue that the additional benefit provided by PIAs may not be such as to justify a further regulatory burden on organisations in all cases. These authorities believe that PIAs should rather be promoted as "best practice".

States to ensure that operators in the RFID sector conduct an assessment of the implications of the application implementation for the protection of personal data and privacy, including whether the application could be used to monitor an individual.

[7] European Commission, A comprehensive approach on personal data protection in the European Union, Communication from the Commission to the European Parliament, the Council, the Economic and Social Committee and the Committee of the Regions, COM (2010) 609 final, Brussels, 4 Nov 2010.

[8] European Parliament, Resolution of 5 May 2010 on the launch of negotiations for Passenger Name Record (PNR) agreements with the United States, Australia and Canada. http://www.europarl.europa.eu/sides/getDoc.do?pubRef=-//EP//TEXT+TA+P7-TA-2010-0144+0+DOC+XML+V0//EN

On the other hand, other authorities believe compulsory PIAs would be a good way forward, at least in the long run. PIAs could, for instance, be made available to the Data Protection Authority at the time of an inspection. Some authorities, while backing a compulsory instrument, believe that it should nevertheless depend on the sector (e.g., administration), size (e.g., big companies) and/or risks involved in data processing (e.g., for sensitive data).

As regards the interaction between PIAs and prior checking, the vast majority of Data Protection Authorities believe that PIAs should complement, but not replace, prior checking – as the pros and cons of PIAs are still unknown. The rationale for considering PIAs as complementing prior checking is generally that it will improve data protection and help determine the appropriate security measures which should be implemented in a system. Indeed, PIAs must include a risk assessment approach in order to give a reasonable assurance that the proposed security measures are adequate or proportionate to the risks. In this scenario, PIAs can either have a role to play before submitting a prior-checking request to ensure an organisation understands shortfalls and addresses privacy implications, or they could be used as an element of prior checking (thus helping to simplify the procedures for prior checking since many aspects evaluated in PIAs may already be shared with prior checking).

However, other authorities argue that prior checking and PIAs are completely independent because the former is a legal obligation and is performed by an independent party (the Data Protection Authority), whereas the latter is carried out on a voluntary basis and is usually either performed or sponsored by the data controller. A couple of authorities consider that PIAs should be subject to their control, at least when dealing with specific prior checking requests. Finally, only one authority believes PIAs represent a serious alternative to prior checking.

4.4.3.4 Impact of PIAs on Data Protection

The vast majority of Data Protection Authorities believe that PIAs have the potential to improve data protection, if carried out with due professionalism and an appropriate level of data protection expertise. A PIA can be seen as an internal privacy evaluation tool for the data controller as well as a "privacy by design" tool.

However, some Data Protection Authorities comment that it will mainly depend on the manner in which a PIA is implemented. They also believe that a PIA should not be a symbol of compliance or assurance that limits the existing risk assessment/control mechanisms, thus creating a risk to hinder data protection.

4.4.3.5 Recognition of PIAs at the European Level

PIAs are gaining popularity at European level. In 2009, the European Commission adopted a recommendation on RFID.[9] Its Article 4 states that "Member States

---

[9] European Commission, Recommendation on the implementation of privacy and data protection principles in applications supported by radio-frequency identification, C (2009) 3200

should ensure that industry, in collaboration with relevant civil society stakeholders, develops a framework for privacy and data protection impact assessments. This framework should be submitted for endorsement to the Article 29 Data Protection Working Party within 12 months from the publication of this Recommendation in the Official Journal of the European Union."

Based on the framework approved by the Article 29 Working Party in February 2011, RFID operators will need to conduct a "Privacy and Data Protection Impact Assessment" before an RFID application is deployed. Operators will also have to make the PIA results available to the "competent authority".[10] As mentioned above, this topic may be of particular importance in the context of the review of Directive 95/46/EC. Indeed, to promote design methods protecting privacy ("privacy by design") and the principle of accountability, this review could include the concept of privacy impact assessment, and the framework, currently set for RFID, could serve as a model for other issues.

In March 2010, the RFID workgroup, composed of industry representatives, submitted a first draft of the privacy impact assessment framework, which was not endorsed by the Article 29 Working Party.[11] In its opinion assessing the industry's framework proposal, the Article 29 Working Party addressed several concerns and in particular highlighted the need for a clear and comprehensive privacy and data protection risk assessment approach in the proposed framework. According to the Working Party, risk assessment is a "key component" of a PIA process and "a satisfactory means to give the RFID Operator or the competent authority a reasonable assurance that the proposed measures are adequate or proportionate to the risks, since these risks have not been identified in the first place". The absence of risk assessment in the framework proposed by the industry is the central issue raised in the Opinion.[12]

After several revisions, the industry submitted a new RFID PIA Framework to the Article 29 Working Party in January 2011. The new proposal addressed most issues that were highlighted in Opinion 5/2010 and the Article 29 Working Party endorsed the revised PIA Framework on 11 February 2011.

4.5 Conclusion

It follows from Article 20 of Directive 95/46/EC, which provides that Member States shall carry out "prior checking" for processing operations likely to present specific risks, that most Member States use prior checking in practice. While the

---

final, Brussels, 12 May 2009. http://ec.europa.eu/information_society/policy/rfid/documents/recommendationonrfid2009.pdf

[10] The manner in which the PIA should be made available (e.g., on request or not) will be determined by the national Data Protection Authorities. In particular, the risks related to the application may be taken into account, as well as other factors such as the presence of a data protection official.

[11] http://ec.europa.eu/justice/policies/privacy/workinggroup/index_en.htm

[12] See Chapters 15 and 16 of this book for further discussion of the RFID PIA Framework.

implementation of this measure is not homogeneous, regarding for instance the categories of processing operations, the scope of exemptions or the various shapes it takes at national level, prior checking is seen as an important element of data protection.

Prior checking is also at the very heart of the activities of the majority of Data Protection Authorities: it allows authorities to monitor and assess "risky" developments and to exercise a control ex ante as in the vast majority of countries processing operations cannot start before a decision of the Data Protection Authority is received by the controller. Also, authorities have been developing specific instruments and procedures for processing operations subject to prior checking. In this context, privacy impact assessments are increasingly considered as a complement to prior checking.

Today, authorities use "PIA-like activities" (such as audit or assessment activities) and very often PIAs carried out by organisations are seen as voluntary internal self-assessment instruments. Yet, on the one hand, some authorities are considering making use of PIAs and, on the other, the precedent set up by the EC RFID Recommendation, which requires RFID operators to conduct a "Privacy and Data Protection Impact Assessment" before an RFID application is deployed, may well accelerate the current trend. In addition, the upcoming review of Directive 95/46/EC is expected to give more weight to PIA as a tool to complement prior checking and as a means to improve the enforcement of data protection.

While it may be difficult to assert that prior checking is a forerunner to privacy impact assessments, one may consider that, due to their complementary nature, prior checking is playing a dynamic role in the development of privacy impact assessment.

Acknowledgements This study could not have been conducted without the help of the national Data Protection Authorities who kindly accepted to respond to the questionnaire sent by the authors. The views and conclusions presented in this article do not necessarily represent those of Data Protection Authorities (including CNIL) or of the Article 29 Working Party.

Part II
Five Countries Lead the Way

Chapter 5
PIAs in Australia: A Work-In-Progress Report

Roger Clarke

Privacy impact assessment (PIA) has a long history in Australia, and some degree of maturity has been achieved. This chapter provides historical background to privacy laws in Australia and the emergence of PIAs as a tool of government and business. It then evaluates the available guidance documents and indicates likely directions of future development.

Privacy laws in Australia are in the process of being significantly weakened. As a result, merely complying with privacy laws will provide organisations with no assurance that their schemes will be acceptable to citizens and consumers. PIAs are, therefore, highly likely to assume increasing importance, as government agencies and corporations alike seek understanding of how to avoid negative media coverage and public opposition.

5.1 Introduction

In Australia, assessments of the privacy impacts of new projects can be traced back to about 1990. The momentum has been markedly greater since about 2000, and several guidance documents exist.

The purpose of this chapter is to review the development of PIAs in Australia, and the adequacy of the guidance documents published by Australian government agencies. In order to set the scene for that analysis, it is first necessary to clarify the features of PIAs as the term is used in this chapter.

R. Clarke (✉)
Xamax Consultancy Pty Ltd, Canberra, Australia
e-mail: Roger.Clarke@xamax.com.au

D. Wright, P. De Hert (eds.), *Privacy Impact Assessment*, Law, Governance and Technology Series 6, DOI 10.1007/978-94-007-2543-0_5,

5.2 The Nature of PIAs

The term privacy impact assessment (PIA) is used to refer to activities of widely varying scope. This author has catalogued a number of definitions of the term.[1]

In a guidance document published in 1998, the author defined a PIA as "a process whereby the potential impacts and implications of proposals that involve potential privacy-invasiveness are surfaced and examined".[2] Those documents made clear that the scope was much more than an audit of compliance with the law, and that the activity needed to address all dimensions of privacy. Consultation was described as central to the process: "The objectives of a PIA cannot be achieved if the process is undertaken behind closed doors. In a complex project applying powerful technologies, there are many segments of the population that are affected. It is intrinsic to the process that members of the public provide input to the assessment, and that the outcomes reflect their concerns."[3]

The term is used in this chapter in a manner that sustains the key elements identified in 1998, and precludes narrow interpretations of the nature of mere legal compliance checks:

> Privacy impact assessment (PIA) is a systematic process that identifies and evaluates, from the perspectives of all stakeholders, the potential effects on privacy of a project, initiative or proposed system or scheme, and includes a search for ways to avoid or mitigate negative privacy impacts.

The author has drawn distinctions between a PIA and several other business process methods.[4] These features are presented in revised form in Exhibit 5.1.

These features are reflected in the sections below that outline the history of PIAs in Australia and provide critiques of the available guidance documents.

5.3 The History and Status of PIAs in Australia

This section focuses on the conduct of privacy impact assessments, with consideration of PIA guidance documents for the most part deferred until later. The development path can be usefully separated into the periods before and after 2000. The third sub-section summarises the position in 2010 in each of the nine jurisdictions of the federation together with the complex situation in non-government sectors.

---

[1] Clarke Roger, "Privacy Impact Assessment: Its Origins and Development", *Computer Law & Security Review*, Vol. 25, No. 2, April 2009, pp. 123–135. Preprint at http://www.rogerclarke.com/DV/PIAHist-08.html

[2] Clarke, Roger, "Privacy Impact Assessments", Xamax Consultancy Pty Ltd, February 1998. http://www.rogerclarke.com/DV/PIA.html.

[3] Clarke Roger, "Privacy Impact Assessment Guidelines", Xamax Consultancy Pty Ltd, February 1998. http://www.xamax.com.au/DV/PIA.html

[4] Clarke, 2009, op. cit. fn. 1.

Exhibit 5.1 – PIAs Distinguished from Other Privacy-Related Processes

- **Activities conducted prior to a PIA**

    - *Privacy strategy formulation* considers privacy from a corporate perspective, whereas **a PIA focuses on a particular initiative, scheme, program or project**. In this chapter, the term "project" is used to encompass all such categories of activity.
    - *Privacy issues analysis* is a preliminary, internal assessment of the potential issues that may arise during the life-cycle of a project, whereas **a PIA is performed at depth, through the project life-cycle, and involves engagement with stakeholders.**

- **Activities with narrower scope than a PIA**

    - *A privacy impact statement* is a declaration by the organisation, whereas **PIA is a process.**
    - *Legal compliance assessment* is an analysis of the extent to which the project complies with relevant laws, whereas **a PIA assesses a project against the needs, expectations and concerns of all stakeholders, including but not limited to legal requirements.**
    - *Data privacy impact assessment* is a study of the impacts of a project on only the privacy of personal data, whereas **a PIA considers all dimensions of privacy.**
    - *Internal cost/benefit analysis* is an assessment of the costs and benefits of a project from the viewpoint of the organisation alone, whereas **a PIA adopts a multi-perspective approach, taking into account the costs and benefits as perceived by all stakeholders.**
    - *Internal risk assessment* is an assessment of the risks arising in relation to a project from the viewpoint of the organisation alone, whereas **a PIA adopts a multi-perspective approach, taking into account the risks as perceived by all stakeholders.**

- **Activities conducted subsequent to a PIA**

    - *A privacy policy statement (PPS)* declares the organisation's undertakings in relation to privacy, whereas **a PIA is a process used to establish what undertakings an organisation needs to give.**
    - *Privacy management planning and control* is a systematic process of ensuring that a privacy management plan is articulated and implemented, in order to give effect to the privacy-relevant decisions made during the project, whereas **a PIA is the process that identifies the problems and identifies solutions to them.**
    - *Privacy audit* is an assessment conducted after a project is implemented, whereas **a PIA is conducted before and in parallel with a project, and ensures that harmful and expensive problems that an audit would later expose are avoided, and that unavoidable negative impacts on privacy are minimised and harms mitigated.**

5.3.1 Pre-2000

The earliest activity in Australia that has been identified as being of the nature of a PIA was the "program protocol" required from 1990 onwards by the Data-Matching Program (Assistance and Tax) Act and expressed in Schedule 1 of the Act. These requirements were specific to the so-called "Parallel Data-Matching Program".[5] Generic guidelines for data matching programs, which also had a program protocol at the core, were published subsequently.[6] The most recent revision was in February 1998, so they have remained unrevised for over a decade. The generic guidelines were not, and still are not, in any way binding on the agencies that conduct matching programs.

The next activity that has been located is an April 1993 strategy devised by this author as part of a consultancy assignment for a smartcard-based loyalty scheme for Card Technologies Australia Ltd (subsequently re-structured as the NASDAQ-listed Catuity Inc.).

The earliest mention of the term "PIA" found in Australian sources appears to be a 1995 acknowledgement by the Telecommunications Industry Ombudsman that PIAs had a role to play.[7] Articles published by the Deputy New Zealand Privacy Commissioner in the Australian *Privacy Law & Policy Reporter* provided a stimulus to developments.[8] In mid-1996, Blair Stewart organised a discussion session on PIAs in Christchurch.[9]

---

[5] Clarke Roger, "Matches Played Under Rafferty's Rules: The Parallel Data Matching Program Is Not Only Privacy-Invasive But Economically Unjustifiable As Well", Xamax Consultancy Pty Ltd, November 1993. http://www.rogerclarke.com/DV/PaperMatchPDMP.html. Versions published in *Privacy Law & Policy Reporter*, Vol. 1, No. 1, February 1994, and in *Policy*, Autumn 1994.

[6] Office of the Australian Privacy Commissioner, "The Use of Data Matching in Commonwealth Administration – Guidelines", 1992, revised February 1998. http://www.privacy.gov.au/publications/dmcomadmin.pdf. Note that the title of the Office has been, between 1989 and 2010, variously the Office of the Privacy Commissioner (OPC), the Office of the Federal Privacy Commissioner (OFPC) and the Office of the Australian Privacy Commissioner (OAPC), and from 1 November 2010, it has been absorbed into the Office of the Australian Information Commissioner (OAIC). To distinguish it from other similarly named entities at the State and Territory level, Office of the Australian Privacy Commissioner (OAPC) is used here.

[7] See the reference in Dixon, Tim, "Communications Law Centre Wants IPPs Revised in Line with Australian Privacy Charter", *Privacy Law and Policy Reporter*, Vol. 3, No.9, January 1997. http://www.austlii.edu.au/au/journals/PLPR/1997/4.html.

[8] Stewart, Blair, "Privacy Impact Assessments", *Privacy Law and Policy Reporter*, Vol. 3, No. 4, July 1996. http://www.austlii.edu.au/au/journals/PLPR/1996/39.html. See also Stewart, Blair, "PIAs – An Early Warning System", *Privacy Law and Policy Reporter*, Vol. 3, No. 7, October/November 1996. http://www.austlii.edu.au/au/journals/PLPR/1996/65.html.

[9] See endnote 3 in Flaherty, David, "Privacy Impact Assessments: An Essential Tool for Data Protection", *Privacy Law and Policy Reporter*, Vol. 7, No. 5, November 2000. http://www.austlii.edu.au/au/journals/PLPR/2000/45.html. See also NZPC, "A Compilation of Materials in Relation to Privacy Impact Assessment", New Zealand Privacy Commissioner, 1997, and Stewart, Blair, "Privacy Impact Assessment Towards a Better Informed Process for Evaluating Privacy Issues Arising from New Technologies", *Privacy Law and Policy Reporter*, Vol. 5, No. 8, February 1999. http://www.austlii.edu.au/au/journals/PLPR/1999/8.html

Also in 1996, this author conducted assignments for the Australian Commission for the Future in relation to smartcard-based payment schemes generally, and for MasterCard International's smartcard-based electronic cash trial (whose international pilot was run in Canberra). Soon afterwards, the Communications Law Centre, a research group, called for PIAs to be conducted in relation to "any new system, technology or practice which may affect personal privacy".[10] The call invoked Stewart's publications, Flaherty's work in British Columbia and the Australian Privacy Charter.[11]

During 1998, this author undertook further assignments relating to patient data linkage by the New South Wales (NSW) Health Commission, the then-emergent Australian Business Number and Register, and a proposed multi-purpose smart identification card for Centrelink. On the basis of the experience accumulated to that point in time, the author published descriptions of the PIA process at lesser and greater depth.[12]

5.3.2   Post-2000

The tempo picked up from this time onwards. Nigel Waters commented, "There [was] nothing particularly new or radical about PIAs – just a new name for a technique of assessment which privacy regulators and consultants have been performing for years. It is essentially just a systematic appraisal of the privacy implications of a new proposal. Some appraisals are limited to assessing compliance with specific privacy rules or standards, but others range more widely over all privacy issues of concern to affected individuals, whether or not they are currently subject to privacy law."[13] Blair Stewart published a collection of "Approaches, Issues and Examples" in 2001,[14] and a further paper in 2002.[15]

In December 2001, the then federal Privacy Commissioner, Malcolm Crompton, issued guidelines relating to a specific category of projects, which included a recommendation that a PIA be performed.[16] Although those guidelines were non-binding, government agencies have heeded them in a number of subsequent projects.

---

[10] Dixon, 1997, op. cit. fn. 7.

[11] The Australian Privacy Charter was launched in December 1994 by a specially-formed group, the Australian Privacy Charter Council (APCC), under the chairmanship of Justice Michael Kirby. http://www.privacy.org.au/About/PrivacyCharter.html

[12] Clarke, 1998, op. cit., fn. 2 and 3.

[13] Waters, Nigel, "Privacy Impact Assessment – Traps for the Unwary", *Privacy Law & Policy Reporter*, Vol. 7, No. 9, February 2001. http://www.austlii.edu.au/au/journals/PLPR/2001/10.html

[14] Stewart, Blair, "Privacy Impact Assessment: Some Approaches, Issues and Examples". http://jeb.cerps.org.tw/files/JEB2002-009.pdf

[15] Stewart, Blair, "Privacy Impact Assessment Roundup", *Privacy Law & Policy Reporter*, Vol. 9, No. 5, September 2002. http://www.austlii.edu.au/au/journals/PLPR/2002/index.html

[16] Office of the Australian Privacy Commissioner (OAPC), Privacy and Public Key Infrastructure: Guidelines for Agencies using PKI to Communicate or Transact with Individuals, December 2001. http://www.privacy.gov.au/materials/types/download/8809/6609

By 2003, the Commissioner had submitted to a parliamentary committee that "Commonwealth agencies [should] be required to undertake privacy impact assessments at the beginning of the development of new proposals and initiatives involving the handling of the personal information of the Australian community. These assessments should be published."[17]

As further discussed below, the Commissioner's Office developed draft PIA guidelines during 2003–2004 and, following a consultation period, published them.[18] During their launch in August 2006, the then Attorney-General Phillip Ruddock said that "as a matter of good business practice, I strongly encourage government agencies to use the guide to assist them in playing a larger role in promoting privacy compliance".[19] This was reinforced in April 2007, when the head of the Attorney-General's Department wrote to all agency heads in relation to privacy issues generally, extolling the benefits of using PIAs early in the project life-cycle.[20]

During the period 2004–2010, PIAs became a mainstream activity among a range of Commonwealth government agencies, but use of the technique remains much more muted in other contexts. The following section provides a summary of the situation.

5.3.3 The 10 Contexts

Australia is a resource-rich nation that occupies the world's largest island and/or smallest continent. It has a population of 22 million people, who live primarily in urban areas around the eastern seaboard. The country is a federation – the Commonwealth of Australia, formed in 1901 – which comprises one national and eight subsidiary geographical jurisdictions. There are six States (whose formation as colonies occurred between 1788 and 1851) and two Territories (which were given self-government by Commonwealth statutes in 1978 and 1988). Each of the nine Crowns is empowered to regulate its own public sector. However, the Commonwealth Parliament retains the power to over-ride the Territory Parliaments, and has occasionally done so, in one relevant instance in relation to euthanasia laws.

For the purposes of privacy law, a tenth context needs to be recognised – the non-government sectors. A major component is "the private sector" comprising for-profit business enterprises – including corporations, unincorporated businesses including sole traders, partnerships and trusts, and many co-operatives. There are also a great many not-for-profit organisations, large and small – including charities,

---

[17] Office of the Australian Privacy Commissioner, Submission to the Joint Committee of Public Accounts and Audit (JCPAA) on Management and Integrity of Electronic Information in the Commonwealth, January 2003, pp. 19–20. http://www.privacy.gov.au/publications/jcpaasubs.doc

[18] Office of the Australian Privacy Commissioner, Privacy Impact Assessment Guide, August 2006. http://www.privacy.gov.au/publications/PIA06.pdf

[19] Attorney-General, "Privacy Impact Assessment Guide and Layered Privacy Policy Launch", Press release, 26 Aug 2006.

[20] Interview with OAPC in 2007.

associations, clubs, unions, political parties and some co-operatives. The third non-government segment is people. The privacy impact of the behaviour of individuals has become much more significant as their ability to electronically publish information emerged in the mid-1990s through websites, and exploded from 2000 through blogging, then social networking services and since about 2005, micro-blogging ("tweeting").

Under the Australian Constitution, the non-government sectors are subject to aspects of both Commonwealth law and the laws of the States and Territories. In relation to some sectors and activities, one is clearly relevant and the other, clearly not; but in a number of contexts, there is considerable uncertainty as to which law would prevail in the likely event of conflict between laws.

The following sub-sections provide brief overviews of each of the 10 contexts, including the size and nature of the jurisdictions, the history and status of privacy law, and the situation in 2010 relating to PIAs.[21]

(1) Federal Public Sector

The Commonwealth public sector is subject to the Privacy Act 1988, which embodies in s. 14 the Information Privacy Principles (the IPPs) and which created the position of Privacy Commissioner and the Office of the Australian Privacy Commissioner (OAPC). From the viewpoint of privacy advocates, the statute was a weak instrument, but somewhat better than nothing at all. With the passage of time and a vast fleet of subsequent laws that over-ride the protections it provided, it has atrophied into a very weak instrument.

Most of the functions of the Privacy Commissioner are specifically limited to information privacy, in particular, as defined by the Information Privacy Principles in the Privacy Act. However, seven of the 24 functions are expressed openly, and empower and require the Commissioner to consider all dimensions of the privacy of individuals, not merely the privacy of personal information. These functions are the examination of proposed enactments [s. 27(1)(b)], research into IT (c), provision of advice (f), examination of proposals for data matching or data linkage (k), educational programs (m), reports and recommendations (r), and anything incidental or conducive to those six functions (s). The first four Commissioners during the two decades from 1989 to 2010 largely avoided the exercise of these functions outside the narrow realm of privacy of personal data as limited by the Information Privacy Principles.

---

[21] The analysis draws on and updates the following: Information Commissioner's Office, "Appendix E: Jurisdictional Report for Australia" in "Privacy Impact Assessments: International Study of their Application and Effects", Wilmslow, UK, December 2007. http://www.ico.gov.uk/upload/documents/library/corporate/research_and_reports/lbrouni_piastudy_appe_aus_2910071.pdf and Clarke, Roger, "Privacy Impact Assessment in Australian Contexts", *Murdoch eLaw Journal*, Vol. 15, No. 1, June 2008. For a preprint, see http://www.rogerclarke.com/DV/PIAAust.html.

A further consideration is occasional hints that a tort of privacy might emerge. However, no court of any consequence has ever handed down a significant decision. An Australian Law Reform Commission (ALRC) report recommended a common-law right of action,[22] but the media wilfully misrepresented the proposal as an attack on freedom of the press, and neither the current nor any future government appears to have the capacity to withstand media assaults; so the chances of a right of action emerging remain low, notwithstanding renewed interest following the Murdoch media scandals.

The Australian Privacy Foundation (APF) has identified a considerable array of laws,[23] which provide incidental protections for various aspects of privacy.

The notion of a PIA emerged in 1990, and PIAs and PIA guidance documents were apparent under that name from 1998 onwards. A PIA guidance document published by the Privacy Commissioner[24] has had considerable influence, and is discussed in the following section.

During 2003–2005, a central agency, the Australian Government Information Management Office (AGIMO), the head of which is the Australian Government Chief Information Officer (AGCIO), conducted PIAs on the succession of sub-projects within the then Australian Government Authentication Framework (AGAF) program (since re-named the National e-Authentication Framework, NeAF), and urged conduct of a PIA at critical points within smartcard projects. During 2004–2007, the benefits-payment agency, Centrelink, conducted a multi-phase PIA relating to speaker authentication. In addition, at least some divisions within a range of Commonwealth government agencies have undertaken PIAs, including the Attorney-General's Department, the Australian Bureau of Statistics (ABS) and the Department of Health and of Human Services (DHS).[25]

The Commonwealth public sector provides a particularly telling example of how the mishandling of the PIA notion can be extremely costly.[26] In April 2006, the then Coalition Government committed $1 billion to the development of an Access Card scheme. The two most senior project executives promptly resigned, citing privacy, information security and accountability concerns. Many independent commentators, experts, newspaper editors and letter-writers expressed similar concerns.

---

[22] Australian Law Reform Commission, "For Your Information: Australian Privacy Law and Practice", ALRC Report 108, August 2008. http://www.alrc.gov.au/publications/report-108

[23] Australian Privacy Foundation, "Resources – The Law", current as at August 2010. http://www.privacy.org.au/Resources. See also the website of the Office of the Australian Privacy Commissioner: http://www.privacy.gov.au/government

[24] Office of the Australian Privacy Commissioner, "Privacy Impact Assessment Guide", August 2006. http://www.privacy.gov.au/publications/PIA06.pdf. The OAPC produced a revised version in May 2010. http://www.privacy.gov.au/materials/types/download/9509/6590

[25] Lists of exemplars can be found in Appendix E within ICO, 2007, op. cit., pp. 15–17.

[26] Australian Privacy Foundation, "The Federal government calls it a 'Human Services Access Card'. We call it for what it is: a National ID Card System", 2007. http://www.privacy.org.au/Campaigns/ID_cards/HSAC.html

A PIA report was prepared by consultants (although it appears to have actually been a privacy issues analysis), but it was suppressed. A Consumer and Privacy "Task force" was announced on 24 May 2006, whose effect, and presumably intention, was to shield the Minister and the agency from contact with privacy advocates. The Task force released an Issues Paper, held public briefings and delivered a report in November 2006, some of which appeared to be strongly expressed. But it made extremely weak recommendations. Despite that, the Minister simply rejected the recommendations that did not fit his agenda.

The privacy advocacy community continued to be held at distance from the agency. In March 2007, however, a Senate Committee report was scathing, recommending withdrawal of the bill, substantial changes and re-submission of the complete package of legislation.[27] This was highly exceptional in that the Government Senators joined in the attack, along with the Opposition and minor parties. The Bill was allowed to lapse, and after the election in November 2007, the incoming Labour Government closed the still-large office.

Estimates of the public funds wasted were in excess of $50 million, but this appeared to exclude the substantial costs associated with the hundreds of staff who had been assembled. Private sector costs also ran into many tens of millions, because scores of companies had responded to several very large tenders, but only (relatively) small preliminary consultancy contracts were ever let. The many misconceptions inherent in the project would have been detected at an early stage if the agency had conducted a first-phase PIA and engaged with civil society.

(2) The Non-government Sectors

Constitutional powers in relation to non-government organisations are somewhat complex. The Commonwealth has legislated in respect of the for-profit and not-for-profit sectors generally – but with exemptions for small business enterprises and associations. The States and Territories appear to have generally accepted that jurisdictional claim. Some States and Territories have, however, passed privacy law in respect of particular activities, particularly the health care sector, which intersects and may conflict with the federal law.[28]

The credit-reporting sector nationwide was subjected to specific provisions enacted in 1989. They are contained in ss. 18A-18B and Part IIIA (ss. 18C-18V) of the Privacy Act. Ever since their enactment, these provisions have been the subject of lobbying by the monopoly credit reference company and the financial services sector. The pleas had met with very limited success. The ALRC's 2008 report, however, gifted the industry an opportunity to at last achieve its desires. If the industry is

---

[27] Senate Finance and Public Administration Committee (SFPAC), "Human Services (Enhanced Service Delivery) Bill 2007 [Provisions]", March 2007. http://www.aph.gov.au/senate/committee/fapa_ctte/access_card/report/index.htm

[28] The Australian Privacy Foundation has identified relevant laws in its text "Resources – The Law", current as at August 2010, at http://www.privacy.org.au/Resources. See also the website of the Office of the Australian Privacy Commissioner: http://www.privacy.gov.au/business

successful in having the provisions changed, the level of intrusiveness into personal data, and the amount of harm caused by errors in the industry, can both be expected to leap.

In 2000, the for-profit and not-for-profit sectors nationwide were brought under the Privacy Act through changes embodied in the Privacy Amendment (Private Sector) Act 2000. This created in Schedule 3 the National Privacy Principles (the NPPs), which are significantly different from the IPPs that apply to the Commonwealth public sector. The Privacy Commissioner's limited oversight powers apply to this segment of the Act as well. The NPPs are much longer than the public sector IPPs (3,300 words cf. 1,600 words). This is because government agencies can, and frequently do, override the IPPs through legislation that they ask their Minister to put before Parliament, whereas the private sector has less direct access to Parliament and hence demanded that a vast array of privacy-invasive practices be authorised as part of the NPPs.

During the decade following 2000, there was considerable unrest among consumers about electronic marketing practices. Consultative processes conducted by the Department of Communications resulted in regulation firstly of unsolicited e-mail by the Spam Act 2003, and secondly of unsolicited tele-marketing calls by the Do Not Call Register Act 2006. The Do Not Call Register attracted more than 200,000 registrations in the first 24 hours it was open, passed 2 million registrations within the first six months, and stood at 5 million in mid-2010, even though the law exempts categories of organisations widely regarded as abusing the medium, including charities, researchers and politicians.

In the telecommunications sector more generally, the Telecommunications Act and the Telecommunications (Interception and Access) Act include provisions relating to security and privacy. The privacy-protective aspects of these laws are utilised much more effectively by the Telecommunications Industry Ombudsman (TIO) and the Australian Communications and Media Authority (ACMA) than the provisions of the Privacy Act are by the Privacy Commissioner.[29]

A range of additional provisions apply in particular non-government contexts, and fall outside or at the boundary of the Privacy Commissioner's purview. Victoria, New South Wales (NSW) and the Australian Capital Territory (ACT) all have laws specifically relating to health care data, and it is far from clear to what extent each of the conflicting laws applies to any given activity by any given organisation. The confusion may not be of much consequence, however, because there are very limited sanctions, and little or no enforcement is undertaken, at either federal or State level.

A further area of conflict of laws is outsourced service providers to State and Territory governments and public-private partnerships. Toll-road operators have blatantly played the federal and state Commissioners off against one another.

---

[29] Cyberspace Law and Policy Centre of the University of New South Wales, "Communications Privacy Complaints: In Search of the Right Path", A consumer research report supported by the Australian Communications Consumer Action Network (ACCAN), Sydney, September 2010. http://www.cyberlawcentre.org/privacy/ACCAN_Complaints_Report/report.pdf

Despite formal complaints, the Commissioners have steadfastly avoided resolving the question of which privacy laws and which sets of Principles apply.

The OAPC's purview includes both the public and the non-government sectors, and its PIA guide has been relevant to corporations since it was first published in 2006. Amendments in 2010 were designed to make clearer the guide's applicability to business enterprises.

PIAs have been conducted in the for-profit and not-for-profit sectors, but are still not widespread. Few have been widely publicised, and the author is aware of no published reports. Areas in which projects are known to the author to have been conducted include toll-roads, transport ticketing, consumer e-commerce applications and participant authentication in health records systems. Coles-Myer, the Australian retail chain, was reported in 2006 as having applied the IPPs to a project to produce a data warehouse relating to retail customers. Given the range of organisations whose operations are seriously privacy-invasive, the PIA notion has a long way to go.

(3) New South Wales

NSW is a State of c. 800,000 sq. km (20 per cent larger than France). It has a population approaching 7 million, almost 75 per cent of whom live in the Newcastle-Sydney-Wollongong conurbation. Its Parliament suffers the lowest repute of the nine in Australia, and its government agencies are widely regarded as being large bureaucracies of, at best, modest competence. Reforms are few, and proceed very slowly.

The Privacy Committee Act 1975 (NSW) created a complaints-investigation and research organisation of broad scope. That statute was rescinded in 1998, when the Privacy and Personal Information Protection Act (PPIPA) was prepared by the bureaucracy for the bureaucracy and passed by the Parliament. It embodies a set of Information Protection Principles in ss. 8-19. It created a Privacy Commissioner and an Office, Privacy NSW. The law is perhaps the least privacy-protective of such statutes anywhere in the world, and the Commissioner perhaps the weakest.

A NSW Health Records and Information Privacy Act was passed in 2002. It affects both public and private sector organisations active in the NSW health care sector. Despite its highly permissive nature, it was inconvenient to the conduct of a major trial of electronic health records in the Hunter Valley called HealtheLink; so the government simply suspended the inconvenient principle. Privacy protections in NSW are nominal rather than real.[30]

No PIA guidance document has ever been published for NSW government agencies, despite statements of intention that date from about 2004 and supportive submissions to parliamentary committees and the Australian Law Reform Commission. Privacy NSW informed the author in 2007 that it is aware that a few

---

[30] Ibid. See also the Privacy NSW website: http://www.lawlink.nsw.gov.au/lawlink/privacynsw/ll_pnsw.nsf/pages/PNSW_nswprivacy_laws

agencies have conducted PIAs. Despite this, and mention in various discussions of PIAs in the health and education spheres, no evidence of any PIA report or process has ever been located.

(4) Victoria

Victoria is a State of c. 230,000 sq. km (about the same as the UK). It has a population of 5.5 million, 75 per cent of whom live in the capital city, Melbourne.

In 2006, Victoria became only the second Australian jurisdiction to provide a degree of generic protection of human rights in the form of the Charter of Human Rights and Responsibilities Act. Under s. 13, "a person has the right (a) not to have his or her privacy, family, home or correspondence unlawfully or arbitrarily interfered with; and (b) not to have his or her reputation unlawfully attacked". The statutory protection is very weak, however, and it is not clear that it has had, or ever will have, any effect on privacy-invasive behaviour.[31]

The Information Privacy Act was drafted by a Data Protection Advisory Council formed by the Minister for Multimedia in 1996. (The author was a member of that Council.) Despite a change of government in the meantime, the Bill was passed virtually unchanged in 2000. It is a straightforward implementation of the 1980 OECD Guidelines, and the approach is, therefore, dated but mainstream. It established a set of Information Privacy Principles, and a Privacy Commissioner and Office, referred to as Privacy Victoria or OVPC.

The Victorian Health Records Act was passed in 2001. This includes a set of Health Privacy Principles which is highly permissive of data disclosures. The law is administered by the Health Services Commissioner (HSC). The law encompasses both public and private sector organisations active in the Victorian health care sector.

In 2005, a further, highly specialised Office was created by the Commissioner for Law Enforcement Data Security Act to address the public disquiet about rampant leakage of personal data from Victoria Police records. The Commissioner (CLEDS) has powers relating to management practices for law enforcement data.

The Privacy Commissioner has published two editions of a PIA guidance document, in 2004 and 2009.[32] This is examined in a later section.

In late 2010, HSC's site still provided no guidance in relation to PIAs in the health care sector. In an interview, HSC stated that it has not developed similar guidelines, but that it believed the frameworks outlined in the Victorian and Federal Privacy Commissioners' guidelines can be used in the health sector, and that it intended linking to the Victorian Privacy Commissioner's guidelines.

---

[31] For relevant laws, see the aforementioned websites of the Australian Privacy Foundation and the Office of the Privacy Commissioner as well as the OVPC website: http://www.privacy.gov.au/law/states/vic

[32] Office of the Victorian Privacy Commissioner (OVPC), *Privacy Impact Assessments – A Guide*, August 2004; OVPC, *Privacy Impact Assessment Guide*, Edition 2, with supporting documents: *Privacy Impact Assessment Report Template* and *Accompanying Guide to the Template*, May 2009. http://www.privacy.vic.gov.au/privacy/web2.nsf/pages/publication-types

It is understood that only a small number of PIAs have been performed by Victorian government agencies, that few have been notified to the Commissioner, and that not only have there been almost no PIA reports published, but most have been conducted in secrecy. Informally, it is understood that a PIA was performed in relation to a pilot health smartcard scheme, but the project as a whole did not proceed to implementation.

The only published documents appear to be those relating to a student database and identifier project conducted by the Department of Education & Training (DET). A preliminary report was published in 2006, citing a privacy issues analysis performed by this author in 2005, followed by another in 2007 and finally what purported to be a PIA report in 2010.[33] However, it appears that this may not have been a PIA as the term is properly used, but merely a data protection law compliance check.

(5) Queensland

Queensland is a State of c. 1.8 million sq. km (equivalent to Spain, France, Germany and Poland combined), ranging from lush coastal lands via rich agricultural country to semi-desert. It has a population of 4 million, of whom about 55 per cent live in the Brisbane-Gold Coast-Ipswich conurbation.

Despite various parliamentary reports, generic privacy legislation and a statutory privacy protection body took a very long time to emerge. From 2001 to 2010, unenforceable codes existed in the form of Government Standard 42,[34] and a variant (42A[35]) for the Department of Health. These Standards reflected the National Privacy Principles (i.e., those applicable to the private sector nationally, rather than the federal public sector Information Privacy Principles). They applied to almost all agencies, but excluding local government. A small Privacy Unit existed within the Department of Justice and Attorney-General. It is unclear whether the Standards and the Unit ever influenced agency practices and, if so, to what extent.

An Information Privacy Act was passed in 2009.[36] This created an Information Commissioner and, subordinate to that role, a Privacy Commissioner, together with

---

[33] Victorian Department of Education and Early Childhood Development, "Privacy Impact Assessment Report: The Ultranet", Melbourne, 19 March 2010. http://www.eduweb.vic.gov.au/edulibrary/public/ultranet/ultranet-pia.pdf

[34] Queensland Government Chief Information Officer (QGCIO), "Information Standard No 42 – Information Privacy", 2001. http://www.qgcio.qld.gov.au/SiteCollectionDocuments/Architecture%20and%20Standards/Information%20Standards/Current/is42.pdf

[35] Queensland Government Chief Information Officer, "Information Standard No 42A – Information Privacy for the Queensland Department of Health", 2001. http://www.qgcio.qld.gov.au/SiteCollectionDocuments/Architecture%20and%20Standards/Information%20Standards/Current/is42a.pdf

[36] For other relevant laws, see the websites of the Australian Privacy Foundation at http://www.privacy.org.au/Resources, and the Office of the Australian Privacy Commissioner, at http://www.privacy.gov.au/law/states/vic.

an Office of the Information Commissioner (OIC). The first Privacy Commissioner was appointed in May 2010.

The Privacy Unit declared several times during 2005–2007 that it was developing a PIA guidance document. A newsletter in December 2005 stated that "[a] Privacy Impact Assessment (PIA) Annotated Questionnaire has been piloted in some Queensland Government agencies in relation to proposed programs and initiatives. Work continues on the questionnaire in relation to expanding use of the PIA process to assess proposed legislation or legislative amendments. PIA guidelines will be available in February 2006 as a decision-making and privacy assessment tool complimentary [sic] to the PIA annotated questionnaire." Further issues of the newsletter in March and December 2006 stated that documents were "in the final drafting stage and will be made available online shortly". No copy of the guidelines has ever been located. The last available copy of the webpage in the Internet Archive in July 2008 suggests that the document may never have been released. In any case, it is apparent from the webpage that the process envisaged was a mere check of compliance with the government Standard, not a PIA.

At some time during 2010, the old domain of privacy.qld.gov.au was deleted, and visitors redirected to the OIC's site. The existing documents were not transferred, and appear to have been simply withdrawn, without a transition period to the new regime.

Slow emergence of the PIA concept was apparent, however. An obscure document of the government chief information officer (CIO) stated that "The implementation of classification processes will have security and privacy implications and a privacy impact assessment should be conducted when any new business processes are being developed, or during the modification of business process to ensure the privacy principles are followed."[37] However, the concept remained limited to compliance with the then Standard 42/42A, and no evidence has been located to suggest that any agency ever took any notice of the CIO's exhortation.

Some months after the effective formation of the new OIC, there was no information on the website concerning PIAs. Based on an interview in 2010, the Privacy Commissioner was understood to be placing priority on the development and publication of a guidance document.

References have been made to the Department of Transport's having a PIA performed on the proposed smartcard-based driver's licence in 2003, but it appears not to have been published. A further study was conducted on the long-running project in 2010.[38] Although nominally a PIA, it was conducted by the Crown Law office; it

---

[37] Queensland Government Chief Information Office, "Queensland Government Information Security Classification Framework", Version 1.0.1, April 2008, p. 56. http://www.qgcio.qld.gov.au/SiteCollectionDocuments/Architecture%20and%20Standards/QGISCF%20v1.0.1.doc

[38] Queensland Transport and Main Roads, "New Queensland Driver Licence – Privacy Impact Assessment", 30 September 2010. http://www.tmr.qld.gov.au/~/media/7496f017-55bb-4853-8c7b-da9150800707/new_qld_licence_privacy_impact_assess.pdf

was only a check of compliance with the law, and there was no meaningful involvement of privacy advocacy organisations. No evidence has been found of any other Queensland government agency having performed a PIA on any project or initiative.

(6) Western Australia

Western Australia is a State of about 2.3 million sq. km (and is the second-largest sub-national entity in the world, after the Sakha Republic, i.e., Western Siberia). It is the size of Spain, France, Germany and the whole of Scandinavia combined. Most of it is desert or semi-desert. It has a population of about 2 million, three-quarters of whom live in the capital city, Perth.

The State has no generic privacy laws, and it appears that no agency has ever had any substantive function that approximates a privacy oversight role.[39]

The Office of e-Government has, however, recognised the risks that privacy-invasiveness entails for the adoption of electronic forms of government service delivery. A PIA was conducted on a proposed whole-of-government employee identifier,[40] following a privacy issues analysis by this author.[41]

No evidence has been found of any other PIA being performed in Western Australia.

(7) South Australia

South Australia is a State of about 1 million sq. km (equivalent to France, Germany, Belgium and the Netherlands combined), most of it arid or semi-arid. It has a population of 1.5 million, 70 per cent of whom live in the capital city, Adelaide.

The State has no generic privacy laws.[42]

A Cabinet Administrative Instruction established a set of Information Privacy Principles which requires agency compliance.[43] Although nominally binding, it is unclear by what means and by whom it could be enforced. A Privacy Committee of

---

[39] For relevant laws, see the Australian Privacy Foundation, "Resources – The Law", current as at August 2010, at http://www.privacy.org.au/Resources. See also the website of the Office of the Australian Privacy Commissioner, at http://www.privacy.gov.au/law/states/wa.

[40] Clayton Utz, Lawyers, "Proposed Western Australian Government Number: Privacy Impact Assessment", prepared for the Western Australian Department of the Premier and Cabinet: Office of e-Government, 19 June 2007, pp. 84–91. http://www.publicsector.wa.gov.au/SiteCollectionDocuments/FINALWAGNPIA.pdf

[41] Convergence e-Business Solutions Pty Ltd, "Identity & Access Management Framework", v.2, prepared for the West Australian Government Office of e-Government, Department of the Premier & Cabinet, Perth, 15 September 2005. http://www.publicsector.wa.gov.au/SiteCollectionDocuments/WA_IAM_Framework_rpt_V2.0.pdf

[42] For relevant laws, see APF, "Resources – The Law", at http://www.privacy.org.au/Resources. See also the OAPC website, at http://www.privacy.gov.au/law/states/sa

[43] South Australian Department of Premier and Cabinet, Cabinet Administrative Instruction No. 1 of 1989: PC012 – Information Privacy Principles Instruction, 1989. http://www.premcab.sa.gov.au/pdf/circulars/Privacy.pdf

South Australia exists, under government proclamation. It is run out of the State Records Office, and appears to have no budget. Its primary function appears to be to approve exemptions to the non-statutory principles. It is unclear whether the Instruction applies to local government.

Privacy Committee documents make no substantive reference to privacy impact assessment. The Executive Officer of the Committee told the author in 2007 that the South Australian Government does not have a centralised program for privacy impact assessment. However, "the Privacy Committee, supported by State Records, does use a rudimentary questionnaire for programs that require Privacy Committee approval, exemption from the Information Privacy Principles, or require consideration of complex personal information handling issues. It is a working document that is adapted to suit the situation at hand. It may be formalised later, and adopt components from other jurisdictions' structured PIAs."

The Department of Health Code of Fair Information Practice makes reference to a PIA methodology tool.[44] The author was given to understand in the same 2007 interview that the Department of Health and the Department of Families and Communities have mandated PIAs for use in the early planning stages of projects involving personal information. The PIA guidelines are broader than information privacy alone, but the PIA "Proforma" is limited to the Information Privacy Principles. Searches on the websites did not locate the documents, however, and it is unclear whether any use has been made of them.

The only evidence found of any South Australian government agency having performed a PIA on any project or initiative was a one-line mention in a 157-page report on a SA Vaccine Safety Data Linkage Project (SAVeS).

(8) Tasmania

Tasmania is an island State of c. 90,000 sq. km (much the same as Portugal). Much of the island is mountainous and forested. It has a population of close to 0.5 million, about 40 per cent of whom live in the capital city, Hobart.

The Personal Information Protection Act 2004 came into effect on 5 September 2005. It applies to the public and local government sectors and the University of Tasmania. The Act is a weakened form of the OECD model. It did not create a statutory office responsible for privacy matters, nor did it assign such responsibilities to any existing agency.

A complaints-handling function was created, and assigned to the Ombudsman. The practice in the State has been to consolidate all forms of review in the Ombudsman's Office, including freedom of information (FOI), police and health matters. The Ombudsman has no powers to enforce decisions. The privacy powers are not mentioned on the Ombudsman's home-page. The Annual Reports are

---

[44] South Australian Department of Health (SADOH), Code of Fair Information Practice, July 2004. http://www.health.sa.gov.au/Portals/0/Health-Code-July04.pdf

almost devoid of substantive information about privacy, and mentions of privacy on the website are apparent only well down the menu hierarchy.[45]

The author has found only one mention of "PIA" on government sites, which was a misuse of the term in a report on a consultation process relating to a privacy-intrusive proposal for checking people working with children and other vulnerable people.

(9) The Australian Capital Territory

The Australian Capital Territory (ACT) was formed in 1911 by transfer of the area from the State of NSW. It was required to govern itself by the Australian Capital Territory (Self-Government) Act 1988. It has a well-educated and high-income urban population of about 320,000.

The ACT is one of only two jurisdictions in Australia that has enacted a Bill of Rights – the Human Rights Act 2004. In s. 12, the Act provides people with a right to not have their privacy, family, home or correspondence interfered with unlawfully or arbitrarily. The Act is administered by a Human Rights Commissioner (HRC), who has a small staff. There is nothing on the HRC's website to suggest that privacy is seen as a significant element of its responsibilities. The law and the Office adopt the weakest possible approach to the protection of human rights, and they have to date had no detectable impact on privacy protection in the Territory.

A decade before the Human Rights Act was passed, the Territory chose to adopt the Commonwealth Privacy Act 1988. The OAPC is supposed to perform the functions of an ACT Privacy Commissioner, but there is little evidence of much actually being achieved. For example, the OAPC's 2008–2009 Annual Report mentions four interactions with ACT government agencies, and the 2007–2008 Report mentions three, one of which was only a briefing by the agency, without advice being provided by the OAPC. Again in 2006–2007, interactions were mentioned with four agencies. Nothing arising from such meetings appears to have been published, and no agency of the ACT government has ever been known to engage with privacy advocacy organisations.

In 1997, the ACT enacted a Health Records (Privacy and Access) Act, which applies to organisations in both the public and private sectors.[46]

There is no evidence that the Privacy Commissioner has ever communicated the existence and relevance of its PIA guide to ACT agencies. There are only incidental mentions of the ACT on the OAPC's website, and there is no mention of the guide on the ACT government's website.

In an interview in 2010, OAPC stated that it was aware of some ACT agencies undertaking PIAs. On the other hand, no evidence could be found of any ACT

---

[45] For relevant laws, see APF, "Resources – The Law", at http://www.privacy.org.au/Resources. See also the OAPC website, at http://www.privacy.gov.au/law/states/tas

[46] Other relevant laws are identified in APF, "Resources – The Law", at http://www.privacy.org. au/Resources, and on the OAPC website, at http://www.privacy.gov.au/law/states/act.

government agency having performed a PIA on any project or initiative. There are many projects for which a PIA would be appropriate. The government handles a great deal of personal data relating to its residents generally. In addition, the Department of Corrective Services initiated the acquisition of technology to impose continuous RFID-based tracking of prisoners, prison officers and prison visitors, without any form of PIA. (However, it appears that the project fell victim to budgetary constraints.)

(10) The Northern Territory

The Northern Territory (NT) was part of the colony of South Australia until 1901, after which it became a Territory of the Commonwealth of Australia. It was granted self-government by the Northern Territory (Self-Government) Act 1978. NT has an area of 1.4 million sq. km (about the same as Portugal, Spain, France and Germany combined). It is mostly desert or semi-desert, and has a population of 200,000, about one-third indigenous, a big proportion of whom are widely and very thinly dispersed. About half of the population lives in the capital city, Darwin.

In 2002, the Northern Territory implemented the Information Commissioner model by means of the Information Act.[47] This was a pragmatic approach to cost minimisation in administering a tiny population scattered across a vast area. The architect of the statute had been deeply involved in the preparation of the Victorian Information Privacy Act, and the privacy aspects of the NT statute are accordingly a clean and practical application of the (now badly dated) OECD 1980 provisions. The Act created a single statutory post of Information Commissioner and an Office of the Information Commissioner (OIC), covering both FOI and privacy functions. The same appointee has since had added to their functions the role of Commissioner for Public Interest Disclosures (Whistleblowers).

No written guidance has been provided to agencies concerning PIAs. However, the Commissioner encourages agencies to discuss matters with the OIC, and some success has been achieved in this area. A "Tip of the Day" during Privacy Awareness Week in May 2010 suggested conducting a PIA "if your workplace is planning a major project", and pointed to the Commonwealth and Victorian PIA guides.

No evidence was found of any NT government agency having performed a PIA on any project or initiative. The author was told in an interview in 2007 that the OIC was involved in discussions about an initiative referred to as "Territory Services". This was considering a common shop front as a way to reduce the number of government offices and consolidate citizen-facing resources. Because this had significant privacy implications, the Commissioner recommended that a PIA be performed, and provided the team developing the initiative with copies of the Australian and Victorian PIA guidelines.

---

[47] Other relevant laws are identified in APF, "Resources – The Law", at http://www.privacy.org. au/Resources, and on the OAPC website, at http://www.privacy.gov.au/law/states/nt.

Under s. 160 of the Act, a review is required after five years, which might have extended to PIA matters. The first review is more than two years overdue, however, and there is no evidence of commencement.

5.4 PIA Guidance Documents

The preceding section has shown that the Commonwealth public sector – which is responsible for a great many of the most inherently privacy-invasive systems in the country – is the sole context in which significant progress has been made. Much more limited progress has been made in the private sector and in Victoria. In the other seven jurisdictions, the conduct of PIAs is at least muted and in many cases non-existent. In those jurisdictions, the performance of parliaments and central government agencies alike has been severely lax, reflecting the sub-professional standard of public services in some States and Territories and/or the low priority accorded by public servants to people's privacy.

The conduct of a PIA is, however, non-obvious and non-trivial. Guidance is necessary to assist organisations to achieve the benefits and avoid the pitfalls. Guidance documents emerged in various countries from the early 1990s onwards.[48] The author published the first set in Australia.[49] Guidance documents were subsequently published by two privacy oversight agencies in Australia, in one case intended specifically for the agencies of a single State,[50] and in the other for agencies of the Commonwealth government, for organisations in the non-government sectors, and nominally at least for agencies of the ACT government.[51]

The purpose of this section is to consider the two available guidance documents that have been published by privacy oversight agencies. It commences by providing an overview of a set of evaluation criteria, and then applies that set to the guidance documents published by the OVPC and the OAPC.

5.4.1 Evaluation Criteria

In a companion paper, the author proposed a set of criteria for PIA guidance documents, and applied them to a dozen documents published by agencies in 10 countries.[52] The criteria are listed in Exhibit 5.2. The cited paper provides a detailed discussion.

---

[48] Clarke, 2009, op. cit. at fn. 1.

[49] Clarke, 1998, op. cit., at fn. 2 and 3.

[50] OVPC, 2004 and 2009, op. cit., at fn. 32.

[51] OAPC, 2006 and 2010, op. cit., at fn. 24.

[52] Clarke, Roger, "An Evaluation of Privacy Impact Assessment Guidance Documents", *International Data Privacy Law*, Vol. 1, No. 2, May 2011. http://idpl.oxfordjournals.org/content/early/2011/02/15/idpl.ipr002.full

Exhibit 5.2 – Evaluation Criteria for PIA Guidance Documents

1. Status of the guidance document
2. Discoverability of the guidance document
3. Applicability of the guidance document
4. Responsibility for the PIA
5. Timing of the PIA
6. Scope of the PIA

   1. The dimensions of privacy
   2. Stakeholders
   3. Reference points

7. Stakeholder engagement
8. Orientation

   1. Process cf. product
   2. Solutions cf. problems

9. The PIA process
10. The role of the oversight agency

The following sub-sections apply the above criteria, and identify the strong and weak aspects of the two guides published by Australian oversight agencies.

5.4.2 The Victorian Privacy Commissioner's Guide

In 2004, the Victorian Privacy Commissioner published a Privacy Impact Assessment Guide.[53] The Australian Privacy Foundation expressed serious reservations about it, stating that "the document may be a guide for Privacy Law Compliance Audit, but not for Privacy Impact Assessment".[54] In 2009, the Commissioner published a significantly amended version.[55] An assessment of the 2009 version against the criteria outlined in Exhibit 5.2 gives rise to the following observations.

There is no formal requirement to conduct a PIA, but the Guide exists, is readily discoverable and reflects both the human rights and privacy laws that apply to Victorian government agencies. It is comprehensive, extending beyond legal requirements to encompass public concerns and implications for all dimensions of privacy. It stresses the importance of public consultation. It adopts a checklist

---

[53] OVPC, 2004, op. cit., at fn. 32.

[54] In a letter dated 15 Feb 2005 to the Privacy Commissioner. http://www.privacy.org.au/Papers/OVPC-PIA-0502.rtf

[55] OVPC, 2009, op. cit., at fn. 32.

approach, but the checklists incorporate advice on the process needed to satisfy the requirement.

The Privacy Commissioner has communicated the existence of the PIA guidelines through its network of privacy officers in government agencies, conducted training sessions and mentioned the PIA guidelines in various presentations. It is understood that the Department of Justice used the Guide as a basis for a practical document suitable for practitioners in the Department's organisational sub-units. This appears to have been one of the stimuli for the upgrade of the Guide in 2009.

A weakness exists, in that, at several points, it would be feasible for an agency to interpret a PIA as being a report, rather than as a process. In addition, the Guide contemplates the possibility of a PIA being conducted by an independent organisation such as a consultancy. This would have the effect of shielding the agency from the relevant public, and prevent assimilation of information by the agency's executives and staff. The Guide lacks visibility in the health care sector, which is subject to a separate Commissioner who appears to place no emphasis on PIAs.

On the other hand, the Template[56] and the Accompanying Guide[57] draw the assessor well beyond mere legal compliance, place considerable emphasis on consultation and solution-orientation, and provide instruction without permitting the assessor to abandon intellectual engagement with the work. The Guide's comprehensiveness, quality and practicality are all high, and it represents one of the three most useful guidance documents available in any jurisdiction, anywhere in the world, along with those produced by the UK Information Commissioner's Office (ICO)[58] and the Ontario government.[59]

5.4.3 The Australian Privacy Commissioner's Guide

The potential impact of this guidance document is very substantial, because it applies to the large federal public sector – which is the source of a large number of proposals that are inherently highly privacy-intrusive – to the non-government sectors throughout Australia, and in principle at least to the ACT public sector. There are, accordingly, benefits in tracing the considerable history behind the current, 2010 version.

---

[56] Office of the Victorian Privacy Commissioner, "Privacy Impact Assessments Report Template", May 2009. http://www.privacy.vic.gov.au/privacy/web2.nsf/pages/publication-types

[57] Office of the Victorian Privacy Commissioner, "Privacy Impact Assessments – Accompanying Guide", May 2009. http://www.privacy.vic.gov.au/privacy/web2.nsf/pages/publication-types? opendocument&Subcategory=Guidelines&s=2

[58] Information Commissioner's Office, *Privacy Impact Assessment Handbook*, Wilmslow, UK, December 2007. ICO published a revised version in June 2009. http://www.ico.gov.uk/for_ organisations/topic_specific_guides/pia_handbook.aspx

[59] Management Board Secretariat, Government of Ontario, *Privacy Impact Assessment: A User's Guide*, 1999, revised 2001. http://www.accessandprivacy.gov.on.ca/english/pia/index.html

In December 2001, the then Australian Privacy Commissioner, Malcolm Crompton, issued *Guidelines for Agencies using PKI to communicate or transact with individuals*.[60] Public Key Infrastructure (PKI) is the means whereby digital signature schemes are supported. Guideline 3 stated that "Agencies should undertake a Privacy Impact Assessment before implementing a new PKI system or significantly revising or extending an existing PKI system" (p. 29). A PIA was depicted as "a method of identifying privacy risks so that these can be highlighted and addressed when … systems or … business applications are being designed, implemented, revised or extended. A PIA may be part of a larger risk assessment and management procedure. Properly done, this assessment will include an understanding of which parties will bear what risks" (p. 35).

Throughout the world, the extent of implementation of PKI schemes has fallen far below the inflated expectations of the mid-to-late 1990s.[61] On the other hand, many of the government projects involving PKI that have been conducted in Australia have taken at least some account of the OAPC's document.

Work on general PIA guidelines during Crompton's period as Privacy Commissioner culminated in the release by his successor, Karen Curtis, of a draft for public consultation in 2004. The Guide was based on considerable research into the experiences of and guidance provided in other jurisdictions, particularly New Zealand, Canada and Ontario, and on experience within Australia. It was published in final form two years later.[62]

Under the current statutory regime, the performance of a PIA is not mandatory. However, in an interview in 2007, the Commissioner's office stated that communications with agencies and the private sector in relation to schemes that have privacy implications routinely contain segments of text along the following lines: "The Office suggests that a privacy impact assessment be undertaken as part of the further development of the proposal. The Office has released a Privacy Impact Assessment Guide for Australian Government and ACT Government agencies."

In the same interview, it was stated that, during 2006–2007, the Guide attracted 23,000 hits and downloads. It quickly became common for requests for tender for consultancy support for PIAs to explicitly require that the Guide be at least reflected, and in many cases complied with. On the other hand, many agencies do not yet perform PIAs as a matter of course, even for projects with significantly privacy-invasive features.

In 2010, a lightly-revised version of the Guide was published.[63] This was intended to be more obviously applicable to the private sector as well as government

---

[60] OAPC, December 2001, op. cit., at fn. 24.

[61] Reasons why this is the case can be found in Clarke, Roger, "The Fundamental Inadequacies of Conventional Public Key Infrastructure", *Proceedings of the Ninth European Conference on Information Systems (ECIS 2001)*, Association for Information Systems, Bled, Slovenia, 27–29 June 2001. http://www.rogerclarke.com/II/ECIS2001.html

[62] OAPC, 2006, op. cit., at fn. 24.

[63] OAPC, May 2010, op. cit., at fn. 24.

agencies. An assessment of the 2010 version against the criteria outlined in Exhibit 5.2 gave rise to the following observations.

The OAPC's Guide scores reasonably well against many of the criteria outlined earlier in this paper. It is process-oriented and practical, and indicates the need for broad scope. There are, however, some weaknesses that result in it being a less appropriate basis for conducting PIAs than the Victorian Guide, the UK Handbook and the Ontario Guide.

Most critically, although it recognises the significance of the views of the affected public, it fails to provide clear advice on how to treat them as stakeholders, lacks practical advice on consultation processes and fails to mention advocacy groups as a means of gaining an appreciation of the views of the relevant public. In an interview in 2010, the OAPC excused the absence of such guidance on the basis that this is consistent with an approach to privacy law based on Principles, which gives agencies the flexibility to determine an approach to consultation that is appropriately tailored to each project.

The Guide is strongly problem-oriented (frequently mentioning "impacts" and "issues"), but creates only limited momentum towards solutions – the word "solution" only appears twice, the concept of avoidance only four times and the concept of mitigation not at all. The OAPC acknowledged this weakness, but again justified it in terms of the law being Principles-based.

It is entirely feasible to interpret the Guide as requiring an assessment of broad scope, and some PIAs conducted using it have extended beyond information privacy, and beyond extant data protection law. Unfortunately, narrow interpretations are also possible, and some agencies have performed what they have called PIAs, but which were no more than checks of compliance with the Information Privacy Principles. Examples include a cut-down Privacy Impact Checklist published by the Department of Defence,[64] a report by Medicare[65] and a report for the Attorney-General's Department.[66]

The OAPC defended the limited stress on "privacy in the broad" by stating that the PIA Guide is appropriately focused on those aspects of privacy that are within the scope of the Privacy Act. This is, however, a patently incorrect reading of the Act. As indicated earlier in this chapter, seven of the Commissioner's 24 functions

---

[64] Department of Defence (DoD), "Defence Privacy Impact Checklist", Canberra, February 2008. http://www.defence.gov.au/fr/Privacy/defence-piachecklist-Feb08.doc

[65] Medicare Australia, "Privacy Impact Assessment (PIA) – Increased MBS Compliance Audits", Canberra, 28 April 2009. http://www.health.gov.au/internet/main/publishing.nsf/Content/C010759A8FB2E35DCA25759300011241/$File/Privacy%20Impact%20Assessment%20for%20the%20IMCA%20initiative.pdf

[66] Attorney-General's Department/Salinger Privacy, "Privacy Impact Assessment – The Aus Check Amendment Bill 2009 and the National Security Background Check", Canberra, 3 March 2009. http://www.ag.gov.au/www/agd/rwpattach.nsf/VAP/(712B446AA84F124A6F0833A09BD304C8)~AusCheck+PIA+-+Final+report.pdf/$file/AusCheck+PIA+-+Final+report.pdf

as defined in s. 27 are expressed openly, and empower and require the Commissioner to consider all dimensions of the privacy of individuals, not merely the privacy of personal information. These functions include the one most relevant to the PIA Guide – s. 27(1)(f) relating to the provision of advice.

Further concerns are that there appears to be no webpage that provides a brief explanation of PIAs, why a guidance document has been published and who it is for. In addition, the document is not as easy to find within the business sub-site as would be desirable. Even within the document, there is only weak encouragement for agencies and corporations to apply the Guide.

The OAPC defended the Guide's accessibility on the basis that there are many links to it, and that it routinely receives the second highest number of hits for a publication on the Office's website. However, the OAPC did not respond to any of the specific criticisms regarding the lack of an introductory index-page, its limited visibility on the webpages for business, and the weakness of expression about the need to apply it.

5.5 Future Developments

It appears quite possible that more PIAs – as the term is used in this paper – have been performed in Australia than in any other country. On the other hand, the vast majority of them have been performed in the federal public sector, and there remain some shortfalls even in that context. The evidence presented in the preceding sections shows inadequate application of the excellent Victorian Guide, significant shortfalls in the non-government sector, and abject failure in the other seven Australian jurisdictions. This section considers the prospects for improvements.

5.5.1 The States and Territories

There is substantial in-principle support for the conduct of PIAs among privacy oversight bodies. For example, a submission by Privacy NSW to a committee reviewing NSW legislation stated that: "We believe that PIAs are the best means by which government agencies can aim for best privacy practice as well as legislative compliance. It is our submission that ideally, a PIA would be a statutory requirement for any new Bill, regulation, or project significant enough to require Cabinet consideration."[67] No progress has been made within NSW, but the Office's submission to the ALRC review was emphatic: "Privacy legislation should make it mandatory for all Commonwealth agencies and private organisations to provide and

---

[67] Privacy NSW, "Submission on the Review of the Privacy and Personal Information Protection Act 1998", 24 June 2004, p. 31. http://www.lawlink.nsw.gov.au/lawlink/privacynsw/ll_pnsw.nsf/ vwFiles/sub_ppipareview.pdf/$file/sub_ppipareview.pdf#target=%27_blank%27

publish Privacy Impact Assessments (PIAs) for all new programs, policies and draft legislation which impacts on the handling of 'personal information'".[68]

Similarly, the Northern Territory Commissioner's submission to the ALRC on the matter said that "The preferred approach would be to allow the [OAPC] to consider the need for a privacy impact assessment, discuss the issue with the agency, and direct that an assessment be undertaken if necessary".[69] The Victorian Privacy Commissioner submitted to a Senate inquiry into DNA that "It is essential to conduct a Privacy Impact Assessment before biometrics are introduced."[70]

In Victoria, the scope exists for the application of the Privacy Commissioner's clear and helpful guidance document more assiduously, and far more frequently, than has been the case in the past. Further impetus could arise from the 2010 review of inappropriate arrangements for the passing of personal data from Victoria Police to various organisations: "The Commissioner [for Law Enforcement Data Security] highlights the need for Victoria Police to undertake an Information Sharing Risk Assessment – made up of a proportionality assessment, a Privacy Impact Assessment, a security Threat and Risk Assessment and a Human Rights Impact Assessment – for all major information sharing initiatives."[71]

The Victorian document is visible to privacy oversight and central agencies in other jurisdictions. In Queensland, the Privacy Commissioner appointed in mid-2010 is understood from an interview in late 2010 to regard publication of a guidance document as a priority, although whether it will achieve any greater application than the phantom guide of some years earlier is unclear.

The other jurisdictions, however, show no signs of overcoming their torpor. There appears to be no commitment in NSW (which is culpable, given that it is the largest State), nor in the ACT. In the Northern Territory, resource constraints hinder the performance of PIAs. In Western Australia, South Australia and Tasmania, there appears not even to be any prospect of meaningful privacy laws.

A further spectre hangs over privacy protection in the States and Territories. As discussed below, the ALRC recommended the creation of a single set of "unified privacy principles" (UPPs), and their adoption in all jurisdictions. As is explained below, these will be a lowest common denominator, and much weaker than the strongest of the provisions that are currently in place. Compliance checks in 5–10 years' time will likely be against very weak legal requirements.

---

[68] Privacy NSW, "Submission in response to the Review of Privacy Issues Paper of the Australian Law Reform Commission", Privacy NSW, February 2007, p. 12. http://www.lawlink.nsw.gov.au/lawlink/privacynsw/ll_pnsw.nsf/vwFiles/sub_alrc2007.pdf/$file/sub_alrc2007.pdf

[69] Northern Territory Information Commissioner, "ALRC Review of Privacy: Submissions on Issues Paper 31", January 2007, p. 25.

[70] Office of the Victoria Privacy Commissioner, "Submission to the Commonwealth Senate Legal and Constitutional Committee on its Inquiry into the Privacy Act 1988 (Cth)", March 2005, p. 4. http://www.privacy.vic.gov.au/dir100/priweb.nsf/download/ED6E906311CA2570110019833A/$FILE/Sen%20Leg%20Con%20Ctte%20sub.pdf

[71] Commissioner for Law Enforcement Data Security (CLEDS), "Review of Victoria Police Major Project Development MOUs Under s11(1)(e) of the Commissioner for Law Enforcement Data Security Act 2005 Commissioner for Law Enforcement Data Security", August 2010. http://www.chiefexaminer.vic.gov.au/retrievemedia.asp?Media_ID=60421

5.5.2 The OAPC/ICO

During the period 2005–2010, the tenure of Karen Curtis, the OAPC was markedly close to government and business, and hostile to civil society. Among many other deficiencies, Curtis undermined the Office's independence by entering into Memoranda of Understanding (MoUs) with particular agencies. The Office accepted funding from those agencies in return for the performance of a fundamental function of the Office under s. 27(1)(f): "to provide ... advice to [an] agency ... on any matter relevant to the operation of this Act". Advice provided to agencies has been unpublished, and unavailable to civil society. Advocacy organisations were kept at arm's length by both OAPC and the agencies with which the Office consulted.

Moreover, such PIA processes as the Office induced agencies to undertake were generally conducted behind closed doors and excluded public participation, or an intermediary was introduced in order to buffer the agency from the public and public interest advocates. The OAPC's guidance document has many good features, but if they are not even respected by the oversight agency that issued them, they are unlikely to gain any currency among agencies more generally.

The organisation is in transition from an independent Office to a subsidiary segment of the Office of the Australian Information Commissioner (OAIC). With effect from November 2010, many functions of the Privacy Commissioner are functions of the Information Commissioner. The Information Commissioner's perspective is much broader and there is a considerable risk that the low valuation of privacy that was established under Curtis' regime will become entrenched.

It remains to be seen whether the new Commissioner, Timothy Pilgrim, previously Curtis' Deputy, will recover the credibility of the Office. To do so, there is a need to avoid compromise of the Office's intended independence from government and business, to accord civil society recognition at the same level as government and business, to promote effective PIAs far more actively than in the past, to stress the importance of direct consultation with the public, and to strengthen the Office's PIA guidance document by overcoming the shortfalls against the evaluation criteria outlined earlier in this paper.

5.5.3 The ALRC's Recommendations

The Australian Law Reform Commission's report on its review of the Privacy Act made two recommendations in relation to PIAs:

Recommendation 47-4
The Privacy Act should be amended to empower the Privacy Commissioner to:

- direct an agency to provide to the Privacy Commissioner a Privacy Impact Assessment in relation to a new project or development that the Privacy Commissioner considers may have a significant impact on the handling of personal information; and
- report to the ministers responsible for the agency and for administering the Privacy Act on the agency's failure to comply with such a direction.

Recommendation 47-5
The Office of the Privacy Commissioner should develop and publish Privacy Impact Assessment Guidelines tailored to the needs of organisations. A review should be undertaken in five years from the commencement of the amended Privacy Act to assess whether the power in Recommendation 47-4 should be extended to include organisations.[72]

Superficially, this appears to represent progress in the use of PIAs in at least government, and perhaps business. On closer inspection, however, the picture is not so positive.

Firstly, despite mentioning important aspects of PIAs in the text, the notion of a PIA reflected in the ALRC's recommendations was seriously deficient, because it was treated as a product rather than a process ("provide ... a [PIA]"). The expression fails to reinforce the need for consultation with affected parties. It also fails to specify the publication of both information in advance of consultation and the PIA report.

Secondly, the refusal to recommend that the power to require a PIA extend to the private sector ignored both submissions and a Senate Committee recommendation. It stated that "the strongest argument in favour of not directing organisations to undertake a PIA is that the [OAPC] has not yet issued voluntary guidelines for private sector PIAs" (para. 47.82). Yet the Privacy Commissioner needed to make very few changes to deliver a workable version for private sector organisations, as shown by its revised Guide in 2010, and could have easily done so during the 28-month course of the ALRC study.

Added to that, the ALRC's recommendation to wait for a further five years was simply irresponsible. The problem has been apparent for 40 years, it has worsened considerably as technology and rationalist management have exploded, and it has very clearly not been solved, and will not be solved, without parliamentary intervention.

Among the ALRC's 294 recommendations (many of them multi-partite) was a proposal to consolidate the two current, very different sets of principles into Unified Privacy Principles (UPPs), and apply them across all of the 10 contexts discussed earlier.[73] Clearly, both the public and private sectors would argue that they should not have the more onerous requirements of the other set thrust upon them. The effect, therefore, would inevitably be that the less onerous of the two alternatives will be selected in every case. In addition, three State Privacy Commissioners would be expected to argue for minimal inconsistency with their existing Principles, and separate Commissioners who administer vast numbers of exceptions created for health services would be expected to argue the same. Further, the enormous complexity of the new scheme provides great scope for additional loopholes to be created and disguised.

---

[72] ALRC, 2008, op. cit., fn. 22.

[73] ALRC, 2008, op. cit., fn. 22, Recommendations 18–1, 18–2.

The conventional processes of policy formation and preparation of legislation in Australia involve only the recognised stakeholder groups, that is to say, government agencies and industry associations. Public interest advocacy groups may be permitted to make submissions, but they are entirely excluded from the detailed discussions that give rise to legislative drafting instructions. The policy agency and its favoured advisers have control over the agenda. They are in a position to devise a weakening of the Privacy Principles, and are able to do so out of public view. If the proposal to create the UPPs is enacted, it is inevitable that privacy protections in Australia, in all jurisdictions, will be greatly weakened.

Hence, even if the ALRC's sole positive proposal in relation to PIAs is implemented, it will represent only the tiniest step forward in privacy protection in Australia, and will be swamped by the reductions in privacy protections achieved by means of the consolidation of privacy principles.

5.5.4 The Government's Response

In October 2009, the Government signalled its agreement with the ALRC's recommendations in relation to PIAs:

> The Government agrees that a Privacy Impact Assessment (PIA) is a best practice tool which can provide a valuable evaluation of how a project or policy may impact on an individual's privacy and possible solutions to address those issues. In line with the principles-based approach of the Privacy Act, PIAs allow agencies and organisations to consider how to best put the Privacy Principles into practice and it is appropriate that PIAs are voluntary in nature.

> The Government supports this recommendation. It is important that the Privacy Commissioner have the discretion to direct an agency to undertake a PIA where it is considered that it is crucial to ensuring that a policy or project is appropriately balanced against an individual's right to privacy. This is in line with the Privacy Commissioner's role in enforcing the requirements of the Privacy Act and with the strong need to ensure that Government policy is appropriately balanced against privacy requirements.

> This discretionary power is not intended to reduce the voluntary nature of PIAs nor mean that PIAs should only be conducted where there is a direction from the Privacy Commissioner. It will still be necessary for agencies to determine when developing a policy whether it will impact on privacy and whether a PIA is required. This is intrinsically linked with the agency's obligation to comply with the Privacy Principles.[74]

At the time of writing, no draft legislation to give effect to the government's commitment had yet emerged, four and a half years after the ALRC commenced its review, more than two years after it published its report, and more than one year after the government published its response.

---

[74] Cabinet Secretary to the Australian Government, "First Stage Response to the Australian Law Reform Commission Report 108", October 2009, pp. 86–87. http://www.pmc.gov.au/privacy/alrc_docs/stage1_aus_govt_response.pdf

In June 2010, however, an "Exposure Draft" of what are now referred to as the Australian Privacy Principles (APPs) was released.[75] The draft was produced without civil society involvement. The draft APPs comprise in excess of 6,000 words (compared with the 1,600 of the IPPs and the 3,300 of the NPPs). The majority of the wordage authorises exceptions to the Principles, which undermine privacy and advantage business and government.

The government agency that negotiated the draft buffered itself from privacy advocacy groups not only during their preparation, but also subsequently. The sole channel for public submissions is a Senate Committee, and the Committee handling the matter (Finance and Public Administration) is attuned to government efficiency and intrinsically hostile to privacy interests. Given that background, it is of little surprise that civil society identified vast problems with the draft.[76]

5.6 Conclusions

For many years, there has been ongoing, slow filtration of the PIA notion through agencies, corporations and consultancies. The technique is projected as being a positive approach to risk management and as being supported by all central agencies and opposed by none. Guidance documents of good quality exist, and a small number of consultancies are experienced in assisting organisations to apply them. Public interest advocacy organisations press for PIAs to be conducted. Some Senate Committees increasingly expect legislation that comes before them to have been the subject of a PIA, and query the absence of public consultation if none has been performed.

A significant incentive for the conduct of effective PIAs is the visibility of project failures due at least in part to privacy issues. Some agencies have tried to avoid PIAs, or have conducted sham processes by interposing another organisation between themselves and the public. Those agencies have failed to understand the messages, and have suffered negative media coverage and ignominious project failures. On the other hand, agencies that have conducted effective processes have assimilated the public's views, found ways to address the risks, avoided negative publicity and brought their projects to successful conclusions.

Government agencies and the business sector are endeavouring to grossly weaken privacy protection in Australia through a new set of APPs and accompanying legislation, with the expectation that this will be to the advantage of business and

---

[75] Senate Finance and Public Administration Committee, "Australian Privacy Principles – Exposure Draft", June 2010. http://www.aph.gov.au/Senate/committee/fapa_ctte/priv_exp_drafts/guide/exposure_draft.pdf

[76] See, for example, Cyberspace Law and Policy Centre of the University of New South Wales, "Necessary Improvements to the Australian Privacy Principles", August 2010, https://senate.aph.gov.au/submissions/comittees/viewdocument.aspx?id=9b3bffed-935d-4ea7-8a8a-123433c9eaec and Australian Privacy Foundation, "Submission re Exposure Draft of Australian Privacy Amendment Legislation", August 2010. http://www.privacy.org.au/Papers/Sen-APPs-100818.pdf

government activities. If they are successful, organisations will indeed find it very easy to achieve compliance with such exception-ridden privacy laws.

In the emergent, very-soft-touch regulatory context, agencies and corporations in Australia will be free to design and implement privacy-abusive schemes. They will include features that extend beyond the threshold of acceptability to the categories of people whom they deal with and affect. They will encounter push-back from the citizens and consumers over whom they seek power. They will also suffer negative media coverage. Public relations disasters will occur more often. The incidence of scheme rejection and loss of investment will increase.

To cope with these problems, organisations will appreciate the need for risk management. They will discover a ready-made technique called privacy impact assessment. Hence, in the emergent context of privacy-hostile law, the significance of PIAs in Australia looks set to increase.

Chapter 6
Privacy Impact Assessment – Great Potential Not Often Realised

Nigel Waters

6.1 Introduction

Since privacy impact assessment (PIA) first emerged as a recognised tool in the 1990s, it has quickly become a part of the standard privacy protection toolkit in many jurisdictions. While it is mandatory in a few jurisdictions,[1] it mostly remains merely a recommended step in the consideration and approval processes for major personal information-handling projects.[2] Data protection authorities typically exhort data users to undertake PIA and issue guidelines in support. In most jurisdictions, PIA is seen primarily as a tool for use by public sector agencies, although there is no obvious reason why the technique cannot also be valuable for privacy sector initiatives.[3]

This chapter reflects on the experience of PIAs from the perspective of a practitioner who has conducted many PIAs, mostly in Australia but also in New Zealand and Hong Kong, and has closely observed PIA experience around the world as both a civil society privacy advocate and an academic. I freely acknowledge the potential conflict of interest between these roles, but having successfully balanced them for more than 12 years, I feel able to comment perhaps with more insight on the strengths and weaknesses of PIA as part of the privacy protection toolkit.

---

[1] US E-Government Act 2002, Treasury Board of Canada PIA Policy 2002.

[2] See, for instance, Guidance on PIAs issued in Australia by the Federal and Victorian Privacy Commissioners, by the New Zealand Privacy Commissioner and by the UK Information Commissioner. For a comprehensive list, see Information Commissioner's Office, *Privacy Impact Assessments: International Study of their Application and Effects*, Appendix I, Information Commissioner's Office, Wilmslow, UK, December 2007. http://www.ico.gov.uk/upload/documents/library/corporate/research_and_reports/privacy_impact_assessment_international_study.011007.pdf

[3] The 2010 edition of the Australian Privacy Commissioner's PIA Guide includes a separate section on private sector application, although there are as yet no public examples.

N. Waters (✉)
Pacific Privacy Consulting, Nelson Bay, NSW, Australia
e-mail: nigelwaters@pacificprivacy.com.au

D. Wright, P. De Hert (eds.), *Privacy Impact Assessment*, Law, Governance and Technology Series 6, DOI 10.1007/978-94-007-2543-0_6,
© Springer Science+Business Media B.V. 2012

6.2 A Useful Analogy?

Analogies are drawn throughout the chapter to environmental impact assessment of physical development applications. At least in Australia, and probably elsewhere, environmental assessment has a longer track record than PIA, and has shown many of the same strengths and weaknesses.[4]

6.3 What Is PIA?

Privacy impact assessment comes in many different shapes, sizes and flavours. This fact reflects the wide range of motives and objectives for undertaking PIA; the identity, status and experience of both the client and the assessor; the stage of the subject project at which the PIA is undertaken; the involvement of third parties and the development and approval process into which the PIA is inserted.

There are as yet no recognised certification standards for PIA. Anyone is free to "pitch" or bid for PIA work, and while there are some specialised firms and sole practitioners, more and more PIA is being performed by mainstream legal, accounting and consulting practices. PIA practitioners have varying qualifications and levels of experience. The privacy community, and potential clients, currently have to rely on an informal peer review process whereby aspiring assessors are recommended, or not, by regulators, pressure groups or previous clients. Attempts have been made to establish a privacy profession, with associated standards and certification processes,[5] but most experienced PIA practitioners do not currently see any need to belong, relying instead on their track record and reputation.[6]

6.4 PIA and Privacy by Design

PIA can contribute to ensuring that privacy is designed into new systems,[7] but the link is not as direct as might be thought. PIA of individual projects is typically undertaken well after the main design parameters have been set, an organisational structure committed and significant costs incurred. While a thorough PIA should

---

[4] There is a very extensive literature concerning environmental impact assessment – for a starting point, see the Wikipedia entry at http://en.wikipedia.org/wiki/Environmental_impact_assessment

[5] See International Association of Privacy Professionals (IAPP), founded in the US but now with chapters in other parts of the world. www.privacyassociation.org

[6] In Australia, specialised practitioners include Aulich & Co; Galexia Consulting; Information Integrity Solutions (IIS); Pacific Privacy Consulting; Privacy Law Consulting; Salinger Privacy; and Xamax Consultancy. In Canada, David Flaherty; Linden Consulting; PrivaTech Consulting.

[7] The concept of "privacy by design" has been championed in recent years by Ontario Privacy Commissioner Ann Cavoukian but has a long pedigree, including pioneering work in the 1980s and 1990s by a number of Data Protection Authorities. An early summary of work in the area of privacy by design, by Dr Roger Clarke, is at http://www.rogerclarke.com/DV/CFP2000.html

seek to identify alternatives that may be less privacy intrusive, these will usually be at the margins. Clients will rarely welcome a recommendation that an entire project be taken back to the drawing board and fundamentally re-designed, and it is unrealistic to expect PIA practitioners to make such recommendations even where it is obvious to them that a different direction at an earlier stage would have been preferable.

True "privacy by design" will only be achieved when the instigators and designers of new systems recognise privacy at the outset as one of the variables that they need to consider, alongside functionality, cost and other factors. Where PIA can contribute most to privacy by design is in the cumulative retrospective effect of projects proceeding more smoothly and with less controversy where they have minimised adverse effects on privacy. Conversely, where projects have encountered difficulties as a result of privacy intrusion, weak security of personal information, etc., organisations and professionals involved will hopefully learn the lesson and be more conscious of the benefits of "building in" privacy from the outset in future work.

In the longer term, it would be desirable for privacy experts to be engaged at much earlier stages, when policies are being formulated and key choices are being made about how to meet organisational objectives. This could reduce the need for PIA at later stages of project implementation, although periodic compliance reviews will still be desirable, as there is considerable scope for privacy intrusive elements, or security weaknesses, to be introduced inadvertently as someone comes up with a bright idea to deal with operational problems.

6.5 PIA and Privacy Auditing

PIA differs from privacy auditing or privacy compliance review both in timing and potentially in scope. Privacy audits or compliance reviews will typically look at a personal information-handling system in operation, whereas a PIA should be prospective, assessing a system before it commences operation. In practice, of course, this distinction is often less clear, as organisations are often only persuaded to commission a PIA late in the development process and the conduct of the PIA often overlaps with the commencement of operations. This can have advantages such as the PIA being used as a tool to judge whether anticipated effects do actually happen and whether recommended measures do bring the intended benefits.

Privacy audits and, as the name suggests, compliance reviews typically focus more narrowly on compliance with applicable privacy laws, regulations or other rules to which the data user is subject. PIAs in contrast look also at wider privacy implications, including how the project may be perceived by data subjects or the wider community. A PIA that only looks at strict compliance will be of limited service to the project proponent unless they are only interested in the letter of the law and impervious to public opinion or potential reputational damage. Most privacy laws have significant exemptions and exceptions to specific requirements, which will often mean that a project can technically comply whilst still not meeting common expectations. A thorough PIA will identify privacy issues that the proponent will need to manage, even though they are not breaches of any applicable rules.

6.6 Who Should Be the Client?

The typical model adopted for engaging and funding a PIA is that the proponent of the scheme to be assessed both engages the assessor and pays for the PIA. It is perhaps surprising that there has been little commentary on or criticism of this model. This is particularly so given the widespread criticism of the same model in the field of environmental assessment of physical development proposals.

The model unavoidably involves a conflict of interest. There is an inherent tendency for the assessor to tailor their findings to the client's expectations – to put it more bluntly, to tell the client what they want to hear. Depending on how ethical and principled the assessor, they may be more or less successful in resisting this tendency, but any individual with practical experience of PIA cannot credibly deny that the pressure is always there, even if not expressed, or that they have not on occasion (or perhaps more regularly?) tempered their analysis and recommendations in the knowledge that the client would find certain conclusions too unpalatable.

This observation is not intended as a criticism – except where an assessor leans so far towards pragmatism that they omit to draw the client's attention to significant implications. It is simply an honest recognition of practical realities.

It is easy for assessors to "self-justify" some tailoring of their PIA reports to the expressed or perceived expectations of their clients. They can argue that the client is more likely to be receptive to recommendations if they are more pragmatic and less principled, and that "lecturing" the client will be counter-productive and lead to shutters being closed.

These arguments are legitimate, and it may well be that in PIA as in so many other areas, "the best is the enemy of the good", and that a pragmatic approach can often achieve more effective practical privacy protection than holding out for a more ideal outcome.

But it is equally legitimate to ask if the pressure to qualify or water down analysis and recommendations could be reduced if a different model were adopted.

In the field of physical development planning and approval, the detailed environmental assessment of a project is generally carried out by consultants hired by the project proponent – preparation of such an assessment, against legislated criteria, is generally a requirement under planning law. There are requirements for assessments to be placed on public exhibition alongside the proposal, for public comment. However, the lack of independence inherent in this arrangement is usually balanced by a separate assessment by officers of the consent authority, such as a local council, which can focus on whether the main assessment has met professional standards and not overlooked major implications. This model seeks to ensure that the bulk of the work, and associated cost, is borne by the project proponent, while retaining the safeguard of a disinterested "peer review".

It should be noted that, at least in Australia, this model of environmental assessment has come under pressure in recent years from governments seeking to cut costs and speed development approvals. At least for minor developments, the process has been entirely privatised, with "private certifiers" – supposedly independent but employed by the developer – able to sign off all necessary approvals. This variant of the model relies on professional standards in the assessment or certification marketplace, and on after-the-event investigations of complaints, with an oversight body able to sanction assessors who do not meet the required standards. Unsurprisingly, it has been widely criticised, not least because any redress or sanction will typically come, if at all, too late for individuals and communities damaged by sub-standard assessments.

Back in the privacy world, the practical reality is that privacy regulators will never be given the resources to carry out a "second assessment" (or audit) of every PIA, and are unlikely even to be able to adequately supervise private sector assessors who are engaged directly by project proponents.

6.7 In an Ideal World . . .?

Ideally, PIA would be commissioned by a privacy regulator or third party intermediary, who would determine the brief, and engage and pay the assessor, using funds reclaimed from the project proponent. This would insulate the assessor from the pressures involved in a direct relationship with the project proponent as a client.

It would, of course, be appropriate for the regulator or intermediary to consult the project proponent in drawing up the PIA brief and establishing a budget. But the project proponent should have neither the final say, nor a veto.

Proposals could still be invited from a range of potential assessors, i.e., a competitive tender, but with cost being only one of the selection criteria (provided it was within an acceptable budget range).

Various models could be considered for payment. There could be case-by-case funds transfers for individual projects, or a pool scheme with proponents paying into a common fund. In either model, payments could be based on a fixed levy – perhaps a percentage of the estimated or budgeted project cost, or a sliding scale of fixed amounts for projects falling into different ranges of cost.

While such a model may be achievable in the long term, in the interim most PIAs will continue to be produced by assessors engaged directly by the project proponent, and consideration must be given to how best to make use of the PIA reports, in full knowledge that they may not be entirely comprehensive or objective.

6.8 Using PIA Findings to Effect Change

Most PIA reports will have only a limited ability to effect change, on their own, in the design or implementation of a major project.

Because of the factors discussed above, most PIA reports will only go some way towards specifying changes to project design and implementation that will reduce privacy intrusion and enhance privacy protection and safeguards.

Because of the pressures on the assessor already discussed, PIA reports will often only hint at potential problems. Assessors trying to fully document adverse privacy effects, or to suggest alternatives or safeguards, but constrained in their ability to do so too bluntly, can often nevertheless include clues which can be detected and interpreted by experienced readers. Those who have faced this dilemma will recognise the frustration of having left what they think are obvious clues, or potential ammunition, only to watch regulators, non-government organisations and legislators fail to detect the clues and follow up accordingly.

I suggest that all concerned should become more realistic in their expectations as to what a PIA report can achieve on its own without other interested parties becoming involved, reading the clues and making use of the report to influence the outcome.

Privacy regulators in particular need to become more active in following up on PIA reports. They should ask project proponents which recommendations in a PIA they accept and, if they don't accept all, to explain why they do not do so. Where recommendations are accepted, there also needs to be follow-up to ascertain if they have actually been implemented and, again, if they have not been implemented, then why not? It is all too easy for project proponents to say initially that they accept and will implement suggested changes, only to find reasons later to backslide, and either partially or wholly abandon their initial commitment.

There is a perception that privacy regulators have too often seen the issuance of PIA guidance, and the subsequent take-up of PIA by agencies and organisations as "mission accomplished". They may see PIA activity in response to guidance as a way of relieving them of responsibility for proactive work in relation to the projects concerned. In an environment where financial and staff resources available are always constrained, regulators understandably can be tempted to focus those resources on projects where there has been no PIA, or on other areas of work altogether, such as complaint handling. But this can be a false economy, if PIA activity does not result in actual changes to project design and implementation.

As with all areas of their work, privacy regulators may get a better return for the deployment of scarce resources by following through at least some exemplar PIAs, and publicising the outcomes as a way of demonstrating the value of PIA (or alternatively of demonstrating the risks of not addressing privacy implications).

Even if the conduct of PIA becomes mandatory, as has been suggested in some jurisdictions,[8] it would be impracticable to mandate the adoption of all PIA recommendations. There are, after all, always other interests to be balanced against

---

[8] E.g., Australian Law Reform Commission, "For Your Information", Report 108, August 2008, Recommendation 47–4. http://www.austlii.edu.au/cgi-bin/sinodisp/au/other/alrc/publications/reports/108/_3.html#Heading403; House of Lords, Constitution Committee – Second Report, Surveillance: Citizens and the State, January 2009, paragraph 30. http://www.publications.parliament.uk/pa/ld200809/ldselect/ldconst/18/1808.htm#a56

privacy protection, and circumstances will change, such that it will not always be appropriate to implement all recommendations. But regulators can at least follow through and require project proponents to justify why they have not accepted or implemented PIA recommendations.

Many public sector projects require legislative authorisation, and PIA can and should be an important input to legislative processes. Unfortunately, legislative authority is often granted before a PIA is undertaken, which limits the scope for PIA findings to influence project design, even if they can still contribute to implementation safeguards.

Ideally, PIA should be undertaken in time for the report to be made available to legislators before they are called on to debate authorising legislation.

6.9 Some Examples of PIA

Five examples from three different jurisdictions illustrate the importance, and interplay, of the factors discussed above.

6.9.1 Online Authentication for e-Government in New Zealand

In 2003–2004, the New Zealand government, through its State Services Commission, was considering options for online authentication for e-government services. On the advice of the NZ Privacy Commissioner, the Commission engaged specialist consultants (the author and a colleague, in partnership) to conduct a PIA. Because the PIA was commissioned at a very early stage in the consideration of options, and because the project team were committed to addressing privacy issues, both the initial report in December 2003 and a subsequent update report in April 2004 had significant influence on the choice of approach – as the e-Government website explains:

> The EGU has been working closely with the Office of the Privacy Commissioner and other stakeholders to determine the most appropriate action to take in relation to each of the recommendations in the PIA... A number of the report's recommendations are being "taken up" in continuing design development. A further 20 of the total of 39 recommendations have been identified as only requiring further action if a decision is made in the future to proceed further with a full implementation of all-of-government authentication.[9]

In this case, warnings in the PIA about the privacy risks inherent in the more ambitious options appear to have resulted in much more focussed, and less privacy intrusive, programs. The current e-government website promotes the concept of federated identity and managing multiple identities – a key recommendation

---

[9] The PIA reports were available online but now appear to have been removed, leaving only an archived discussion of how the government has responded to the recommendations. See http://www.e.govt.nz/plone/archive/services/authentication/privacy-faqs.html

of the 2003 PIA, and incidentally encourages agencies adopting the whole of government framework to conduct their own PIA before implementing identity federation solutions.[10]

6.9.2 Retention and Linkage of Australian Census Data

In April 2005, the Australian Bureau of Statistics (ABS) issued a Discussion Paper on a proposed census data enhancement project which would involve a departure from the long established practice of irrevocably de-identifying census records after a relatively short period of processing, although this change could be effected without legislative amendments. The ABS commissioned a PIA (from the author) and made the report publicly available,[11] together with its response to the PIA recommendations, in June 2005, and invited comments. Eight submissions were received (and published), including three from privacy regulators and four from interested non-government organisations. The ABS subsequently implemented a significantly modified version of the project, involving longitudinal records of only a small sample of census respondents. This is arguably the best example to date of an open PIA process which allowed key stakeholders to provide timely input, and resulted in a significant improvements in the project design from a privacy perspective (although not all of the PIA recommendations were implemented).

6.9.3 The Australian Financial Reporting Regime

In 2006, major changes to Australian federal anti money-laundering legislation were introduced. A privacy impact assessment was commissioned and the report[12] was made public in time for the Senate Committee Inquiry into the Bill only six weeks later.[13] Interested parties making submissions were able to draw on the up-to-date PIA, and the Committee devoted a section of its report to the issues raised by the PIA, and to the Attorney-General's Department (the proponent)'s response. As in

---

[10] See http://www.e.govt.nz/standards/authentication/security-assertion-messaging-framework/benefits-of-identity-federation

[11] See http://www.abs.gov.au/websitedbs/D3110124.NSF/f5c7b8fb229cf017ca256973001fecec/fa7fd3e58e5cb46bca2571ee00190475!OpenDocument

[12] Salinger & Co, "Privacy Impacts of the Anti-Money Laundering and Counter-Terrorism Financing Bill and Rules, 2006, A Privacy Impact Assessment for the Australian Government Attorney-General's Department", 15 September 2006. http://www.ag.gov.au/www/agd/rwpattach.nsf/VAP/(CFD7369FCAE9B8F32F341DBE097801FF)~88Privacy+impact+assessment+aml-06.pdf/file/88Privacy+impact+assessment+aml-06.pdf

[13] Senate Standing Committee on Legal and Constitutional Affairs, "Provisions of the Anti-Money Laundering and Counter-Terrorism Financing Bill 2006, and the Anti-Money Laundering and Counter-Terrorism Financing (Transitional Provisions and Consequential Amendments) Bill 2006", Report, November 2006, Chapter 4. http://www.aph.gov.au/senate/committee/legcon_ctte/completed_inquiries/2004-07/aml_ctf06/report/index.htm

the NZ example, the PIA led to some significant improvements, particularly in terms of privacy safeguards, governance and accountability.

6.9.4 Individual Identifiers for e-Health in Australia

In contrast, the controversial issue of unique health identifiers, in the context of Australian e-health initiatives, saw a significant investment in PIA almost completely wasted. The proponent, in this case the National E-Health Transition Authority (NeHTA), commissioned three separate PIAs from different assessors[14] over a period of three years, at a total cost that must have approached $1 million. Despite calls from concerned non-government organisations, the three PIAs, conducted in 2006, 2008 and early 2009 respectively, were only publicly released (as a batch and with NeHTA responses) in November 2009.[15] All three PIAs raised very significant issues, but by late 2009 NeHTA was able to claim that the project design had significantly changed, reducing the relevance and value of the PIAs.

An exposure draft Healthcare Identifiers Bill 2010 was made publicly available on 10 December 2009 (just before Christmas and the long summer holidays), and comments invited by 7 January – a typical timing tactic by governments wishing to minimise input. The final Bill was introduced in February 2010, and referred to a Senate Committee on 24 February with an unusually short consultation period.[16] The Committee held hearings in March, at which the Australian Privacy Foundation, and others, referred to the failure to adequately address more than 30 key recommendations from the PIAs. The PIAs are not referred to at all in the majority report, but only in the dissenting minority report in support of some proposed amendments. Most of these amendments were not accepted by the government and the Bill was enacted in June 2010.

Interestingly, *The Australian* newspaper, in a report on the Senate Inquiry, stated that "The federal Privacy Commissioner's Office yesterday responded to questions on the issue, saying it was 'not our role to approve PIAs or their recommendations'."[17]

The experience of this controversial legislation, with major privacy implications,[18] shows how the failure to release PIAs closer to the time of their completion, the failure of key interested parties to follow up effectively and the failure to provide

---

[14] Galexia Consulting, 2006; Clayton Utz, 2008; and Mallesons, Stephen Jacques, 2009. The author was engaged as a sub-contractor in the 2009 PIA.

[15] http://www.nehta.gov.au/connecting-australia/privacy/pias

[16] Senate Community Affairs Legislation Committee, "Healthcare Identifiers Bill 2010 and Healthcare Identifiers (Consequential Amendments) Bill 2010", Report, March 2010. http://www.aph.gov.au/senate/committee/clac_ctte/healthcare_identifier/report/index.htm

[17] Dearne, Karen, "Reject e-Health Identifier Bill, Says Law Professor", *The Australian*, 16 Mar 2010.

[18] Submissions to the Senate Committee invoked comparisons with previous highly controversial attempts to introduce a universal national identification scheme. Many believe that the Individual

adequate opportunity for debate all contribute to limiting the effectiveness of PIA in influencing project design.

Another relevant feature of the health identifier PIA process was that all three PIAs emphasised that the full privacy implications of the identifier scheme could not be assessed in the absence of more information about the proposed use of the identifiers in e-health initiatives. The insistence of NeHTA, and subsequently of the government, on presenting the identifier scheme and legislation as a "stand-alone infrastructure" initiative, effectively prevented proper and useful PIA, despite the hundreds of thousands of dollars spent on the three assessments.

6.9.5 Hong Kong Smart Identity Card

The Immigration Department of the Hong Kong Special Administrative Region (HKSAR) commenced a project in the late 1990s to replace the previous Territory identity card, introduced in 1987, with a new HKSAR "smart" identity card (SMARTIC), to contain a microchip and biometric information.[19]

In 2000, a consortium led by the author was commissioned to undertake a PIA of the SMARTIC project. A generous budget (at least by Australian and New Zealand standards) allowed for a comprehensive and detailed assessment, but the client did not welcome many of the recommendations, and there was considerable tension during the finalisation of the report, leading to a final product which did not highlight key recommendations, leaving them to be "discovered" by readers in the body of a lengthy document. As predicted in the general discussion above, this unsurprisingly meant that the PIA work was not used as effectively by potential critics, or in the course of the political process, as it could have been, had the assessors been able to present their findings differently.

The PIA recommendations, together with the government's response following discussions with the Privacy Commissioner, were presented to the Legislative Council (LegCo) Security Panel, thereby becoming public, in February 2001,[20] although the full PIA Report was not made public until some time in 2002.[21] A meeting of the Panel in December 2001 was given a list of the privacy-related

---

Health Identifier has in effect now introduced the essential infrastructure for such a multi-function ID system, with inadequate safeguards against "function creep".

[19] The history of the SMARTIC project can be traced from an index to Legislative Council policy papers on the project at http://www.legco.gov.hk/database/english/data_se/se-hksar-identity-card-project.htm and a critical overview of the entire programme is provided in Greenleaf, Graham, "Hong Kong's 'Smart' ID Card: Designed to be Out of Control", Chapter 5 in Colin J. Bennett and David Lyon (eds.), *Playing the Identity Card: Surveillance, Security and Identification in Global Perspective*, Routledge, 2008. Chapter available separately at http://www.austlii.edu.au/au/journals/ALRS/2008/10.html

[20] Paper at http://www.legco.gov.hk/yr00-01/english/panels/se/papers/b752e04.pdf

[21] Report (abridged version) at http://www.legco.gov.hk/yr00-01/english/fc/esc/papers/esc27e1.pdf

measures and actions taken by the Project to that date with a re-assurance on the government's decision to limit non-immigration functions for the new card, and to make any such functions available on a voluntary basis – consistent with the PIA recommendations.[22] However, in early 2002, amendments to the Registration of Persons Ordinance were introduced to allow for multiple non-immigration uses of the SMARTIC, contrary to the PIA report which had recommended legislative barriers to function creep.

The Department subsequently commissioned a second PIA as "an assessment on how the technical design has addressed the key data privacy recommendations in the first PIA report". The recommendations of the second PIA, again together with the government's response and taking account of the Privacy Commissioner's views, were also made available to the LegCo Panel, in 2002.[23] A third PIA remains unpublished, while a fourth and final PIA, sometime in 2004–2005, provided "an overall post-implementation review of data privacy protection relating to system controls, functionalities and manual procedures to ascertain that all privacy protection measures have been suitably implemented and are operating effectively in practice".[24]

The presentation of the fourth PIA to the LegCo panel states that "The Consultant finds that ImmD is privacy conscious and has a strong commitment to addressing privacy issues and concerns arising from the SMARTICS project. ImmD has also been responsive in implementing the recommendations arising from the various PIAs."[25]

The second, third and fourth PIAs were carried out by different consultants from the first (it is not known if the same consultant was responsible for the last three). Whilst it is not uncommon for agencies to use different consultants for different stages of PIA (see also the Australian e-health identifier project discussed above), it does mean a loss of continuity and experience, and it may be questioned whether the initial assessors would necessarily have the same confidence that their recommendations had been implemented as the "new" assessors appear to have in the HK case. There are, however, potential benefits in "peer review" and it is arguably just as likely that a second assessor would pick up weaknesses in the initial report or identify additional issues, as that they will provide a less rigorous assessment. The potential for different conclusions to be drawn from the same facts strengthens the case for maximum transparency – if all PIA reports are made public, then interested parties can compare them and form their own judgement about their relative strengths.

Comparison of the three published sets of PIA recommendations for the HKSAR Smart ID card also illustrates another predictable trend – that in the later stages of a project, attention focuses on detailed systems design and procedural safeguards,

---

[22] Paper at http://www.legco.gov.hk/yr01-02/english/panels/se/papers/itbse1220cb1-666-1e.pdf

[23] Paper at http://www.legco.gov.hk/yr01-02/english/panels/se/papers/se0710cb2-2433-7e.pdf

[24] Paper at http://www.legco.gov.hk/yr04-05/english/panels/se/papers/secb2-858-1e.pdf

[25] Paper at http://www.legco.gov.hk/yr04-05/english/panels/se/papers/secb2-858-1e.pdf

compared to the consideration of "big picture" issues, such as justification for privacy intrusion, alternatives and risks of function creep, that is possible and justifiable at earlier stages. Once key decisions on project scope and design have been made, it is unreasonable to expect PIA assessors to revisit issues that have been effectively closed through the political process. That does not, of course, prevent interest groups continuing to pursue wider issues and it is worth noting that questions from HK legislators about wider uses of the ID card have continued, with the government giving assurances about future consultation.

6.10 Conclusion

This chapter has made suggestions, based on the author's personal experience and observations, as to how PIA can be made more effective. All interested parties need to develop a more sophisticated understanding of the practical and political realities, and take these into account when commissioning, reading and using PIA reports.

PIA has great potential as a privacy protection tool, but that potential will only be realised if it is accepted that a PIA report is not an end in itself and will not generally lead unaided to better privacy outcomes. Assessors carrying out PIAs operate under significant constraints and are subject to many pressures that may prevent them from achieving as much with the processes and reports as others might expect.

As in the much more familiar field of environmental assessment of physical development projects, PIA can at least provide useful information for others to use in the bureaucratic and political environments where project designs are formed and where decisions on whether, when and how to implement are made.

Chapter 7
Privacy Impact Assessments in Canada

Robin M. Bayley and Colin J. Bennett

7.1 Introduction

Over the last 20 years or so, a range of new policy instruments has entered the "toolbox" of those regulators charged with implementing and enforcing information privacy and data protection policy. During the earlier history of these policies, it was generally assumed that law alone, codifying the information privacy principles and establishing independent oversight, would be both necessary and sufficient to regulate the collection, use and dissemination of personal data by organisations. The assumptions have shifted. Now, it is generally assumed that law is necessary, but not sufficient. A variety of other mechanisms, both self-regulatory and technological, are also necessary. There is now a complicated toolkit of instruments that is expected to supplement legal enforcement.[1]

Privacy impact assessments (PIAs) are one of these new tools, introduced at a time when the policy community was looking for more innovative ways to make privacy and data protection law more effective (referred to as privacy law in Canada). It is probable that some organisations have always conducted prospective assessments of whether new services, proposals and products have privacy implications and were consistent with relevant legal norms. As a separate instrument, however, institutionalised in organisational processes, recommended by data protection authorities (DPAs, usually called privacy commissioners in Canada), and, in some cases, required by law, PIAs are of quite recent vintage. Various trends and influences seem to have converged in the mid-1990s when experts and officials in Canada, New Zealand and Australia began to think seriously about PIAs in a more systematic way as an essential tool for data protection. The idea then spread quite

---

[1] Bennett, Colin J., and Charles Raab, *The Governance of Privacy: Policy Instruments in Global Perspective,* Ashgate Press, Aldershot, UK, 2003. Second and revised edition, MIT Press, Cambridge, MA, 2006.

R.M. Bayley (✉)
Linden Consulting, Inc., Victoria, BC, Canada
e-mail: rmbayley@shaw.ca

D. Wright, P. De Hert (eds.), *Privacy Impact Assessment,* Law, Governance
and Technology Series 6, DOI 10.1007/978-94-007-2543-0_7,
© Springer Science+Business Media B.V. 2012

rapidly around the policy community as a way to demonstrate legal compliance, to allow organisations to develop better policy, to save money, to develop a culture of privacy protection, to prevent adverse publicity and to mitigate risks in advance of resource allocation.[2] They contribute to the "ounce of prevention" reasoning that has been part of the rhetoric of data protection authorities and privacy commissioners for a long time.

Canada was one of the first countries to take up the idea of PIAs at both national and provincial levels. This experience is probably, therefore, as thorough and instructive as anywhere in the world. We start by summarising the legal framework for privacy protection in Canada, followed by a discussion of how PIAs are conducted at the national and provincial levels in Ontario, British Columbia (BC) and Alberta. It is more difficult to find evidence of the use of PIAs in the private sector, but we do describe where they are conducted how they might be done differently than in the public sector. We conclude by drawing some lessons from the Canadian experience.

7.1.1 The Canadian Privacy Legislative Framework

The development of privacy law in the decentralised federal structure of the Canadian political system is complicated, shifting and incremental. The legal framework, whilst now quite comprehensive, was not always so. Laws for both public and private sectors, at national and provincial levels, have evolved pragmatically and in response to a variety of local, national and international pressures.

The first privacy legislation at the national level was contained in Part IV of the 1977 Canadian Human Rights Act, which established the office of the Privacy Commissioner, then a member of the Canadian Human Rights Commission. Parallel debates over an access to information statute for the national public sector in the early 1980s raised immediate questions about the compatibility between such legislation and the privacy standards within Part IV of the Human Rights Act. The current 1982 Privacy Act, therefore, flows from a belief that the protection of personal information should be a corollary to freedom of information (FOI) and that the various exemptions in both pieces of legislation should be consistent. These new laws thus institutionalised the Canadian innovation of legislating access to information and privacy protection within the same statutory framework.

The practice of legislating both policy areas within one statute was later copied by each of the provinces and territories and, most notably, by Quebec in 1982, Ontario (1988), Saskatchewan (1992), BC (1993), Alberta (1995) and Manitoba (1997). An independent privacy commissioner now oversees each law (although the two functions have since split, and the Privacy Commissioner of Canada has no FOI

---

[2] Bayley, Robin M., "Appendix C, Jurisdictional Report for Canada", in *Privacy Impact Assessments: An International Study of their Application and Effects*, Report to the UK Information Commissioner, December 2007, p. 64. http://www.rogerclarke.com/DV/ICOStudy-2007-Apps.pdf

responsibilities). All privacy commissioners are primarily ombudsmen whose primary duty is to receive and investigate complaints, and legislation tends to specify in considerable detail the procedures and powers for receiving, investigating and reporting the results of complaints. They differ in the degree to which their decisions are binding and how they are enforced. Much of the work, then, is reactive and commands a significant amount of the often limited personnel and resources. The privacy commissioners also conduct investigations and audits of government agencies. These may be part of a formal audit program (as in Ottawa), or more ad hoc "site visits" to public bodies (as in BC).

Most commissioners are also authorised to comment on the privacy implications of pending legislation and other initiatives, and attempt to inject a privacy perspective at the earliest stages of the legislative process, technology development or service delivery. High-profile legislative changes that involve radical implications for the processing of personal information are often the circumstances under which consultation is the most serious, and attended by the most significant media interest. On many occasions, however, privacy commissioners have complained that privacy protection is a last minute "add-on" and that their staff are not consulted early enough in the policy development process. In this context, PIAs were seen as a way to encourage agencies to consider privacy in a more systematic and pro-active manner.

The aforementioned legislation applies only to national and provincial public agencies. The passage in 1993 of Quebec's Act respecting the protection of personal information in the private sector gave effect to the information privacy rights incorporated in the new Civil Code and made Quebec the first jurisdiction in North America to produce comprehensive data protection rules for the private sector. The privacy commissioner, the Commission d'Accès à l'Information du Québec, a body established under the 1982 public sector access and privacy law, oversees implementation of the Act, hears complaints and renders binding decisions. This was followed in 2000 by the Personal Information Protection and Electronic Documents Act (PIPEDA) of Canada, obliging the private sector to abide by the principles in the 1996 Canadian Standards Association Code for the Protection of Personal Information, and overseen by the Privacy Commissioner of Canada. Because of constitutional limitations, however, this law only applies to the nationally regulated sectors (e.g., banking, telecommunications and transportation) and to personal information transmitted across interprovincial and international borders for a commercial purpose. A controversial provision, however, made PIPEDA apply to all other private enterprises unless the province had substantially similar private sector legislation. To date, only Quebec, BC and Alberta have passed such laws. In addition, there are a number of provincial sectoral statutes, most notably for the protection of personal health information, and Ontario has a separate statute covering municipal governments. Constitutional and tort law applies in certain instances as well.

In addition to the privacy commissioner, each government has a unit with privacy policy responsibilities, sometimes established under specific legislative authorities or stemming from ministerial responsibility for the statute. In this paper, the term "central agency" is used to describe a unit of government with expertise and overall responsibility for Canadian privacy law, subordinate legislation and policy and for producing tools and information. Both the privacy commissioner and the central agency have a significant role to play with regard to the implementation of PIAs in Canada.

7.2 The Conduct of PIAs in Canada

7.2.1 The Legal Basis for Privacy Impact Assessments

"The Privacy Act and Privacy Regulations[3] provide the legal framework for the collection, retention, use, disclosure, disposition and accuracy of personal information in the administration of programs and activities by national government institutions. The Act is modelled on internationally accepted standards, which are based on the principles that every individual retains ownership of his or her personal information and has the right to know what personal information is being collected about him or her, how it will be used, to whom it will be disclosed, and when and how it will be disposed of."[4] The Act gives the Treasury Board Secretariat administrative responsibility for the Act and that central agency introduced the original PIA policy in May 2002,[5] replacing it with the current Directive, effective July 2010. This makes PIAs mandatory for government institutions in given circumstances.

Within Canada, BC alone has an explicit legislative requirement for ministries to conduct PIAs. PIAs must be conducted by government ministries, but not by all public bodies subject to the Act. As of April 2002, section 69(5) of Freedom of Information and Protection of Privacy Act (FOIPPA) requires ministries to conduct PIAs for "a new enactment, system, project or program", to determine their compliance with Part 3 of FOIPPA, governing the collection, use, disclosure, protection and retention of personal information by public bodies. The minister responsible for the Act has authority to develop mandatory policy with regard to PIAs for ministries. Originally, the central agency introduced a PIA policy in December 1998, last updated in 2008. Further, the minister has not-yet-used authority to require any other public bodies to comply with PIA policy.

In Alberta, most PIAs are completed to satisfy the requirements of section 64 of the Health Information Act, under which "custodians" [of personal health information] must conduct PIAs whenever they plan to implement new administrative

---

[3] Privacy Act, R.S., 1985, c. P-21. http://laws.justice.gc.ca/eng/P-21/index.html and Privacy Regulation, OR/83-508. http://laws.justice.gc.ca/en/showtdm/cr/SOR-83-508/?showtoc=&instrumentnumber=SOR-83-508

[4] Treasury Board of Canada Secretariat, Directive on Privacy Practices, s. 3. http://www.tbs-sct.gc.ca/pol/doc-eng.aspx?section=text&id=18309

[5] Treasury Board of Canada Secretariat, Archived – Privacy Impact Assessment Policy [superseded]. http://www.tbs-sct.gc.ca/pol/doc-eng.aspx?id=12450&section=text#cha1

practices or information systems that collect, use or disclose health information about identifiable individuals, or where there are changes to existing systems.[6] Other bodies are encouraged to use the tool, but modify it according to their governing legislation.[7] PIAs are not required by other public bodies, but are recommended for major projects that involve the collection, use or disclosure of personal information.[8] This policy is issued under the authority of the minister responsible for Alberta's FOIPPA.[9] In 2001, the Office of the Information and Privacy Commissioner (OIPC) of Alberta introduced its first PIA questionnaire, which was used for more than eight years, during which the practice of conducting privacy impact assessments matured considerably and the volume of PIAs handled by the OIPC increased dramatically.[10] New PIA requirements, with their focus on health information, replaced the questionnaire in September 2010.

The mandate to complete PIAs in the Ontario public service derives from the Corporate Policy on Protection of Personal Information,[11] the Procurement Directive[12] and information technology project review processes. In December 2010, Ontario's central agency, the Office of the Information and Privacy Officer[13] released a revised PIA guide, replacing the 2001 version. The guide provides an overview of the PIA methodology and outlines the privacy activities required throughout a project's lifecycle. It also explains how to integrate a PIA into project management and use the results to meet the corporate governance requirements. Three PIA tools were also released at that time and provide detailed instructions, checklists, templates and other resources to help projects complete the PIA process.[14] It is too early to draw conclusions on their use.

---

[6] Office of the Information and Privacy Commissioner of Alberta, *Privacy Impact Assessment Requirements*, 2009, p. 10. http://www.oipc.ab.ca/Content_Files/Files/PIAs/PIA_Requirements_2010.pdf

[7] OIPC of Alberta website, *PIA Requirements* webpage. http://www.oipc.ab.ca/pages/PIAs/PIARequirements.aspx

[8] OIPC of Alberta website, *PIAs*. http://www.oipc.ab.ca/pages/PIAs/default.aspx

[9] Revised Statutes of Alberta 2000, Chapter F-25. http://www.qp.alberta.ca/570.cfm?frm_isbn=9780779743568&search_by=link

[10] OIPC of Alberta, *Privacy Impact Assessment Requirements*, 2010. http://www.oipc.ab.ca/Content_Files/Files/PIAs/PIA_Requirements_2010.pdf

[11] Ontario, Ministry of Government Services, Corporate Policy on Protection of Personal Information, effective 25 July 2011.

[12] Ontario, Ministry of Government Services, Procurement Directive, 7.5, Protection of Personal and Sensitive Information, April 2011. http://www.doingbusiness.mgs.gov.on.ca/mbs/psb/psb.nsf/Attachments/PDApril2011-RelatedPolicies/$FILE/07-otherrelatedpolicies-e.html

[13] Effective 11 April 2011, OCIPO merged with Archives of Ontario to form Information, Privacy and Archives (IPA) Division, Ministry of Government Services.

[14] These four tools developed by the Office of the Chief Information and Privacy Officer and dated December 2010 are the Preliminary Analysis, Privacy Design Analysis, Privacy Impact Assessment Guide and Privacy Risk Analysis.

Further, the Privacy Commissioner developed two specialised PIA tools that are not required under legislation, nor is there an expectation of submitting PIAs to the Privacy Commissioner for review.[15]

The province of Quebec has enjoyed privacy law for both public and private sectors for longer than any jurisdiction in North America. Indeed, the passage of Bill 68 in 1992 was one of the main reasons why private sector privacy protection reached the federal agenda in the 1990s; Canada had become a jurisdiction where the level of protection in one of the provinces was higher than that at the federal level. Despite this experience, however, there is not much evidence that PIAs have been promoted within either the Quebec government, or within the provincially regulated businesses covered by Bill 68. PIAs represent a pro-active and self-regulatory approach which is somewhat at odds with the civil law tradition upon which these statutes are based. The culture of the privacy community in Quebec tends to be one of technical and legal compliance. The approach to enforcement within the Commission d'Acces à l'Information (CAI) tends to be quite legalistic.

Quebec has a formal procedure for public agencies to obtain the opinion of the Commission on proposed systems that have implications for the protection of personal information.[16] Guidance published by the Commission has many of the features of a PIA. But the process seems to be confined to large-scale projects such as the introduction of biometrics.[17]

Because the Quebec Commission has tended to look for lessons more from the European data protection tradition in continental Europe, rather than to the privacy protection tradition prevalent in the rest of Canada,[18] we focus on Ontario, BC and Alberta in this chapter.

7.2.2 Who Conducts PIAs?

Typically, the organisation itself undertakes the analysis and produces the final PIA document(s), usually at the program or project level. The locus of responsibility differs by organisation, but often entails a team approach, with privacy, program and systems staff participating. Analysts working under the direction of a project team leader may be assigned unless significant privacy issues are expected. By the

---

[15] Anderson, Ken, "You can get there from here: *IPC tools and approaches for privacy compliance in Ontario"*, speech by the Assistant Commissioner of the OIPC of Ontario, 27 April 2006. http://www.ipc.on.ca/images/Resources/up-2006_04_26_PIPA_Presentation.pdf

[16] Commission d'accès à l'information du Québec, *Cadre de référence concernant l'Obtention d'un avis de la Commission pour un dossier technologique*, February 2004. http://www.cai.gouv.qc.ca/06_documentation/01_pdf/cadre_reference.pdf

[17] Commission d'accès à l'information du Québec, *Biometrics in Québec: Application Principles – Making an Informed Choice*, July 2002. http://www.cai.gouv.qc.ca/home_00_portail/01_pdf/biometrics.pdf

[18] LaPerrière, René, "The 'Quebec Model' of Data Protection: A Compromise between *Laissez-Fair* and Public Control in a Technological Era", in Colin J. Bennett and Rebecca Grant (eds.), *Visions of Privacy: Policy Choices for the Digital Age*, University of Toronto Press Toronto, 1999.

time a PIA is completed, it should have been reviewed and approved throughout the organisation's hierarchy and have drawn on widespread expertise. Sometimes external consultants will also be contracted. Beyond this, there is some different guidance within the various Canadian jurisdictions.

At the national level, the Directive requiring PIAs applies to "government institutions" as defined in the Privacy Act. This includes departments or ministries, or any scheduled body or office and Crown corporations, and their subsidiaries. The Schedule includes a lengthy and diverse list of public organisations including marketing boards, research institutes, tribunals, labour relations and safety boards, independent oversight offices, regional development agencies, charitable foundations, etc.[19] The OPC's fact sheet on PIAs stipulates that "individual government departments and agencies conduct their own PIAs. An assessment team often includes experts in several areas, including legal services, privacy, access to information and information technology."[20]

In BC, a PIA process overview states: "Even though the revised PIA has been designed with a view to being completed, at least in part, by program staff, there are a number of questions in the PIA where consultations with privacy experts are recommended if not required" (indicated by an asterisk in the margin of the template).[21] Though brief, this guide also provides some basic information about privacy to novices and links to other sources of information. Depending on the scale and potential privacy impact of the initiative, a larger team may be assembled for the PIA. The process of fleshing out the initiative and completing the PIA go hand in hand. The PIA author may bring issues to the project committee or management for decision and may also identify potential barriers to implementing the initiative such as lack of legislative authority. After the PIA is completed, a series of briefings of officials in the hierarchy can result in questions being raised which result in further analysis.

In Alberta, a training program aimed at new public body privacy officers includes a section on PIAs in its Managing a FOIP Program course. As in BC, program staff members conduct the PIA with a team which may include a project or senior manager, privacy officer and specialists in records management, IT, legal services and communications. The team should be led by "someone who understands the FOIP Act and privacy principles and issues, has technical writing skills, has project management experience and can synthesise input from a variety of sources".[22] As the vast majority of PIAs conducted in Alberta concern health information systems,

---

[19] Privacy Act, (R.S., 1985, c. P-21), Schedule 3. http://laws.justice.gc.ca/eng/P-21/20090723/page-11.html#anchorsc:1

[20] Office of the Privacy Commissioner of Canada, Fact Sheet on Privacy Impact Assessment. http://www.priv.gc.ca/fs-fi/02_05_d_33_e.cfm

[21] Ministry of Citizens' Services, *Privacy Impact Assessment Process* webpage. http://www.cio.gov.bc.ca/cio/priv_leg/foippa/pia/pia_index.page

[22] Service Alberta, *FOIP Guidelines and Practices (2009)*, section 9.3 Privacy Impact Assessments. http://www.servicealberta.gov.ab.ca/foip/documents/chapter9.pdf

many private sector information technology consultants are developing expertise and leading the PIA exercise as part of system design.

The "business owner", the program manager responsible for privacy compliance and program records, is responsible for ensuring the PIA process is undertaken, if required.

Generalisations cannot be made about the type of position held by the individual who completes the PIA. The Guide recommends a team approach requiring "different subject matter experts to identify, evaluate and address privacy risks at different times in the project." It cites expertise in the business process, privacy, policy, information management and technology, security, legal, stakeholder management, procurement, risk assessment as well as in the privacy requirements of partner organisations.[23]

7.2.3 Private Sector PIAs

No Canadian jurisdiction requires the conduct of PIAs under private sector privacy legislation, but they are occasionally conducted as part of good business practices. The privacy commissioners of Canada and Ontario are particularly vocal advocates of PIAs, with the latter including PIAs in her emphasis on a proactive "privacy by design" approach. However, no governments have developed PIA methodologies specifically for the private sector, although specialised PIAs for the health and justice information sectors may be used for public and private entities in those fields.

Some companies conducting PIAs use proprietary methodologies they are reluctant to share, either because they are the property of consultants or because they were developed in-house and are seen as a competitive advantage. Major consulting firms and some training firms offer PIA services or training.[24] Using techniques from information management disciplines, private sector PIAs are most frequently conducted for information technology projects. PIAs have been conducted by telecommunications companies, those providing back-room services in human resources and payment processing, banks and other financial institutions, international energy companies and major retailers. PIAs are also spreading from public to private sectors through contracting out, public-private partnerships and other joint initiatives, particularly in the health care field with shared information systems. PIAs may also be conducted by those seeking access to publicly held information as a due diligence exercise before information sharing agreements are concluded.

---

[23] Ontario, Office of the Chief Information and Privacy Officer, *Privacy Impact Assessment Guide for the Ontario Public Service*, December 2010, p. 4 and Appendix C.

[24] Examples include Deloitte Canada, which has an active privacy practice and conducts PIAs as part of enterprise risk services, and Priva-C, which provides PIA training. http://www.priva-c.com/corporate/training_pia.asp

Where PIAs are conducted in the private sector, the methods and considerations can be different. Some organisations recognise that privacy can give them a strategic advantage. Others conduct PIAs as a risk management process, recognising that business can be affected by privacy incidents such as breaches and complaints.[25]

Alberta is the only jurisdiction where PIAs are prescribed for some private organisations under its health privacy law which applies to "custodians" of personal health information.[26] This includes private companies such as those running nursing homes, the private practices of physicians, pharmacists, opticians, optometrists, midwives, podiatrists, dentists, dental hygienists, denturists and any other health services providers named in the regulations.[27]

7.2.4 When PIAs Are Required

At the national level, government departments and agencies should conduct PIAs when new programs or services raise privacy issues or when changes to programs or services affect the collection, use or disclosure of personal information. Information systems are included, but the Directive is explicit about not applying to proposals for legislation. Senior officials or executives are responsible for compliance and must initiate a PIA for a program or activity in the following circumstances:

- when personal information is used for or is intended to be used as part of a *decision-making* process that directly affects the individual;
- upon substantial modifications to existing programs or activities where personal information is used or intended to be used for an *administrative purpose*; and
- when *contracting out or transferring* a program or activities to another level of government or the private sector results in substantial modifications to the program or activities [emphasis added].

Further, senior officials must consult with their privacy officer to determine when to conduct a PIA and whether the institutions' privacy protocol is adequate to deal with privacy risks, and to document those decisions. The Directive addresses PIAs for multi-institution initiatives (in s. 6.3B), setting responsibilities for the lead institution and inter-institution co-ordinating committees and approvals.

In BC, FOIPPA requires ministries to conduct PIAs for "a new enactment, system, project or program". "System" covers information systems and introduction of new technology. PIAs should also be conducted for significant changes to an initiative. Unique to BC, PIAs are not limited to initiatives including personal information. The first step of a PIA is to determine if personal information is involved and, if not, one goes no further. Further, only BC requires PIAs for all legislative

---

[25] Wright, David, Trilateral Research & Consulting, "Should privacy impact assessments be mandatory?", presentation at the ENISA summer school, 17 Sept 2009. http://www.nis-summer-school.eu/nis09/presentations/18-wright.pdf

[26] Section 1(1)(f) of the HIA and the Health Information Regulation defines "custodians".

[27] OIPC of Alberta, *Privacy Impact Assessment Requirements for use with the Health Information Act*, p. 7. http://www.oipc.ab.ca/Content_Files/Files/PIAs/PIA_Requirements_2010.pdf

proposals. The recent report of an all-party review of the public sector privacy law made recommendations for amending the law to specify that "privacy impact assessments must be completed at the conceptual, design and implementation phases of databases." Not only would the recommendation ensure that PIAs were conducted early, it would also extend the requirement to conduct PIAs out of core government and into regional health authorities.[28] The recommendation was proposed by the Privacy Commissioner, and is currently under consideration by government.

Because PIAs are conducted under the FOIPPA and health information privacy statutes in Alberta, the variety of initiatives on which PIAs are conducted is broad and includes information systems, applications of new technologies and other initiatives. Examples include the DNA Testing Services program, the Public Guardian Information System, the Canadian Agricultural Injury Surveillance Project, the National Hockey League Players Tax, facial recognition software and individual doctors' offices' electronic medical record information systems. A registry with hundreds of PIA summaries is available online on the Privacy Commissioner's website.[29] Under health privacy legislation, the main focus is on information systems. Custodians must conduct a PIA and submit it for review by the Privacy Commissioner's Office before "making changes to an existing practice or information system relating to the collection, use or disclosure of individually identifying health information".[30] PIAs conducted by government departments can relate to any type of initiative.

In Ontario, Corporate Policy requires a PIA to be conducted whenever there is a substantial change in the collection, use or disclosure of personal information, including the creation or substantial modification of an information system or database containing personal information. The PIA Guide advises ministries and agencies to complete a PIA for any "substantive change in the collection, use, or disclosure of personal information, including the creation or modification of a database containing personal information or its associated application, or where the processing and storage of personal information may be out-sourced to an external service provider".[31] The Procurement Directive requires ministries to do a PIA prior "to undertaking any procurement of goods and/or services that may result in the release of personal or sensitive information."

The Preliminary Analysis Tool enables projects without personal information or privacy risk to be quickly identified. For those projects entailing personal information, that Tool helps them start to identify factors that may create privacy risks (e.g.,

---

[28] See Recommendation 25 of the Report of the Special Committee to Review the Freedom of Information and Protection of Privacy Act, Legislative Assembly of BC, May 2010. http://www.leg.bc.ca/cmt/39thparl/session-2/foi/reports/PDF/Rpt-FOI-39-2-Rpt-2010-MAY-31.pdf

[29] OIPC of Alberta, PIAs, Registry. http://www.oipc.ab.ca/pages/PIAs/Registry.aspx. Recent PIA summaries are on the *What's New* page. http://www.oipc.ab.ca/pages/PIAs/WhatsNew.aspx

[30] OIPC of Alberta, webpage overview, *PIA Requirements*. http://www.oipc.ab.ca/pages/PIAs/PIARequirements.aspx

[31] Ontario, Office of the Chief Information and Privacy Officer, *Privacy Impact Assessment Guide for the Ontario Public Service*, December 2010, p. 6.

scope of project, number of partners, use of unique identifiers, cross-jurisdictional flow of data, etc.) Collectively, the guidance tools repeatedly stress the need to conduct the PIA and related exercises early and throughout the project planning, approval, implementation and evaluation cycle.

7.2.5 PIAs Involving State Security, Law Enforcement and International Projects and Agreements

The entire national government, which has constitutional responsibility for foreign relations, is subject to the PIA policy. Thus, a PIA would be completed for any initiative involving personal information and state security, crime prevention or an international project or agreement, if it were captured under the Directive, and the other parties to which personal information was disclosed would be named. However, the exceptions to release under FOI legislation allow information to be withheld by redaction where it is harmful to federal-provincial affairs, international affairs and defence, law enforcement and investigations, and security.

The Privacy Act covers both national intelligence and police services. The executive summaries of 17 PIAs conducted by the national police force are available on its website.[32] The force participated in multi-agency PIAs including multilateral information agreements regarding immigrants. The national intelligence service appears to be under-reporting its PIAs. It has only mentioned the initiation of one PIA in an annual report (2009/2010) and no PIA summaries are available on its website. Twelve PIA summaries were available on Citizenship and Immigration Canada's website in mid-2010.[33] Examples include a biometrics field trial for border security and a multinational initiative regarding information sharing among it, the US Immigration and Naturalization Service and the US Department of State. Another security-related program to have undergone a PIA is full body scanning at airports, described in the Privacy Commissioner's annual report.[34] This report also describes the OPC's review of an e-passport, a biometric identifier on visas of foreigners, the Anti-Money Laundering/Anti-Terrorist Financing Regime and an integrated law enforcement information-sharing regime. The report described the Privacy Commissioner's outstanding concerns that these PIAs were not sufficiently comprehensive or cumulative.

Again, in the provinces, the type of project, rather than the policy area, determines whether a PIA must be completed. Provinces do not have responsibility for international affairs but their provincial and municipal police forces may share personal information with their counterparts in other jurisdictions. In Ontario, the

---

[32] Royal Canadian Mounted Police (RCMP), Privacy Impact Assessment Executive Summaries. http://www.rcmp-grc.gc.ca/pia-efvp/index-eng.htm

[33] Citizenship and Immigration Canada, Access to Information and Privacy, Privacy Impact Assessment Summaries, webpage. http://www.cic.gc.ca/english//department/atip/pia.asp

[34] Office of the Privacy Commissioner of Canada (OPC), Annual Report to Parliament 2008–2009, Report on the Privacy Act. http://www.priv.gc.ca/information/ar/200809/200809_pa_e.cfm

Privacy Commissioner produced a guide to PIAs for justice information systems. BC does not have a provincial police force, but municipal police services are covered by public sector legislation and have conducted PIAs on surveillance systems. Alberta has also conducted PIAs in the field of security. For example, in 2003, the Privacy Commissioner reviewed a PIA for the Security Screening Directive, under which security reviews are required for some positions in the public service.[35] Further, an investigation report addressing a city's police service's use of public video surveillance as a tool against rioting referenced a previously-submitted PIA. It appears from this investigation report that the Privacy Commissioner took the PIA's description of what was being done at face value, as opposed to verifying it independently.[36]

7.2.6 PIA Characteristics and Methodology

In most jurisdictions, PIAs are part of the larger system for privacy management and governance in the public sector. There has also been a great deal of cross-jurisdictional lesson-drawing about good practices. Jurisdictions use others' tools as starting points for developing their own, and some PIAs even point to consultations with other governments who have previously implemented similar initiatives.

The Privacy Commissioner for Canada published a PIA fact sheet in which it describes the key steps in a PIA. While intended to describe the Canadian process, it also generally summarises the methodologies used in the provinces. These include:

- Identifying all of the personal information related to a program or service and then looking at how it will be used;
- Mapping where personal data is sent after it is collected;
- Identifying privacy risks and the level of those risks; and
- Finding ways to eliminate or reduce privacy risks.[37]

The central agency's Directive is not as prescriptive about format as those in the provinces, although it does describe a core PIA's minimum content, with standard sections for a project overview, risk identification and categorisation (into a four-point risk scale), identification of specific data elements and their flow, the authority for the planned collection, use, disclosure of personal information and technical and administrative safeguards. While the Directive does not require public consultation, it can be read in conjunction with the Communications Policy, which requires

---

[35] OIPC of Alberta, "Commissioner Accepts Privacy Impact Assessment for the Alberta Security Screening Directive", press release, 16 Jan 2003. http://www.oipc.ab.ca/pages/NewsReleases/default.aspx?id=519

[36] OIPC of Alberta, Investigation Number 2777, para. 9.

[37] Office of the Privacy Commissioner of Canada, Fact Sheet on Privacy Impact Assessment. http://www.priv.gc.ca/fs-fi/02_05_d_33_e.cfm

ministries to "provide the public with timely, accurate, clear, objective and complete information about its policies, programs, services and initiatives".[38] Further, "To communicate about risk effectively, institutions must demonstrate interest and concern for all opinions and positions, understand different perspectives, and respect their underlying premises. Effective risk management requires open and transparent communication among differing or even opposing interests."[39]

The BC PIA methodology is outlined in a website overview and a mandatory report template. The template requires contact information, a description of the initiative and the completion of a detailed compliance checklist with questions relating to the core privacy requirements of the public sector privacy legislation. It ends with management signatures and tick box attestations from the official responsible for privacy in the ministry. The format requires identification of data elements and depiction of data flows in narrative or diagram form. There are some free text fields. For instance, legislative authority for collection of personal information must be cited, so others can confirm the author's interpretation. Organisations are told to "provide details of the original purpose for which the personal information was obtained or compiled. Include, if applicable, details of the consistent/secondary use." Some answers require further documentation to be appended, as in the case of an individual having consented to disclosure of personal information. A consent form or similar evidence would be appended. An expert reviewer would have the basis on which to make a judgement as to whether the standards for meaningful consent were met.

The BC PIA process is also designed as an educational tool, since participation in privacy impact assessments will promote privacy awareness. Further tips and "best practices" on maximising PIA benefits include: providing as much detail as possible, consulting widely to identify issues, avoiding hiding problems, doing the work early and thinking ahead and treating the PIA as a living document.[40]

The Ontario government defines a PIA as a business process involving multiple activities and deliverables – not as a single end-product. The guidance stresses the need for projects to be proactive in order to ensure that appropriate and effective privacy protections are designed into their processes and systems. Ontario positions the PIA as part of its broader risk management framework. In addition, the PIA process is mapped to Ontario's required project management methodology. Reporting and accountability mechanisms are integrated in the information systems development and approval methodology.

The Preliminary Analysis Tool is a screening tool that helps determine if personal information is involved and the applicable privacy legislation. The Privacy

---

[38] Treasury Board of Canada Secretariat, Communications Policy of the Government of Canada, Policy Statement, November 2004. http://www.tbs-sct.gc.ca/pol/doc-eng.aspx?id=12316&section=text#sec5.10

[39] Ibid., Risk Communication, s. 10.

[40] Province of BC, "Privacy Impact Assessments: Mitigating Risks – Maximizing Benefits", Presentation for Private Sector Privacy in a Changing World, PIPA Conference 2007, Vancouver, 20–21 Sept 2006, p. 13. http://www.verney.ca/pipa2007/presentations/420.pdf

Risk Analysis Tool assists in identifying privacy, organisational and legal risks and mitigations. The Privacy Design Analysis Tool helps determine how to comply with the public sector privacy law, evaluate risks and develop mitigations.

In the privacy assessment guidelines for the Ontario Personal Health Information Act, the Privacy Commissioner describes criteria for a high quality PIA. These include an accurate and detailed description of the personal information collected, used, disclosed and retained; an informed, critical perspective on identifying risk; and not sacrificing this analysis in order to push an initiative through.[41] This methodology and information is similar to other Canadian instruments, with a checklist questionnaire about the treatment of personal information, and the opportunity to describe mitigations of risks or make other notes and to append additional material. Authors are encouraged to explain their choices of Yes, No, In Progress or Not Applicable/Not Available in the checklist.[42] Another tool developed by the Ontario Commissioner is a specialised PIA for justice information systems.[43] This tool uses an information mapping technique entailing red, yellow and green light classifications for information disclosure. The question-driven methodology is principles-based and extensive. Guidance is given on the types of personal information for each category and the risks discussed. It suggests training for staff in the requirements and ethics for protecting personal information. It deals with preventing unauthorised use and disclosure and gets organisations to consider what to do if that happens.

The primary Alberta methodology is contained in the PIA Requirements, produced by the Privacy Commissioner. According to it, "The PIA process requires a thorough analysis of potential impacts on privacy and a consideration of measures to mitigate or eliminate any such impacts. The privacy impact assessment is a due diligence exercise, in which the organisation identifies and addresses potential privacy risks that may occur in the course of its operations . . . While PIAs are focused on specific projects, the process should also include an examination of organisation-wide practices that could have an impact on privacy."[44] The Requirements also point to the need to review privacy risks throughout the project life cycle. Organisations are advised to periodically review their PIA to ensure any risks caused by these changes are mitigated and to inform the Privacy Commissioner.

The Alberta PIA format is prescribed in detail in the Requirements. Apart from cover letter, contact information and signatures, it must contain a project overview, description of organisational privacy management structure and policies (appending policy and procedures), project privacy analysis (information flows, data elements,

---

[41] Cavoukian, Ann, *Privacy Impact Assessment Guidelines for the Ontario Personal Health Information Protection Act,* OIPC of Ontario, October 2005, p. 7. http://www.ipc.on.ca/images/Resources/up-phipa_pia_e.pdf

[42] Ibid., p. 10.

[43] OIPC of Ontario and the United States Department of Justice, Office of Justice Programs, *Privacy Impact Assessment for Justice Information Systems,* August 2000. http://www.ipc.on.ca/English/Resources/Discussion-Papers/Discussion-Papers-Summary/?id=326

[44] OIPC of Alberta, PIAs webpage. http://www.oipc.ab.ca/pages/PIAs/default.aspx

parties with access, legislative and other authorities, etc.), description of privacy risks and mitigation measures (to be as detailed as possible), and project privacy risks and mitigation plans.[45]

PIA guidelines under FOIPPA are published as policy by the Alberta central agency. Consultation features significantly, because "focused public discussion conducted early in the process can help program or system designers anticipate public reaction to proposals or help to eliminate options that meet with significant resistance".

PIAs conducted in both the public and private sectors often entail cost-benefit analyses of various mitigation strategies in order to arrive at decisions, although these considerations may not be described in PIA reports. Cost-benefit considerations have driven the development of PIA methodologies, particularly in technology and large consulting firms. Information systems have common privacy risks, particularly in the health information sector, which avail themselves to common effective mitigation strategies. Those conducting large numbers of PIAs have been able to compile privacy risk and control/mitigation matrices to improve the efficiency with which PIAs may be completed as well as the quality of the PIA product. With this approach, knowledge is accumulated and passed on within an entity or from consultant to client in a cost-effective manner.

7.2.7 The Audit and Review of PIAs

Reviews, rather than audits, are the norm in Canada. Reviews are an effective part of the PIA system in Canada and provide much additional value. Where reviews are not required or recommended, less formal, voluntary consultations may take place. PIAs are reviewed externally to the organisation in:

- BC, where the central agency reviews and "accepts" PIA reports on certain types of higher-risk and profile initiatives,
- Ontario, where the central agency reviews the Preliminary Analysis and some IT committees review reports,
- Alberta, where the privacy commissioner reviews and "accepts" PIA reports and
- Canada, where the privacy commissioner reviews, but does not accept or reject them.

Thus, a review may be conducted outside the organisation that conducted the PIA, but may still occur within government. Where an independent privacy commissioner reviews the PIA, the organisation may also have voluntarily shared the PIA and consulted with the central agency. Where there is no obligation to submit the PIA to the privacy commissioner, this may be done voluntarily for high-profile and initiatives that raise new issues because the privacy commissioner usually

---

[45] Service Alberta, *FOIP Guidelines and Practices (2009)*, section 9.3 Privacy Impact Assessments. http://www.servicealberta.gov.ab.ca/foip/documents/chapter9.pdf

has the ability to comment publicly on programs. Despite BC's widely-applicable PIA policy, the BC privacy commissioner received only 12 PIAs for review in 2009–2010 and three in 2008–2009.[46]

In no Canadian jurisdiction is the routine external review as stringent as connoted by the term audit. Information in the PIA tends to be taken at face value, or questions may be asked and clarification sought, but independent confirmation is not obtained. However, privacy commissioners have conducted audits of pilots and fully implemented initiatives whose PIAs they have reviewed or investigations or audits resulting from complaints lodged by an individual. An example includes the Privacy Commissioner of Canada's self-initiated audit of Transport Canada's Passenger Protect Program.[47]

At the national level, public agencies are required to share their PIAs with the Privacy Commissioner of Canada. In a speech on its website, a representative of the Office indicated what it expects: "We will want to make sure that the department has the legal authority to collect and use personal information; We will want to ensure that the PIA is very clear about the amount and type of personal information that will be collected, how it will be used, and to whom it will be disclosed; We will want to satisfy ourselves that all the privacy risk associated with the project have been identified; We will want to satisfy ourselves that all the mitigating measures proposed are reasonable and appropriate, and We will want to know what the department ultimately intends to do to mitigate the risks identified."[48] When the Privacy Commissioner has outstanding issues after review of a PIA and discussions with the institution, she has been known to publish her concerns. In the instance of millimetre wave screening technology for airports, the PIA identified risks and stated that audits would be undertaken. The Privacy Commissioner's published response recommended that the institution supply her with the results and recommended a multi-media public information campaign and a number of other specific measures for the program's implementation.[49]

After a few years of reviewing PIAs, the Privacy Commissioner of Canada found that for initiatives involving the electronic delivery of services to individuals through the Internet (the bulk of PIAs it had received), it was able to identify a number of

[46] Office of the Information and Privacy Commissioner for British Columbia, *2009–2010 Annual Report*, July 2010, p.11.

[47] Office of the Privacy Commissioner of Canada (OPC), Audit of the Passenger Protect Program, Transport Canada, November 2009. http://www.priv.gc.ca/information/pub/ar-vr/ar-vr_ppp_200910_e.cfm

[48] Bloomfield, Stuart, "The Role of the Privacy Impact Assessment", speech for Managing Government Information, 2nd Annual Forum, OPC of Canada, Ottawa, 10 March 2004. http://www.priv.gc.ca/speech/2004/sp-d_040310_e.cfm

[49] OPC of Canada, Letter in response to the Privacy Impact Assessment (PIA) completed by the Canadian Air Transport Security Authority (CATSA) in anticipation of the deployment of millimetre wave (MMW) screening technology at selected Canadian airport, October 2009. http://www.priv.gc.ca/pia-efvp/let_20100108_e.cfm

common privacy risks and share common mitigating measures for those risks on its website.[50]

In addition to public sector agencies, some organisations subject to the national private sector privacy law ask the Privacy Commissioner's Office to review a PIA. In such instances, the Office takes great care to ensure that policy, and not investigation, staff do so, to ensure impartiality should the initiative be the subject of a later complaint to that office. More often though, such consultations take place in the absence of a PIA, and are not as fruitful.

Reporting on her office's activities and accomplishments in 2008–2009, the Commissioner stated that PIA "review resources are being used in a more effective manner to offer more timely interventions, resulting in more focused guidance to departments and institutions." They have introduced a new triage process to give precedence to the review of PIAs that either deal with one of the Office's four priority privacy issues, or are particularly sensitive. The PIA unit also began offering higher-level advice to departments to reduce the time needed to respond to PIA submissions.[51]

The government of Canada developed a PIA Audit Guide, "intended as a reference tool for Internal Auditors in the Government of Canada and may also be of assistance to the privacy community, including PIA Coordinators".[52] It was developed before the PIA policy was replaced by the current PIA Directive. Further, an important audit of compliance with the Canadian PIA policy was conducted by the Privacy Commissioner in 2007.[53] Its findings were not positive, and concluded that:

> Although the Government of Canada's PIA Policy is beginning to have the desired effect of promoting awareness and understanding of the privacy implications associated with program and service delivery, five years after the Policy was first issued, we would have expected departments to be further along in supporting the initiative. Overall, there are varying degrees of commitment to the Policy.... Based on our audit work, we believe that there are a number of main factors that have contributed to this performance gap....

- Lack of management support and infrastructure
- Limited integration into decision making and assessment of effects
- Resources are stretched
- PIA requirements need to be streamlined
- More training capacity is needed
- Absence of internal audit evaluation.[54]

---

[50] Bloomfield, op. cit.

[51] OPC of Canada, "Message from the Privacy Commissioner of Canada" [regarding 2008–9] Contribution of Priorities to the Strategic Outcome. http://www.tbs-sct.gc.ca/dpr-rmr/2008-2009/inst/nd6/nd601-eng.asp

[52] Treasury Board Secretariat of Canada, Privacy Impact Assessment Audit Guide, as archived. http://www.collectionscanada.gc.ca/webarchives/20071211001631/www.tbs-sct.gc.ca/ia-vi/policies-politiques/pia-efvp/pia-efvp_e.asp

[53] Privacy Commissioner of Canada, *Assessing the Privacy Impacts of Programs, Plans, and Policies*, Audit Report, October 2007. http://www.priv.gc.ca/information/pub/ar-vr/pia_200710_e.cfm

[54] Ibid., s. 1.79.

Two and half years later, the government introduced the new PIA Directive.

The Privacy Commissioner has also commented in investigation reports on the need for PIAs to be conducted on more initiatives. For example, in a decision of the Privacy Commissioner of Canada in a complaint about the Canadian Firearms Program, she found that program "officials agreed that a Privacy Impact Assessment, in this instance, may have assisted in assuring senior officials that all privacy issues had been identified and resolved or mitigated with respect to the contracting of this service".[55]

At the provincial government level, PIAs are reviewed by central agencies responsible for privacy within government or the privacy commissioner or both, although the policy or legal requirement is usually for review by either and, in the case of Ontario, is not mandatory.

The reviewing agency generally accepts but does not "approve" the PIA or may only note that consultation has taken place. During the review process, there is generally some back and forth communication. Probing questions may be asked, further privacy issues identified, and mitigation strategies may be found lacking. PIAs may be sent back to the originating organisation for clarification, further work on the specifics of personal information collection and handling, or for more fundamental program redesign to address privacy risks. Or further information may be requested and put on file and the PIA itself not altered.

In BC, for instance, ministries must submit certain types of PIAs to the central agency for review. The initiatives which must be submitted for review include alternative service delivery and outsourcing projects, corporate systems (cross-government, whether automated or not), information-sharing and data linkage agreements, and legislative proposals. Ministries often make revisions to the PIA and changes to the initiative as a result of input. Following its review, the central agency issues a letter to the ministry stating that the initiative is compliant with FOIPPA or expressing unresolved concerns. Most suggestions are well-taken but there may be resistance if the PIA is started late in the initiative's life cycle.[56]

In Alberta, health privacy legislation "requires that the Information and Privacy Commissioner receive a privacy impact assessment for review and comment before a custodian of personal health information implements proposed administrative practices and information systems relating to the collection, use or disclosure of individually identifying health information".[57]

Conversely, review of PIAs under Alberta's public sector privacy law is voluntary, but organisations are motivated to do so by the Commissioner's legislative

---

[55] OPC of Canada, *Investigation finds that RCMP handled polling appropriately*, Report of Findings, Complaint under the Privacy Act. http://www.priv.gc.ca/cf-dc/pa/2009-10/pa_20091216_e.cfm

[56] Bayley, Robin M., "Appendix C, Jurisdictional Report for Canada", in *Privacy Impact Assessments: An International Study of their Application and Effects*, Report to the UK Information Commissioner, December 2007, p. 64. http://www.rogerclarke.com/DV/ICOStudy-2007-Apps.pdf

[57] OIPC of Alberta, PIAs webpage: http://www.oipc.ab.ca/pages/PIAs/default.aspx

authority to "comment on the implications for FOI or for protection of privacy of proposed legislative schemes or programs of public bodies". Such public comment can cause program delay and political embarrassment. The process and meaning of review are discussed on the Commissioner's website. "Because the onus always remains on the organisation to ensure adequate levels of privacy protection, as required in the applicable legislation, the Commissioner will not 'approve' a PIA submitted to him by an organisation. Once satisfied that the organisation has addressed the relevant considerations and is committed to the provision of the necessary level of privacy protection, the Commissioner will 'accept' the PIA. Acceptance is not approval; it merely reflects the Commissioner's acceptance that the organisation has made reasonable efforts to protect privacy. A PIA cannot be used to obtain a waiver of, or relaxation from, any requirement of the relevant legislation."[58] The review process is iterative and may involve an invitation to present to the Office.

In instances where a complaint has been made and the Privacy Commissioner investigates, the first priority is reviewing the PIA, to gather information about the organisation's privacy practices. Then the investigation determines whether the mitigations outlined in the PIA were actually implemented and implemented effectively. The results of some such comparisons have brought to light discrepancies that give the Office reason to believe that it would discover more unmet PIA undertakings if it were to audit PIAs proactively.[59] However, this is not always the case. In a published investigation report regarding the Edmonton Police Service's use of video surveillance in a public place, the Commissioner referred to the PIA previously submitted by the local public body as a basis for his findings. He referenced its submission and review by his Office, commented on its good quality, read the PIA into the investigation report, used the PIA as evidence that the police had properly considered the issues and upheld the surveillance.[60]

In Ontario, of the four guidance tools, only the Preliminary Analysis Questionnaire and project background are to be submitted to the central agency. However, it is open to reviewing other PIA documents if asked to do so by projects. This review allows the central agency to verify the organisation's conclusions and help them identify next steps.[61]

In Ontario, there is no requirement for the central agency to review PIAs. However, PIAs are reviewed by various committees as part of the approval and funding process for information technology projects. The Privacy Commissioner does not require health custodians to submit PIAs for review. However, as in other

---

[58] Ibid.

[59] Interview, LeRoy Brower, OIPC of Alberta, August 2010 (Brower interview).

[60] OIPC of Alberta, Investigation Report F2003-IR-005, Edmonton Police Service, 6 August 2003. http://www.oipc.ab.ca/downloads/documentloader.ashx?id=2081

[61] The Questionnaire is an appendix to the Preliminary Analysis tool and contains numerous examples of personal information that should be useful for privacy novices, and many questions that will help the program and central agency determine the degree personal information linkages and potential areas of privacy risk.

jurisdictions, it is common for the Privacy Commissioner to ask an organisation to complete a PIA to aid discussion of an initiative when consulted in early stages. Review provides the Privacy Commissioner the opportunity to ask probing questions which may not have been raised, and suggest other models for achieving objectives.

7.2.8 The Publication of PIAs

Generally in Canada, only PIA summaries are published (by posting on an organisation's website), and individuals wanting to see the entire PIA must apply under FOI legislation. Under that process, applicants may face delays of a month or more, fees and severing or redacting of information. Commonly, information relating to security controls would be withheld. Other exceptions to release relate to policy advice, legal privilege and executive confidence and harm to intergovernmental relations, international affairs and defence, law enforcement and financial, economic or third-party business interests. Jurisdictions have slightly different wording and precedents regarding the interpretation of these exceptions.

The timeliness of posting of summaries varies as does compliance with the basic requirement to publish and the descriptiveness of the summary. Of the jurisdictions studied, Ontario is the only one with no requirement to publish PIAs or summaries. The most fulsome summaries are provided by government of Canada public institutions but even those can be brief and do not generally confer a full understanding of the privacy issues and mitigation strategies. Most provincial summaries describe the initiative in a paragraph or two and serve only as a notice that a PIA has been completed.

Exceptions exist and some organisations post entire PIAs or very detailed summaries.[62]

At the national level, under the Directive, government institutions must make PIA summaries public in English and French.[63] The 2007 Privacy Commissioner's audit of compliance with government PIA policy found poor compliance with this requirement. Now, executive summaries are generally published as links from one page on a departmental or agency website. They are usually published after the program is announced and implemented. Some of the more fulsome Canadian government summaries are published by Public Works and Government Services Canada. These provide much better than average descriptions of the personal information involved and how it is handled, as well as risk mitigation strategies, and some

---

[62] For example, the PIA for the Ontario Laboratory Information System, by the Smart Systems for Health Agency, where 12 specific risks were named, mitigation strategies described and target completion dates provided in more than 20 pages. http://www.ehealthontario.on.ca/pdfs/Privacy/OLIS_PIA_Summary.pdf

[63] Treasury Board of Canada Secretariat, Directive on Privacy Impact Assessment, Ottawa, 1 Apr 2010. http://www.tbs-sct.gc.ca/pol/doc-eng.aspx?id=18308&section=text. See especially section 6.3.16 of the Directive as well as sections 1 and 2 of Appendix C to the Directive, which details what is to be made public.

contain target dates for implementing mitigations.[64] However, it is more common, in other organisations' PIA summaries, to find meaningless statements that risks were identified and appropriate mitigations implemented or planned, with no hint to what those might be. In the case of multi-jurisdictional or multi-party initiatives, one can often find out more from one party than another.[65]

In BC, despite policy requiring it, only a small percentage of summaries are published by ministries. Even when posted, they are not timely or descriptive of the PIA, but briefly describe the initiative in one or two paragraphs. No audit has been conducted of compliance with the publication requirement, but many implemented initiatives are announced for which no PIA summary exists. However, some organisations which undertake PIAs voluntarily readily release them, even if not posted, and it "pays to ask".[66]

In Alberta, where the Privacy Commissioner posts the summaries, they are timely, usually posted before the initiative is implemented. After reviewing the PIA, it posts a notice on its website, saying that it has "accepted" an organisation's PIA, with a link to the summary. These PIAs may have been conducted by organisations subject to health privacy or public sector privacy legislation, although the vast majority (85–90 per cent) are health PIAs. They are usually less than two pages and describe the initiative rather than the PIA process and findings. Persons wanting to see the full PIA must make a FOI request.

In Alberta, there is little utility in publishing the entire PIA because organisations are not required to update them as a result of communications and additions during the Privacy Commissioner's review. Thus, the PIA would only be the starting point, and would not be current. The Alberta Privacy Commissioner is not aware of demand for full PIA reports. Those who have expressed interest have been professionals hoping to gain insight into PIA methods used by others. Alberta's Privacy Commissioner has never had a FOI complaint regarding access to PIAs, which may mean that they are not often requested, or that organisations release them upon request without overzealous redaction of information under the exceptions allowed by legislation.

---

[64] All of Public Works and Government Services Canada's PIA summaries can be found on its website. http://www.tpsgc-pwgsc.gc.ca/aiprp-atip/efvp-pia/efvp-pia-eng.html

[65] For instance, the government of Canada published a standard PIA summary for the Enhanced Drivers' Licence (a US-driven, Canada-wide initiative to increase the reliability of drivers' licences as a form of identification), whereas BC's 24-page PIA is available online from the Insurance Corporation of British Columbia. http://www.cic.gc.ca/english/department/atip/pia-eic.asp and http://www.icbc.com/cs/Satellite?blobcol=urldata&blobheader=application%2Fpdf&blobheadername1=Content-Disposition&blobheadervalue1=filename%3D%22edl-privacy-impact.pdf%22&blobkey=id&blobtable=MungoBlobs&blobwhere=1233968011097&ssbinary=true

[66] An example of a quality, readily-released PIA is the Population Data BC's, Population Data BC Privacy Impact Assessment, September 2009. This PIA was for a complex multi-agency initiative to facilitate access to population health data from a number of sources by university researchers. http://www.popdata.bc.ca/privacy/pia

Ontario does not require PIAs or summaries to be published, although some may be found online, especially in the health sector. Unlike the other jurisdictions, the government of Ontario has not published its new PIA tools online, but the Commissioner publishes her tools. It is difficult to see how the benefits of the methodology will spread to the private sector, when these models are not readily available.

7.3 Conclusions

It is evident that PIAs are useful in two ways: first, for the analysis they force an organisation to undertake during the development of new programs and services, often resulting in program modifications and privacy improvements; and second, in their use by regulators, including central agencies charged with privacy responsibilities, those who allocate funds and independent privacy commissioners. Regulators use PIAs as a basis for discussions about the privacy implications of certain initiatives and can often instigate improvements or publicly comment if they feel that privacy concerns are not adequately addressed. PIAs can act as an accountability mechanism when their review results in a requirement to submit specific mitigation tools as they are completed and as a starting point in complaint-driven or self-initiated investigations by a privacy commissioner. Further, PIAs can be used in internal and external audits to determine if planned mitigations have been implemented.

The likelihood of PIAs being conducted is related to the degree of policy compulsion to conduct them and to accountability for their completion. Accountability can arise from a requirement that a completed PIA be included in the program and funding approval processes. Accountability for PIA completion can also be enhanced by mandatory reporting requirements.

PIA policies, procedures, guides, formats and models (collectively called "tools") cannot be viewed in a vacuum. They must be seen as part of a broader framework for privacy management and accountability. The requirement to conduct a PIA may ensure that proper privacy and security policies and strategies are put in place in an organisation, particularly where they must be appended.

Our analysis has, however, identified some key areas for improvement. First, there is room for improvement in the scope of analysis for complex initiatives, such as those involving new technologies, sensitive personal information or vulnerable groups or where there is coercive collection of personal information.[67] In a 2004 speech, an official at the Office of the Privacy Commissioner described some of the common deficiencies in PIAs: confusing privacy with security and confidentiality, and thereby overlooking broader issues such as consent, excess collection of personal information and so on; attention limited to the disclosure of information

---

[67] These criteria are discussed more fully by Roger Clarke in the PIA Handbook developed for the UK Information Commissioner's Office (ICO).

outside the organisation, rather than access controls within; seeing the PIA process as a legal compliance audit; the failure to link identified risks with the specific design elements of a project; and the proposed mitigating measures often not appropriate to the risks identified, for instance, using public communications to allay fears instead of directly addressing the risks from which such fears might arise.[68]

As expertise has spread, practitioners and organisations have learned that standard mitigations will be accepted for certain privacy risks. There is a risk that complacency will set in and that a cookie-cutter approach rather than serious analysis of a particular initiative will take place, especially when a large number of similar PIAs are completed for different organisations using a common framework. Such analysis might not take into account peculiar aspects of an individual application such as the physical setting.

Another challenge to quality comes with universality. When a great number of initiatives require a PIA, this necessarily leads to those PIAs being completed by people with little knowledge of privacy, or stretching the resources of qualified staff. It can take experience and a good deal of knowledge to recognise a privacy issue. In part, this is addressed by review of draft PIAs by the organisation's specialised privacy officers, but there is a chance that some issues will be missed or understated, as privacy novices will not have knowledge of privacy commissioner decisions, past incidents and all available mitigation options. One way to address this is by providing specialised PIA training such as that offered by the government of Canada.[69] Another is to ensure that all staff have some basic privacy training. Most jurisdictions offer some sort of privacy training – the key will be to ensure that those who conduct or participate in PIAs have received it.

This challenge can further be addressed by classifying PIAs into two types and ensuring that knowledgeable people are assigned to PIAs for initiatives with higher privacy risks.

Canadian PIAs seldom involve public consultation, opinion polling or other means of gauging the privacy values of the Canadian public. They tend to focus on legal compliance rather that doing the right thing and asking larger questions. Although most methodologies include guidance about considering these issues, the end product, and that which gets reviewed, tends to resemble a compliance checklist and does not require documentation of deliberations. Issues of quality can arise when those who are convinced of the need for a particular initiative conduct the privacy analysis without benefit of the perceptions of the people whose personal information are affected. Clarke suggests that a preparation stage be undertaken which includes developing a consultation plan, stating that "Any project that is sufficiently complex and potentially privacy-threatening that it requires a full-scale

---

[68] Bloomfield, Stuart, "The Role of the Privacy Impact Assessment", Speech, OPC of Canada, Ottawa, 10 March 2004. http://www.priv.gc.ca/speech/2004/sp-d_040310_e.cfm

[69] Examples may be found in the government of Canada's PIA e-learning tool. http://www.tbs-sct.gc.ca/pgol-pged/piatp-pfefvp/course1/outline/outline3-eng.asp

PIA is likely to affect many parties."[70] Further, he recommends embedding PIA consultations into the project stakeholder management strategy.

A related shortcoming relates to publicity. There is no common practice with regard to the publication of either the full PIAs or their summaries. Central PIA registers would overcome organisations not posting their PIA summaries, and allow organisations publicly to seek consultation.

With regard to implementation, Canadian PIAs also fall short. The extent to which the PIAs are revisited and revised and the promised mitigation measures implemented is unknown. However, privacy regulators have reason to believe that PIA plans are not always carried out. The system would benefit from increased accountability for implementation of PIA plans. Currently, there is no reporting mechanism in Canada for the implementation of PIA plans, except in the rare instance where the process of review yields instructions to organisations to provide the actual mitigation measures. In instances of high-risk proposals which rely on a limited number of mitigation measures, reviewers could more frequently require organisations to return and demonstrate how the mitigations were implemented, or even submit draft measures for review where that is possible. The PIA system might also be improved if PIAs were regularly used as a project management tool, and updated as mitigations are implemented and risks changed. A requirement to conduct post-implementation reviews could be added or made more explicit in Canadian PIA policies and guides. This would work in conjunction with a requirement to submit for review the amended PIAs and post-implementation reports, as a way of demonstrating full implementation. However, this would work only if there were sufficient resources dedicated for meaningful and ongoing review within a system that entailed mandatory, independent review of PIAs and focused on high-risk initiatives.

Finally, Canadians would clearly benefit if more private sector organisations completed PIAs, to possibly stave off later complaints and investigations. The newer private sector privacy laws are generally more outcome or principles-based, so private sector organisations have more freedom to determine how they will comply. In no jurisdiction in Canada are PIAs mandatory in the private sector. Alberta is the exception in legislatively requiring PIAs to be conducted by "private" healthcare organisations. For PIAs to be adopted by more companies, however, private sector organisations must know about PIA methodologies, have tools that work for their organisations and believe that the benefits will outweigh the cost. They will likely conduct PIAs differently, or consider different risk management factors. Economic factors may outweigh compliance motivation, but market forces could mean that private organisations consider public perception and reputational risk as more important than their public counterparts. Whether the shortcomings observed in public sector PIAs are generalisable from the public sector to private sector is

---

[70] See "Part II – The PIA Process, Chapter IV – Full-scale PIA, 2. Preparation Phase", written by Roger Clarke, in *Privacy Impact Assessment Handbook*, Version 2, Information Commissioner's Office, UK, June 2009. http://www.ico.gov.uk/upload/documents/pia_handbook_html_v2/html/2-Chap4-2.html

unknown, however. Industry organisations could play a role in developing PIA tools for their own sectors, but would likely need to be urged to do so and avail themselves of expertise centred in privacy central agencies and privacy commissioners' offices.

In conclusion, therefore, Canadian PIAs are widespread and institutionalised, and periodically refined, at least in the public sector. Expertise at conducting PIAs has spread, and some private sector organisations, particularly in large management consulting firms and in the electronic systems area, have developed specialisations. Further, PIA tools are subject to continuing refinement, amendment and benefit from lessons in other jurisdictions, both Canadian and international. The governments of Canada, Ontario, BC and Alberta have all updated their primary PIA instruments in the last three years. Changes were made to address the ambiguity in previous requirements and common deficiencies in the level of detail in the appended documentation. Whether these more refined processes add up to better privacy protection for Canadians, however, is still an open question. Ultimately, the effectiveness of PIAs should be judged according to whether or not they generate a higher level of organisational responsibility for the processing of personal information, and thereby advance the privacy rights of Canadian citizens.

Chapter 8
Privacy Impact Assessment in New Zealand – A Practitioner's Perspective

John Edwards

8.1 Introduction

This chapter takes a non-scholarly look at privacy impact assessment from the perspective of a law practitioner with some experience in undertaking such assessments. It starts with a history of the concept in New Zealand, and looks at the regulatory and administrative environment in which it emerged.

The rest consists of a number of observations on the conduct of privacy impact assessments, and some of the practical issues an assessor might expect to confront. The principal challenge this author has found is different assumptions among clients, regulators and others as to what the assessment process is intended to do and is capable of delivering. The key to maintaining the integrity and credibility of the process is to ensure that the client is fully informed as to the options, and the implications of each of his or her choices.

The chapter offers some assistance to assessors when they accept their brief.

I conclude that, although a very useful concept and methodology, "privacy impact assessment" is not yet a term of art. It is a process undertaken by practitioners from a variety of different disciplines all of whom approach the task with different backgrounds, values and expectations. Add into that mix the varied expectations of different clients and you have the ingredients for considerable misunderstandings and unmet expectations. Much of this chapter is intended to guide the practitioner to avoid these pitfalls.

J. Edwards (✉)
Barrister and Solicitor, Wellington, NZ
e-mail: jedwards@actrix.gen.nz

D. Wright, P. De Hert (eds.), *Privacy Impact Assessment*, Law, Governance
and Technology Series 6, DOI 10.1007/978-94-007-2543-0_8,
© Springer Science+Business Media B.V. 2012

8.2 Background

Privacy impact assessment has really taken off as a methodical means of assessing the effects on privacy of any given proposal or innovation since Assistant Privacy Commissioner Blair Stewart first mooted, then effectively proselytised for the adoption of the concept in the mid-1990s.

He and others had been impressed by the environmental impact assessment model, by which those proposing a new or expanded use of natural resources might undertake or commission a kind of self-audit of the downstream effects of the proposal if realised. One of the attractions of the model presumably was the assistance that it might give to a regulator with limited resources and virtually unlimited demands on those resources. An agency with a policy or technological idea involving a novel use of personal information might seek the Privacy Commissioner's "sign-off", or endorsement. Quite often, a Privacy Commissioner's formal response might well be: "I can't give a ruling in advance. I might have to investigate a complaint arising from this innovation." Behind the scenes, however, the Commissioner's office has always recognised the importance of engaging, particularly when government proposals are involved, and being as helpful as possible.

The suggestion or requirement to undertake a privacy impact assessment provides the Commissioner with a template and standardised format in which proposals can be presented and assessed. Here arises a potential point of confusion. The sales job has been wildly successful. Privacy impact assessments are now commonplace, being commissioned and prepared in respect of a wide range of innovations and proposals. But who are they for? What are they for? These are the first questions I ask a client who calls and tells me they "need" a PIA.

This chapter looks at the different types of privacy impact assessment, the different purposes they serve and some of the implications of those variables in the way in which the work is undertaken. It may serve as a guide or warning to practitioners to ensure that unchecked assumptions about the clients' needs are avoided, and expectations are effectively managed.

8.3 A Short History of Privacy Impact Assessment in New Zealand

The New Zealand Privacy Act 1993 is based, like many of its data protection counterparts around the world, on the 1980 Recommendation of the Council of the Organisation for Economic Co-operation and Development Concerning Guidelines Governing the Protection of Privacy and Transborder Flows of Personal Data ("the OECD guidelines").

Section 13 of the Act bestows a somewhat unwieldy number of functions on the Privacy Commissioner[1] including:

- Conducting audits of personal information against the information privacy principles
- Examining proposed policies or legislation that might affect the privacy of any individuals and reporting to the Minster of Justice
- Providing advice on the operation of the Privacy Act.

Early on, the Commissioner ensured that his office was inserted into the Cabinet policy-making process. Ministers taking proposals to Cabinet had to certify, on the cover sheet known as the CAB100, that the Privacy Commissioner had been consulted.

Subsequent amendments and simplifications of that form have seen that obligation dropped, but the Cabinet office guidelines for public servants on Cabinet processes still retains the requirement:

> Departments preparing papers must ensure that they consider the interests both of other departments and of other government agencies including the Privacy Commissioner, Officers of Parliament – the Controller and Auditor-General, Office of the Ombudsmen and the Parliamentary Commissioner for the Environment – and consult them at the earliest possible stage.[2]

The Cabinet Manual, which sets out the constitutional conventions, procedures and rules of Cabinet and central executive government, also contains the requirement, at para 5.19; it confirms and cross-references the guideline:

> Almost all policy proposals have implications for other government agencies. The initiating department or other agency with policy responsibility and the portfolio Minister must ensure that all other agencies affected by a proposal are consulted at the earliest possible stage, and that their views are reflected accurately in the paper. Consultation may sometimes be needed with agencies that have an advisory role, for example, the Office of the Privacy Commissioner.

Further, Ministers must certify consideration of privacy implications. Paragraph 7.60 requires

> when submitting bids for bills to be included in the legislation programme. In particular, Ministers must draw attention to any aspects of a bill that have implications for, or may be affected by:

(a) the principles of the Treaty of Waitangi;
(b) the rights and freedoms contained in the New Zealand Bill of Rights Act 1990 and the Human Rights Act 1993;
(c) the principles in the Privacy Act 1993;
(d) international obligations;
(e) the guidance contained in the *LAC Guidelines*

---

[1] http://bit.ly/hopBZ8

[2] http://bit.ly/gX0f1v

One of the implications of a principle-based Privacy Act, dealing as it does with all personal information (broadly defined without any qualitative restrictions as "information about an identifiable individual"), is that almost any proposal will "have implications for, or be affected by the principles of the Privacy Act". Whether those implications will be trivial or significant is sometimes difficult for Ministers and officials to assess, focused as they are on the public benefits of the primary policy with which they are concerned. An assessment of whether a given proposal is lawful often does not advance the discussion. Similarly, certifying that the proposal complies with the principles will often not be sufficient. The shortcomings of a "compliance" enquiry are discussed further below, however, in this context, when the proposal might be given effect by legislation (which will therefore override the Privacy Act) asking whether anything in the proposal "breaches" the Act does not necessarily identify privacy implications. Similarly, the information privacy principles contain a number of exceptions within them. Therefore, it is easy to say a new initiative that allows law enforcement agencies to access, use or disclose personal information in a novel way is consistent with information privacy principles which themselves contain provisions for non-compliance where necessary to avoid a prejudice to the maintenance of the law.

Privacy impact assessment is one means by which those implications can be assessed, presented and weighed against the asserted public benefit of the primary policy. Uniquely, in New Zealand, the process was enshrined in statute from the very beginning of data protection regulation before it was known by its catchy handle "PIA".

As is often the case, New Zealand's privacy law originated in a desire by government to act in a more intrusive manner with personal information. The Privacy Commissioner Act 1991 was in fact passed principally to allow information matching between government departments. A potentially rich source of information about who was defrauding the welfare system was anticipated in the combined revenue and welfare payment records. If you could match a list of everyone from whom income tax was being deducted by his or her employer, against a list of everyone who was receiving a welfare payment, you would know who was double dipping, being fraudulent or had merely forgotten to notify the authorities of their changed status (or, as happened in many cases, who had notified authorities, who then failed to act on that information).

The problem was that the tax system in New Zealand is founded on the concept of "voluntary compliance". It is assumed that voluntary compliance only works where taxpayers have near absolute confidence that their information will be retained in secrecy. Those assumptions are enshrined in the tax laws, which impose strict secrecy on the Commissioner of Inland Revenue and his or her staff. It is an offence for any person in the Inland Revenue Department to breach that secrecy requirement, on pain of imprisonment.

Therefore, legislation was needed to carry out the matching, and the Privacy Commissioner Act was the result. That Act was intended as an interim measure only, to allow information matching, and to appoint a Privacy Commissioner to oversee it. In the following year, the Commissioner worked with the Parliamentary Select Committee to prepare a new Act, this one with principles (the first Privacy

Commissioner, Sir Bruce Slane was fond of repeating the joke that he was, for a time, the only privacy or data protection commissioner in the world without principles). The addition of information privacy principles (derived from the OECD data protection principles, and repeated in summary below) meant that the Privacy Act 1993 had a different focus to its predecessor, but the information matching imperative was still there. Part 10 of the Act was (and remains) dedicated to regulating such programmes. Section 13(1)(f) imposes a duty on the Privacy Commissioner

to examine any proposed legislation that makes provision for—

(i) the collection of personal information by any public sector agency; or
(ii) the disclosure of personal information by one public sector agency to any other public sector agency,—

or both; to have particular regard, in the course of that examination, to the matters set out in section 98, in any case where the Commissioner considers that the information might be used for the purposes of an information matching programme; and to report to the responsible Minister the results of that examination.

Section 98 tells the Commissioner what he or she has to take into account in assessing any potentially new information matching programme:

...the Commissioner shall have particular regard, in examining any proposed legislation that makes provision for the collection of personal information by any public sector agency, or the disclosure of personal information by one public sector agency to any other public sector agency, in any case where the Commissioner considers that the information might be used for the purposes of an information matching programme:

(a) whether or not the objective of the programme relates to a matter of significant public importance;
(b) whether or not the use of the programme to achieve that objective will result in monetary savings that are both significant and quantifiable, or in other comparable benefits to society;
(c) whether or not the use of an alternative means of achieving that objective would give either of the results referred to in paragraph (b);
(d) whether or not the public interest in allowing the programme to proceed outweighs the public interest in adhering to the information privacy principles that the programme would otherwise contravene;
(e) whether or not the programme involves information matching on a scale that is excessive, having regard to—

(i) the number of agencies that will be involved in the programme; and
(ii) the amount of detail about an individual that will be matched under the programme;
(f) whether or not the programme will comply with the information matching rules.

From 1993 then, New Zealand law provided for privacy impact assessment, although not by that name. Before long, however, the reports the Privacy Commissioner sought from officials in order to discharge his responsibilities under this section became known as Information Matching Privacy Impact

Assessments, or IMPIAs, for short. These documents required a cost bene-fit analysis (costs and benefits here being hard cash, the economic cost of setting up and running the programme, measured against the projected sav-ings to be made from catching fraudsters and stopping their payments), con-sideration of alternative methods of achieving the same result, and other justifications for, and mitigations of the inherent insult to privacy that any such scheme constitutes.

Early efforts at objective and methodical evaluation of privacy impacts produced varied results. Some were little more than sales pitches, with benefits hyperbolically overstated, projections hopelessly optimistic, and negatives glossed over, barely touched, or simply dismissed as small, private and insignificant incidents of the greater public good that would be served.

Perhaps in response to this variety in quality and usefulness, perhaps to fur-ther promote the use of this analytical tool, the Privacy Commissioner produced a handbook for the preparation and use of privacy impact assessment in 2002. The handbook formalised and institutionalised the concept of privacy impact assessment as part of the legal and policy landscape of data protection in New Zealand. In his forward to the handbook, then Privacy Commissioner Bruce Slane opened by saying:

> Organisations frequently approach my office asking "Will my project comply with the Privacy Act?" Sometimes this leads to the wider and perhaps more valuable, questions:
>
> • How will my project affect individuals?
> • Can I achieve my objectives while also protecting privacy?
>
> This handbook provides the tools to help answer those questions.

From that time on, privacy impact assessment became part of the mainstream and its popularity has continued to grow to the extent that such undertakings became common prerequisites to Cabinet reports, and even became an express legislative requirement in one recent Act. Section 32 of the Immigration Act 2009 says

(1) The Department must complete a privacy impact assessment in respect of the collection and handling of biometric information under this Act to—

    (a) identify the potential effects that the Act may have on personal privacy; and
    (b) examine how any detrimental effects on privacy might be lessened.

(2) The Department must consult the Privacy Commissioner—

    (a) on the terms of reference developed for the assessment; and
    (b) when completing the assessment.

(3) The Department must review its privacy impact assessment if changes are made to this Act, regulations made under it, or operational policy in respect of the collection or handling of biometric information and, if the review establishes that new or increased privacy impacts have resulted from the changes, must—

    (a) amend or replace the privacy impact assessment; and
    (b) consult the Privacy Commissioner on the amended or replacement assessment.

(4) The Department must ensure the current privacy impact assessment is—

    (a) available on the Department's Internet site; and
    (b) available or readily obtainable for inspection, free of charge, at—

    (i) offices of the Department; and
    (ii) New Zealand government offices overseas that deal with immigration matters.

In one sense, this approach seems wrong-headed. Shouldn't government have considered and addressed privacy implications before passing the law? However, it can also be seen as a recognition that, in some cases, statutes can only paint the broad policy objective, and go so far into regulating the contingent effects of the implementation of the policy. A requirement to thoroughly investigate the privacy impacts as a core part of a proposal that potentially has profound effects on individual privacy and liberty is a way of balancing the government's need to move on the primary policy, while seeking to do so in a way that takes into account and mitigates the effects on privacy to the greatest extent possible.

One of the risks though, in legislating for a process, or the production of a document called a privacy impact assessment, is that it assumes a community of understanding and consensus as to what that relatively recently devised form entails.

From the preceding narrative, at least two different purposes of privacy impact assessment are evident. One is to describe any given initiative in a standardised way, to assist the Privacy Commissioner to discharge his or her obligations in terms of participating in a consultation on that proposal. Secondly, it can be a mechanism to make privacy values and consequences transparent for officials and Ministers (or in the private sector, senior managers and the Board), so those costs can be explicitly weighed against the benefits they are hoping to achieve with their policy. Also flagged is the confusion in those commissioning such work, who believe they will receive a report telling them whether or not their project complies with the Privacy Act.

8.4 Undertaking Privacy Impact Assessments

For the practitioner, the most important thing is to not rely on assumptions that, just because the client uses the phrase "privacy impact assessment" in their instructions, they know what they mean or they mean the same thing as you understand.

Sometimes obtaining clear instructions can be problematic. The person commissioning a privacy impact assessment is quite often a generic project manager, particularly in relation to information technology initiatives, and is working from a checklist of requirements or dependencies in his or her project. In New Zealand, many IT projects in the justice and health sectors require privacy impact assessments as part of the suite of documentation required for management "sign-off". How many privacy impact assessments this has resulted in is impossible to know. I have prepared two or three per year for at least 10 years, and have seen at least as many prepared by other consultants, or in-house. There is no central register of PIA reports, and no requirement that they be shared with the Privacy Commissioner or published anywhere.

The project manager often reports to a steering group. The steering group oversees the project at a high level, but also requires regular reports that the project manager and his or her team are meeting the tasks they have been set.

A common misconception in the project manager's mind is that a requirement to address privacy issues, even if clearly expressed as a privacy impact assessment, means that they are getting a legal sign-off that the project is not illegal or otherwise contravenes some aspect of the Privacy Act. The most important role of the assessor is to disabuse the project manager of this assumption. A report on whether the project is lawful will be very short indeed. It is rare for a project to be so misconceived as to be plainly illegal. Therefore, if this is the kind of report the project manager is really looking for, it can be provided for in a single sentence: "The proposed collections and uses of personal information in this project do not breach any law." Such an assessment does not tell the organisation that as a result of poor consideration of privacy issues, there is a potential litigation risk or risk of serious reputational harm. It does not differentiate between privacy risks which are a direct and unavoidable consequence of the initiative, and those that are created unnecessarily by poor planning or design. The mitigation of the latter is one of the principal concerns of a process of thorough privacy impact assessment.

A single line report assuring the project manager that the proposal is not unlawful is unlikely to assist the project manager when he or she is asked to report to the steering committee on the recommendations of the privacy impact assessment, or to satisfy media queries about the extent to which the project has taken into account privacy issues.

The most important issue for the assessor is to have very clear instructions, and all assumptions explicit. I try to attend to this at the very first meeting with a client. The following paragraphs address some of the elements I try to cover.

8.5 Timing

What a privacy impact assessment can achieve depends on where in the project it is commissioned. There are merits in different approaches. For example, if someone has a bright idea about a new IT project, or policy which makes a new use of personal information, there is often value in testing the underlying assumptions against good privacy practice at a high level so that the client can get an understanding, in general terms, of the issues they are likely to encounter as the project progresses. Left too late, many key decisions with unnecessarily privacy adverse consequences might have been made and be difficult or costly to reverse.

However, the adage or cliché about the devil being in the detail is often true. Once an information system to support the proposal is being designed, or business processes developed, a great many decisions, with varying degrees of impact on privacy, will need to be made.

Waiting until these practical considerations are known can mean that the cost of mitigating adverse privacy impacts later, when a vendor has already been selected, and a price for the project accepted, is considerably higher than would otherwise have been the case.

Often the best approach is to invite the person commissioning the assessment to regard the process as an iterative, dynamic one that changes as more is known about the project. In some cases, I have begun an assessment with the barest outline of what the initiative is intended to achieve, and that has then grown into a detailed analysis of security and access settings and the like. If the process of privacy impact assessment is linked to the development of the project, one objective can be to raise issues and make recommendations in an early version, and as those are adopted into the project, remove them from the PIA. This can lead to a final report which is very bland, and contains reassurances about the project without the context of how bad things could have been had the privacy impact assessment not been running alongside the development of IT solutions and business processes. Which leads to another important issue – the intended audience, to which I will return after addressing another matter which needs to be raised early on.

8.6 The Cost of Privacy Impact Assessment

The number of variables present at the outset of the project makes it difficult for the assessor to answer those other two key questions that the project manager will inevitably have: "How long will it take, and how much will it cost?"

As a consultant, one tries to maintain a customer service focus, so the estimates of duration of the task will most likely be linked to the project milestones. The assessor ought to work with the project manager to identify sensible points in the project at which a report might be helpful, or critical dates beyond which a report will not be able to be implemented (or not without great cost and disruption).

Similarly, the question of cost will be largely in the hands of the project team. Sadly, I have yet to be engaged on a project where money is no object, and the assessor is given free rein (and a blank cheque) to chase down all of the privacy implications, wherever they lie. More commonly, at least an indication of cost will be sought, and the assessor will provide a range. If the top end of that range is beyond the budget allocation of the project manager, another conversation about the scope of the assessment will be required. A report on a large project involving new technology or a significant new policy potentially affecting a large number of people could easily cost in excess of $20,000 (NZD, about €10,000) to prepare. Often an assessor for projects of that scale will be commissioned by way of a public tender. However, I have reported to clients at the first meeting after reviewing project documentation that no privacy impact assessment is necessary, that that statement constitutes the report, and a reading fee of $500 will be sufficient for us all to get on with other work. It can go against the grain somewhat, but if the "checklist" approach has led to the commissioning of a privacy impact assessment for a project which, for example, simply involves upgrading a software system without changing any functionality or business processes, it is pointless to spin it out for the sake of form and income.

8.7 For Whom Is the Report Prepared?

The tangible output of a process of privacy impact assessment is the privacy impact report.

If the report is to inform the project staff of privacy issues as they arise and to make recommendations which are then taken up and incorporated into the design, it will look different at the end of the project than a report prepared for a regulator or steering group. Where the assessor is working alongside the team, issues will be identified and analysed, and possibly become the subject of an ameliorating recommendation. If that recommendation is picked up and incorporated into the design, the matter need not be raised in the next iteration of the report. The path of this evolving document will trace an arc from its inception to the project's implementation, and will undergo many changes over the course of the project. It will be a living document, informing decision-makers at all critical points, and at the end, will be largely spent, its purpose fulfilled.

A report for the steering group will be making trade-offs between privacy and other considerations (such as cost, "functionality" and the like) transparent so the steering committee can consider, and either accept or reject, recommendations, and later be able to be held to account for those decisions.

A report that is being prepared for the Privacy Commissioner, in order to fulfil a statutory or administrative obligation, or to forestall an anticipated adverse Privacy Commissioner's report to Ministers, the Prime Minister, Parliament or, worse still, the press, will be assuming no prior knowledge, and will laboriously record all the accommodations to privacy made as a result of the privacy impact assessment, and may conclude with a series of recommendations that the Minister, steering group or whoever can, in a subsequent report of their own, attest have been fully accepted (or give their reasons for not doing so, as the case may be).

8.8 Problems with Privacy

One of the first things the privacy impact assessor must do is consider what privacy issues are within the scope of his or her report.

In New Zealand, the emphasis is, as in many other OECD-principle-based jurisdictions, on informational privacy or data protection, as it is called elsewhere. As mentioned above, the data protection principles have been transformed into "information privacy principles". Because of the undoubted familiarity of readers with the origins of principles only the briefest summary, to show their domestic expression, is required here:

Principle 1 – Purpose of collection of personal information
Personal information shall not be collected by any agency unless—
(a) the information is collected for a lawful purpose connected with a function or activity of the agency; and
(b) the collection of the information is necessary for that purpose.

Principle 2 – Source of personal information
(1) Where an agency collects personal information, the agency shall collect the information directly from the individual concerned (exceptions apply).

Principle 3 – Collection of information from subject
(1) The individual from whom personal information is collected must be properly informed as to the purpose, intended recipients and the like (exceptions apply).

Principle 4 – Manner of collection of personal information
Personal information shall not be collected by an agency—
(a) by unlawful means; or
(b) by means that, in the circumstances of the case,—
   (i) are unfair; or
   (ii) intrude to an unreasonable extent upon the personal affairs of the individual concerned.

Principle 5 – Storage and security of personal information
An agency that holds personal information shall ensure—
(a) that the information is protected, by such security safeguards as it is reasonable in the circumstances to take, against—
   (i) loss; and
   (ii) access, use, modification, or disclosure, except with the authority of the agency that holds the information; and
   (iii) other misuse.

Principle 6 – Access to personal information
(1) Where an agency holds personal information in such a way that it can readily be retrieved, the individual concerned shall be entitled—
   (a) to obtain from the agency confirmation of whether or not the agency holds such personal information; and
   (b) to have access to that information (exceptions apply).

Principle 7 – Correction of personal information
(1) Where an agency holds personal information, the individual concerned shall be entitled—
   (a) to request correction of the information; and
   (b) to request that there be attached to the information a statement of the correction sought but not made.

Principle 8 – Accuracy, etc., of personal information to be checked before use
An agency that holds personal information shall not use that information without taking such steps (if any) as are, in the circumstances, reasonable to ensure that, having regard to the purpose for which the information is proposed to be used, the information is accurate, up to date, complete, relevant, and not misleading.

Principle 9 – Agency not to keep personal information for longer than necessary
An agency that holds personal information shall not keep that information for longer than is required for the purposes for which the information may lawfully be used.

Principle 10 – Limits on use of personal information
An agency that holds personal information that was obtained in connection with one purpose shall not use the information for any other purpose (exceptions apply).

Principle 11 – Limits on disclosure of personal information
An agency that holds personal information shall not disclose the information to a person or body or agency (exceptions apply).

Principle 12 – Unique identifiers

An agency shall not assign a unique identifier to an individual unless the assignment of that identifier is necessary to enable the agency to carry out any one or more of its functions efficiently. Two agencies should not assign the same unique identifier to an individual.

It is evident that a privacy impact assessment based solely on compliance (in spirit or in law) is hardly going to be a comprehensive review of privacy issues. Data protection or information privacy is just a subset of the innate integrity, autonomy and dignity possessed by all humanity, which is capable of being compromised by the thoughtless actions of others and which we sometimes call "privacy".

However, the assessment presents definitional challenges even if we do limit the scope to data flows. If disregarding a "compliance based" approach makes sense in order to ensure the issues are widely canvassed, it presents another challenge, that of subjectivity. "Complies with"/"does not comply with" reports are crude, but at least have the virtue of objectivity. The activity is being measured against the standard set in law. To go beyond those bounds requires the assessor to bring his or her own values into the process and, in the absence of empirical evidence on the weightings to be attached to various privacy values, to make a number of assumptions and assertions about what factors are to be taken into account, and how serious they are. An anecdote from another part of my practice illustrates the issue. I once gave a seminar to a group of health professionals, including many nurses. One asked whether the charts that traditionally hang over the end of patients' beds, within clear view of anyone visiting the ward, were a breach of privacy, or contrary to the Privacy Act. At first, I dodged the question, as the answer, based on application of the need to apply reasonable security, could only be "it depends". However, I was curious to gauge the views of the group, so I asked what personal information was on the clipboard. The woman who had raised the question, gave the example of date of birth, and said that she would not want everyone wandering in off the street to have access to that information. A colleague spoke up and said that she didn't care if people knew how old she was, but in no way wanted strangers knowing her weight, which was also on the sheet!

If those women were each asked to undertake a privacy impact assessment of the new ward personal information policy, each would assign a different weight and value to the different information items. This can have important implications. It might be very costly for the organisation to adopt a recommendation to promote privacy, or doing so might create other risks. One assessor might say that the information on the bed-end clipboard is so sensitive the only solution is for it to be locked in a drawer in a secure room. There will be cost then, in the extra time taken to access the charts to read or update them. There will be risks that a doctor, unfamiliar with her patient, will act on the basis of the wrong chart, with potentially disastrous results.

The report must ensure that subjective assessments are clearly flagged as such, and be couched in terms of a "sensitivity analysis" to reduce the effect of the subjectivity. In other words, an assessor must recognise the bias and subjectivity that he or she brings to the task, declare that in the report, seek empirical backing for any position taken (e.g., public surveys on attitudes) and present a range of scenarios with different consequences evident for decision-makers.

8.9 Independence

Independence is often unquestioningly assumed to be a requisite virtue of any process of purportedly objective assessment; however, the precise meaning of the word often goes unexamined.

Independence in this context should be considered as a range of alternatives existing on a continuum. A person actively involved in the design or marketing of the project would not usually be considered independent. An in-house legal adviser should be able to provide an independent and objective view, as might an internal person with audit responsibilities. However, those people owe a number of other ethical and legal duties to the commissioning organisation. The project promoter and the assessor have a common employer.

Often, for large or complex projects involving novel collections or uses of personal information, external assistance is called upon, as few organisations retain suitably qualified or experienced staff on a full-time basis.

Where a project is potentially controversial, and is likely to attract media interest, a measure of independence of the assessor often adds to the credibility of the output.

However, if the independence of in-house staff can be impugned by regulators or opponents of a particular project, why should a consultant, whose livelihood and reputation depend on delivering work which pleases, rather than annoys those who pay him or her, have any extra credibility?

If the client truly wants to have an independent report, and is prepared to take the risks associated with such an approach, they have a number of options. They can ask the regulator to undertake the assessment for them. Alternatively, they can ask the regulator to recommend and instruct a person to be funded by them.

Further down the independence continuum, they can agree terms of reference with the "independent" consultant that guarantee a free rein to the assessor to make any such findings as he or she sees fit.

Beyond that, the level of independence is a measure of the reputation of the assessor, and the rigour of his or her analysis.

Which leads to another important factor.

8.10 Givens

What can be done when the fundamental tenets of the policy or proposal under review are themselves anathema to privacy protection, a policy that to a privacy advocate would seem abhorrent *ab initio*? Take, for example, a suggestion that every citizen would be issued an identity card coded with all their health information, which could in turn be accessed by readers held by any number of officials.

As a private practitioner, the word "no" is not one that I often engage in response to a suggestion that I should be paid a handsome sum of money to undertake a particular task that is within my area of expertise. And policy-makers are unlikely to have any enthusiasm for a lengthy diatribe on the reasons the basic policy is so fundamentally flawed.

Having said that, it is not a privacy impact assessor's job to apply lipstick to a pig, to use a colourful local phrase, never mind that industrial quantities of cosmetics would be required to render the hypothetical policy above less porcine.

If the proposal is non-negotiable, such as one that was a central plank of an election campaign, railing against it in a privacy impact report is pointless, never mind the fact that it will not endear the assessor to the person he hopes will pay his bill.

Nonetheless, an assessor will want to maintain his or her integrity.

The objection in principle can be dealt with in a paragraph, in language as strong as the author desires or dares; however, then the serious work begins. It will be essential to obtain an understanding from the client about just which aspects of the project are non-negotiable. What are the key features that cannot be tampered with or given away? Once these have been identified, the author can identify them as "givens" and clearly state that his or her silence on those aspects of the proposal in no way detracts from the privacy impact, but that the remainder of the assessment is predicated on the sentence "If we must have this policy, how can privacy impacts be mitigated?". Another construction might be "What is the *least worst* outcome for privacy from this project proceeding?". In the case of the hypothetical situation above, that might include a robust statutory regime, including penalties for misuse, and tight constraints on permitted uses of the personal information. At the detailed operational level, the report will include recommendations related to internal policies, staff training, public notification, and the security of and permitted access to IT systems. Thus, privacy is promoted to the greatest extent possible, notwithstanding that the principal policy still goes "oink" and rolls in the mud.

8.11 Scope Constraints

On several occasions, I have been asked to review a proposal which, on a cursory reading, seems innocuous. A system is being upgraded or a data warehouse is being created into which all the data from a business system will be extracted, for easier analysis.

In such a case, there is little incremental change to the current privacy practices. It will be easier and more efficient for the organisation concerned to access its own data to do things it is already entitled to do. However, the new system might provide a platform on to which other functions can be more readily bolted than is the case with the legacy system. This creates a contingent privacy risk. In other words, there is no measurable privacy risk with what the project is proposing, except that it will engender greater risks down the line. For example, it might make it far easier for a Minister to access unit level data about identifiable individuals from a departmental system, or it may enable the creation of what analysts are fond of calling a "longitudinal record" of individuals' interactions with an organisation over time.

Here the assessor has two options. He or she can forecast the infinite possibilities for offending privacy that exist contingent on new future applications being introduced, and comment upon those. This approach seldom endears the assessor to the well intentioned project sponsor who might justifiably comment that such conjecture has no place in a document about a project that has no intention of expanding in the predicted direction. One response to this objection is that the system and its potential will remain long after the project manager, commissioning officials and privacy-committed Minister have moved on, and it is important for opportunities for Orwellian exploitation of information to be clearly marked at the outset.

It will be a matter of judgement as to which approach should be adopted. One of the difficulties of the former is that it can be hard to identify useful and realistic recommendations based on such conjured hypotheticals, and even less likely that officials will adopt any recommendations that bear no relationship to the project scope as currently understood.

In many cases, the preferable option will be to record the contingent risk in broad terms, and recommend that the organisation adopt policies to ensure that any further increments are subject to fresh and robust privacy impact assessment as they are proposed.

What is most important for the assessor is to ensure that the scope constraints are clearly identified in the report, and that the report notes that it is based on that description. This protects the assessor when scope creep (or function creep or mission creep) infects the system or organisation, and project owners respond that no one need be concerned "because we got a privacy impact assessment from John Edwards, and he told us it was okay". Actually, what I told you was okay was something quite different, as you can see from page 1 of my report.

8.12 Legal Professional Privilege Applies

Privacy impact assessment is not the domain solely of law practitioners. Many disciplines have valuable perspectives to bring, and in fact there may be tasks such as complex IT initiatives with which law practitioners are quite ill-suited to assist.

One of the advantages in instructing legal counsel to undertake the assessment is that in the event that the organisation commissioning the report does not wish to make it publicly available (for any number of reasons, not all of which necessarily involve a cover-up), it can claim that the document is subject to legal professional privilege.

Legal professional privilege applies to all communications between a solicitor and client for the purposes of eliciting or giving legal advice. One question that has arisen in relation to one of my reports was whether a privacy impact assessment report constituted legal advice.

I had prepared a report for a client, and the report described the proposal in detail, and in equal detail pointed out a number of implications for privacy that the architects of the scheme had not anticipated. The proposal did not proceed in that form.

Some time later, a journalist sought a copy of my report from the organisation under New Zealand's freedom of information law, the Official Information Act. That law requires public sector agencies to make information available unless there is good reason to withhold it. The "good reasons" are all listed in the Act, and include, where withholding is necessary, the information to maintain legal professional privilege.

The Parliamentary Ombudsman, whose task it is to review such decisions initially considered that the document could not be said to be legal advice. It was, he thought, more in the nature of policy advice or some new specialty field, privacy advice. He wrote to me to let me know his thoughts, and to seek my views, which I provided to him at length. Ultimately, he revised his opinion and accepted that the document was subject to privilege, as it had been prepared by a solicitor, on instructions from a client, and that it did contain legal advice, and that other advice therein was of a nature a client would expect to obtain from legal counsel with experience in a specialty area. Advice on technical means of mitigating privacy impacts, for example, might not strictly be seen as legal advice, but considered in the whole, the document was privileged, in the same way the advice of a lawyer specialising in natural resource management might be privileged, notwithstanding that it might also include some reference to practical engineering or political means of mitigating an environmental impact.

8.13 After the Assessment?

My practice is always to submit a report in draft, as a means of checking facts, and ensuring that any assumptions or subjectivities that I have brought to the process are contestable. A cynic might say that this undermines the independence of the report, giving, as it does, the agency an opportunity to influence the outcome, and potentially dilute any of its adverse findings. I have no time for such criticisms. Giving an opportunity to comment can only improve the quality of the final product. An assessor should be able to be challenged on his or her findings, and required to justify or explain conclusions where those are not immediately apparent from the preceding analysis.

As for compromising the independence of the report, the assessor should have the judgement to know when to concede that a bow has been drawn too long, and when to simply respond "That is my conclusion, you are free to accept or reject it as you wish".

In any case, a final report should not be a document that includes surprises for the client.

Where a report is intended to be submitted to the Privacy Commissioner, my preferred practice is to give that office an opportunity to review a draft before the client is given the finalised report. In this way, the Privacy Commissioner can indicate areas which he or she thinks warrant further analysis, while the client can distance himself or herself from the draft findings or recommendations on the basis that the analysis in some way misrepresents the project.

Where a report is to be made to a steering group or oversight committee of some sort, and is to be referred to in public discussions about the project, I usually suggest that they make a formal response to the recommendations, so that interested parties can clearly see what was recommended, which of those recommendations were accepted and implemented, and which were not (and why). This provides transparency and accountability in the project, and nicely concludes the process of privacy impact assessment.

8.14 Conclusion

Privacy impact assessment has been a useful tool for standardising an approach to what is after all a fundamentally subjective set of values. It has limitations, and is only a tool. It should not be seen as a panacea for the incorporation of privacy sensibilities into technology or policy initiatives. Nor should it be a static form. Each exercise will require an approach suited to the subject matter and the client and other stakeholders. The unthinking inclusion of a requirement to undertake privacy impact assessment on every project will not necessarily promote privacy, or the interests of the commissioning party.

Done properly, a privacy impact assessment can assist policy-makers and system developers to critically examine the merits of their proposal, given the adverse effect on privacy, and to avoid adverse privacy impacts which are an unnecessary incident of poor design. A good report can improve systems, and contribute to public confidence in the organisation undertaking the initiative.

Until a consensus as to form and content emerges (if it is possible given the variables mentioned in this chapter), the critical thing is to ensure that all assumptions are transparent and that all parties understand the scope and intended audience and purpose of the project.

Having gently criticised a "checklist" approach to privacy impact assessment, I leave you with my own.

A checklist for assessors
How advanced is the project?
Ask the client, which of these questions do you want the report to answer?

- Can we do what we want to do?
- How can we do what we want to do? (More coarsely, "what will the law let us get away with?")
- How do we do what we want to do in a way which best reflects good privacy practice, and mitigates any adverse effects?
- All of the above?
- None of the above?

What level of PIA is required, a high level critique of the broad policy settings, or a detailed examination of the operational components?
Should the PIA be a one-off, an ongoing process or one of a series?

Should the assessor "take as read" the organisation's current policies and processes, and just examine the increment represented by the new initiative, or start afresh?

Is the report to be published, or will it be just for the use of the project team?

Are there aspects of the design or policy which are "not negotiable"?

Why is a PIA being commissioned? To provide a "tick" on a checklist? To improve the product? To provide assurance of lawfulness? To give to the regulator?

Chapter 9
Privacy Impact Assessment in the UK

Adam Warren and Andrew Charlesworth

9.1 Introduction

The adoption of PIAs in the UK is a recent development. Both it, and related initiatives such as "privacy by design", pioneered by the Ontario Information and Privacy Commissioner, Ann Cavoukian[1] (discussed further below), can be seen as indicative of a disenchantment amongst some regulators, including the UK's national data protection regulator, the Information Commissioner's Office (ICO), with the largely reactive approach to regulation adopted by the EU Data Protection Directive and the national legislation which implements it. As has been argued elsewhere,[2] that regime, which depends heavily upon data subjects acting proactively via the subject access mechanism, both to ensure data controller compliance and to provide the regulator with information, has proven to be ineffectual in the face of contemporary technological developments. When one considers established technologies such as the World Wide Web, or developing technologies such as cloud computing, neither of these disaggregated data environments lend themselves to effective regulation via the Directive's largely post hoc processes.

In addition, the ubiquity of information technology, the ease and speed of data transfers and the devolving of control over information within organisations have resulted in commercial and governmental data environments where significant personal data losses can result from the relatively minor actions of low-level employees or of data processors. The loss of 25 million child benefit records by HM Revenue and Customs, resulting from the actions of a junior civil servant, demonstrates clearly the problems that the incremental and unmonitored development of internal

---

[1] Ontario Information and Privacy Commissioner (OIPC), *Privacy by Design*, Toronto, 2009. http://www.ipc.on.ca/images/Resources/privacybydesign.pdf

[2] Charlesworth, Andrew, "The Future of UK Data Protection Regulation", *Information Security Technical Report*, Vol. 11, No. 1, 2006, pp. 46–54.

A. Warren (✉)
Department of Geography, Loughborough University, Leicestershire, UK
e-mail: A.P.Warren@lboro.ac.uk

D. Wright, P. De Hert (eds.), *Privacy Impact Assessment*, Law, Governance and Technology Series 6, DOI 10.1007/978-94-007-2543-0_9,
© Springer Science+Business Media B.V. 2012

practices and procedures relating to personal data holdings can pose for effective organisational data protection compliance.

With these issues in mind, in 2007 the UK's ICO commissioned a report on the development and use of PIAs in other jurisdictions, notably Australia, Canada, Hong Kong, New Zealand and the United States.[3] Commissioned in tandem with the report was a practitioner handbook for PIAs.[4] Both report and handbook were officially launched in December 2007 at the ICO's conference "Surveillance Society: Turning Debate into Action". In July 2010, the ICO published its *Annual Report*. In a chapter entitled "Educating and Influencing", a small paragraph noted that "over 300 Privacy Impact Assessments have been started across central government and their agencies".[5] Yet, despite this ostensible policy success for a tool that had been launched less than three years earlier,[6] very few UK privacy impact assessment (PIA) reports have reached the public domain. Moreover, evidence of private sector activity in this field is almost non-existent, being restricted to the occasional report[7] or citation.[8] It is perhaps, therefore, not surprising that academic interest in PIAs has been limited.

This chapter aims to stimulate interest in this topic, and address some of the gaps identified above, through an investigation of PIAs being processed in the UK. In order to investigate this topic, it is important to start with a clear definition. The meaning ascribed to the term "PIA" has varied over time and across most jurisdictions.[9] In this chapter, we use the following definition, synthesised from descriptions given in various international guidance material for PIAs:

---

[3] ICO, *Privacy Impact Assessments: International Study of Their Application and Effects*, Information Commissioner's Office, Wilmslow, 2007. http://www.ico.gov.uk/upload/documents/library/corporate/research_and_reports/privacy_impact_assessment_international_study.011007.pdf

[4] ICO, *Privacy Impact Assessment Handbook,* Information Commissioner's Office, Wilmslow, 2007.

[5] ICO, *Information Commissioner's Annual Report 2009/10*, Information Commissioner's Office, Wilmslow, 2010, p. 23. http://www.ico.gov.uk/upload/documents/library/corporate/detailed_specialist_guides/annual_report_2010.pdf

[6] Warren, Adam, Robin Bayley, Colin Bennett, Andrew Charlesworth, Roger Clarke and Charles Oppenheim, "Privacy Impact Assessments: International Experience as a Basis for UK Guidance", *Computer Law & Security Report,* Vol. 24, No. 3, 2008, pp. 233–242.

[7] For example: 80/20 Thinking Ltd., *First Stage (Interim) Privacy Impact Assessment for Phorm Inc*, February 2008. http://blogs.guardian.co.uk/technology/Phorm%20PIA%20interim%20final%20.pdf

[8] ESRC Seminar Series, *Mapping the Public Policy Landscape: Assessing Privacy Impact,* 2009.

[9] See ICO, *Privacy Impact Assessments: International Study. . .*, op. cit., fn. 3, and Tancock, David, Siani Pearson and Andrew Charlesworth, *The Emergence of Privacy Impact Assessments*, HP Labs Technical Report (HPL-2010-63), 2010. http://www.hpl.hp.com/techreports/2010/HPL-2010-63.html

A *Privacy Impact Assessment (PIA)* is a systematic process for identifying and addressing privacy issues in an information system that considers the future consequences for privacy of a current or proposed action.[10]

Our analysis commences with an overview of the UK legislative and policy framework, and the extent to which this influenced the development of a methodology for the conduct of PIAs within the UK. We then consider the UK PIA process, drawing from examples of PIAs undertaken since the publication of the ICO's PIA handbook. The practicalities of conducting a PIA are illustrated through a case study of the UK 2011 census, informed by empirical research conducted by the authors during July and August 2010. This is followed by a discussion of lessons learnt from the national experience to date, identifying potential pitfalls, misconceptions and gaps in understanding. We then discuss possible future directions for PIAs in the UK, paying attention to the drive towards a proactive approach to regulation, the influence of cross-jurisdictional technologies and the involvement of the private sector in creating and using systems to facilitate accountability and compliance. Finally, conclusions are drawn.

9.2 Legislative and Policy Framework

As noted above, the methodology for the conduct of PIAs in the UK was officially launched in December 2007 by the Information Commissioner's Office. It took the form of a practitioner handbook (available electronically and, later, in hard copy), supported by a study investigating the use of PIAs overseas and the lessons learnt from their experiences.[11] When developing the methodology for the UK, the team commissioned by the ICO were mindful of the fact that no previous official guidance had been published and that, at the time, there was no formal legislative basis, or governmental support, for the process. Consequently, the potential benefits to organisations had to be explicitly stated, and the tool itself had to be sufficiently flexible so as to be capable of being integrated within existing business processes. In addition, the project team, in their study, recommended that the ICO aim for a "structured and timetabled roll-out" of PIAs, encouraging organisations to develop internal expertise in PIA processes.[12]

A quarter century of increasingly rigorous UK data protection legislation has encouraged the development of strong networks of knowledgeable data protection officers (for example, NADPO[13] and the Data Protection Forum[14]), creating regular

---

[10] Tancock et al., op. cit., fn. 10, p. 22.

[11] The authors of this chapter were involved in this research project, which was commissioned by the UK Information Commissioner's Office in 2007. Other members of the research team were Charles Oppenheim (Project Director), Colin Bennett, Robin Bayley and Roger Clarke.

[12] ICO, *Privacy Impact Assessments: International Study...*, op. cit., fn. 3, p. 31.

[13] National Association of Data Protection Officers. http://www.nadpo.org.uk/

[14] Data Protection Forum. http://www.dpforum.org.uk/

opportunities for cross-organisational learning. There is also a long history of developing codes of practice within related sectors through umbrella groups (for example, ACPO[15] and the CCTV User Group[16]). In theory, such groups could have influential roles in the introduction and promotion of PIAs.

9.2.1 Legislation

Since 1984, the UK has had overarching data protection legislation covering both public and private sectors. The most recent iteration, the Data Protection Act 1998 (DPA 1998), implemented the EU Data Protection Directive (95/46/EC). This extended the prior regime under the Data Protection Act 1984 to include, amongst other changes, extension of coverage to manual files; creation of a new category of sensitive personal data, subject to more rigorous processing preconditions; additional security requirements; increased, and stronger, rights for individual data subjects; and the prohibition of transfers of personal data to countries outside the European Economic Area, subject to certain conditions being satisfied.[17]

At the European level, Art. 20 of the Data Protection Directive requires that processing operations likely to present specific risks to the rights and freedoms of data subjects should be examined prior to their start, an intervention described as "prior checking":

1. Member States shall determine the processing operations likely to present specific risks to the rights and freedoms of data subjects and shall check that these processing operations are examined prior to the start thereof.
2. Such prior checks shall be carried out by the supervisory authority following receipt of a notification from the controller or by the data protection official, who, in cases of doubt, must consult the supervisory authority.
3. Member States may also carry out such checks in the context of preparation either of a measure of the national parliament or of a measure based on such a legislative measure, which define the nature of the processing and lay down appropriate safeguards.

S. 22 of the DPA 1998 provides for a version of prior checking by requiring that, as part of the notification process, certain processing might be assessed by the ICO for compliance with the provisions of the Act before the processing begins. The

---

[15] Various iterations, most recently: ACPO, *Guidance on the Management of Police Information*, Second Edition, 2010. http://www.acpo.police.uk/documents/information/2010/201004INFMOPI01.pdf

[16] CCTV User Group, *Model Code of Practice and Procedures Manual*, 2002. http://www.cctvusergroup.com/index.php

[17] Charlesworth, Andrew, "Implementing the European Union Data Protection Directive 1995 in UK Law: The Data Protection Act 1998", *Government Information Quarterly*, Vol. 16, No. 3, 1999, pp. 203–240.

type of processing must be specified in an Order made by the Secretary of State, if it is considered that processing would be particularly likely to cause substantial damage or substantial distress to data subjects or otherwise significantly to prejudice the rights and freedoms of data subjects. While the UK government identified three possible categories of processing that might be covered by such "preliminary assessment" (data matching, processing involving genetic data and processing by private investigators), to date, no such order has been made in the UK. Indeed, Elizabeth France, while Information Commissioner:

> ...was of the opinion that "no 'assessable processing' should be designated", i.e. that no processing operations should be made subject to a prior assessment at all.[18]

This rejection of prior assessment likely stemmed from the lack of necessary in-house technology expertise at the ICO which would have been required in order for such "prior assessments" to have constituted a meaningful oversight mechanism. Other EU Member States have adopted prior checks for particular types of processing relating, for example, to sensitive data, offences and criminal convictions, and genetic data.[19]

Previous research undertaken for the ICO[20] suggested that the UK should reconsider its position on prior checking. It is possible that wider use of PIAs could form part of such a process as they would:

- facilitate the process of prior checking by allowing the supervisory authority to draw upon the results of PIAs incorporated into organisational processes, such as risk assessments for new or redesigned projects;
- broaden the pool of organisational privacy understanding and expertise such that organisations will be more readily aware of the need for prior checking when it is appropriate, and better able to supply the supervisory authority with appropriate information about the project or process for an appropriate prior-checking assessment or decision to be made efficiently.

It is clear, however, that while supervisory authority prior checking in specific circumstances may be provided for in the UK data privacy regime, it is not in itself synonymous with the PIA process, as currently understood.

Thus, while they are capable of supporting a legislated (if largely unused) prior checking process, PIAs themselves have no statutory footing in the UK, and thus cannot be made a legally mandated process for either the public or private sector, without further legislative enactment. However, as in other jurisdictions, recent

---

[18] Foundation for Information Policy Research (FIPR), *Children's Databases – Safety and Privacy: A Report for the Information Commissioner*, March/August 2006, p. 187. http://www. cl.cam.ac.uk/~rja14/Papers/kids.pdf

[19] ICO, *Privacy Impact Assessments: International Study...*, op. cit., fn. 5, Appendix H, pp. 5–9. See also Chapter 4 of this book: Le Grand, Gwendal, and Emilie Barrau, "Prior Checking, a Forerunner to Privacy Impact Assessments".

[20] FIPR, op. cit., fn. 21.

developments in the UK have resulted in a requirement being placed on some parts of the public sector (and anecdotally it appears, indirectly on quasi-public and private organisations exercising public sector functions) to adopt PIAs, as a required element of internal project development processes.

9.2.2 Policy

Although the introduction of PIAs into the UK was primarily promoted by the production of the ICO-commissioned handbook, further impetus was added by a number of data handling scandals involving public and private sector organisations.[21] Arguably the highest profile incident, the loss of 25 million child benefit records by HM Revenue and Customs, resulted in a Cabinet Office review. The resulting report, *Data Handling Procedures in Government* (the "Data Handling Review"), mandated the use of PIAs in central government departments from July 2008. The Data Handling Review drew attention to the benefits of this process, stating the ICO had made "a powerful case" for government to adopt PIAs, which, if carried out at an early stage

> enable organisations to anticipate and address the likely impacts of new initiatives, foresee problems, and negotiate solutions. Risks can be managed through the gathering and sharing of information with stakeholders. Systems can be designed to avoid unnecessary privacy intrusion, and features can be built in from the outset that reduce any impact on privacy. The Privacy Impact Assessment adopts a risk management process approach, periodic reports from which [Privacy Impact Assessment Reports] may be published or distributed to stakeholders.[22]

In addition, the review called for the process to be built into existing government reviews of information and technology projects.[23] The ICO has incorporated this advice into its own policy approach, eschewing the production of templates and instead encouraging organisations to "embed" PIAs within existing processes, for example, when seeking information assurance accreditation or engaging on public consultations.[24]

In this context, PIAs support accountability, efficient management and effective incorporation of risk assessments into key decision-making processes. In the private sector, further motivations may be at play, for example, conferring competitive advantage, demonstrating legal compliance, saving money and preventing adverse

---

[21] Private sector data losses included bank and insurance details by financial institutions. See, for example, the Financial Services Authority report, *Data Security in Financial Services*, April 2008. http://www.fsa.gov.uk/pubs/other/data_security.pdf

[22] Cabinet Office, *Data Handling Procedures in Government: Final Report*, Cabinet Office, London, 2008, p. 19. http://www.cabinetoffice.gov.uk/media/65948/dhr080625.pdf

[23] Known as the "Gateway", the review process is managed by the Office of Government Commerce. It delivers a "peer review" in which independent practitioners from outside the programme and project examine its progress and the likelihood of successful delivery. http://www.ogc.gov.uk/what_is_ogc_gateway_review.asp

[24] Telephone conversation with ICO representative, July 2010.

publicity. In short, PIAs can be regarded as more beneficial to organisations than to individuals. The need to convince agencies and businesses that they are the right thing to do for "business" reasons trumps the ostensible goal of protecting and advancing privacy rights.[25]

9.3 The UK PIA Process

The UK PIA process is outlined in the ICO handbook, updated in June 2009.[26] As the size of projects and the degree of privacy risk involved vary enormously, the ICO guidance seeks to direct organisations to conducting the most appropriate level of assessment. The processes consist of the following (Table 9.1):

Table 9.1   UK PIA process: an overview

Process	Action
Initial assessment	Examines the project at an early stage, identifies stakeholders, assesses privacy risks and decides whether a PIA is necessary and, if so, what level of PIA is required.
Full-scale PIA	An in-depth internal assessment of privacy risks and liabilities, consisting of five phases usually conducted in sequence. They include the following: i. *Preliminary:* establishes and ensures a firm basis for the PIA, so that it can be conducted effectively and efficiently. ii. *Preparation:* makes the arrangements needed to enable the following phase (i.e., consultation and analysis) to run smoothly. iii. *Consultation and analysis:* identifies problems early on, discovers effective solutions and ensures that the design is adapted to include those solutions. iv. *Documentation:* documents the PIA process and the outcomes and delivers a PIA report. v. *Review and audit:* ensures that the undertakings arising from the consultation and analysis phase are actually within the running system or implemented project.
Small-scale PIA	Similar to a full-scale PIA, but less formalised and requires less exhaustive information-gathering and analysis and usually focuses on specific aspects of a project.
Privacy law compliance check	Examines compliance with statutory powers, duties and prohibitions in relation to the use and disclosure of personal information.
Data protection compliance check	Checks for compliance with the Data Protection Act of 1998. An organisation usually conducts this check when the project is more fully formed.

[25] For a more in-depth discussion of privacy policy and governance, see Bennett, Colin J., and Charles D. Raab, *The Governance of Privacy: Policy Instruments in Global Perspective*, MIT Press, Cambridge, MA, 2006.

[26] ICO, *Privacy Impact Assessment Handbook: Version 2.0*, Information Commissioner's Office, Wilmslow, 2009. http://www.ico.gov.uk/upload/documents/pia_handbook_html_v2/index.html

To be effective, a PIA needs to be conducted at a stage where it can "genuinely affect the development of a project".[27] It therefore needs to be seen as a separate process from compliance checks or data protection audits, both of which comprise analyses of systems already in place "against a prevailing legal, management or technology standard".[28] Conversely, a PIA aims to prevent problems arising, and hence to avoid subsequent expense and disruption.[29] The ICO advises that responsibility for PIAs be placed at a senior executive level – ideally, the lead for risk management, audit or compliance – in order to reflect the strategic importance of the exercise. The guidance recommends a team or committee approach, with the PIA usually conducted by a senior member of the project team. This can include, with varying degrees of participation, the following personnel:

- Programme and project managers
- Privacy policy advisors
- Legal advisors
- Records management staff
- Information technology or data security experts
- Communications staff
- Other functional specialists, as appropriate.[30]

Examples of PIAs conducted in the UK are outlined in Table 9.2, below.

Some organisations employ external consultants to carry out a PIA, either because they believe that they do not possess the necessary skills in-house, or they wish the PIA to be perceived as being as independent as possible from potential influences within the organisation. Some examples are outlined in Table 9.3, below.

External consultants often bring considerable experience to the PIA process, lending impartiality to the process. They can offer frank advice when initiatives are deemed to be unwise or ill-conceived, and tend to have greater expertise and familiarity with relevant legislation.[31] Yet, there are disadvantages. Smaller organisations may find them prohibitively expensive. Moreover, there is scepticism about consultants using "cookie cutter" PIAs whereby the same templates are used for vastly different clients.[32] There is also a risk that organisations will seek to use external consultants to attempt to "legitimise" controversial projects or applications. For example, a "PIA" conducted in 2008 by the consultancy group 80/20 Thinking Ltd for Phorm, a company specialising in targeted online advertising, generated considerable debate among privacy experts, and in sections of the mainstream media, about

---

[27] Ibid., p. 3.

[28] ICO, *Privacy Impact Assessments: International Study...*, op. cit., fn. 3, p. 1.

[29] ICO, *Privacy Impact Assessment Handbook*, op. cit., fn. 4.

[30] Tancock et al., op. cit., fn. 10.

[31] ICO, *Privacy Impact Assessments: International Study...*, op. cit., fn. 3.

[32] Ibid.

Table 9.2   PIAs conducted in the UK

Organisation	Project/procedure assessed	Type of PIA
UK Anti-Doping (2010[a])	The disclosure of personal data to UK Anti-Doping by the Serious Organised Crime Agency	Small-scale
Northern Ireland Statistics and Research Agency (NISRA) (2010)	2011 census for Northern Ireland	Full-scale
Office for National Statistics (ONS) (2009)	2011 census for England and Wales	Full-scale
UK Border Agency (2009)	Exchange of fingerprint information with immigration authorities in Australia, Canada, United States and New Zealand	Small-scale
National Policing Improvement Agency (2009)	Electronic exchange of police intelligence across England and Wales via the Police National Database	Full-scale

[a] The year in this column relates to the year of publication of the PIA report.

Table 9.3   Examples of PIAs outsourced to consultants

Organisation	Type of privacy impact assessed	Consultancy employed
Aegate (Pharmaceutical authentication services)	Use of RFID technologies to authenticate prescription pharmaceuticals at the point of sale	Enterprise Privacy Group
Department for Transport	National time-distance-place road pricing policy[a]	Enterprise Privacy Group
Phorm Inc.	Behavioural targeted advertising	80/20 Thinking Ltd

[a] In this system of road pricing, vehicle owners are charged based on when, where and how much they drive.

the motivations behind the exercise.[33] In practice, the exercise undertaken by 80/20 Thinking Ltd cannot be accurately described as a PIA, given that the technology and its applications were already fully developed and in use in business operations, and Phorm was clearly seeking to retrospectively validate those applications rather than

---

[33] See, for example, Arthur, Charles, "Simon Davies (of Privacy International, and 80/20 Thinking) on Phorm", Technology Blog, *The Guardian*, 20 March 2008. http://www.guardian.co.uk/technology/blog/2008/mar/20/simondaviesofprivacyintern. See also BBC News, "Phorm Needs 'Better Protection'", 18 March 2008. http://news.bbc.co.uk/1/hi/technology/7303426.stm

to establish any potential impact on privacy with an eye to proactive mitigation. A more accurate description of the exercise undertaken would thus be a privacy audit or compliance check.[34]

We will now consider the processes involved in the conduct of a PIA at the Office for National Statistics (ONS), which is responsible for producing official statistics and conducting surveys on behalf of the UK government.

9.4 Case Study: Office for National Statistics (ONS), 2011 Census

The ONS, as the executive arm of the UK Statistics Authority, is responsible for conducting the census in England and Wales. Scotland and Northern Ireland are subject to separate censuses carried out by their devolved agencies. The census is compulsory throughout the UK, and is conducted every 10 years. The most recent survey was carried out in 2011 and, according to the ONS, the data collected will be used "solely for the production of statistics and statistical research".[35] The legal basis for conducting a national census was established by the Census Act 1920. This is supported by the Census Order (directing that a particular census of the population shall be taken) and Census Regulations (covering procedural and practical arrangements for the census). Both the Order and the Regulations are laid before both Houses of Parliament.[36] The census provides three broad categories of information:

- Counts of population units – people, households and dwellings;
- Population structures – e.g., family and household relationships, ethnic groups;
- Population and housing characteristics – e.g., health, employment and qualifications.[37]

As these statistics are published for small population groups (down to approximately 125 households or 250 people) and are cross-tabulated with other variables, effective privacy safeguards governing the collection and use of personal data are paramount. Accordingly, publication of the results of the census is subject to additional statutes including the DPA 1998 and the Statistics and Service Registration Act 2007. This legislative framework is supported by a detailed procedural review, undertaken by the ONS over the last four decades, of the methods and processes underpinning each census.[38] Thus, the review process prior to the 2011 census

---

[34] 80/20 Thinking Ltd., op. cit., fn. 7.

[35] ONS, *Report of a Privacy Impact Assessment Conducted by the Office for National Statistics in Relation to the 2011 Census England and Wales*, Office for National Statistics, London, 2009, p. 4. http://www.ons.gov.uk/census/2011-census/2011-census-project/commitment-to-confidentiality/privacy-impact-assessment--pia--on-2011-census.pdf

[36] The National Assembly for Wales is consulted in the making of any census order. Moreover, Welsh Ministers are now responsible for the Regulation in Wales.

[37] ONS, op. cit., fn. 38, p. 4.

[38] Much of the information in this section is based on a telephone conversation with an ONS representative (August 2010).

commenced in 2002 by posing the question: "Is there a need for another census?". Once that question was answered in the affirmative, preparations began in earnest, with a series of consultations over the census design (to ensure accurate population counts, maximise overall response, provide high quality statistics) and questionnaire content (so that it produced useful outputs, catered for small population groups, served the UK as a whole). As a result, the ONS were fully cognisant of the process-orientated approach advocated in the ICO's PIA handbook. As the internal processes assessing the 2011 census were well advanced by the time the handbook was published in 2007, the ONS conducted its "PIA" on work that had largely been done. Although this approach runs counter to the prospective nature of the PIA, it is nevertheless instructive to follow the processes enacted by the ONS as it sought to identify privacy risks inherent in conducting the census, and develop solutions to "accept, mitigate or avoid them".[39]

Perhaps the greatest difficulty encountered by the ONS was in locating appropriate expertise on PIAs. Following the ICO's publication of the PIA handbook, and its subsequent promotion of the tool, the ONS met with representatives from the data protection regulator during 2008 and 2009. These meetings could be deemed successful in that they reinforced the need for the ONS to build on its existing internal review process to consider, in greater detail, new arrangements for the 2011 census compared with the 2001 census; highlight any changes that raised new privacy concerns; and describe the safeguards put in place to protect the privacy of all census respondents.[40] Moreover, the ONS was clearly persuaded during these discussions that it "had little choice" but to conduct the PIA. It immediately elected for the full-scale PIA (without considering the screening process outlined in the handbook) as (i) the census programme was "so important" and (ii) it "would be expected" of them. Yet, although the ONS found the PIA handbook to be helpful, especially in outlining the processes to be enacted and requiring it to check legal compliance, it was unable to make contact with anyone with direct experience of conducting PIAs in the UK. The handbook "contained a lot of processes but did not tell [the ONS] what to do".[41] This proved to be the greatest stumbling block. In the absence of a referral from the ICO, exemplar PIA reports conducted by other UK government departments or a list of approved consultants with suitable expertise, the ONS resorted to consulting PIA reports conducted by public bodies in New Zealand and the United States.[42] At the time, there appeared to be a clear PIA "skills gap" within UK organisations and a need for PIA processes to be incorporated within the professional training of those responsible for leading the assessment, for example, through

---

[39] ONS, op. cit., fn. 38 p. 6.

[40] Ibid., p. 5.

[41] Telephone conversation, ONS representative, August 2010.

[42] The ONS representative was aware of a PIA report conducted by the Department of Finance and Personnel in Northern Ireland. However, it related to a vastly different topic – a review of domestic rating systems, with a view to encouraging various groups to take up domestic rate reliefs. See Department of Finance and Personnel (Northern Ireland), *Review of Domestic Rating Data Sharing Privacy Impact Assessment (PIA)*, Bangor, 2008.

Managing Successful Programmes, a project management course taught at the UK's National School of Government.

In addition, the ONS expressed disappointment with the response to its stakeholder consultation. In spite of receiving a list of civil society organisations from the ICO, and issuing direct invitations to these and related bodies, representatives from only two groups attended the consultation event (with another individual contributing via e-mail) and neither provided particularly meaningful feedback. This experience suggests the need for a clearer, more consistent process for ensuring wider societal engagement with PIAs, particularly in the early stages of projects. This could be achieved through more innovative means of publicising ongoing PIAs, possibly via a dedicated portal or one-stop shop. This would raise the profile of PIAs, particularly if organisations are also encouraged to publish Plain Language PIA reports, and increase the obligation for civil society groups to participate in policy processes affecting citizens' personal privacy.

On the whole, the ONS reported that conducting the PIA process did not cause it to uncover anything "unexpected" in its approach to the 2011 census. In part, this may be due to its existing adherence to a series of rigorous, well-established rolling consultation processes in preparation for each upcoming census. Nevertheless, the PIA did prove helpful in "pulling together" various strands of the ONS's work and providing further evidence (through publication of a PIA report) that, as an organisation, it was taking privacy seriously. This was reflected in the section in the ONS PIA report relating to the legal basis for the 2011 census, which was stated to owe the most to the ICO PIA handbook.[43] Finally, the ONS was conscious of the largely retrospective nature of the PIA conducted. In some respects, this was unavoidable due to the PIA handbook being published so far into the ONS's own internal review process for the 2011 census. Nevertheless, the ONS stated that, with hindsight, it would have consulted with the ICO and engaged with stakeholders at a much earlier stage in process, recognising that there is little point in involving these groups unless they have a realistic opportunity to alter the design and implementation of the project.

9.5 Lessons Learnt

The report commissioned by the ICO[44] noted that PIAs were generally perceived to be more effective when

- they offer a prospective identification of privacy risks *before* systems and programmes are put in place;
- they assess the proposed initiatives within a framework which takes into account the broader set of community values and expectations about privacy;

---

[43] Telephone conversation, op. cit., fn. 44.

[44] ICO, *Privacy Impact Assessments: International Study...*, op. cit., fn. 3, pp. 29–30.

- they refer to an entire process of assessment of privacy risks rather than a statement or end-product;
- they have, and are perceived to have, the potential to alter proposed initiatives in order to mitigate privacy risks;
- their scope and depth are sensitive to a number of crucial variables: the size of the organisation, the sensitivity of the personal data, the forms of risk, the intrusiveness of the technology;
- they are part of a system of incentives, sanctions and review, and/or where they are embedded in project workflows or quality assurance processes, as is common with other forms of risk assessment;
- the individuals charged with completing PIAs not only have good programme knowledge, but also have access to multidisciplinary expertise from a variety of perspectives – privacy law and practice, information security, records management and other functional specialists as appropriate;
- the PIA tool is accessible, readily available and easy to access, and the process involved is flexible;
- there is a process of formal or informal external review either by central agencies or privacy oversight bodies;
- there is a strong advocacy role played by the relevant oversight body;
- there is external consultation with outsiders affected by the initiative. Public consultation is often advised;
- there is transparency, and the resulting statements or reports are published. Openness of process and output enhances trust in the initiative being proposed.

Some initial observations on these points from the UK context can be made. The available evidence suggests that ICO has clearly worked very hard, both in public and behind the scenes, to promote the use of PIAs; to seek and utilise feedback to make the handbook more user friendly; and to encourage government agencies which have undertaken PIAs to make their reports public. The focus of the ICO's work has been government, and it appears that there has been relatively little interaction with the private sector. Criticism could perhaps be levelled at the ICO with regard to the review of Phorm's business undertaken by 80/20 Thinking Ltd. (see above), where a clear public statement why an *ex post facto* review of an existing business practice should not be viewed as a PIA would have been useful, but was not forthcoming. The Phorm example also suggests that there was, initially at least, a paucity of expertise on PIAs available to organisations wishing to undertake them, and that this, depending on one's perspective on that particular instance, could mean that an organisation might misunderstand the purpose of the process, or might cynically seek to mischaracterise it. The last three years have seen a considerable upturn in consultants claiming PIA expertise, and organisations such as the Enterprise Privacy Group have been instrumental in helping government departments tackle PIAs for complex and potentially controversial projects.

In terms of guidance, the Ministry of Justice is responsible for advising government departments, and has recently published a short guidance document on handling PIAs.[45] However, the Ministry of Justice does not itself review departmental PIA processes or reports, and may not be informed when PIAs are undertaken. As such, detailed data protection responsibilities, including establishing PIA processes, are routinely devolved to individual departments. There does not currently appear to be any central co-ordination of officials or civil servants with PIA experience across government departments; any central guidance as to the type of projects that would fall within the "mandatory" PIA requirement; or any central guidance on appropriate or approved consultants. Based on the experience of organisations in other jurisdictions, particularly the Canadian federal jurisdiction, it seems likely that there will continue to be a PIA skills gap both within UK organisations and in the consultancy market going forward. Encouraging departments to share PIA tools, templates and frameworks across government will help to overcome that gap and hasten the spread of PIA good practice and innovation.

The UK has no formal process of external review by central agencies or by the ICO. As noted above, the ICO has played a key advisory role, but would unlikely be able to take on a formal scrutiny role, at least in the form the regulator currently takes. As a result, its role has been primarily in advising on methodology and helping organisations to embed PIA processes in existing practices. Following the Data Handling Review, the Cabinet Office has responsibility for monitoring the use of PIAs in government, although it is not clear exactly how it intends to carry out this monitoring and/or enforcement role. As such, there is insufficient evidence at present to determine whether or not the ad hoc processes of review currently in place are, or will be, effective at ensuring that government agencies fully engage, or engage effectively, with the PIA process. While any move to a mandatory review of PIAs is highly unlikely, a requirement that government departments provide notification and/or submission of outputs including PIA reports to either the Cabinet office, or the ICO, would facilitate oversight by allowing them to request and review selected PIAs of particular interest, and to engage in more targeted departmental, sectoral or government-wide compliance audits.

The focus on departmental responsibility, the apparent lack of PIA cross-fertilisation across departmental boundaries, and what appears to be relatively "hands-off" oversight raise questions about the current ability of governmental PIA processes to deal with privacy issues at a strategic level. In other words, how would a department approach a decision to create or adapt a system or policy, which arises from the actions of a higher level of government, e.g., the Executive or Parliament, or a decision where the carrying out of policy requires inter or multi-departmental input? For example, the policy behind plans to share data across government departments in the UK may come from the Executive, and require implementing measures across a number of departments. If each department is responsible for its own PIA process, then there is a risk that privacy failures that arise directly from the Executive decision, or from issues that are not the specific responsibility of any

---

[45] Ministry of Justice, *Undertaking Privacy Impact Assessments: The Data Protection Act 1998,* London, 2010. http://www.justice.gov.uk/guidance/docs/pia-guidance-08-10.pdf

one department, are not appropriately addressed. Another problem may arise where the cumulative effect of programmes initiated by different departments upon the individual are not addressed. For example, Department A seeks to initiate a project involving an individual's personal data. Before doing so, they carry out a departmental PIA. Their PIA alerts them to the privacy risks for individuals of their particular project but, in the absence of knowledge about projects in other Departments, may not take account of the cumulative risk posed by that collection in combination with the collections of personal information by Departments B, C and D.

Although the value of "inward-facing" use of PIAs to inform management risk assessments appears to be increasingly established, at least in government agencies, the use of PIAs for "public-facing" activities seems much less developed. This may be due to the fact that the ICO has emphasised the self-assessment nature of PIAs, with the focus on process and not on generating documentation for public review. Currently, obtaining information about the conduct of PIAs, or information relating to specific PIA outcomes, is far from easy. There may well be "over 300 Privacy Impact Assessments ... started across central government and their agencies",[46] but there is little evidence of that activity available to the public. Equally, it appears that the paucity of PIA-related information and reports is depriving other government agencies of a potentially valuable source of information, which may result in departments having to "reinvent the wheel" when setting up PIA processes. There are some publicly available PIA reports, for example:

- The UK Border Agency's PIA report on the exchange of fingerprint information with immigration authorities in Australia, Canada, New Zealand and the United States (38 pages) is readily available from their website, and it is clearly envisaged that continuing public feedback will be part of the "evergreening" process for the document, i.e., it is intended that the document will be used as a focus for ongoing privacy evaluation[47];
- The National Policing Improvement Agency's PIA report on the Police National Database (42 pages) is available from their website, and was published with the intent that it might stimulate further input, as the initial PIA process received "a low number of responses" from a "narrow range of organisations"[48];
- The Office for National Statistics' PIA report on the 2011 Census in England and Wales (62 pages) is available from their website. This report is less obviously geared towards continuing public engagement, possibly due to the ONS's existing policy of engaging in ongoing consultation on the census.[49]

But these examples seem to be the exception rather than the rule across government. While it is possible that information on ongoing and completed PIAs

---

[46] ICO, *Information Commissioner's Annual Report 2009/10*, op. cit., fn. 5, p. 23.

[47] UKBA, *Report of a Privacy Impact Assessment conducted by the UK Border Agency in relation to the High Value Data Sharing Protocol amongst the immigration authorities of the Five Country Conference*, UK Border Agency, London, 2009.

[48] NPIA, *Police National Database – Privacy Impact Assessment Report*, National Policing Improvement Agency, London, 2009. http://www.npia.police.uk/en/docs/Privacy_Impact_Assessment.pdf

[49] ONS, op. cit., fn. 38.

could be obtained by the public via freedom of information requests,[50] the apparent reluctance on the part of government agencies to promote and disseminate their PIA outcomes would seem to run counter to the public engagement ethos that underpins the ICO's initiatives.

In the public sector, more thought needs to be given to developing a coherent approach to PIA consultation and dissemination. A key weakness in other jurisdictions has been the generally unstructured approach to these issues. At present in the UK, as elsewhere, there is:

- no consistent process for ensuring effective consultation with stakeholders, notably the general public, e.g., a register of ongoing PIAs, consultation periods and relevant contact details;
- no consistency in reporting formats for PIAs, whether in draft or completed, e.g., a PIA might be reported in a detailed 62-page document, or simply mentioned in a paragraph in a general impact statement[51]; and,
- no strategy for ensuing that, where PIA decisions and reports are made publicly available, they are easily accessible, perhaps from a centralised point, e.g., the UK Office of Public Sector Information (OPSI) or the ICO.

If the public are unaware of consultations, are unable to effectively parse reports or compare the relative quality of reports from different agencies, or are unable to easily access reports, then poor public engagement and ineffective tripartite regulation (i.e., through the interaction of the regulator, the regulated entity and the public or public representative bodies) of agency practices are almost inevitable.

The issues raised above are not exclusive to the UK experience of PIAs. In fact, they are virtually all issues that have arisen in other jurisdictions, enhanced in some cases by the peculiarities or particularities of the UK governmental and regulatory systems. Nor are these issues insurmountable, although overcoming them will likely involve a considerable degree of political will, careful administrative co-ordination and thoughtful public engagement.

---

[50] Subject, of course, to the wide exemptions granted to government departments in the FOI Act 2000.

[51] See, for example:

- Department of Communities and Local Government, *Making Better Use of Energy Performance Data: Impact Assessment*, Consultation, March 2010. http://www.communities. gov.uk/documents/planningandbuilding/pdf/1491281.pdf
- Department for Transport, *Impact Assessment on the Use of Security Scanners at UK Airports*, Consultation, March 2010. http://www.dft.gov.uk/consultations/closed/2010-23/ia.pdf

9.6 Future Developments

We would be on rather firmer ground when assessing the future of PIAs in the UK if there was greater certainty about the situation in the present. However, there are several potential drivers that could significantly influence the future role and scope of PIAs:

- The international drive for data privacy mechanisms that encourage proactive regulation via targeted and appropriate systems of accountability;
- The influence of globalisation, combined with jurisdiction-dissolving technologies, such as the World Wide Web, social networking tools and cloud computing;
- The interest of the private sector in creating and using systems to facilitate accountability and compliance.

It is no secret, as noted in the Introduction above, that there is dissatisfaction with the current EU data privacy framework. Both the UK ICO[52] and the European Commission[53] have recently produced reports examining possible future developments in the EU approach to data privacy. One heavily promoted approach is the concept of "privacy by design", defined as "the philosophy and approach of embedding privacy into the design specifications of various technologies".[54] Privacy by design (PbD) is premised on several key principles, notably:

1. Recognition of the core privacy principles as the default position in a system or process;
2. Recognition of the organisational benefits of addressing privacy interests and concerns proactively and pre-emptively;
3. Early mitigation of privacy concerns when developing IT systems and business practices, throughout the entire information life cycle;
4. Embedding of privacy as a core component in the design and architecture of IT systems and business practices, so as to enhance both privacy and system functionality;
5. Keeping the interests of the individual uppermost by offering strong privacy defaults, appropriate notice and empowering user-friendly options such as privacy-enhancing technologies (PETs);

---

[52] Robinson, N., H. Graux, M. Botterman and L. Valeri, *Review of the European Data Protection Directive*, Information Commissioner's Office, Wilmslow, 2009. http://www.ico.gov.uk/upload/documents/library/data_protection/detailed_specialist_guides/review_of_eu_dp_directive.pdf

[53] Korff, Douwe, and Ian Brown, *Different Approaches to New Privacy Challenges in Particular in the Light of Technological Developments*, European Commission, DG Justice, Freedom and Security, Brussels, 2010. http://ec.europa.eu/justice/policies/privacy/docs/studies/new_privacy_challenges/final_report_en.pdf

[54] OIPC, op. cit., fn. 1.

6. Business practices and technologies should be operated according to stated promises and objectives, and subject to independent verification;
7. Knowledge of the organisation and of the related privacy sub-domains (legal compliance, technology, business operations, customer relations) is critical and requires qualified leadership and professional input.

As such, PbD as a philosophy appears very much in tune with the light-touch approach that the UK ICO has tended to adopt as a regulator (although the lack, until recently, of a "big stick" may have played a role in this), and the ICO has already indicated support for the PbD approach. Creating a regulatory system premised on PbD would be simpler if PIAs were to have already become a familiar part of the UK data privacy regime, not least because there would be a greater pool of expertise and organisational and technical support to draw upon. Such a regime would also be attractive to organisations seeking to utilise developing information technologies such as cloud computing.

> Cloud computing is essentially Internet-based computing, whereby a large pool of easily usable and accessible virtualised resources (such as hardware, development platforms and/or services) can be dynamically reconfigured to adjust to a variable load (scale), allowing for an optimum resource utilisation.[55]

While cloud computing technology is potentially extremely cost effective, the nature of the technology means that a data controller processing personal data "in the cloud" will often:

- not have control over the machine and software that is being used (outsourcing);
- not be able to control and may not know where in the world the data is being processed (offshoring);
- not be the sole user of the hardware, platform or service (multi-tenancy/virtualisation);
- be in a position where they may be switched automatically between systems owned by different suppliers automatically according to demand (autonomic technology).

These features of cloud computing clearly present a significant challenge to data controllers seeking to adhere to the requirements found under current legislation, notably the restrictions on cross-border data transfer. A PbD regulatory framework underpinned by effective PIAs could be the basis for a regime based on the use of a combination of privacy policies and contractual terms to create accountability in the

---

[55] Tancock, David, Siani Pearson and Andrew Charlesworth, "A Privacy Impact Assessment Tool for Cloud Computing", in *Proceedings of the Second IEEE International Conference on Cloud Computing Technology and Science (CloudCom 2010)*, Indiana University, USA, 30 November – 3 December 2010, pp. 667–676. http://ieeexplore.ieee.org/xpl/freeabs_all.jsp?arnumber=5708516

form of transparent, enforceable commitments to responsible data handling.[56] The tools that might support such a framework are already under development, ranging from automated decision-support tools to aid organisations in undertaking effective PIAs,[57] to trusted computing tools for security and audit[58] and trusted virtual platforms.[59] There is thus an incentive for the private sector to build upon the early work on PIAs conducted by the public sector in the UK to the potential benefit of both.

9.7 Conclusion

The UK Information Commissioner's Office's championing of the incorporation of PIAs into public and private sector management processes, via its commissioning of the initial research and the incremental development of its PIA handbook, has come at a particularly fortuitous time. A "perfect storm" of technological and business innovation, high profile and large-scale personal data leaks, and decreasing public confidence in existing data protection and privacy laws has led to increasing international interest in seeking more effective and efficient means to protect personal data and privacy. The ICO's work has thus been at the forefront of the next generation of PIA process development, and is being drawn upon by early PIA adopters, such as the Ontario Information and Privacy Commissioner (OIPC), when they come to review their existing models and guidance. The ICO has also been keen not to rest on its laurels, with the second iteration of the PIA handbook appearing after only two years as the ICO seeks to draw upon and incorporate feedback from its users.

In terms of adoption of PIAs, it appears that this has primarily, if not exclusively, occurred in the public sector, as a result of the post-Data Handling Review policy. Whilst some private sector companies do engage in PIA-like processes, in general, the private sector has up till now shown little enthusiasm for the ICO's handbook. Examples from other jurisdictions (e.g., the Royal Bank of Canada) suggest that the process envisaged in the handbook is considerably more detailed than current private sector requirements.

To the outside onlooker, the PIA picture within the public sector appears still to be fragmented and confused. In contrast to the activities of the ICO, the Cabinet Office and Ministry of Justice have been slow to establish a framework to enable

---

[56] Pearson, S., and A. Charlesworth, "Accountability as a Way Forward for Privacy Protection in the Cloud", in M.G. Jaatun, G. Zhao and C. Rong (eds.), *CloudCom 2009: Proceedings*, Lecture Notes in Computer Science, 5931/2009, Springer, 2009, pp. 131–144.

[57] Tancock et al., op. cit., fn. 60.

[58] Pearson, S., "Trusted Computing: Strengths, Weaknesses and Further Opportunities for Enhancing Privacy, Trust Management", in Peter Herrmann, Valérie Issarny and Simon Shiu (eds.), *iTrust 2005, Proceedings*, Lecture Notes in Computer Science, 3477/2005, Springer, 2005, pp. 305–320.

[59] Dalton, C., D. Plaquin, W. Weidner, D. Kuhlmann, B. Balacheff and R. Brown, "Trusted Virtual Platforms: A Key Enabler for Converged Client Devices", *Operating Systems Review*, Vol. 43, No. 1, 2009, pp. 36–43.

departments to plan, conduct and review PIAs in a manner which is consistent across government. This is problematic on two levels. First, the current situation appears to be an inefficient use of government resources, with departments apparently unable to draw effectively upon each other's prior experience and outputs. Second, if there is a lack of cross-governmental communication regarding PIAs, then their use as an effective mechanism for strategic review of privacy risks is significantly decreased.

Given the relative paucity of evidence currently available, it is difficult to provide a clear assessment of the state of play with regard to PIAs in the UK. The apparently inward-facing nature of the majority of PIAs suggests that, as with PIAs in some other jurisdictions, e.g., those carried out within the Ontario provincial government, PIAs are going to be used primarily as risk assessment tools. If this becomes the primary function of UK PIAs, then it is likely that the UK will fail to capture the wider public benefits of more open PIA processes.

It is particularly important that organisations carrying out PIAs are not discouraged by low response rates to, or lack of wide public engagement with, early stage PIAs. Previously, the public have had no great expectation of consultation in many areas covered by PIAs, so it is unsurprising that current participation is limited. Wider availability of user-friendly PIA reports, combined with innovation in public engagement strategies should, over time, create a greater expectation amongst the public of involvement in policy decisions which affect their privacy. Seeking more extensive public engagement in both consultation and dissemination may also help to prevent PIAs from devolving into yet another administrative "box-ticking" exercise.

Chapter 10
PIA Requirements and Privacy Decision-Making in US Government Agencies

Kenneth A. Bamberger and Deirdre K. Mulligan

10.1 Introduction

It is notoriously difficult to make organisations take into account "secondary mandates" – values at best orthogonal to, and at worst in tension with, the institution's primary mission.[1] This is true when the goal is to force business organisations to prioritise legal goals such as market fairness or consumer safety along with their pursuit of profit. It is equally true when the aim is to force government agencies primarily responsible for security, transportation or the efficient administration of social benefits, to consider secondary goals, such as environmental protection or policy-making transparency.[2]

This difficulty arises in force in the context of legislative attempts to force administrative agencies to promote privacy protection while they pursue their primary policy objectives. In the US legal context, such attempts have taken the form of the requirement, enacted as part of the E-Government Act of 2002,[3] that administrative agencies conduct privacy impact assessments (PIAs) when developing or procuring information technology systems that include personally identifiable information.[4] Recognising that "rapid evolution of information technology has raised questions

---

[1] Bamberger, Kenneth A., "Regulation as Delegation: Private Firms, Decisionmaking and Accountability in the Administrative State", *Duke Law Journal*, Vol. 56, No. 2, November 2006, pp. 377–468 (discussing systemic barriers to incorporating secondary goals in organisational decision-making).

[2] See generally DeShazo, J.R., and Jody Freeman, "Public Agencies As Lobbyists", *Columbia Law Review*, Vol. 105, No. 8, December 2005, pp. 2219 (discussing the tension between primary and secondary mandates).

[3] Pub L No 107-347, 116 Stat 2899.

[4] 44 USC § 3501 note (2000 & Supp 2002) (requiring agencies to conduct a PIA before "developing or procuring information technology that collects, maintains, or disseminates information that is in an identifiable form").

K.A. Bamberger (✉)
University of California, Berkeley, CA 94720-7200, USA
e-mail: kbamberger@law.berkeley.edu

D. Wright, P. De Hert (eds.), *Privacy Impact Assessment*, Law, Governance and Technology Series 6, DOI 10.1007/978-94-007-2543-0_10,
© Springer Science+Business Media B.V. 2012

about whether personal information is adequately protected",[5] the US Congress imposed a PIA requirement both to new technology systems and to "new privacy risks" created when changing existing systems. The Office of Management and Budget (OMB) guidance promulgated pursuant to the statute mandates that PIAs include a risk assessment that specifically identifies and evaluates potential threats to individual privacy, discusses alternatives, identifies appropriate risk mitigation measures and articulates the rationale for the final design choice.[6]

The PIA requirement embodies an approach intended explicitly to "mitigate agency tunnel vision or mission orientation" by requiring that agencies consider privacy goals that are not directly within their primary statutory purpose.[7] Yet this process-based approach faces particular problems with agency reluctance to comply. At a minimum, an agency's organic statute may embody a variety of goals – some that conflict directly with the secondary concern – to which administrators may legitimately point in justifying their actions internally and externally.[8] More significantly, process directives alone may make little headway in redirecting agency structures, cultures and decision-making routines geared to maximising the agency's primary mission.[9]

This chapter begins an inquiry into lessons from the US experience regarding ways in which the PIA requirement might, in fact, be implemented so as to "mitigate agency tunnel vision" and begin to integrate meaningful consideration of privacy concerns into agency structures, cultures and decision-making. It does this by considering the implementation of the PIA requirement by two different federal agencies considering the adoption radio frequency identification (RFID) technology, which allows a data chip – one that can be accessed remotely by wireless technology – to be attached to or inserted into a product, animal or person. The two different approaches reflect the highly inconsistent adherence to the PIA mandate across agencies, and even between programs within a single agency.

---

[5] Great Falls Historic District Study Act of 2001, S Rep No 107-74, 107th Congress, 2nd Session 8, 2002.

[6] Office of Management and Budget, *OMB Guidance for Implementing the Privacy Provisions of the E-Government Act of 2002*, 26 September 2003 (providing information for heads of executive departments and agencies regarding the requirements of the E-Government Act of 2002). http://www.whitehouse.gov/omb/memoranda/m03-22.html

[7] Mashaw, Jerry L., "Norms, Practices, and the Paradox of Difference: A Preliminary Inquiry into Agency Statutory Interpretation", *Administrative Law Review*, Vol. 57, No. 2, 2005, p. 509 (arguing that agencies, like courts, must fit statutory language into the overarching legal framework).

[8] See DeShazo Freeman, op. cit., fn. 2, p. 2220 (citing examples of "[a]gencies frequently resolv[ing]... interstatutory conflicts by prioritizing their primary mission and letting their secondary obligations fall by the wayside"); Clarke, Jeanne Nienaber, and Daniel C. McCool, *Staking Out the Terrain: Power Differential among Natural Resource Management Agencies*, second edition, State University of New York Press, 1996, pp. 4–5 (noting that some agencies may not easily incorporate the purposes of new legislation, even when they accord with the agency's original mission).

[9] See discussion at fn. 25–28 below.

In the first example, the Department of State (DOS), proposed a Rule incorporating RFID technology into US passports. Its one and one-half page "e-Passport" PIA, consisting of seven paragraphs, failed to discuss the technical aspects of the program, alternative technologies, risks or their mitigation. The program was ultimately adopted with significant modifications late in the process of program development, but with criticism as to its security vulnerabilities and privacy risks.

By contrast, the Department of Homeland Security (DHS) produced a 48-page, single-spaced PIA during its adoption of the same technology[10] in the United States Visitor and Immigrant Status Indicator Technology (US-VISIT) program. The PIA, produced early enough in the process to influence design decisions in addition to policies, detailed the system architecture, privacy threats and mitigation methods, an explanation of the design choice, and a plan for implementing any necessary additional privacy and security measures on an ongoing basis. The program, though later abandoned for other reasons, was adopted as proposed and reflected these assessments.[11]

---

[10] The particular standards used varied (e-passport ISO 14443, US-VISIT) but the basic technology is the same.

[11] Section 7208(d) of the Intelligence Reform and Terrorism Prevention Act of 2004 required US-VISIT to collect biometric exit data from all individuals who are required to provide biometric entry data. Pub L No 108-458, 118 Stat 3638, 3819, codified at 8 USC § 1365b(d) (Supp 2004). In response, DHS proposed Increment 2C, which intended to use passive RFID tags embedded in the I-94 arrival/departure form to track entry and exit of foreign visitors at land border point-of-entry crossings. DHS, *Notice of Privacy Act System of Records*, 70 Fed Reg 38699, 38699–700 (2005). The embedded tag stored no personally identifiable data; instead, each tag contained a unique identifier that was linked to a traveller's information in the US-VISIT database. DHS conducted a feasibility study (final report issued 21 January 2005) and commenced testing of the proposed system. See Government Accountability Office (GAO), *Homeland Security: Prospects For Biometric US-VISIT Exit Capability Remain Unclear*, GAO-07-1044T, 28 June 2007, p. 10 (pointing to reliability problems in tests of the proposed system at five points of entry). http://www.gao.gov/new.items/d071044t.pdf. DHS, US-VISIT Increment 2C RFID Feasibility Study Final Report, 21 January 2005 (proposing recommendations based upon the feasibility study). http://www.dhs.gov/xlibrary/assets/foia/US-VISIT_RFID feasibility_redacted-051106.pdf. A GAO Report issued in January 2007 noted that in addition to technical deficiencies with the proposed system, "the technology that had been tested cannot meet a key goal of US-VISIT—ensuring that visitors who enter the country are the same ones who leave." GAO, *Border Security: US-VISIT Program Faces Strategic, Operational, and Technological Challenges at Land Ports of Entry*, GAO-07-378T, 31 January 2007, p. 21 (claiming that DHS's proposed RFID system cannot provide the needed biometric-matching capability). http://www.gao.gov/new.items/d07378t.pdf. DHS Secretary Michael Chertoff announced in February 2007 while testifying before the House Homeland Security Committee that DHS was abandoning the program due to its inability to meet its primary objective of identifying the flow of I-94 carriers across borders. See UPI, "Chertoff: RFID program to be abandoned", 9 February 2007. The authors believe the intense examination of the program's objective, performance and risks that led to its abandonment was greatly facilitated by the PIA process and the ongoing examination and attention to the privacy and security issues posed by the program by the Privacy and Integrity Advisory Committee, Congress and the public.

An examination of the practices of these two US agencies, interviews with agency decision-makers involved in these processes and insights from the US experience with the parallel context of environmental impact statements offer a starting point for developing hypotheses about the role of internal agency structure, culture, personnel and professional expertise in whether the PIA process can be meaningfully integrated as an element of bureaucratic decision-making. Specifically, they suggest the importance of continued research into the role of alternate methods of external accountability as a means for strengthening the hand of privacy officers internally, the importance of substantive experts combined with internal processes for insinuating privacy into daily practice, and the need for status and structures that respect the different roles privacy professionals play in protecting privacy during policy-making and integrating privacy into the bureaucracy.

10.2 The US PIA Requirement and Its Implementation

In the face of increased digitisation of information, Congress created a PIA requirement in the 2002 E-Government Act. The PIA provisions mandated, in the words of the bill's Senate Report, that agencies publicly "explain" – by means of a PIA – how they "take. . . into account privacy considerations when purchasing and creating new information systems, and when initiating collections of information".[12] "[T]he greater personalization of government services," the Report continued, "need not impinge on personal privacy, if the federal government takes steps to address privacy concerns when first designing systems."[13]

Specifically, the Act required that PIAs be conducted prior to the adoption of new technology, that they be reviewed by an agency's chief information officer or equivalent official and that they be made available to the public online if "practicable".[14] It directed OMB to establish guidelines to ensure that PIAs are commensurate with the size of the information system, the sensitivity of information and the privacy risk.[15] The resulting guidance mandated that PIAs, in addition to providing a public description of the system, contain a risk assessment that specifically identifies and evaluates potential threats to individual privacy, discusses alternatives and identifies the appropriate risk mitigation measures for each, articulates the rationale for the final design, and identifies what choices the agency made "as a result of performing

---

[12] S Rep No107-74, op. cit., fn. 5, pp. 28–29.

[13] Ibid., p. 28 (addressing one of two major concerns in privacy policy, the other being clarity of privacy notices).

[14] See 44 USC § 3501 note.

[15] Ibid.

the PIA".[16] The guidance further provides that PIAs be submitted to OMB as part of the agency's budget review process.[17]

Congress's inclusion of the PIA requirement engendered significant optimism. PIAs, the Senate Report stated, "are increasingly being recognized as an important means of ensuring that privacy protection is being taken into account".[18] Echoing that language, then-OMB Director Josh Bolten declared that PIAs – in combination with other existing requirements – would "ensure" that information "is handled in a manner that maximizes both privacy and security".[19] By both requiring agencies to weigh privacy concerns along with their primary substantive mandates and rendering their decision processes more transparent to outsiders, privacy advocates believed the PIA requirement would "force" agencies to "act responsibly . . . [and] ultimately lead to better-designed and more user-oriented government IT projects".[20]

Despite these lofty goals, however, implementation of the PIA requirement has been neither swift nor uniform. The self-reported agency data included in OMB's most recent report to Congress indicated that only 56 per cent of those agencies reporting had developed and documented an adequate PIA policy, and fully implemented it, and was managing and operating a process for performing adequate PIAs.[21]

Moreover, more individualised analyses suggest that these self-reported figures mask deeper qualitative non-compliance issues with the PIA mandate. GAO reports, for example, have documented: (1) a number of specific failures to comply with privacy requirements for programs covered by the E-Government Act's terms,[22] (2)

---

[16] Office of Management and Budget, op. cit., 2003, fn. 6, p. 4 (providing PIA implementation details for administrative agencies). The guidance further specifies that PIA requirements apply not just to new information systems, but also when systems are converted from paper-based to electronic, when anonymous information is converted to an identifiable form, and when new uses of an existing IT system, including application of new technologies that significantly change how information is managed.

[17] Ibid., p. 1 (imposing a deadline for PIAs for purposes of budgetary requests).

[18] S Rep No 107-74, op. cit., fn. 5, pp. 28–29 (noting the importance of PIAs to supplement the Privacy Act of 1974).

[19] OMB Guidance, op. cit., fn. 6, p. 1 (noting that the primary objective of the E-Government Act complements the National Strategy to Secure Cyberspace).

[20] Center for Democracy and Technology, Statement before the Senate Government Affairs Committee, 11 July 2001 (arguing that the Privacy Act of 1974 had become obsolete and that PIAs could help reassure users of online government services). http://www.cdt.org/testimony/010711cdt.shtml

[21] Office of Management and Budget, Fiscal Year 2009 Report to Congress on Implementation of The Federal Information Security Management Act of 2002, p. 22. http://www.whitehouse.gov/sites/default/files/omb/assets/egov_docs/FY09_FISMA.pdf

[22] Government Accountability Office, *Homeland Security: Continuing Attention to Privacy Concerns is Needed as Programs Are Developed* ("Homeland Security Report"), GAO-07-630T, 21 March 2007, pp. 10–15 (concluding that "DHS did not assess privacy risks in developing a data mining tool known as ADVISE . . . as required by the E-Government Act of 2002," which created the "risk that uses of ADVISE in systems containing personal information could require costly

insufficient consideration of privacy concerns in existing PIAs that fail to satisfy the statute,[23] and (3) highly "uneven" compliance on basic Privacy Act requirements.[24]

10.3 Challenges Inherent in the PIA Model

The inconsistency in agency implementation of the PIA requirement is not surprising, as both procedural and substantive elements pose challenges to oversight of such an approach's effectiveness. First, PIAs, like many process-oriented reforms, must be incorporated into agency decision-making and often require effective oversight to ensure compliance. Second, oversight of PIAs is difficult because of the opacity of technological decisions and possible conflict between privacy and politics; in this way, the substantive context in which privacy decisions arise frequently interferes with those decisions' accountability.

10.3.1 Limits of Process

Organisational theory suggests numerous ways that externally-imposed process requirements face high hurdles as means to ensure the robust and consistent integration of secondary values, like privacy in an agency's decisions about its primary mission.

In general, organisations shape their behaviour in order to secure external resources.[25] Through compliance with procedural requirements, agencies convey the legitimacy of their behaviour to outsiders. External perception of legitimacy expands the agencies' social licence – a basic "resource" – providing it with greater freedom to self-direct its operations.

---

and potentially duplicative retrofitting at a later date to add the needed controls"). http://www.gao. gov/new.items/d07630t.pdf. See also ibid., pp. 18–19 (noting that DHS's failure even to comply with Privacy Act notice for "Secure Flight", a program to evaluate passengers before they board an aircraft on domestic flights).

[23] Government Accountability Office, *Data Mining: Agencies Have Taken Key Steps to Protect Privacy in Selected Efforts, but Significant Compliance Issues Remain*, GAO-05-866, August 2005, pp. 24–27 (noting that IRS, Small Business Administration, and Risk Management Agency PIAs did not adequately address the statutory requirements regarding their data mining efforts and that the FBI conducted no PIA, in violation of agency regulations). http://www.gao.gov/new.items/ d05866.pdf. See also Government Accountability Office, *Homeland Security Report*, op. cit., fn. 22, pp.17–18 (reporting that privacy guidelines developed for implementation of The Intelligence Reform and Terrorism Prevention Act of 2004 "provide only a high-level framework for privacy protection").

[24] Government Accountability Office, *Privacy Act: OMB Leadership Needed to Improve Agency Compliance*, GAO-03-304, June 2003, p. 14 (reporting compliance with requirements as low as 70 per cent). http://www.gao.gov/new.items/d03304.pdf

[25] Pfeffer, Jeffrey, and Gerald Salancik, *The External Control of Organizations: A Resource Dependence Perspective*, Harper and Row, 1978, pp. 51–52.

Yet the signalling value of a PIA – as with other externally process mandates – is coupled with the reality that meaningful engagement with the PIA process "may be disruptive to the internal workings of the organization".[26] Indeed, disruption of business as usual and substantive reorientation are among Congress's goals in legislating the PIA process in the first place. However, the tension between agency mission and external mandates can result in the "ceremonial" performance of mandated processes, whereby an organisation adapts external mandates in ways that most easily achieve the appearance of legitimacy, while minimising the dislocation of existing practices and priorities.[27] At its worst, external process mandates may result in procedures that signal formal compliance but, because they are treated as an "add-on" distinct from other functions or because they are assigned to a sub-unit that is detached from core agency policy-making, avoid fundamental behavioural change. In this way, process directives in and of themselves may make little headway in redirecting agency structures, cultures and decision-making routines geared to maximising the agency's primary mission.[28]

10.3.2 Substantive Barriers to Oversight

Several factors specific to the PIA context, moreover, create obstacles to the type of public monitoring that can facilitate traditional oversight by the political branches and the courts: the contemporary politics of privacy, a lack of decision openness and the opacity of decisions about technology.[29]

10.3.2.1 Political Barriers to Implementation

Expending political capital on privacy can be risky. While polls consistently reveal deep concern about information abuse and support for privacy protections in general,[30] individual decisions frequently counterpose privacy against two other

---

[26] Heimer, Carol A., "Explaining Variation in the Impact of Law: Organizations, Institutions, and Professions", in Austin Sarat and Susan S. Silbey (eds.), *Studies In Law, Politics, And Society*, Vol. 15, 1995, pp. 29–59 [41].

[27] Meyer, John W., and Brian Rowan, "Institutionalized Organizations: Formal Structure as Myth and Ceremony", *American Journal of Sociology*, Vol. 83, 1977, pp. 340–363 [pp. 340–41].

[28] Bamberger, Kenneth A., "Regulation as Delegation: Private Firms, Decisionmaking and Accountability in the Administrative State", *Duke Law Journal*, Vol. 56, No. 2, November 2006, pp. 377–468 (discussing systemic barriers to incorporating secondary goals in organisational decision-making).

[29] Simitis, Spiros, "Reviewing Privacy in an Information Society", *University of Pennsylvania Law Review*, Vol. 135, No. 3, 1987, pp. 707–746 (discussing reasons why individual rights of action through the courts and executive and legislative oversight are insufficient to effect privacy protection with government, pointing to particular problems with access, technical knowledge and intensity of supervision).

[30] See, for example, Electronic Privacy Information Center, *Public Opinion on Privacy* (summarising various public opinion polls on the importance of privacy and concluding that there is "strong

powerful values: efficiency and security. The ideological and political pressures supporting each run deep. Technology is adopted, in large part, as a seemingly value-neutral means for promoting efficient and effective pursuit of already-legitimised public goals. Because of the presumption in favour of technology, it is politically risky to oppose new developments on grounds of privacy concerns.

Placing privacy in conflict with security raises even greater political hazard because of the immense risk of even a low-probability security event. The experience of former Deputy Attorney General Jamie Gorelick, blamed for the set of directives creating a "wall" prohibiting FBI and CIA co-ordination in light of civil liberties concerns – an act former Attorney General John Ashcroft called "the single greatest structural cause for September 11"[31] – stands as a salient cautionary tale. As one news network reminds, "no one wants to be the one who dropped the ball when, as predicted, terrorists strike again."[32]

The conflicts between privacy concerns and national security were heightened during the Bush administration. After taking office, President Bush did not preserve the chief privacy counsel position in OMB despite calls for a renewal of the position by advocacy groups.[33] The relegation of privacy to lower level policy analysts may help explain early inefficacies of the PIA program.

10.3.2.2 Lack of Decision Openness and Public Participation

Oversight of the PIA program is further weakened by the lack of public involvement in the PIA implementation process. A multi-country review of PIAs prepared for the UK Information Commissioner's Office echoed earlier findings of scholars in the context of the National Environmental Policy Act (NEPA) of 1969, concluding that external consultation with key stakeholders and the public enhances the effectiveness of PIAs. Noting divergence around consultation and publication requirements, the authors concluded that openness and transparency of process and publication of reports "enhances trust in the initiative being proposed".[34]

---

support among Americans for privacy rights in law to protect their personal information from government and commercial entities"). http://www.epic.org/privacy/survey/

[31] National Commission on Terrorist Attacks upon the United States, Tenth Public Hearing: Law Enforcement and the Intelligence Committee, Testimony of Attorney General John Ashcroft, 13 April 2004. http://www.9-11commission.gov/hearings/hearing10/ashcroft_statement.pdf

[32] Assuras, Thalia, and Joie Chen, "House and Senate Committees Will Begin Rare August Hearings", CBS News Transcripts, 24 July 2004 (discussing increased attention to intelligence reform following the release of the 9/11 Commission Report).

[33] Center for Democracy and Technology, "Public Interest Groups and Academics Call on Bush Administration to Fill Privacy Position", Press release, 16 April 2001 (reporting on concern from privacy advocacy groups over the vacant position). http://old.cdt.org/press/010416press.shtml

[34] Linden Consulting, *Privacy Impact Assessments: International Study of their Application and Effects*, prepared for the [UK] Information Commissioner's Office, October 2007, p. vii. http://www.ico.gov.uk/upload/documents/library/corporate/research_and_reports/privacy_impact_assessment_international_study.011007.pdf

Yet despite the US E-Government Act's explicit commitment to the production of PIAs before developing or purchasing technology systems, and to the publication of PIAs, it fails to provide for public consultation at any point in the PIA production. The development or procurement of information systems is often treated as a management issue and accomplished through means that do not require notice and comment. In those contexts, if the PIA is not made available to the public prior to development or procurement of the system, there is no vehicle for public participation before the technology has been purchased and implemented. Any participation after this point is, arguably, too late to be greatly effective. Additionally, a federal court has rejected the single Freedom of Information Act (FOIA) request by a privacy advocacy group for draft PIAs developed in advance of a proposed rulemaking on the very ground that those documents were "predecisional", and therefore fell within one of the established FOIA exemptions.[35]

Further, the lack of explicit mechanisms for public participation in the PIA process limits the opportunities for outside experts to assist the agency in identifying the privacy implications of often complex technological systems. Absent external direction or internal efforts to engage the public through a comment process or other means, public input is limited to the stage in which proposals and programs are already well developed. Relegated to this late stage, the comments – whether by experts or the general public – are more likely to result in revisions on the margins rather than fundamental switches in technology or architectural design.

Obscuring these decisions from public participation also makes it more difficult for the public to raise the alarm required for congressional activism. Not surprisingly, while the GAO – Congress' oversight arm – has issued a number of reports criticising privacy decisions ex post, Congress itself has not engaged, on the whole, in active monitoring of privacy decision-making.[36]

---

[35] See *Electronic Privacy Information Center v Transportation Security Administration*, 2006 WL 626925, *10 (DDC 2006) (rejecting a FOIA request by Electronic Privacy Information Center to obtain a PIA associated with the development by the Transportation Safety Authority of the Computer Assisted Passenger Profiling System (CAPPS II)).

[36] A LEXIS search of the *Congressional Record* database over the past 10 years for "privacy impact assessment" yields 53 hits; there are no colloquies or discussion of PIAs on the floor, and most of these hits are mentions in passing, or texts of bills and amendments. Only two hearings have even included any sustained discussion of PIAs, both in colloquy with DHS Privacy Officers. See Protection of Privacy in the DHS Intelligence Enterprise, Hearings before the Subcommittee on Intelligence, Information Sharing, and Terrorism Risk Assessment of the House Homeland Security Committee, 109th Congress, Second Session, 2006, in CQ Congressional Testimony (statement of Maureen Cooney, Acting Chief Privacy Officer, Department of Homeland Security) (describing how "the Privacy Office has worked to build privacy into the sinews of" DHS); Privacy in the Hands of the Government: The Privacy Officer for the Department of Homeland Security, Hearings before the Subcommittee of Commercial and Administrative Law of the House Committee on the Judiciary, 108th Congress, Second Session, 2004, in CQ Congressional Testimony (discussing the unavailability of PIAs for meaningful notice and comment). However, Senator Lieberman, author of the E-Government Act of 2002, and his staff have engaged in some oversight activities, the majority of which occurred at the staff level and off the public record. Some of the senator's work in this area is evident in press releases. See Senate Committee on

10.3.2.3 Opacity of Technical Decisions

Transparency concerns also arise from the technical nature of the information systems whose adoption the PIA process was designed to influence. In general, the problem of bureaucratic discretion increases along with information asymmetries between expert agencies and their overseers, including the general public.[37] These asymmetries can be particularly pronounced in this area because the debates that raise privacy concerns frequently involve technical standards that can be both procedurally and linguistically inaccessible.[38] These asymmetries are especially concerning because technology is often positioned as neutral with respect to values when, in fact, it can create and implement value decisions at least as effectively as more traditional forms of regulation.[39] Decisions about the design and deployment of technical systems can permit bureaucrats to cloak policy decisions and mask the exercise of discretion behind claims of technical neutrality and complex jargon.[40]

Homeland Security and Governmental Affairs, "DHS Violates Privacy Impact Requirements with US Visit Technology", Press release, 4 December 2003 (reporting Senator Lieberman's correspondence with then–DHS Secretary Tom Ridge and raising DHS's failure to conduct and make public privacy impact assessments for biometric technology). http://hsgac.senate.gov/public/index.cfm?FuseAction=Press.MajorityNews&ContentRecord_id=8103bcce-8436-4e87-82f4-fe04642e6db2&Region_id=&Issue_id=; Senate Committee on Homeland Security and Governmental Affairs, "Government Privacy Protections Fall Short, Lieberman Calls for Leadership, Greater Commitment of Resources", Press release, 30 July 2003 (reporting Senator Lieberman's criticism of the GAO for failing to protect privacy rights and his call to the Bush administration to show a greater commitment to privacy policy). http://hsgac.senate.gov/public/index.cfm?FuseAction=Press.MajorityNews&ContentRecord_id=96af45f1-8460-4a3b-aea0-7ef37c689403&Region_id=&Issue_id=

[37] Lupia, Arthur, and Mathew D. McCubbins, *The Democratic Dilemma: Can Citizens Learn What They Need to Know?*, Cambridge University Press, New York, 1998, pp. 215–226 (highlighting the lack of common interest and information discrepancies between agents and principles).

[38] Schwartz, Paul, "Data Processing and Government Administration: The Failure of the American Legal Response to the Computer", *Hastings Law Journal*, Vol. 43, 1992, pp. 1321–1399 [pp. 1380–1381] (discussing the difficulty of congressional oversight in light of the growth in data processing as the source of privacy issues).

[39] Lessig, Lawrence, *Code and Other Laws of Cyberspace*, Basic Books, New York, 1999, pp. 107–108 (noting the importance of structure in determining the ability of agencies to regulate and the danger that courts will back away from new and technical regulatory issues); Winner, Langdon, "Do Artifacts Have Politics?", in Donald MacKenzie and Judy Wajcman (eds.), *The Social Shaping of Technology*, second edition, Open University Press, Philadelphia, 1999, pp. 28–40 (discussing technology's impact on the structure of power and authority and its often inherently political nature); Reidenberg, Joel R., "Lex Informatica: The Formulation of Information Policy Rules through Technology", *Texas Law Review*, Vol. 76, No. 3, February 1998, pp. 553–584 [pp. 553–54] (arguing that technological capabilities and system design choices can impose rules on network participants, adding to or supplanting traditional forms of regulation); Nissenbaum, Helen, "Values in the Design of Computer Systems", *Computers in Society*, Vol. 28, No. 1, March 1998, pp. 38–39 (arguing that values, including public policy values, are embedded in design choices and asking who should control the undemocratic values embedded in designs).

[40] See Winner, op. cit., fn. 39, p. 31 (providing examples from architectural and city planning choices of political decisions made by way of seemingly neutral aesthetic choices). As an example, systems of identification can be designed with a higher or lower propensity for false positives and

The problem is exacerbated by the fact that the privacy concerns created by information systems are frequently analysed in the abstract and may depend upon testing an agency's specific – and often idiosyncratic – technological implementation.

Unlike the type of expert information on which administrative policy more traditionally relies – the safe level of atmospheric chemical discharge, for example – privacy effects of system design have only recently become the subject of regular public scientific analysis and often depend upon system-specific implementation details unknown to the public.[41] The PIA and other public documentation of DOS's e-Passport program discussed below, for example, did not provide the exact specifications of the system under consideration. Understanding the specifics of the technology DOS was seeking to employ – which is a prerequisite for meaningful participation in the notice-and-comment process accompanying its roll-out – would have required a detailed analysis of the e-Passport proposal, access to and analysis of an enormous amount of free-standing technical documentation and specifications[42] and, ideally, the ability to test the technology independently.

10.4 Seeking Ways to Overcome Barriers to PIA Success: Learning from the US Experience

Although the PIA approach to the integration of privacy concerns into administrative decision-making faces significant hurdles, the US regulatory experience offers some lessons regarding elements that may mitigate such barriers. The first is experience with the statute on which the PIA process was roughly modelled – the National Environmental Policy Act (NEPA) of 1969,[43] which mandates the completion of environmental impact statements (EISs) for federal government action significantly affecting environmental quality.[44] The second is the success on the part of some US agencies in incorporating the PIA requirement and its goals into agency decision-making.

---

false negatives. Depending upon the context of use, a decision to prefer errors in one direction or the other has profound policy consequences, for example, purging eligible voters from the rolls.

[41] This might be a context in which adherence to the standards of the Data Quality Act could possibly be helpful, as it could force agencies to provide research support for privacy and security claims. Such a requirement could, of course, cut in the opposite direction.

[42] Meingast, Marci, Jennifer King and Deirdre K. Mulligan, "Embedded RFID and Everyday Things: A Case Study of the Security and Privacy Risks of the U.S. e-Passport", *Proceedings of IEEE International Conference on RFID*, 2007, pp. 4–5 (discussing the e-Passport project's failure to address security and privacy risks to passport holders, in part because of insufficient information). http://www.truststc.org/pubs/157/Meingast_King_Mulligan_RFID2007_Final.pdf

[43] Pub L No 91-190, 83 Stat 852, codified as amended at 42 USC §§ 4321–47 (2000).

[44] See 42 USC § 4332(2)(C) (requiring EISs to report the environmental impacts of the proposed action, alternatives to the proposed action and any adverse environmental impacts which cannot be avoided should the proposal be implemented).

10.4.1 Lessons from NEPA

NEPA's initial focus on decision processes alone permitted widespread resistance in many agencies, resulting in widely inconsistent implementation[45] and was, accordingly, subject to strong early criticism.[46] The statute is now, however, considered by many in and out of agencies to have successfully "institutionaliz[ed] environmental values in government".[47]

Scholars and policy-makers have identified several elements critical to this transformation. First, they cite the development of mechanisms for accountability to external oversight. Indeed, perhaps the most surprising element in NEPA's evolution was the development of robust judicial and executive oversight unanticipated by the initial legislation. The year after the Act's passage, the oversight powers of the Council on Environmental Quality (CEQ), the body tasked with the statute's co-ordination, were enhanced by executive order[48] and the CEQ worked with agencies to direct consistent NEPA implementation.[49] At the same time, courts took an active role in review of the EIS process, ordering agencies to implement NEPA's procedural reforms, adopting broad constructions of many of the Act's provisions and imposing meaningful sanctions for non-compliance in the form of costly and time-consuming injunctions and adverse publicity.[50] This combination of external

---

[45] Wichelman, Allan F., "Administrative Agency Implementation of the National Environmental Policy Act of 1969: A Conceptual Framework for Explaining Differential Response", *Natural Resources Journal*, Vol. 16, 1976, pp. 296–300 (studying the implementation of NEPA across 20 different federal agencies).

[46] Sax, Joseph L., "The (Unhappy) Truth About NEPA", *Oklahoma Law Review*, Vol. 26, May 1973, pp. 239–278 [p. 248] ("Until we are ready to face… hard realities, we can expect laws like NEPA to produce little except fodder for law review writers and contracts for that newest of growth industries, environmental consulting.").

[47] Taylor, Serge, *Making Bureaucracies Think: The Environmental Impact Statement Strategy of Administrative Reform*, Stanford University Press, Stanford, CA, 1984, p. 251 ("Since the advent of NEPA, environmental concerns have been officially incorporated into every agency's charter."). See also Council on Environmental Quality, *The National Environmental Policy Act: A Study of Its Effectiveness after Twenty-Five Years*, Jan. 1997 (discussing NEPA's "success" in making federal agencies take a "hard look" at the potential environmental consequences of their actions). http://ceq.hss.doe.gov/nepa/nepa25fn.pdf. But see Karkkainen, Bradley C., "Toward a Smarter NEPA: Monitoring and Managing Government's Environmental Performance", *Columbia Law Review*, Vol. 102, No. 4, May 2002, pp. 904–906 (describing the positions of both proponents and critics of NEPA).

[48] See Executive Order 11514, 35 Fed Reg 4247 (1970).

[49] See Wichelman, op. cit., fn. 45, pp. 275–276 (discussing the CEQ's role as an overseer that provided "the coordination necessary to assure implementation of specific court decision across the administrative process" and that became a focus to which agencies could turn voluntarily for informal guidance).

[50] Scholars point to judicial review as a particularly important element in NEPA's success. See, for example, Yost, Nicolas C., and James W. Rubin, "Administrative Implementation of and Judicial Review under the National Environmental Policy Act", in Sheldon M. Novick, Donald W. Stever and Margaret G. Mellon (eds.), *The Law of Environmental Protection*, West Publishing, 2007, § 10.01(2) at pp. 10–32 ("Judicial review, coupled with the action-forcing provisions that so neatly

oversight of the EIS requirement is credited with catalysing a "wide range of internal agency adaptations", resulting in the integration of environmental concerns in agency decisions.[51]

Second, they cite the importance of the NEPA process for involving the public and scientific community. The NEPA process, as it has evolved, "gives other agencies, public interest groups, and the general public the opportunity to express alternative views and debate significant issues" and, in particular, involves scientists in the process.[52] Finally, they suggest certain elements that can drive a shift in agency culture from inclinations towards ceremonial and formal satisfaction of impact-assessment requirements to meaningful integration of privacy into decision processes. Specifically, these include "'front-loading' the NEPA process through the early, active participation of key staff", the hiring of experts in the substantive policy the impact of which is being assessed and initiating ongoing NEPA training programs.[53] Case studies of different agencies have demonstrated the ways that these elements have made NEPA compliance an "operational objective of the agency", integrating environmental impact concerns in discussion early on; they also suggest – of particular importance to the PIA context, in which not a single court challenge has been brought to a PIA – that while these changes have occurred as a result of litigation in some agencies, in others they resulted because of other external pressures (in this case, by Congress).[54]

10.5 Suggestions from the US PIA Experience: The RFID Cases

Despite the inherent challenges in implementing the PIA requirement, some agencies have successfully incorporated the PIA requirement and its goals into agency decision-making. The inconsistency of PIA implementation is epitomised by examples from two different agencies – DOS in the case of the e-Passport program and

---

lent themselves to enforcement in the courts, assured the success of NEPA"). See also *Kleppe v Sierra Club*, 427 US 390, 421 (1975) (Marshall concurring in part and dissenting in part) ("[T]his vaguely worded statute seems designed to serve as no more than a catalyst for development of a 'common law' of NEPA. To date, the courts have responded in just that manner and have created such a 'common law.'... Indeed, that development is the source of NEPA's success.").

[51] See Wichelman, op. cit., fn. 45, p. 278 (describing initial resistance and eventual capitulation by agencies to EIS requirements).

[52] Hildebrand, Stephen G., and Johnnie B. Cannon, *Environmental Analysis: The NEPA Experience*, Lewis Publishers, Boca Raton, FL, 1993, p. 5.

[53] Bryant, Beth C., "NEPA Compliance In Fisheries Management: The Programmatic Supplemental Environmental Impact Statement On Alaskan Groundfish Fisheries And Implications For NEPA Reform", *Harvard Environmental Law Review*, Vol. 30, No. 2, 2006, pp. 441–479 [p. 459].

[54] Ibid., pp. 459–460 [discussing the ways that the US Forest Service "(thanks in no small part to litigation pressure) has managed to integrate NEPA into its decision process", and the parallel accomplishments of the National Oceanic and Atmospheric Administration Fisheries pursuant to their "Regulatory Streamlining Project"].

DHS with respect to its US-VISIT initiative – considering the adoption of RFID technology in travel documents. Together with the preceding discussion of oversight obstacles, these case-specific compliance experiences can suggest factors to overcome and elements to reproduce in the future institutionalisation of privacy policy.

10.5.1 The Cases in Brief

10.5.1.1 The e-Passport Program

In February 2005, DOS published a proposed rulemaking setting forth a program for an e-Passport, an enhanced version of the traditional passport featuring an embedded electronic chip containing the information from the data page of the passport and a digital copy of the bearer's photo. The chip, a radio frequency (RF) transponder, is readable without physical contact through wireless technology. The agency had concluded the previous year that the e-Passport would provide "significant security benefits" in that it was more tamper-resistant and harder to forge than traditional passports.[55] Yet neither the proposed rule nor the summary PIA that was made public addressed the privacy (and security) risks to the bearer whose personal information the RFID chips contained.[56] The two-page PIA omits most of the critical elements specified in the OMB guidance: it does not mention RFID technology; it neither identifies nor addresses any potential privacy risks it might create; and it provides no information about the range of testing, let alone the data that formed DOS's technical decisions.[57] The proposed rule, without considering the effect of technology on data access and collection, summarily rejected data protection concerns, because "the personal data stored on the passport's electronic chip consists simply of the information traditionally and visibly displayed on the passport data page."[58]

---

[55] Department of State, *Abstract of Concept of Operations for the Integration of Contactless Chip in the U.S. Passport*, Abstract of Document Version 2.0, 2004, pp. 3, 28 (describing the specification and benefits of new passport technology). http://www.statewatch.org/news/2004/jul/us-biometric-passport-original.pdf

[56] Meingast, King and Mulligan, op. cit, fn. 42, p. 4. Department of State, *2006 Summary Privacy Impact Assessment*, 2006.

[57] Compare DOS, *2006 Summary Privacy Impact Assessment*, op. cit., fn. 56, with OMB, *OMB Guidance*, op. cit., fn. 6 (setting out PIA content requirements). The Center for Democracy and Technology has sought, as has the Samuelson Law, Technology & Public Policy Clinic and the American Civil Liberties Union, access to PIAs conducted in relation to the e-Passport project. At this point, we believe it is quite possible that a full PIA was not conducted and, if it was, it seems highly likely that it occurred after the development of the system rather than before as directed by the law. See Center for Democracy and Technology, "Letter to Secretary of State Condoleezza Rice Re: State Department Release of Privacy Impact Assessments", 2007, pp. 1–2. http://www.cdt.org/security/identity/20070502rice.pdf

[58] Department of State, Electronic Passport, 70 Fed Reg 8305, 2005 (proposed rule), p. 8306.

This silence on risks is particularly striking in light of the threat inherent in RFID technology. Internal DOS documents from as early as January 2003 discuss concerns over "skimming" – unauthorised wireless access of the data on the transponder without the owner's knowledge or consent – yet tests to examine the e-Passport's vulnerability were not requisitioned until February 2005, several months after the PIA was completed.[59] The results of those tests, performed by the National Institute of Standards and Technology (NIST), have still not been released to the public at the time of publication.[60] Some of the privacy concerns were ultimately addressed in the revised Final Rule (specifically, the incorporation of an anti-skimming material in the cover of the passport, a locking code limiting data access to authorised readers and transmission encryption). However, the question of whether RFID was the appropriate technology was never addressed in the first instance.

10.5.1.2 The US-VISIT Program

DHS chose similar RF technology when piloting the US-VISIT program pursuant to the Intelligence Reform and Terrorism Prevention Act of 2004. DHS proposed the use of passive RFID tags embedded in the I-94 arrival/departure form to track entry and exit of foreign visitors at land border point of entry crossings. The embedded tag would store no personally identifiable data, but would contain a unique identifier linked to a traveller's information in the US-VISIT database.[61]

The two PIAs DHS published for the US-VISIT project are eight and 33 pages long respectively.[62] They contain relatively detailed information about the system architecture, data flows and access controls, and lay out the privacy threats and mitigation techniques in clear charts. To further advance public participation in the PIA process, the DHS Chief Privacy Officer (CPO) held meetings with privacy and immigration organisations to further explore privacy concerns. Issues identified through these meetings, and by experts' comments on the PIA, were reflected in subsequent PIAs and in the ultimate design of the project.[63] While the PIA process

---

[59] See Meingast, King and Mulligan, op. cit., fn. 42, p. 2 (outlining the timeline of the e-Passport Project).

[60] NIST did provide guidance on security in RFID systems generally. See Karygiannis, Tom, Bernard Eydt, Greg Barber, Lynn Bunn and Ted Phillips, *Guidelines for Securing Radio Frequency Identification (RFID) Systems*, NIST Special Publication 800-98, National Institute of Standards and Technology, Gaithersburg, MD, April 2007.

[61] Department of Homeland Security, Privacy Act of 1974; Systems of Records, 1 July 2005, p. 2. http://www.dhs.gov/xlibrary/assets/privacy/privacy_sorn_usvisit_aidms.pdf

[62] Department of Homeland Security, US-VISIT Program, Increment 1, Privacy Impact Assessment, Washington, DC, 18 December 2003. (The initial privacy impact assessment was published in the *Federal Register* of 4 January 2004, but was amended to correct a technical error on 16 January 2004.) http://www.dhs.gov/xlibrary/assets/privacy/privacy_pia_usvisit_inc1. pdf. Additional privacy impact assessments have occurred as the system underwent testing. These PIAs can be found here; http://www.dhs.gov/files/publications/gc_1281125467696.shtm

[63] See Dempsey, James X., Executive Director, Center for Democracy and Technology, "Privacy in the Hands of the Government: The Privacy Officer for the Department of Homeland Security",

was not entirely without criticism of its timing and substantive conclusions,[64] it was generally lauded as "a high-quality PIA" that can "serve as a model for upcoming PIAs of other national security-related systems".[65]

10.5.2 Possible Elements of Variance

The RFID case studies illuminate three areas of significant variance between the agencies – each consistent with the broader literature concerning internal and external forces on compliance within the public and private sector – that we hypothesise contribute to the disparate levels of compliance with the PIA mandate: (1) the status and independence of a privacy expert embedded within the agency; (2) the decentralised distribution, disciplinary diversity, prior experience and expertise of the privacy staff; and (3) the creation of an alternative external oversight structure, which proved particularly significant given the lack of systematic congressional and administrative privacy oversight. In the process of developing our initial hypotheses, we interviewed Nuala O'Connor Kelly, the first Chief Privacy Officer at DHS. We later conducted confidential interviews with three former employees of the DHS's privacy office to explore the validity of our hypotheses and identify other factors viewed as important by those on the ground. The confidential interviewees largely confirmed the importance of these factors, but they offered some additional nuance and qualification to the issue of independence and the merits of advisory bodies as quasi-oversight mechanisms. In addition, they flagged the importance of de-politicising the operationalisation of privacy protection – an issue largely inseparable from the question of independence – particularly in an evolving environment, like DHS during this time period, where the opportunity to impact new systems and processes requires both an insider's seat at the policy-making table and an insider position within the day-to-day bureaucratic processes.

Testimony before the Subcommittee on Commercial and Administrative Law of the House Committee on the Judiciary, 108th Congress, Second Session, 2004 ("Dempsey Testimony", reporting that advocates expressed their concerns about issues such as the lack of information on redress issues for visitors who believe that information held about them may be incorrect or incorrectly interpreted and the unclear nature of the data quality and data retention rules). http://old.cdt.org/testimony/20040210dempsey.shtml

[64] See Senate Committee on Homeland Security and Governmental Affairs, "Government Privacy Protections Fall Short, Lieberman Calls for Leadership, Greater Commitment of Resources", Press release, 30 July 2003 ("In order for the privacy impact assessment to serve its intended purpose, the PIA must be conducted before the agency develops or procures information technology for the program."). http://hsgac.senate.gov/public/index.cfm?FuseAction= Press.MajorityNews&ContentRecord_id=96af45f1-8460-4a3b-aea0-7ef37c689403&Region_id= &Issue_id=

[65] Center for Democracy and Technology, Comments of the Center for Democracy and Technology on US-VISIT Program, Increment 1, Privacy Impact Assessment (December 18, 2003), 4 February 2004. http://old.cdt.org/security/usvisit/20040204cdt.pdf

10.6 Status and Independence of Embedded Privacy Experts

The most visible difference between the two agencies at the time of the RFID PIA processes was the existence of a high-status privacy expert within DHS, a CPO, specifically charged with advancing privacy among competing agency interests, located in a central position within the agency decision-making structure, able to draw on internal relationships and external sources of power, and operate with relative independence. The existence of such an embedded expert was not fully predetermined by statute or agency culture, but resulted instead from the confluence of structural, personal and context-contingent factors. Nonetheless, the status and independence proved determinative in the compliance – and "beyond compliance" – choices surrounding the US-VISIT program.

The statute that established DHS provided the basic predicate for these developments. In addition to consolidating several security functions into one cabinet level department, the Homeland Security Act of 2002 specifically established a privacy officer within the agency, the first statutory privacy officer position at the federal level in the United States.[66] The legislation directed the Secretary of Homeland Security to appoint a senior official with broad responsibility for ensuring that the use of technologies sustains, and does not erode, privacy protections; ensuring compliance with the Privacy Act of 1974; evaluating legislative and regulatory proposals involving personal information; and conducting privacy impact assessments.[67]

In response to his statutory mandate, Secretary Tom Ridge appointed Nuala O'Connor Kelly, then Chief Privacy Officer of the Department of Commerce, as CPO at DHS. Kelly was a respected professional in the privacy community and enjoyed a high level of visibility and support from Secretary Ridge, reported directly to him and was part of his senior leadership team.

The role of the new DHS CPO office and its first occupant developed alongside the routines, cultural presumptions and working relationships negotiated more broadly within the newly organised DHS and its leadership. Because of a combination of internal agency structure mandated by external statutory mandate, Kelly's experience as a respected professional in the privacy community, and her legitimacy as a result of Secretary Ridge's commitment to privacy issues generally and to his appointee in particular, DHS had a privacy oversight function characterised by its legitimacy and strength from its inception.

Kelly, moreover, used the relative autonomy provided by the status of her appointment, as well as the trust invested in her by Secretary Ridge, to reframe DHS's agency mission to include the privacy goals embodied by her office. Relying

---

[66] Pub L No 107-296, 116 Stat 2135.

[67] 6 USCA § 142 (2007).

on arguably ambiguous language[68] in the DHS Act discussing annual CPO reporting to Congress, Kelly, with Secretary Ridge's support, pushed for a forward-leaning
interpretation of her office's independence. In particular, Kelly framed her office's
direct-Congressional-reporting function as both a right and an obligation and
emphasised the function's importance as a signal of structural independence. Kelly
successfully prevented other offices within the Department or the White House
from exercising editorial control over the reports and PIAs issued by her office,
although her annual report did go through a review.[69] She sought opportunities to
speak directly to potential oversight bodies – construed broadly to include Congress,
the press and the public – even when her communications and reports showed the
agency failing in its obligation to protect privacy. The ability to use an external
reporting mechanism both as a threat and a means for inviting external oversight,
provided particularly effective means for enhancing her office's legitimacy within
the organisation,[70] tools that would be used to great effect during the period of
the US-VISIT privacy evaluation. Finally, Kelly leveraged her status and independence so as to play a singular role in the creation of the Data Privacy and Integrity
Advisory Committee (PIAC), an external oversight body discussed below, which
played an important role in the depth of the US-VISIT PIA.

None of the individuals who can be said to be responsible for spearheading privacy policy at DOS had the status or the independence of Kelly. The senior DOS
official designated as responsible for privacy matters is the Assistant Secretary for
Administration – a high-level position, no doubt, but one differently situated than
a CPO. Indeed, the position was held by William A. Eaton, a career foreign service officer, from July 2001 through May 2005, when he was confirmed as US
Ambassador to Panama, after which the post was vacant for over a year. Formal
privacy compliance activities are managed and overseen by civil servants, some of
whom have substantial and impressive experience with privacy,[71] but none of whom
possess comparable status or authority to the DHS CPO.[72]

---

[68] The statute directs the privacy officer to assume primary responsibility for privacy policy, including "preparing a report to Congress on an annual basis on activities of the Department that affect
privacy, including complaints of privacy violations, implementation of the Privacy Act of 1974,
internal controls, and other matters". See 6 USCA § 142(a)(6) (2007). In other instances, however, Congress has more clearly created direct reporting obligations. For example, in creating the
Privacy and Civil Liberties Oversight Board, Congress explicitly created an independent reporting
requirement stating, "the Board shall prepare a report to Congress". See Intelligence Reform and
Terrorism Prevention Act of 2004, Pub L No 108-458 § 1061(c)(4), 118 Stat 3638, 3684 (2004),
codified at 5 USC § 601 note (2000 & Supp 2004).

[69] Telephone Interview with Nuala O'Connor Kelly, former DHS CPO ("Kelly Interview"), 1 June
2007.

[70] Pfeffer and Salancik, op. cit., fn. 25, pp. 104–106 (arguing that publicly visible behaviours,
including the disclosure of information, are easier to influence than private behaviours).

[71] See Dempsey Testimony, op. cit., fn. 63 (describing the evolving status of privacy officers in
federal agencies).

[72] Swire, Peter, "The Administration Response to the Challenges of Protecting Privacy", 8 January
2000, p. 22 (concluding, based on his experience as the first Chief Counselor for Privacy, that

Because of these structures, neither high-level officials for whom privacy tasks are grafted onto existing responsibilities nor civil service privacy compliance officers are likely to possess means to achieve a comparable level of independence as the DHS CPO. Reports regarding the treatment of personally identifiable information are issued to the inspector general, an intermediate entity within the DOS. This precludes any independent relationship with Congress through which such staffers could enlist such an external, legitimacy-enhancing oversight function.

The comparison between the DHS and DOS experiences underscores scholarship that emphasises independence in action and reporting as essential components of effective government data-protection offices.[73] In the case of DHS at the time of the US-VISIT PIA, that independence enabled the CPO to argue that privacy was an integral component of the institution's core mission.[74] It enabled the CPO to act relatively autonomously, particularly with respect to issuing reports on agency actions and investigations, thereby establishing an independent voice and relationships with external oversight bodies. Finally, it provided the political capital and access necessary to create a new independent external quasi-oversight mechanism comprising privacy and security experts, thereby securing an additional mechanism to ensure that agency actions and commitments affecting privacy were examined.

During confidential interviews, former DHS privacy office employees discussed their sense of the importance of the status of the privacy office in privacy activities generally and the PIA process specifically. An indicator of the CPO's status

---

because "privacy debates have a significant political dimension, and there are advantages to having a political appointee rather than a civil servant articulate the privacy issues, both within the Administration and in public"). www.peterswire.net/stanford7.doc

[73] Gellman, Robert, "A Better Way to Approach Privacy Policy in the United States: Establish a Non-Regulatory Privacy Protection Board", *Hastings Law Journal*, Vol. 54, April 2003, pp. 1183–1226 [pp. 1208–10] (emphasising the importance of independence for the success of the Privacy Protection Board); Berman, Jerry, and Deirdre K. Mulligan, Comments of the Center for Democracy and Technology on the Draft "Options for Promoting Privacy on the National Information Infrastructure", 29 July 1997 (recommending a body for privacy oversight that would be an independent voice empowered with the scope, expertise and authority to guide public policy) http://old.cdt.org/privacy/ntia.html; Schwartz, op. cit., fn. 38, pp. 1379–1384 (arguing that an independent data protection body could develop expertise and specialisation currently missing in congressional oversight); Flaherty, David H., *Protecting Privacy in Surveillance Societies*, University of North Carolina Press, 1989, p. 381 (concluding that independent agency oversight is "essential" to make a data protection law work in practice); Simitis, op. cit., fn. 29, p. 742 ("Efficient regulation presupposes the establishment of an independent control authority. Experience confirms what was argued in the earlier debates: a mandatory framework for data processing is not sufficient."); US Department of Health, Education and Welfare, Secretary's Advisory Committee on Automated Personal Data Systems, *Records, Computers and the Rights of Citizens*, 1973, pp. 42–43 (concluding that agency oversight was the strongest option for protecting privacy but rejecting it due to lack of political support).

[74] In fact, OMB guidance left it up to the agency to decide whether to conduct a PIA at all where the personal information at issue was about aliens. See *OMB Guidance*, op. cit., fn. 6 ("Agencies may, consistent with individual practice, choose to extend the protections of the Privacy Act and E-Government Act to businesses, sole proprietors, aliens, etc.").

and power included participation in top-level deputy meetings and other decision-making meetings with the Secretary. As a general matter, having "enough authority and trust internally and externally" was considered critical to the CPO's success. The clout of the CPO was considered particularly important during the agency's formative days; as one former employee explained, "It was war everyday, but you felt good about being there, you made a difference. You can't do this without a strong CPO."

DHS's "very robust position on where PIAs are required" was attributed directly to the CPO's status, which conferred power and access within the agency. One interviewee discussed a disagreement between the Office of Policy, the Office of the General Counsel and the Privacy Office about whether PIAs should be conducted for body-scanning systems. The status and trust the Privacy Office had developed within the Department allowed the CPO to argue that PIAs should be conducted for such systems *regardless* of whether it was legally required. This "beyond-compliance" orientation was deeply tied to the legal status – yet bolstered by the institution-building and strong people skills – of the CPO, according to our interview subjects. They claimed that the lower-level civil service employees in charge of privacy at other agencies lacked the access required to make such arguments and the clout to win them.

The interviewees also suggested important qualifications on the value of CPO independence distinguishing the mix of insider and outsider status required to affect privacy practices in various roles. Influencing policy requires access to high-level policy meetings typically associated with political appointees and the inner circle of decision-making. Presence at these meetings is necessary, yet it drives home the perception that privacy is a policy decision with unavoidable connections to politics. Access to and impact at such meetings strongly supports the interviewees' belief that the CPO should be a political appointee.

Yet, while an independent agency for privacy might be useful as an oversight mechanism, a venue to handle complaints and for taking on larger policy issues, the operationalisation of privacy requires an inside position. According to interviewees, as mentioned above, protecting privacy in the context of the agency's activities requires privacy to be "de-politicised" and incorporated into the bureaucracy. The interviewees all spoke of the high-level policy perspective necessary for policy impact as somewhat in tension with the daily practice of privacy. In discussing PIAs specifically, one interviewee explained that the iterative nature of PIAs, the need to be in the room with "legal, program and technical people" at the "formulation of the project", and the "trust and access" required for an effective PIA demand an insider position. In the words of another, "you can't get in the tent if you are totally independent" and unless you are in the tent, you can't "work to salvage privacy interests in implementation" where Congress has made a decision generally adverse to privacy interests. Ultimately, all three concluded that a privacy office charged with carrying out PIAs and attempting to advance privacy in the context of broader agency goals requires a "balance of independent oversight, while not being outside. . .you want the privacy person in up front, and with enough status and experience." Advancing privacy through tools such as PIAs required the privacy office to "build trust internally, then insinuate [privacy] into the bureaucratic process". The goal was for others in the agency to say "Where's privacy?" when a new system or program is under discussion. "Privacy needs to be in the room as a bureaucratic matter." "The political appointee CPO's job is to bridge the gap between political/policy and career/bureaucracy", for both are essential to protecting privacy.

10.7 Expert Personnel, Integrated Structure and the PIA Tool

Kelly further leveraged her individual capacity to affect decision-making within the agency through decisions about both personnel and structure. In particular, Kelly assembled a staff of demonstrated privacy professionals with diverse disciplinary skills and not only located these employees in the central DHS privacy office, but embedded them within operational units throughout the agency. This combination of privacy expertise, varied training and perspective, and decentralised integration throughout decision-making structures, was particularly well suited to take advantage of the privacy impact assessment mechanism, an inherently interdisciplinary tool for affecting decision-making from the "bottom up".

Like Kelly, several key privacy office staff had held prior positions that required them to identify emerging privacy issues proactively and engage a wide range of businesses in the development of privacy policy and implementation of privacy management strategies.[75] Several members of the staff had been involved in negotiations with the European Union about the adequacy of United States privacy law and practice, which provided them with a deep familiarity with the larger trade and political context of agency privacy decisions. Kelly specifically identified the breadth of her core privacy staff – lawyers, technologists, government insiders, implementation and education experts – and their connections and experiences as essential to the success of her office.[76]

Kelly believed it essential to embed privacy personnel within the operational units of DHS. In addition to her core privacy staff, each of the operational divisions – and even particular programs that raised heightened privacy concerns, such

---

[75] For example, Maureen Cooney, Chief of Staff and Director of International Privacy Policy, was Legal Advisor for International Consumer Protection at the US Federal Trade Commission where she worked on international privacy and security issues; Elizabeth Whitnell, Chief Counsel to the Privacy Office, was a lawyer at the Office of Information and Privacy at the Department of Justice; Peter Sand, Director of Privacy Technology, was the Chief Privacy and Information Officer for the Pennsylvania Office of the Attorney General; Toby Levin, the Senior Advisor to the Department of Homeland Security Privacy Office, was a Senior Attorney in the Division of Financial Practices at the Federal Trade Commission, where she worked on children's privacy and financial privacy, among other issues; and Rebecca Richards, Director of Privacy Compliance at the Department of Homeland Security, was Director of Policy and Compliance at a privacy certification program (TRUSTe) and worked on the US–European Union Safe Harbour accord while an international trade specialist at the US Department of Commerce.

[76] See Kelly interview, op. cit., fn. 69.

as US-VISIT – had dedicated privacy officers.[77] Privacy professionals in the private sector interviewed by the authors, as well as other privacy professionals, stress the importance of embedding expertise within business units and establishing specific staff who are personally responsible for privacy – typically through indirect reporting mechanisms – as essential to institutionalising privacy considerations in large decentralised organisations.[78] Literature on the relationship between formal structures and successful decentralised decision-making, moreover, further supports this claim,[79] as do studies of cognition and decision-making, which emphasise "interaction with others whose thought processes are not governed by the same culture or knowledge structures as the decision maker" as a principal means of forcing integration of secondary concerns that are in tension with an organisation's existing focus.[80]

---

[77] See, for example, Department of Homeland Security, Privacy Impact Assessment for the Naturalization Redesign Test Pilot, 17 January 2007, http://www.dhs.gov/xlibrary/assets/privacy/privacy_pia_uscis_nrtp.pdf; Department of Homeland Security, Transportation Security Administration (TSA), Airport Access Control Pilot Project Privacy Impact Assessment, 18 June 2004, p. 6 (providing contact information for Lisa S. Dean, Privacy Officer, TSA), http://www.dhs.gov/xlibrary/assets/privacy/privacy_pia_aacpp.pdf; Department of Homeland Security, US-VISIT Program, op. cit., fn. 62, p. 10 (providing contact information for Steve Yonkers, US-VISIT Privacy Officer, Border and Transportation Security).

[78] Bamberger, Kenneth A., and Deirdre K. Mulligan, "New Governance, Chief Privacy Officers, and the Corporate Management of Information Privacy in the United States: An Initial Inquiry", *Law & Policy*, Vol. 33, No. 4, October 2011, pp. 477–508; Kelly interview, op. cit., fn. 69; see also Flaherty, David H., "Privacy Impact Assessments: an essential tool for data protection", Presentation at the 22nd Annual Meeting of Privacy and Data Protection Officials, Venice, 27-30 September 2000 ("I conclude that the ideal privacy impact assessment of any project is prepared by someone from inside the project and with an up-front demonstration of just how it works or is supposed to work."). http://aspe.hhs.gov/datacncl/flaherty.htm; Stewart, Blair, "Privacy impact Assessment Towards a Better Informed Process for Evaluating Privacy Issues Arising from New Technologies", *Privacy Law and Policy Reporter*, Vol. 5, No. 8, February 1999 ("PIA needs to be integrated into decision-making processes. For a government proposal, PIA might be integrated into departmental decision-making and appropriate cabinet processes. The important thing is that PIA not be divorced from decision-making processes."). http://www.austlii.edu.au/au/journals/PLPR/1999/8.html

[79] Scott, W. Richard, *Organizations: Rational, Natural and Open Systems*, fourth edition, Prentice Hall, 1998, pp. 262–263 (discussing scholarship suggesting that centralisation and formalisation may be viewed as alternative control mechanisms: more formalised arrangements permit more decentralised decision-making).

[80] Bamberger, op. cit., fn. 28, p. 443 (citing Heath, Chip, Richard P. Larrick and Joshua Klayman, "Cognitive Repairs: How Organizational Practices Can Compensate for Individual Shortcomings", *Research in Organizational Behavior*, Vol. 20, No. 1, 1998, pp. 1–37 [p. 20] ("Often, organizations ensure that individuals weigh information effectively by forcing them to interact with others who might weigh the information differently."); Walsh, James P., "Managerial and Organizational Cognition: Notes from a Trip Down Memory Lane", *Organization Science*, Vol. 6, No. 3, May–June 1995, pp. 280–321 [p. 291] ("[R]esearch on the process of knowledge structure development suggests that a dramatically altered information environment is often the locus of knowledge structure change.").

Kelly's personnel decisions, then, reflected an attempt to break down traditional boundaries, both disciplinary and institutional. Particularly, as here, where the secondary mandate requires expertise outside the realm of the agency culture, the introduction of specialised personnel – a privacy infrastructure – is a necessary prerequisite for success.

The other former employees we interviewed in confidence suggested the importance of Kelly's decision to hire experienced privacy professionals from a range of backgrounds. This amounted to "Personnel as policy", as stated by one interviewee, who sought to highlight the distinction between privacy offices in other agencies that are staffed with "technicians" who approach privacy with a "compliance mindset" and DHS where privacy is led by an experienced team of "experts" and a "policy orientation" dominates. The experts were important for their own impact on specific matters, but perhaps more importantly for processes they established that embedded privacy into the bureaucracy's daily business. The interviewees emphasised that the Office was staffed by "people with experience not only putting together solid policy, but making privacy actionable and integrating it into the operations of an organization". "Operationalizing [privacy] was at the...core...of who and what the Privacy Office was and is." Each interviewee discussed the efforts of the privacy office staff to create privacy structures to ensure the reasoned consideration of privacy throughout the agency. The privacy officers – now embedded in nearly every unit of DHS – combine these standardised tools with their detailed knowledge of the people, program and mission to influence programs at the outset.

The ability of expert personnel to effect programmatic decisions, several described, is aided by compliance with the timing envisioned by the E-Government Act, which requires agencies to conduct a PIA *before* "developing or procuring IT systems or projects that collect, maintain or disseminate information in identifiable form...or initiating...a new electronic collection of information in identifiable form". The timing requirement "front-loads" privacy activities, forcing the consideration of privacy into the design phase and precluding a compliance or audit approach. This shift is significant according to a recent report on the use of PIAs that concluded "To be valuable, PIAs need to offer a prospective identification of privacy risks before systems and programmes are put in place." Indeed that same report found that, "In every jurisdiction, PIA processes have been designed to be prospective." And that PIAs "refer to an entire process of assessment of privacy risks" rather than the static reports they produce.[81] This form of "front-loaded" process combined with substantive experts on staff reflects similar elements emphasised as important to the success of environmental impact assessments under NEPA.[82]

---

[81] Linden Consulting, op. cit., fn. 34, p. vi.

[82] See Bryant, op. cit., p. 459, fn. 53 and accompanying text.

10.7.1 Creating Accountability in the Absence of Oversight: The Privacy and Integrity Advisory Committee

Finally, the US-VISIT process was conducted in the context of a third important factor unique to DHS: the DHS Privacy and Integrity Advisory Committee, a federal advisory committee established in 2004 to oversee DHS's privacy activities.[83] The enhanced accountability made possible through the creation of this external quasi-oversight board strengthened and publicised DHS's privacy office's processes and substantive decisions, thus enabling the office to further its subgoal within the agency.

Faced with a relative void of external oversight mechanisms geared to ensure compliance with privacy directives and the need to strengthen privacy's position within the conflicting DHS missions, Kelly requested Secretary Ridge's support to establish the DPIAC early on. She credits him with understanding that the creation of a "structure for consistent oversight by privacy and security experts" was essential for the office and the agency as a whole to both establish credibility and formalise the conversation about "what is a reasonable amount of government data collection even in the most extreme circumstances".[84]

The Committee, which met quarterly and set its own agenda, comprised privacy and security experts from the public and private sectors with sophisticated knowledge of technology and privacy. With the exception of one individual, none of the members fell into the category of privacy "advocates". Rather, they were respected individuals within corporate America and academia with sound privacy and security credentials.[85] Their ties to industry, the defence sector and academia gave them particular force when they spoke to a privacy or security issue.

The DPIAC created a consistent form of oversight, pulling in DHS officials from various departmental units to discuss privacy and security issues within specific projects. Importantly, the ability of the DPIAC to engage in a rather freewheeling review of DHS's activity introduced an external expert quasi-oversight body to whom agency personnel, including those within operational divisions, had to account for their actions and decisions. Research into the psychology of accountability indicates the benefits of this type of review, in which decision-makers are required to explain themselves to others whose views they do not know in

---

[83] Department of Homeland Security, Privacy Office, Data Integrity, Privacy, and Interoperability Advisory Committee, 69 Fed Reg 18923 (2004).

[84] Kelly interview, op. cit., fn. 69.

[85] See Department of Homeland Security, "Department of Homeland Security Announces Appointments to Data Privacy and Integrity Advisory Committee", Press release, 23 February 2005 (listing initial appointees and noting that "members of this Advisory Committee have diverse expertise in privacy, security, and emerging technology, and come from large and small companies, the academic community, and the non-profit sector. . . . and also reflect a depth of knowledge on issues of data protection, openness, technology, and national security"). http://www.dhs.gov/xnews/releases/press_release_0625.shtm

advance.[86] In particular, such accountability "motivates" people "to anticipate the counterarguments that potential critics could raise to their positions".[87] It develops tolerance for cognitive inconsistency, so that a decision-maker recognises good features of rejected policies and bad features of accepted policies. It fosters a greater awareness of the cognitive processes underlying the decision. Finally, it counters the reliance on "existing knowledge structures in interpreting new information", making decision-makers more willing to revise initial impressions of the situation in response to changing evidence.[88]

In confidential interviews, former employees described a shifting relationship between the privacy office and the DPIAC. Early on, the DPIAC was given relatively free rein to determine what issues to address, but later on, it was asked to give advice and guidance on issues the office brought before it. These former employees felt that the DPIAC's free-ranging inquiries antagonised DHS and complicated the inside work of insinuating privacy into the bureaucracy. The external attacks risked "politicising" privacy and undermining the ability of the privacy office to build privacy into the practices of the agency.

When the DPIAC focused on activities and projects brought forward by the CPO, interviewees pointed to two distinct methods in which its contributions were influential and significant. At times, the DPIAC's utility was in "giving an outside voice to what the CPO was already saying" and "amplifying the voice for privacy". "Each published DPIAC paper identified a policy concern that the CPO was grappling with and provided support for pushing privacy concerns and ways to address them." "It strengthened [the privacy office's] hand." At other times, the diverse background of DPIAC board members provided additional "expertise on how to solve a privacy problem" and identified novel strategies pulling from "private sector experiences". Here, the board acted as an independent source of knowledge allowing the privacy office to pull from the broader privacy community's resources and knowledge base.

10.8 Directions for Further Inquiry

The DHS PIA case study suggests several questions regarding the conditions for meaningful privacy impact assessments for future inquiry.

Specifically, it suggests the role of alternate methods of external accountability as a means of strengthening the hand of privacy officers internally, the importance of substantive experts combined with internal processes for insinuating privacy

---

[86] See, for example, Tetlock, Philip E., "Accountability: The Neglected Social Context of Judgment and Choice", in Barry M. Staw and L.L. Cummings (eds.), *Research in Organizational Behavior*, Vol. 7, 1985, pp. 297–332 [pp. 314–21] (reviewing research on heuristics and stating that accountability can cultivate sensitivity to complex thinking practices under certain circumstances).

[87] Ibid., at pp. 314, 316.

[88] Ibid.

into daily practice, and the need for status and structures that respect the different roles privacy professionals play in protecting privacy during policy-making and integrating privacy into the bureaucracy.

More generally, these elements suggest the limits of formal law in operationalising privacy. The successful integration of privacy concerns into agency decision-making poses, at least in part, a challenge to management – of personnel, structures and processes. While independence may be essential in policy debates, it is viewed as a barrier to the infiltration and embedding of PIAs and other efforts to institutionalise privacy within bureaucracies. Further inquiry is warranted into the tension between these elements and possible structural solutions to assure privacy fares well in policy debates as well as during implementation. Enhancing privacy function independence, for example, is inherently in tension with both integrating that function within teams and units, and increasing its status within the agency by creating direct agency-head reporting. Moreover, strong monitoring mindsets tend to cancel out more co-operative impulses towards co-ordination between disciplines and units.[89] The case study suggests that privacy personnel within DHS were acutely aware of this tension and the tightrope they walked as they sought to influence policy while infiltrating the bureaucracy. At a minimum, these preliminary indicators of barriers and aids to PIA performance – through status, expertise, embeddedness and external accountability – strongly recommend broader qualitative and context-dependent analysis of PIAs in practice and broader efforts to implement privacy in the shadow of privacy politics.

Acknowledgments Much appreciation to Colin Bennett, Malcolm Crompton, Peter Cullen, Lauren Edelman, Robert Gellman, Chris Hoofnagle, Robert Kagan, Jennifer King, Anne Joseph O'Connell, Fred B. Schneider, Ari Schwartz, Paul Schwartz, and the participants at the University of Chicago Law School Conference on Surveillance for insight, comment and discussion; Nuala O'Connor Kelly and Peter Swire for consenting to be interviewed about their experiences as the first individuals to hold path-breaking privacy roles within the United States government; Sara Terheggen, Marta Porwit Czajkowska, Rebecca Henshaw and Andrew McDiarmid for their able research. This chapter draws from Bamberger, Kenneth A., and Deirdre K. Mulligan, "Privacy Decisionmaking in Administrative Agencies", *University of Chicago Law Review*, Vol. 75, No. 1, 2008, pp. 75–107, and reflects insights from the authors' research on corporate Chief Privacy Officers and practices discussed in Bamberger, Kenneth A., and Deirdre K. Mulligan, "New Governance, Chief Privacy Officers, and the Corporate Management of Information Privacy in the United States: An Initial Inquiry", *Law & Policy*, Vol. 33, No. 4, October 2011, pp. 477–508.

---

[89] See Langevoort, Donald C., "Monitoring: The Behavioral Economics of Corporate Compliance with Law", *Columbia Business Law Review*, Vol. 2002, No. 1, pp. 71–118 [p. 96].

Part III
PIA in the Private Sector: Three Examples

Chapter 11
PIA: Cornerstone of Privacy Compliance in Nokia

Tobias Bräutigam

11.1 Introduction

Nokia designs, operates, manufactures and sells mobile telephones, smart phones and online services. With a market share of around 35 per cent, Nokia is the market leader in mobile phones and has customers in virtually every country on Earth. Millions of customers will gain Internet access for the first time in their life by using a Nokia phone. Nokia's services include e-mail delivery, music, navigation, application stores and management of contacts.[1] Globally, 55.000 employees work for Nokia in all major markets. Countries such as Finland, India, China, Germany, the United States, Brazil, Hungary, UK, Mexico and Poland each have sites with about 2,000 employees.[2]

Privacy is crucial for Nokia in many ways. First, privacy is an important part of legal compliance which must be assured in different markets. This includes typical data protection questions such as the following: For how long is the personal data being stored? Who has access to it? On which servers and in which countries does the personal data reside? Without good answers to these questions, doing business becomes impossible. Second, data protection authorities are becoming increasingly aware of the importance of privacy as a fundamental right and hardly a month

---

This chapter represents the author's own opinions and should not be interpreted to reflect those of Nokia.

[1] See http://www.ovi.com/services/worldwide. This website shows Nokia's main services. Thousands of applications are available through the ovi-store, Nokia's online application shop: http://store.ovi.com.

[2] Nokia, "Nokia in 2009, Review by the Board of Directors and Nokia Annual Accounts". http://phx.corporate-ir.net/External.File?item=
UGFyZW50SUQ9NDE1NDZ8Q2hpbGRJRD0tMXxUeXBlXBlPTM=&t=1

T. Bräutigam (✉)
Nokia Corporation, Espoo, Finland

Affiliated Research Fellow at the Erik Castrén Institute of International Law and Human Rights, Helsinki. http://www.helsinki.fi/eci/Staff/affiliated_research_fellows.html
e-mail: tobias.brautigam@nokia.com

D. Wright, P. De Hert (eds.), *Privacy Impact Assessment*, Law, Governance and Technology Series 6, DOI 10.1007/978-94-007-2543-0_11,
© Springer Science+Business Media B.V. 2012

goes by without a new legislative initiative on privacy.[3] The last question about the location of servers already points to a second set of privacy questions concerning international data transfers. For a global company, free data flow is an essential element of doing business. However, many countries restrict the flow of personal data to other countries or require notifications to authorities about such personal data flows. A third reason why privacy is important for Nokia is that Nokia's employees are located in many different countries; it is not unlikely that a manager resides in a different country from the employee. While Nokia's headquarters are in Finland and most of the personal data is controlled through the Finnish entity, often there is local legislation with which Nokia needs to comply. This becomes relevant when global human resource (HR) systems, such as those marketed by SAP, or an internal phonebook, are used. Finally, not only does Nokia have businesses and employees in many countries, but also it has production sites in countries such as China, India, Hungary, Romania, Brazil and Finland. This makes Nokia a truly global company as it is established in many countries in terms of employment management, operations and manufacturing. Thus, Nokia faces privacy questions that are different from those faced by pure Internet companies. Finally and most importantly, privacy is immediately relevant for Nokia's business model to connect people to what matters most to them. Nokia's mobile Internet services offer opportunities for consumers, such as location sharing with friends or getting relevant information from local services just in time.[4] However, sensible consumers will only use those services if they feel safe and if they trust the service. They will only trust a service when there are no data breaches or losses, when the personal data is not sold to third parties without their consent and when they know what happens with their personal data. Privacy is all about trust. And consumer trust is essential for Nokia's success. That is why privacy is a key consideration in Nokia's business.

In order to ensure best privacy practices, Nokia uses privacy impact assessments. This chapter will describe how Nokia manages privacy assessments. There are a few caveats here. First, this chapter will not only cover privacy, but also security to a certain degree, both of which are assessed in a process called privacy impact and security assessment. Further, this chapter will focus on two distinct privacy assessments, privacy impact and security assessment (PISA) and privacy impact assessment (PIA). Second, there are numerous other assessments done in Nokia. Those other assessments, such as the security threat analysis, are idiosyncratic to a location or a particular business unit or designed to assess third parties' compliance with basic privacy rules. Third, as is natural with companies that provide services in the Internet age, implementation changes quickly. This chapter describes the process of conducting privacy assessments as of 2010.

---

[3] Recent initiatives include the passing of the first data protection law in Mexico; the proposal of the German government for an act on data protection in an employment relationship and the Boucher-Stearns bill on online privacy in the United States.

[4] What is meant here is not only very specific advertisement, but information on opening hours of shops or updated bus schedules.

Following this introduction, I define important terms. The chapter then goes on to describe Nokia's approach to privacy and how privacy assessments fit therein. This is important as I will argue that privacy assessments only make sense when they are embedded in a governance model that supports the implementation of the results. After that, the process and the content of privacy assessments will be described. To provide value for readers, I will also identify areas for improvement. A conclusion sums up the main findings by listing the top 10 lessons learned for companies that plan to implement privacy impact assessments.

This chapter was written with the help of Nokia's privacy expert network. In order to get a wider perspective, I conducted 15 interviews with experts on different levels in the company who helped me gain better insight into how the privacy assessment process works in practice. My intent was to interview people with very different perspectives and experiences concerning privacy assessments.[5]

11.2 Definitions

11.2.1 Privacy

While we each might have a sense of what "privacy" means, at least to each of us, the reality is that "there is no overarching conception of privacy".[6] In this contribution, privacy is seen predominantly from a consumer perspective. This concerns questions such as: What kind of data will the company process about me? What will they do with it – share it, combine it, lose it?[7] This means that, in addition to some core privacy issues (e.g., data sharing with third parties, profiling), many questions are common with security issues.[8] This is also the reason why the most common assessment done at Nokia is called a privacy impact and security assessment.

---

[5] I want to explicitly thank Frank Dawson, Mikko Hämäläinen, Matti Jussila, Henri Kujala, Mikko Larikka, Kari-Pekka Lifländer, Matti Malinen, Mohamed Maricar, Ralf Maruhn, Mikko Niva, Kirsi-Marja Salmela, Tony Spires, Riikka Turunen, Antti Vähä-Sipilä and Pauli Wihuri from Nokia and Jarno Vanto from Vanto Law PLLC for their valuable contributions. Without those contributions, the article could not have been written. Of course, any inaccuracies are my own.

[6] Solove, Daniel, *Understanding Privacy*, Harvard University Press, Cambridge, MA, 2008, Preface. The author later shows that there is an abundance of concepts of privacy and proposes his own model.

[7] In Solove's taxonomy, most relevant for businesses are the concepts of information processing (e.g., aggregation, identification, insecurity, secondary use) and information dissemination (e.g., disclosure, exposure, increased accessibility).

[8] Even requirements (such as deletion of data when there is no purpose for the processing) are in equal measure security questions.

11.2.2 Personal Data

When the term personal data is used here, it means personally identifiable information (PII), i.e., all information that allows the identification of a person. Nokia uses the broad definition of the EU Data Protection Directive[9] to determine if a processing concerns personal data. In other countries, the term PII is used to describe the same concept.

11.2.3 PCI DSS

The Payment Card Industry Data Security Standard[10] is a commonly used standard for ensuring protection of credit card information. PCI DSS includes extensive requirements concerning information security.

11.2.4 PIA, PISA

PIA stands for privacy impact assessment, and PISA for privacy impact and security assessment. When both assessments are intended, privacy assessment is used.

11.2.5 Nokia

For the purpose of this chapter, Nokia refers to the Nokia Corporation, including its affiliates. NAVTEQ and Nokia Siemens Networks' practices concerning PIAs, however, are not meant when the term "Nokia" is used in this chapter. Some affiliates might have additional practices, which focus on certain aspects of compliance.

11.3 Nokia's Approach to Privacy

After taking a look at Nokia's privacy governance, this section describes other measures supporting privacy assessments and explains why Nokia conducts privacy assessments.

---

[9] Article 2 (a) of the European Data Protection Directive 95/46/EC of the European Parliament and of the Council of 24 October 1995 on the protection of individuals with regard to the processing of personal data and on the free movement of such data [Data Protection Directive], Official Journal L 281, 23/11/1995, pp. 0031–0050.

[10] Payment Card Industry Security Standards Council, Payment Card Industry Data Security Standard. https://www.pcisecuritystandards.org/security_standards/pci_dss_download.html

11.3.1 Governance Model

Nokia manages privacy through requirements. What does that mean? It means, first, that Nokia manages privacy on different levels, centrally and distributed. There is – as compared to many other blue-chip companies – a relatively small team of experts to manage privacy requirements full time with a company-wide view. This team mainly consists of part of the legal department and an organisation called "Privacy". The privacy legal team is responsible for drafting Nokia-wide policies, guidelines and requirements. The organisation called Privacy oversees the implementation of the guidelines, instructions and privacy requirements and verifies compliance. Above those teams are two high-level steering groups, which make operational decisions on Nokia-wide consumer privacy matters. These steering groups decide also on Nokia-wide privacy processes.

Furthermore, there are organisational unit specific roles, such as the unit privacy officers and unit privacy managers. These staff interpret Nokia's privacy approach for the specific unit and define a unit-specific privacy strategy, mode of operation, implementation guidelines and related practices.

To complement the relatively few resources who deal full-time with privacy, there are literally thousands of employees who take care of privacy implementation in concrete projects. These employees are regularly trained and typically work as:

- product managers, who are responsible for following privacy requirements;
- sourcing managers, who negotiate agreements (e.g., hosting, co-marketing);
- solution architects, who are responsible for interpreting privacy requirements as product requirements and embed privacy into the IT product concept (lead developer or concept owner);
- business lawyers, who are responsible for legal compliance of a particular project or service;
- IT managers, who are responsible for implementing the privacy-derived requirements in IT products;
- production managers, who manage and maintain privacy in the use phase.

Responsibilities in this governance model need to be defined. For example, in IT, responsibilities are defined through the ARCI model,[11] which describes in matrix form who is accountable, responsible, and needs to be consulted or informed at a certain project step.

Privacy is managed through *requirements*. Privacy requirements are generic prerequisites with which all of Nokia's products and services need to comply. An example of a privacy requirement is: "[...] must use the least sensitive type of personal data to satisfy the identified business purpose". This means that whoever assesses a product, service or application must find out – with the help of privacy

---

[11] For a brief introduction, see Campbell, Clark A., *The one-page project manager for IT projects*, John Wiley & Sons Inc., New Jersey, 2008, pp. 77–79.

experts – what data is necessary for the business purpose and what the alternatives are. This comes back to the management of requirements in the units. The requirements are not – at least, in most cases – controls that could be answered immediately by giving a number or by ticking a box. They need to be applied in the units and need to be tailored to the specific needs of the business in question. Units might have specific standards, guidelines and/or instructions, which explain more and give concrete advice to implement requirements.

These requirements apply to, for example, Nokia's mobile devices, and Internet services as well as to customer care and applications that employees use on a daily basis. Privacy requirements are relevant in all of Nokia's operational units and other Nokia organisations. They must be integrated into each unit's management systems and processes. The units are responsible for compliance with such requirements. They must proactively drive the inclusion of privacy considerations into the design of their products and services.

The sources for requirements are, amongst others:

- BS 10012:2009[12]
- ISO 22307[13]
- Information Security Forum (ISF)'s Fundamental Information Risk Management (FIRM)[14]
- Payment Card Industry Data Security Standard[15]
- European Privacy Seal Criteria Catalogue[16]
- European privacy directives 95/46/EC and 2002/58/EC including information on their implementation and interpretation (e.g., Article 29 Working Party documents)
- UK Information Commissioner's Privacy Impact Assessment guidelines
- Information Security Forum: Standard of Good Practice.[17]

---

[12] British Standards Institution, 10012:2009 Data protection. Specification for a personal information management system, London, May 2009. http://shop.bsigroup.com/en/ProductDetail/?pid=000000000030175849

[13] International Organization for Standardization, ISO 22307:2008 Financial services – Privacy impact assessment, Geneva, 2008. http://www.iso.org/iso/iso_catalogue/catalogue_tc/catalogue_detail.htm?csnumber=40897

[14] https://www.securityforum.org/services/publictools/publictoolsfirm/

[15] Payment Card Industry Security Standards Council, op. cit.

[16] Public version available at: https://www.european-privacy-seal.eu/criteria/EuroPriSe%20Criteria%20Catalogue%20public%20version%201.0.pdf

[17] Information Security Forum, Standard of Good Practice for Information Security. http://www.isfsecuritystandard.com/SOGP07/index.htm

11.3.2 Other Measures in Support of Privacy

Respect for consumer and employee privacy is a key value for Nokia. Without the right culture, assessments will not be done consistently. So what is done to foster that culture? Since a few years, privacy has been included in the code of conduct and the general e-learning that every employee needs to take. This section describes other aspects of developing a privacy-sensitive culture: training, awareness campaigns, blogs and the company's intranet.

11.3.2.1 Training

Key functional employees in Nokia are regularly trained in privacy compliance. Training falls into several categories: One is longer specialist training, usually delivered on demand to a targeted audience. The content is tailored to address specific questions. A good example of this first group is training such as "Privacy for sourcing specialists". This type of training might take about a day. Second, training is given to those who need to know about privacy compliance in general. The audience ranges from software designers to HR specialists. This type of training is focused more on awareness-building than on teaching specific skills. The idea behind this type of training is that managers can influence their subordinates so that important decisions are not taken without taking privacy into account.

Screenshot: *Privacy Pursuit*

Finally, Nokia has designed and deployed several types of e-learning.[18] Two of these are specifically designed for HR specialists; another one introduces eight key aspects of privacy compliance to a general audience. The screenshot above shows a quiz question in the fantasy privacy game called *Privacy Pursuit*. This unusual approach was chosen to spread core privacy-related information to thousands of employees.

11.3.2.2 Awareness Campaigns, Blogs and the Intranet

Nokia runs privacy awareness programs from time to time. A recent example concerns the 2010 screensaver campaign, which brought privacy-related core messages to every employee's computer as a screensaver. These messages informed employees about good security practices, the importance of trust in online services and questions specific to Internet services such as sharing location data with friends. Nokia management decided to deliver this campaign as a screensaver because it was the best way to reach everyone in this truly global company.

Another channel to raise privacy awareness is the internal privacy blog. The blog informs employees about what is happening in the world of privacy, and it is tightly linked to the privacy intranet – an extensive site which covers topics such as requirements, instructions, training, frequently asked questions (FAQs) and contacts.

11.3.3 Reasons for Conducting Privacy Assessments

There are four main reasons for conducting privacy assessments:

The primary reason for conducting privacy assessments is to measure the implementation of privacy requirements, to get an understanding of the current status (risks, controls, root causes, etc.).

Second, Nokia sees the assessments as part of its technical and organisational measures.[19] PIAs and PISAs are the main way to find out if new projects follow the privacy requirements. Furthermore, the assessments can be used in project management – they help to communicate about the fulfilment of requirements. They also help to generate status reports for management teams. They have proven to be an effective tool for assigning responsibility and fixing problems.

Third, an assessment, once done, serves as a repository for information requests from authorities and consumers. Consumers might ask Nokia where and for how long their data is stored. A data protection authority might, for example, ask how consumers are informed about privacy practices or who the controller of the data

---

[18] These are online training courses delivered directly to users' desktop computers. Completing an e-learning lesson usually takes between 30 minutes and 1 hour.

[19] Compare Article 17 of the EU Data Protection Directive.

is. Privacy assessment might also be used to prepare notifications for data protection authorities (i.e., filings that indicate Nokia's processing practices in different countries).

Fourth, the assessments are well recognised in Nokia as a means to improve general awareness. The assessment process slowly builds up competencies and privacy awareness, as it offers an extensive set of questions that might be relevant for privacy compliance.

11.4 The Process, or How Privacy Assessments Are Conducted

This section will characterise the two kinds of privacy assessment and describe how PISAs and PIAs are conducted. The section ends by discussing the resources needed to perform these assessments.

11.4.1 Two Kinds of Privacy Assessments

At Nokia, two kinds of privacy assessments are conducted; one can be seen as a subset of the other. The main template or questionnaire is used for the PISA. This template, with free text fields and the possibility to attach information, focuses on security and it includes a section on privacy. A PISA is required for all consumer-facing applications before they go into production or before existing applications undergo a major upgrade. The PISA is used to evaluate the organisational and technical security level of Nokia's consumer services from both a consumer and a Nokia perspective. Among other things, it aims to ensure compliance with industry security standards and consumer data regulations.

Sometimes, only the introductory and privacy sections of the PISA template are used. This shorter assessment is a PIA. The privacy section is applicable to all services and products (internal and external) and assesses the level of compliance against Nokia's core privacy requirements. The PIA is mainly used for applications that deal with employee data or by research groups to conduct a first self-assessment. The purpose of a self-assessment is to raise awareness of questions that are likely to come up at later stages. If the PIA identifies a need for additional assessment categories, other parts of the PISA template may be used. Nokia fundamentally renewed its assessment process in the last three years and continuously seeks to improve it. The catalogue of key questions in the template has more than doubled in those years and extra fields have been added.

11.4.2 Undertaking a PISA

The PISA process can be divided into five steps: initiation, validation, execution, delivery and monitoring.

11.4.2.1 Initiation

Any Nokia business unit may initiate the PISA process by submitting a request to the privacy assessment team. In most cases, the request will come from a product manager, who is responsible for overall legal compliance. The request might come through the supporting business lawyer or through a team member of the project manager, who happens to be trained in privacy compliance.[20] The knowledge about the need for assessment is growing rapidly as management teams ask for privacy assessments as part of the overall project management process.

11.4.2.2 Validation

In this step, the unit scopes the assessment based on a privacy scenario, and agrees an organisation of the assessment and a preliminary schedule. This information forms the scope of the assessment. *Scenario* in this context means to find out what kind of testing is needed and whether a PIA is enough or if there should be a full-scale PISA. The scope concerns the application, product or service in question.[21] The process might end here if it is determined at this stage that no assessment should be made. That could be the case if the application handles data only in anonymous or pseudonymised form.

A complete PISA is conducted if the consumer service is new, if there are fundamental changes to the service or if there have been serious attacks by hackers. Applications that process employee data will usually only use PIAs. A self-assessment is the right approach if the application is still under development. At this stage, the assessment is planned, i.e., the persons that should be involved are identified and the schedule for interviews, workshops and testing is determined.

11.4.2.3 Execution

There are often different experts involved in the security and the privacy parts; the interviewers are chosen from a group of about 10 people according to the skill set needed.

The execution phase takes approximately three weeks. It includes a technical kick-off, workshops and technical security testing and is designed to assess the adequacy of technical controls [e.g., application, network, database and operating system (OS) configurations]. Results of these activities are consolidated into a report. Senior peers perform quality assurance. Usually the product manager, architect, service transitioning and the production or service delivery manager are involved from the service side. Often specialists from other areas are consulted. Subject matter experts are utilised for the technical PISA testing. The testing

---

[20] This underlines the importance of regular training. Privacy officers and privacy managers typically contact units proactively.

[21] This covers related organisation and production hosting sites as well.

includes application and network vulnerability testing, as well as platform and database level audit. The toolset contains both automated and manual testing.

11.4.2.4 Delivery

The findings arising from the PISA and recommendations for mitigating controls are consolidated into a final report and delivered to the product team. They are also entered into an online repository for tracking and follow-up. In some cases, especially when there are critical findings, the report will be discussed in management teams, as these findings might delay the launch of a service.

11.4.2.5 Monitoring

A product security manager will follow up on compliance. If there is a fundamental change to a product or service, then a new PISA should be conducted. If there are only minor changes compared to the assessed version, the product security manager must decide if the assessment needs to be updated.

11.4.3 The PIA Process – Deviations from PISA

While a PIA follows basically the same steps as a PISA, there are some differences:
One big difference between the processes is the way the applications are prioritised. As there are many more applications handling employee data, IT staff use the following methodology to prioritise assessments: First, they assess the amount of personal data that might be involved in an application. Second, they group applications according to the sensitivity of the personal data.[22] The third criterion might be the most surprising. They look at the life cycle: Is the application at the end of the lifecycle, just launched or in design? The rationale behind this criterion is to make sure that resources are spent on those applications that will have the most impact in the future. Typically, the costs of corrective actions are a thousand times more costly when a service is in the operational phase compared to the design phase. All application owners are regularly asked to fill in a specifically designed tool, which is used for prioritisation of applications to be assessed.

Another important difference is that the PIA process does not include any testing. This means that the information provided by the product manager is taken at face value. As the applications are available to all employees, the assessors might already be familiar with them.

Finally, a PISA and PIA differ in the people involved. The IT unit privacy managers have a strong role in PIAs, but not always in PISAs. They are responsible for planning and organising the PIAs, interviewing the product team, suggesting corrective actions and following up on those actions.

---

[22] Nokia classifies information as public, company confidential, confidential or secret.

11.4.3.1 Resources

As Nokia's products and services are very different in scope, it is hard to give any specific estimate of the cost and time involved in performing a PIA. For PIAs, the costs are purely internal (roughly two or three employee-days in total). Self-assessments take even less time. A PISA will usually involve an external party assessing the service. Costs will be about €10,000 in addition to the employee-days needed. While this might appear high at first sight, all interviewees have confirmed that they think the process is necessary and cost-effective.

PIAs can be concluded – from beginning to end – within a few hours. This is the exception, however, as usually not all information is available and monitoring is necessary. PISAs are targeted to be completed within three weeks; in practice, they can take up to five weeks and in extreme cases up to three months, depending on how long it might take to perform technical testing.

11.5 The Content of Privacy Assessments

This section describes the content of the PISA and PIA templates.

11.5.1 The PISA Template

11.5.1.1 Overview

The PISA template includes 17 sections. One section deals with privacy and is used for the PIA assessment. That part is described in more detail below, even though it is an integral part of the PISA process. While the rest of the template focuses on different aspects of security, the distinction between privacy and security is not crystal clear; many of the questions in those sections can be considered as privacy questions too. This is why the privacy section refers to six security sections: access management, business continuity planning, network security, physical security, platform security, third-party management and training.

Describing in detail all of the more than 100 privacy and security questions in a PISA is beyond the scope of this chapter. The following description is merely an overview of the 16 sections dealing with security. The structure of the 16 sections is almost the same (with the exception of the cover section): Most of the PISA template is in the form of a matrix. The questions are in different rows; additional information, guidance and space for answering and commenting are provided in columns. As part of the guidance, the risk and the impact are explained and classified. The latter is useful for awareness raising and as guidance for higher levels of management. The modular structure of the template allows scoping the assessment according the needs of the service. For example, not every application needs to be assessed on network security or change management, but for some products and services, these modules may be the most important for privacy compliance.

11.5.1.2 Introductory Cover Section

This section requires five types of basic data. First, administrative information is documented: who is the assessor, when was the assessment made, etc. Second, the type of personal data is identified: Is this assessment dealing with employee or consumer data? How sensitive is the data? Third, important contacts are addressed: Who is the supporting legal counsel? Who is the privacy manager assigned to this project, etc? Next, data flows are addressed and, last, are questions concerning server hosting.

11.5.1.3 Access Management

In this section of the PISA, most of the access control metrics are standard metrics derived from the PCI DSS. Other questions address the strength of passwords, the use of shared accounts and audit trails.

11.5.1.4 Business Continuity Planning

This section contains basic questions concerning business continuity, such as removal of single points of failure and management of back-up arrangements.

11.5.1.5 Change Management

The term *change management* as employed here covers how new procedures, versions and upgrades are handled: Is there a documented change management process used for all changes in the environment? Are changes tested prior to being applied to the "live environment"? Does the process include handling of emergency fixes?

11.5.1.6 Incident Management

The purpose of this section is to align services and applications with Nokia-level incident response management. Staff assess whether the product or service in question has reactive capabilities for privacy and security incidents.

11.5.1.7 Log Management

Which audit trails exist? Are audit trails secured so they cannot be altered and can only be viewed by those with a job-related need? The last question is in itself crucial for good privacy compliance towards employees and collaborators, while the first question helps, for example, to discover the course of actions taken by a hacker in an incident-handling case.

11.5.1.8 Network Security

This section aims at making sure that networks used by Nokia are secure. It includes questions about basic encryption processes and security configurations. It also addresses requirements, such as encryption during transmission over public or open networks and monitoring of network traffic.

11.5.1.9 Physical and Platform Security

The questions on physical security deal mainly with facility entry controls, i.e., whether there are systems in place to limit and monitor physical access to systems that store, process or transmit classified data. The requirements are taken from the PCI standard. The same is true for platform security. An example of a question that may be asked in this part of the assessment is whether file integrity monitoring software exists.

11.5.1.10 Risk and Security Management

The risk management section asks whether information risk analyses have been done and whether the process is repeatable and structured. Security management questions concern the roles and responsibilities related to information security and privacy.

11.5.1.11 Security Testing

This part of the assessment tests whether internal and external network vulnerability scans are run regularly and after fundamental changes, such as new system component installations or changes in network topology. It also asks about penetration testing and how it is assessed. A penetration test is a highly defined test with specific parameters regarding unauthorised access to information assets.

11.5.1.12 Systems Development

There are several questions pertaining to systems development security. They concern, for example, the methodology of system development, the need for testing and the reviewing of code before going live.

11.5.1.13 Third-Party Management

From supplier selection, contract creation and monitoring suppliers, this section assesses whether the product or service checks that third parties follow Nokia's privacy requirements.

11.5.1.14 Training

It is imperative that all personnel supporting the product or service have been trained on privacy and security. The training should include the communication of the information security policy and data privacy requirements.

11.5.1.15 Vulnerability Management

The vulnerability management section seeks to find out whether the product or service makes sure that latest software updates and anti-virus programs are run on all systems commonly affected by viruses.

11.5.2 The PIA Template

As stated above, the PIA template is part of the PISA template. A PIA usually includes an introductory section, a section dealing with third-party management, questions concerning PCI and a privacy section. If needed, other sections, such as that concerning training, can be included. The PIA form uses the privacy requirements as its backbone. In the template, the same standard fields exist, i.e., control questions, guidance, risk and impact, reference to the source of the requirement and an auditor's assessment. The privacy section asks 49 core questions.

Control Question	Guidance	Risk	Impact (In the absence of mitigating controls)	Source/Reference	Response	Auditor's Assessment
Is storage of special categories of personal data kept to minimum and is storage amount and retention time limited to that which is required for business, legal, and/or regulatory purposes?	Should avoid collection and storage of so called special categories of personal data (e.g., data revealing racial or ethnic origin, political opinions, religious or philosophical beliefs, trade-union membership, and the processing of data concerning health or sex life).	Nokia may face corrective costs when forced by individual or regulatory complaint. Or there may be local damage to our reputation and we loose trust of individuals and their business.	Medium	Nokia Privacy Requirement 2.2		
Are there controls in place to distinguish what information being collect is required and what is optional? And that only mandatory data fields are collected?	If the user provides his personal data e.g. through a web-form, must identify the mandatory and voluntary data fields. Only such data fields may be mandatory that are necessary in order to provide the product or service. However, optional parameters can be collected if they have been communicated to the users as optional.	Should Nokia fail to gain consent for processing and location of personal data from users and not have capabilities to handle personal data according to requirement (anonymously, location, deletion) and face privacy breach, it may potentially cause Nokia to face huge liability costs to build them into services when forced by law enforcement. Also, Nokia may face world-wide damage to reputation and loose trust of consumers causing losses of consumer business.	Medium	Nokia Privacy Requirement 2.2		

Screenshot: Two questions in the PIA as examples

Screenshot: Two questions in the PIA as examples

In the following paragraphs, I describe 18 sets of questions from the PIA template. I pick some from each set to give an idea of what is assessed.

The first set of questions concerns documentation, as part of technical and organisational matters. Outdated documentation could lead to confusion as to the current status and responsibilities of key individuals. In addition, the product or service must ensure that relevant personnel are aware of the privacy requirements.

The second set of questions assesses the principle of data minimisation, i.e., the obligation to minimise data collection; data should only be processed for identified, fair and lawful purposes. This part assesses as well whether there is a life-cycle defined for the data and how the information is updated.

The third set of questions concerns the information given to the data subject. These requirements are assessed to make sure the data subject knows what kind of data processing is going on and has a chance to easily retrieve more information, e.g., by consulting the service terms or the privacy policy. Typically, this concerns online content; in rare cases, other channels of communication are assessed as well.

The fourth set of questions covers the collection of data by the product or service. Especially these features are assessed: Is it possible to opt out of the collection of data? What are the purposes for the collection?

A particularly sensitive aspect, which is assessed separately in the next set, is location data. One important aspect concerning location data and as well general data sharing is addressed in the following section on privacy settings. These features allow users to exercise control over how their personal data is shared or otherwise used.

Next, a number of questions evaluate whether the application or service has appropriate security measures to protect personal information. This concerns access control, encryption and the process of taking data extracts.

Section eight covers the incident response mechanism in the event of a breach of privacy and/or security – to make sure breach notification rules are followed. This section helps to raise awareness. By asking whether there is a defined process to address personal data breaches or other privacy-related security incidents, the product manager is taught that there is actually an incident response mechanism. A section on third-party management follows, which mainly refers to the section in the PISA template on third-party selection and assessment. The key point here is to find out whether the product manager has chosen suppliers carefully.

The questions in section 10 on user choices for privacy and security are very much derived from the privacy-by-design movement,[23] as product managers need to address the security architecture when the product or system is still in development. The next section deals with authority requests, followed by a section on international data transfers. These questions are asked to make sure a valid mechanism for data export is used, such as the Standard Contractual Clauses. This is usually quite easy to assess.

Section 13 on the protection of children is much harder to assess, as there might be different ways to fulfil this requirement due to the open nature of the subject area. The next section assesses whether user messages, call logs or other such information protected by confidentiality of communications are only accessible with the user's consent. This is important, as telecommunication operators might provide Nokia with traffic data to be used in the provision of the product or service. The following set of questions concern direct marketing activities.

Section 16 determines whether notifications need to be made to data protection authorities. This section often leads to escalation to the legal department. Section 17 assesses whether the application complies with local employment-related privacy requirements, the Nokia global employment privacy policy and the Nokia privacy policy for "externals", i.e., those persons who are not employed by Nokia but who are engaged in external resourcing for Nokia, such as subcontracting, service

---

[23] See Schaar, Peter, "Privacy by Design", *Identity in the Information Society*, Vol. 3, No. 2, April 2010, pp 267–274 with concrete examples.

provisioning for Nokia, external temporary labour, and thus part of the Nokia value chain. The last set of questions address privacy in mergers and acquisitions.

11.6 Areas for Improvement

No process is perfect. Privacy is an area where all companies are learning, and so is Nokia. The following paragraphs identify seven areas where improvements can be made, based on the interviews I have conducted.

11.6.1 Quality of the Requirements That Are Assessed

An assessment is only as good as the metrics employed. So if the "privacy requirements" are unclear, the results will be less useful. This is especially a problem with self-assessments: People who are not trained in information security and privacy compliance are confronted with questions that need a substantial level of knowledge.[24]

This is an important point, and there are regular reviews in both processes to improve the templates, including adding new requirements as well as explaining what a certain requirement means. The good side of confronting hundreds of employees with detailed privacy requirements is that the level of knowledge of the employees will rise and there will be a push for more detailed guidance. However, the task of the unit privacy officer will always remain, as the units need someone to "translate" the meaning of general requirements.

The PISA and PIA templates are designed for consumer applications; therefore, employees who are charged with doing PIAs for applications that process employee data do not always understand the level of detail in the questionnaire. Some sets of questions might not be relevant for PIAs done for applications that process employee data.

One way to improve the quality of the requirements is to add a description of privacy requirements in form of a brief story or vignette. A vignette means that a requirement will not just read:

> In case of privacy violation or other privacy incident, staff must check with Nokia legal counsel whether a notification to the users is required and, if so, make the necessary notifications.

A vignette would say something along these lines:

> A consumer asks you: I have heard a lot about privacy violations of Internet companies. I am concerned. How do you make sure that I hear from Nokia when something unplanned happens to my data? Do you know who are the right people to make the decision to inform me according to the law?

---

[24] One example is terminology: Product managers in IT do not usually know what "data subject" means. So it is better to avoid this term.

The difference might seem small for the seasoned privacy professional. The "vignette" approach explains why a certain requirement is relevant for consumers, which makes it easier to understand (and implement!) for business teams. First experiences with this approach have shown that parts of the organisation will implement requirements faster if they are presented in a more approachable way.

11.6.2 Resources

While the product managers interviewed for this chapter were generally satisfied with the number of PIAs conducted each year, some pointed out that by having a less "heavy" process, more assessments could be conducted. Use of resources for privacy and security is an issue in all companies, but all experts asked have stated that the benefits of PIAs far outweigh the costs. Generally speaking, product managers were very willing to improve their products; it was more difficult to get the time needed from other people involved with the assessments, e.g., the supporting lawyers and IT architects.

Resource planning is always difficult. Self-assessments are one way to decrease the costs, another way is to have the right scope for the assessment – not every new version of a service needs a complete PISA.

11.6.3 Awareness

Most of the specialists interviewed for this chapter found that the PIA process is sufficiently known and have stated that they feel privacy awareness has increased over the last two years.[25] However, keeping up awareness about privacy in general and PIAs in particular is hard, probably best compared to swimming upstream. After all, what could sound more boring than "privacy impact assessment"? The problem all privacy and security professionals face is that it takes only one product manager not aware of the privacy requirements and assessment structure to cause a privacy incident.

Nokia addresses this question with different levels of training and by relying on the network of privacy officers within the company, who work closely with their units. The target is that all product managers in the company know that, when handling personal information, the privacy requirements apply and a PIA might be needed. One way to address this in the coming years is to make self-assessments more common at earlier stages in the product or service development cycle.

---

[25] According to one representative privacy manager, the PIA and PISA process is well known in the product management community and among legal staff. Awareness could be improved with developers.

11.6.4 Evaluating Findings

Some interviewees have found it difficult to evaluate the findings of a PISA or PIA. As described above, the assessments ask for a classification of the risk. Risk evaluation is something that ultimately depends on personal judgement. While seasoned interviewees did not even mention this issue, it seemed to be a problem for those who are new in their role. An easy and cost-effective remedy is that new assessors are coached by more experienced ones.

11.6.5 Information Not Available

The main factor that slows execution of assessments is lacking documentation in the project. This is in particular the case with legacy cases or when third parties are involved. Sometimes, incomplete information is passed on when projects move from research and development units to the business units.

11.6.6 Corrective Actions

Assessing is not a self-serving function. It is done for a reason, namely to identify potential privacy impacts. Nokia has learned that having the findings alone is not enough; the key is to have a supporting structure that follows up on the status of those findings. This sounds obvious; however, implementation requires different people with different roles in the company to be aware of the findings. Almost all persons interviewed for this chapter saw implementation of reported findings as one of the core challenges. Nokia has been addressing the problem by involving some management teams in the PIA reporting process. Implementation is made easier if the assessments are available to the relevant experts.

11.6.7 Speed of Execution

Usually, big companies do not see anything negative in fast execution and reaction to the market; on the contrary, it is regarded as a key competitive skill. However, an ever-changing business environment is challenging for privacy compliance. Project managers move on to new roles and development cycles get shorter. Nokia reacts to this challenge through general awareness raising and by trying to include privacy compliance in the product or service development at a very early stage.

11.7 Conclusion and Summary: 10 Recommendations

PIA and PISA are the cornerstones for privacy compliance in Nokia. The general opinion in Nokia is that they are a cost-effective way to ensure privacy compliance. The assessments are mainly seen as a way to reduce risk and to provide business with better visibility of privacy and security concerns. Privacy assessments have helped Nokia to decrease the risk of financial loss caused by compensation and penalties. They also decrease the risk of damage to reputation, which is the consequence of every privacy incident. PISAs and PIAs are part of implementing privacy-by-design principles. This is why it is so important to have (self-) assessments at a very early stage, when changes can easily be implemented.

PISAs and PIAs are no panacea and even the best process cannot guarantee that companies steer clear of privacy incidents. There are other dangers such as industry espionage and social engineering, issues all larger corporations have to deal with. New employees might not necessarily know how important privacy is for Nokia. That is why PIAs are only one of several measures in privacy compliance. They are complemented by awareness campaigns and training of all kinds. Even if assessments are conducted, there is a lot of work to do in implementing the findings. It is best to think of privacy governance as an interlinked system which needs to be constructed in a way that information is shared freely, both bottom-up and top-down.

Instead of a conventional summary, here is Nokia's list of 10 recommendations to those other companies who see the value of undertaking privacy impact assessments and are just beginning to use them.

11.7.1 Start Small, But Start

Designing a PIA program is a huge task, but this should not stop any company from starting with a process that can be improved step by step. Without real-life experience, a process cannot be improved.

11.7.2 Awareness

Assessments will only be done if product managers know about the process. General awareness campaigns should go hand in hand with targeted training. Culture and awareness need time to grow. Privacy assessments are in themselves a step towards changing corporate cultures.

11.7.3 Privacy Assessments Need to Be Supported by a Governance Model

Privacy assessments should be part of a governance system that makes sure that roles and responsibilities are clear. One good way to do this is the RACI model[26] and assigning implementation tasks to privacy officers that are embedded in the business.

---

[26] RACI is an acronym derived from the four key responsibilities – Responsible, Accountable, Consulted and Informed – used in a Responsibility Assignment Matrix (RAM), also known as a

A central function should be responsible for creating guidelines and monitoring the assessment process.

11.7.4 Definitions of Requirements Must be as Self-Explanatory as Possible

Assessments should be written from the point of view of the person who is interviewed, not from the point of view of the interviewer. One good idea is to add different forms of explanations to the question, for example, a source, an example or a consumer vignette.

11.7.5 Include Open Questions in the Assessments

It is not advisable to rely only on closed questions, such as yes/no type of questions or questions that let the interviewee choose from a set of given answers. While closed questions are needed, as they are easier to evaluate and help with the scoping, open questions are essential to find hidden privacy problems.

11.7.6 Specialisation

Privacy assessments are a process, repetitive over time. As people tend to get better at things they do more than once, it makes sense to have a core team of specialists who concentrate on conducting the interviews, writing reports and following up with the findings. This helps as well to deal with open questions.

11.7.7 Cultivate a Culture of Continuous Improvement and Open Communication

The more an organisation performs privacy assessments, the more new problems are discovered. It is necessary that feedback from the field is effectively communicated to a central function, managing, for example, the requirements. An example is the need for escalation to higher level managers when the interviewer notices that there is no appropriate training for a certain business team. By listening to feedback, managers can continuously improve the assessment process.[27] The assessor

---

RACI matrix, which describes the participation by various roles in completing tasks or deliverables for a project or business process. For more, see http://en.wikipedia.org/wiki/Responsibility_assignment_matrix

[27] For more on the concept of continuous improvement, see Maurer, Robert, *One Small Step Can Change Your Life: The Kaizen Way*, Workman, New York, 2004.

should as well have the right attitude: Her role is to improve things, to help – not to judge and condemn. This will help in getting people to be open about the possible problems with a product or service.

11.7.8 Prioritisation

It is advisable to have criteria to prioritise the assessment of tools and applications, e.g., taking into account the amount of data, its sensitivity and life cycle. A first come, first serve approach might be appropriate in bars, but cannot be considered good practice for companies assessing tools and applications.

11.7.9 Effective Resource Management

Privacy assessment templates tend to get more complex over time. Therefore, it is important to scope the assessment appropriately. Spending too much time on one application might prevent other applications from being assessed.

11.7.10 Inclusion of PIA and PISA When Managing Projects

One key lesson from Nokia's experience is that privacy assessments need to be part of the project management methodology in each business line. Unit privacy officers are responsible to ensure that "do a PISA/PIA" is on all relevant checklists and is followed up by management teams. Continuous reporting is needed to ensure they are ingrained in corporate practice.

Chapter 12
How Siemens Assesses Privacy Impacts

Florian Thoma

12.1 Siemens at a Glance

To understand Siemens' approach to data protection in general and to privacy impact assessments in particular, it is helpful to provide some insight into the corporate structures and markets in which the company is operating. In fact, the size of Siemens creates some unique challenges in implementing, operating and auditing a privacy framework:

- With three main business sectors – industry, energy and healthcare – and additional businesses, in particular, information technology (IT) solutions and services, financial services and real estate, Siemens operates in nearly every country on the globe and provides a broad range of products and solutions to customers – among which are light bulbs, diagnostic and imaging systems as well as turnkey power plants. The annual turnover is about €76 billion (2010).
- Siemens staff is highly diverse and, as of December 2010, comprises 410,000 employees working for about 1,000 legal entities. About 129,000 of the staff are located in Germany, about 62,000 in all states of the US.
- As a consequence, IT systems and processes show a broad range – from unified global systems through regional systems used in a number of countries within regional clusters to systems deployed in single countries, entities or even sites (e.g., production plants).

The following can, therefore, provide only an overview of the company's approach and is far from being complete. Rather, most of the description focuses on central programs and processes.

F. Thoma (✉)
Siemens AG, Munich, Germany
e-mail: Florian.Thoma@siemens.com

D. Wright, P. De Hert (eds.), *Privacy Impact Assessment*, Law, Governance
and Technology Series 6, DOI 10.1007/978-94-007-2543-0_12,
© Springer Science+Business Media B.V. 2012

12.2 Terminology

Siemens has not yet found a globally consistent approach to privacy impact assessments (PIA) or even used this terminology a lot – and will probably not start using the terminology in the foreseeable future, but rather will focus on increasing the sharing of practices and implementing common policies across its business sectors across all countries and regions. Therefore, the author hereinafter discusses a range of concepts that fall within the broader category of PIA but typically are not introduced specifically as such in the company.

When referring to PIA, Siemens tends to apply a rather comprehensive definition covering a broad range of processes, styles and concepts that have in common a systematic approach for

- identifying and understanding actions likely to have effects on privacy-related rights and freedoms of individuals (and, in some cases, corporate and collective entities),
- identifying the company's interests and individuals' rights and freedoms, as well as the legal framework applying to such actions,
- evaluating the effects and in particular the risks and other adverse impacts rising from actions,
- defining means to mitigate such risks and impacts, and thereby
- assisting management in deciding if, and how, to move forward.

"Actions" used in the in the sense above cover, among other things, the creation and deployment of changes to and the decommissioning of IT systems, the use of personal data and changes to the original purpose for which data were collected and processes, as well as the establishment of policies, processes and procedures that govern the collection, processing and use of personal data within an entity. In some circumstances, the term "actions" also covers decisions not to take an action, where this is a realistic alternative.

12.3 Some Challenges

One practical challenge in introducing regular privacy checks within the company's processes, in particular in the IT and compliance arenas, is in the terminology: while those in privacy functions typically have a sound understanding of who a data subject is and of core concepts such as data quality, adequacy and legitimacy, this is not equally true for the intended addressees – those having responsibility for data in human resources (HR), sales, IT and other functions and those devising, implementing and operating systems that process personal data.

As the language derived from directives and the law does not transport the message particularly well, we have frequently found that significant efforts were, and are, needed to translate the abstract concepts into understandable, concise and practicable rules and policies. This has resulted in a kind of "in-house commentary" and in (constantly revised) templates and intranet pages. Still, the need for practical advice and training remains high, but this is a must to familiarise staff with privacy and avoid its being seen as a field that is best left exclusively to the experts.

This is particularly true for those countries that have not experienced a mature data protection regime. The function of a data protection co-ordinator was new to many of the Siemens group companies when it was introduced on a company-by-company basis from 2003 onwards, and we could not build on the same fundamental principles and values in all parts of the globe. Since then, our training program (comprising both onsite and web-based trainings and other elements) has acquainted major parts of the data protection organisation and, subsequently, the legal, compliance, IT and HR functions with insight into the rights and freedoms and the underlying values. Realistically though, this will be a long-term program requiring significant resources.

Finally, some remarks on the data protection officer (DPO) function: while it is conceived as a function reducing the burden placed on companies (e.g., waiving requirements of notice to, and approval of, the data protection authorities) and allowing a self-control of businesses to some extent, not everyone has full insight into this function and thus may be tempted to perceive the DPO function as itself being a burden placed on businesses. Similarly, in the initial stage, we found that the policies and procedures that were introduced were sometimes perceived as overly burdensome, even bureaucratic, and while we revised the documents and templates with the aim of making them more self-explanatory and short, we also discovered an increasing interest in our work, in particular, in the transparency and details that became available through the process documentation and IT services descriptions. The IT services descriptions led to a steep increase in interaction, in particular within the data protection organisation and between it and other functions (HR, Legal, IT).

12.4 The Data Protection Officer's Tasks

With the group headquarters located in Germany, the development of data protection started early and for many years was influenced largely by German legislation and its requirements. Siemens created a privacy function – which soon became the Data Protection Officer's organisation – already in 1976 and thereby even ahead of the German Federal Data Protection Act (FDPA), which came into force in 1977.

This long history, however, led to a strong focus on the specific German requirements for many years, based partly on the assumption that if we would only embed German standards, we would easily also meet or even exceed the standards in what at that time was a very limited number of other countries with developed approaches to privacy. It was only around 2001 that Siemens undertook concrete steps to approach privacy with a dedicated international strategy. Many elements have survived this change, and the assessments we run today are influenced by the German tradition:

- The Data Protection Officer is a function mandatory for most German private companies collecting, processing and using personal data, except for very small companies. This function is designed as a strong element of self-regulation and self-control within the company. Therefore, the main task assigned to the DPO by law is to "work towards compliance with data protection requirements" as defined by the FDPA, specific legislation and/or additional rules set, e.g., by intra-company agreements with the employees' representation, the Works Councils. The DPO role is therefore not devised as a primarily operational one but as a function encouraging, urging and controlling those who collect, process and use personal data.
- "Working towards compliance" comprises two main elements: (a) to acquaint management and employees – on a level commensurate with the respective tasks of the target groups – with the requirements of data protection, and (b) auditing and controlling the systems deployed to process personal data of employees, customers and suppliers, other business partners and shareholders. It must be understood, though, that the law does not require the DPO to assess compliance of the systems with the law in all cases prior to the deployment of such systems. Rather, the FDPA limits such mandatory controls to what it defines as "Vorabkontrolle" ("prior checking"), i.e., an anticipated control of systems that could create specific risks to the fundamental rights and freedoms of individuals. Typically, this is the case when sensitive data [as defined by s. 3 para. 9 FDPA and Art. 8 of the EU Data Protection Directive (95/46/EC)] is processed, or where the system allows for performance or behavioural monitoring.
- Due to these limitations, there are no requirements in Germany to always conduct PIAs for IT systems: only where the requirements for an anticipated control are met or where a third-party processor is involved are specific privacy-related measures required. As an example, if the company establishes a new IT system to keep track of its IT assets, including software licences assigned to, and used by, employees, this would neither require a "prior checking" nor a processor audit; rather it would be reported to the Data Protection Officer and documented in the company's IT systems inventory. In this case, a privacy assessment would only occur ex post.

12.5 Prior Checking

Prior checking, as defined by Article 20 of the EU Data Protection Directive, can be seen as a sub-type of privacy impact assessments: such prior checking is meant as a means to ensure compliance of high-risk processing operations with the law, and effectively limit or even exclude such risks to data subjects. It is required for processing operations that are likely to pose specific risks due to their nature, scope and purpose (cf. recitals 53 and 54 of the EU Data Protection Directive 95/46/EC).

In Germany, the Federal Data Protection Act (in s. 4d para 5) requires a "Vorabkontrolle" for automated processing operations that cause particular risks to data subjects and assigns this task to the company's data protection officer, who is obliged to refer the matter to the competent data protection authority in case of doubt (cf. s. 4d para. 6 of the Act). The scope is therefore limited. In addition, the Act refers to "Prüfung", i.e., an examination or assessment, but does not define in detail the means, extent or depth of the examination.

We are convinced that prior checking provides benefits to both the individuals and the company. The idea behind this approach is simply that prevention is better than cure, and if conducted early enough, it is an efficient means to protect the privacy of individuals in directing projects onto the right tracks. It offers the company significant advantages because it can ensure its compliant behaviour, foster employees' and customers' trust, achieve a higher degree of quality, transparency and security and avoid incurring additional costs and delay that could result from non-compliant actions, in particular, in the design of IT systems. While reliable data on these effects seems to be rare, we are convinced that this will outweigh the resources consumed for the assessment itself in nearly all cases.

12.6   Processor Audits

A complementary approach is implemented in our system of processor audits, which are mandatory under German legislation. Following a legal change in 2009, data processors must not only be chosen diligently and bound by detailed written contracts, but in particular need to be audited on a regular basis throughout the contract term. In particular, the law requires a first audit prior to the commencement of processing. On the other hand, it does not define additional requirements for such pre-processing audits, so we need to define in each case whether to do an on-site audit, rely in full or in part on audits of trusted third parties or obtain written statements and supporting documentation.

Siemens plans those audits based on its corporate IT system inventory that lists all IT systems that process personal data. This inventory is a fundamental means of maintaining an overview over the IT landscape and data flows and keep track of changes. Beyond the legal requirements, we have complemented this inventory with additional information. It now provides us with fundamental data on the systems, lists the individuals responsible for each system, provides an overview over the technical and organisational measures taken to protect the data, the amount of data processed, the number of individuals with access rights and other metrics. Also, it provides a per-system assessment of the overall criticality based on the purpose, sensitivity, amount of data, access rights and other elements.

For PIA and processor audit purposes, the inventory also lists the processors (if any) involved, including information regarding the contracts that govern such processing. This is not limited to non-Siemens processors but includes in-house entities, which are treated in the same way. Based on the overall criticality derived from the inventory, we require each provider to be audited prior to the commencement of its operations, and then in defined intervals thereafter (between one and five years). These audits are contained in the rolling five-year audit plan and documented appropriately.

The content of the audits may change from time to time, depending on the case: while the legal minimum requires the company to convince itself that all technical and organisational measures are met, we use these audits in a broader way. Typically, the first two audits include a detailed contract audit with somewhat different purposes: The first audit ensures that the legal requirements are met (written contract, detailed technical and organisational measures, adequacy of these measures and other elements as required by s. 11 FDPA). Complementing this, the second audit is necessary to assure us that the requirements really have been met: in the initial audit, in most cases, we cannot fully check all measures in sufficient detail, because it necessarily takes place prior to the commencement of the actual processing.

We do not limit these audits to the technical and organisational measures and their contractual basis, though, but regularly also check other important aspects – when we anyway collect data and look at certain aspects of a system, it makes sense not to stop there but also evaluate the legitimacy of the process or system as such, including the purpose, the principles of data avoidance and data minimisation and concepts for data access, retention and deletion. Frequently, there is also a need to update the IT system inventory as a result of such activities. The additional burden seems to be quite small, compared to full checks that would otherwise be necessary.

12.7 Group IT System Assessment: Inter-company Agreements

On a group level, a significant number of the IT systems have been consolidated over time and are typically planned, designed and implemented in the context of projects that span the global operations or at least more than one of the regional clusters. Most of these corporate systems are run under headquarters' responsibility and are documented and controlled in the context of the ICA framework – a system of Inter Company Agreements including all legal entities that use, or contribute data to, at least one of these corporate systems.

Siemens AG, as the entity running the operations and maintaining the systems, has entered into these agreements with all of the group's companies that use central IT systems for their business purposes. This has resulted in far more than 1.000 contracts, given the size of the group.

The Inter Company Agreement itself contains the abstract principles and requirements of data protection that are not system-specific. It defines processes to be followed and the typical split of responsibilities between controller and processor and defines the group-internal audit rights that Siemens entities have vis-à-vis the internal data processor. Also, the ICA defines the way in which new processes or services can become part of the framework and how legal compliance is ensured.

The ICA is complemented by documents that describe each system in detail, including its processes, data fields, technical and organisational measures, the purpose of processing, responsibilities (including the entities and individuals responsible for data protection), data flows to and from other systems and much more. Those documents, the "Process and Service Descriptions" (PSDs), follow a single template and are drafted by those setting up the system and assuming responsibility for the processing. It is no surprise that such PSDs can become rather extensive, and we have recently taken steps to structure the templates provided differently in order to concentrate on the key factors.

Following the completion of the draft, the PSDs are sent to the Corporate Data Protection Office for approval. The data protection organisation then conducts a full assessment of all aspects – frequently, this assessment results in clarifying questions and thereafter in requiring changes to the IT systems. As a part of this assessment, we consider both the legal framework and existing agreements with the Siemens works councils (i.e., bodies representing the employees and their interests vis-à-vis the management). Sometimes, such works council agreements are concluded as a result of the assessment.

Once the assessment is completed, the PSDs are sent to defined contact persons within all entities that will use the system to process their data. As the entities are in control of the data they feed into the system, they need to assess themselves whether the intended processing and use of data complies with their own local requirements. In general, this task is co-ordinated at the country level to avoid multiple checks of the same legal framework. The contact persons will consider the comments that Corporate Data Protection provides as part of the PSD but are in particular required to regard further, even deviating from or exceeding local legal require-ments. Where there is a need for changes, the controller and processor then enter into system-specific supplementary agreements that implement further requirements. As an example, there are agreements excluding the provision, or the use, of certain data fields, and others require specific processes or information or notice given to the respective controller.

The PSDs are also published on a dedicated intranet site maintained by Corporate Data Protection. However, we do not publish the full PSD but exclude both the comments which we provide to the contact persons and the description of technical and organisational measures for security reasons. The full text, however, is available upon request.

12.8 Assessment of Offshoring and Outsourcing Projects

A central program has recently been established to ensure an early assessment of projects that would result in data being processed in other countries or by non-Siemens processors. The overall reason is to manage associated risks, and the approach includes general legal risks, compliance and export control risks, data pro-tection, IT security and corporate security aspects. It is, therefore, a cross-functional approach involving the data protection function at its core. As it is a single process, it brings a "one stop" experience to those starting to implement a project. Involving a range of functions, it ensures a consistent and integrative assessment with high man-agement attention. Finally, bringing the risk-managing functions to a round table ensures that relevant projects are brought to those functions' attention in due time and don't slip through inadvertently.

The initiators of a project are required to provide basic information in the first step to allow the central team to assess whether the project is in or out of the scope of the program. This initial questionnaire includes items focusing on personal data, on the purposes pursued by the project, the involvement of processors and any cross-border aspects. As a consequence, the project is either referred to a regional or country level or dealt with in more detail by the central team. In the latter case, the project will be presented and additional documentation needs to become available before the final recommendation can be made.

The representatives of each risk-managing function then prepare their assessments, which highlight any challenges and legal limitations and discuss the involved risks. It is vital that these assessments are independent, i.e., a negative data protection assessment cannot be overturned by an exceedingly positive statement from the representative of another function. The assessments and recommendations – which can be anywhere between "no significant risks, proceed as proposed" or "project cannot be realised for legal reasons" – are made available to the initiators who are then expected to report back on how they intend to proceed. Frequently, this assessment is the starting point for a close co-operation between the project and the data protection organisation over the full project lifetime.

12.9 Advantages of Privacy Impact Assessments

What are the advantages of privacy impact assessments? Clearly, part of the assessments fulfils legal requirements in some countries, e.g., the pre-processing audit requirements related to data processors under German law (cf. s. 11 FDPA).

- Legal requirements to conduct specific checks are one reason for PIA. Obtaining certainty about compliance with data protection legislation is necessary. However, PIAs can and should go further: in particular, where other laws and regulations require the collection, processing and use of data, a PIA helps to understand what really is required by such other rules, how they interact with data protection legislation and to what extent they mandate not only the collection of data but are prescriptive or flexible regarding the means.
- PIAs can support transparency and trust to a very high degree. We have seen many situations where some project teams' initial reluctance to work with us in documenting and assessing privacy aspects (typical arguments were missing resources, expected delays, additional cost, lack of need) changed completely within a short time. The transparency achieved through documented processes and the broad availability of such documentation both showed that there was nothing to hide but supported an open discussion and helped to make stakeholders understand in more detail what the aims of a project were. Also, a PIA documents that privacy aspects have been taken into account appropriately.
- Avoiding risks to individuals, to the company's operations and reputation because they support privacy-friendly technologies and behaviour and over time might even encourage the development of privacy enhancing technologies to address issues found repeatedly in PIAs.

- Avoiding unnecessary cost to the company by ensuring that systems are developed in conformity with data protection requirements, thus preventing more expensive last-minute changes to systems and preventing risks that a system gets stopped by authorities for data protection violations.
- Protecting the company through an increased level of IT security (because the technical and organisational measures to protect personal data will – at least partly – also apply to sensitive company data).

12.10 Involvement of Data Protection Authorities

Currently, there is no formalised process by which the competent data protection authorities would be involved on a regular basis. The regulatory landscape in the privacy arena is quite fragmented, and in Germany in particular due to the federal structure. As a multinational, we are in constant contact with many authorities in different countries; still the Bavarian Data Protection Authority plays a major role for Siemens, as Bayern is where the headquarters and a major part of our German workforce are located.

Siemens does not share on a regular basis the results of privacy assessments with the authority, and the filing of documents would in itself not provide any benefits to individuals, the company or authorities, but only consume the authorities' scarce resources – it necessarily needs to be complemented by processes that ensure additional benefits. In this spirit, we involve the authorities on a regular and on an ad hoc basis. This includes discussion and advice in case of persistent doubt following a prior checking as well as a broad range of topics of mutual interest, including the overall privacy-related developments within the company.

12.11 Moving Forward

We have shown that Siemens applies a number of different programs that contain elements of PIA. Given the benefits of PIA discussed above, what could be the next steps forward?

- Further harmonise existing different approaches (of our business units and regional organisations) to PIA, including first steps in those of our focus countries that do not use PIA yet.
- Establish tools to be used in a more modular approach to PIA, i.e., to reduce complexity by breaking down the full PIA concept into a combination of modules that can be combined depending on project specifics (e.g., specific modules for contract assessments, for the assessment of legal requirements, for specific technical and organisational measures applying to typical technical concepts, and for cross-border transfers).

- In the context of our current project to revise the Siemens Binding Corporate Rules (BCRs),[1] implement a more uniform approach to PIA, including further steps towards a harmonised understanding of PIA, to ensure a minimum level of assessments occurs throughout the company. Using a standardised assessment methodology will help to intensify documentation of BCR compliance.
- Develop some metrics to get a better understanding of the cost and benefits associated with PIA. Ultimately, effective PIA that shows clear results can also help to support the role and function of the in-house data protection officer and thereby businesses' self-regulation.

We believe that the benefits of a methodical approach towards PIA are clearly visible. In a complex environment involving about 1,000 companies and nearly every country on the globe, however, the implementation and full development of the concept needs to occur step by step. The results are encouraging.

---

[1] BCR are intra-organisational privacy codes aiming to establish an adequate level (in the sense of EU Directive 95/46/EC) of protection of personal data within the members of the organisation. This adequate level is a prerequisite for many cross-border transfers of personal data to most non-EU countries.

Chapter 13
Vodafone's Approach to Privacy Impact Assessments

Stephen Deadman and Amanda Chandler

13.1 Introduction

To put privacy and Vodafone's approach to privacy impact assessments into context, we begin by describing Vodafone, how it is governed, what it does and where it's going.

Vodafone's approach to privacy has three main drivers:

Trust – For a communications company, user trust is an essential ingredient for providing a trusted network and environment for customers and users as they spend more of their lives connected to Vodafone's networks, platforms and services. Respect for privacy is an essential element in building trust.

Reputation – The maintenance of Vodafone's reputation with its key external stakeholders is also a key driver. Shareholders, civil society, policy-makers and the media expect Vodafone to have high ethical standards and Vodafone is cognizant of the fundamental importance and sensitivity of privacy within an increasingly connected digital world.

Regulation – Finally, compliance with law and regulation plays an important role, particularly as Vodafone has to grapple with multiple national legal frameworks and operates in a regulated sector.

S. Deadman (✉)
Vodafone Group, London, UK
e-mail: stephen.deadman@vodafone.com

D. Wright, P. De Hert (eds.), *Privacy Impact Assessment*, Law, Governance
and Technology Series 6, DOI 10.1007/978-94-007-2543-0_13,
© Springer Science+Business Media B.V. 2012

13.2 Vodafone's Core Business Operations

Vodafone[1] operates mobile networks and provides related services in 30 countries and has partners[2] in more than 40 other countries. As of June 2011, it had approximately 382 million subscribers.[3] In addition, Vodafone operates fixed DSL networks, cable, IPTV and satellite networks, and is developing new services such as mobile payments and money transfer, m-health, enterprise IT services, cloud computing and telephony, machine-to-machine ("M2M") services, and digital content and social media.

As a consequence, Vodafone's operations raise a wide and complex set of privacy challenges. Vodafone's most fundamental privacy obligation is to protect the confidentiality of communications. It carries a vast volume of personal information in various forms (subscription, communications traffic data, web logs, search queries, transactional data, etc.). It increasingly manages data on behalf of others. Its enterprise customers have many thousands of users using an array of networks, devices, applications and connected services.[4]

The rapid evolution of technology raises continual challenges, especially in the field of privacy. This evolution blurs boundaries between communications services and the content carried over them, and between the public and private domains. It raises complex issues relating to the generation and use of sensitive information, such as geo-location – a necessary component in cellular communications – which can be generated, used and made available via alternative technologies (see below).

With the convergence of the Internet and mobile, and "anywhere, anytime" broadband connectivity, Vodafone users are becoming active participants in the creation and sharing of Internet content through mobile and personal devices supported by applications, services and data running on remote servers, in the "cloud". This personal and potentially more open social Web[5] also raises complex new perspectives on privacy.

---

[1] Further information about the Vodafone group of companies can be found here: http://www. vodafone.com/start/investor_relations/vodafone_at_a_glance0/fact_sheet.html

[2] A Vodafone "partner" is a mobile network operator in a market where Vodafone does not hold an equity stake but has an arrangement to co-operate in the marketing of Vodafone global products and services with varying levels of brand association. http://www.vodafone.com/start/about_vodafone/ partner_markets.html

[3] Across controlled and jointly controlled operations.

[4] Vodafone Global Enterprise is one of the world's leading providers of managed mobility services, device management and solutions to global enterprise customers: http://enterprise.vodafone.com/ home/

[5] Some organisations are beginning look towards a Web that is both social and open, enabling individuals to take control over their own personal information and privacy. See a recent report from the W3C Incubator Group at: http://www.w3.org/2005/Incubator/socialweb/XGR-socialweb-20101206/ and Vodafone's R&D project on the social Web at: http://onesocialweb.org/

13.3 The External and Industry Environment

Vodafone operates in a regulated sector, characterised by spectrum licensing, tele-coms authorisation regimes, obligations to provide lawful interception and surveil-lance assistance, which is of strategic importance for the protection of national security and critical infrastructure. This regulation is largely responsible for the corporate structure of the Vodafone Group, i.e., a federation of discrete, nationally regulated businesses. The laws of each market vary, a fact which adds complexity to the development and roll-out of global products, services and technologies and, correspondingly, for privacy and other aspects of regulatory and legal compliance.

At the time of writing, many countries are developing new privacy laws and reg-ulations or revising existing ones, including the European Union with its review of the Data Protection Directive,[6] adding a degree of uncertainty to the complexity of varying national laws. At the same time, many of Vodafone's products and technolo-gies raise important privacy issues for regulators, advocates and policy-makers, e.g., social media, e-health, smart grid, intelligent transport, cloud computing, "Internet of things", geo-location, data retention, human rights and so on.

Aside from the regulatory environment, Vodafone also operates in highly dynamic and competitive markets. In addition to its traditional competitors, i.e., other mobile or fixed line operators, it faces competition from new market entrants, such as Internet companies, software and application providers and social media companies. Competition introduces its own challenges for privacy. Consider the offering of services by Internet companies using an advertising-funded business model, i.e., where services are offered without charge to the consumer. While these services have proved popular with consumers, they have also raised significant concerns about consumer privacy, particularly in regard to the use of behavioural and demographic factors to increase the relevancy of advertising to the user. This has presented a competitive challenge to the subscription-based models adopted by Vodafone and other telecoms operators.

As well as a highly dynamic and competitive environment, the telecoms industry, including Vodafone, has a tradition of collaboration on technical standards to ensure interoperability. This collaboration extends to social and legal issues such as child protection and privacy.

13.4 Vodafone's Policy and Approach to Privacy Risk Management

Vodafone adopted its global privacy policy in 2005, and every controlled entity within Vodafone is required to adopt and implement it. The privacy policy aims to achieve three objectives:

---

[6] http://europa.eu/rapid/pressReleasesAction.do?reference=IP/10/1462&format=HTML&aged=1&language=EN&guiLanguage=fr

1. To establish respect for privacy as a core corporate value, beyond simply meeting legal obligations, and embed privacy management deeply within the business;
2. To encourage appropriate and consistent privacy standards across the industry wherever possible by working with its partners, competitors and industry and technology standards bodies;
3. To be trusted by its customers and staff alike as a guardian of their privacy.

Essentially, the last of these three objectives – being trusted – can only be met by achieving the first two, i.e., embedding privacy as a corporate value, above and beyond regulatory compliance, and recognising that the protection of Vodafone's customers' privacy also depends upon, and is influenced by, the actions of others, e.g., its partners, those who build the technologies it uses and its competitors.

To meet these objectives, Vodafone's policy includes the following elements:

13.4.1 Governance and Accountability

The policy allocates clear governance and accountability for implementing the policy. At a Vodafone Group level, the policy is "owned" by a member of Vodafone's most senior executive committee, and "championed" by the Group Privacy Officer. The Group Privacy Officer is responsible for co-ordinating and aligning the Group's overall strategic direction and for managing the implementation of the global privacy programme. The CEO of each Vodafone entity is accountable for the appropriate implementation of the policy within his/her organisation. Responsibility for implementation at an operating entity level reflects the Group structure, with each Vodafone operating entity identifying a board sponsor and appointing a privacy officer with operational day-to-day responsibility.

13.4.2 Principles

The policy provides a principles-based framework, rather than a prescriptive, rules-based approach. The nature of privacy risk is not fixed, nor is privacy easily defined. While data protection regulation seeks to provide a framework for the protection of personal data, this only reflects a portion of privacy harms, particularly as new forms of privacy risk emerge with new technologies and services. Vodafone's privacy principles provide a simple but flexible framework to help manage the company's response to a variety of privacy risks across diverse markets, where perceptions of privacy are shaped by social and cultural factors, and where the legal and operational contexts vary widely. The federated nature of Vodafone's operations and the autonomy of Vodafone's local businesses in most day-to-day operational decisions also favour a more distributed form of privacy governance in keeping with Vodafone's overall governance ethos and approach, which is reflected in the principle of "one company, local roots".

13.5 Privacy Impact Assessments

Vodafone's policy expressly requires the conduct of privacy impact assessments. The inclusion of privacy impact assessments as a formal policy requirement was a recognition that the privacy impacts of activities, services or technologies provided by Vodafone and the solutions for addressing or mitigating them cannot be determined at the outset or by simply following prescriptive rules. One of the benefits of privacy impact assessments is that they can encourage consideration of creative solutions to privacy risks in a way that a rules-based compliance approach does not, e.g., engineering solutions through "privacy by design". Privacy impact assessments require the judgement of competent privacy professionals using clear principles and an established risk assessment methodology to ensure Vodafone is able to pursue its commercial strategy while satisfying people's expectations regarding their privacy and meeting its legal and ethical obligations.

Vodafone's privacy policy framework is implemented and managed through a privacy programme and a support structure for its privacy professionals.

13.6 Vodafone's Privacy Programme

Designed to be consistent with the internal governance structures and operational culture of Vodafone, the Vodafone privacy programme seeks to leverage the company's strengths, such as depth and reach of local knowledge, while providing greater support in areas identified as being of particularly high risk or complexity. There are three tiers to this:

1. *Building programme maturity* – A core objective of the programme is to attain a level of "programme maturity" in privacy risk management commensurate with Vodafone's global scale, market position and brand. The expression "programme maturity" means the degree to which accountability and operational controls and processes for privacy risk management are embedded into Vodafone's business, and managed by competent and trained privacy professionals. The management system used to deliver this is the privacy risk management system (PRMS), described below.
2. *Providing leadership* – While developing overall programme maturity will help ensure Vodafone has the competence to manage many day-to-day privacy risks, the complex and fast-changing nature of the business environments in which Vodafone operates means that it needs to take a more focused position in certain high-risk and high-profile areas. The Group Privacy Officer and Group privacy team, working closely with Group and local stakeholders and experts, provide leadership on certain privacy issues with policy implications for the Group. The management tool used to identify and prioritise these critical issues is the critical privacy issues register (CPIR), also described in more detail below.

3. *Maintaining local sensitivity* – In accordance with the "one company, local roots" principle, Vodafone must not lose focus on the importance of its local markets and the standards that are set there. Hence, Vodafone's local teams are required to ensure they address local privacy concerns and are not out of step with best practices or behaviours of our primary peer-group companies in any particular local market.

13.7 The Role of the PIA in the Vodafone Privacy Programme

Privacy impact assessments play a critical role in the Vodafone privacy programme. There is not, however, a single model or form of privacy impact assessment, as privacy impact assessments are used in different contexts. Here we provide a brief overview of privacy impact assessments used in two contrasting contexts: the strategic and the operational.

13.7.1 Strategic Privacy Impact Assessment

The CPIR is a privacy impact assessment that addresses the major strategic privacy challenges facing Vodafone and the wider industry of which it is a part. It is a tool used to identify areas where greater focus is needed, i.e., areas requiring leadership. Essentially, it adopts a macro view and looks at the wider external and industry environment to gauge where the major challenges may come from. A significant part of addressing many of these more strategic issues is the need for engagement of external stakeholders to help shape and inform opinion, conduct research or seek to agree standards with other industry players, as well as provide feedback to shape Vodafone's internal policy.

There are three main inputs into the CPIR:

1. Vodafone's corporate strategy – The trajectory of Vodafone's business and the major strategic drivers of new business opportunities, such as technology, product and service development.
2. The external regulatory and policy environment – Both existing legal and regulatory regimes, but also emerging areas of concern or debate.
3. The competitive landscape – The impact of the competitive markets in which Vodafone operates, the behaviour of its competitors and partners, new entrants and disruptive forces.

The CPIR is formally reviewed biannually by the Vodafone Group privacy team, in conjunction with local privacy teams, and a programme of actions identified following engagement with key internal functions. External inputs to this process include a quarterly review of the regulatory landscape from Vodafone's external law firms, plus input received through Vodafone's engagement with external stakeholders through its corporate sustainability programme. The CPIR and individual risk areas are then reviewed and positions approved through a senior cross-functional steering committee.

The risk identification for the CPIR is relatively straightforward. As with most risk management methodologies, it consists of an assessment of both the likelihood of an identified risk, and the impact that risk will have. However, as the CPIR is concerned with the wider strategic risks that may impact not just Vodafone directly but the industry as a whole or a technology, business model or type of product, it also includes an assessment of its proximity to Vodafone. This question of proximity seeks to position the risk by reference to the degree of control or influence Vodafone has over a particular risk. The degree of proximity can range from complete control to shared control to minimal control.

Finally, identified risks are prioritised into tiers, with tier 1 risks receiving the greatest attention.

13.7.2 Case Study – Location Services

Vodafone started to develop location services and technology in the late 1990s and began to think about how to manage location-related privacy. Around this time, policy-makers began to raise concerns around location privacy and in 2002, the EU e-Privacy Directive[7] introduced measures aimed at regulating the use of location data. In 2003, the early emergence of location services in the UK, particularly those that emphasised the utility of tracking the whereabouts of others, such as parents keeping tabs on their children, began to cause concerns among child protection groups in particular. In September 2004, an industry working group, including Vodafone, published a code of practice for the use of mobile phone technology for what were termed "passive" location services in the UK.[8]

While a reasonably tight self-regulatory framework was in place for network-enabled location services, by 2006, innovative start-up companies were offering a variety of new location-aware services based on the availability of new forms of positioning data, such as GPS and innovative techniques using open sourced mobile cell ID and wifi hotspot positioning.

13.7.2.1 Identified Risk Factors

Vodafone identified various risk factors associated with location services, as follows:

> *Corporate strategy*: Vodafone's ability to provide real-time location to partners has long been and remains a key enabling capability and the company continues to develop its own range of location-aware applications and services. For Vodafone as a network-location services provider itself, and as

---

[7] European Parliament and the Council, Directive 2002/58/EC of 12 July 2002 concerning the processing of personal data and the protection of privacy in the electronic communications sector, Brussels.

[8] www.mobilebroadbandgroup.com/.../UKCoP_location_servs_210706v_pub_clean.pdf

a company that was adopting and incorporating new positioning techniques and technologies into its services, these developments presented a significant privacy risk.

External environment: The early interest and concern around location privacy and safety that led to the 2004 UK code of practice was reignited with the advent of new location services, particularly those that combined location with a social or sharing element. At the time of writing, there continues to be increasing concern from policy-makers, civil society and regulators about how location services should be regulated.[9] If those concerns are not adequately addressed within an effective regulatory framework, there remains a significant risk of further adverse regulatory, policy-maker and, importantly, consumer reaction.

Competitive landscape: Mobile operators are no longer the sole viable source of location information (as they arguably were at the time of the 2004 UK code); new market entrants are now able to offer location services without the self-regulatory controls exerted by operators. They are also able to bypass regulatory controls, such as those introduced under the e-Privacy Directive, as they use unregulated technologies. This has resulted in regulatory asymmetry between different services based upon the type of technology used.

13.7.2.2 Risk Assessment

Taking the above factors into account, Vodafone assessed the risk as follows:

Impact – high. Geo-location invokes highly sensitive, privacy-related concerns, combining the more traditional concerns surrounding collection of sensitive data, to the potential for unauthorised surveillance and fears about physical safety. Failing to manage location privacy risk was identified as high across all three of the main drivers for Vodafone's approach to privacy:

1.   Trust – Failing to address location privacy risks would undermine trust in Vodafone, impede the adoption of new services and potentially cause customers to turn off their devices altogether for fear of being tracked without their authorisation.[10]

2.   Reputation – Having been an author and signatory to the UK code of practice on location services, there was an existing expectation from

---

[9] In July 2010, Peter Schaar, the Germany Federal Privacy Commissioner, called for further regulation to address concerns with new location services: http://www.dw-world.de/dw/article/0,,5771196,00.html. In May 2011, the Article 29 Working Party issued Opinion 13/2011 on geo-location services on smartphone devices, in response to rising concerns surrounding use of wifi access points to geo-position passing smartphones.

[10] Research conducted in 2009 at Carnegie Mellon University supported the view that users have concerns about sharing their location information online. http://cups.cs.cmu.edu/LBSprivacy/files/TsaiKelleyCranorSadeh_2009.pdf

stakeholders that Vodafone would adopt principled standards for new location services at least consistent with those adopted in the UK code.

3. Regulation – Vodafone's status as an operator and therefore the impact of the e-Privacy Directive in the EU leaves it more vulnerable to national regulatory action than non-operators. The potential for further regulatory action was assessed to be high.[11]

Likelihood – high. With previous experience of the first generation of location services in the UK, Vodafone assessed as high the likelihood that the impacts that had been identified would materialise.[12] The combination of location capabilities within highly social applications, and in an increasingly open handset and application development environment, were seen as exacerbating the already heightened concerns around privacy within social networking.

Proximity – high. Vodafone has been offering its own suite of services and applications that utilise location for many years and, in 2009, acquired a navigation and location services business[13] to support further product development. In addition, location is an important network-based "enabler" (i.e., Vodafone offers network-based capabilities to third-party developers to enhance their own location-enabled services and applications). Even where the location data itself is based on GPS or other non-Vodafone sources, Vodafone may be supporting the application by providing the underlying platform[14] or the application store from which it is marketed[15] and therefore supporting the distribution and billing for the application. Finally, for services not supported in any way by Vodafone, Vodafone sells the device and provides ongoing customer support, so there often remains a strong perception that Vodafone has some degree of control. Hence, the issue of location privacy was highly proximate to Vodafone's business activities.

Responding to the risk – Having identified location as a strategic privacy risk, Vodafone developed a programme of activities and actions to mitigate and manage the risk. This included these elements:

---

[11] Legislative changes introduced in Germany to the Federal Telecommunications Act in April 2009 bear this risk out, as new regulations were introduced that only related to geo-location services using location derived from mobile telecommunications networks, but did not cover non-mobile forms of geo-location.

[12] By early 2009, there was a steady rise in attention given to location privacy by civil society, policy-makers, regulators and the media. For instance, articles such as this were appearing in mainstream media: http://www.dailymail.co.uk/news/article-1166844/Privacy-risk-new-mobiles-away-location-stored-details-marketing-firms.html

[13] Wayfinder ceased operations in March 2010. Vodafone created the Vodafone Wayfinder Open Source Software project to contribute the software to the open source community. Details are accessible here: http://oss.wayfinder.com

[14] In 2009, Vodafone launched 360, a smartphone software platform for third party application developers that gave developers access to the Vodafone 360 smartphone's GPS positioning capabilities.

[15] Such as Vodafone 360 Shop: http://www.vodafone360.com

External engagement – Vodafone explained to stakeholders how location services, technologies and industry players had changed, and what steps Vodafone was taking to address privacy risk for the new location-aware services. This continues to be done through a series of external engagement activities, including dialogue with national regulators, civil society organisations and policy-makers.[16]

Industry action – In May 2009, Vodafone convened an industry dialogue on location services. It sought out major global players, including device manufacturers, Internet and social media companies, whose co-operation would be needed to find effective solutions for addressing location privacy. The group met in 2009 and 2010 and Vodafone presented the work of the group to the European Commission's second workshop on child safety and mobile phones in June 2010, part of the Commission's Safer Internet Programme.[17] Throughout 2010, Vodafone also worked with other mobile operators to develop privacy principles to ensure consumers' privacy could be respected and protected when using mobile applications and services that access, use or collect their personal, including location, information, that led to the publication on 27 January 2011 of the GSMA Mobile Privacy Principles.[18]

Internal policy articulation – In 2007, Vodafone developed a set of location "privacy design" principles that could be built into new forms of location services. The principles are applied to its location services and applications as well as third-party applications and services using Vodafone's location enablers or platforms. The company also held workshops with partners that utilise Vodafone's location-enabling service, such as start-ups and developers in the social media and location services sectors, to discuss the concerns and solutions for addressing location privacy, including Vodafone's location privacy design principles.

Product development – Vodafone Group's privacy team worked closely with its product development teams to ensure that its location privacy design principles were incorporated into products such as Find&Go, its successor Vodafone Navigator, Vodafone Locate and Vodafone 360. The location privacy design principles were also incorporated into the developer requirements for the Vodafone 360 platform, and included in the tutorials and other materials provided to developers in Vodafone's Developer Zone, and are an important part of the application approval process.[19]

---

[16] For example, in October 2010, Vodafone hosted an event in Brussels to draw the attention of European policy-makers to some of the inherent challenges in reforming EU privacy regulation in the face of emerging technology and social trends: http://www.vodafone.com/content/index/about/about_us/privacy/brussels_roundtable.html

[17] http://ec.europa.eu/saferinternet

[18] http://www.gsmworld.com/our-work/public-policy/mobile_privacy.htm

[19] Vodafone initially published its location design principles for review by developers on its Betavine developer site in early 2010 (http://www.betavine.net/bvportal/resources/location), and

13.8 PIA and the Privacy Risk Management System (PRMS)

13.8.1 Strategic Aims and Objectives of the PRMS

The Vodafone PRMS takes as its inspiration the definition of a "management system" from BS EN ISO 9000:2005[20] – a "system to establish policy and objectives and to achieve those objectives". The same definition is used in British Standard 10012:2009 – Data protection: Specification for a personal information management system, and in BS 25999, which is the British standard specification for business continuity management. The PRMS is based on the management system implemented by Vodafone in the UK for its certification against BS 25999 for the second and third-generation voice and data networks. It is, therefore, based on an externally recognised methodology that has been successfully tested and implemented in Vodafone, building on experience and knowledge, and ensuring a consistency in approach to delivering compliance.

As the standard model for delivering privacy risk management in Vodafone entities across the globe, at both a local and global level, the PRMS aims to ensure that Vodafone's personal information-handling practices and activities comply with privacy and data protection legislation, where these exist, and implement Vodafone's privacy principles in a manner that achieves the correct balance between commercial strategy and peoples' privacy expectations.

For Vodafone, therefore, the PRMS plays a key role in the management of personal information and privacy-impacting activities and in supporting information governance, which is a wider framework for handling information in a secure and confidential manner to appropriate business and quality standards. By adopting a management system similar to those used by other compliance teams in Vodafone, particularly those that have a relationship with privacy management, such as information security management and business continuity management, Vodafone can ensure that all these activities are aligned and consistent. This helps Vodafone get the most effective and efficient results from those compliance teams by reducing duplication of compliance activity, and protecting the business functions from being continually monitored by numerous different compliance teams, which can be very disruptive to their business-as-usual activities.

The PRMS aims to ensure that privacy risk management is built into the organisational culture of the business, and delivers tangible benefits. Experience with implementing the business continuity management system (BCMS) in Vodafone in the UK has shown that this approach is successful in getting the business and commercial teams to participate in, and provide support and resource for, delivering compliance activities. It is essential that these teams are fully engaged because

---

subsequently incorporated these into guidance for developers on the Vodafone Developer Zone (http://developer.vodafone.com/develop-apps/privacy/)

[20] BS EN ISO 9000:2005 describes the fundamentals of a quality management system, which are the subject of the BS EN ISO 9000 family, and defines related terms. See http://shop.bsigroup.com/en/ProductDetail/?pid=000000000030093429

privacy risks arise through and out of their business and commercial activities and projects. These teams also have the budget and resources to mitigate or remedy identified privacy risks through amending their processes or practices, or by designing privacy management into their products and services.

The Global Privacy Manager, under the auspices of the Group Privacy Officer, determined the privacy risk controls required by the PRMS, and developed a series of high level manuals that explain each privacy risk control – their aims and objectives, the required inputs and outputs – and give guidance on how the local privacy officer can implement each privacy risk control within his or her organisation. They are not prescriptive in the sense that they set out exactly how each control should be designed locally or who should be involved. Each Vodafone entity is structured or organised differently, and may have different privacy challenges depending on their local market. The PRMS therefore seeks to deliver on the principle of "one company, local roots" by recognising that the local privacy officer is better placed in identifying, assessing and managing their privacy risks, but that privacy risk management needs to be carried out according to a robust and methodical standard.

The PRMS, the privacy risk control manuals, templates (such as questionnaires, checklists, etc.), guidance (e.g., how to use the Vodafone risk assessment matrix) and examples of standards are all available electronically via the internal Privacy Officers' Forum intranet page. Although the Global Privacy Manager has created many of the documents for use, the global privacy officer community are also encouraged and able to upload their own tools such as their supplier review questionnaire, so that best practice and experience can be shared – thus, the approach is collaborative and mutually supportive.

13.8.2 Key Operational Controls in the PRMS

Vodafone's audit group[21] defines "control"[22] as the policies, procedures, practices and organisational structures designed to provide assurance that a risk is managed (i.e., reduced or eliminated), and that undesired events are prevented (preventative control) or detected and corrected (detective control). At an operational level, the PRMS is the model for controlling privacy risk and requires each Vodafone entity to ensure that a number of standard or required processes are implemented that identify, assess and manage privacy risks.

Some of these control processes are described below:

13.8.2.1 Privacy Impact and Risk Assessment Control Process

This control requires the privacy officer to agree a programme of privacy impact and risk assessments with their board sponsor for privacy. It is based on industry

---

[21] "Vodafone Risk Management – Risk Assessment Process", version 1, October 2009.

[22] There are currently eight required privacy risk controls in the PRMS, some of which are discussed here.

best practice from the business continuity management (BCM) profession, which requires an organisation to identify their mission critical activities, and then carry out a business and site impact assessment of by whom, where and how those mission critical activities are delivered, so that threats and risks can be identified and planned for. The Vodafone Group privacy team has identified privacy sensitive activities such as targeted mobile advertising, location aware services, use of network traffic monitoring techniques or remote management of mobile devices, and a number of privacy sensitive categories of information such as credit card information, content of communications, mobile browsing logs, which can be used to identify business areas or activities that need to be prioritised for privacy impact and risk assessment.

According to BCM practice, an impact assessment should be carried out at a high level across the organisation to identify mission critical activities, but for the purposes of the PRMS, experience among the senior privacy professionals and a range of other internal stakeholders is used to identify the privacy sensitive activities and categories of personal information outlined above. This is also informed by the outputs from the CPIR (see above).

Carrying out a privacy impact assessment or a programme of privacy impact assessments is the first and most important step in the PRMS because:

- It is an important tool for providing data about issues and risks that need to be treated, and provides a methodology for agreeing and prioritising treatment actions. It is also useful in identifying the correct people within the business who are responsible for treating those issues and risks, as they are likely to be the privacy risk owners rather than the privacy officer or manager.
- It is an important tool for providing data that will assist in developing other control processes required by the PRMS such as the personal information location register, retention policies and disclosure processes.
- It can be used to identify existing third-party suppliers whose services or activities may also need to be assessed for their impact on privacy.
- The process of carrying out a privacy impact assessment can help to raise awareness of the concept and importance of privacy in the business functions covered by the privacy impact assessment.

Privacy impact assessment is a process which combines two activities – information gathering and risk assessment. It looks at specific operational or business activities prioritised according to what the privacy officer and his or her board sponsor for privacy deem to be the highest privacy risks in their organisation. A privacy officer may therefore carry out:

- A business or functional privacy risk assessment by looking at one particular operational area of the business, such as the customer contact centre or the marketing department, and assessing all of their activities for privacy risks; or
- A privacy risk assessment of a particular privacy-sensitive activity such as network monitoring and reviewing this activity across the whole Vodafone operating

entity to identify where it happens, why and what controls currently exist to minimise privacy risk and where more controls may be required; or

- A privacy risk assessment of use of a particular privacy-sensitive category of information such as browsing behaviour, and reviewing how all operational areas use this category of information; or
- A combined privacy risk assessment, for example, reviewing how the marketing department uses or plans to use browsing information.

Having defined the privacy impact assessment to be undertaken, the privacy officer works with the relevant senior management and team leaders to identify which members of staff can provide the relevant operational information that will enable the privacy officer to understand what is happening "on the ground". The privacy officer can use a range of techniques to gather information such as questionnaires, workshops or simply one-to-one interviews with key operational staff. Once those activities have been completed, the privacy officer compiles the outputs from the information-gathering exercise into a business unit report that sets out the impacts that its activities have on the privacy of customers and/or employees, together with a suggested prioritised action plan for treating or mitigating those impacts. The privacy officer shares this report with the board sponsor for privacy and the head of the relevant business or functional area, activity owners or data users so that everyone involved in both creation and management of the privacy risk are aware of what has been identified and what needs to be done by way of mitigation action.

The reasons for preparation of a privacy impact assessment are:

- As an element of accountability, in order to demonstrate that the privacy impact assessment process was performed appropriately and in accordance with the programme of privacy impact assessments agreed with the board sponsor for privacy;
- To provide a basis for post-implementation review, i.e., to ensure that any privacy risks identified have been allocated a business owner and a timetable for delivering mitigating actions, thus providing the privacy officer with a mechanism for ensuring that those agreed actions are delivered within the agreed timescales;
- To provide a basis for audit. The PRMS distinguishes between "review", which is undertaken by the privacy officer who is responsible for ensuring that the PRMS is implemented and the controls required are delivered, and "audit", which is an objective and neutral assessment undertaken by the Vodafone Group or local audit function or by any other suitably qualified audit function that is *not* part of delivering the PRMS;
- To provide "corporate memory", ensuring that the information gained is available to those completing new privacy impact assessments if original staff have left or for use as part of a subsequent privacy impact assessment of the same business or commercial unit or activity; and
- To enable the experience gained during the project to be shared with future privacy impact assessment teams and others outside the organisation.

The following are key elements of a privacy impact assessment report:

- The scope of the privacy impact assessment undertaken,
- A summary of the consultative processes undertaken,
- The project background paper(s) provided to those consulted (in appendices),
- An analysis of the privacy issues and risks arising from the privacy impact assessment,
- The business case justifying privacy intrusion and its implications, where treatment or mitigating action has not been recommended and/or agreed,
- A description of agreed treatment or mitigating actions together with timelines for implementation,
- References to relevant laws, codes and guidelines, including internal Vodafone local or group policies.

The privacy officer is required to log all privacy risks and associated management information (such as business owner, description of mitigating action, deadline for implementation, decision to accept risk, etc.). Where the relevant Vodafone entity has an established enterprise-wide risk management process, the privacy officer can use this existing structure to record privacy risks. Where that is not the case, the privacy officer is required to maintain his or her own privacy risk register which can be shared with the board sponsor for privacy and other senior management.

The key message for this control is that it is not a one-off exercise. The information captured is only accurate for the date that it was collected. It is, therefore, imperative that not only are the outputs kept under review by the privacy officer, but that the privacy impact assessment is repeated on a regular basis to capture any new privacy risks that may have arisen due to a re-organisation of the business or commercial teams, or because of a change in commercial or business strategy. The regularity with which the privacy impact assessment is repeated will depend on the privacy sensitive nature of the personal information involved and/or the privacy intrusive nature of the activity. Thus, for a high privacy risk, the privacy impact assessment may need to be repeated on a six-monthly basis until the agreed mitigating actions have been implemented and therefore have reduced the likelihood of the privacy risk materialising, while for a low privacy risk activity, the privacy impact assessment may only need to be repeated every two years unless there is a relevant legislative change or a major re-organisation in the business and commercial arrangements.

The PRMS also requires that other specific privacy risk control processes be implemented, but these may not always be processes that are owned or managed by the privacy officer. These include the following:

13.8.2.2   Supplier Assessment

The supplier assessment control process requires the privacy officer to engage with the procurement and supply chain management (SCM) teams to ensure that a privacy impact assessment of each new supplier is carried out either at the time of vendor selection or during the process of negotiating the commercial terms. The privacy officer needs to ensure that during this control process, the SCM team engages with the technology and information security teams to ensure that a proper assessment of the supplier's information security handling systems and processes can be undertaken. In addition, the privacy officer needs to ensure that a risk assessment of the geographical location of the processing facilities is undertaken as they may be in a sensitive political jurisdiction where legal control by government or law enforcement agencies is not compatible with Vodafone's privacy risk appetite.

This control process does not envisage that a full privacy risk assessment will be made of each new supplier, but rather requires the privacy officer to adopt a prioritisation approach that takes into account a range of risk factors, such as the nature of the service to be provided; support and maintenance requiring remote access to Vodafone systems versus hosting which requires the transfer of Vodafone privacy sensitive information to the supplier's facilities; a managed service which requires Vodafone customers to interact directly with the supplier; the location of the supplier, as well as consideration of whether the pre-defined categories of privacy intrusive activities or privacy sensitive categories of personal information are impacted. Depending on the level of privacy risk, an onsite review of the supplier's hosting or processing facilities by the information security team may be required before the processing may begin. Alternatively, should the privacy risk be assessed as low, the privacy officer may simply require sight of the supplier's privacy or information security policy.

13.8.2.3 New Product and Service Assessment

The new product and service assessment control process requires the privacy officer to interface with his or her business's defined process for product and service development to ensure that project teams engage the privacy officer at the right gate or milestone in the project development lifecycle. This will ensure that privacy risks arising from the proposed product or service are identified and mitigated by design or other measures implemented or, where appropriate, are accepted by the product or project sponsor. Because product or service design is an iterative process, a privacy risk assessment may be required at different gates or milestones and the privacy risk mitigating actions may change as the product or service evolves.

Both of these control processes require that a record of the privacy risks identified are recorded on the appropriate risk register. Where the Vodafone entity has an enterprise-wide risk management structure, the privacy officer can use that to record identified privacy risks. Where there is no formalised risk management structure, the privacy officer is required to maintain his or her own privacy risk register.

The maintenance of a record of identified and assessed privacy risks is an essential element of the next privacy risk control to be discussed.

13.8.2.4 Review and Reporting

An annual management review (AMR) is a required control process that is an essential tool for demonstrating to senior and executive management that:

- the PRMS as a whole as well as the required control processes that make up the PRMS are delivering on their objectives;
- where weaknesses or challenges are identified, they have been assessed and, where appropriate, corrective actions are being taken;
- privacy risks are being appropriately treated or mitigated; and
- changes in legal, regulatory or contractual obligations impacting Vodafone's privacy management strategy, policy or activities have been addressed.

The AMR control process results in a report based on the following inputs:

- privacy risks identified and assessed including any residual and accepted risk, mitigating or remedial action plans, completed or otherwise,
- other outcomes and recommendations contained in privacy impact assessment reports,
- findings and feedback including recommendations for remedial action from any privacy audit carried out by the organisation's internal audit function,
- feedback provided by the privacy community including developments in industry best practice or changes in legal requirements,
- feedback or findings from assessment of new products and services,
- feedback or findings from assessment of suppliers,
- status of any preventive or corrective actions other than those identified above,
- findings and recommendations from the previous annual management review, including a review of the implementation of actions for improvement.

The AMR report therefore provides the board sponsor for privacy with a status review of the effectiveness of the PRMS as implemented locally, recommendations for improvements to the PRMS, a business case for more resources where required and, where appropriate, recommended policy changes to be ratified by the board.

Not only does this provide the necessary reassurance to management that both legal and policy compliance is being delivered, but it also helps to maintain their awareness of the subject, thus encouraging their continued support for privacy risk management activities as well as ensuring that they play a privacy risk assessment role at the highest management level.

13.9   The Role of the Privacy Officer

The privacy officer plays a central role in the overall management of operational privacy risk. However, the various control processes that make up the PRMS do not need to be wholly or solely delivered by the privacy officer. For example, the data gathering part of the privacy impact assessment process could be carried out by the BCM manager or team, provided with the right questions, during their business and/or site impact process, with the privacy officer subsequently carrying out the privacy risk assessment. The information security team could gather the relevant privacy-related information in regard to new suppliers during their information security review, again with the privacy officer carrying out the privacy risk assessment. Information about the privacy implications of new products and services can be collated by properly trained business analysts employed to gather the business requirements during the new product and service development lifecycle, with the privacy officer making the required risk assessment at the relevant gates or milestones.

Thus, at a high level and in relation to the PRMS, the role of the Vodafone privacy officer is to:

- manage the local deployment of Vodafone's global privacy strategy and policy across their organisation through the implementation of the PRMS,
- build and maintain positive cross-functional relationships with other teams and people in their organisation that play a key role in delivering compliance with policy and legal requirements as reflected in the PRMS,
- act as the privacy champion for customers and employees, particularly through the privacy risk assessment element of the various PRMS control processes, and
- play a constructive role in the governance mechanisms set out in the PRMS through privacy risk assessment and regular reviews including the delivery of the AMR.

13.10 The Role of Privacy Impact Assessment in the PRMS

Privacy impact assessment is the bedrock of managing privacy risk through the control system of the PRMS. It is not one prescribed and defined all-encompassing process that sits outside the commercial activities of the organisation, but rather is a flexible tool embedded in existing governance and compliance structures, as well as the business structures that have been developed to ensure proper management of a commercial organisation – for example, the supply chain management function and the product development lifecycle process designed to manage technology-supported implementation of new products and services and the costs and budgetary constraints of their build and delivery, as well as the risk management structures where they exist in the organisation.

Prior to the implementation of the PRMS, privacy impact assessments were carried out in an inconsistent manner – for example, some privacy officers had some involvement in their organisation's development of new product and services, whilst others were involved in reviewing suppliers to ensure that the proper contractual controls were in place. However, there was no clear means of measuring when and where privacy impact assessments were carried out, whether the outputs were of a consistent quality and resulted in effective change. The consistent use of privacy impact assessment tools in the context of a mature PRMS not only delivers tangible privacy outcomes, but because the PRMS can be measured and assessed in its own right, can also demonstrate positive change and improvement in the way in which privacy risks are managed and mitigated. Because this change and improvement is "business as usual", there is no need for lengthy, complex enterprise-wide and, thus, costly privacy audits to be carried out. At the same time, the overall level of privacy risk awareness is raised throughout the commercial and business functions, particularly amongst those whose decisions and actions could have the biggest impact on customers and employees' privacy.

Privacy impact and risk assessment controls as required by the PRMS are essential to moving Vodafone to a higher, or more "mature", level of operational privacy management, moving away from being seen as solely a matter for the legal and regulatory function of the organisation and into the commercial and business reality, where privacy risks are generated and must be addressed.

13.11 Conclusion – The Value of Privacy Impact Assessments

Our understanding of privacy is continually changing. As technology continues to augment people's relationship with enterprises, government and with each other, new privacy risks will emerge and some privacy risks may recede. Perceptions of privacy will also continue to be shaped by social and cultural factors that shift over time and across borders. In the business sectors in which Vodafone operates, regulation is often playing catch-up. Increasingly, it is apparent that the treatment of privacy risks will require the collaboration and involvement of other organisations, including Vodafone's partners and competitors.

As Vodafone has sought to re-position its approach to privacy risk as being more than complying with legal and regulatory obligations, it has become necessary to adopt an approach that supports this wider assessment of privacy risk, tackling concerns that may be on the outer periphery of regulatory requirements or in areas that have simply yet to attract the attention of policy-makers. If one of Vodafone's drivers is trust, then it isn't enough to wait to be told what it must do by regulation; it is often imperative to take the initiative.

Privacy impact assessments encourage and require initiative, and can be an effective means of encouraging solutions to privacy risks that would less likely be developed from a rules-based compliance approach. Privacy impact assessments and "privacy by design" often go hand in hand, as the former identifies the possibilities and potential for the latter. Vodafone also uses privacy impact assessments to look beyond the corporate boundary and identify external factors that are needed to help address privacy risks. Its public policy and stakeholder engagement, and work with industry, are shaped and influenced by the use of privacy impact assessments.

To be most effective, a privacy impact assessment must be used to guide and build a structured privacy risk management programme. Without such a programme, an organisation will most likely:

- simply be "shooting the wolf nearest the door", i.e., responding to privacy risks when they have become privacy threats.[23] The response to a privacy threat may

---

[23] In risk management, a threat is a risk that has materialised.

well require a privacy impact assessment to be made during the incident or crisis management process to prioritise the remedial actions, but in general lack of planning will lead to an ineffective or a lengthy response to a threat, which in turn means that the time to return to business as usual from the threat will take longer and thus be more costly. The negative impact on brand and reputation that results from a perceived lack of immediate and robust response to a crisis is also potentially costly.[24]

- be identifying privacy risks without having any agreed structures for managing them. This may be the first step in developing a privacy risk management programme, but an organisation that simply knows what its privacy risks are without having a programme or timetable for addressing them will be in an invidious position with the courts, regulators and other stakeholders should one of those privacy risks become a privacy threat.

- be failing to make the most of its resources and people through lack of prioritised and targeted action. The organisation could be wasting money by addressing the wrong privacy risks, duplicating compliance, review and auditing activities, and losing valuable working hours because employees are responding to or participating in numerous reviews and audits rather than being able to deliver their own duties and responsibilities.

The value to Vodafone of the privacy impact assessment is the creation of a holistic approach to privacy risk management, from the strategic to the operational, from the local to the global, where competent privacy professionals are empowered to exercise judgement in the evaluation of privacy harms and to develop tailored, and sometimes innovative, responses to privacy risks, such as by designing products to minimise privacy harms. The privacy impact assessment, therefore, provides an essential foundation for addressing the three drivers of Vodafone's approach to privacy[25] – trust, reputation and regulation.

---

[24] Witness negative media coverage and political comment on BP's response to the oil crisis in the Gulf of Mexico during May and June 2010.

[25] For more information about Vodafone's approach to privacy, see: www.vodafone.com/privacy

Part IV
Specialised PIA: The Cases of the Financial Services Industry and the RFID PIA Framework

Chapter 14
The ISO PIA Standard for Financial Services

John Martin Ferris

14.1 Introduction

This chapter examines the International Organization for Standardization (ISO) PIA standard 22307:2008 Financial services — Privacy impact assessment, its development and what it means as an ISO voluntary consensus standard for the financial services industry. The chapter has been written from the perspective of both the convenor of the ISO 22307:2008's development and the chairman of the American National Standards Institute's (ANSI) Accredited Standards Committee X9 working group where much of the ISO 22307:2008 early content was developed.

The ISO 22307:2008 was developed for the international financial services industry through the ISO and its Technical Committee 68 (TC 68). ISO TC 68 has developed and continues to develop standards in support of the financial services industry which seeks to safeguard the privacy of their customers' financial data when it is processed by automated, networked information systems.

The development of ISO 22307:2008 recognised that:

- A privacy impact assessment is a tool which, when used effectively, can identify risks associated with privacy and help organisations to mitigate those risks.
- The frameworks for providing privacy protection among the members of the financial services industry as well as within each country where a financial services industry member may reside or conduct business may be different.
- The internationalisation of privacy impact assessments is critical for global banking, in particular, for cross-border financial transactions.
- One way of proactively addressing privacy principles and practices across the financial industry is to follow a standardised privacy impact assessment process for a proposed financial system (PFS).

J.M. Ferris (✉)
Ferris & Associates, Inc., Washington, DC
e-mail: jmferris@erols.com

D. Wright, P. De Hert (eds.), *Privacy Impact Assessment*, Law, Governance
and Technology Series 6, DOI 10.1007/978-94-007-2543-0_14,
© Springer Science+Business Media B.V. 2012

14.2 Overview of the ISO 22307:2008 Voluntary Consensus Standard

ISO 22307:2008 is a voluntary consensus PIA standard for the financial services industry. It defines for those financial services industry members who choose to apply it those aspects of a PIA that are common and defined as normative requirements across PIAs conducted for the financial services industry. The normative requirements are supported with guidance to specifically assist financial services industry members in conducting a PIA in their institutions.

ISO 22307:2008 is intended to be a tool for the internal processing of personally identifiable information (PII) during development of a proposed financial system (PFS) and for mitigating risks during the development of information systems used for processing the financial data of customers and consumers, business partners and citizens.

The standard is also intended to be a tool to be used as a good practice for an individual bank as well as a tool to assist in reaching agreements among financial services industry members for the appropriate sharing of information among themselves or their customers.

ISO 22307:2008 is based on some key concepts:

- A PIA is useful during any phase of a system's life cycle.
- A PIA requires a process including a plan.
- A PIA needs adequate description of the system processing PII.
- A PIA standard should be neutral on frameworks that support a PIA development.
- A PIA is not a privacy audit.

14.2.1 A PIA Is Useful During Any Phase of a System's Life Cycle

ISO 22307:2008 provides normative requirements and informative guidance for developing a PIA for either a new financial information system or changes to an existing financial information system. The ISO 22307:2008 defines the term *Proposed Financial System* (PFS) to mean all of the components of a financial system assessed in a privacy impact assessment. A component of a financial system is defined for the purposes of this standard as any service, facility, business process and data flow or combination thereof used by financial institutions to implement or perform financial transactions. So the standard applies to a broad range of proposed financial systems or subsystems, and where in their life cycle they might currently be. It also assumes a life cycle without specifying a particular life cycle methodology.

14.2.2 A PIA Requires a Process Including a Plan

Performing a PIA is a process and the process requires a plan.

ISO 22307:2008 establishes for the financial services industry a set of PIA objectives which the PIA process should minimally achieve including:

- ensuring that privacy protection is a core consideration in the initial considerations of a PFS and in all subsequent activities during the system development life cycle;
- ensuring that accountability for privacy issues is clearly incorporated into the responsibilities of respective system developers, administrators and any other participants in the development of a financial system, including those from other institutions, jurisdictions and sectors;
- providing decision-makers with the information necessary to make fully informed policy, system design and procurement decisions for proposed financial systems based on an understanding of the privacy implications and risks and the options available for avoiding and/or mitigating those risks;
- reducing the risk of having to terminate or substantially modify a financial service after its implementation in order to comply with privacy requirements;
- providing documentation on the business processes and flow of personal information for use and review by departmental and agency staff and to serve as the basis for consultations with clients, privacy officers and other stakeholders.

The PIA plan should indicate the scope of the PIA and systematically establish the steps to be followed, questions to be answered and options to be examined. This scope should guide the PIA process for a specific PFS by stating

- the business objectives of the PFS;
- the privacy policy compliance objectives of the PIA, which as a minimum should comply with the OECD privacy principles and any financial sector agreements regarding compliance with OECD privacy principles (e.g., international standards addressing the financial sector and security);
- the life cycle phase of the PFS.

Prior to the assessment, the PIA practitioner should follow these steps:

- Provide a description of the PFS and, if necessary, a description of the existing financial systems relevant to the PFS;
- Identify the competent expertise needed to perform the PIA and develop the PIA report within the defined scope;
- Agree how the PIA report should be integrated into decision-making processes affecting development of the PFS;
- Identify known and relevant risks to personal information associated with the PFS, its business processes and any relevant existing systems.

14.2.3 A PIA Needs an Adequate Description of the System

According to the ISO 22307:2008, the description of a PFS should include:

- documented business objectives of the PFS and consideration of alternative systems to the proposed financial system as approved by the appropriate management;
- a description of how the PFS will use and process personal information;
- information about whether the PFS is intended to add to or modify an existing financial system described in the scope of the proposal;
- details about the proposed collection, generation or obtaining of personal information through its holding, storage, security, use and disclosure. Details could be depicted through the use of business process and data flow diagrams, data models and information access models;
- details about the supporting infrastructure to be used to process personal information which includes telecommunications, help desk operations and use or reuse of common services shared both within jurisdictions and across jurisdictions.

The ISO 22307:2008 guides the user to other standards for describing the financial system to be assessed. These includes architectural standards such as the International Security, Trust and Privacy Alliance (ISTPA) privacy framework and applicable industry privacy frameworks, e.g., IEEE 1471:2000 (which is now ISO/IEC 42010:2007) for architectural descriptions of software intensive systems.

14.2.4 A PIA Standard Should Be Neutral on Frameworks That Support a PIA Development

14.2.4.1 System Development Life Cycle

Systems that conform to frameworks such as those that describe system development life cycles (SDLC)[1] and security practices provide useful and descriptive information about a system and its controls and, consequently, provide useful information for a PIA. There is no one correct SDLC methodology but they typically consist of several phases. Most often, these include gathering requirements and the design, implementation and post-implementation support phases. They guide the

---

[1] Wikipedia defines the systems development life cycle (SDLC), or software development life cycle in systems engineering, information systems and software engineering, as "the process of creating or altering systems, and the models and methodologies that people use to develop these systems. The concept generally refers to computer or information systems. In software engineering the SDLC concept underpins many kinds of software development methodologies. These methodologies form the framework for planning and controlling the creation of an information system." http://en.wikipedia.org/wiki/Systems_Development_Life_Cycle#cite_note-0

system development process and prescribe various work items and "artefacts" (e.g., engineering documents such as design documents) for each phase. Each successive phase of an SDLC leverages the documentation and knowledge gained from the previous phases and provides milestones for managing systems from cradle to grave.

Depending on whether the PFS is a new system or a change to an existing system, there is an opportunity for the PIA process to be integrated into the SDLC or security processes. These processes can be the source of useful information to describe the PFS and its operating environment. This is particularly true during the requirements and design phases.

14.2.4.2 Gathering and Analysing Requirements

The goal of system analysis is to determine where a problem exists in an attempt to fix the system. This step involves analysing the different components of a system. It helps to understand what needs to be fixed. Involving users helps in the definition of requirements. The PIA process should begin here. Gathering requirements is the most crucial aspect. Inadequate communication with users often leads to gaps in this phase which may, in turn, lead to validation errors and bugs in software programs.

14.2.4.3 Design and Design Artefacts

In systems, design functions and operations are described in varying levels of detail depending at what level of design. Design artefacts provide logical and physical descriptions of PFS components and subsystems, business rules, process diagrams and other documentation. The output of this stage will describe the new system or the changes to an existing system and should provide transparency of information flow and controls.

The design stage takes as its initial input the requirements identified in the approved requirements document. For each requirement, a set of one or more design elements can be produced through team meetings, workshops and/or prototype efforts.

Interface control documents (ICDs) may also provide useful information about the PFS to be examined during a PIA, particularly in authoritatively defining:

- the systems or components being interfaced,
- the type of components being interfaced (e.g., application software, system software, hardware component),
- the types of information to be handled by the interface,
- the interface protocol type in terms of the primary mechanism used to implement the interface (e.g. HTTP, FTP, WSDL-defined web services).

While the known SDLC and security frameworks may be useful or even important considerations in a privacy impact assessment, they are not essential as normative requirements in a voluntary consensus PIA standard. Requiring one of the many frameworks could be cost prohibitive to members of the financial services industry, and it is unlikely that there would be a consensus in the industry to include one as a normative requirement. There are non-sector-specific voluntary consensus standards that describe SDLC and security frameworks. Members of the financial service community are, of course, free to adopt them for their use.

14.2.4.4 Security Frameworks

As we all know, privacy and security are not the same thing. They are related but different. It is useful for the PIA practitioner to understand the security frameworks (e.g., policies, standards and processes) that govern a PFS. Some standard security frameworks can help the practitioner to understand how an organisation applies compliance and regulatory requirements to the PFS and the risk management approach used to address overlapping or conflicting requirements. Examples of security frameworks include:

- Cyber security program management, e.g., the ISO/IEC 27000 family of Information Security Management Systems (ISMS) standards,
- Cyber security systems of controls, e.g., ISACA Control Objectives for Information and related Technology (COBIT)[2]
- Cyber security process management, e.g., CERT's Resiliency Management Model,[3]
- Cyber security system and software development, e.g., SEI Capability Maturity Model Integration (CMMI)[4]; ISO/IEC 21827 Systems Security Engineering – Capability Maturity Model; OWASP Software Assurance Maturity Model.[5]

A PFS could also be a financial services organisation which serves the health care industry, which has adopted emerging security frameworks such as:

---

[2] ISACA standards for Information Systems Audit and Control Association, however, ISACA now goes by its acronym only. http://www.isaca.org. A copy of the COBIT document can be downloaded from http://www.isaca.org/KNOWLEDGE-CENTER/COBIT/Pages/Downloads.aspx

[3] CERT stands for Computer Emergency Response Team, which is based at Carnegie-Mellon University. See http://www.cert.org/

[4] SEI is the Software Engineering Institute. Details of the Capability Maturity Model Integration (CMMI) can be found at http://www.sei.cmu.edu/cmmi/

[5] OWASP is the Open Web Application Security Project. Details of the Software Assurance Maturity Model can be found at https://www.owasp.org/index.php/Category:Software_Assurance_Maturity_Model

- eXtensible Access Control Markup Language (XACML) Version 2.0 OASIS Standard, 1 February 2005,
- Cross-Enterprise Security and Privacy Authorization (XSPA) Profile of Security,
- Assertion Markup Language (SAML) for Healthcare Version 1.0 OASIS Standard, 1 November 2009,
- Cross-Enterprise Security and Privacy Authorization (XSPA) Profile of XACML v2.0 for Healthcare Version 1.0 OASIS Standard, 1 November 2009.[6]

14.2.5 A PIA Is Not a Privacy Audit

A privacy compliance audit differs from a PIA, in that the compliance audit tries to determine a particular business system's current level of compliance with the law and identify steps to avoid non-compliance with the law in the future. While there are similarities between PIAs and privacy compliance audits, in that they use some of the same skills and they seek to avoid privacy breaches, compliance audits are primarily directed towards existing systems in order to validate their compliance with required policies, standards and law. By contrast, a PIA is used at an early stage in the development of a PFS and is useful in identifying optimum privacy options and solutions. If a PFS is a change to an existing system, the most recent privacy compliance audit may provide useful information for assessing the impact of the PFS.

14.3 History of ISO 22307:2008

The history of ISO 22307:2008 begins with ANSI X9.99.[7] The interest in developing ANSI X9.99 began in 2000 while I was involved with security and privacy engineering for a major modernisation effort of the information systems of the US Internal Revenue Service (IRS). The IRS had adopted PIAs as a mandatory activity for all information systems and included these activities in their systems development life cycle processes.

The IRS takes privacy seriously. The IRS has had a history of unauthorised access to tax information by either system failures, employees or others (e.g., the US Privacy Act was passed into law in the wake of revelations that the Nixon White House had used confidential IRS files against political enemies). The Internal Revenue Code prohibits the disclosure of most of the information about individual taxpayers which the IRS has stored in various media forms. Unauthorised access to taxpayer information applies to all employees regardless of their position. If there is not a business need to access, view or discuss taxpayer and employee information, then an employee should not be looking at it. The Internal Revenue

---

[6] See the OASIS website for details of all of these four items: http://www.oasis-open.org/standards
[7] ANSI is the American National Standards Institute. www.ansi.org

Code imposes civil and criminal penalties for violations of the disclosure prohibitions. Unauthorised access could lead to disciplinary action which could include termination of employment.

The IRS security and privacy program has a history of ensuring that controls are in place to protect against employee browsing and ensuring improvements to those controls as necessary. The adoption of PIAs as a mandatory activity for their information systems was an extension of IRS efforts to ensure that privacy controls are in place. The PIA process started early in systems development (i.e., in identifying business requirements) and was updated, reviewed through each milestone and served as part of the exit criteria for a project to advance from one development life cycle milestone to the next.

At the time, I had never heard of a PIA and was impressed with its usefulness in the systems development life cycle, particularly in defining requirements and tracking whether those requirements are satisfied. Inspired by the IRS experience, I began researching the topic of PIAs in general and what other PIA-like activities were being pursued within and outside the US. The result at that time was that PIA activities seemed to be occurring exclusively outside the US – except for the IRS and the US Health and Human Services.

As I had an ongoing relationship with the financial service community in regard to security standards via the Accredited Standards Committee X9,[8] I discussed the idea of a PIA standard with various X9 committee members to see if there was interest. There was interest, particularly if such a standard could be a tool that the financial service community members could use to assist in identifying privacy requirements for financial information systems. In the US, there are approximately 8,000 banks as well as other financial services institutions.

The IRS PIA process was specific to the IRS, its adopted system development life cycle methodology and its security program which is governed by both US government law and US Treasury policies. It was useful to have an example of one organisation's PIA standard even if it was specifically tuned for IRS purposes. Although it would not be appropriate for other organisations, it would nevertheless serve as a basis for identifying that which is in common in other PIAs and that which is not but could serve as useful background information.

So, in 2002, a new standards development work proposal was submitted to and approved by ASC X9. In 2004, the ASC X9 approved ANSI X9.9:2004, its PIA standard.

ASC X9 routinely shares its work with the ISO Technical Committee (TC) 68 for consideration as an ISO standard. ASC X9 submitted ANSI X9.99 for consideration as an ISO standard. It was approved with the comment that the ISO standard would not be specific to US privacy considerations. The work was assigned to the core banking subcommittee of TC 68 as a new ISO work activity and, in 2008, ISO TC 68 approved ISO 22307:2008. The ISO voluntary standard is

---

[8] The US-based Accredited Standards Committee X9, Inc. or more simply X9, develops technical financial industry standards. http://www.x9.org/home/

essentially the same as ANSI X9.99 but has more specifics and adjustments to reflect the requirements of the international financial services industry. ASC X9 later adopted ISO 22307:2008 as ANSI X9.99:2009 which replaced the previous version ANSI X9.99:2004.

14.4 Voluntary Consensus Standards

In order to understand the development of ISO 22307:2008 and its context within the financial services industry, it is necessary to explain what a voluntary consensus standard is. To that end, it is useful to parse the expression "voluntary consensus standards". The "voluntary" part refers to the use of the standard. A voluntary standard is a type of standard the adoption and interpretation of which are the responsibility of the organisation that uses it. Any organisation may mandate its use within its organisation. The "consensus" applies to how the standard was developed.

As mentioned above, ISO and ANSI were the two voluntary consensus standards organisations involved with this development. The foremost aim of international standardisation is to facilitate the exchange of goods and services through the elimination of technical barriers to trade. The International Organization for Standardization, located in Geneva, promotes the development and implementation of voluntary international standards. All ISO standards are developed through a voluntary, consensus-based approach. Each member country of ISO develops its position on the standards and these positions are then negotiated with other member countries. Draft versions of the standards are sent out for formal written comment and each country casts its official vote on the drafts at the appropriate stage of the process. Within each country, various types of organisations can and do participate in the process including industry, government and other interested parties.

The American National Standards Institute has been administrator and coordinator of the United States private sector voluntary standardisation system for more than 90 years. Founded in 1918 by five engineering societies and three government agencies, the Institute remains a private, non-profit membership organisation supported by a diverse constituency of private and public sector organisations.

ANSI facilitates the development of American National Standards (ANS) by accrediting the procedures of standards-developing organisations such as ASC X9. ASC X9 operates under its own procedures as well as those prescribed and approved by the American National Standards Institute.

For both ISO and ANSI accreditation, standards developers are required to consistently adhere to a set of requirements or procedures that govern the consensus development. The standards are developed in an environment that is equitable, accessible and responsive to the requirements of various stakeholders. The open and fair process ensures that all interested and affected parties have an opportunity to participate in a standard's development. It also serves and protects the public interest since standards-accredited developers must meet the requirements for openness, balance, consensus and other due process safeguards.

Distinctive characteristics or attributes of this process include the following:

- Consensus must be reached by representatives from materially affected and interested parties.
- Standards are required to undergo public reviews when any member of the public may submit comments.
- Comments from the consensus body and from the public review must be responded to in good faith.

14.4.1 ISO TC 68

ISO TC 68 is the ISO standards development committee designated to develop standards and technical reports for the financial services industry. The financial services industry includes credit institutions, which traditionally are recognised as banks, non-depository institutions or finance companies, consumer and commercial lenders that raise funds in the capital markets, the buy-and-sell side of the securities markets, private equity firms, mutual fund complexes, central banks, electronic clearing networks and other financial intermediaries, and mortgage and insurance companies.

Consequently, the ISO TC 68 standards development aims to reduce technical barriers to international financial transactions by improving interoperability, reliability, confidence, security and universal usage.

Most of the standards developed by ISO TC 68 are adopted by member countries as their domestic standard for their financial services industry. The standards have helped countries achieve interoperability across businesses and systems, reduce fraud, overcome legal obstacles in the use of electronic "financial transactions" communications through the use of uniform rules and information security technologies, facilitate global funds transfers and funds availability for consumers, and protect monetary transfer systems (such as retail and bankcard networks) from electronic attack. Thus, ISO TC 68 has had success in meeting the objectives of ISO standards for the financial service industry.

14.4.2 Business Challenges of ISO TC 68 and Voluntary Consensus Standards

Consistent with the voluntary consensus standards criteria of ISO, TC 68 deliverables need to be developed and maintained to overcome obstacles to adoption in member countries with different economic, regulatory and social systems. The global business environment significantly influences what standards are needed, how these standards are developed and how the standards are used and applied. ISO TC 68 has existed since 1948, so one can imagine that the business environment has changed over time and has contributed to the life cycle of ISO TC 68 standards. That life cycle includes the creation, maintenance and, as appropriate, withdrawal of

ISO TC 68 standards. Currently, there are about 50 ISO TC 68 standards addressing protocols that the international financial services community can use for reliable and secure transactions as well as for agreement on the business elements, terms and definitions needed to complete financial transactions.

Below are some of the current economic, political, regulatory, social and technical dynamics associated with the financial services environment and that drive the current ISO TC 68 considerations for their programme of work and the environment to which a voluntary consensus standard needs to be responsive in regard to the performance of PIAs.

14.4.2.1 Economic Dynamics

Changes in supply and demand factors for financial products have resulted in new trends in financial transactions. The primary demand factors have included increased risk and convenience for existing products and increased acceptability of newer products. The globalisation of the financial market (resulting in part from cross-border mergers and acquisitions) has helped facilitate the emergence of a broader range of products and significant changes to the delivery, pricing and processing arrangements for financial transactions. At the same time, disparate products and services are being developed and integrated into this market which creates the need for common solutions and processes for continued services in the new markets.

14.4.2.2 Technological Changes and Major Product Innovation

Some of the technology changes and major innovations that may have an impact on the development of markets include the following:

- Emergence of cheaper, more convenient delivery alternatives for both consumers and business users (for example, the Internet and other open, non-proprietary networks, wireless handheld devices, mobile telephones and contact-less bank-issued transaction cards),
- Regional and national management of disparate security and privacy requirements,
- Increased collaboration of the various stakeholders in the value chain,
- Emergence of a commonly agreed way of modelling businesses and representing business and financial transactions.

14.4.2.3 Regulatory Activities

The financial services industry is highly regulated both domestically and internationally. Regulation has a continuous and profound effect and can drive the need for standards. Important factors in this area include the following:

- Several EU regulatory initiatives have committed to using ISO standards for the payments and the securities industry.

- There is an increased playing of regulatory environments against each other (e.g., hedge fund relocation).
- Regulations aimed at money laundering and terrorism both at the global and national levels increase the constraints and consequently the costs of banking and raise the issue of privacy.

14.4.2.4 Payments Industry Impacts

Retail payments are experiencing increased experimentation and innovation. Also, the growth of electronic payments has caused the more traditional forms of payment instruments, technology and banking arrangements to evolve resulting in changes to payment practices with the objective of increased efficiency and convenience in retail payment systems.

While banking institutions are still the primary providers to end-users for most retail payment services, payment applications are no longer their exclusive business. These services are now provided by a wider range of service providers including non-traditional financial institutions.

International payments supported since the 1970s by SWIFT proprietary standards are now moving to XML-based ISO 20022 messages for customer-to-bank and bank-to-bank messages.[9]

Also, international payments are under continual pressure from regulators to increase the level of transparency of the transactions in adding more mandatory information concerning the parties involved including the ordering and beneficiary customers as well as their banks and the intermediaries. This could sometimes appear as contradictory with data privacy constraints, in particular, if such messages should fall into some external hands (e.g., US requirements regarding SWIFT traffic[10]).

14.4.2.5 Growth in Mobile Payments

There is growth in international mobile payment applications in developing countries. Developing countries are using mobile text messaging and short messaging services (SMS) for remittances and money transfers between people.

14.4.2.6 Identity Theft

Identity theft, associated with fraud, continues to grow and has become a worldwide phenomenon. Some industry estimates suggest that over half of probable fraud losses are classified as credit losses. Furthermore, fraud is difficult to prosecute as most legal systems require that fraud be proven beyond a reasonable doubt.

---

[9] SWIFT is the Society for Worldwide Interbank Financial Telecommunication. Its headquarters are in Brussels. http://www.swift.com

[10] Lichtblau, Eric, and James Risen, "Bank Data Is Sifted by U.S. in Secret to Block Terrorism", *The New York Times*, 23 June 2006.

Both consumers and lending institutions experience the problem. The international financial service community has sought help in reducing the risk of fraud from technology and global standards.

14.4.3 ISO TC 68 Security and Privacy Work

For the financial services industry, the barriers to trade often include a lack of protocols that the international financial service community can use for reliable and secure transactions as well as lack of agreement on the business elements, terms and definitions needed to complete financial transactions.

With regard to security and privacy, ISO TC 68 continues to support standardised protection of financial services transactions, particularly the protection of customer account and transaction data with the following considerations:

- The financial services industry is impacted by many and disparate business influences, as noted above.
- Financial services span both existing and mature financial transactions and their life cycle as well as new and emerging financial transactions (e.g., mobile banking).

ISO TC 68 work addresses standardised protection of financial services transactions. In this regard, it supports the security and protection of the privacy of customer information required for financial services transactions. Table 14.1 identifies the work TC 68 has produced and maintains.

14.4.4 Choosing Voluntary Consensus Standards

Some organisations need to choose effective security and privacy policies and standards that bridge common problems across the disparate sub-organisational elements of their domains of governance. These choices allow for each sub-organisation to own their variations to meet their particular business need with specific solutions but with the ownership of any associated risk. Similarly, for other organisations, the choice of security and privacy policies and standards is to bridge common problems with peer organisations that share similar risks but, for a variety of reasons, they must choose variations to meet their particular business needs with the associated risk ownership.

While there may be other mandatory standards, financial services organisations may find it useful to select voluntary consensus standards that align their organisation with their business peers and their experiences and practices.

As mentioned above, I have been involved in the development of security standards for the financial service community via the ANSI Accredited Standards Committee X9. From the mid-1980s through the mid-1990s, I led information security policy and programs for the US Treasury and its many bureaus. In particular, as

Table 14.1 Financial security standards produced and maintained by ISO TC 68 – as of October 2011

Standard number	Title
ISO 9564-1:2011	Financial services – Personal Identification Number (PIN) management and security – Part 1: Basic principles and requirements for PINs in card-based systems
ISO 9564-2:2005	Banking – Personal Identification Number management and security – Part 2: Approved algorithms for PIN encipherment
ISO/TR 9564-4:2004	Banking – Personal Identification Number (PIN) management and security – Part 4: Guidelines for PIN handling in open networks
ISO 11568-1:2005	Banking – Key management (retail) – Part 1: Principles
ISO 11568-2:2005	Banking – Key management (retail) – Part 2: Symmetric ciphers, their key management and life cycle
ISO 11568-4:2007	Banking – Key management (retail) – Part 4: Asymmetric cryptosystems – Key management and life cycle
ISO 13491-1:2007	Banking – Secure cryptographic devices (retail) – Part 1: Concepts, requirements and evaluation methods
ISO 13491-2:2005	Banking – Secure cryptographic devices (retail) – Part 2: Security compliance checklists for devices used in financial transactions
ISO 13492:2007	Financial services – Key management related data element – Application and usage of ISO 8583 data elements 53 and 96
ISO/TR 13569:2005	Financial services – Information security guidelines
ISO/TR 14742:2010	Financial services – Recommendations on cryptographic algorithms and their use
ISO 15782-1:2009	Certificate management for financial services – Part 1: Public key certificates
ISO 15782-2:2001	Banking – Certificate management – Part 2: Certificate extensions
ISO 16609:2004	Banking – Requirements for message authentication using symmetric techniques
ISO/TR 19038:2005	Banking and related financial services – Triple DEA – Modes of operation – Implementation guidelines
ISO 19092:2008	Financial services – Biometrics – Security framework
ISO 21188:2006	Public key infrastructure for financial services – Practices and policy framework

part of an information systems modernisation effort, the Treasury adopted a method to serve as an electronic signature for financial transactions. This method used private key cryptography applying message authentication codes as expressed by ANSI X9.9 (note: this predates acceptable public key standards). Critical to that adoption was a method to securely manage cryptographic keys as expressed by ANSI X9.17. The US Secretary of Treasury at that time adopted those voluntary consensus standards as a matter of internal policy. The standards provided the basis for satisfying electronic signature requirements specified by the government's auditor, the US General Accounting Office, as well as by other partners (e.g., the Federal Reserve and US private commercial banks that performed contracted services for the US Treasury) and providers of security products. The choice of those standards created a small and short-lived controversy when the financial services industry perceived, incorrectly, that by adopting those standards, the US Treasury was creating a de facto regulation. After a few conversations, the financial services industry was persuaded that the US Treasury had no interest in regulating the adoption of the standards and was merely adopting the standards for its own internal use.

This experience launched a long-term relationship with the voluntary consensus standards community of the financial service industries and in collaborating with them in the development and use of such standards, a relationship that continues to this day.

14.5 Summary

ISO 22307:2008 is a voluntary consensus standard for the financial services industry. ISO 22307:2008 provides a tool for that community to normalise PIAs. It provides visibility to PIAs within that community as a good practice. The business constraints of the financial services industry or any other business sector play a major role in the sector's agreement on and use of a standard. ISO 22307:2008 evolved out of voluntary consensus processes of both ANSI and ISO.

It took about seven years' effort to achieve ISO 22307:2008. The consensus process included several internal reviews and at least two public reviews. In the beginning of that effort, there was little awareness of PIAs, at least in the US. Since then, PIAs have evolved to become a best practice with some PIA guidance mirroring that of ISO 22307:2008. ISO and ANSI sell copies of their standards as a source of income for their organisations. As of 2010, they had sold about 80 copies of the voluntary consensus standard.

And, of course, there is always more that might be done to enhance or supplement ISO 22307:2008. ISO JTC 1 [the Joint Technical Committee 1 of ISO and the International Electrotechnical Commission (IEC)] is pursuing privacy frameworks and possibly other privacy-related standards. If that work results in improving the routine description of privacy controls within systems in general, that will be useful.

There already exists an ISO standard (i.e. ISO/IEC TR 24774:2010) intended to promote uniformity in process reference models. Also, there already exists an ISO standard establishing a common framework for describing the life cycle of systems (i.e., ISO/IEC 15288:2008). ISO/IEC 15288:2008 provides a set of development life cycle processes and associated terminology for all of the processes required in the system development life cycle. While it does not make normative what the process should be, it does describe the essential elements that a complete system engineering process should have. ISO/IEC 15288:2008 is accompanied by a technical report ISO/IEC TR 19760: "Systems engineering – A guide for the application of ISO/IEC 15288 (System life cycle processes", which, as its title suggests, provides additional informative guidance.

The potential for the harmonisation of these future ISO privacy standards and framework initiatives with these existing ISO engineering standards is exciting and could complement the financial services industry's ISO 22307:2008 nicely as well as provide significant benefits for PIA standardisation in general.

The work goes on.

Chapter 15
The RFID PIA – Developed by Industry, Endorsed by Regulators

Sarah Spiekermann

15.1 Introduction – The History of the RFID PIA

With more technologies penetrating our everyday lives, maintaining the privacy of personal information has become an issue of growing concern. A recent global survey showed that, when prompted, 88% of consumers say that they are worried about who has access to their data; 84% worry about where their data is stored. Most importantly, such concerns are on the rise: 89% state in the same survey that they are becoming more security conscious with their data.[1]

Despite these growing concerns, privacy is not holistically regulated or even legally addressed in some countries. Instead, privacy regulation is an international patchwork that fails to establish a common trust framework for people while often forcing companies to incur a high transaction cost for compliance. In times of constant technical evolution, regulation often comes too late, lacks practical enforcement mechanisms and finds itself charged with crippling innovation. In response to this legal dilemma, regulators seek new ways to regulate privacy. Globally integrated, timely and effective privacy protection would be more feasible if global industry players, associations or whole sectors committed to institute common privacy procedures and integrate privacy-friendly architectures and defaults into their systems ("privacy by design").

One promising way to achieve this goal is to avoid regulating the dos and don'ts of specific technologies at a national level; instead, global industry players and sectors could embrace privacy impact assessments (PIA). "A PIA is a systematic process for evaluating the potential effects on privacy of a project, initiative or

---

[1] Fujitsu Research Institute, "Personal Data in the Cloud: The Importance of Trust", Tokyo, 2010, pp. 8, 13. Fujitsu gathered its data from 500 consumers from each of Australia, Brazil, Canada, China, Finland, Germany, India, Japan, Singapore, Switzerland, the UK and US, for a total of 6,000. The data was gathered between June and September 2010. http://ts.fujitsu.com/rl/visit2010/downloads/Fujitsu_Consumer_Data_Privacy_Report_part2.pdf

S. Spiekermann (✉)
Vienna University of Economics and Business (WU Wien), Vienna, Austria
e-mail: sspieker@wu.ac.at

D. Wright, P. De Hert (eds.), *Privacy Impact Assessment*, Law, Governance and Technology Series 6, DOI 10.1007/978-94-007-2543-0_15,
© Springer Science+Business Media B.V. 2012

proposed system or scheme and finding ways to mitigate or avoid any adverse effects."[2] If PIAs were mandatory, companies would be forced to proactively investigate and prepare for potentially disadvantageous social implications of the technologies they build and deploy.

PIAs are seen as a particularly promising way to confront the privacy challenges inherent in ambient computer services. PIAs enforce creative thinking about how the ethical challenges of ubiquitous, "always-on" technologies could be addressed; as a result, they stimulate innovation around socially attractive technologies instead of stifling their launch. One ambient technology that has stirred up particularly strong privacy debates and, as a result, became one of the first to be regulated with the help of a PIA, is radio frequency identification (RFID). With other wireless technologies such as Bluetooth or wireless LAN, RFID is a major building block of the "Internet of Things" or "ubiquitous computing environment", envisioned by computer science researchers.[3] RFID tags embed "smart" chips that communicate with readers and transfer their information to a back-end infrastructure for processing and analysis. The wireless transfer of item information or object-to-object communication is vital for many current services and products, new home and after-sales services, real-time logistics, intelligent manufacturing, and more. In the next decade, it has been estimated that some 87 billion passive tags and 6 million readers will be deployed in Europe.[4]

The reason why RFID has caused particularly strong privacy debates is the combination of three of its technological traits that raise consumer fears: First, humans have always been afraid of the invisible. And this invisibility is manifest in many kinds of RFID that use chips too tiny to be recognised by the human eye, communicating information through fabrics and at long distances (6–8 metres for UHF frequencies) without a line of sight. Second, and unlike many other forms of IT, RFID cannot be "switched off". For mobile phones and PCs, users can opt out of participation, go offline or switch off the device. For RFID – at least for the time being – this is not the case. And last but not least, RFID technology is expected to be ubiquitously deployed and present on or embedded in all products and product components carrying barcodes today, which means that the technology will be very pervasive very soon.[5]

---

[2] Wright, David, "Should Privacy Impact Assessment Be Mandatory?", *Communications of the ACM*, Vol. 54, No. 8, August 2011, pp. 121–131. http://cacm.acm.org/magazines/2011/8

[3] Weiser, Marc, "The Computer for the 21st Century", *Scientific American*, Vol. 265, No. 3, Sept 1991, pp. 94–104.

[4] GS1 and Logica CMG, European passive RFID Market Sizing 2007-2022, Report of the BRIDGE Project, February 2007, p. 8. BRIDGE (Building Radio frequency Identification solutions for the Global Environment) was an Integrated Project funded by the European Commission. http://www.bridge-project.eu/data/File/BRIDGE%20WP13%20European%20passive%20RFID%20Market%20Sizing%202007-2022.pdf

[5] Another "political" reason why RFID has led to such intense privacy debates is the industry's strong push for RFID roll-out and perfection. In particular, the intent to make it the carrier medium of the future barcode has caused privacy rights organisations to become more alert to RFID than other technologies that penetrate markets slowly.

Because RFID is a highly promising building block of innovative service delivery, regulators at the EU level have avoided passing the kind of technology-specific "RFID Law" that was considered in the US.[6] The risk of strangling RFID-related innovations was too great. Therefore, calling for PIAs for RFID has been regarded as the ideal political route. In May 2009, the European Commission issued a Recommendation in which it established a requirement for endorsement by the Article 29 Data Protection Working Party of a framework for personal data and privacy impact assessments of RFID applications.[7] This framework was to be developed by industry, but "in collaboration with relevant civil society", according to Article 4 of the Recommendation. The resulting process framework (or "process reference model") "is designed to help RFID Application Operators uncover the privacy risks associated with an RFID Application, assess their likelihood, and document the steps taken to address those risks".[8]

The road to agreement on this PIA framework, finally endorsed by the Art. 29 Working Party in February 2011,[9] was a rocky one. The 18 months of political battle can be characterised by two PIA construction phases: Phase 1 led to the submission of an initial PIA Framework draft (PIA I) written under the auspices of GS1.[10] It introduced a distinction between a *PIA framework* as a general outline for RFID PIA and *PIA templates* as concrete implementation guidelines.[11] The draft fell victim to many of the typical pitfalls a PIA design can have: It focused on

---

[6] Schmid, Viola, "Radio Frequency Identification Law Beyond 2007" in Christian Floerkemeier, Marc Langheinrich, Elgar Fleisch, Friedemann Mattern and Sanjay E. Sarma (eds.), *The Internet of Things*, Proceedings of IOT 2008, LNCS 4952, Springer-Verlag, Berlin, 2008, pp. 196–212.

[7] European Commission, Recommendation on the implementation of privacy and data protection principles in applications supported by radio-frequency identification, C(2009) 3200 final, Brussels, 12 May 2009. http://ec.europa.eu/information_society/policy/rfid/documents/recommendationonrfid2009.pdf

[8] Privacy and Data Protection Impact Assessment Framework for RFID Applications [the "PIA Framework" hereafter], 11 February 2011, p. 3. http://cordis.europa.eu/fp7/ict/enet/policy_en.html

[9] Art. 29 Data Protection Working Party, Opinion 9/2011 on the revised Industry Proposal for a Privacy and Data Protection Impact Assessment Framework for RFID Applications, Brussels, Adopted on 11 February 2011. http://ec.europa.eu/justice/policies/privacy/docs/wpdocs/2011/wp180_en.pdf

[10] GS1 is an international association dedicated to the development of global barcode numbering standards and the electronic management of these. It was formed by a merger of the European Article Number (EAN) Association and the Unified Code Council (UCC). GS1 chose RFID as the carrier medium for the barcode system and contributes strongly to the development of the technology. It wrote and edited the initially submitted PIA Framework (called "PIA I" by PIA Framework stakeholders and authors) in co-operation with the European retail industry (represented by the European Retail Round Table Association), a German association called "RFID Informationsforum" (later re-named 'GS1') and a group of other companies.

[11] The Recommendation called for a "framework" and not concrete PIA guidelines. The PIA "Framework identifies the objectives of RFID Application PIAs, the components of RFID Applications to be considered during PIAs, and the common structure and content of RFID Application PIA Reports" (PIA Framework, p. 4). The Framework "could be used as a basis for the development of industry-based, sector-based, and/or application-based PIA templates" (p. 3).

the general reporting of privacy issues only, avoided any kind of risk identification process, failed to link to any legal system already governing privacy in Europe and was written as a barely structured pamphlet in a language that Norbert Wiener would probably recognise as "forensic discourse".[12] Unsurprisingly, the Article 29 Data Protection Working Party (Art. 29 WP hereafter) rejected the piece as unacceptable.[13]

In Phase 2 of the PIA Framework development, a European group from a variety of industries and academic backgrounds forced the initial authors to outline a methodology that identified privacy risks and mitigation strategies. This group also insisted that the PIA report provide enough details about an RFID application and its back-end infrastructure to allow for a comprehensible identification and judgement of such risks.

As one of the co-authors of the RFID PIA Framework, I describe in this chapter the details of the methodology that was finally endorsed as well as means to apply it. I comment on the purpose and scope of RFID PIAs, the most important procedures, the reasoning behind them, and the meaning of details, definitions, formulations and structure. I also report on the stakeholder challenges overcome, the compromises reached and the lessons learned about PIA construction, at both a technical and political level.

The structure of this article is based on four phases of a privacy impact assessment process for RFID (see Fig. 15.1). Some preliminary considerations lead to two main PIA process phases: initial analysis and privacy risk assessment. The initial analysis and privacy risk assessment are accompanied by documentation and reporting.

In this chapter, I define and explain the terms and concepts of the RFID PIA Framework as I understand them as a co-author.[14] Stakeholder discussions are tricky

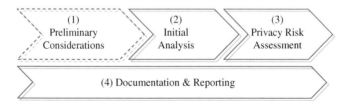

Fig. 15.1 Process phases of a privacy impact assessment (PIA) for RFID

---

[12] In his influential work on cybernetics, Norbert Wiener distinguishes between two types of language: "one of which is intended primarily to convey information and the other to primarily impose a point of view against a wilful opposition". See Wiener, Norbert, *The Human Use of Human Beings: Cybernetics and Society*, Houghton Mifflin, New York, 1950.

[13] Readers interested in the concrete criticisms of PIA I can also consult the collection of documents published by the European Digital Rights Association (EDRI): http://www.edri.org/edrigram/number8.15/article-29-no-to-rfid-pia

[14] My role in this negotiation was that of rapporteur for the European Commission in the first phase of the PIA Framework development. I then led the negotiations for a German industry group in the second phase of the PIA Framework development and co-authored the PIA III Framework.

in that conflicting interests can result in "language" (usage of terms) in the final documents that leave room for interpretation. Any material that might be regarded as personal opinion or backroom information is included in the footnotes so it is not confused with the more factual frame of the main text. When I use the term "PIA Framework" in this chapter, I refer to the specific RFID PIA Framework endorsed on 11 February 2011. Official terminology from the RFID PIA Framework appears in *italics* the first time it is used in the text; the spelling of terms also matches the official document. If I excerpt a definition from the Framework, I provide the exact wording and details of the Framework's text in the footnote section. For further information, the reader should refer to the official RFID PIA Framework published by the European Commission.[15]

15.2 Preliminary Considerations Before Engaging in a PIA

Before engaging in the PIA core processes (initial analysis, privacy risk assessment), one must consider a few key points. These include the status of a company deploying RFID as an "RFID operator" in the sense of the PIA Framework (who), the scope of the relevant RFID application (what) and the timing of the PIA (when).

The Commission's Recommendation indicates that *all* RFID operators should assess the impact of their operations on privacy and data protection. It defines an RFID application operator as a "natural or legal person, public authority, agency, or any other body, which, alone or jointly with others, determines the purposes and means of operating an application, including controllers of personal data using an RFID application".[16] Yet, RFID is a widely used technology that is already embedded in many of today's products and service architectures. Automobiles, for example, contain various RFID applications. RFID gates regularly support manufacturing processes. Ski resorts, public transport companies, toll collectors and event organisers use RFID infrastructures to efficiently manage access controls. As a result, the question is whether all of these RFID operators now and in the future need to immediately consider the privacy implications of their operations. What about tiny retailers or kiosks that may soon use RFID readers only to check out customers, replacing traditional barcode scanners with an RFID system? Are they all equally in need of a PIA? Will every car leaving the factory require a PIA prior to sale, just because it uses RFID for anti-theft protection? The *scope* of the PIA roll-out was a prominent issue in the preparation of the PIA Framework.

The compromise embedded in the PIA Framework is that its procedures will have *no retrospective effect* and *only apply if "significant changes in the RFID application" are made.* The most significant changes are those that "expand beyond the

---

[15] The European Commission has posted the PIA Framework document as well as key documents that led to the final version on the Web. See http://cordis.europa.eu/fp7/ict/enet/policy_en.html as well as http://ec.europa.eu/information_society/policy/rfid/pia/index_en.htm

[16] Recommendation, op. cit., Art. 3(e).

original purposes" of the application, or lead to new "types of information processed; uses of the information that weaken the controls employed".[17] For example, if a fitness club uses lockers with RFID keys and later personalises the keys so that premium members can benefit from the use of their preferred lockers, then the upgrade of the RFID functionality would justify the need for a PIA. The PIA would be needed because the upgrade supplements the original locking function of the system with a customer-relationship function.

In the context of this fitness club example, another aspect of scope becomes apparent: whether the fitness club is the RFID operator responsible for conducting the PIA. After all, fitness clubs are not technology providers; the function and technical architecture of the systems they use are often pre-determined by system vendors. As the goal of a PIA is not only to identify privacy risks, but also to mitigate them technically, can customers implementing an "out-of-the-box" RFID system be held responsible for privacy controls because they are the ones "operating" it? At this point, the definition of the RFID operator becomes important. *The RFID operator is the entity determining the purposes and means of operation.*[18] This is indeed primarily the entity running the RFID application in its premises. However, in view of the fact that in many cases these commercial entities are not technically prone, it would often need to be the system vendor or system implementer and not necessarily the customer (such as the fitness club owner) who would carry the bulk of responsibility for conducting a PIA. The responsibility of *system* vendors also becomes important when they offer turnkey RFID systems. In this case, system vendors need to conduct PIAs, because they are the ones who determine the purposes and means of those applications. The authors also thought that in cases where RFID systems are tailored to customer needs, then system vendors would have the prime responsibility to inform their customers of the privacy implications of the RFID application and to use (potentially standardised) PIA templates to check for the privacy risks together with them.

Another important issue to consider is *when* a PIA needs to be conducted. What constitutes a significant change of an RFID application? Here the definition of an RFID application becomes important because it outlines the breadth of the system landscape to be watched. An RFID application is "An Application that processes data through the use of tags and readers, and which is supported by a back-end system and a networked communication infrastructure" [PIA Framework, p. 23]. *The consideration of RFID back-end systems' links and sharing networks is important*

---

[17] The factors that would require a new or revised PIA include "significant changes in the RFID Application, such as material changes that expand beyond the original purposes (e.g., secondary purposes); types of information processed; uses of the information that weaken the controls employed; unexpected personal data breach with determinant impact and which wasn't part of the residual risks of the application identified by the first PIA; defining of a period of regular review; responding to substantive or significant internal or external stakeholder feedback or inquiry; or significant changes in technology with privacy and data protection implications for the RFID Application at stake" (PIA Framework, p. 5).

[18] See the glossary at Appendix B of the PIA Framework.

for a PIA kick-off. It is important because privacy problems often result from the "secondary" processing of data somewhere at the back-end of a system and outside of the particular application that initially collects and uses the data for a specific purpose. For example, a retailer may initially collect, store and process uniquely identified purchase item data for his RFID-enhanced inventory control application. These activities do not cause any privacy concerns. However, when the retailer decides that purchase data items should be forwarded to a back-end loyalty-card system containing customer identities, a privacy problem is created and a PIA or PIA upgrade is warranted. Thus, *the RFID application borders considered for the PIA analysis and kick-off should be understood as the initial application collecting the RFID data* plus *all those networked communication infrastructures that receive the RFID-based data for additional purposes.*

Finally, a strong concern among stakeholders was whether a PIA would need to be conducted for *every* system and thus potentially *every* product that embeds an RFID application supported by a back-end infrastructure. For example, the automotive industry questioned whether each car containing an RFID-enabled anti-theft functionality supported by dealers' car-owner databases would need a PIA. This would create an unjustifiable cost load to complete manufacturing. The PIA Framework therefore specifies that PIAs need to be done only once for a product series: "If RFID Application Operators reuse one RFID Application in the same way for multiple products, services or processes, they may create one PIA Report for all products, services or processes that are similar" (PIA Framework, p. 6).

15.3 Initial Analysis to Determine the Scope of PIA

Some companies *are* RFID operators in the sense of the Framework but still don't need to conduct a PIA because they simply don't have a privacy problem. These RFID operators have RFID data that is never used for personal data processing or profiling. One only needs to think of a farmer using RFID for tagging his cattle. Furthermore, RFID applications differ in the *degree* to which they entail a privacy risk. For these reasons, an initial analysis can be used by RFID operators to assess whether and at what level of detail they need to conduct a PIA. The decision tree in Fig. 15.2 depicts the principal questions an RFID operator needs to consider in documented form for initial analysis.

The key question at the outset of the initial analysis is whether the RFID application actually processes personal data or whether the RFID application links RFID data to personal data. The issue of linking must be understood in the context of the RFID application definition outlined above: Because the RFID application in the RFID PIA Framework is a broad system infrastructure that includes a data-sharing network at the back-end, one must ask whether that level contains links between RFID data and personal data. For example, a manufacturer may use RFID in manufacturing and for employees' access control. The question is whether these two data sources could be linked at some point to investigate who had access to the manufacturing unit at a specific point in time.

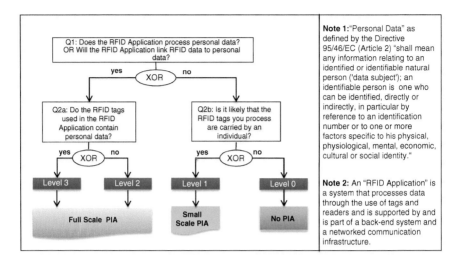

Fig. 15.2 Initial decision tree on PIA necessity and scope

For those who are not privacy experts, it is crucial to note that in the initial analysis phase, "personal data" is understood in a legal sense. A layman would think of personal data as being information about an identified individual – a known person. In the legal sense, however, the definition of personal data is much broader. According to the EU Data Protection Directive, personal data is "any information relating to an identified or identifiable natural person ('data subject'); an identifiable person is one who can be identified, directly or indirectly, in particular by reference to an identification number or to one or more factors specific to his physical, physiological, mental, economic, cultural or social identity".[19]

If a company does not handle personal data (right side of the decision tree), it may not need to conduct a PIA (Level 0, no PIA). Companies that do not handle personal data must conduct a PIA only if individuals will carry RFID tags that the companies process. This consideration (Q2b) was developed with a view to retailers who may process tags in their retail outlets that are passed on to their customers. The thinking here is that *the process of using and passing on tags alone creates a responsibility for RFID operators* to check whether they create privacy problems outside their own premises.

If a company does handle personal data (left side of the decision tree) in conjunction with its RFID application (e.g., a retailer using unique purchase identifiers in conjunction with identifiable loyalty card data or a health care system involving patient data in a hospital), it must answer a second question (Q2a) about the personal

---

[19] European Parliament and the Council, Directive 95/46/EC on the protection of individuals with regard to the processing of personal data and on the free movement of such data, 24 October 1995, Art. 2(a).

data on the tags. If personal data is stored in tags, the privacy analysis requires more detail. In fact, *the terminology of "levels" was introduced as an indicator for the level of detail expected for privacy analysis.* The threat environment for privacy breach is enlarged in situations where personal data is not only stored at the back-end of an RFID application, but also directly on the tag. PIAs for these situations need to look at both domains: the back-end and the front-end. *The level terminology does* not *refer to the level of risk inherent in an RFID application.* In fact, future smart card applications may even benefit from storing more of an individual's information directly on the tag and thus potentially under user control. Even though this kind of RFID application would require a careful a priori privacy analysis (level 3, full-scale PIA), it could be the more privacy-friendly system. After all, privacy scholars agree that decentralised data-processing architectures (ideally under user control) are more privacy friendly than centralised ones.[20]

A recurring question on the initial decision tree is how a full-scale PIA differs from a small-scale PIA. The UK and Canada make a distinction between small scale and full scale for PIAs.[21] This distinction has been made because companies (in particular, small and medium enterprises) that do not process personal data in relation to RFID data should not be overburdened with a privacy analysis, even if they have to take some responsibility for passing tags that are then carried by individuals. An earlier version of the PIA Framework (dubbed "PIA II"[22]) actually contained separate process charts for small-scale and full-scale PIAs. Wright comments: "The phases in a small-scale PIA mirror those in a full-scale PIA, but a small-scale PIA is less formalized and does not warrant as great an investment of time and resources in analysis and information-gathering."[23] During the Framework development discussion, stakeholders suggested that responsibility for conducting a small-scale PIA could probably remain with the person or team who introduced the RFID application; furthermore, a small-scale PIA could dispense with the stakeholder process recommended for a full-scale PIA. Stakeholders also argued that entities developing PIA templates for whole sectors or product and service lines should certainly run through a full-scale PIA.

Ultimately, the initial analysis must be reported. One pitfall involved in the negotiation of PIA reports with industry is the difficulty of establishing consensus on what needs to be reported in the different phases of analysis. Companies often want

---

[20] Spiekermann, Sarah, and Lorrie Faith Cranor, "Engineering Privacy", *IEEE Transactions on Software Engineering*, Vol. 35, No. 1, January/February 2009, pp. 67–82.

[21] See respectively Information Commissioner's Office (ICO), *Privacy Impact Assessment Handbook*, Version 2.0, Wilmslow, Cheshire, June 2009, and Office of the Privacy Commissioner of Canada, *Assessing the Privacy Impacts of Programs, Plans, and Policies*, Audit Report of the Privacy Commissioner of Canada, Ottawa, 2007.

[22] Spiekermann, S., *PIA II – A Proposal for a Privacy Impact Assessment Framework for RFID Applications*, Vienna University of Economics and Business, 2011, http://cordis.europa.eu/fp7/ict/enet/policy_en.html, published there under the title: German Industry Alternative Proposal on the RFID Privacy and Data Protection Impact Assessment Framework [21 October 2010].

[23] Wright, op. cit.

to avoid a description of data flows, push for the publication of just a summary about the results of a PIA (as is the case in Canada), or both. Indeed, a major achievement for the RFID PIA Framework is that all of these common pitfalls were avoided. Europe's PIA for RFID now states that the "initial analysis must be documented and made available to data protection authorities upon request" (PIA Framework, p. 6) and that this documentation not only describes the RFID application at a superficial level, but contains all information needed to judge the potential privacy impact of the system. This requirement implies that the RFID application description must contain detailed information about the method and purpose of data storage, processing and transfer. Table 15.1 shows what reporting elements must be contained in an RFID application description according to Annex 1 of the RFID PIA Framework. Most of these information elements are not specific to RFID and may be used in other system contexts.

Table 15.1 Reporting elements of the initial analysis of an RFID application according to Annex I of the RFID PIA Framework

RFID application operator	• Legal entity name and location • Person or office responsible for PIA timeliness • Point(s) of contact and inquiry method to reach the Operator
RFID application overview	• RFID Application name • Purpose(s) of RFID Application(s) • Basic use case scenarios of the RFID Application • RFID Application components and technology used (i.e., frequencies, etc.) • Geographical scope of the RFID Application • Types of users/individuals impacted by the RFID Application • Individual access and control
PIA report number	• Version Number of PIA Report (distinguishing new PIA or just minor changes) • Date of last change made to PIA Report
RFID data processing	• List of types of data elements processed • Presence of sensitive information in the data being processed (health, for instance)
RFID data storage	• List of types of data elements stored • Storage duration
Internal RFID data transfer (if applicable)	• Description or diagrams of data flows of internal operations involving RFID data • Purpose(s) of transferring the personal data
External RFID data transfer (if applicable)	• Type of data recipient(s) • Purpose(s) for transfer or access in general • Identified and/or identifiable (level of) personal data involved in transfer • Transfers outside the European Economic Area (EEA)

15.4 PIA Risk Assessment Process

One of the biggest challenges for the PIA stakeholder process was to gain industry consent to a *process* for privacy risk assessment. Running through a proper process and reporting on its individual steps is more time-intensive and costly for companies than writing a report with less stringent requirements. Scholars agree that if PIAs "are conducted in a mechanical fashion for the purpose of satisfying a legislative or bureaucratic requirement, they are often regarded as exercises in legitimization rather than risk assessment".[24] Coming up with the *right* process for PIAs was difficult because few publicly available, proven examples exist. The difficulty in developing the PIA risk assessment process was that it needed to be concrete enough to help uncover *all* (or at least most) privacy risks while being generic enough to cover all of the ways that RFID technology can be deployed. As with many modern quality management or business continuity activities, "completeness" for this process could only be achieved through a process reference model that enforced the identification of privacy risks and mitigation strategies with its *procedure*.

If the initial analysis concludes that a PIA is necessary and the RFID application description is completed (as described in Table 15.1), the first step of the risk analysis is also completed. The relevant material is gathered and status quo information is available (see Fig. 15.2). The next step (step 2) is to identify the privacy risks associated with the RFID application.

Laymen associate many meanings with the term "risk". But for professional risk assessments, it is vital to embrace a precise and established definition. Most security risk assessments and respective ISO standards used as references[25] for the PIA Framework agree on the following definition of risk: "a function of the likelihood of a given threat-source exercising a particular potential vulnerability and the resulting impact of that adverse event on the organization".[26] This definition sees the *extent* of risk as a result of three main factors: (1) threats, (2) the likelihood of these threats and (3) their impact magnitude (see left side of Fig. 15.2). It is therefore vital to understand whether RFID applications actually *threaten* privacy and with what effects. When risks are assessed, the next step (step 3) in the risk assessment procedure calls for the RFID operators to identify controls that mitigate these risks. The

---

[24] Wright, op. cit.

[25] These included: International Organization for Standardization (ISO), ISO/IEC 27005 Information technology – Security techniques – Information Security Risk Management, Geneva, 2008; Bartels, C., H. Kelter, R. Oberweis and B. Rosenberg, "Technische Richtlinie für den sicheren RFID-Einsatz", in TR 03126, B.f.S.i.d. Informationstechnik, Bundesamt für Sicherheit in der Informationstechnik, Germany, 2009; European Network and Information Security Agency (ENISA), Emerging and Future Risks Framework – Introductory Manual, Heraklion, 2010; Stoneburner, Gary, Alice Goguen and Alexis Feringa, National Institute for Standards and Technology (NIST), Risk Management Guide for Information Technology Systems, Recommendations of the National Institute of Standards and Technology, NIST Special Publication 800-30, July 2002.

[26] Stoneburner, Goguen and Feringa, NIST, op. cit., July 2002, p. 8.

final step (step 4) results in documentation and reflection on what has been done to reduce privacy risks and what remains to be done later (residual privacy risk).

15.4.1 How Is the Risk Assessment Done Step By Step?

Even though Fig. 15.3 suggests a relatively easy way to conduct the PIA risk assessment, putting this process into practice is not a trivial task. In fact, in order to reach consensus among the negotiating parties of the PIA Framework, a relatively high level of abstraction was chosen in the official document depicting the risk assessment process (Fig. 15.3). That said, there are existing international risk assessment standards that can now be used to translate this overview process (Fig. 15.3) into a practical step-by-step methodology (for example, the method proposed by the National Institute for Standards and Technology (NIST) 2010) can be helpful, even if this process relates exclusively to security assessments).[27] One of the most usable and recognised methodologies to handle the details of the RFID risk assessment has been proposed by the German Federal Office for Information Security (BSI) [BSI2007]. By adhering to the BSI PIA standards outlined hereafter, a company signals its commitment to optimise its security and privacy operations according to timely standards in security management and EU data protection regulation.

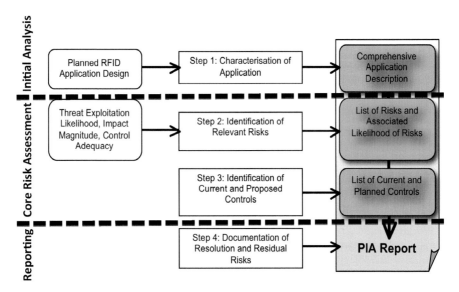

Fig. 15.3 PIA risk assessment process [PIA Framework, p. 8]

---

[27] National Institute of Standards and Technology, Guide for Applying the Risk Management Framework to Federal Information Systems: A Security Life Cycle Approach, NIST Special Publication 800-37, Revision 1, Gaithersburg, MD, Feb 2010. http://csrc.nist.gov/publications/nistpubs/800-37-rev1/sp800-37-rev1-final.pdf

Risk Assessment Methodology for RFID Deployments adopted from the IT security concept of the German BSI*

① Characterisation of the Application		
② Definition of Privacy Targets (P)	→ Table I	Based on EU 95/46/EC as well as other relevant laws, operator specifies privacy targets and defines their meanings for his proper operations.
③ Evaluation of Degree of Protection Demand for each Privacy Target (P)	→ Table II	Operator evaluates the degree of protection demand, which may be low, medium or high depending on the impact of potential privacy breaches.
④ Identification of Threats (T) for each Privacy Target (P)	→ Table III	For each privacy target potential threats are identified and their likelihood is determined.
⑤ Identification and Recommendation of existing or new Controls (C) suited to protect against Threats (T)	→ Table IV	For each threat an adequate control is chosen. The level of control varies according to the degree of protection demand identified in step 3.
⑥ Assessment and Documentation of Residual Risks		

Fig. 15.4 Full-scale PIA process in detail

The step-by-step process that a company would need to run through is depicted in Fig. 15.4. Here it becomes clear that an organisation needs to first understand its *privacy targets*, then analyse how these targets are threatened and finally judge risks based on the situation and existing control landscape (Fig. 15.4). Each step is supported by an explicit keying scheme as well as tables which ensure the rigour of the methodology. The next section will outline how to conduct a PIA according to this standard.

15.4.1.1 Defining Privacy Targets

The purpose of the risk analysis is to understand what is at risk. What is the privacy protection target? The UK's Privacy Impact Assessment Handbook regards the following aspects of privacy as being at risk and worth protecting: (1) privacy of personal information, (2) privacy of the person, (3) privacy of personal behaviour, and (4) privacy of personal communications.[28] Yet, instead of putting these four

---

[28] ICO, op. cit.

privacy targets at the centre of the risk assessment, the PIA Framework consortium opted to take legislation as the starting point of risk analysis. Framed in a legal way, the Data Protection Directive formulates the nine privacy targets summarised in Table 15.2 (and included in Annex II of the RFID PIA Framework). Note that every privacy target can have a key associated with it (P1, P2, ... P_N). These keys can later be linked to threats and controls (see Fig. 15.5).[29] The use of a key structure facilitates systematic risk assessment and is often employed by both privacy and security assessments.[30]

Table 15.2 Privacy targets identified in Annex II of the PIA Framework

Description of privacy target (taken and updated from the respective EU Privacy Directive(s); here Directive 95/46/EC)	
Safeguarding quality of personal data	Data avoidance and minimisation, purpose specification and limitation, quality of data and transparency are the key targets that need to be ensured.
Legitimacy of processing personal data	Legitimacy of processing personal data must be ensured either by basing data processing on consent, contract, legal obligation, etc.
Legitimacy of processing *sensitive* personal data	Legitimacy of processing sensitive personal data must be ensured either by basing data processing on explicit consent, a special legal basis, etc.
Compliance with the data subject's right to be informed	It must be ensured that the data subject is informed about the collection of his data in a timely manner.
Compliance with the data subject's right of access to data, correct and erase data	It must be ensured that the data subject's wish to access, correct, erase and block his data is fulfilled in a timely manner.
Compliance with the data subject's right to object	It must be ensured that the data subject's data is no longer processed if he or she objects. Transparency of automated decisions vis-à-vis individuals must be ensured especially.
Safeguarding confidentiality and security of processing	Preventing unauthorised access, logging of data processing, network and transport security and preventing accidental loss of data are the key targets that need to be ensured.
Compliance with notification requirements	Notification about data processing, prior compliance checking and documentation are the key targets that need to be ensured.
Compliance with data retention requirements	Retention of data should be for the minimum period of time consistent with the purpose of the retention or other legal requirements.

---

[29] The keys were part of PIA II, but omitted from the official and final PIA Framework document to avoid giving the impression that the Annex tables represent the complete methodology.

[30] Bartels, Cord, Harald Kelter, Rainer Oberweis and Birger Rosenberg, TR 03126 – Technische Richtlinie für den sicheren RFID-Einsatz, Bundesamt für Sicherheit in der Informationstechnik,

Table I

Privacy target code and name	
P1	Safeguarding quality of personal data
P2	Legitimacy of processing personal data
P3	Legitimacy of processing *sensitive* personal data
P4	Compliance with the data subject's right to be informed
P5	…

Table II

T7	Threat codes and names	P2	…
T8	Invalidation of consent		Consent has been obtained under threat of disadvantage. Example: Cannot return/exchange/use warranties for products when RFID tag is deactivated.
T9	Invalidation of explicit consent	P3	Consent has not been given explicitly. Example: Must accept an RFID based access control system to sensitive locations such as labor union offices, toilets, smoking areas, etc.
T10	Secret data collection	P4	Some data is secretly recorded and thus unknown to the data subject, e.g. movement profiles. Example: Consumer is read out while walking in front of stores or in a mall and no Logo or Emblem is warning him or her about RFID readouts.
T11	Incomplete information	P4, P8	The information provided to the data subject on the purpose and use of data is not complete. Example: RFID Information posters that lack clear information on how RFID data is processed and used.

Fig. 15.5 Deriving privacy threats from privacy targets systematically

The PIA Framework consortium took the articles of the Data Protection Directive as its privacy targets for several reasons. Most importantly, it is very useful and sensible to draw privacy threats from existing legal frameworks and thereby combine a PIA with a legal compliance check. While scholars tend to distinguish PIAs from compliance checks and privacy audits,[31] the stakeholder negotiation over RFID PIAs cast doubt on the value of this distinction: taking privacy legislation as a starting point for privacy threat analysis saves companies cost and time.[32] *If a company commits to invest in a (potentially cost intensive) PIA, the minimum outcome it expects is the legal compliance of its operations.* It should be noted that the PIA

Bonn, 2009; ENISA, Emerging and Future Risks Framework – Introductory Manual, op. cit.; ENISA, Flying 2.0 – Enabling automated air travel by identifying and addressing the challenges of IoT & RFID technology, Heraklion, 2010.

[31] Wright, op. cit.

[32] In fact, combining the RFID PIA process with a legal privacy compliance check was an important reason why major industry bodies got involved in the RFID PIA Framework definition in its second phase. The argument was that, especially for small and medium enterprises, investing in privacy issues twice – once for PIA and again for legal compliance – was unjustifiable.

Framework stakeholder group did not view the EU's Data Protection Directive as the only valid privacy target; the group also considered that its RFID PIA approach was sufficiently flexible to take into account other relevant jurisdictions, depending on where PIA will be used (e.g., in the US). An alternative set of rules could, for example, be the OECD Guidelines on the Protection of Privacy and Transborder Flows of Personal Data.[33] Taking current privacy laws as privacy targets makes the risk assessment process timely and adaptable for various regions.

Making legal privacy rights the targets of privacy analysis also has practical benefits: Many PIA processes start with a difficult discussion of what privacy actually is in order to define what needs protection. Yet, as Lillian R. BeVier notes, "Privacy is a chameleon-like word, used denotatively to designate a range of wildly disparate interests – from confidentiality of personal information to reproductive autonomy – and connotatively to generate goodwill on behalf of whatever interest is being asserted in its name."[34] As a result, stakeholder discussions about privacy targets can be lengthy and frustrating. Such discussions also risk producing an incomplete list of privacy issues that is more compromised than complete. The law, in contrast, is an undisputable common denominator that leads to acceptance of the resulting risk assessment.

Taking legislation as a central starting point to define privacy targets also produced some valuable insight on how a PIA is different from a security risk assessment. In fact, security agencies such as the German BSI have been among the first organisations to look into the security of RFID systems and means to identify security risks.[35] They tend to confine privacy targets to those data protection issues that are found in the security domain. Here privacy is typically manifest in four targets: the guarantee of anonymity, pseudonymity, unlinkability and unobservability.[36] Yet, are these privacy targets suited to embrace the privacy rights manifest in European privacy law, such as the *legitimacy* of processing personal data or *data subjects' right* to be informed and have access to her data? No. *Security and data protection targets as found in security risk assessments often do not constitute viable privacy targets as such. However, they may offer the technical means to ensure the*

---

[33] Organisation for Economic Co-operation and Development (OECD), Guidelines Governing the Protection of Privacy and Transborder Flows of Personal Data, OECD, Paris, 23 September 1980. http://www.oecd.org/document/18/0,3343,en_2649_34255_1815186_1_1_1,00.html

[34] BeVier, Lillian R., "Information About Individuals in the Hands of Government: Some Reflections on Mechanisms for Privacy Protection", *William & Mary Bill of Rights Journal*, Vol. 4, No. 2, 1995, pp. 455–506 [p. 458]. Cited also in Solove, Daniel J., "A Taxonomy of Privacy", *University of Pennsylvania Law Review*, Vol. 154, No. 3, January 2006, pp. 477–560.

[35] Bartels, Cord, Harald Kelter, Rainer Oberweis and Birger Rosenberg, TR 03126 – Technische Richtlinie für den sicheren RFID-Einsatz, Bundesamt für Sicherheit in der Informationstechnik, Bonn, 2009. As previously mentioned, the German BSI published PIA templates that provide a detailed description of how PIAs for RFID can be conducted for e-ticketing applications in public transport and for events, as well as how they can be used for retail logistics and employee cards. These templates can be accessed for initial guidance at: https://www.bsi.bund.de/cln_165/EN/Topics/ElectrIDDocuments/RadioFrequencyIdentification/TR_RFID/trfid_node.html

[36] See p. 51 in Bartels et al., *supra*.

safeguarding of confidentiality and security of processing (as outlined in Articles 16-17 of the EU Data Protection Directive 95/46/EC) *or of the quality of personal data* (Article 6). Consequently, for the purpose of PIAs, security targets can be described as nested within privacy targets. Many privacy targets can be met only if security targets are met.

As mentioned above, legislation was used to constitute the privacy targets in the RFID PIA Framework. Yet taking legislation as the privacy target for PIA also has drawbacks. One is that data protection laws may not cover all of the privacy issues inherent in RFID. Laws often lag behind current technological developments and have varying foci and strengths. For example, focus group studies on privacy concerns around RFID revealed that people are afraid of being restricted, criticised or exposed through automatic object reactions.[37] This concern relates to the possibility that RFID technology could be used to "paternalistically" regulate behaviour by observing and correctively influencing interactions with objects. This practice might breach the *physical* right to be let alone[38] as a form of privacy. However, this right is not explicitly regulated by the EU Directive (although it is recognised in US common law); as a result, PIAs using the EU's legal framework as the sole privacy target would probably fail to identify this risk. Some PIA experts therefore advise using the legal framework as a starting point to define PIA targets[39] before questioning whether the list is really complete.

15.4.1.2   Defining Protection Demand and Importance Categories

Even though all privacy targets are equally important vis-à-vis the regulator, some of them will have different degrees of urgency from a company perspective. In security assessments, it is common practice that security targets (i.e., the confidentiality of data) are ranked according to the loss or damage that would result from their potential breach. Such a ranking of targets or formation of protection demand categories is important, because companies or regulators need to be aware of their most important points of system failure and they need to be able to prioritise security investments in those areas.

However, the judgement of the relative priority of security targets is a challenge. The extent of damage can often not be evaluated solely in financial terms. In those cases, "soft" factors must be considered, such as the potential loss of a company's reputation or the social implications for people in their roles as citizens or customers. An informed qualitative judgement of experts is therefore often used to estimate the amount of damage resulting from a security breach. According to this judgement, protection demand categories are formed (for a similar approach, see also BSI2008).

---

[37] Spiekermann, S., *User Control in Ubiquitous Computing: Design Alternatives and User Acceptance*, Shaker Verlag, Aachen, 2008.

[38] Warren, Samuel, and Louis D. Brandeis, "The Right to Privacy", *Harvard Law Review*, Vol. IV, No. 5, 15 December 1890.

[39] ICO, op. cit.

When protection demand categories are formed for *privacy* targets, a challenge is that even fewer of them can be represented in monetary terms. For example, it is hard to judge how customers or citizens will react in cases where companies or regulators are not transparent enough, don't describe data processing practices to an adequate extent, etc. Nevertheless, the extent of consequences of privacy breaches should be anticipated for RFID operators as well as for customers of the RFID operator (the "data subjects") in order to get a feeling for the importance and priority of different privacy measures. Customers could lose their social standing, money or even their personal freedom as a result of a privacy breach. But regardless of whether this actually happens or not, companies can also damage their reputation and brand when privacy breaches become known to their customers or the public at large through negative press coverage. RFID operators should, therefore, carefully consider how the breach of different privacy targets could differentially impact their market reputation or lead to financial compensation payments. Based on this judgement, they can prioritise the different privacy targets for their operations. For example, they can form protection demand categories "low – 1", "medium – 2" or "high – 3". In a later state of the risk assessment, such a categorisation can help to choose privacy controls that correspond in strength and vigour.

15.4.1.3 Deducing Privacy Threats from Privacy Targets

Once privacy targets are identified and prioritised as to their protection demand, they can be used to systematically deduce threats. The core question is how a privacy target is threatened. For example, compliance with a person's right to be informed (P4) may be threatened by secret data collection (T10) or incomplete information about the data collection's purpose (T11). Again, keys (P_4, T_{10}) can be used to systematically link privacy targets to privacy threats. Annex III of the PIA Framework contains a relatively extensive but incomplete list of potential threats with RFID-specific examples. Depending on the industry and the RFID application at hand, RFID operators can pick and comment on the potential threats from this list that are relevant to their operations. Alternatively, RFID operators may also need to add other threats that are more meaningful to them. Sector-specific PIA templates, which will be developed from this framework and for use in different industries, may inform threat identification in greater detail. Figure 15.5 visualises the link between privacy targets and threats with the help of keys.

Not all threats given as examples in the PIA Framework Annex III may be equally probable. Many of them will not materialise at all from a specific operator's perspective. An RFID operator must therefore identify those threats that are *likely* to occur in the respective organisation. Threats can occur from within and outside of the particular system at hand and derive from likely uses and possible misuses of the information. A full-scale PIA would typically involve a stakeholder group identifying threats and determining their likelihood. This group should include the technical staff responsible for the RFID roll-out, managers who will benefit from RFID data, those responsible for data protection of the respective RFID operator (if there is one) and end users of the RFID service. Potentially, additional external stakeholders, such as privacy rights groups, may be consulted. But obviously many companies will be reluctant to do so.

In security risk assessments, threats and their likelihood are identified and judged based on the vulnerability of a system.[40] Vulnerability analysis identifies the technical weaknesses of a system that may be exploited by an attacker. Yet, can this methodology be transferred to a PIA? How does a vulnerability relate to a privacy threat? In preparing the PIA Framework, the authors found that RFID operators may fail to meet the privacy targets of the legal environment due to two kinds of threats: (1) threats caused by neglect of privacy-friendly practices and (2) threats caused by the exploitation of a RFID system's technical vulnerability. Consequently, in the privacy context, threats can originate in the technology or stem from poor privacy management. The threat analysis of a PIA can benefit by systematically distinguishing between these two kinds of threats.

One threat of particular concern in the RFID context is the potential *secrecy of data collection* that may undermine a data subject's right to be informed that an RFID is being used. The rating of privacy threats should therefore consider the read-range difference, which depends on the type of RFID technology used. Different frequencies make it more or less likely that secret tracking of RFID tags can take place and therefore cause a greater or lesser number of privacy threats. For example, the UHF frequency entails a potentially higher privacy threat than HF or LF. Proximity technology (ISO/IEC 14443) causes fewer privacy threats than vicinity technology (ISO/IEC 15693). Nevertheless, independent of the technology, it is also necessary to consider how easy it is to get the reader in the vicinity of the tag without drawing attention to it.

Finally, a prime subject of debate is the threat that RFID tags could be used to profile or track individuals.[41] The RFID tag's information – in particular its identifier(s) – could be used as a sort of "cookie" to re-recognise, profile and track an individual. Retailers who pass RFID tags to customers without automatically deactivating them at check-out *may* unintentionally enable this threat. For this reason, the EC's Recommendation contains a special retail section that is repeated in the RFID PIA Framework. It states:

> A risk that has caused a prime subject of debate is that RFID Tags could be used for the profiling and/or tracking of individuals. In this case the RFID Tag's information – in particular its identifier(s) – would be used to re-identify a particular individual. Retailers who pass RFID Tags on to customers without automatically deactivating or removing them at the checkout *may* unintentionally enable this risk. A key question, though, is whether this risk is likely and actually materialises into an *undismissable* risk or not. According to point 11 of the RFID Recommendation, retailers should deactivate or remove at the point of sale tags used in their application unless consumers, after being informed of the policy in accordance with this Framework, give their consent to keep the tags operational. Retailers are not required to deactivate or remove tags if the PIA report concludes that tags that are used in a retail application and would remain operational after the point of sale do not represent a

---

[40] Stoneburner, Goguen and Feringa, NIST, op. cit.

[41] Guenther, Oliver, and Sarah Spiekermann, "RFID and the Perception of Control: The Consumer's View", *Communications of the ACM*, Vol. 48, No. 9, 2005, pp. 73–76.

likely threat to privacy or the protection of personal data as stated in point 12 of the same Recommendation. Deactivation of the tags should be understood as any process that stops those interactions of a tag with its environment which do not require the active involvement of the consumer [PIA Framework, p. 9].

The PIA Framework authors and stakeholders debated at length about whether and how the PIA Framework should contain clear guidance for the retail sector on when to deactivate. All agreed that the "likelihood" of this profiling and tracking risk depends on three main factors: (1) the volume of RFID readers that RFID operators use officially outside a retailer's premises that gather RFID tags' data in a way the individual cannot control, (2) the volume of RFID tags passed on to customers that are "left on" and (3) the number of malicious attackers that will regularly and personally spy on consumers' assets. Furthermore, all retail stakeholders involved in the negotiations agreed to abstain from the reading of "foreign" tags as part of their PIA controls. If foreign tags were processed, they agreed that they would need to use privacy-by-design methods to mitigate the creation of personally identifiable data from tag information. They argued that either of these two control methods would sufficiently mitigate the threat of uncontrollable profiling or tracking, making the risk "dismissible" (not likely enough to require deactivation). This agreement was supposed to be included in a separate "Deactivation Annex" in the PIA Framework.

What retail stakeholders could not agree on, unfortunately, was a threshold level at which the volume of left-on RFID tags is so high that deactivation becomes a necessity. One retailer suggested that the threshold level would be reached when retailers use RFID tags for anti-theft purposes and thus embed dual-functionality RFID tags in all products that they seek to protect. At this point, (most) retailers will heavily invest in the RFID infrastructure at their checkout systems; it must be assumed that they would do so only for a reasonably large volume of tags. However, not all retail stakeholders could agree to this "anti-theft" threshold suggestion. Consequently, it was not included in the Annex, leaving this Annex with relatively little material that addresses the "deactivation dilemma". As a result, informal feedback from the WP 29 Technical Subgroup viewed the Annex as an attempt by retailers to get around the deactivation provision. As a further result, the "deactivation decision" was postponed and no information on it was included in the PIA Framework except for a repetition of what was already agreed in the May 2009 EC Recommendation (see above).

15.4.1.4 Identifying and Implementing Controls to Mitigate Privacy Risks

The crucial step in the privacy risk assessment process is to identify controls that can help to "minimise, mitigate or eliminate the identified privacy risks" [PIA Framework, p. 10]. First, controls are considered that are implemented already or available for implementation. This helps operators judge real threats and their likelihood. Then, the identified threats as well as the protection demand level of the respective privacy target should guide the decision on which of the identified controls are relevant and thus need to be implemented. Figure 15.6 visualises this relationship.

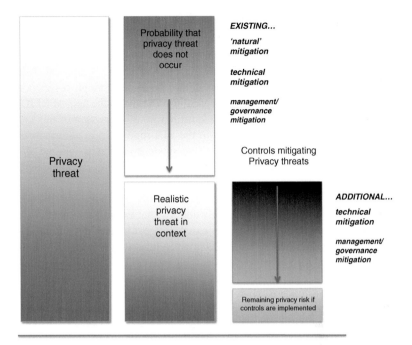

Fig. 15.6   Assessing and controlling privacy risks

Controls are either of a technical or non-technical nature. Technical controls are incorporated into an application, e.g., access control mechanisms, authentication mechanisms and encryption methods. Non-technical controls, on the other hand, are management and operational controls, e.g., policies or operational procedures. Controls can be categorised as being preventive or detective. Preventive controls inhibit violation attempts, while detective controls warn operators about violations or attempted violations. In the privacy context specifically, it is important to note a category of "natural" privacy controls created by the environment. Natural privacy controls are physical or social artefacts in the environment that enforce privacy-sensitive behaviour simply through the force of their existence. For example, if no readers that can conduct a tracking of items or individuals are physically installed (i.e., because there is no business case for it), then "naturally" there is also no (likely) threat to privacy. Similarly, a social rule to avoid staring at people also acts as a natural privacy control. A list of control examples for RFID is included in Annex IV of the PIA Framework. Many of them were drawn from the catalogue of EuroPrise,[42] an entity that helps companies understand how privacy friendly their systems are.

---

[42] https://www.european-privacy-seal.eu/ See also Unabhängiges Landeszentrum für Datenschutz Schleswig-Holstein, EuroPrise Criteria, Version 1.0, Kiel, Germany, 2009.

15.5 PIA Reporting

To save companies' time, the RFID application description, as outlined in Annex I of the PIA Framework, always constitutes the first part of a more complete PIA report. If this first part reveals that the RFID application under scrutiny processes personal data in relation to RFID or allows for personal profiling with the help of RFID, then a privacy risk analysis must be completed; furthermore, every step of this analysis must be fully documented and included in the PIA report. From an organisational perspective, it is sensible to report conclusions made at each step outlined above in Fig. 15.3. Just publishing a summary of the risk analysis is *not* acceptable under the RFID PIA Framework.

That said, a major point of debate in the PIA negotiation process was the question of who would receive the privacy analysis and to what extent such detailed reports would need to be public. In Canada, for example, government institutions have to post PIA summaries on their website. Companies involved in the RFID PIA negotiations were strongly opposed to the idea that internal data flows and processing operations might leak outside the company or even be exposed to competitors. This issue is of particular concern where RFID is used to enable product functionality through the technology's object-object recognition capability (e.g., in-car communication). Here company-internal innovation processes and legitimate competitive secrecy conflict with the ambitions of privacy reporting.

The compromise reached for RFID PIAs is that *PIA reports will not be public, but must be made available to competent authorities* in line with section IX of the Directive 95/46/EC. This requirement means that, in most cases, a company's data protection official or the department responsible for the RFID deployment will prepare the PIA report for authorities.

The PIA Framework contains an important distinction between reporting and scheduling the PIA process: "Scheduling of the PIA process [shall be] so that there is sufficient time to make any needed adjustments to the RFID Application" [PIA Framework, p. 4]. In contrast, the "PIA Report [shall be made] available to the competent authorities at least six weeks before deployment" [PIA Framework, p. 4]. This distinction is made because the whole purpose and goal of PIAs is "to run through (a) risk assessment phase well before final decisions on an RFID Application's architecture are taken so that technical privacy mitigation strategies can be embedded into the system's design, and do not need to be 'bolted on' later" [PIA Framework, p. 8]. This implies that PIAs need to be kicked off in the early requirements definition phase of an application design or upgrade; the need is also recognised for security engineering (as the above-cited NIST guide makes clear).

15.6 Conclusion

The development and endorsement of the RFID PIA Framework is a great achievement for the European privacy landscape on many grounds. First, one of the technologies that has the most potential to intrude on personal privacy can be controlled through a procedure that promises a relatively complete, holistic and proactive tackling of the problem. The methodology will help RFID operators assess whether, why and to what extent their RFID applications entail a privacy risk; it will also help them identify viable strategies for minimising these risks. Second, the methodology outlined in the Framework leaves companies enough room to adapt it to their industry or their specific conditions. This adaptability, along with the ability to ensure legal compliance by using privacy legislation as the target of analysis, promises a wide acceptance of the PIA Framework methodology. Third, the RFID PIA guide is, to my knowledge, the first PIA guide developed by industry instead of data protection authorities. It is a result of a true and difficult stakeholder process. It may therefore find wider backing from the industry than a top-down PIA or regulation would receive. Most importantly, it was a true international effort. The Framework was motivated and edited mostly in the EU, but US technology policy-makers influenced it heavily. For this reason, the Framework contains no terminology in the main text that would limit it to European borders. Consequently, some US companies and industry bodies will probably promote its use as well. Finally, the RFID PIA is generic enough to be adaptable to other technologies of the Internet of Things. It can be taken as a starting point or even a blueprint for how to do privacy impact assessments generally.

Despite these promising facts, some challenges lie ahead. The PIA Framework will enter a proof-of-concept phase. All industries using RFID will need to develop PIA templates. Tools are needed to support the methodology. Industry associations will need to set standards for how to go about PIAs in their respective domains. All of this will take time and effort on the part of companies. At this point, the question becomes: to what extent are companies really willing to comply with the rules that they have set for themselves? So far, it is unclear where in an organisation a PIA would be kicked off. Who would typically have the responsibility? And at what points in time do specific criteria require a PIA upgrade?

An open question is also what will happen if companies do not comply with the PIA Framework methodology. Will there be any sanctions? Or could this PIA Framework become mandatory for RFID operators? If not, how can companies be rewarded for their willingness to embrace PIA? Will established privacy seals or auditing companies incorporate the PIA Framework methodology into their controlling operations?

The trade associations who have developed and, most importantly, signed the RFID PIA Framework – GS1, the German Association for IT, Telecommunications and New Media (Bitkom), the Association of Automatic Identification and Mobility (AIM), the European Retailers Round Table (ERRT) and the European-American Business Council (EABC) – will undoubtedly come back with some answers in due course.

Acknowledgements I particularly want to thank Wolf-Rüdiger Hansen and Frithjof Walk (Association of Automatic Identification and Mobility, AIM Global), Heinz-Paul Bonn (Federal Association for Information Technology, Telecommunications and New Media, BITKOM), Harald Kelter (Federal Office for Information Security, BSI), Christian von Grone (Gerry Weber), Markus Sprafke (Volkswagen), Gerald Santucci (Directorate General Information Society,

European Commission), Johannes Landvogt (Federal Office for Data Protection and Freedom of Information), Barbara Daskala and Udo Helmbrecht (European Network and Information Security Agency, ENISA) as well as Andreas Krisch (European Digital Rights Association, EDRI) and Marie Ötzel (Vienna University of Economics and Business, WU Wien) for their support in the PIA Framework development process. I also want to thank Elizabeth Board (GS1 US) and Marisa Jimenez (formerly GS1) for their co-authorship of the PIA Framework and Paul Skehan (European Round Table, ERRT), Pierre Blanc (Carrefour), Joseph Alhadeff (Oracle, US), Veronique Corduant (Deutsche Post) and Daniel Caprio Jr. (McKenna Long & Aldridge, US) for their active stakeholder involvement.

Chapter 16
Double-Take: Getting to the RFID PIA Framework

Laurent Beslay and Anne-Christine Lacoste

16.1 An Introduction to the RFID Recommendation

The Radio Frequency Identification (RFID) tag is based on a principle defined and developed more than 70 years ago. A chip is attached to an object and offers the possibility through an electromagnetic signal to identify and discriminate electronically this object from others. Even if this basic principle is not new, it has recently triggered growing activities and concerns as some new technological trends are now facilitating its massive adoption.

Indeed, the Information Society is mainly built on a continuous quest for an almost unlimited storage capacity, ubiquitous network access points and nearly unlimited bandwidth. Data can be produced and communicated endlessly from anywhere. These three asymptotic trends underpin the simultaneous management of billions of tags and the processing of an ocean of data produced by the identification of tags attached to objects and the interactions with these objects.

Recent developments – such as new tracing procedures in the food sector, notably after the outbreak of the so-called mad cow disease (Bovine Spongiform Encephalopathy); the policy of large companies, such as Wal-Mart, to tag the billions of products they are processing and selling; or the obligation imposed by the US Department of Defence on its more than 14,000 suppliers to tag all their products – have contributed strongly to the mass production of RFID. But the real ingredient in the success of RFID implementation is the new added value RFID offers compared to more traditional ways of managing products. In a Communication issued in 2007,[1] the European Commission identified the potential RFID technologies could offer to the European Information Society as well as the possible drawbacks and risks they could produce regarding privacy and data protection.

---

[1] European Commission, Radio Frequency Identification (RFID) in Europe: steps towards a policy framework, Communication to the European Parliament, the Council, the European Economic and Social Committee and the Committee of the Regions, COM(2007) 96 final, Brussels, 15 Mar 2007.

L. Beslay (✉)
European Data Protection Supervisor (EDPS), Brussels, Belgium
e-mail: laurent.beslay@jrc.ec.europa.eu

D. Wright, P. De Hert (eds.), *Privacy Impact Assessment*, Law, Governance and Technology Series 6, DOI 10.1007/978-94-007-2543-0_16,
© Springer Science+Business Media B.V. 2012

This Communication was followed by a Recommendation issued in May 2009[2] which aimed at providing an implementation framework for the use of RFID in order to mitigate some legal uncertainties and promote its usage without adopting new legislation.

The development of this Recommendation was fuelled by the contributions of an RFID expert stakeholders group launched and managed by the Commission since 2007 and with a two-year mandate. Composed of more than 25 members, this group represented a great diversity of stakeholders from industry, civil society as well as national and European data protection authorities (DPAs) and standardisation bodies.

Point 4 of the RFID Recommendation introduced the need for a privacy and data protection impact assessment (PIA) framework: it asked the Member States to "ensure that industry, in collaboration with relevant civil society stakeholders, develops a framework for privacy and data protection impact assessments". This point was the result of intense discussions between industry, the European Commission and DPAs. It presents an interesting combination of self-regulatory measures (under certain conditions, a PIA should be conducted by the application owner) and of the involvement of national data protection authorities (the results of the PIA have to be made available to them).

The need to conduct a PIA offers also a flexible approach for the application of the "opt-in" principle. Indeed, as stated in point 11 of the Recommendation, RFID tags shall be deactivated by default at the point of sale. However, the application owner has the opportunity through a PIA to demonstrate that the level of risk of the system is low enough and as a consequence allows him not deactivate the tag if a set of appropriate safeguards can be implemented. This possibility can be seen as a compromise between a strict application of the principle of deactivation except if the individual opts in and the reverse situation where RFID data will be processed unless the individual opts out. The essential element to determine whether RFID tags will be deactivated by default or not is the privacy impact assessment.

In order to consolidate this possibility and introduce the necessary trustworthiness for its success, a PIA framework had to be endorsed by the Article 29 Working Party, as detailed hereafter.

16.2 Conditions of Involvement of the Art. 29 WP

The Article 29 Data Protection Working Party (hereafter Art. 29 WP) is an advisory body to the European Commission, composed of national data protection authorities, the European Data Protection Supervisor (EDPS) and the Commission. The Art. 29 WP has four major competences including contributing to the uniform application of data protection legislation in the Member States, giving opinions on the

---

[2] European Commission, Recommendation on the implementation of privacy and data protection principles in applications supported by radio-frequency identification, C(2009) 3200 final, Brussels, 12 May 2009.

level of protection in the EU and in third countries, advising on Community measures affecting data protection rights and giving opinions on codes of conduct drawn at Community level.[3]

The evaluation of a PIA framework represents a new task for the Art 29 WP: it is in line with its advisory role but goes further: compared to the work of the Art. 29 WP on codes of conduct such as those of the International Air Transport Association (IATA) or the Federation of European Direct and Interactive Marketing (FEDMA), the consultation of the Art. 29 WP is integrated here in a specific regulatory procedure. Besides, it led to "endorsement" by the group which gives a binding force to its decision. Without endorsement by the Art. 29 WP, the RFID framework would have lacked the required legitimacy. As developed below, this would not in itself prevent the deployment of RFID tags but without endorsement by the Working Party, such a deployment would happen outside a clear framework: it would be harder for the private sector to demonstrate that sufficient safeguards are in place, which would be an incentive for the adoption of hard law, via a Regulation or a Directive on RFID proposed by the Commission.

16.3 The Different Actors Involved in the Recommendation

16.3.1 The European Data Protection Supervisor

The EDPS delivered already in 2007 an Opinion[4] which took into account not only the Commission Communication issued the same year but also the activities of the RFID expert stakeholders group as well as the forthcoming Recommendation. In this Opinion, the EDPS stressed the need to introduce stringent safeguards for the use of RFID together with the need for a flexible approach regarding the implementation of the opt-in principle: the obligation to deactivate the tag by default. The EDPS was also informally consulted by the Commission on the Recommendation. As a member of the Art. 29 WP, he took part in the evaluation of the PIA framework submitted by the industry.

16.3.2 The European Network and Information Security Agency

As suggested in the EDPS Opinion,[5] the involvement of ENISA was introduced in recital 17 of the Recommendation where it is proposed that the agency be consulted for the definition of technical implementing measures. ENISA is rightly considered as the centre of excellence or the European "hub" for exchange of information,

---

[3] Article 30 of Directive 95/46/EC.

[4] http://www.edps.europa.eu/EDPSWEB/webdav/site/mySite/shared/Documents/Consultation/Opinions/2007/07-12-20_RFID_EN.pdf

[5] Ibid., point 53 of the Opinion.

best practices and knowledge in the field of information security. The fact that the PIA framework should be built around risk assessment made the involvement of the European agency necessary and logical. The aim was to obtain an expert, independent and reliable input on the way to introduce and develop a risk assessment scheme in the PIA framework.

16.3.3 Industry

An EU Recommendation is traditionally addressed to Member States. Point 4 of the Recommendation on RFID confirms this principle as it starts with "Member States should ensure that the industry...". Accordingly, we assume that industry representation at the occasion of the drafting of the PIA was triggered by Member States, or that industry was at least invited by Member States to contribute. An informal RFID stakeholders group[6] including industry representatives was set up accordingly and hosted by the Commission.

16.3.4 National Authorities and Agencies

In addition to data protection authorities involved de facto in the building process of the PIA framework with the Art. 29 WP, other public organisations contributed directly within the informal group or indirectly with targeted publications. The German Federal Office for Information Security (Bundesamt für Sicherheit in der Informationstechnik: BSI) published a series of guidelines for the implementation of RFID applications in various fields. On several occasions, it provided concrete and operational inputs to the RFID stakeholders group before the recommendation was adopted and latterly to the informal group for the PIA framework.

16.4 From a Negative Opinion of the WP29 to a Positive One

16.4.1 The July 2010 Opinion of the Art. 29 WP and the Issue of Risk Analysis

On 31 March 2010, industry stakeholders submitted to the Art. 29 WP a first Privacy and Data Protection Impact Assessment Framework for RFID applications. The Art. 29 WP adopted a negative opinion on this proposed framework on 13 July 2010. The reasons for the negative opinion were not related to the concept of a PIA framework: on the contrary, the Art. 29 WP indicated in the beginning of its opinion that it foresaw major advantages in this process, including the development of privacy by

---

[6] http://ec.europa.eu/information_society/policy/rfid/documents/participateinworkgroup.pdf

design (by "helping data controllers to address privacy and data protection before a product or service is deployed"), the reduction of legal uncertainty and loss of public trust and finally the fact that PIAs may give DPAs as well as controllers more insight into the privacy and data protection aspects of RFID applications.

The proposed framework, however, did not meet the Art. 29 WP's expectations. The three major reasons which led to a negative opinion were as follows: the absence of an effective procedure for risk assessment; the absence of taking into consideration the risks linked with tags carried by individuals; and the lack of clear analysis of the need for tag deactivation in the retail sector.

16.4.1.1 Risk Assessment

The first critical comment of the Art. 29 WP on risk assessment was decisive. The Art. 29 WP considered that, in order to be assured that measures taken by an operator are adequate or proportionate to the risk, it is essential that a procedure be developed that allows an identification and assessment of the risks linked with the processing of RFID data. Therefore, the Art. 29 WP said that a methodology had to be developed in this regard. In its reaction to the proposed framework, ENISA made a similarly critical comment.[7]

As mentioned in recital 17 of the Commission's Recommendation, the development of the PIA Framework "should build on existing practices and experiences gained in Member States, in third countries and in the work conducted by the European Network and Information Security Agency (ENISA)", in view of the expertise and experience of the agency in risk assessment methodologies. ENISA was not consulted by the industry in the process of elaborating the framework proposed in March 2010, but the agency issued an opinion at the request of the Commission, to which the Art. 29 WP referred in its opinion.

Before coming back to the other critical comments of the Art. 29 WP, we briefly reflect upon ENISA's input on this risk assessment issue. ENISA said that PIAs should present the right information, with two different actors in mind: the competent authority, who will receive the PIA reports, and the RFID application owners, who would be performing the PIA process. ENISA called for a structured approach based on existing methodologies, especially on risk management. ISO/IEC 27005 as well as existing practice developed in several countries were given as references of established methodology. In its opinion, ENISA recommended that the following steps be included as part of the PIA process:

- *Identifying the system of reference*: the scope and objectives of the RFID applications, the stakeholders involved and their roles, all of the assets involved in the application;

---

[7] European Network and Information Security Agency, ENISA Opinion on the Industry Proposal for a Privacy and Data Protection Impact Assessment Framework for RFID Applications [of March 31, 2010], Heraklion, July 2010. http://www.enisa.europa.eu/media/news-items/enisa-opinion-on-pia

- *Setting the criteria against which the impact on privacy is determined*, especially if different from the ones identified in the PIA document;
- *Identifying and evaluating the risks*: this would mean identifying the vulnerabilities and threats, and estimating a risk value;
- *Identifying the levels of risk acceptance*: levels that determine whether the risks can be accepted or not; this means that some risks might be considered as acceptable;
- *Identifying appropriate mitigation strategies*: identification of controls and countermeasures to address the risks that are not accepted (through mitigation or transfer).

The aspects which were considered as unsatisfactory in the proposed framework related in particular to the procedure for identifying risks. In fact, the proposal went directly to the step of protection and controls without developing an assessment of risks which would lead to a determination of which protections and controls exactly would be needed.

ENISA's opinion clearly referred to the need to identify vulnerabilities and threats. Risks could arise from vulnerabilities in the RFID scheme (a lack of security safeguards, for instance, or the fact that sensitive information is processed), but also from external threats (such as theft or misuse of data). In the view of the authors, the risk assessment should also take into account the dimension of the impact on the individual: this impact may vary depending on different criteria, such as the nature of the data concerned: tags on a pharmaceutical product, for instance, could affect the individual in a much greater way if reused than a tag on a pack of mineral water. Depending on the nature of the risk, the measures to be adopted in order to mitigate them may differ.

16.4.1.2 Tags Carried by Individuals

The second comment of the Art. 29 WP related to the specific issue of tags carried by individuals. Although the framework proposed by industry identified the need for a privacy impact assessment in such a case, it did not take the consequences into account in terms of risk assessment. The requirement to evaluate the risks of unauthorised monitoring based on the unique identifier carried by the individual should have been taken into account in the proposed framework, as well as the steps to be taken to address those risks.

The issue of the use of unique identifiers was of particular importance for the Art. 29 WP. Such use is related to the notion of personal data and the scope of application of the EU's Data Protection Directive (95/46/EC), issues on which the Art. 29 WP has dedicated substantial work. Before the Commission issued its Communication and Recommendation on RFID, the Art. 29 WP had already put out a working document in January 2005[8] identifying the data protection aspects related to the use of RFID, and concentrating on the issue of personal data. This document was

---

[8] Article 29 Data Protection Working Party, Working document on data protection issues related to RFID technologies, WP105, 19 Jan 2005. http://ec.europa.eu/justice/policies/privacy/workinggroup/wpdocs/2005_en.htm

followed by a public consultation[9] which showed clearly the diverging views of the retailers on the one hand and consumers, universities and the security industry on the other hand on the scope of application of data protection principles. The Working Party was, and is, of the view that tags carried by individuals trigger the application of the Directive and raise privacy risks even if, for instance, no name of an individual is attached to the tag: "The use of the RFID technology to track individual movements which, given the massive data aggregation and computer memory and processing capacity, are if not identified, identifiable, also triggers the application of the data protection Directive." In its working paper, the Art. 29 WP gave examples of the targeting of individuals based on the tags on the objects they carry, such as books, medicines or banknotes. "Belongings of a person are very personal and hold information whose knowledge by third parties would invade the privacy of the person who owns the object." For these reasons, the Art. 29 WP insisted in its Opinion on the need for a thorough analysis of the risks linked with tags carried by individuals, to be developed in the Framework proposal.

16.4.1.3 Tags in the Retail Sector

The third issue highlighted by the Art. 29 WP related to the use of tags in the retail sector. The Commission's Recommendation clearly indicated in point 11 that the default obligation is the deactivation of the tag at the point of sale. An exception to this rule allows keeping the tag active if it does not "represent a likely threat to privacy or the protection of personal data". The Art. 29 WP criticised the lack of granularity of the proposed Framework in this respect: instead of limiting the analysis to a binary choice of applications which are – or are not – ready for deployment, it considered that an analysis of the potential threat should be performed to identify, on a case-by-case basis, whether the RFID tag can remain active beyond the point of sale. The Art. 29 WP indicated that this may be justified or required by the application.

The Art. 29 WP criticised the binary assessment made in the proposed Framework as it could prevent any tag from remaining active beyond the point of sale. We support the call for more granularity, but we would have favoured also a stronger requirement for compliance with the necessity test: even if the tag is not likely to present a threat to privacy or data protection, it should not remain active beyond the point of sale if there is no need for it: in addition to the requirements of the Commission's Recommendation, the necessity test is an essential requirement of the Data Protection Directive.

If the proposed Framework maintained a "black or white" approach to risks at the point of sale, the absence of granularity in the assessment could have as a consequence that all tags are deactivated, but it could also have the undesirable reverse

---

[9] Article 29 Data Protection Working Party, Results of the Public Consultation on Article 29 Working Party Document 105 on Data Protection Issues Related to RFID Technologies, WP 111, Adopted on 28 September 2005. http://ec.europa.eu/justice/policies/privacy/workinggroup/wpdocs/2005_en.htm

consequence: in the view of the authors, there is a risk that no tag is deactivated because goods in the retail sector are considered as harmless, or the possibility to read information beyond the point of sale is considered, on a general basis, as too rare to present an effective threat. As mentioned already in point (a) above, it is important that the risk assessment takes into account a wide range of possible factors, including not only the number of existing readers outside the point of sale (which is a dynamic criterion) but also the nature of the goods (medical or luxury products, for instance) and the possible profiling or targeting of the individual on that basis.

These were the major reasons which led to the Working Party's not endorsing the first PIA framework proposed by industry.

If, eventually, there had been no endorsement at all, there would be no general framework to guide the development and use of RFID applications and to provide for practical orientations to stakeholders. Two nuances should, however, be noted here: first, the fact that the Art. 29 WP did not endorse the first proposed framework did not mean that it was distancing itself from the issue of RFID applications: nothing prevents the Art. 29 WP from issuing opinions on its own initiative, which would complement the working document adopted in 2005, and from giving its views on the way RFID applications should be developed and implemented. Second, the data protection framework remains applicable, with or without an endorsed framework for impact assessments. This means notably that the principles of necessity and proportionality must be complied with, as well as the obligation to inform individuals about the processing of their data.

The added value of a framework is more obvious in cases where there are diverging views among stakeholders on the application of the principles, as is the case for tags carried by individuals. The framework could definitely bring more legal certainty here, to the benefit of the private sector as well as individuals. Had this happened to become a practical issue in the absence of a framework, the Commission would still have had the possibility to legislate and impose clear and binding rules.

16.5 Endorsement of the Art. 29 WP: Consequences and Further Steps

As mentioned above, the fact that the Art. 29 WP subsequently adopted a positive opinion following industry's revision of their framework was not a *condicio sine qua non* to the deployment of RFID applications in compliance with the existing framework, but it is still an essential element supporting the legitimacy of the deployment of the applications.

This observation was obviously an incentive for industry to amend the proposed framework and come back with a new enhanced proposal.

The best case scenario, which actually happened, was a proposal for an updated framework with a wider group of stakeholders, bringing added value to the original proposal. Not only does the revised framework guarantee a higher level of data protection, but its implementation should be facilitated by a greater legitimacy.

The proposal endorsed by the Working Party on 11 February 2011 meets the recommendations issued by the Working Party when it gave its opinion on the previous version. The new framework notably includes a review of the internal procedures that are relevant to the execution of a PIA such as:

- scheduling and reviewing the PIA,
- compiling relevant documentation,
- determining relevant persons in the organisation to support the PIA process, identifying conditions which might trigger a revision of the PIA in the future,
- and including a stakeholder consultation, an element missing in the previous text, and stressed by the Working Party.

The revised Framework proposed a PIA in two phases:

I. A pre-assessment phase that classifies an RFID application according to a scale including several levels, based on a decision tree. The result of this evaluation allows one to determine if a PIA is required or not, and to choose between a "Full Scale PIA" and a "Small Scale PIA".
II. The risk assessment phase, which includes four steps:

   (1) Characterisation of the application (data types, data flows, RFID technology, data storage and transfers, etc.);
   (2) Identification of the risks to personal data;
   (3) Identification and recommendation of controls, in response to previously identified risks;
   (4) Documentation of the results of the PIA.

Risk management is now at the core of the assessment. Each step in this risk assessment phase is supported by documented elements, including:

- a template to describe key characteristics of the RFID application (the assets);
- a list of nine privacy targets for the RFID application, derived from Directive 95/46/EC;
- a list of typical privacy and data protection risks, with descriptions and examples;
- a list of examples of controls and mitigating measures that can be used in response to previously identified risks.

The Working Party endorsed the new Framework while adding a few comments. The Working Party approved in particular the fact that the new text requires RFID operators to evaluate the risks that may arise when tags are used outside the operational perimeter of an RFID application and/or are carried by persons, especially if a third party uses tags for unintended purposes. The opinion of 11 February 2011 recalls that this concern is particularly valid "in the retail sector, where it is feared that tagged items bought by individuals could be misused by retailers or third parties for tracking or profiling purposes".

With relation to this observation, the Working Party recalled the broad scope of the notion of personal data: "If a tag containing a unique ID is destined to be carried by a person, then the tag ID should be considered as personal data". This has important implications to determine a more or less extensive impact assessment.

16.6 PIA in Perspective

16.6.1 PIA for RFID Applications and Impact Assessments in a Regulatory Process

The privacy and data protection impact assessment process, as initiated by the Commission in its Recommendation, presents some specificities if compared with traditional impact assessments performed notably by European institutions in a regulatory framework.

In the RFID context, the objective is to develop a methodology to assess privacy and data protection risks linked with the deployment of RFID applications. The impact assessments have a practical rather than theoretical dimension, linked with the development of technologies and in a co-regulation perspective. On the other hand, impact assessments conducted by EU institutions are a mandatory step in the legislative process. The same tool is therefore used in two different contexts: in the first case, it represents a possible alternative to the adoption of a specific and binding regulation on RFID, while in the second case, it is part of the regulatory process, as a pre-condition to assess whether legislation is needed.

16.6.2 The Issue of Representativeness of the Industry Group

Right after the publication of the Recommendation, an informal RFID stakeholders group was launched. Its activities were facilitated by the Commission which hosted its different meetings. In other words, the Commission was encouraging the industry to accomplish its task but without any official recognition or blessing of the quality or adequacy of its representatives. We can wonder if all the relevant RFID stakeholders were appropriately represented in this group.

A difficult issue for the Art. 29 WP was indeed to receive guarantees on the real representativeness of the industry stakeholders who submitted the draft Framework. According to the Recommendation, Member States were supposed to ensure that industry proposed a framework. Implicitly, those Member States should have made sure that this group of industries was representative enough; however, throughout the process that led to approval of the Framework, this guarantee of representativeness was never demonstrated clearly to the Art. 29 WP. Even if the exchanges between the Art. 29 WP and the Commission took place in a completely trustworthy and constructive atmosphere which can be considered to a certain extent as an element of guarantee, one can challenge this dimension of the procedure.

Although it actually did not happen, the Art. 29 WP could have received an alternative draft produced and promoted by another group of industry players. Considering the global dimension of RFID as well as the origin of the main actors in this field (some of whom came from outside the EU), it is also true that Member States might not have been in a position to provide these expected guarantees. On the other hand, a resolution of the Council, for example, could have more officially introduced and mandated a specific group of industry players for creating and submitting this draft framework.

In the end, the risk is that independent of a proper endorsement of the PIA framework by the Art. 29 WP, a non-negligible part of the industry actors would not recognise the procedure and would not apply it in their business.

16.6.3 PIA Procedure: A Voluntary Action

The need to conduct a PIA is promoted by the Recommendation but it is clearly not mandatory. Such policy measures are usually called "soft law" and constitute incentives for actors related to the field at stake, in this case RFID applications.

Although a PIA is not an obligation in itself, it is still mandatory for the application owner to be in compliance with the law and especially with the data protection regulatory framework. The PIA as it is defined in the Recommendation and detailed in the endorsed Framework should be considered as a tool, a determinant one for this compliance.

From the point of view of the RFID application owner, a PIA will drive and facilitate its compliance with the national regulatory framework and will mitigate greatly the legal uncertainties around the deployment of such applications.

In the case of data protection authorities, the use of this tool by industry will contribute to a higher level of trust and ultimately will also facilitate the legal procedure by demonstrating the level of risk and the corresponding mitigation measures.

A similar mechanism of levelling the playing field of trust has been developed by the Commission in the environmental field for assessing the level of authorised pollution emissions.[10] Sector-specific best available techniques (BATs) are commonly defined between the European legislator and the main industry stakeholders. The implementation of these BATs is not an obligation for the industry. However, their implementation, which is technologically neutral, should guarantee a level of pollution emission which will be below the ones authorised. This procedure could be adapted to the RFID field. The European Commission together with representatives from the industry could produce and adopt reference documents on best available techniques. These reference documents would be then used by the industry as guidance to implement RFID applications in compliance with the legal

---

[10] European Parliament and the Council, Directive 2010/75/EU on industrial emissions, 24 November 2010. http://eur-lex.europa.eu/LexUriServ/LexUriServ.do?uri=OJ:L:2010:334:0017: 0119:EN:PDF

framework. They could be used as well by data protection authorities in order to facilitate their evaluation of those implementations if needed.

16.6.4 The PIA Framework for RFID: An Example for Other Technological Fields?

There is no reason to believe that the procedure applied to RFID in order to produce a PIA framework could not be applied as well to other fields which might present similarities. Intelligent transport system applications, biometric systems and smart metering seem to constitute good candidates for such a framework. The objectives are still the same: limiting the legal uncertainties related to their respective implementation and contributing to a more streamlined way or soft way from a regulatory point of view to their compliance with an existing legal framework.

Of course, for each of them, the approach will be different, as the risk assessment will not produce the same results. In the case of a biometric system, for example, the quality of the enrolment procedure, the error rates of the system as well as the fallback procedures implemented will constitute determinant parameters in the selection of the safeguards to be applied.

The possibility of setting up a dedicated mechanism involving the Art. 29 WP for the analysis and possible endorsement of such PIAs would then trigger a broader discussion on the possible need for a revision of the role of the Working Group. In such a configuration, how would the independence of the group be preserved? Today's resources of the Art. 29 WP will obviously need to be adapted to ensure an effective reply to more frequent and systematic requests. More systematic involvement of the industry should also be promoted as is already the case when BATs related to pollution emission are defined.

16.7 Conclusion: Efficiency of PIA and Residual Risk: A Difficult Compromise

This contribution gives an "instant picture" of the developments taking place today with regard to privacy impact assessment of RFID applications. Further developments linked with the implementation of this Framework will allow an assessment of how far the debate can be enlarged, on this basis, to other frameworks.

In particular, the efficiency of this PIA scheme will need to be measured, and the way it will be measured has yet to be defined.

One of the end products of a risk assessment is the identification of residual risk for the application. This residual risk needs to be considered as acceptable and to be communicated in a transparent and appropriate way to the DPAs as well as to the end users. The acceptance mechanism (and its results) will have to be recognised by the data protection authorities as a trustworthy way of offering better legal certainty to the RFID application owner. In other words, if a DPA has approved or at least did not challenge the result of a PIA, the RFID application owner should not be blamed if an incident from this residual risk occurs. This incident, however, should be analysed in order to review the PIA and gain experience for better mitigating those risks.

The precise role of data protection authorities and data protection officers in this assessment also needs clarification.

In particular, the question of harmonisation of criteria for the assessment of PIA reports will undoubtedly arise. It is not yet completely clear if an assessment (positive or negative) made in one Member State will be recognised de facto by the DPA of another Member State or if the RFID system owner will have to go through the whole process again for each Member State where a decision is required. Mutual recognition of DPAs' decisions on PIA reports is among the future points which will also have to be elaborated and clarified.

Further reflection is needed on the desirability or utility of some sort of certification, and on possible ways to organise feedback from data protection authorities on the usefulness of PIAs in practice. Among other tools, a centralisation of complaints and of investigations and inspections could be developed. There is also a need to develop a clear chain of responsibilities, from developers to users of RFID applications.

There are, however, limits to such an evaluation exercise. The future will show, on the basis of available reporting, whether there is still a need for a stricter regulation, or if the system put in place via this impact assessment procedure keeps its promises.

Part V
Specific Issues

Chapter 17
Surveillance: Extending the Limits of Privacy Impact Assessment

Charles Raab and David Wright

17.1 Introduction

Privacy impact assessment (PIA) can be used to investigate the impact upon privacy that surveillance, using new information and communications technologies (ICTs) or information systems, might have before these applications are fully developed and implemented. PIA requires that an organisation subject its plans to more or less rigorous screening through the lens of privacy or data protection, to identify weaknesses in the innovation's compliance with relevant laws or principles, and to indicate how these might be eliminated. Myriad stakeholders potentially affected by the innovation may also be involved in this investigation. In an extreme situation, a project could be abandoned if its PIA indicated irremediable shortcomings.

As other chapters in this book show, a variety of PIA models exist across the world, in terms of their scope, procedures, the involvement of bodies such as regulatory agencies or civil society organisations, and transparency requirements. Some focus on information privacy (data protection) only, while others say that PIAs should address all types of privacy. PIA differs from privacy audits and other inspections and analyses of organisational data processing in that the latter are usually performed on systems and technologies already in use. As a fairly recent addition to the array of tools and methodologies that can be used to avoid or mitigate the negative impacts upon privacy of a new technology or service, PIA is required in some countries and strongly urged upon data collectors in others. Handbooks, guidance materials and examples of PIA are readily available.[1] PIA plays a part in an organisation's procedures for compliance with privacy and data protection laws and good

---

[1] For a compendium and analysis of PIA methodologies from seven countries and of 10 PIA reports, see Wright, David, et al. (eds.), *A Privacy Impact Assessment Framework (PIAF) Deliverable D1*, a report of the PIAF consortium prepared for the European Commission, September 2011. www.piafproject.eu

C. Raab (✉)
University of Edinburgh, Edinburgh EH8 9LD, Scotland
e-mail: c.d.raab@ed.ac.uk

D. Wright, P. De Hert (eds.), *Privacy Impact Assessment*, Law, Governance and Technology Series 6, DOI 10.1007/978-94-007-2543-0_17,
© Springer Science+Business Media B.V. 2012

practice. These important contributions to privacy protection are likely to spread further in future, and PIA – especially if legally mandated to be carried out – may become one of the key instruments available to privacy policy-makers, regulators and practitioners themselves.

On the other hand, PIA is subject to a number of objections and limitations. This chapter briefly reviews them and offers some rebuttals before looking more closely at surveillance practices and their users: the what and who of surveillance. It then indicates some analytical dimensions of surveillance – their visibility, legality, power implications and targets – that raise ethical concerns. Following that, it reflects upon one of the main limitations of PIA: its nearly exclusive focus on privacy, to the neglect of a range of other individual and societal values, rights or freedoms that may be impacted by surveillance. In the light of this, the chapter finally considers how PIA could be extended to assess the impact of surveillance on this broader range.

17.2 Objections to Subjecting Surveillance to PIA

Sceptics and critics have often resisted the application of PIA techniques to surveillance projects on a variety of grounds. This section considers and rebuts some of these arguments.

17.2.1 A Brake on Technical Progress

Information and communication technologies – although themselves shaped by social processes – are among the most powerful drivers of today's economy and society. An argument can be mounted that the pace of technological development ought not to be slackened by the "interference" that PIA might represent, and that any adverse effects can be controlled by appropriate responses and resilience rather than through *ex ante*, or precautionary, application of PIA. This argument seems to prevail in the training and education of technologists as well as in the philosophy of those who use their products, so that special effort has been required in very recent years to insinuate the merits of PIA and "privacy by design" into the thinking and practice of the laboratory and boardroom.

Against this is the argument that to separate technical progress from other social phenomena is to create, without sufficient warrant or reason, a zone of exception in which other values cannot enter, thus altering the nature of society and the possibility of individual privacy through a form of political and economic fiat. Simply because there are precedents for this is no reason for sealing the issues off from deliberation and action that might reconfigure the relationship between technology and society. PIA takes its place alongside other techniques associated with technology assessment in seeking a different point of departure.

17.2.2 Some Surveillance Involves Central Functions of the State

It is often argued that the maintenance of public order, the enforcement of law and national security should exempt information activities from restrictions applied to systems that do not perform these functions, or that are in the private sector. It is held that the intensive and extensive use of personal data, video surveillance, interception of communications and biometric devices must be regarded as legitimate means to the paramount end of keeping us safe. Data protection law already provides exceptions from certain provisions and requirements where the prevention and detection of crime, and the safety of the state are at stake in the activities of certain organisations.[2] Therefore, it would inhibit the efficiency and effectiveness of the performance of these functions if the technologies and information systems involved in their pursuit had to be subject to privacy impact and other forms of assessment, and if their use would be limited or proscribed unless they met the recommendations exhorted in these assessments. Moreover, exposing details of surveillance systems to the public for scrutiny would damage the operations in which their use is intended. Overall, much of the argument is, because these functions of the state are essential to the national or public interest, they therefore trump the individual interest in, or right to, privacy.

This is a powerful argument, especially in the climate of terrorist threat and public fears of disorder and crime. It would be a brave or foolish politician who would set her face against this mood and the realities of national security and law enforcement that accompany it. Revelation of technical details and operations in a PIA might indeed have adverse consequences for legitimate surveillance; this point is discussed further below, as a variant of it also applies in the commercial environment. On the other hand, the rule of law, the living legacy of human rights, and the workings of the system of justice are equally central to the national interest. Even the US Department of Homeland Security has recognised this, saying: "A PIA should be conducted for *all* systems handling personally identifiable information *including classified or law enforcement sensitive programs.*"[3] [Italics added.] Where surveillance breaches the boundaries of necessity and proportionality, it must be subjected to checks whether anticipatory or remedial. Moreover, systems should be put in place – including PIA – to help determine whether a particular technological or information-management system is, in fact, necessary and not excessive if the objective is to be reached. While the hoary mottoes, "you can never be too safe" or "better safe than sorry", are poor guides to policy and practice where privacy and

---

[2] Until the Lisbon Treaty came into force in December 2009, the EU Data Protection Directive (95/46/EC) exempted second and third pillar issues from data protection scrutiny. The Lisbon Treaty now makes such scrutiny possible. With the planned revision of the Data Protection Directive, data controllers processing sensitive data, including surveillance systems, may be obliged to subject them to PIA.

[3] Department of Homeland Security, *Privacy Impact Assessments: The Privacy Office Official Guidance*, Washington, DC, June 2010, p. 7. http://www.dhs.gov/files/publications/gc_1209396374339.shtm

other crucial values are threatened by surveillance, PIA – a technique rooted in risk analysis and discourse – could open up the question "how much safety do we need?" to serious scrutiny in specific instances.

If the security concerns are truly serious, these could be addressed by conducting a PIA with a non-disclosure agreement so that a representative group of stakeholders could be engaged in the process of evaluating the impacts on privacy of new security proposals. Furthermore, budget submissions for new security initiatives could be accompanied by a PIA as a condition of funding. In Canada, government agencies must include a PIA with their budgetary submissions and deputy ministers must approve the final PIA reports, which must be sent to the Office of the Privacy Commissioner of Canada.[4] The funding agency could be given the power to turn down a budgetary submission if it judged the PIA to be inadequate; the Treasury Board in Canada has such a power. Post-PIA audits carried out by an independent third party could ensure the PIA recommendations were actually implemented. Such measures could be put in place to ensure that new security initiatives were subjected to a PIA without actually compromising security.

17.2.3 Some Surveillance Involves Commercial Sensitivity

Companies could argue that, for competitive reasons or in the interests of protecting intellectual property, at least some of their activities should not be subject to a PIA. A PIA may violate security, the commercially sensitive nature of certain technical information, or the business case for an innovation, and exposure to external participants in the PIA process should therefore be avoided. Against this is the argument that ways can still be found to protect what needs to be protected for commercial or security reasons while still allowing the aims of a PIA to be achieved satisfactorily, including the transparency that publication of the PIA would ensure. In the United Kingdom, the Information Commissioner's Office (ICO) advises that sensitive details can be placed in a less widely distributed appendix and protected by confidentiality constraints, but counsels that such suppression should be limited to what can be justified, and that the concealment of poor thinking at the design stage could damage stakeholders' trust.[5] Maintaining or increasing public confidence in the legitimacy of properly regulated surveillance is, after all, an important objective of PIA. In any event, PIA is being taken up by the private sector: see the chapters in this book on Nokia, Siemens and Vodafone.

---

[4] "Federal organizations seeking preliminary project approval (PPA) from the Treasury Board pursuant to the Project Management Policy must include the results of the Privacy Impact Assessment (PIA) in the body of the submission or project brief, where applicable." Treasury Board of Canada Secretariat, "A Guide to Preparing Treasury Board Submissions", Annex D, section 4. http://www.tbs-sct.gc.ca/pubs_pol/opepubs/TBM_162/gptbs-gppct09-eng.asp#d4. See also the TBS Privacy Impact Assessment Policy, section on accountability, 2 May 2002. http://www.tbs-sct.gc.ca/pol/doc-eng.aspx?id=12450&section=text

[5] Information Commissioners Office (ICO), *Privacy Impact Assessment Handbook*, Version 2.0, Wilmslow, Cheshire, June 2009, pp. 33, 34, 40.

The International Organization for Standardization (ISO) has developed a PIA for financial institutions (see Chapter 14), and an industry-developed PIA framework for radio frequency identification (RFID) has been endorsed by the Article 29 Data Protection Working Party (see Chapters 15 and 16). In Australia, the revised PIA guide has been developed to be applicable to the private sector[6] and the European Commission may oblige data controllers (including those in the private sector) who process sensitive data to carry out a PIA.[7]

17.2.4 Some Surveillance Involves More Than One Country

A further argument resisting PIA in circumstances of sensitive and secure operations is that the flow of personal data involved in the surveillance and information systems often takes place across national boundaries and is likely to involve objectives related to law enforcement and counter-terrorism, this time in an international or global setting. It could be claimed that the nature of these operations should rule out exposing their privacy and other impacts: the "trump card" justification, but with potentially more at stake than in many merely domestic environments. Moreover, conducting a PIA would seem to be somewhat difficult in procedural and organisational terms, as well as with regard to the applicable law with which the innovation should comply. This argument might seem difficult to rebut. However, although conducting a transnational PIA might be problematic, the countries involved in an international surveillance operation could nevertheless conduct their own PIA and, following its recommendations, negotiate with the other countries as necessary to ensure the surveillance operation was proportionate and necessary or to determine whether certain measures should be undertaken to ensure that the operation was subject to the oversight of, for example, a parliamentary committee and/or a court of law. New Zealand's *Privacy Impact Assessment Handbook* foresaw this situation some years ago:

> Certain projects will have significant privacy implications in more than one jurisdiction. Indeed, some initiatives will have truly global implications. In such cases, comment might be invited from the privacy commissioners of several countries before finalising the privacy impact report. A significant objective of a PIA in such projects may be to ensure that the project meets or exceeds the data protection and information privacy requirements in all the relevant countries and achieves a level of trust amongst consumers and regulators.[8]

---

[6] Office of the Privacy Commissioner, *Privacy Impact Assessment Guide*, 2006, revised May 2010. http://www.privacy.gov.au.

[7] European Commission, A comprehensive approach on personal data protection in the European Union, Communication from the Commission to the European Parliament, the Council, the Economic and Social Committee and the Committee of the Regions, COM(2010) 609 final, Brussels, 4.11.2010. http://ec.europa.eu/justice/news/intro/news_intro_en.htm#20101104

[8] Stewart, Blair, *Privacy Impact Assessment Handbook*, Office of the Privacy Commissioner, Auckland, June 2007, p. 14. http://privacy.org.nz/privacy-impact-assessment-handbook/ A first edition of the Handbook appeared in 2002.

The message here is that transnational projects should not escape the scrutiny of a PIA, simply because they are transnational. Even if government agencies have not yet put this in hand, transnational PIA has attracted some attention in the corporate world. The international consultancy Deloitte & Touche published a guide to cross-border privacy impact assessment as long ago as 2001,[9] although aimed at companies with cross-border operations rather than government agencies. More recently, a PIA has been performed for a transnational medical information project in Europe.[10] Robin Bayley and Colin Bennett (Chapter 7) refer to a PIA of a biometrics field trial involving the Canadian Citizenship and Immigration department, the US Immigration and Naturalization Service and the US Department of State.

17.2.5 Ineffectiveness Would Be Revealed by a PIA

Officials may not want to subject surveillance projects to a PIA lest system effectiveness be questioned in damaging ways, especially where the system is likely to be very costly. Politicians and the public, not to mention the suppliers of equipment and owners of premises, may have set great store by the supposed ability of a surveillance technology to achieve popular objectives. In the UK, closed-circuit television (CCTV) has been the single most heavily funded crime prevention measure operating outside the criminal justice system. The Home Office funded two major independent studies that cast serious doubt upon the effectiveness of CCTV, which had not produced the expected benefits, although improved performance might result from proper management and design.[11] The police themselves have questioned the utility of CCTV, and the Home Office and the Association of Chief Police Officers outlined a new CCTV strategy in 2007.[12] Although a PIA is not a retrospective audit, and conducting one for a changed system would aim primarily at assessing the impact on privacy and other values rather than functional effectiveness, it might also help to avoid such mistakes in future through the information that would be gathered and analysed about how the system works. With hindsight, if a PIA had been conducted from the inception of the British "love affair" with CCTV

---

[9] Karol, Thomas J., *A Guide To Cross-Border Privacy Impact Assessments*, Deloitte & Touche, 2001. http://www.isaca.org/Knowledge-Center/Research/ResearchDeliverables/Pages/A-Guide-To-Cross-Border-Privacy-Impact-Assessments.aspx

[10] Di Iorio, C.T., F. Carinci, J. Azzopardi et al., "Privacy Impact Assessment in the Design of Transnational Public Health Information Systems: The BIRO Project", *Journal of Medical Ethics*, Vol. 35, 2009, pp. 753–761. http://jme.bmj.com/content/35/12/753.abstract

[11] Welsh, Brandon C., and David P. Farrington, *Crime Prevention Effects of Closed Circuit Television: A Systematic Review*, Home Office Research, Development and Statistics Directorate, August 2002; Gill, Martin, and Angela Spriggs, *Assessing the Impact of CCTV*, Home Office Research, Development and Statistics Directorate, Feb 2005, pp. 120–121.

[12] Gerrard, Graeme, Garry Parkins, Ian Cunningham et al., National CCTV Strategy, Home Office and Association of Chief Police Officers, London, October 2007. http://www.bhphousing.co.uk/streetcare2.nsf/Files/LBBA-24/$FILE/Home%20Office%20National%20CCTV%20Strategy.pdf

that is carried on by local authorities, central government, the media and the general public, it might have had beneficial effects on performance as well as minimising the impact on privacy and legitimate social behaviour in public places.

17.2.6 PIA Is Too Narrowly Focused

This is a further objection, which is taken up at a later point. It is not that PIA is irrelevant, but that its scope in regard to surveillance currently is too limited because it mainly concerns impacts on individual privacy, not other rights and values. Therefore, it is unlikely to address the significance of surveillance for society as well as for individuals' lives and behaviour more broadly conceived, or to regulate its impact. This objection is rarely heard, but is important if the impact of surveillance is to be more fully assessed. This chapter builds on this objection in arguing that the range of impacts or risks to be considered should be extended. Before that point in the argument is reached, it is important to review various types of surveillance as well as the kinds of actors who engage in surveillance practices and the purposes served.

17.3 Types of Surveillance

With the development of new technologies, surveillance has become a much more complex set of processes than the literal meaning – to watch over – suggests. The many types of surveillance include watching, listening, locating, detecting and personal data monitoring[13] (or *dataveillance*, in Clarke's coinage[14]). In this section, we briefly describe the variety of surveillance types, some of which overlap, and then identify the main purposes and functions of these applications as well as the variety of surveillance users or "surveillants". The distinction between well-tried operational systems and those still undergoing development is important in describing examples of surveillance. So, too, is the distinction between ICTs that perform their intended and more or less discrete functions and those that have "crept" to new functions where regulatory understandings and rules, and social and individual impacts, may be less clear.

---

[13] For a more detailed discussion, see Ball, Kirstie, David Lyon, David Murakami Wood, Clive Norris and Charles Raab, *A Report on the Surveillance Society*, for the Information Commissioner by the Surveillance Studies Network (SSN), September 2006. http://ico.crl.uk.com/files/Surveillance%20society%20full%20report%20final.pdf. Raab, Charles, Kirstie Ball, Steve Graham, David Lyon, David Murakami Wood and Clive Norris, *The Surveillance Society – An Update Report on Developments Since the 2006 Report on the Surveillance Society*, Information Commissioner's Office, Wilmslow, Cheshire, November 2010. http://www.ico.gov.uk/news/current_topics.aspx. Monahan, Torin (ed.), *Surveillance and Security: Technological Politics and Power in Everyday Life*, Routledge, New York, 2006.

[14] Clarke, Roger, "Information Technology and Dataveillance", *Communications of the ACM*, Vol. 31, No. 5, May 1988, pp. 498–512.

17.3.1 Watching

The visual connotation of surveillance is probably the most prominent one recognised by the public today. Visual surveillance is practised in public spaces and in private premises such as shops and office buildings, but this is not the place to ponder the legal or cultural distinction between "public" and "private". In many countries – perhaps especially the United Kingdom – the CCTV camera "stands for" surveillance. CCTV is used for automatic number-plate recognition (ANPR) – in some cases, also recording passengers' facial images – as well as for recognising suspicious or "abnormal" behaviour. It has been reported that software called Intelligence Pedestrian Surveillance "analyses clusters and movements of pixels in CCTV footage in search of 'behavioural oddities'", and that gait-recognition facilities are being developed. There are developments of intelligent software and a theoretical model to detect deviations from pre-defined "normal" patterns of behaviour,[15] as well as technologies that can "see" through clothing but supposedly not show anatomical details.[16] Small spy drones watch crowds at public events and are likely to play an important role in future, perhaps along with recognition technologies, for identifying individuals.[17]

17.3.2 Listening

Surveillance by eavesdropping or wiretapping (and wireless-tapping) – with or without judicial authorisation – usually targets individuals rather than groups. These practices have become much more difficult now that calls are packet-switched, when millions of people use Voice over Internet Protocol (VoIP), and when more calls than ever are encrypted. Watching and listening may merge in certain ICT applications: some scientists are developing artificial intelligence technology to enable CCTV cameras to "hear" sounds that suggest a crime is taking place and to capture it on film.[18]

17.3.3 Locating

Location tracking is being built into many products and services, including social networking, mobile telephony, control of convicted criminals or wayward school

---

[15] *ScienceDaily*, "Intelligent Surveillance System to Detect Aberrant Behavior by Drivers and Pedestrians", 21 Sept 2009. http://www.sciencedaily.com/releases/2009/09/090918100010.htm

[16] Leake, Jonathan, "Strip Search: Camera That Sees Through Clothes from 80ft Away", *The Sunday Times*, 9 Mar 2008. http://www.timesonline.co.uk/tol/news/uk/science/article3512019.ece

[17] Randerson, James, "Eye in the Sky: Police Use Drone to Spy on V Festival", *The Guardian*, 21Aug 2007. http://www.guardian.co.uk/uk_news/story/0,,2152983,00.html

[18] Williams, Rachel, "CCTV Cameras to be Given 'Ears'", *The Guardian*, 24 June 2008. http://www.guardian.co.uk/uk/2008/jun/24/ukcrime1

pupils, and vehicle safety systems, often anonymously but sometimes with discriminatory effects.[19] The European Data Protection Supervisor has cautioned that the technology for vehicle tracking would have "great impact on rights to privacy and data".[20]

Smart phones allow users to "geotag" images, indicating where and when the photo was taken, and then to upload them to their own websites or to those of social networks such as Facebook. Social networking through mobile phones or other devices can enable movable locations to be mutually known – a form of "participatory surveillance". Apple has built into its terms and conditions, and its privacy policy, a provision allowing the tracking of the user's precise location "anonymously in a form that does not personally identify" the user.[21]

17.3.4 Detecting

Some forms of surveillance involve detection by means of various technologies. These include those of ubiquitous computing or ambient intelligence, e.g., networking sensors and actuators, sometimes referred to as "smart dust", and RFID devices. RFID's many uses include machine-readable passports, identity cards, loyalty cards and travel cards.[22]

Other technologies – still experimental – can detect "abnormal" behaviour of suspicious characters, for example, passing through airports, by scrutinising pulse and breathing rates, and fleeting "micro-expressions".[23] Terrorists are often trained

---

[19] See Phillips, David, and Michael Curry, "Privacy and the Phenetic Urge: Geodemographics and the Changing Spatiality of Local Practice", in David Lyon (ed.), *Surveillance as Social Sorting: Privacy, Risk, and Digital Discrimination,* Routledge, London, 2003.

[20] Lewis, Paul, "Big Brother Is Watching: Surveillance Box to Track Drivers is Backed", *The Guardian,* 31 March 2009. http://www.guardian.co.uk/uk/2009/mar/31/surveillance-transport-communication-box. See also Bennett, Colin, Charles Raab and Priscilla Regan, "People and Place: Patterns of Individual Identification within Intelligent Transportation Systems", in Lyon, 2003, op. cit., fn. 18.

[21] Quoted in Myslewski, Rik, "Apple Tweaks Privacy Policy to Juice Location Tracking", *The Register,* 22 June 2010. http://www.theregister.co.uk/2010/06/22/apple_location_terms_and_conditions/.

[22] For more on RFID applications and their implications, see, for example, OECD, *RFID Guidance and Reports,* OECD Digital Economy Papers, No. 150, OECD publishing, Paris, 2008; van Lieshout, Marc, Luigi Grossi, Graziella Spinelli et al., *RFID Technologies: Emerging Issues, Challenges and Policy Options,* European Commission, Joint Research Centre, Institute for Prospective Technological Studies, Office for Official Publications of the European Communities, Luxembourg, 2007; Ontario Information and Privacy Commissioner, *Privacy Guidelines for RFID Information Systems,* June 2006.

[23] Marks, Paul, "'Pre-crime' Detector Shows Promise", *New Scientist,* 23 September 2008. http://www.newscientist.com/blogs/shortsharpscience/2008/09/precrime-detector-is-showing-p.html. See also *The Economist,* "Surveillance Technology: If Looks Could Kill", 23 Oct 2008. http://www.economist.com/science/displaystory.cfm?story_id=12465303; and Sample, Ian, "Security Firms Working on Devices to Spot Would-Be Terrorists in Crowd", *The Guardian,* 9 Aug 2007. http://www.guardian.co.uk/science/2007/aug/09/terrorism

to conceal emotions; micro-expressions, however, are largely involuntary and are accentuated by deliberate attempts to suppress facial expressions. Research has been conducted into compiling physiological data, correlated with data on the subject's emotional and mental state to identify people intent on committing serious crimes.[24]

17.3.5 Dataveillance

Dataveillance involves activities that use collections of personal data – databases – in extensive and intensive ways for many purposes. It is a defining characteristic of the modern bureaucratic state, and of huge swathes of the modern economy. An array of dataveillance applications, including data monitoring, sharing, aggregation and mining, are used in the provision of public services and in marketing. Online monitoring of what people download or of which websites they visit is also a form of dataveillance. So, too, is the retention and analysis of electronic records of telephone calls and Internet usage for law-enforcement and counter-terrorism purposes, as in the European Union's (EU) Data Retention Directive 2006/24/EC. The Directive's financial and civil liberties implications have generated controversy.[25]

Another controversial instance of dataveillance concerns the monitoring of financial transactions to spot transfers made by criminals and terrorists through the Brussels-based Society for Worldwide Interbank Financial Telecommunication (SWIFT) system, thus allowing the CIA, the FBI and other agencies to examine large numbers of transactions.[26] Dataveillance is involved when governments and firms attempt to counter piracy on the Internet. Dataveillance also uses international travel data that are recorded and stored on government databases for many years in order to tighten border controls and fight terrorist threats. But among the main uses of extensive dataveillance are those in the operations of states and companies carrying out myriad everyday dealings with citizens or customers. The drive for joined-up service provision and for efficient marketing, especially online, has placed a premium on the collection and processing of large quantities of detailed personal data in the "database state".

17.3.6 Assemblages

Stand-alone surveillance technologies or systems can be combined into "assemblages": for example, digital CCTV combined with facial recognition or

---

[24] See, for example, *The Washington Post*, "Gallery: Anti-deception Technologies", 18 July 2010. http://projects.washingtonpost.com/top-secret-america/articles/a-hidden-world-growing-beyond-control/

[25] Article 29 Data Protection Working Party, "European Data Protection Authorities find Current Implementation of Data Retention Directive Unlawful", Press release, Brussels, 14 July 2010. http://ec.europa.eu/justice_home/fsj/privacy/news/index_en.htm

[26] Lichtblau, Eric, and James Risen, "Bank Data Is Sifted by U.S. in Secret to Block Terror", *The New York Times*, 23 June 2006.

video content analysis. Smart CCTV has developed software that analyses the movements of people or vehicles; the CCTV operator checks the image and, if concerned, rings the police. Other possible uses of algorithmic systems concern the detection of suspicious behaviour and packages on public transport.

Assemblages can also involve the pooling or aggregation of data. The accuracy of assemblage technologies can be doubted, for there may be many false positives flagging up innocent people as suspicious. This inaccuracy, as shown in technical trials, is one reason why the UK government has moved away from "voice-risk analysis" of eavesdropped telephone calls to catch "benefit cheats".[27]

17.3.7 Surveillance: Causes of Concern

In sum, the technologies and applications of surveillance are legion, and many more examples could be given of their variety and combination.[28] Suffice it to say that surveillance throws up many causes of concern about its effect on persons, groups and society, and that impact assessment – in the form of PIA – is a valuable instrument for mitigation. At this point, it is relevant to identify three causes of concern about surveillance that are important in analysis and in considering regulatory measures.

The first is its *visibility*: surveillance can be visible or invisible from both a technological and a human point of view. Some surveillance is invisible because the surveillants do not want a target to know of the surveillance; for example, where law enforcement authorities intercept a suspect's communications or where a company bugs politicians.[29] The second is *legality*: it is not always apparent whether a particular surveillance practice is legal or not. The grounds for legality vary across jurisdictions. Some practices may be declared illegal if, for example, their operators have failed to get the necessary warrants, perhaps especially if the surveillance is covert, such as in planting a global positioning system (GPS) device in a suspect's car.[30] Some practices may be thought to be of dubious legality, leading to legal challenges as to their proportionality, necessity or compatibility with the target's "reasonable expectation of privacy".

The third is the *power implications* of surveillance. Surveillance implies a power relationship between the surveillants and the surveilled, where the latter is at a power disadvantage to the former, resulting in other adversities flowing from the

---

[27] Sample, Ian, "Government Abandons Lie Detector Tests for Catching Benefit Cheats", *The Guardian*, 9 November 2010. http://www.guardian.co.uk/science/2010/nov/09/lie-detector-tests-benefit-cheats

[28] See Ball, Lyon et al., op. cit., fn. 12, and Raab, Ball et al., op. cit., fn. 12.

[29] Goslett, Miles, "Your Office May Have Been Bugged by BAE, Investigators Told MP", *Daily Mail*, 3 Oct 2009. http://www.dailymail.co.uk/news/article-1217919/Your-office-bugged-BAE-investigators-told-MP.html.

[30] *The New York Times*, "GPS and Privacy Rights", Editorial, 14 May 2009. http://www.nytimes.com/2009/05/15/opinion/15fri3.html

surveillance itself. However, the relationships between surveillants and surveilled are much more complex and nuanced. Power implications will be particularly relevant to the later discussion about surveillance impact assessment.

17.4 Who Are the Surveillants, and Why Do They Use Surveillance?

With reference to the types of surveillance reviewed above, the ubiquity of technologies and the influence of complex motivations mean that there is a large variety of surveillants, in both the public and private sectors. In the following paragraphs, we identify three main groups of surveillants and their major purposes. Many surveillants use all types of surveillance to target specific individuals and groups, while others use a narrower range depending on the means available, the purpose and the desired target. It is not a question of what "they" are doing to "us": with the willingness of so many people to put so much personal data on social networks, some experts have described the phenomenon as "participatory surveillance":[31] the witting or unwitting involvement of the surveilled in surveillance practices. It should also be borne in mind that – beyond the intended purposes – surveillance involves many unintended side-effects that would need close examination in an application of PIA.

17.4.1 Public Sector

Governments conduct surveillance for many purposes. These range from security, policing, checking benefits entitlement and preventing fraud or (at the local level) detecting misdemeanours, charging vehicles in traffic-congested inner cities, checking up on dubious school catchment-area residents or catching owners whose dogs foul the pavement. Intelligence and law-enforcement agencies typically use surveillance of electronic communications, often with the support of telecom carriers and ISPs. Covert surveillance is frequent: police forces usually argue that this is necessary to investigate paedophiles, Internet fraudsters, identity thieves, terrorists and other "cybercrime" suspects. Surveillance, and particularly information practices associated with dataveillance in the widest sense, is often used by the "welfare" parts of the state, and in health and care services, to underpin a variety of precautionary or responsive practices aimed at people in need or at risk. Thus, surveillance is used in the public sector, and at all levels of the state from local to central – and indeed, beyond state borders – for purposes of sanctioning as well as benefitting

---

[31] "Online social networking seems to introduce a participatory approach to surveillance, which can empower – and not necessarily violate – the user." Albrechtslund, Anders, "Online Social Networking as Participatory Surveillance", *First Monday*, Vol. 13, No. 3, 3 March 2008. http://firstmonday.org/htbin/cgiwrap/bin/ojs/index.php/fm/article/viewArticle/2142/1949

the general public or sections of the population. Different government agencies may also share the data they amass.[32] Some surveillants may operate either in the public or the private sector. In controlling the behaviour of pupils, students or visitors, education institutions use CCTV as a precautionary or investigatory tool for purposes of maintaining order or fighting crime. They also use biometric devices to control entry and exit to premises, and in schools' catering and library facilities. Managers of hospitals, airports, rail stations and networks, and other infrastructure or service facilities use surveillance to prevent and detect not only malfunctions and criminal behaviour, but also disruptive or malicious attacks such as may be involved in terrorist activity. Surveillance thus plays an important role in the protection of critical infrastructures, whether public or private.

17.4.2 Private Sector

Companies' commercial purposes have been highlighted in the discussion of types of surveillance. Profiling of customers through the intensive analysis of information plays a central part in modern marketing. ISPs and search engines have tracked users' surfing habits by a variety of means, including cookies, giving an important business capability and, in particular, selling advertising space. Receivers installed around a shopping centre or trade show allow a company to pick up communication between individuals' mobile phones and base stations, and thereby track visits and re-visits to exhibits or shops, and how long a visitor spends in each. Journalists have engaged in sometimes illegal surveillance and interception of telephone calls, for example, in pursuit of "investigative" stories concerning celebrities.[33] Surveillance of employees has long been controversial, pitting employee privacy against employer interests in ensuring employees are doing what they are paid to do, and not misusing company facilities such as e-mail and the Internet.

17.4.3 Society

Surveillance is widespread in society, used by a wide variety of people. Major examples include those intending to carry out criminal or terrorist acts: burglars, for example, may use Web-based surveillance techniques to monitor the whereabouts of targeted individuals or activity in their households. Stalkers and extortionists can insert a Trojan or other virus on users' computers. Others engage in corporate espionage for business, national or military advantage. In today's safety-oriented

---

[32] Thomas, Richard, and Mark Walport, *Data Sharing Review Report*, 11 July 2008. www.justice.gov.uk/docs/data-sharing-review-report.pdf

[33] Davoudi, Salamander, "Newspaper Phone-Hacking Scandal Widens", *The Financial Times*, 14 Mar 2011. http://www.ft.com/cms/s/0/4dbe102c-4e28-11e0-a9fa-00144feab49a.html#axzz1Gdl4ObsB

culture, parents may track their children as the latter travel to and from school or around the world. Surveillance may be endemic because many people are naturally suspicious: survey evidence has shown the extent to which, among married couples, spouses snoop on each other's e-mails, text messages and patterns of Internet use.[34] In addition, the recreational or entertainment use of surveillance cannot be discounted. Surveillance of others is "fun" for some people, as the popularity of social networking and reality TV suggests; surveillance powerfully shapes, if not defines, our culture. This indicates a shortcoming of PIA: while it can be applied to many types of surveillants in the public and private sectors, surveillance used more generally and amorphously in society cannot be subjected to its rigours; other regulatory instruments, including the application of the law, are more appropriate – even if they are weak in the circumstances of societal surveillants as well as in the global flow of personal information.

17.5 Assessing Surveillance Effects: Privacy and Beyond

PIA presupposes a perspective on some dimensions of privacy that might be affected by surveillance; this section explores some considerations on that issue. It then moves towards a new way of thinking about PIA by placing it in the innermost of several concentric circles of impact analysis of surveillance and describing the wider dimensions that might be affected, and that should therefore be taken into account. This yields a suite of PIAs ranging from PIA_1 to PIA_4. For analytical purposes, this formulation refines and differentiates the approach taken in a prominent report on surveillance, in which "surveillance impact assessment" (SIA) was seen as a development of PIA in the direction of recognising wider impacts, but it amends the terminology.[35] "Impact Assessment" (IA) is the root of these evaluations; the prefix "privacy" in conventional PIA suggests that the impact under consideration is the privacy of the individual, but this is not so straightforward. Although, in the EU, privacy is seen as both a fundamental right and a societal value, there is no universally agreed definition of privacy, and diverse ways in which privacy can be understood.

Privacy has been defined in different ways, but a widely agreed definition remains elusive. It is a difficult term to define because it means different things to different people in different contexts at different times. Many privacy scholars have commented on the difficulty of defining privacy. James Whitman, for example, has observed that "privacy, fundamentally important though it may be, is an unusually slippery concept. In particular, the sense of what must be kept 'private,' of what

---

[34] The survey was part of a larger project. See Oxford Internet Institute, "Me, My Spouse and the Internet: Meeting, Dating and Marriage in the Digital Age", January 2008. http://www.oii.ox.ac.uk/research/projects/?id=47.

[35] Ball, Lyon et al., op. cit., fn. 11, p. 93. "Surveillance impact assessment" is a misleading term if – paralleling the meaning of PIA as the assessment of impact on privacy – it is construed as the assessment of impacts on surveillance, which would be meaningless.

must be hidden before the eyes of others, seems to differ strangely from society to society." The "slipperiness" of privacy is compounded by virtue of the fact that the "ideas of privacy have shifted and mutated over time".[36] To cite another example, Daniel Solove describes privacy as "a concept in disarray. . . . Currently, privacy is a sweeping concept, encompassing (among other things), freedom of thought, control over one's body, solitude in one's home, control over personal information, freedom from surveillance, protection of one's reputation, and protection from searches and interrogations."[37] Solove therefore eschews any search for a single definition, essence or common denominator and adopts a Wittgensteinian approach, seeing "family resemblances" in the plurality of contexts in which privacy *problems* are said to arise, so that privacy becomes an "umbrella term".[38] In this perspective, context becomes an important key to understanding and protecting privacy, as Helen Nissenbaum's analysis shows.[39]

A pluralistic approach is useful in that it allows the retention of "privacy" as a general prefix to IA while enabling distinctions between the different kinds and extents of impact that different kinds of surveillance may bring about. $PIA_{1, 2, 3}$ and $_4$ therefore map onto these various meanings and associations within privacy's conceptual family, resembling but framing differently, the useful delineation of types of privacy found in other writing. For example, corresponding to well-grounded approaches to understanding privacy, the ICO usefully identifies four conventional but overlapping dimensions of privacy: privacy of personal information, privacy of the person, privacy of personal behaviour and privacy of personal communications.[40] Privacy can be taken to have intrinsic worth, connected with ideas of dignity, autonomy and a sense of being a person. Privacy involves being "let alone", being forgotten when desired or where desirable, and being able to exert some control over one's personal information. Privacy can also be justified on more instrumental or utilitarian grounds. Without it, individuals would find it difficult to develop their personalities, engage in social relationships, separate their personal and public lives, or enjoy important freedoms, including freedom of religion, freedom of expression and freedom of association.[41]

---

[36] Whitman, James Q., "The Two Western Cultures of Privacy: Dignity Versus Liberty", *The Yale Law Journal*, Vol. 113, 2004, pp. 1151–1221 [pp. 1153–1154].

[37] Solove, Daniel J., *Understanding Privacy*, Harvard University Press, Cambridge MA, 2008, p. 1.

[38] Solove, ibid., ch.3.

[39] Nissenbaum, Helen, *Privacy in Context: Technology, Policy, and the Integrity of Social Life*, Stanford University Press, Stanford, CA, 2010. See also her earlier paper: "Privacy as Contextual Integrity", *Washington Law Review*, Vol. 79, No. 1, 2004, pp. 101–139. http://www.nyu.edu/projects/nissenbaum/main_cv.html

[40] ICO, PIA *Handbook*, p. 14. These four types of privacy draw on Roger Clarke's categorisations. See Clarke, Roger, "What's Privacy?", 2006. http://www.rogerclarke.com/DV/Privacy.html

[41] For a range of writings across the spectrum of meanings, see Schoeman, Ferdinand D. (ed.), *Philosophical Dimensions of Privacy: An Anthology*, Cambridge University Press, Cambridge, UK, 1984.

These other utilities, rights and freedoms are reflected in the further circles identified below because they embody values that are vital to individuals, but also have important implications for others, and for society. They tap the dimension of *sociality* in individual behaviour as well as the dimension of the public interest in mitigating the impacts of surveillance for the sake of preserving the values of society and the political system. An increasing number of scholars have pointed to the social value of privacy. Priscilla Regan was one of the first to develop an argument showing its importance to society, commenting that

> Privacy has value beyond its usefulness in helping the individual maintain his or her dignity or develop personal relationships. Most privacy scholars emphasize that the individual is better off if privacy exists; I argue that society is better off as well when privacy exists. I maintain that privacy serves not just individual interests but also common, public, and collective purposes. If privacy becomes less important to one individual in one particular context, or even to several individuals in several contexts, it would still be important as a value because it serves other crucial functions beyond those that it performs for a particular individual.[42]

The range of surveillance forms described earlier can be seen as affecting privacy in one or more of these connotations of the term. It is hard to find ways to be let alone if one is subjected to listening and watching, tracking and detecting. It is not easy to maintain a sense of personal dignity when faced with body scanning, fingerprinting and electronic tagging. Autonomy is affected by behavioural monitoring and database profiling, and the sense that one is able to associate freely with others – socially and politically – is reduced by video surveillance, eavesdropping on communications and long-term retention and sharing of information by organisations. These and other effects may be the more insidious to the extent that surveillance is covert, or thought to be taking place without knowing when, how or why.

For all its admirable qualities, PIA tends only to concern surveillance's impact on individual privacy, not on other rights and values pertaining to the individual or its impact on other targets and entities, intended or not. These other impacts are not normally recognised in the risk analysis that PIA prescribes. As was mentioned earlier, this can be seen as an objection to conducting a PIA, albeit in the sense that a PIA is necessary but insufficient to address all of the impacts that surveillance may have. Surveillance scholars plausibly argue that privacy incursion is not the main concern to highlight in evaluating the effects of watching, detecting, data-mining and other surveillance techniques. It would follow that PIA as conventionally conceived, while useful, leaves a great deal out of account – or out of accountability. This is not to deny the crucial importance of privacy to the individual, making its protection imperative as a human right. However, PIA tends mainly to assess the prospective compliance of new technologies or systems involved in surveillance

---

[42] Regan, Priscilla M., *Legislating Privacy: Technology, Social Values, and Public Policy*, University of North Carolina Press, Chapel Hill, 1995, p. 221. See also Raab, Charles, "Privacy, Social Values, and the Public Interest" and Rössler, Beate, "Soziale Dimensionen des Privaten", both in *Politische Vierteljahresschrift*, Special Issue 46 (2011) on "Politik und die Regulierung von Information".

with the canonical, though limited, inventory of "fair information" principles or practices pertaining to "personal data" – itself an ambiguous and controversial concept. These principles are enshrined, with variations, in every information privacy law and in international documents,[43] and are likely to persist through the likely revisions of these laws and instruments. Data protection principles are an essential bedrock, but they do not fully address the range of questions that should be asked about surveillance, especially the "new surveillance" brought about through new technologies and information systems.[44]

By focusing only, or mainly, on the privacy of the individual data subject, PIA has little directly to say about the effects of particular surveillance forms upon wider and cumulative circles of individual and civic values that may not necessarily be inherent in, or commonly understood as part of, the concept of privacy. Conventional PIA, therefore, constitutes the first, innermost circle, which can be called "PIA_1", but there are three further kinds of orientation for an IA that goes beyond PIA (see Fig. 17.1 and Table 17.1). The rest of the PIA suite would assess the form or technology in question against other meanings of privacy that take wider ranges of impact into serious consideration.

Impact assessment in the second, wider circle – called "PIA_2" – remains close to the realm of individual values and rights, but does not stop at considering the most conventionally understood privacy impacts. It takes into account the risk posed by surveillance to the individual's social and political relationships, and her relative position within society and the market, as the potentially impacted objects.

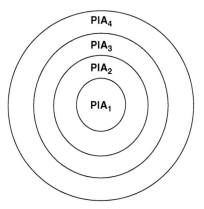

Fig. 17.1 Circles of PIA

[43] Bennett, Colin J., and Charles D. Raab, *The Governance of Privacy: Policy Instruments in Global Perspective*, The MIT Press, Cambridge, MA, 2006.
[44] Marx, Gary T., "What's New About the 'New Surveillance'? Classifying for Change and Continuity", *Surveillance & Society*, Vol. 1, No. 1, 2002, pp. 9–29. http://www.surveillance-and-society.org/journalv1i1.htm

Table 17.1 Extending the limits of PIA

PIA$_1$	PIA$_2$	PIA$_3$	PIA$_4$
Focuses on individual privacy	Focuses on PIA$_1$ + other impacts on individual's relationships, positions and freedoms	Focuses on PIA$_2$ + impacts on groups and categories	Focuses on PIA$_3$ + impacts on society and political system

Among them are also the individual's freedom of speech and association: political and social values that are enshrined as foundational in western-style liberal democracies and in conceptions of the nature of society and interpersonal relationships at several levels of scale. These freedoms might well be infringed by ICTs and information processing, as when video surveillance or electronic eavesdropping makes it risky for people to communicate with one another or to join associations whose activities are monitored closely. This is the much-discussed "chilling effect" of public-space surveillance or of communications monitoring upon sociability and legitimate political participation.

The third circle of IA – "PIA$_3$" – incorporates the first and second, but is also concerned with surveillance's effect on the groups and categories to which individuals belong, or to which their membership is attributed by others. Individual privacy may be affected by the way individuals are thought of, or are treated, as members of wider categories, classes or groups. How these trans-individual entities are administratively or socially constructed, or individually self-selected, is important in understanding the impact of surveillance, but is somewhat outside the scope of this chapter to explore in detail. However, PIA needs to take account of these broader reaches in terms of who might be affected. The ICO, for example, enumerates those whose safety is at risk if their personal data are disclosed: people who are under the direct threat of violence; celebrities, notorieties and VIPs; and people in security-sensitive roles. Then there are "vulnerable populations", including young children or adults who are incapable of providing consent, the homeless, ex-prisoners, refugees and those with certain health conditions.[45]

But this catalogue is too constrained: one might want prominently to add groups or categories identified by characteristics that include ethnicity, race, religion, national origin, political affiliation and sexual orientation, all of which might be the subject of surveillance techniques performed on these groups or categories as such, led by suspicions about the propensity of such persons to endanger the state or society. The profiling of individuals and social groups through the intensive analysis of digitised data in order to make decisions about their treatment by the state or the market provides another example of these effects. The principles of equality and non-discrimination could be negated by the profiling activities of commercial or state organisations. These employ techniques that target not only certain individuals, but also groups or categories of persons through an intensive analysis of collections

---

[45] ICO, PIA *Handbook*, p. 19.

of personal data. On the basis of the analysis, decisions or judgements are made about the role of individuals or groups and categories in the market, their potential to commit crimes, or their creditworthiness – and thus, colloquially, their moral character – that have consequences for their lives or well-being. Thus, beyond having a privacy impact as such, profiling and classification – possibly through obscure and opaque analytical processes – can affect the access to goods and services, and the power to act and participate as social beings, that may be experienced by individuals sharing a similar fate, and the adversity is compounded if the classification is erroneous or arbitrary.[46] The involvement of stakeholders in PIA, or in any other form of IA, is more likely to bring these matters to the surface if collectivities of individuals are recognised as having a stake in the implementation of surveillance technologies and systems.

Whether or not one is particularly concerned about the loss of one's own privacy, the reduction in society's ability to sustain privacy as a general good and a constitutive value has consequences for citizenship and the relation between the individual and the state or other organisations. Going even further than an assessment of impacts on privacy and a range of other individual or group values, on the outermost circle – "PIA$_4$" – the effects of surveillance on the workings of society and the political system as such would be assessed. This chapter falls short of elaborating such a wide-ranging "societal impact assessment" but is in sympathy with attempts to do so. This is because the social and political value of privacy is coming to be recognised as important, or – putting it another way – the effects of surveillance are felt in ways that go beyond the conventional paradigm of what "privacy" means, even taking into account the variety of traditional meanings as well as the distributive justice implicit in critiques of social sorting, to involve yet further values that recent authors emphasise.[47] These effects are felt in terms of what they portend for the texture of society and the constitutive properties of liberal, democratic political systems. Taken together, these trans-individual values form some of the most important fundamentals of these societies and polities. If surveillance through ICTs and information processing potentially affects the ability to realise these values, as well as individuals' ability to enjoy well-established rights, it would seem important to implement assessment techniques – including privacy but widening the focus to take in impacts beyond it – and to link them to remedial or preventive action to mitigate these effects. The effect of surveillance upon society and the polity, and not only on individuals as entities to whom rights pertain, is likely to be missed in the performance of PIA unless it is repositioned to assess the impact of surveillance in broad terms.

---

[46] See Lyon, David (ed.), *Surveillance as Social Sorting: Privacy, Risk, and Digital Discrimination*, Routledge, London, 2003, and Vedder, Anton, *The Values of Freedom*, Aurelia Domus Artium, Utrecht, 1995, Chapter 4, re "categorial privacy". More generally on the consequences of classification, see Bowker, Geoffrey C., and Susan L. Star, *Sorting Things Out: Classification and Its Consequences*, MIT Press, Cambridge, MA, 1999.

[47] See Regan, 1995, op. cit., fn. 39, Chapter 8; Goold, Benjamin J., "Surveillance and the Political Value of Privacy", *Amsterdam Law Forum*, Vol. 1, No. 4, August 2009; Rössler, op. cit., fn. 42, and Raab, op. cit., fn. 42.

Of course, *what kind* and *how much* privacy and in what contexts it is important are endlessly debatable questions, but so too are what kind and how much surveillance and in what contexts. Not all of the effects on privacy occur to the same degree of severity, and different kinds of surveillance affect privacy differently, as a PIA would show. As indicated earlier, an understanding of contexts[48] is crucial if PIA is to result in usable recommendations for improving information systems and technologies, rather than in black-and-white judgements. Contexts mediate the effects – mitigating or amplifying them – and may enable individuals to influence the ways in which their privacy is, is not, or is less severely eroded by a particular surveillance technology operating in a particular place at a particular time. These nuances contribute powerfully to the lived experience of being under surveillance, and may arbitrate the need for more reliable safeguards to be built into information systems – one of the outcomes of PIA – or for more stringent control mechanisms found in the law and other instruments of regulation.

17.6 Conclusion

PIA by itself, on whatever circle, is not a silver bullet for privacy protection, but it can exert a strong influence on the culture, structure and behaviour of organisations that deploy surveillance. Maximising that influence depends on how securely PIA is embedded in organisational routines and in the information governance strategies adopted for the handling of personal data. That, in turn, may depend on internal and external leadership and on the requirements and sanctions that are brought to bear to improve privacy orientation and practice. PIA cannot engineer these components, but can contribute to making their necessity more palpable.

However, there are other shortcomings within PIA itself. One is the extent to which a particular form of PIA emphasises the importance of privacy rights and values as the rationale for the PIA approach and the solutions it recommends, rather than the risks to the organisation itself. Selling PIA to a government department or a commercial firm may require a business or policy case to be established as an inducement to undertake PIA, but the assessment will be caught short if the impression is given that PIA is about protecting the organisation's reputation, balance sheet or legality, more than about protecting the privacy of those affected by the information or surveillance system and practice that is being assessed. A PIA should address both aspects.

In the perspective of this chapter, however, the most important shortcoming would be the restriction of PIA largely to assessing the impact on individuals, even if its recognition that categories and groups might be at risk takes a step into the field of considering wider impacts, and ultimately impacts on society as a whole. As mentioned earlier, this recognition is more likely to be reinforced if the participation of stakeholders reflects and represents important segments of the population

---

[48] Nissenbaum, 2010, op cit., fn. 38. See also Solove, op. cit, fn. 36.

who may be especially affected by surveillance. The effects to be investigated by a PIA that goes one or more steps beyond the entry level of a PIA would include social exclusion and categorical discrimination, by which choices and life-chances for individuals and groups are limited beyond any incursion of privacy that surveillance may cause, thus adversely shaping the nature and texture of society. If taken into consideration, the criteria for assessment would bring PIA closer to ethical impact assessment, discussed in Chapter 19 in this volume. It would also underline the importance of privacy as a human right, seen not only in terms of its value for the individual alone, but for a society made up of privacy-protected individuals who are capable of, and empowered to, engage in a variety of social and political relationships at various levels of scale – or refrain from such engagement, if they choose – free of the restrictions imposed or implied by certain forms and degrees of surveillance.

Further afield, PIA_4 would address some of the most subtle and neglected dimensions of the discourse and practice of privacy invasion through surveillance: matters concerning society, the polity and the public interest broadly conceived. How this kind of assessment would be constructed is not only unfinished business, but has scarcely begun. Whether the analytical distinctions made in this chapter can be translated into practice is the proof of the pudding, but the ingredients themselves may nevertheless be of practical worth in developing ways of assessing the impact of new technologies and systems of surveillance.

Chapter 18
The Madrid Resolution and Prospects for Transnational PIAs

Artemi Rallo Lombarte

If a field were to be identified that would exemplify an area in which the law has difficulties in keeping up with reality, it would have to be the Internet. The concepts of sovereignty and territoriality, traditional limitations to the international application of laws, are being superseded every day by a reality in which interconnection and globalisation are no longer the exception but the norm against a background of vast telecommunications networks. In this respect, the profusion of international flows of data in the "information age" has highlighted the need for privacy legislation that is consistent at a global level.

Legislation relating to the protection of privacy and personal data differs substantially from one State to another, to the point that there are still many legal systems in which these rights, considered as fundamental in a large part of the world, lack an appropriate framework of guarantees. The consequences are easy to understand: information is not uniformly protected, people find it increasingly difficult to assert their rights and data exchanges are therefore at risk – something that would not occur if a universally accepted set of rights, principles, obligations and procedures, applicable to all processing of personal data, were to exist.

18.1 The Madrid Resolution

18.1.1 Origin of the Document

The first international document to address this issue was the Guidelines on the Protection of Privacy and Transborder Flows of Personal Data, approved on 23 September 1980 by the Organisation for Economic Co-operation and Development (OECD). In its explanatory memorandum, the text acknowledges that "for a number of reasons, the problems of developing safeguards for the

A. Rallo Lombarte (✉)
Former Director of the Spanish Data Protection Agency (2007–2011) and Constitutional Law
Professor at Universitat Jaume I, 12071 Castelló de la Plana, Spain
e-mail: rallo@dpu.uji.es

D. Wright, P. De Hert (eds.), *Privacy Impact Assessment*, Law, Governance
and Technology Series 6, DOI 10.1007/978-94-007-2543-0_18,
© Springer Science+Business Media B.V. 2012

individual in respect of the handling of personal data cannot be solved exclusively at the national level" – a statement that is particularly relevant in the electronic communications age.

Data protection authorities were aware of this reality and in 1979 established what has now become the largest worldwide forum dedicated to this subject: the International Conference of Data Protection and Privacy Commissioners. The Conference could be called *the* global event for data protection issues thanks to the large number of accredited authorities (around 100), and the fact that they represent the diverse legal and cultural environments that exist around the world. Indeed, its annual meetings, the first of which was held in Bonn, not only involve different regulators but also the private sector and civil society.

In its search for a pragmatic approach to the problems derived from the global application of data protection, each edition of the Conference adopts one or more resolutions related to important international issues. These documents aim to reflect not only the concerns of the data protection authorities, but also to provide guidelines or discussion points that contribute to achieving balanced solutions to the difficulties identified. Nevertheless, their consensual nature really provides added value to these resolutions, since they represent the agreement between authorities of very diverse origins. During the last few years, numerous issues have been tackled through these documents: the retention of telecommunications traffic data, the use of biometric data in travel documents, RFID tags, etc. Of remarkable relevance is the ongoing appeal that was first made in 2004 to disseminate and strengthen privacy and data protection rights, through two resolutions in particular: the "Montreux Declaration" (2005),[1] and the "Resolution on the Urgent Need for Protecting Privacy in a Borderless World" (2008).[2]

- Through the Montreux Declaration, members of the Conference recognised the need for global recognition of the rights to personal data protection and privacy, expressly choosing to approve an international agreement that includes and develops them. They therefore confirmed "their will to strengthen the international recognition of the universal character of these principles", declaring their desire "to collaborate in particular with the governments and international and supranational organisations for the development of a universal convention for the protection of individuals with regard to the processing of personal data". Similarly, they expressly appealed "to the United Nations to prepare a legal binding instrument which clearly sets out in detail the rights to data protection and privacy as enforceable human rights".

---

[1] "The Montreux Declaration – The protection of personal data and privacy in a globalised world: a universal right respecting diversities", adopted by the 27th International Conference of Data Protection and Privacy Commissioners in Montreux, Switzerland, on 16 September 2005.

[2] "Resolution on the Urgent Need for Protecting Privacy in a Borderless World, and for Reaching a Joint Proposal for Setting International Standards on Privacy and Personal Data Protection", adopted by the 30th International Conference of Data Protection and Privacy Commissioners in Strasbourg, France, on 17 October 2008.

- With regard to the second of the aforementioned resolutions, it expresses their concerns regarding "the persisting data protection and privacy disparities in the world, in particular due to the fact that many states have not yet passed adequate laws", which harms "the exchange of personal information and the implementation of effective global data protection". It also highlights that "the development of cross-border rules that guarantee in a uniform way the respect for data protection and privacy has priority". Aware of the importance of starting this work as soon as possible, the Conference took the important decision to create a working group "to draft and submit to its closed session a joint proposal for setting international standards on privacy and personal data protection".

The creation and co-ordination of this working group was the responsibility of the Spanish Data Protection Agency (AEPD) as the organising authority of the International Conference in 2009. Following the Conference's mandate, it based its work on existing principles and rights in diverse geographical regions around the world, with particular emphasis on texts that might benefit from a wide consensus in their respective regional or international forums. Based on this starting point, the objective was to create a document that, while drawing on and complementing the existing texts, could achieve the highest level of international acceptance, while also ensuring a high level of protection.

The working group carried out its work throughout 2009, with a high level of participation from public and private entities and organisations from all of the social and economic sectors involved. It was able to draft successive versions of the document, incorporating contributions from data protection authorities, companies, academics and representatives from civil society. The result was the "Joint Proposal for International Standards on the Protection of Privacy with regard to the Processing of Personal Data", presented at the 31st International Conference held in Madrid between 4 and 6 November, and approved by means of the Madrid Resolution on International Standards of Privacy. Despite the fact that this was not an international agreement, nor legally binding legislation, this document still had a clear value and relevance as an international reference text and as a possible precursor to a universal convention on this matter. And not only for its specific content, but also because it carefully integrated elements present in all existing data protection systems and due to the unanimous support of the authorities composing the International Conference.

18.1.2 The Contents of the Madrid Resolution

The Madrid Resolution has two very different parts. One "provides a set of principles, rights, obligations and procedures that any legal system of data protection and privacy should strive to meet". The other welcomes the Joint Proposal (which it includes as an annex), and invites members of the Conference to disseminate and support it.

The Proposal has two key objectives. First, it aims to promote internationally the right to data protection and privacy, offering a model for regulation that, while guaranteeing a high level of protection, could also be incorporated by any country, with minimum adaptation, depending on each region's legal, social and economic culture. Second, it seeks to facilitate the smooth international flows of personal data. At present, the coexistence of different national legislations means that the transfer of data between countries in different geographical regions requires complex authorisation systems. Indeed, compliance by a specific entity with its own national regulations to export data does not necessarily mean that the requirements to receive data established by the legislation of the destination country are also met. The situation can be even more complex for multinational corporations, which have to abide by several different regulatory systems, depending on the countries in which their various offices are based. This not only generates obstacles and delays in international data flows, but also makes it difficult for individuals to exercise their rights and for supervisory authorities to act to protect them.

Aimed at both the public and the private sector, and at all types of data processing, whether automated or not, the Proposal is designed to represent the minimum level that all regulations in relation to privacy protection must provide, but which can be improved or supplemented through the national or regional instruments that implement it. This means that those legal systems that decide to adopt it or that have superior protection measures compared to those in the Madrid Resolution perfectly conform with the proposed model; however, it also requires mechanisms to be implemented that reconcile relations between those legal systems that opt for this reinforced regulation and those that just transpose the level of protection offered by the Proposal, which is rigorous in itself.

The simplification of the data flows intended by the document is therefore achieved, acknowledging that its provisions constitute a sufficient basis to enable international transfers of data. In this sense, by establishing a universal model that can be considered as providing an appropriate level of protection, the Proposal seeks to enable these transfers with a minimum of formalities between the countries or entities that have protection systems that comply with this model.

Another of the challenges tackled by the document was to harmonise definitions. Within these, it is especially worth noting the new way in which the subjects involved in data processing are defined, differentiating between the person that carries out the processing of the personal data (called the "responsible person") and the person that provides a data processing service on behalf of the "responsible person". It therefore seeks to overcome the difficulties derived from differentiating the classic concepts of "data controller" and "data processor", something that is increasingly complicated nowadays.

With the concepts, purpose and scope all defined, the Standards deal with the core principles of the right to privacy and data protection. They acknowledge that the processing of personal data must be carried out in a fair, lawful and proportionate way in relation to the specific, explicit and legitimate purposes of the "responsible person", which must also guarantee that the data being processed are accurate, sufficient and kept up to date. Following on from these principles, it also establishes the need to limit both the data being processed and the period during which they are retained to the essential minimum.

Transparency in the data processing is also strengthened in this document. The information to provide to data subjects is incorporated in detail, including a special case regarding the need to use particularly clear and plain vocabulary when dealing with minors, and recognising the validity of those privacy policies that are accessible through electronic communications networks, such as the Internet. These obligations are especially important when the basis used to legitimise the processing of the data is consent, which must be freely given, unambiguous and informed. Therefore, a failure of the duty to inform could nullify the consent and result in unlawful processing.

Consent is one way of legitimising data processing, just as important as other equally valid issues, such as the legitimate interest of the responsible person or compliance with the obligations derived from the applicable legislation or from the legal relations that might connect the responsible person and the data subject. However, consent has its own unique characteristics: it can be withdrawn at any time and freely.

Similarly, the document tackles the need to establish additional guarantees in relation to the processing of sensitive information, defining this sort of data as information that affects the most intimate aspects of the individual or that may give rise to discrimination or carry a serious risk to the data subject in the event of misuse.

The subcontracting of services and international data transfers also have an important place in the Madrid Resolution. Subcontracting is considered as the "provision of processing services", establishing the need to agree a contract between the service provider and the responsible person, and to guarantee the level of protection established in this contract, in the Resolution itself and in national legislation. With regard to transfers, it establishes the level of protection defined in the Proposal of Standards as general criteria, in order to enable the circulation of data. This level of protection can be provided by States by establishing solid legislation, as well as through mechanisms to ensure that it is effectively used[3] or by the recipient of the transfer by means of signing the appropriate contractual clauses, or "internal privacy rules, compliance with which is mandatory". The Resolution thus adopts a flexible approach regulated by the control tasks performed by the supervisory authorities, whether before or after the transfer.

The rights of data subjects also enjoy a privileged position in the Resolution. Three of its sections establish and govern the access, rectification, deletion and objection to the processing of personal data, while the common aspects of these rights are included in an additional section. That section states, for example, that procedures must be established that enable the exercising of these rights in a simple, fast and efficient way, without causing delays or excessive costs, and without

---

[3] Working Document WP12, adopted by the Article 29 Data Protection Working Party on 14 July 1998, states: "It is therefore necessary to consider not only the content of rules applicable to personal data transferred to a third country, but also the system in place to ensure the effectiveness of such rules."

generating any gain whatsoever for the responsible person. This is especially important in the Information Society as a basis for the effective application of the right to "digital oblivion", which could be defined as the right of every citizen to assert their rights in the event that their personal data is disseminated via networks such as the Internet.[4]

To ensure the integrity, confidentiality and availability of information is another of the objectives tackled in the Standards, which establish a series of criteria to determine the technical and organisational security measures that are appropriate at any time. The Standards include a duty to notify data subjects in the event that a breach of security significantly affects their pecuniary or non-pecuniary rights, a notification that must be made with sufficient notice to enable them to react in defence of these rights.

The role of the supervisory authorities is also examined in detail. It provides for the obligation that each State, according to its internal legislation and legal tradition, establish one or more authorities to supervise compliance with the principles included in the Standards. Independence and impartiality will be essential characteristics of these authorities, which will have sufficient authority and resources to carry out their functions. One of these functions expressly includes dealing with claims filed by data subjects and carrying out the investigations and interventions that may be necessary to guarantee respect for the right to data protection – and all of this without compromising the individuals' right of access to justice. Similarly, the necessary co-operation between these authorities, especially in relation to the exchange of data, the co-ordination of investigations and participation in joint working groups, is appropriately covered.

Finally, a section has been included that deals with the liability derived from the illegal processing of data, both in relation to pecuniary and non-pecuniary damages caused to data subjects, and in relation to the legally established criminal, civil or administrative sanctions.

18.2 Privacy Impact Assessments in the Madrid Resolution

The Madrid Resolution is the first international document with a global scope that includes the concept of "privacy impact assessments", which are specifically tackled in paragraph f) of section 22:

22. Proactive measures

States should encourage, through their domestic law, the implementation by those involved in any stage of the processing of measures to promote better compliance with applicable laws on the protection of privacy with regard to the processing of personal data. Such measures could include, among others...

---

[4] Rallo Lombarte, Artemi, "El derecho al olvido y su protección", Fundación Telefónica, Revista TELOS, No. 85, October–December 2010, pp. 104–108.

f) The implementation of privacy impact assessments prior to implementing new information systems and/or technologies for the processing of personal data, as well as prior to carrying out any new method of processing personal data or substantial modifications in existing processing.

Inclusion of PIAs in the section of the Standards dedicated to "Proactive measures" is derived from the eminently practical nature of these assessments, from their usefulness as an instrument to determine the precautionary actions to take in processing personal data and from a desire to encourage their use without making any kind of imposition. In this sense, the inclusion of PIAs recognises the fundamental importance that self-regulation has had at an enterprise and sector level in the development of the protection of privacy in jurisdictions in which internal legislation does not explicitly refer to these guarantees, as well as in those in which specific laws do exist.

The text of the section is aimed directly at States, urging them to provide a series of measures through their national laws. This structure has a dual purpose: first, it tries to make the incentives offered clear and recognisable by the legal system, guaranteeing the legal certainty required in any State governed by the rule of law and, second, it provides the system with flexibility, enabling each legislator to decide how to implement them, according to its own culture, legal and constitutional traditions and legislative and political model. Aspects such as the size of organisations or the risk of the processing that they carry should therefore be taken into account when definitively implementing these incentives in national law.

These measures must have a clear objective: to promote compliance with the applicable legislation in relation to data protection issues. In so far as how this should be promoted, it will once again be the legislator who decides on the most appropriate means, although there is an initial suggestion in paragraph four of section 25 of the Standards:

25. Liability

4. The implementation of proactive measures such as those described in section 22 of this Document shall be considered when determining the liability and penalties established in this section.

Subsequently, section 22 offers a list of eight proactive measures, which include, as stated above, privacy impact assessments. It is an open list, meaning it is only illustrative and not exclusive, which includes a set of good practices generally accepted as being effective when improving personal data protection. Despite referring to practices covered in a different section to the one that includes security measures, they are largely complementary. Equally, the isolated application of just one or two proactive measures would be inconceivable due to their ineffectiveness. It is therefore important to highlight the need that these measures encourage compliance with legislation, and that this is only possible when they are included in a coherent and systematic plan designed to promote this compliance. For example: it would make little or no sense to appoint a privacy official in an organisation that does not implement the most basic information security measures and, likewise, it would be illogical to incentivise this. The coexistence of the classic data protection mechanisms and these proactive measures therefore makes it necessary to assess their suitability and to examine whether the corresponding incentives resulting from their establishment would be appropriate.

Similarly, these practices must be contrasted with the obligation to adopt the necessary measures to comply with the principles and obligations established both in the Standards and in legislation, included in section 11 of the text and known as the "principle of accountability". This requirement is supplemented by the need to provide the necessary mechanisms to demonstrate compliance, of which PIAs are a perfect example, by providing written evidence of the analysis of the feasibility of a specific project in terms of privacy.

PIAs could be extremely useful in the context of international transfers of data, precisely due to the appropriateness of this instrument to generate evidence demonstrating due diligence. According to section 15(2) of the Standards, transborder flows could be carried out, as has been previously noted, if the responsible person guarantees that the recipient affords, at a minimum, the level of protection provided for in the document. Those assessments could be used, to a certain extent, to provide a clear record that the transfer was intended to be carried out with the necessary care, a relevant factor in order to determine liabilities in case of non-compliance.

If we look at the subsection on PIAs, we should first highlight the purely descriptive notion attributed to them, moving away from doctrinal characterisations that might restrict the concept unnecessarily. This establishes that the determining factor in considering this measure will be its "implementation", therefore excluding those activities that are limited to merely planning or designing a protocol for action. Implementation must come before the launch of any of the following projects:

- the implementation of new information systems or technologies (which can be defined as any type of program, support, equipment or database), which are used for the processing of personal data;
- the carrying out of new methods of processing personal data;
- the carrying out of significant modifications to existing processing.

As already explained elsewhere in this book, timing is one of the essential characteristics of this type of assessment, since this is the only way that its ultimate objective can be achieved: to adapt the project in question to the results obtained, improving it from the moment that it is conceived and preventing certain risks from even occurring.

18.3 Reception of the Madrid Resolution

18.3.1 Towards a Binding International Instrument

In a globalised world, the problems arising from the existence of different protection systems in different geographical regions, including countries or zones where there is no regulation of the protection of data or of privacy, can only be a cause of constant concern. And not only due to the differences that arise when adequately guaranteeing a fundamental right, which may be alarming in themselves, but also due to the subsequent difficulties in relation to international exchanges of personal data. Achieving harmonisation between the multitude of existing legal systems while also guaranteeing a high level of protection in data processing is the ambitious challenge that underlies the drafting of the Madrid Resolution.

As it states in its explanatory note, "the resolution expresses the conviction of the Conference [the International Conference of Data Protection and Privacy Commissioners] that recognition of these rights requires the adoption of a universal legally binding instrument establishing, drawing on and complementing the common data protection and privacy principles laid down in several existing instruments, and strengthening the international cooperation between data protection authorities". However, the adoption of a document, such as the one proposed, requires a climate of international consensus to be created regarding the need and the opportunity to negotiate a convention, treaty or agreement of similar characteristics, and to do it successfully. The Resolution therefore also exists as a means of achieving a more immediate objective: the incorporation of its underlying set of principles, rights, obligations and procedures to the internal legislation of States.

Several entities and organisations have endorsed the qualities of the Madrid Resolution as a document likely to achieve this purpose. Through its paper on "The Future of Privacy",[5] a contribution to the consultation of the European Commission on the legal framework for the fundamental right to protection of personal data, the Article 29 Working Party (which brings together the data protection authorities of the EU) recognised that "global standards regarding data protection are becoming indispensable", affirming that the Madrid Resolution "deserves support". Therefore, it called upon the Commission to promote the development of legislation providing an adequate level of protection of personal data, stating that the principles of data protection "as laid down in the Madrid Resolution, should be the universal basis for such legislations".

In the same vein, both the Congress of Deputies and the Senate, the parliamentary chambers composing the legislature in Spain, urged the Government, through two separate resolutions, "to institutionally support the activities of dissemination and promotion of international standards on privacy, and particularly the Joint Proposal adopted by the International Conference of Data Protection Authorities (Madrid Resolution), as well as promote them within the European Union, the Ibero-American Community and the relevant international organisations".[6] A similar initiative is currently pending in the National Assembly of France.

---

[5] Document WP168, adopted by the Article 29 Working Party on 1 December 2009.

[6] Non-legislative proposal adopted by the plenary of the Congress of Deputies on 13 April 2010, and Motion adopted by the plenary of the Senate on 28 April of the same year.

Thus, the Madrid Resolution has achieved wide support as a regulatory model, which is sufficiently rights-based to ensure a high level of protection flexible enough to be adapted to the different legal, social or economic cultures of each region.

18.3.2 Mexico: First Country to Incorporate the Resolution into Its Legal System

Reflecting the spirit of the document, several States whose legislation is being drafted or amended have shown an interest in the contents of the Madrid Resolution. A case in point is Mexico: its Federal Act on the Protection of Personal Data Held by Private Parties (published in the Official Gazette of the Federation on 5 July 2010) is the first legally binding text that incorporates the Standards into its provisions. This is expressly recognised by the Opinion of the parliamentary commissions on Governance and on Legislative Studies of the Mexican Congress, which states in its fifth recital that:

> This is the reason why our Co-legislator placed special emphasis on fully guaranteeing each and every one of the principles included in the document entitled "International Standards on Privacy and Personal Data Protection", commonly known as the Madrid Resolution, approved in November 2009, through the joint work of the personal data protection entities in fifty countries, and the participation of the industry at a global level and organised civil society.

In that sense, the Federal Act recognises, among the competences of the Federal Institute for Access to Information and Data Protection, the Mexican supervisory authority:

> To carry out privacy impact assessments prior to the implementation of any new method of processing of personal data or substantial modifications in existing processing.

Insofar as this provision is still being developed, through Regulations expected to be adopted in the next few months, it is not possible yet to opine on how this competence will be implemented by the Institute. In any case, those organisations, such as the Spanish Data Protection Agency, that actively engaged in the drafting process of the Standards should feel really proud when confirming that this and other proposals have been properly incorporated in the Mexican legislation.

18.3.3 Europe: Influence of the Madrid Resolution on the "Future of Privacy"

The aforementioned document by the Article 29 Working Party, on "The Future of Privacy", includes not only references to the value of the Madrid Resolution as a text of reference "to promote an international framework for data protection". It also uses it as a source of inspiration for many proposals addressed to the Commission, some of them of particular importance, because they are intended to feed into the revision of the current Community data protection law.

Privacy impact assessments occupy an important place among these proposals. Thus, in the chapter dealing with embedding data protection in organisations, an express mention was included about the usefulness of carrying out privacy impact assessments, "particularly for certain data processing operations deemed to present specific risks to the rights and freedoms of data subjects, for example, by virtue of their nature, their scope or their purpose". It also suggested that the outcomes of these assessments should be brought together as part of notifications, which would be limited, precisely, to those processings deemed to present specific risks.

Moreover, the Opinion of the Article 29 Working Party on the principle of accountability[7] states that, as a complement to this important principle, specific additional requirements aiming at putting into effect data protection safeguards or at ensuring their effectiveness could be set up. In that sense, it expressly states that "one example would be a provision requiring the performance of a privacy impact assessment for higher risk data processing operations" – a complementary role that is also ascribed to data protection officers.

As a result of the Working Party's initiatives, the Commission also included reference to privacy impact assessments in its Communication on a comprehensive approach on personal data protection in the European Union.[8] Its section dealing with enhancing data controllers' responsibility proposes to examine the appropriateness of "including in the [data protection] legal framework an obligation for data controllers to carry out a data protection impact assessment in specific cases, for instance, when sensitive data are being processed, or when the type of processing otherwise involves specific risks, in particular when using specific technologies, mechanisms or procedures, including profiling or video surveillance". This wideranging statement gives rise to predictions about where the imminent new European legislation is heading and confirms the increasing relevance that PIAs have in the Community framework.

18.4 Conclusions

To those that understand data protection and privacy as fundamental rights of every person, the Madrid Resolution is itself a key achievement. It is a first step towards a relevant internationally binding agreement, which guarantees an appropriate protection to these rights all around the world and allows simultaneously for the free flow of information needed by the society in which we live today. And it offers a

---

[7] Article 29 Data Protection Working Party, Opinion 3/2010 on the principle of accountability, Adopted on 13 July 2010.

[8] European Commission, A comprehensive approach on personal data protection in the European Union, Communication from the Commission to the European Parliament, the Council, the Economic and Social Committee and the Committee of the Regions, COM(2010) 609 final, Brussels, 4.11.2010. http://ec.europa.eu/justice/news/intro/news_intro_en.htm#20101104

robust, solid and efficient regulatory model to provide legal certainty to individuals, organisations and public bodies.

It is no coincidence that privacy impact assessments are part of the set of principles, rights, obligations and procedures that make up the Standards. There is no doubt about their usefulness in adequate decision-making and subsequent effective management of the processing of personal data. This worth deserves appropriate international promotion, to expand its take-up on the five continents, not through impositions, but through support and encouragement. The Madrid Resolution contributes to this promotional effort.

The facts suggest that the joint effort of regulators, companies, academia and civil society is starting to pay off. Time will allow us to consider its long term results, but it already appears that the Madrid Resolution has been a resounding success.

Acknowledgments The preparation of this text was possible thanks to the invaluable help from José Leandro Núñez García, to whom I would like to express my gratitude.

Chapter 19
Privacy and Ethical Impact Assessment

David Wright and Emilio Mordini

19.1 Introduction

The development and deployment of new information and communications technologies and applications fuelled by the use of personal information may raise not only privacy concerns, but also ethical issues. In this chapter, we propose and describe an ethical impact assessment framework (EIA),[1] which could complement a privacy impact assessment. Indeed, the two forms of impact assessment could be carried out concurrently. Like a PIA, an EIA could be used as a way to ensure ethical implications are adequately examined by stakeholders before deployment so that mitigating measures can be taken as necessary.

One of the objectives of an ethical impact assessment is to engage stakeholders in order to identify, discuss and find ways of dealing with ethical issues arising from the development of new technologies, services, projects or whatever. Stakeholders may have some information or ideas or views or values which the project manager had not previously considered. They may be able to suggest alternative courses of actions to achieve the desired objectives. They may be able to suggest some safeguards which would minimise the ethical risks that might otherwise explode after a technology or project is launched. By consulting stakeholders before launch, the project manager may be able to lower his liability and avoid some nasty surprises. As a minimum, the policy-maker or project manager will earn some good will by consulting stakeholders who might otherwise be among his chief critics.

The idea or need to consider ethics in context is not new. In his 1985 essay, "What is Computer Ethics?", Moor observed that "A typical problem in computer ethics arises because there is a policy vacuum about how computer technology should be used. . . . A central task of computer ethics is to determine what we should do in such

---

[1] This chapter is based on Wright, David, "An Ethical Impact Assessment Framework for Information Technology", *Ethics and Information Technology*, Vol. 13, No. 3, September 2011, pp. 199–226.

D. Wright (✉)
Trilateral Research & Consulting, London W8 5JB, UK
e-mail: david.wright@trilateralresearch.com

D. Wright, P. De Hert (eds.), *Privacy Impact Assessment*, Law, Governance and Technology Series 6, DOI 10.1007/978-94-007-2543-0_19,
© Springer Science+Business Media B.V. 2012

cases, i.e., to formulate policies to guide our actions."[2] He added, "Computer ethics requires us to think anew about the nature of computer technology and our values." An ethical impact assessment would be a way of addressing Moor's concerns.

Helen Nissenbaum, author of the influential essay "Privacy as contextual integrity", argued along somewhat the same lines. She presented a model of informational privacy in terms of contextual integrity, namely, that in determining privacy threats, one needs to take into account the nature of a situation or context: what is appropriate in one context can be a violation of privacy in another context.[3] Again, given the need to consider ethical issues in context, an ethical impact assessment would be more appropriate than prescriptive rules.

If a prescriptive ethical guidance is problematic because contextual factors influence the ethics, then a better approach would be to ask questions, which is what the European Commission and others do, and which is the approach adopted here too.[4] Questions aimed at identifying issues also feature in the privacy impact assessment models in countries such as Canada[5] and the UK.[6] Scholars such as Gary T. Marx have also formulated sets of questions aimed at uncovering ethical issues.[7] In preparing the ethical impact assessment framework presented in this chapter, the authors drew on the approach and questions presented by these and other sources.

The collection of essays brought together by Paul Sollie and Marcus Düwell in their book *Evaluating New Technologies* has advanced the state of the methodological art of ethical assessment of new technologies.[8] In their introductory chapter, the editors note that "Although technology is easily one of the most permeating and consequential features of modern society, surprisingly, an ethics of technology is still in its infancy. Important reasons for this 'underdevelopment' of a methodology for morally evaluating technology development are related to its complex, uncertain, dynamic, and large-scale character that seems to resist human control." [9]

---

[2] Moor, James H., "What is Computer Ethics?", in Terrell Ward Bynum (ed.), *Computers & Ethics*, Blackwell, 1985, pp. 266–275.

[3] Nissenbaum, Helen, "Privacy as Contextual Integrity", *Washington Law Review*, Vol. 79, No. 1, 2004, pp. 101–139.

[4] Those making proposals for funding under the Commission's Framework Programmes of research and technological development must respond to a set of ethical questions. http://cordis.europa.eu/fp7/ethics_en.html#ethics_cl

[5] Treasury Board of Canada Secretariat, *Privacy Impact Assessment Guidelines: A Framework to Manage Privacy Risks*, Ottawa, 31 Aug 2002.

[6] [UK] Information Commissioner's Office (ICO), *Privacy Impact Assessment Handbook*, Version 2.0, June 2009. http://www.ico.gov.uk/for_organisations/topic_specific_guides/pia_handbook.aspx

[7] Van Gorp also proposed a list of questions "that helps researchers doing research in technological fields to identify ethical aspects of their research". Van Gorp, Anke, "Ethics in and During Technological Research: An Addition to IT Ethics and Science Ethics", in Paul Sollie and Marcus Düwell (eds.), *Evaluating New Technologies*, Springer, Dordrecht, 2009, p. 35.

[8] Sollie, Paul, and Marcus Düwell, *Evaluating New Technologies: Methodological Problems for the Ethical Assessment of Technology Developments*, Springer, Dordrecht, 2009.

[9] Sollie and Düwell, p. 4.

The ethical impact assessment framework proposed in this chapter is primarily aimed at those who are developing or intend to develop an information technology project, policy or programme that may have ethical implications. More specifically, this would include industry players when they are developing a new technology or planning a new service as well as policy-makers and regulatory authorities when they are considering a new policy or regulation. In addition, the ethical impact assessment framework should be of interest to civil society organisations, so that when they become aware of proposals or plans for new technologies, they can advocate the framework's use and their involvement in the decision-making process. Other stakeholders, such as academics, may find the ethical impact assessment framework of interest too and, as a consequence, may be able to suggest improvements or to analyse its use. It might also be of interest to the media as background to any stories they prepare on the introduction of a new technology or service, which in turn will help raise the awareness of the public and other stakeholders about the associated ethical issues.

The construction of an ethical impact assessment framework, as proposed here, draws on various sources with regard to values, different types of impact assessment and the role that IT plays.

With specific regard to values, it draws on those stated in the EU Reform Treaty, signed by Heads of State and Government at the European Council in Lisbon on 13 December 2007, such as human dignity, freedom, democracy, human right protection, pluralism, non-discrimination, tolerance, justice, solidarity and gender equality.[10] These values are also stated in the Charter of Fundamental Rights of the European Union,[11] and constitute the key frame for design and implementation of all EU policies.[12]

With regard to impact assessment, this chapter draws on the work that scholars, experts and policy-makers have done, especially over the last 20 years or so. There are various types of impact assessments, including

- environmental impact assessment (which includes the notion of the precautionary principle which was given its impetus at the UN Rio Conference or "Earth Summit" in 1992),
- risk assessment, which changed from purely technical analysis to an assessment involving stakeholders, those interested in or affected by a risk,[13]
- technology impact assessment,

---

[10] http://eurlex.europa.eu/JOHtml.do?uri=OJ:C:2007:306:SOM:EN:HTML

[11] http://www.europarl.europa.eu/charter/pdf/text_en.pdf

[12] European Commission, The European Research Area: New Perspectives, Green Paper, COM (2007) 161 final, Brussels, 4 Apr 2007.

[13] For a state-of-the-art review, see Renn, Ortwin, *Risk Governance: Coping with Uncertainty in a Complex World*, Earthscan, London, 2008.

- regulatory impact assessment or simply impact assessment,[14]
- privacy impact assessment.

All of these impact assessments, at least in their more progressive manifestations, have in common a recognition of the need to involve stakeholders in the assessment process. That is also a key feature of the ethical impact assessment proposed here too.

These different types of impact assessments need not be seen as alternatives. Beekman et al. view the ethical assessment of the application of new technologies as complementary rather than as an alternative to scientific risk assessments and economic cost-benefit assessments. Taken together, these ethical, scientific and economic assessments should provide a sound basis for socio-political decision-making.[15]

Regarding the role that IT plays, in conducting an ethical impact assessment of a new technology, one should not treat the technology as a kind of black box. "Technologies always help to shape human actions and interpretations on the basis of which (moral) decisions are made," comments Verbeek. "When technologies are always influencing human actions, we had better try and give this influence a desirable and morally justifiable form."[16]

Technologies are neither neutral nor value free. Hofman agrees: "Technology expresses and influences the norms and values of its social context".[17] Orlikowski and Iacono rightly say that "because IT artefacts are designed, constructed, and used by people, they are shaped by the interests, values, and assumptions of a wide variety of communities of developers, investors, users, etc."[18] While it may be impossible to foresee all of the ethical and other consequences of an emerging technology, nevertheless, an ethical impact assessment, involving different stakeholders from different disciplines and backgrounds, may be a good way of avoiding the traps discerned by Orlikowski and Iacono – i.e., of not seeing the context specificity of a technology and of not examining its critical implications for individuals, groups, organisations and society.

---

[14] For a good overview of developments in this area, see Kirkpatrick, Colin, and David Parker (eds.), *Regulatory Impact Assessment: Towards Better Regulation?*, Edward Elgar, Cheltenham, UK, 2007.

[15] Beekman, Volkert, et al., Ethical Bio-Technology Assessment Tools for Agriculture and Food Production, Final Report of the Ethical Bio-TA Tools project, LEI, The Hague, February 2006, p. 13. http://www.ethicaltools.info.

[16] Verbeek, Peter-Paul, "The Moral Relevance of Technological Artifacts", in Paul Sollie and Marcus Düwell (eds.), *Evaluating New Technologies: Methodological Problems for the Ethical Assessment of Technology Developments*, Springer, Dordrecht, 2009, pp. 63–78 [p. 67, 71].

[17] Hofmann, B., "On Value-Judgements and Ethics in Health Technology Assessment", *Poiesis & Praxis*, Vol. 3, No. 4, December. 2005, pp. 277–295 [p. 289]. He further observes (p. 288) that there appears to be broad agreement among scholars that technology is value-laden.

[18] Orlikowski, Wanda J., and C. Suzanne Iacono, "Research Commentary: Desperately Seeking the 'IT' in IT Research – A Call to Theorizing the IT Artifact", *Information Systems Research*, Vol. 12, No.2, June 2001, pp. 121–134 [p. 131].

In addition, we must recognise that the (ethical) complexity of a technology multiplies as it converges with other technologies. The Internet, as it was originally conceived as a way for scientists to exchange documents, has changed beyond recognition as it has brought together and "absorbed" new broadband technologies, high speed servers, the multiplicity of low cost, high performance user devices, the vast storage capacity of cloud computing, GPS, networking sensors and actuators, ambient intelligence, the so-called Internet of Things. In less than the time span of a single generation, the Internet has gone from something few people had even heard of to a point where broadband access to it is increasingly and widely described as a fundamental right. We can assume that even DARPA could not have imagined the immeasurable benefits, nor the dangers of a virtually ubiquitous Internet – the reductions in privacy, the proliferation of ID theft, child grooming, spam and other cybercrime and cyberterrorism, nor the extent to which our society and economy are underpinned by what has become a critical infrastructure.

Thus, an ethical impact assessment must not only focus on the ethics of a technology, but on the technology itself, its values, how it is perceived and how it is used or might be used in the future, not only by itself but as a component in a larger technological framework.

19.2 Governance Issues in the Practice of an Ethical Impact Assessment

This section aims at providing an overview of the governance issues in the practice of the ethical impact assessment of IT. To help decision-makers in their consideration of the utility and relevance of these governance aspects, a set of questions follows each of them. In some instances, there is no one correct answer to the questions. The applicability and relevance of some questions may depend on the context and on the willingness of the decision-maker to employ these practices.

19.2.1 The Role of Ethics

Information and communication technologies are constantly evolving and transforming our society. As ICTs permeate more and more our lives, crucial ethical, social and political issues are emerging. The ICT-related ethical debate mainly refers to making choices that preserve our well-being, the respect for principles such as autonomy and justice, as well as the ability to innovate quickly. This process might result in radical changes to the concept of privacy itself.

The crucial ethical, privacy-related issue seems to be the one of control, the risk individuals bear as they automatically lose control of their personal information. Individuals' awareness and genuine consent is lacking in many circumstances. The issue of control is also crucial in the emergence of new, powerful, embedded technologies, ubiquitous surveillance techniques and cloud computing services, which could deeply affect individuals' autonomy and freedom of choice, as well as the control over their personal data. An ethical enquiry into these processes and ethical assessment of these technologies can help to clarify such issues in a rational way.

19.2.2 Consulting and Engaging Stakeholders

An ethical impact assessment should not consist of questions only. A process for engaging and consulting with stakeholders should be put in place to help policy-makers, technology developers and project managers in ensuring that ethical issues are identified, discussed and dealt with, preferably as early in the project development as possible.

There are various reasons why project managers should engage stakeholders and undertake a consultation when developing new technologies or projects. For one thing, Article 41 of the Charter of Fundamental Rights of the European Union, entitled the Right to good administration, makes clear that this right includes "the right of every person to be heard, before any individual measure which would affect him or her adversely is taken. . .", which suggests that consultation with stakeholders is not only desirable but necessary.

But there are other reasons too. Stakeholders may bring new information which the project manager might not have considered and may have some good suggestions for resolving complex issues.[19] Also, technology development is often too complex to be fully understood by a single agent, as Sollie and others have pointed out.[20] Palm and Hansson state that "It would be delusive to believe that technology developers are conscious of all the effects of their products. In many cases, negative side effects come as a surprise to technology developers themselves. If they could have anticipated the negative consequences, they would, in the vast majority of the cases, have done their best to avoid them out of social concern or for commercial reasons, or both."[21] Furthermore, by engaging stakeholders, project managers may avoid subsequent criticism about a lack of consultation. Engaging stakeholders before the project is implemented may be a useful way of testing the waters, of gauging the public's reaction to the project. In any event, "A central premise of democratic government – the existence of an informed electorate – implies a free flow of information."[22] Even if participation does not increase support for a decision, it may clear up misunderstandings about the nature of a controversy and

---

[19] Stern, Paul C., and Harvey V. Fineberg (eds.), *Understanding Risk: Informing Decisions in a Democratic Society*, Committee on Risk Characterization, National Research Council, National Academy Press, Washington, DC, 1996.

[20] Sollie, Paul, "Ethics, Technology Development and Uncertainty: An Outline for Any Future Ethics of Technology", *Journal of Information, Communications & Ethics in Society*, Vol. 5, No. 4, 2007, pp. 293–306 [p. 302]. Moor, 2005, op. cit., p. 118, also supports better collaboration among ethicists, scientists, social scientists and technologists.

[21] Palm and Hansson, p. 547.

[22] National Research Council, Committee on Risk Perception and Communications, *Improving Risk Communication*, National Academy Press, Washington, DC, 1989, p. 9. http://www.nap.edu/openbook.php?record_id=1189&page=R1

the views of various participants. And it may contribute generally to building trust in the process, with benefits for dealing with similar issues in the future.[23]

The process of identifying, discussing and dealing with ethical issues should be ongoing throughout the project and perhaps even after it has been implemented, if only because new ethical issues may arise that were not evident at the outset of the project development. Moor has made this point: "Because new technology allows us to perform activities in new ways, situations may arise in which we do not have adequate policies in place to guide us." Ethical problems can be generated at any point, says Moor, "but the number of ethical problems will be greater as the revolution progresses".[24]

The process of engaging stakeholders in consideration of ethical issues that may arise from the development of a new technology or the new use of an existing technology or a new policy or programme is arguably as important as the result. While stakeholders can make a substantial contribution to the decision-making process, at the end of the day, however, it is the policy-maker or technology developer who must take a decision whether to proceed with the technology or to modify it or to build some safeguards into its use in order to accommodate the concerns raised by stakeholders. It is the policy-maker or technology developer alone who will be held accountable for the decision.

Palm and Hansson caution that "the search for consensus in controversial issues should not be overemphasized since it may lead to the closure of issues at a too early stage. In ethical Technology Assessment, conflicts and different opinions should be highlighted rather than evened out." They also urge that the assessment "should seek to identify all relevant stakeholders, i.e., a broad spectrum of agents and therefore also a broad spectrum of responsibilities". They see the task of an ethical assessment as being "to delineate and analyze the issues and point out the alternative approaches for the final analysis that are available".[25]

Questions

Has the policy-maker or technology developer developed a process for identifying and considering ethical issues?

Will the project engage in consultations with stakeholders? If so, when?

Have all relevant stakeholders (i.e., those affected by or with an interest in the technology or project) been identified?

Have they been invited to participate in a consultation and/or to provide their views on the project or technology?

---

[23] Stern and Fineberg, op. cit., pp. 23–24.

[24] Moor, James H., "Why We Need Better Ethics for Emerging Technologies", *Ethics and Information Technology*, Vol. 7, 2005, pp. 111–119. In his paper, Moor proposes the following hypothesis, which he calls "Moor's Law: As technological revolutions increase their social impact, ethical problems increase."

[25] Palm and Hansson, pp. 550–551.

Is the process by means of which decisions are made clearly articulated to stakeholders?

Are stakeholders and citizens presented opportunities to raise concerns about values or non-technical impacts?

Will there be sufficient time for stakeholders to conduct any research which they may need to do in order to represent their views to the project manager (or technology developer or policy-maker, as the case may be)?

How will conflicting views of stakeholders be taken into account or resolved? Are some stakeholders (e.g., industry) given more weight than others (e.g., civil society organisations)?

Has the project manager made known to the public the options – and the pros and cons of each option – available with regard to the development or deployment of the project, technology, service, etc.?

Is there a process in place for considering ethical issues at later stages in the project or technology development that may not have been considered at the outset?

19.2.3 Accountability

The EU Data Protection Directive says the data controller should be accountable for complying with the principles stated in the Directive. In the development of new technologies and services, however, it may be increasingly problematic to ascribe accountability to any single individual or organisation. Many individuals and organisations may be involved in the development and deployment of different pieces of a technology or system or service. Vedder and Custers say this too: "Many of the actors and stakeholders involved only have a very restricted insight into the opportunities and risks involved. Moreover, many of them have restricted means to respond. For instance, engineers are involved in the first phases [of research and development], but have limited influence on the introduction of new technologies into the market/society. End users may have effect on how the new technologies are introduced into society and how the new technologies are actually used. However, end users have restricted means to influence research, development and production of new technologies."[26] Vedder and Custers argue that it is undesirable to assign all responsibilities to just one group of stakeholders. Instead, they argue in favour of "joint responsibilities". "Instead of creating gaps in the responsibilities, i.e., parts of the research and development process where nobody is responsible, this may create joint responsibilities. We consider overlapping responsibilities an advantage rather than a drawback in these cases."[27]

---

[26] Vedder, Anton, and Bart Custers, "Whose Responsibility Is It Anyway? Dealing with the Consequences of New Technologies", in Paul Sollie and Marcus Düwell (eds.), *Evaluating New Technologies*, Springer Science, Dordrecht, 2009, p. 30.

[27] Ibid., p. 32.

René von Schomberg also argues along these lines. He claims that the idea of role responsibility cannot be used any longer in the complex society in which we live. No one person has an overview of all consequences of a technological development and therefore he argues for an ethics of knowledge policy and knowledge assessment and says that citizens should be involved in the assessment and policy-making.[28]

Questions

Does the project make clear who will be responsible for any consequences of the project?

Who is responsible for identifying and addressing positive and negative consequences of the project or technology or service?

Does the project make clear where responsibility lies for liability, equality, property, privacy, autonomy, accountability, etc.?

Are there means for discovering violations and penalties to encourage responsible behaviour by those promoting or undertaking the project?

Is there a fair and just system for addressing project or technology failures with appropriate compensation to affected stakeholders?

19.2.4 Providing More Information, Responding to Complaints and Third Party Ethical Review

An important consideration in undertaking an ethical impact assessment is to provide (proactively) information to stakeholders. The results of an ethical impact assessment should be communicated as widely as possible. The choice and design of future technologies should not be restricted to a well-educated and articulated elite.[29] It is also important that the project manager respond to complaints about either the way the ethical assessment has been conducted or the way in which a particular ethical issue has been considered. The name and contact details of the person responsible for conduct of the ethical impact assessment should be made publicly available (for example, on the project manager's website). An ethical review and audit by a third party would ensure that an ethical impact assessment has been effectively carried out. A third-party review and/or an audit is a way of ensuring that responses to the questions are not merely perfunctory.

Questions

Has the project taken steps to provide information about the project to the public, not simply in response to requests, but proactively?

---

[28] von Schomberg, René, "From the Ethics of Technology Towards an Ethics of Knowledge Policy & Knowledge Assessment", Working document from the European Commission Services, January 2007.

[29] Palm and Hansson, p. 550.

What steps will the project manager take to make relevant information available to relevant stakeholders as soon as possible?

Are relevant stakeholders aware of the findings of ethical assessments and how they were generated?

Has the project instituted a procedure whereby persons can lodge complaints if they feel that they have been mistreated by the project?

Are there procedures for challenging the results, or for entering alternative data or interpretations into the record?

If an individual has been treated unfairly and procedures violated, are there appropriate means of redress?

If anyone objects to the project, does the project make clear whom they can contact to make known their objection?

Have the contact details been published or posted on the relevant website where a person may obtain further information about the ethical impact assessment?

Has the project, its objectives and procedures in regard to treatment of ethical issues been reviewed by independent evaluators to ensure that ethical issues have been adequately considered?

Has the decision-maker considered evaluation of the ethical impact assessment with a view to improving the process of conducting such an assessment?

19.2.5 Good Practice

Examples of good practice in ethical assessments may be strategically important from a policy point of view in the sense that they might encourage other organisations to undertake similar assessments, which might also be an objective of policy-makers. Examples of good practice are also practically important in that they provide guidance on how to undertake ethical assessments. The utility of good practices depends on how well information about such good practices is disseminated and how easy it is for project managers to find relevant good practices.

Questions

Would the project, technology or service be generally regarded as an example of ethical good practice?

Will the technology or project inspire public trust and confidence?

Have the designers or proponents of the project examined other relevant good practices?

19.3 Ethical Principles

The framework provided in this chapter is structured on a set of ethical principles which are followed by some brief explanatory text and a set of questions aimed at the technology developer or policy-maker to facilitate a consideration of the ethical issues which may arise in their undertaking. Values and issues are clustered together because of their relation to the overarching principles and because they may generate debate among stakeholders. For example, everyone would subscribe to the shared value of dignity, but dignity could also become an issue in particular contexts – i.e., does an emerging technology respect the dignity of the individual? Is dignity compromised?

The framework draws on various sources in compiling these questions. No doubt more issues and questions could be added and some of the questions could be framed differently and, if so, so be it. The issues and questions set out here should be regarded as indicative, rather than comprehensive.

19.3.1 Respect for Autonomy

Autonomy is a right enshrined in Article 6 of the European Charter of Fundamental Rights as well as Article 3 of the UN's Universal Declaration of Human Rights of 10 December 1948.[30] Autonomy encompasses two essential conditions: (1) liberty (independence from controlling influences) and (2) agency (capacity for intentional action). When assessing ethical impacts, autonomy cannot, however, be considered in an abstract and theoretical way; it has to be replaced in a "human society" context. Indeed, we can argue that only fictional agents are autonomous and that real-life people are dependent on several external and internal factors.

Questions

> Does the technology or project curtail a person's right to liberty and security in any way? If so, what measures could be taken to avoid such curtailment?
>
> Does the project recognise and respect the right of persons with disabilities to benefit from measures designed to ensure their independence, social and occupational integration and participation in the life of the community?
>
> Will the project use a technology to constrain a person or curtail their freedom of movement or association? If so, what is the justification?
>
> Does the person have a meaningful choice, i.e., are some alternatives so costly that they are not really viable alternatives? If not, what could be done to provide real choice?

19.3.2 Dignity

The idea of human dignity refers to the status of human beings that entitles them to respect and which has to be taken for granted. Protected by the most important international legal instruments as a fundamental human right, the definition of

---

[30] www.un.org/Overview/rights.html

dignity remains elusive, however, as it is a versatile concept that touches the inner and deeper spheres of the human condition.

Questions

Will the technology or project be developed and implemented in a way that recognises and respects the right of citizens to lead a life of dignity and independence and to participate in social and cultural life? If not, what changes can be made?

Is such a recognition explicitly articulated in statements to those involved in or affected by the project?

Does the technology compromise or violate human dignity? What measures can be put in place to minimise or avoid compromising human dignity?

Does the project require citizens to use a technology that marks them in some way as cognitively or physically disabled? If so, can the technology be designed in a way so that it does not make them stand out in a crowd?

Does the project or service or application involve implants? If so, does it accord with the opinion of the European Group on Ethics (EGE)?[31]

19.3.3 Informed Consent

Informed consent is addressed in Article 7 of the EU Data Protection Directive as follows: "Member States shall provide that personal data may be processed only if: (a) the data subject has unambiguously given his consent". Informed consent is given freely after the person is informed of the nature, significance, implications and risks of a given process, and is evidenced in writing, dated and signed, or otherwise marked, by that person so as to indicate his consent, or is given orally in the presence of at least one witness and recorded in writing.

Questions

Will the project obtain the free and informed consent of those persons to be involved in or affected by the project? If not, why not?

Will the person be informed of the nature, significance, implications and risks of the project technology?

Will such consent be evidenced in writing, dated and signed, or otherwise marked, by that person so as to indicate his consent?

---

[31] For ethical considerations re implants, see the European Group on Ethics in Science and New Technologies (EGE), Opinion No. 20 on Ethical Aspects of ICT Implants in the Human Body, Adopted on 16 March 2005.

If the person is unable to sign or to mark a document so as to indicate his consent, can his consent be given orally in the presence of at least one witness and recorded in writing?

Will people be made aware that personal data may be collected? And why?

Will consent be sought of the person whose data is to be collected?

Does the consent outline the use for which data are to be collected, how the data are to be collected, instructions on how to obtain a copy of the data, a description of the mechanism to correct any erroneous data, and details of who will have access to the data?

If the individual is not able to give informed consent (because, for example, the person suffers from dementia) to participate in a project or to use of a technology, will the project representatives consult with close relatives, a guardian with powers over the person's welfare or professional carers? Will written consent be obtained from the patient's legal representative and his doctor?

Will the person have an interview with a project representative in which he will be informed of the objectives, risks and inconveniences of the project or research activity and the conditions under which the project is to be conducted?

Will the project ensure that persons involved in the project give their informed consent, not only in relation to the aims of the project, but also in relation to the *process* of the research, i.e., how data will be collected and by whom, where it will be collected, and how the results are to be used?

Are persons involved in or affected by the project able to withdraw from the project *and* to withdraw their data at any time right up until publication?

Does the project or service collect information from children?

Is consent given truly voluntary? For example, does the person need to give consent in order to get a service to which there is no alternative?

Does the person have to deliberately and consciously opt out in order *not* to receive the "service"?

19.3.4 Justice

19.3.4.1 Equity and Fairness

The norm of justice is one of the most complex in ethics, even if we all have some intuitive sense of what the term means in our daily lives. As a commentator has pointed out:

Taken in its broader sense, justice is action in accordance with the requirements of some law. Some maintain that justice consists of rules common to all humanity that emerge out of some sort of consensus. This sort of justice is often thought of as something higher than a society's legal system.... In its narrower sense, justice is fairness. It is action that pays due regard to the proper interests, property and safety of one's fellows. While justice in the broader sense is often thought of as transcendental, justice as fairness is more context-bound. Parties concerned with fairness typically strive to work out something comfortable and adopt procedures that resemble rules of a game. They work to ensure that people receive their "fair share" of benefits and burdens and adhere to a system of "fair play".[32]

Questions

> Will the service or technology be made widely available or will it be restricted to only the wealthy, powerful or technologically sophisticated?[33]
>
> Does the project or policy apply to all people or only to those less powerful or unable to resist?
>
> If there are means of resisting the provision of personal information, are these means equally available or are they restricted to the most privileged?[34]
>
> Are there negative effects on those beyond the person involved in the project or trials and, if so, can they be adequately mediated?
>
> If persons are treated differently, is there a rationale for differential applications, which are clear and justifiable?
>
> Will any information gained be used in a way that could cause harm or disadvantage to the person to whom it pertains? For example, could an insurance company use the information to increase the premiums charged or to refuse cover?

19.4 Social Cohesion

19.4.1 Nonmaleficence (Avoiding Harm)

The principle of nonmaleficence asserts an obligation not to inflict harm on others. Rules of nonmaleficence, therefore, take the form of "Do not do X".[35] In the context of ICT applications, this principle can be useful to assess the ethical impact of a project in terms of safety, of isolation or substitution of human contact, and of discrimination and social sorting, thus going beyond what is purely stipulated in the criminal code. Under this broad principle, this framework includes several ethical values and issues, as follows.

19.4.1.1 Safety

Article 38 of the EU Charter of Fundamental Rights deals with consumer protection: "Union policies shall ensure a high level of consumer protection." It is the subject

---

[32] Maiese, Michelle, "Principles of Justice and Fairness", Beyond Intractability.org, July 2003. http://www.beyondintractability.org/essay/principles_of_justice/

[33] Marx, Gary T., "Ethics for the New Surveillance", *The Information Society*, Vol. 14, 1998, pp. 171–185 [p. 174].

[34] Marx, p. 174.

[35] Beauchamp, Tom L., and James F. Childress, *Principles of Biomedical Ethics* (5th ed.), Oxford University Press, New York, 2001, p. 113 and p. 115.

of Article 153 of the EC Treaty: "In order to promote the interests of consumers and to ensure a high level of consumer protection, the Community shall contribute to protecting the health, safety and economic interests of consumers, as well as to promoting their right to information, education and to organise themselves in order to safeguard their interests."

Questions

Does the technology or project affect consumer protection?

Is there any risk that the technology or project may cause any physical or psychological harm to consumers? If so, what measures can be adopted to avoid or mitigate the risk?

Have any independent studies already been carried out or, if not, are any planned which will address the safety of the technology or service or trials? If so, will they be made public?

To what extent is scientific or other objective evidence used in making decisions about specific products, processes or trials?

Will the project take any measures to ensure that persons involved in or affected by the project will be protected from harm in the sense that they will not be exposed to any risks other than those they might meet in normal everyday life?

Can the information be used in such a way as to cause unwarranted harm or disadvantage to a person or a group?

19.4.1.2 Isolation or Substitution of Human Contact

Isolation is the objective condition of having too few and too poor social ties, of not being in any relevant social network. New forms of communication help to alleviate, if not overcome, isolation. By the same token, however, new communication tools may become a substitution for face-to-face contact and could, thereby, make social isolation worse. Palm and Hansson rightly observe that "even if communication is facilitated, it is not self-evident that this will bring people together. There is a tendency for electronically mediated contacts to substitute face-to-face contacts."[36]

Questions

Will the project use a technology which could replace or substitute for human contact?

Is there a risk that a technology or service may lead to greater social isolation of individuals? If so, what measures could be adopted to avoid that?

---

[36] Palm and Hansson, p. 552.

19.4.1.3 Discrimination and Social Sorting

Article 21 of the European Charter of Fundamental Rights prohibits "Any discrimination based on any ground such as sex, race, colour, ethnic or social origin, genetic features, language, religion or belief, political or any other opinion, membership of a national minority, property, birth, disability, age or sexual orientation". Profiling technologies have raised a host of ethical, legal and other issues including privacy, equality, due process, security and liability. Profiling technologies make possible a far-reaching monitoring of an individual's behaviour and preferences and allow unparalleled kinds of social sorting[37] and segmentation which could have unfair effects.

Questions

Is there a risk that use of the technology will be seen as stigmatising, e.g., in distinguishing the user from other people?

Could the project be perceived as discriminating against any groups? If so, what measures could be taken to ensure this does not happen?

Does the project or service use profiling technologies?

Does the project or service facilitate social sorting?

Will some groups have to pay more for certain services (e.g., insurance) than other groups?

19.4.2 Beneficence

Principles of beneficence potentially demand more than the principle of nonmaleficence, because they refer not merely to "not harming" but to acting to benefit another person. We must, however, acknowledge practical limits to the principle of beneficence in regard to assessing a project or policy's ethical impact. Indeed, only projects stemming (directly or indirectly) from public authorities can be asked to comply with this principle in a certain respect (for instance, if those public authorities want to be re-elected); on the other hand, private operators are by no means accountable in the field of morality as a general trend in developing ICT applications. The principle of beneficence is thus to be considered as a somewhat idealistic guiding principle which encourages taking into consideration the following ethical values: universal service, accessibility, value sensitive design and social solidarity.

---

[37] Social sorting is a process of classifying people and populations according to varying criteria, to determine who should be targeted for special treatment, suspicion, eligibility, inclusion, access and so on. See Lyon, David (ed.), *Surveillance as Social Sorting: Privacy, Risk, and Digital Discrimination*, Routledge, London, 2003, p. 20.

Questions

Who benefits from the project and in what way?

Will the project improve personal safety, increase dignity, independence or a sense of freedom?

Does the project serve broad community goals and/or values or only the goals of the data collector?

What are the consequences of not proceeding with development of the project?

Does the project or technology or service facilitate the self-expression of users?

19.4.2.1 Universal Service

Universal service means an obligation imposed on one or more operators of electronic communications networks and/or services to provide a minimum set of services to all users, regardless of their geographical location within the national territory, at an affordable price.[38] Now the notion of universal service in Europe encompasses broadband and Internet access for all. The European Commission and various Member States have recognised that it makes economic and social sense to extend broadband Internet access to all citizens. It is also the ethically correct thing to do. They have made commitments with specific deadlines to achieving this objective.[39] Finland has recently made broadband access to the Internet a basic right.[40]

Questions

Will the project or service be made available to all citizens?

Will training be provided to those who do not (yet) have computer skills or knowledge of the Internet?

Will the service cost the same for users who live in remote or rural areas as for users who live in urban areas?

19.4.2.2 Accessibility

The accessibility (user-friendliness) of devices and services are prerequisites for the e-inclusion of citizens in the Information Society. Markets tend to overlook the

---

[38] Directive 2002/22/EC of the European Parliament and of the Council of 7 March 2002 on universal service and users' rights relating to electronic communications networks and services (Universal Service Directive), Official Journal L 108 of 24 April 2002.

[39] On 28 January 2009, the European Commission announced its aim to achieve 100 per cent high-speed Internet coverage for all citizens by 2010. See European Commission, "Commission earmarks €1bn for investment in broadband – Frequently Asked Questions", Press release, MEMO/09/35, Brussels, 28 January 2009. http://europa.eu/rapid/pressReleasesAction.do?reference=MEMO/09/35

[40] Johnson, Bobbie, "Finland Makes Broadband Access a Legal Right", *The Guardian*, 14 Oct 2009. http://www.guardian.co.uk/technology/2009/oct/14/finland-broadband

needs of disadvantaged people such as senior citizens and the disabled: there are few guidelines, voluntary or mandatory standards and related regulatory frameworks.[41] Others have said that commitment to accessibility is widespread throughout the ICT industry, that there is a strong willingness on the part of software and hardware vendors to create accessible products; however, vendors' ability to develop and deploy accessible products is held back by the need to comply with multiple standards. Thus, there needs to be greater convergence between the accessibility standards in force in different areas – such as Europe and the US – so that vendors can develop products that can be marketed and sold worldwide.[42]

Questions

Does the new technology or service or application expect a certain level of knowledge of computers and the Internet that some people may not have?

Could the technology or service be designed in a way that makes it accessible and easy to use for more people, e.g., senior citizens and/or citizens with disabilities?

Are some services being transferred to the Internet only, so that a service is effectively no longer available to people who do not (know how to) use computers or the Internet? What alternatives exist for such people?

19.4.2.3 Value Sensitive Design

Some experts have argued that technology is not neutral with respect to values. Among those that argue in favour of value sensitive design, Flanagan, Howe and Nissenbaum say that the design of technologies bears directly and systematically on the realisation, or suppression, of particular configurations of social, ethical and political values.[43] They also observe that "the values of members of a design team, even those who have not had a say in top level decisions, often shape a project in significant ways as it moves through the design process. Beliefs and commitments, and ethnic, economic, and disciplinary training and education, may frame their perspectives, preferences, and design tendencies, resulting eventually in features that affect the values embodied in particular systems."[44]

---

[41] European Commission, *Ageing well in the Information Society, Action Plan on Information and Communication Technologies and Ageing*, An i2010 Initiative, Communication from the Commission to the European Parliament, the Council, the European Economic and Social Committee and the Committee of the Regions, COM(2007) 332 final, Brussels, 14 June 2007.

[42] See the statement by Oracle, "Oracle Welcomes New EU Policy on e-Inclusion". http://www.oracle.com/global/eu/public-policy/fs/new-e-inclusion-policy.html

[43] Flanagan, Mary, Daniel C. Howe and Helen Nissenbaum, "Embodying Values in Technology: Theory and Practice", in Jeroen van den Hoven and John Weckert (eds.), *Information Technology and Moral Philosophy*, Cambridge University Press, Cambridge, 2008, pp. 322–353.

[44] Flanagan, et al., p. 335.

Questions

Is the project or technology or service being designed taking into account values such as human well-being, dignity, justice, welfare, human rights, trust, autonomy and privacy?

Have the technologists and engineers discussed their project with ethicists and other experts from the social sciences to ensure value sensitive design?

Does the new technology, service or application empower users?

19.4.3 Social Solidarity, Inclusion and Exclusion

The European Council's Lisbon Strategy adopted the notion of e-inclusion which "refers to the actions to realise an inclusive information society, that is, an information society for all".[45] To achieve this objective, which is a manifestation of the value of social solidarity, Europe must tackle the root causes of exclusion and e-exclusion. There are various reasons why some people are excluded from the Information Society, but cost and knowledge are among the principal ones.

Questions

Has the project taken any steps to reach out to the e-excluded (i.e., those excluded from use of the Internet)? If not, what steps (if any) could be taken?

Does the project or policy have any effects on the inclusion or exclusion of any groups?

Are there offline alternatives to online services?

Is there a wide range of perspectives and expertise involved in decision-making for the project?

How many and what kinds of opportunities do stakeholders and citizens have to raise value concerns with the project proponents?

19.4.4 Sustainability

Sustainability, as used here, refers to a condition whereby a project or service can be sustained, can continue into the future, either because it can generate the financial return necessary for doing so or that it has external support (e.g., government funding) which is not likely to go away in the foreseeable future. In addition to economic and social sustainability, more conventional understandings of sustainability should also be considered, i.e., decisions made today should be defensible in relation

---

[45] European Council, Resolution of 8 October 2001 on "e-Inclusion" – exploiting the opportunities of the information society for social inclusion, 2001/C 292/02, *Official Journal of the European Communities*, 18 October 2001. http://eur-lex.europa.eu/JOHtml.do?uri=OJ:C:2001:292:SOM:en: HTML

to coming generations and the depletion of natural resources. Often new technological products can be improved, for instance, through the use of more recyclable materials.[46]

Questions

> Is the project, technology or service economically or socially sustainable? If not, and if the technology or service or project appears to offer benefits, what could be done to make it sustainable?
>
> Will a service provided by means of a research project continue once the research funding comes to an end?
>
> Does the technology have obsolescence built in?
>
> Has the project manager or technology developer discussed their products with environmentalists with a view to determining how their products can be recycled or how their products can be designed to minimise impact on the environment?

19.5 Conclusions

This chapter has proposed an ethical impact assessment framework that could be used by those developing new technologies, services, projects, policies or programmes as a way to ensure that their ethical implications are adequately examined by stakeholders before possible deployment and so that mitigating measures can be taken as necessary.

It argues that an ethical impact assessment is needed of new and emerging technologies because technologies are not neutral, nor value free. Technologies, how they are configured and used, reflect the interests and values of their developers and owners. Over time, other stakeholders, including users, may become developers too by developing new applications for the technology or by adapting the technology for uses unforeseen when the technology was originally developed. These possibilities should be considered at the design stage. An ethical impact assessment is also needed because ethical considerations are often context-dependent. What may be ethically acceptable in one context may not be acceptable in another context.

It is in the interests of policy-makers, technology developers and project managers to conduct an ethical impact assessment involving stakeholders interested in or affected by the technology, as early in the development cycle as possible in order to minimise ethical risks that may arise once the technology is launched. In some sense, an ethical impact assessment, like a privacy impact assessment, can be regarded as a form of risk management – i.e., the purpose of conducting the exercise is to avoid any nasty fall-out from consumers or policy-makers who might feel that

---

[46] Palm and Hansson, p. 553. See also Anke van Gorp who also includes sustainability in his checklist of ethical issues and also in this sense. van Gorp, op. cit., p. 41.

the technology as implemented works to the detriment of generally accepted social values.[47]

The framework proposed here consists of a set of ethical principles, values and issues followed by a set of questions the aim of which is to facilitate ethical consideration of the new technology. The key to a successful ethical impact assessment is finding a way to engage stakeholders effectively. While some decision-makers may think engaging stakeholders is a hassle or risks delaying development, the benefits of engaging stakeholders are numerous and should outweigh any such thoughts. Stakeholders may have some information or ideas or views or values which the project manager had not previously considered. They may be able to suggest alternative courses of actions to achieve the desired objectives. They may be able to suggest some safeguards which would minimise the ethical risks that might otherwise explode after a technology or service is launched. By engaging stakeholders, the technology developer has a better chance of minimising liability. The sooner stakeholders are brought into the process, the better. It will avoid subsequent criticisms and, possibly, costly retrofits downstream.

While consulting and engaging stakeholders is important, ultimately in most cases the decision-maker – the technology developer or policy-maker – will need to take the final decision about whether or how to proceed. If he or she takes a decision at variance with the generally accepted ethical considerations of stakeholders, he or she may (will) need to explain his or her reasons for doing so.

The ethical impact assessment framework proposed here builds on work by other researchers and policy-makers. Even if the exact words – "ethical impact assessment" – have not yet gained currency, others have seen the need for something like it. Verbeek, for example, has emphasised that "Technologies are morally significant; they help human beings to do ethics, by informing our moral decisions and by giving shape to our actions. In order to deal adequately with the moral relevance of technology, therefore, the ethics of technology should broaden its scope. Rather than approaching ethics and technology as belonging to two radically separated domains, the interwoven character of both should be central".[48] Palm and Hansson have noted that new technologies often give rise to previously unknown ethical problems and argued in favour of a continuous dialogue and repeated assessments as preferable to one single large-scale assessment since moral implications may arise at all stages of technological development.[49] Furthermore, they add, "Predicting the future of a

---

[47] Verbeek indirectly offers at least two reasons supporting an ethical impact assessment. "Two forms of designer responsibility can be distinguished here. First, designers can anticipate the impact, side-effects and mediating roles of the technology they are designing. On the basis of such anticipations, they could adapt the original design, or refrain from the design at all. Second, designers can also take a more radical step and deliberately design technologies in terms of their mediating roles. In that case, they explicitly design behavior-influencing or 'moralizing' technologies: designers then inscribe desirable mediating effects in technologies." Verbeek, p. 70.

[48] Verbeek, op. cit.

[49] Palm and Hansson, op. cit., pp. 547–548, p. 550. Moor, 2005, p. 118, makes a similar point: "We can foresee only so far into the future... We cannot anticipate every ethical issue that will

technology is a vain undertaking with low chances of success. Ethical technology assessment should therefore avoid crystal ball ambitions. The ambition should not be to see as far as possible into the future, but to investigate continuously the ethical implications of what is known about the technology under development."

Building on the work of these and others, the framework proposed here offers a new and structured approach to assessing the ethical legitimacy of new technology. While models and methodologies exist for undertaking privacy impact assessments, environmental impact assessments, policy and programmatic impact assessments, technology assessments, regulatory impact assessments and so on, that has not been the case for ethical impact assessments. Furthermore, the framework can be applied not only to new and emerging technologies, but also to products, services, policies and programmes, indeed virtually any undertaking that is likely to raise ethical issues.

Although it has not been within the scope of this chapter, the authors believe there could be a case for integrating an ethical impact assessment and privacy impact assessment or, at least, conducting them concurrently.[50] Privacy and data protection raise ethical issues, although ethical impact assessment addresses issues beyond simply those of privacy and data protection. Nevertheless, there would seem to be value in further research exploring the possibility of developing an integrated privacy and ethical impact assessment.

---

arise from the developing technology... our ethical understanding of developing technology will never be complete. Nevertheless, we can do much to unpack the potential consequences of new technology. We have to do as much as we can while realizing applied ethics is a dynamic enterprise that continually requires reassessment of the situation."

[50] David Flaherty, the first Information and Privacy Commissioner for British Columbia and one of the PIA pioneers, suggested this: "A privacy impact assessment is a risk assessment tool for decision-makers that can address not only the legal, but also the moral and ethical, issues posed by whatever is being proposed." Flaherty, David, "Privacy Impact Assessments: An Essential Tool for Data Protection", *Privacy Law & Policy Reporter*, Vol. 7, No. 5, October 2000, pp. 85. http://www.austlii.edu.au/au/journals/PLPR/2000/#no5

Chapter 20
Auditing Privacy Impact Assessments: The Canadian Experience

Jennifer Stoddart

20.1 Introduction

In early 2007, the Office of the Privacy Commissioner of Canada (OPC) embarked on a project to measure the extent to which privacy issues arising from government operations were being appropriately managed. The audit, titled *Assessing the Privacy Impacts of Programs, Plans and Policies*,[1] was the first of its kind in Canada and, to the best of our knowledge, the only comprehensive evaluation of the implementation of privacy impact assessments (PIAs) worldwide. It was an important initiative, not only for its findings – many of which can be applied cross-jurisdictionally – but also for its salutary effects on PIA practices government-wide. While the primary objective of the audit was to assess compliance with the government's policy on PIAs, it has served as importantly to promote an understanding of PIAs as an effective risk management tool.

Canada is generally accepted as a leader in privacy impact assessment.[2] Within the general statutory regime governing privacy matters in the public sector, mainly the Canadian Charter of Rights and Freedoms[3] and the federal Privacy Act,[4] PIA remains the most comprehensive model in place to assess the effects of federal initiatives on an individual's privacy. Indeed, PIAs are mandated by government for all new or substantially modified programs involving the creation, collection and

---

[1] Office of the Privacy Commissioner of Canada, *Assessing the Privacy Impacts of Programs, Plans, and Policies*, Ottawa, October 2007 [PIA Audit]. www.privcom.gc.ca

[2] Information Commissioner's Office, *Privacy Impact Assessments: International Study of their Application and Effect,* Wilmslow, UK, October 2007. www.ico.gov.uk

[3] Canadian Charter of Rights and Freedoms, Part 1 of the Constitution Act, 1982, being Schedule B to the Canada Act 1982 (U.K.), 1982, c. 11 [Charter].

[4] Privacy Act, R.S.C. 1985, C. P-21.

J. Stoddart (✉)
Privacy Commissioner of Canada, Ottawa, ON, Canada
e-mail: Lindsay.Scotton@priv.gc.ca

D. Wright, P. De Hert (eds.), *Privacy Impact Assessment*, Law, Governance and Technology Series 6, DOI 10.1007/978-94-007-2543-0_20,
© Springer Science+Business Media B.V. 2012

handling of personal information.[5] As such, they have been – and continue to be – a core component of the federal government's privacy compliance regime.

Notwithstanding Canada's policy requirements, PIAs have not always been performed as and when required.[6] As recently as 2007, nearly 70% of federal government departments reported that they did not have a formal management framework in place to support the conduct of PIAs.[7] Despite the government's aim of ensuring that privacy protection was a key consideration in a project's initial framing, PIAs were often completed well after program implementation. In many cases, PIAs were not completed at all. What explains the paradox of seemingly strong privacy prescriptions and failing federal grades? Had the burden of privacy impact assessments become too great? What other models exist to better promote privacy analysis in the development and scoping of new initiatives involving personal information?

This chapter sets out to answer some of these questions by reference to the results of our audit of PIA practices in Canada. It is both a report on our audit observations – what we found – and an essay on the effects of our review – what we feel has been accomplished. We begin by reviewing the most important findings from our audit. Herein, we share some of the measurement tools we employed in assessing the quality of PIA practices within the Canadian federal government. Next, we revisit some of our key policy recommendations. This section is intended to assist other jurisdictions involved in the development of PIA regimes with lessons learned from Canada. We conclude by reflecting upon the most important outcomes of our audit: better PIA practices, shared insight and expectations regarding PIA outcomes, and greater compliance with what is required. Throughout the chapter, we hope to impress upon the reader the value of audit, not just as an instrument for privacy enforcement, but also as a means of shaping the personal information-handling practices of organisations involved in potentially privacy intrusive programs.

---

[5] The purpose of the audit was to assess the government of Canada's implementation of the 2002 PIA policy. See Treasury Board of Canada Secretariat, Privacy Impact Assessment Policy, Ottawa, May 2002 [PIA Policy]. That policy has since been replaced by an overarching policy on privacy protection. See Treasury Board of Canada Secretariat, Policy on Privacy Protection, Ottawa, April 2008, and Treasury Board of Canada Secretariat, Directive on Privacy Impact Assessment, Ottawa, April 2010 [PIA Directive]. www.tbs-sct.gc.ca

[6] See PIA Audit, *supra* fn. 1 at ¶ 1.1.

[7] Ibid. at ¶ 1.36.

20.2 Supporting the Performance of PIAs

In 2002, the government of Canada introduced a formal policy on privacy impact assessments.[8] Although similar PIA requirements existed at the time provincially,[9] the 2002 Privacy Impact Assessment Policy was the first of its kind involving the federal government. The policy was instituted to assure Canadians that their privacy would be taken into account in the development of all new programs and services involving personal information. In addition to stipulating that PIAs be undertaken and regularly updated, the policy required federal departments to communicate the results of PIAs to both the Privacy Commissioner of Canada and the public. As an Officer of Parliament, the OPC would examine the collection, use and disclosure of personal information by federal institutions, and provide advice (where necessary) with respect to potential privacy risks emanating from new projects – a function the Office continues to perform to this day.

Notwithstanding the role of the Privacy Commissioner in the review of PIAs, accountability for privacy compliance rests squarely with the heads of federal institutions. Within departments, that responsibility is often shared. In most cases, the requirement to develop and maintain PIAs is delegated to a team of professionals, mainly program managers, policy experts, legal advisors and functional specialists. Access to information and privacy (ATIP) personnel also play a critical role in the initiation, review and approval of PIAs, though their involvement is not always well defined. While it is within the mandate of OPC as guardian of Canadian privacy rights to provide recommendations on the privacy impacts of government initiatives, Canada's Treasury Board Secretariat (TBS) is responsible for interpreting government policies, for providing advice to institutions where necessary on policy matters and for monitoring compliance with those policies.

Our audit was completed in October of 2007 – roughly five years following the government's introduction of the PIA policy.[10] The principal focus of the audit was to evaluate federal privacy impact assessment practices and, by extension, adherence to the Privacy Act. While we expected government institutions to have faced early challenges in introducing the policy, we were surprised by how little progress had been made with respect to its implementation. While a few institutions had made serious efforts to apply the policy, many were just beginning to implement the management frameworks required to support PIAs. Although we did not identify instances of pervasive non-compliance in any one department, government institutions were not, by and large, fully meeting their policy obligations. In spirit, the privacy impact assessment process sought to ensure that privacy matters would be considered at program conception or design and that risks identified would be

---

[8] See PIA Policy, *supra* fn. 5.

[9] PIA guidelines were introduced in Ontario, Alberta and British Columbia beginning as early as 1999. See Clarke, Roger, "Privacy Impact Assessment: Its Origin and Development", *Computer Law & Security Review*, Vol. 25, No. 2, April 2009, pp. 123–135 [p. 123].

[10] PIA Audit, *supra* fn. 1 at ¶ 1.23.

mitigated prior to program implementation. In reality, however, application of the policy was far from complete.

In assessing a department's PIA practices, we focused our enquiries on the main responsibilities of institutions under the policy. What we discovered was that, while government institutions were slowly beginning to incorporate some privacy analysis into their overall risk management frameworks, still more effort was required to ensure that the policy was having its desired effect – that is, to promote an awareness and understanding of the privacy implications associated with program deliveries at the time of their conception. The degree of failure to implement the policy varied from institution to institution, but the reasons for such failures could often be traced to one of two root causes: the absence of a privacy management framework to support the completion of PIAs or the absence of key control elements therein. We turn to each of these fundamental issues next.

20.2.1 PIAs Are Only as Good as the Processes That Support Them

How an organisation manages the privacy issues arising from its operations is often a function of the administrative infrastructure it has in place to support and guide the production of PIAs. The absence of any such a framework – or control deficiencies within such a process, where one exists – is likely to have a direct and measurable influence on the effectiveness and quality of PIAs. Once privacy is understood as a strategic variable for organisations, the need to factor privacy analysis into the management of organisational risk becomes increasingly compelling for program managers. Indeed, the TBS requirement for departmental compliance with the government's 2002 Privacy Impact Assessment Policy presupposed the existence of an administrative framework to support the policy's objectives and requirements.[11]

Recognising the importance of a sound administrative infrastructure for PIAs, we considered what such an infrastructure might look like. We studied and compared the PIA infrastructures of nine large departments, all of which were actively involved in the handling of personal information.[12] We also envisioned what an ideal infrastructure might look like. Figure 20.1 provides the outline of a generic process for conducting PIAs, as well as some of the key control elements one might expect to find therein. An optimal model would help encourage and support privacy analysis by establishing clear lines of accountability for PIAs within the organisation; enabling training and awareness programs for program managers involved in PIAs; supporting the development and implementation of a system to track all proposals subject to PIA; and establishing quality control and performance measures for PIAs.

The strength and effectiveness of such an infrastructure is likely to be limited by the human and financial resources in place to support it. Without serious senior

---

[11] See Treasury Board of Canada Secretariat, *Privacy Impact Assessment Audit Guide*, Treasury Board of Canada Secretariat, Ottawa: May 2004. http://www.tbs-sct.gc.ca/pgol-pged/guide/guide-eng.asp

[12] See PIA Audit, *supra* fn. 1 at ¶ 1.25 for a list of audit entities.

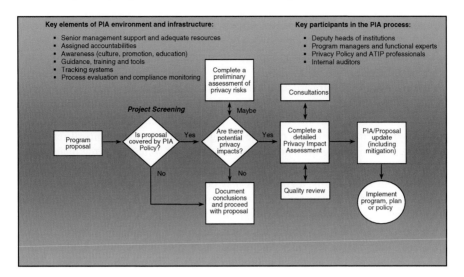

Fig. 20.1   Key elements of a generic privacy impact assessment process

management support, a PIA infrastructure will be difficult to create and sustain. Indeed, the appointment of a privacy leader within the process is often central to privacy accountability and control. Instituting formally defined privacy responsibilities – whether with ATIP staff or with program officials – ensures greater accountability for the management of privacy issues throughout an organisation. It also provides program leaders with the operational clout required to challenge new initiatives where known privacy impacts might have potential operational consequences.

Amongst entities with relatively well defined PIA environments, we observed one of two recurring approaches to privacy and PIA management. In the first case (which may be referred to as a centralised model), privacy or PIA experts within the entity's ATIP unit acted as promoters, educators, advocates and ultimately the compliance authority within the privacy impact assessment process. In the second case (a more decentralised model), the role of ATIP staff is restricted to that of a consultant, who offers advice and guidance only when called upon. In the latter model, all control over the initiation and completion of PIAs rests with program managers.

Although there appear to be operational advantages to each approach, the centralised model seemed to have had much more success in bringing about a general awareness of the policy requirements and in soliciting the support of senior management for PIAs. In many cases, the decentralised model was characterised by the absence of dedicated professionals on PIA teams, often leading to less insightful privacy analysis or a greater reliance on external consultants. Given that federal institutions are different in program and operational structure, it would be difficult to develop or implement any one common model or single administrative framework that would best support PIAs across government. Ideally, however, an organisation's

PIA process should reflect the nature of its operations. While responsibilities within the PIA process may be shared between program managers and privacy professionals, the responsibilities of each group should be clearly defined, well understood and properly enforced.

Inasmuch as PIA infrastructures vary from organisation to organisation, measuring the effectiveness of an entity's infrastructure for the production and support of PIAs can also be difficult. While our experience indicates that a strong process produces good quality PIAs, a premise strongly upheld by the empirical results of our audit,[13] the opposite does not always hold true. In some cases, the quality of a PIA (or its initiation) is dependent on the knowledge and motivation of individual employees. In other words, a good PIA may occasionally result from the dedicated efforts of a single privacy practitioner, working in the absence of any administrative support and with little oversight and control.[14]

In order to establish an objective benchmark for the evaluation of PIA infrastructures within federal departments, we considered both the procedural attributes of such structures as well as their product outputs. In evaluating the procedural attributes of federal infrastructures for PIAs, we looked to the development of a PIA process maturity model.[15] Derived from the Control Objectives for Information and related Technology (COBIT)[16] – and validated against the attributes of an effective administrative infrastructure previously described – the model identified five progressive maturity levels against which entities could be objectively measured.

Five years after the PIA policy's implementation, the PIA environments of most federal departments remained more or less in infancy.[17] Of the nine entities we examined as part of our audit, only three entities had what we would describe as a "well managed and measurable" PIA environment (level 4). In contrast, four of the nine entities examined had PIA processes that we considered largely "ad hoc" or "recognised but intuitive" (levels 1 and 2). The remaining two entities best fit into level 3, a "defined PIA process", having formally introduced PIA guidelines into their overall operations, but lacking adequate controls and oversight. These results were generally consistent with the information we collected as part of our broader audit survey.

---

[13] See PIA Audit, *supra* fn. 1 at ¶ 1.57 ff.

[14] For obvious reasons, this practice is far from ideal. The departure of that employee results in the effective dismantling of the organisation's PIA "process" (at least until his or her replacement by an employee of the same skill and dedication). Likewise, while sound privacy analysis may result from the outsourcing of PIAs to privacy experts, this too is less than sustainable, albeit from a cost management point of view.

[15] See PIA Audit Report, *supra* fn. 1, Exhibit C at p. 13. See also the draft American Institute of Certified Public Accountants and Canadian Institute of Chartered Accountants (AICPA/CICA), Privacy Maturity Model, AICPA/CICA, New York and Toronto, October 2010. www.cica.ca/service-and-products/privacy

[16] See Information Systems Audit and Control Association (ISACA), *COBIT 4.1*, IT Governance Institute, Rolling Meadows, IL, 2008.

[17] See PIA Audit Report, *supra* fn. 1 at ¶ 1.35.

In addition to the detailed audit work conducted on the nine entities referred to above, we conducted a survey of 47 additional institutions subject to the PIA Policy and Privacy Act, asking each to self-assess against the same four evaluation criteria used in our primary review. Of the 47 federal institutions we polled as part of our audit, 89% of respondents indicated that they were actively using personal information in the delivery of programs and services. Yet when asked if the organisation had a formal management framework in place to support the conduct of PIAs, 68% of respondents said no. More notably, 29% of respondents self-assessed at level 1 (initial/ad hoc) on the PIA process maturity model, and 54% self-assessed at level 2 (recognised but intuitive). Only one organisation within our sample self-assessed as having reached a "fully optimised PIA process" (level 5).[18]

Factors contributing to these seemingly failing grades varied as much as the PIA processes we examined. In some cases, departments simply lacked the resources and senior management support to create the infrastructures needed to sustain PIAs. In other cases, the absence of clear lines of accountability for privacy within the organisation precluded the development of a privacy framework around which a PIA process could coalesce. Notwithstanding these differences, we did note several recurring influences in the development of PIA infrastructures. Generally speaking, organisations with strong cultures of confidentiality and an entrenched awareness of privacy issues were more likely to have mature processes for managing the conduct of PIAs.[19] In contrast, those organisations with less sensitivity to the protection of the personal information of their clients tended to have less mature PIA processes. Similarly, entities which had been subject to audit or public scrutiny of their personal information handling practices were also more likely to have conducted internal reviews of their PIA infrastructures aimed at process amelioration. This last finding, we believe, underscores the importance of internal oversight in the conduct of PIAs. Absent appropriate and operational management controls, PIA infrastructures are unlikely to operate as intended.

20.2.2 Frameworks Lacking Critical Control Elements Are More Likely to Fail

So far, this chapter has sought to emphasise the importance of having an administrative infrastructure to support and guide the performance of PIAs. The absence of such an infrastructure, we believe, is likely to have a direct and measurable effect on the privacy analysis emanating from an organisation's operations. Yet simply having a process to manage and support PIAs is often insufficient in ensuring that PIAs are conducted when they should be. Process deficiencies (or the absence of key controls within a PIA infrastructure) often affect the timing of privacy impact assessments, as well as the extent to which privacy risks identified within a PIA are

---

[18] See PIA Audit Report, *supra* fn. 1 at ¶ 1.36.

[19] Ibid. at p. 13.

fully mitigated. The following section examines in greater detail what we found to be three essential control mechanisms for all PIA infrastructures – the initiation, tracking and monitoring of PIAs.

The most common control weakness we identified during our audit was the absence of a regimented screening process to identify potential PIA candidates.[20] Simply put, in order to ensure that PIAs are performed when they should be, an organisation must be aware of the conditions under which a PIA is required, and thereafter have a process in place to initiate a PIA if and when those conditions are met. We might understand such a process as a circuit-breaker of sorts which, once tripped, precipitates the performance of a PIA. Of course, simply instituting a policy which requires a PIA for all projects involving personal information is rarely enough. Such a policy must somehow be made operational.

Of the nine federal entities we audited, fewer than half had mechanisms in place to ensure that a PIA would be conducted for all new initiatives involving personal information.[21] Of those, only one seemed to be operating as intended. Likewise, of the 47 additional federal institutions we surveyed, 64% indicated that they did not have processes in place to identify all activities requiring privacy impact assessment (notwithstanding the requirement to conduct PIAs under government policy).[22] The absence of such a screening process – in essence, the trigger point for any privacy analysis – precluded entities from properly assessing the extent to which privacy risks were associated with a proposal. Absent a formal mechanism to evaluate PIA requirements, government institutions were also able to circumvent the government's policy requirements, deliberately or otherwise, without serious consequence. Indeed, the absence (or poor design) of such a control contributed to the vast majority of PIA omissions we identified as part of our audit. In most cases, these omissions went wholly unnoticed by the heads of institutions as well as by those responsible for privacy compliance.

A Treasury Board submission is an official document submitted by a Minister on behalf of the department to seek approval or authority from Treasury Board to carry out a proposal not covered within the institution's operational budget and requiring extra funding.[23] A submission is also required for approval of Orders in Council that have resource or management implications. This means that federal departments in Canada generally require approval from TBS to carry out major projects or initiatives – certainly those whose costs are expected to exceed a department's delegated authority. As part of the standard Treasury Board submission process, government institutions are required to consider the need for privacy and to reference the results of a PIA report to TBS prior to project funding.[24]

---

[20] See PIA Audit Report, *supra* fn. 1 at ¶ 1.43.

[21] Ibid.

[22] Ibid.

[23] Treasury Board of Canada Secretariat, A Guide to Preparing Treasury Board Submissions, Ottawa, December 2007, p. 73. http://www.tbs-sct.gc.ca/pubs_pol/opepubs/tbm_162/gptbs-gppct-eng.asp

[24] Ibid.

While linking PIA conditions to project funding is intended to serve as a critical external control in enforcing privacy analysis for project proposals, it would be far more effective if the screening of potential PIA candidates were to be more fully integrated into an institution's operational and program planning. Although the PIA requirements associated with a TBS submission help to ensure that major unfunded proposals do not proceed without consideration of potential privacy impacts, the submission process does not provide sufficient coverage over program changes (or the various micro-initiatives often undertaken within larger approved programs). Yet these smaller initiatives or program changes, particularly when combined, might have serious privacy impacts and should therefore have been considered as potential PIA candidates.

Given the inherent complexities of assessing the need for privacy impact assessments within departments, we were convinced that project screening should be viewed as a process in and of itself. A strong screening process would include an ongoing employee awareness program, effectively raising the profile of PIAs and regulatory requirements for their performance with program managers and new hires. An organisation might also look to create and embed administrative linkages between privacy impact assessments and other risk mitigation tools. Here we could imagine the integration of IT threat and risk assessments (TRAs) or other business case documents with a requirement to complete a PIA under certain specified conditions. When one is performed, so is the other. Finally, an organisation might wish to consider the implementation of cross-functional authorities for program approval. This might mean mandating the approval of a privacy head for projects involving personal information or instituting a requirement for their sign-off where a program authority believes that a PIA is not required. All in all, and when combined, these components may prove to be effective instruments in identifying projects that require privacy analysis.

Once adequate systems are in place to trigger the performance of a PIA, there is a need to track and monitor programs with potential privacy impacts. The use of a centralised tracking system for programs involving the use of personal information may assist an organisation in monitoring PIA activities department-wide, and in assessing whether or not it has correctly identified all PIA candidates. Notwithstanding our discovery of PIA omissions in selected federal departments, we were unable to measure the full extent to which privacy impact assessments had not been completed when required. Although we found anecdotal evidence to suggest that the number of omissions was minor in comparison to the total number of government initiatives involving personal information,[25] none of the federal departments we audited had systems in place to track instances where PIAs were required. Although many institutions began introducing such systems over the course of our audit (and/or began

---

[25] In particular, we noted that PIAs had been submitted to the OPC for review for nearly all major crown projects, and noted that instances of omission had declined considerably since the introduction of management control frameworks for PIAs within government institutions. The Treasury Board submission process also provided some assurance that large or extraordinary projects would have been subjected to privacy consideration prior to project funding.

gathering the baseline data required to populate such a system), we believe that the existence of a program repository within departments would have yielded important information regarding potential PIA omissions.[26] They would also serve as an indicator of potential privacy risks associated with programs already in place.

Our audit also considered the potential benefits of a publicly available program inventory of PIAs. In our discussion on alternative PIA governance models, we asked TBS to consider the need for a central database or registry of privacy impact assessments.[27] Its purpose would be to provide a single window of access to PIAs (and thus privacy intrusive projects) across government, regardless of the originating department and program authority. The registry could be used by the public to better understand the substance of government projects and by central agencies such as the Treasury Board Secretariat and the Privacy Commissioner to monitor PIA activities. Such a registry, we believe, might also have enhanced the project management capabilities of institutions and facilitated knowledge sharing between government departments.[28]

Ensuring that PIAs are performed when they should be is as much of a challenge as ensuring that privacy risks identified within PIAs are properly managed. Our audit methodology examined a sample of completed PIAs to assess the extent to which risk mitigation plans, including OPC recommendations, had been implemented. The results of our work indicated that institutions were generally slow in addressing privacy risks associated with new programs and services.[29] Although the majority of what we considered to be "high risk" issues in our sample appeared to be addressed prior to program implementation (or in a reasonable time period thereafter where PIAs were completed post project implementation), a substantial number of issues – qualified by departments themselves as "medium risk" – remained outstanding up to, and in some cases well after, programs were put into place. Some issues marked "high risk" remained similarly outstanding, and departmental progress in addressing such matters was generally unsatisfactory at the time of our review.

Without underestimating the magnitude and complexity of most federal initiatives, or the fact that many recommendations require significant time and investment

---

[26] Our audit revealed that, in some cases, PIAs were not submitted to the Commissioner in a manner which would allow for the provision of advice, if any, to the heads of institutions prior to program or service implementation. The absence of timely notification had a significant impact on the intended monitoring and compliance regime for PIAs government-wide.

[27] See especially PIA Audit Report, *supra* fn. 1 at ¶ 1.103 through 1.112.

[28] The concept of a central index is currently in use in Canada by federal institutions for strategic environmental assessment. The Canadian Environmental Assessment Registry was established in October 2003 pursuant to subsection 55(1) of the Canadian Environmental Act, R.S.C. 1992, c. 37 C-15, to help the public find information related to current environmental assessments conducted by the federal government. www.ceaa.gc.ca

[29] PIA Audit Report, *supra* fn. 1 at ¶ 1.65.

to fully address, institutions did not appear to be actively monitoring the implementation of PIA observations. In some cases, the failure to address known privacy risks left departments and the public open to serious potential harm. Despite the fact that the government's PIA policy encouraged departments to review the implementation of PIA recommendations, we found few objective evaluations conducted by independent investigators.

Whereas ATIP personnel appeared to be assuming some responsibility in the oversight of PIA activities, evidence suggested the use of internal audit resources was likely more effective at enhancing institutional control and oversight over PIA activities. As part of our audit recommendations, we encouraged the internal audit branches of federal institutions to include privacy and PIA related reviews in their plans and priorities for the future. In our view, the conduct of internal audits on privacy management and personal information handling practices is likely to yield significant gains in institutional privacy protection. PIAs are rendered truly effective only when their recommendations are implemented.

20.3 Improving PIA Processes

Until now, this chapter has focused on matters of mostly operational importance: the absence of administrative infrastructures to support PIAs and critical control weaknesses therein. Although the government of Canada's PIA policy had begun to have its desired effect of promoting an understanding of the privacy implications associated with program and service deliveries five years after its introduction, we would have expected departments to be further along in the performance of PIAs at the time of our review. Notwithstanding the importance of issues previously identified, we believe there were a number of other factors contributing to the performance gap.

The following section builds upon the operational issues previously identified with a discussion on matters of PIA policy. Despite Canada's leading presence in the performance of PIAs, we believe that the federal government's privacy impact assessment regime could be improved. The discussion focuses on four primary recommendations derived from our 2007 audit report:

- first, the need for greater integration of PIAs with other regulatory risk management tools;
- second, the streamlining of regulatory requirements so as to ensure that privacy analysis remains commensurate with privacy risks;
- third, the need for strategic and cumulative privacy impact assessment;
- fourth, the importance of enhancing the public reporting requirements for PIAs.

Although these recommendations stem from challenges in Canada's PIA process, they may be just as salient to other jurisdictions involved in the introduction or update of PIA policies and guidelines.

20.3.1 PIAs Should Be Integrated with Other Risk Management Processes

We found that PIAs were viewed as a regulatory obligation independent of an entity's program responsibilities, rather than the sort of specialised and integrated risk management tool they were designed to be. Privacy impact assessments were rarely integrated into the risk management strategies of organisations involved in the handling of personal information. Although we noted the development of formal linkages between privacy professionals and other operations over the course of our audit – most notably in the area of information technology – the government institutions we audited generally viewed PIAs as an administrative burden, to be completed *ex post facto*, rather than in the planning stages of new program and service deliveries.[30]

In order to better encourage the early consideration of privacy risks, we believe there is a need to integrate PIA practices with an organisation's overall approach to risk management. This occurs not only at an operational level – that is, through the PIA triggers or screening devices previously discussed – but by linking existing regulatory requirements with other program activities and their administrative processes. Ideally, senior managers should be using privacy impact assessment, in conjunction with other social and economic analyses, to influence the subsequent development of programs, services, plans and policies. And where privacy impact assessment can be linked to a statutory requirement (irrespective of whether PIAs are made mandatory by law), there is a greater likelihood that they will be employed as a risk management tool prior to a program's deployment. While this is more likely to occur once an organisation deems personal information and privacy as a strategic variable, its importance may be imposed through the integration of PIAs with other operational requirements.

20.3.2 PIA Requirements Need To Be Streamlined

We recommended that the level of effort required of a PIA should be commensurate with the level of privacy risk associated with the program. If PIAs are sometimes performed as an afterthought to program development, it is perhaps in part due to the level of effort required to complete them. Notwithstanding our primary concern for privacy, it stands as a perfectly reasonable contention that conducting a PIA unnecessarily can be a poor use of scarce resources. Likewise, a requirement for institutions to undertake an elaborate privacy analysis for projects of minute risk would not be sensible. That being said, it can be very costly for a public body to uncover privacy risks late in the development or introduction of a project.[31] Indeed,

---

[30] PIA Audit Report, *supra* fn. 1 at ¶ 1.84.

[31] The consequences of poor privacy planning were illustrated in the OPC's 1999–2000 Annual Report with respect to Canada's Longitudinal Labour Force File, a massive information databank

an institution's failure to properly evaluate and mitigate privacy concerns can result in expensive program redesign. In light of the significant resources required to conduct a PIA, and the shortages of such resources across most institutions, there is a need to consider how best to ensure that privacy analysis continues to be conducted while minimising the draw on program and privacy professionals.

In our opinion, PIAs should begin with a preliminary evaluation of risks in order to determine whether or not a full privacy impact assessment is necessary. The same inquiry would also assist in determining the level of effort that ought to be expended in conducting any privacy analysis that ensues. The preliminary analysis of privacy risks would not be time wasted – where a PIA is determined to be unnecessary, the completion of a preliminary assessment of risks would provide the basis and support for proceeding with the project without a PIA. And where a PIA is required, the preliminary assessment could form part of an entity's privacy impact assessment.

One might conceive of such a process as a project gating tool, asking institutions to determine the extent to which a project under consideration is privacy intrusive based on their consideration of a variety of program attributes. A preliminary assessment would consider the overall level of privacy risk emanating from a project by considering a multitude of factors: Is the nature of the activity to be undertaken inherently privacy intrusive? Does the program involve privacy intrusive technologies? Is the data to be collected or used particularly sensitive? Does the program involve project partners who may operate outside the institution's own privacy and statutory framework? The preliminary assessment might also consider public perceptions to the planned program. It might even allow for public bodies to evaluate the capacity of their own administrative infrastructures (or privacy management frameworks) to mitigate the privacy concerns associated with particularly low-risk projects.

Notwithstanding the merits of a gated approach to PIAs, one might conceive of other means of ensuring that the work associated with a PIA remains commensurate with the privacy risks associated with a program. For some jurisdictions, it may be worth considering the implementation of an alternative privacy assessment tool. One might call such an alternative a "privacy review", intended for smaller projects where full PIAs are not economically viable or timely. Whereas this process would not preclude or replace the use of PIAs, they might be used to streamline the administrative requirements of PIAs, balancing the need for some privacy analysis

---

linking information from two federal departments along with provincial and territorial governments. The combination of huge personal databases, powerful computer systems, and growing links with provincial social programs and the private sector created significant privacy concerns. The government's failure to properly evaluate and mitigate such concerns, and to anticipate public reaction to the program, eventually led to the dismantling of the system. See Office of the Privacy Commissioner of Canada, "A Citizen Profile in all but Name—HRDC's Longitudinal Labour Force File", in *Annual Report to Parliament,* Cat. No. IP 30-1/2000, Minister of Public Works and Government Services Canada, Ottawa, 2000, p. 64.

at program conception with other important operational considerations.[32] In other cases, as with shared services or system initiatives where entities use the same or similar approaches to the collection, use and disclosure of personal information, generic assessments might be better employed.[33] Whether jurisdictions introduce scalable PIAs through the introduction of a project gating tool or create alternative and perhaps simplified privacy instruments as alternatives to PIAs, a preliminary process that guides PIA policy requirements (and the risk management strategies which follow) is likely to go a long way in streamlining the reporting requirements surrounding present-day PIAs.

20.4 Need for Strategic Privacy Impact Assessment

At the time of our audit, PIAs in Canada were performed on a project-by-project basis. Little, if any, thought was given to the cumulative and strategic impacts on an individual's privacy by the combination or aggregation of government programs. As such, the privacy analysis emerging from PIAs could at times be rather myopic. Ignoring Orwellian warnings of the intrusive state, few managers ever raised concerns about the long-term changes that were occurring to an individual's privacy from the combined effects of each successive and interdependent government intervention. Indeed, the incremental effects on the integrity of personal information are often significant from a privacy point of view even when the effects of each successive action, independently assessed, are considered insignificant. Despite the benefits of a program-by-program analysis of privacy risks, we believe that there is a serious need to deal with the broader privacy implications of plans and policies, particularly those that may not be easily addressed at a project or service level.

Over the past several years in Canada, we have witnessed the federal government embark on several programs with potentially serious effects on the public's privacy (for example: the Government On-line initiative, the Smart Border Accord, the creation of a "no-fly" list and the establishment of a single point of service kiosk for federal social services, to name but a few). Due to the magnitude of these initiatives, their implementation necessitated an analysis of their combined risks to privacy. While there have been specific privacy impact assessments done by departments on each initiative, there has been no privacy analysis of the overall effects on an individual's privacy.

---

[32] While ideally a PIA would be used as a tool to guide program development, in our view, a PIA report that is issued soon after a project's implementation, and which adequately explains how all privacy risks were identified and mitigated, is likely better than a report which is produced "in time" but which fails to do the same.

[33] Enterprise resource planning (ERP) and standardised records management systems (RDMS) are examples of likely candidates for generic privacy impact assessments, where PIAs can be performed for multiple project deployments involving similar or the same technology (albeit with some customisation).

Although the Office of the Privacy Commissioner, through appearances before parliamentary committees and consultations with government institutions, makes best efforts to comment on large and potentially privacy-invasive programs early in the legislative process, it is often too late when a bill has been introduced into the House of Commons to rethink approaches to information issues. In our view, the public interest would be better served by engaging privacy professionals earlier on in the process and by providing institutions with more time to respond to privacy concerns. What is needed is a strategic assessment of privacy risks that seeks to balance planned program benefits against the erosion of an individual's privacy rights.

Knowing the potential privacy impacts of proposed policies and plans would provide parliamentarians and senior federal executives with an early opportunity to adjust or modify programs to protect the personal information of Canadians. An early intervention on their part might also reduce any future costs associated with program changes. In the absence of a strategic privacy impact assessment tool, we believe the government's privacy policy suite falls short of meeting its promise in guiding policy, planning and program development. Although the assessment of cumulative privacy impacts presents some inherent difficulties, the committee structures employed by many institutions to review PIAs presents an ideal setting in which to begin engaging in inter-departmental consultations. We would note that the assessment of cumulative effects is already seen as representing good practice in conducting environmental assessments, and is now required in federal legislation when an action is subject to review under the Canadian Environmental Assessment Act.

20.5   Enhancing Public Reporting Requirements to Improve PIAs

Enhancing the transparency of the privacy impact assessment process is critical to improving the quality of privacy analysis in government. Greater scrutiny generated by public exposure can prompt greater care in the preparation of PIAs and provide Parliament and the public with the necessary information to inform debates concerning privacy protection. Public disclosure may also provide additional assurance that privacy impacts are being appropriately considered in the development of programs, plans and policies – essentially holding each institution to public account for the adequacy of the privacy analysis that was undertaken.

Canada's Privacy Act requires that federal institutions identify and make public an index of all personal information under their control used or available for use for administrative purposes.[34] This means providing current and comprehensive descriptions of all personal information holdings in the annual federal report, InfoSource. To complement this requirement, and to promote a broader

---

[34] See subsection 10(1) of the Privacy Act.

understanding of how privacy issues related to government programs and services have been addressed, institutions were also required, under the 2002 policy, to make summaries of the results of their PIAs available to the public. These publishing requirements provide institutions with the opportunity to highlight challenges encountered and accomplishments achieved in managing the privacy risks associated with new programs, in effect, providing a window for citizens into the privacy practices of government.

Whereas improved public reporting can be a constructive tool for organisational development and the enhancement of internal privacy practices, poor public reporting may have a profoundly damaging effect on the trust of individuals in their government. At the time of our review, only a minority of the institutions we audited were regularly posting and updating the results of PIA reports to their external web sites.[35] Of the nine entities audited, only four had made PIA summaries publicly available. Worse, in all but one of those four cases, the inventory of summaries available to the public was incomplete. Similarly, of the 47 federal institutions we surveyed, only 25% of respondents indicated that PIA summaries were made accessible to the public through postings to their external websites. Further 50% of respondents indicated that PIA summaries were not being published at all.[36]

Just as the public reporting on PIAs was lacking in completeness, so too was it lacking in quality. Despite the government's recommendation that PIA summaries describe the privacy impacts of all new programs and the measures taken to mitigate them, none of the departmental summaries we reviewed contained more than a simple project description and "privacy disclaimer".[37] In many respects, the PIA summaries seemed more like communication tools than reports on substantive privacy concerns (and not for reasons pertaining to security, legal or confidentiality requirements). Privacy issues were rarely described and action plans were generally missing. One wonders whether the public disclosure standards relative to PIAs provide any value or comfort to individuals seeking to understand the privacy implications of using a specific government service or program.

20.6 Conclusion: Evaluating the Effects of Our Audit

Four years following the publication of our audit report, it remains difficult to take stock of the status of PIA practices in Canada without considering the standards against which such practices might be measured. As part of our contribution to this book, we endeavoured to follow up on the progress departments were making towards our recommendations. Canadian federal PIA directives have, however, changed since 2007, and it was important to first consider the nature of these changes in any post-audit assessment.

---

[35] PIA Audit Report, *supra* fn. 1 at ¶ 1.68.

[36] PIA Audit Report, *supra* fn. 1 at ¶ 1.73 ff.

[37] PIA summaries generally read as follows: "Essential privacy requirements have been addressed and an action plan to further strengthen the privacy of Canadians has been adopted."

At the time of our audit report, the government of Canada was engaged in a comprehensive privacy policy renewal project. While this project was already underway and was not the result of our audit findings, Canada's new privacy policy suite appears to have taken our observations into consideration. While we have expressed concern over certain aspects of Canada's new Directive on Privacy Impact Assessment,[38] the Directive positively addresses several of the problem areas exposed by our audit. In introducing the new PIA Directive, the government of Canada reflects on similar concerns as those expressed in our recommendations:

> Government institutions routinely perform broad risk management activities and develop risk profiles related to their programs and activities. The PIA is the *component of risk management* that focuses on ensuring compliance with the Privacy Act... However, if not properly framed within an institution's *broader risk management framework*, conducting a PIA can be a resource-intensive exercise. [T]he government is committed to ensuring that a PIA is conducted in a manner that is *commensurate with the privacy risk* identified and respects the operating environment of the government institution [italics added].[39]

This statement, which sets the tone for the remainder of the PIA Directive, seems to underscore our most important audit recommendations, mainly the need for PIA integration into an organisation's broader risk management practices, the need for an administrative infrastructure to support PIAs and, finally, the need for a sensible (pragmatic) and risk-based approach to conducting PIAs.

On the matter of PIA integration, the new Directive requires the completion of PIAs in support of the publication of personal information banks,[40] a statutory requirement under subsection 10(1) of the Privacy Act.[41] Thus, whereas completing a PIA is still not required by law, the statutory requirement to identify and describe all personal information holdings is likely to render the failure to complete a PIA highly problematic for departmental heads.[42] The failure to complete a PIA in support of a personal information bank may lead to information omissions under the Act and the potential loss of a department's delegated authority.

Further echoing our audit recommendations is the government's Directive on Privacy Practices,[43] which requires departmental heads subject to the Act to establish effective privacy practices within their institutions. These privacy practices represent the administrative infrastructures or privacy management frameworks we

---

[38] Treasury Board of Canada Secretariat, Directive on Privacy Impact Assessment, Ottawa, April 2010 [PIA Directive].

[39] Ibid. at ¶ 3.3.

[40] Personal Information Bank (PIB) refers to a description of personal information organised and retrievable by a person's name or by an identifying number, symbol or other particular assigned only to that person. The personal information described in the PIB has been used, is being used or is available for an administrative purpose and is under the control of a government institution.

[41] See generally PIA Directive, *supra* fn. 38 at subsections 8.1.1, 6.2.2 and 6.3.14. See also Treasury Board of Canada Secretariat, Directive on Privacy Practices, Ottawa, April 2010 [Privacy Practices], subsection 6.1.4.

[42] Privacy Policy, *supra* fn. 41 at subsection 7.1 ff.

[43] See Privacy Practices, *supra*, fn. 41.

believe are necessary to support PIAs. If properly implemented, these infrastructures are likely to help ensure that an organisation's privacy practices are consistent with those required for compliance with privacy laws.

Some measures were also put in place with a view to ensuring that PIAs remain commensurate with privacy risks.[44] Federal departments are now required to complete a "core privacy impact assessment" as part of every PIA. While we have yet to review any substantial number of PIAs under the new Directive, we hope that the core assessment will be of some assistance to departments in focusing the risk management efforts of program managers on areas of greatest privacy concern.[45] If appropriately supplemented with a detailed analysis of personal information elements, activity flows and compliance review procedures, the federal PIA process should remain quite comprehensive, all the while allowing for an appropriate level of effort to undertake PIAs. It has yet to be seen, however, whether the new Directive will have its intended effect.

Irrespective of the recent changes to Canada's federal privacy policies, the OPC has noted a significant improvement in the quality of PIA submissions over the past several years.

Notwithstanding the fact that PIAs appear to have come into widespread use within Canada's federal government, many challenges remain. PIAs can still be intimidating for infrequent users. The process can still be long and daunting, requirements unfamiliar, and tools complex and confusing. Expertise in conducting PIAs remains hard to find, resulting in a continued reliance on privacy consultants. Despite these challenges, however, PIAs remain one of the most important tools available to government for managing privacy risks.

In consideration of these challenges, the OPC has itself set out to provide guidance on undertaking PIAs. At the time of publication, this guidance was still in development. Given our goal of ensuring that federal programs and services are consistent with the highest standards of privacy protection, we continue to evaluate PIA submissions according to the broader set of fair information practices upon which Canadian privacy laws are based. In conjunction with this evaluation, we hope to promote the need for more strategic privacy analysis in cases where the government embarks on large initiatives with potentially serious privacy impacts. In such cases, a test of necessity and proportionality, where privacy risks are balanced with program benefits, becomes all the more imperative. Our ongoing and active review of privacy impact assessments developed under the new Directive will more fully reveal its impact.

Acknowledgments I would like to acknowledge the contribution of Navroze Austin in the preparation of this chapter.

---

[44] See PIA Directive, *supra* fn. 38 at subsection 6.1.1.

[45] See PIA Directive, *supra* fn. 41, Appendix C – Core Privacy Impact Assessment.

Chapter 21
Privacy Impact Assessment: Optimising the Regulator's Role

Blair Stewart

21.1 Introduction

Privacy impact assessment (PIA) has moved in the last 15 years from being an interesting idea to an integral part of modern information privacy management. PIA is now a tool that regulators may draw upon or, just as frequently, a process that may draw upon the resources of regulators.

David Flaherty in his keynote address to the 22nd International Conference of Data Protection and Privacy Commissioners (ICDPPC) in Venice in 2000 described PIA as "an essential tool" for data protection.[1] Following the 25th International Conference in Sydney, the New Zealand Privacy Commissioner hosted an International Workshop on PIA as a related event.[2] The 29th International Conference in Montreal convened an in-depth workshop on issues and approaches for regulators (for which an earlier version of this paper was prepared as a session overview).[3] The 31st International Conference in Madrid in 2009 resolved to

---

[1] Flaherty, David H., "Privacy Impact Assessments: An Essential Tool for Data Protection", *Privacy Law and Policy Reporter*, Vol. 7, No. 5, Nov 2000. http://www.austlii.edu.au/au/journals/PLPR/2000/

[2] http://www.privacyconference2003.org/revents.asp

[3] 29th International Conference of Data Protection and Privacy Commissioners, *Privacy Impact Assessment Issues and Approaches for Regulators*, Workshop Workbook, Montreal, September 2007, available at http://www.privacyconference2007.gc.ca/workbooks/Terra_Incognita_workbook12_bil.pdf. The workbook includes, in addition to the session overview paper, resources from other PIA experts. In particular, see Nigel Waters, "Getting through Privacy Impact Assessments" and David Flaherty, "Criteria for Evaluating the Adequacy of Privacy Impact Assessments in Canada".

B. Stewart (✉)
Office of the Privacy Commissioner, Wellington, New Zealand
e-mail: Blair.Stewart@privacy.org.nz

D. Wright, P. De Hert (eds.), *Privacy Impact Assessment*, Law, Governance and Technology Series 6, DOI 10.1007/978-94-007-2543-0_21,
© Springer Science+Business Media B.V. 2012

encourage PIA as a "proactive measure" to promote better compliance with privacy laws.[4]

It is not surprising that the ICDPPC, the premier global gathering of privacy regulators, should return to the subject of PIA again and again. The data protection or privacy commissioner model is quintessentially a multi-faceted regulator. Data protection authorities (DPAs) accredited to the ICDPPC all have multiple roles spanning advisory, educative, dispute resolution and investigative functions. Many have additional powers and functions such as rule-making and prior and post-facto compliance-checking. Privacy regulation has required adaptability and innovation and many DPAs have found PIA a flexible addition to their "privacy toolkit".

Exploration of PIA issues has tended to start with a focus upon fundamental questions such as "What is PIA?" and "What are the advantages over other privacy management techniques?". Those that have accepted the case for PIA have tended then to move their attention to how best to introduce PIA into an organisation, government or jurisdiction. The focus, naturally enough, has been on the interests of potential users of PIA (What are the advantages for my organisation? How would I introduce PIA?) and the needs of the potential assessors (How should I undertake an assessment? What standards or guidelines should I follow?). The role of regulators in relation to PIA has been somewhat neglected as a matter for study and debate. This paper seeks to promote further consideration of such issues.

21.2 Approach

There are a number of variations between the models of PIA operated in different jurisdictions. Some are mandated by law – requiring PIAs to be undertaken in certain circumstances – while others may be required under government or company policy or be entirely voluntary. Some schemes focus upon a particular sector – typically public health – while others may seek to embrace all organisations in an economy.

This chapter does not examine the challenges of privacy regulators conducting assessments themselves, as some may do from time to time. It might be expected that such challenges may be similar to those faced by any other assessor. This chapter is interested in an overseeing entity *as regulator* (and as consumer of completed privacy impact reports).

For the purposes of this chapter, regulators are taken to be persons at arm's length from the proposals being evaluated and from the carrying out of the assessment, who have some general or specific responsibility to ensure a level of privacy compliance in the PIA process. The majority of "privacy regulators" in the world are

---

[4] 31st International Conference of Data Protection and Privacy Commissioners, Resolution on International Standards of Privacy, Madrid, November 2009. http://www.privacyconference2009. org/dpas_space/space_reserved/documentos_adoptados/common/2009_Madrid/estandares_ resolucion_madrid_en.pdf. See also Chapter 18 by Artemi Rallo Lombarte.

DPAs. However, there are also other kinds of statutory regulators such as those in specialised areas of, say, e-government, health, consumer protection or financial services who may also be involved with PIAs. (Indeed, the New York Public Service Commission may have been one of the first regulators to require a PIA.[5])

Although this chapter has statutory regulators in mind, some of the issues raised may be relevant to internal arm's-length overseers such as internal control officers in organisations some of whom have a high degree of internal autonomy and semi-independence (for instance, internal auditors and some Chief Privacy Officers). The issues raised may also be relevant to government entities that require PIA by policy (e.g., as an ethical requirement for health research) or as a condition of funding (e.g., for developing new information systems) where those entities perform oversight roles related to compliance or good privacy practice.

The balance of the chapter is in four parts:

- Getting started – the regulator's role at the outset;
- Getting through – the issues for regulators while an assessment is being conducted;
- Getting results – when the privacy assessment report arrives on the regulator's desk;
- Getting value – how the process measures up as a regulatory tool.

The chapter poses a series of questions that could usefully be asked of current arrangements for PIA in a jurisdiction or organisation. The questions focus upon the role of the regulator and are intended to uncover problems, opportunities or scope for improvement. The questions are framed to review an existing scheme but might, with some adaptation, be useful when designing a PIA system from scratch.

The chapter has been written with a firm view that PIA is a valuable process and that regulators have a useful role to play. However, the regulator's role is not always well understood, whether by stakeholders or even by the regulator in some cases. There may be unrealistic expectations in some quarters of what regulators can or should do. Even where the role is relatively well understood, there can be difficulties in performing the role to the satisfaction of all stakeholders. This chapter has been written from a conviction that by further exploring the role – and by pooling experience as to how that role is variously performed – new insights and understandings will emerge enabling adjustment to optimise the privacy outcomes.

The chapter poses dozens of questions but does not attempt to answer any of them. There is no single "right answer" that applies in all cases. However, the process of asking and answering the questions will be helpful in reviewing all existing

---

[5] State of New York Public Service Commission, *Privacy Policy Statement No. 1: A Privacy Impact Statement* in "Statement of Policy on Privacy in Telecommunications", 22 March 1991, reprinted in Longworth Associates, *Telecommunications and Privacy Issues: Report for the Ministry of Commerce*, Wellington, 1992. See also Clarke, Roger, "Privacy Impact Assessment: Its Origins & Development", *Computer Law & Security Review*, Vol. 25, No. 2, April 2009, pp. 123–135.

PIA arrangements that include a regulator. I hope the answers may assist in rethinking the performance of the regulator's role or, if necessary, reforming the underlying processes.

21.3 Part A: Getting Started

Privacy impact assessment doesn't simply happen, someone makes it happen.

In a particular case, this is typically through either:

- the application of a pre-determined rule – such as imposing PIA on projects requiring funding approval or
- an exercise of judgement on an ad hoc basis – "I think this project warrants a PIA".

Sometimes there will be an expectation to undertake PIA as a condition of doing business in a regulated privacy environment.

Deciding to consider the possibility of PIA or positively deciding to undertake an assessment may trigger a series of further decisions for which there may or may not be pre-determined rules. Examples include whether to do further investigations before committing to a full PIA, setting terms of reference, choosing an assessor or assembling a team, setting a timeline, etc.

Aspects of all of these may – but need not – involve a regulator. For instance, in one jurisdiction, the regulator may have set the rules by which PIA generally becomes a mandatory step but is otherwise not involved. In another, the rules may be less rigid with the regulator to be consulted on the decision to undertake an assessment. In a number of jurisdictions, regulators offer model PIA templates.

Questions for consideration:

- What roles do regulators currently perform in relation to PIA?
- Are all of these appropriate? Why so? Why not?
- Are there further roles that should be performed?
- What problems are encountered in these roles?
- Which are the priorities for regulators at this stage?
- What regulatory action most contributes to successful outcomes?
- What causes the most problems?
- Is a PIA required in the right cases? Or do PIA systems miss some important cases? Is a PIA required when it is really not warranted?
- Quality control and appropriate scope of an assessment are clearly important considerations at the outset if the process is to be of value – how can they be ensured?

Getting started in a PIA is a key decision. If this stage is not handled well, there are significant risks. If a PIA is required in circumstances that do not justify an assessment, limited privacy policy or compliance resource may be expended needlessly. If the starting processes are incapable of focusing the assessment on the key issues, there is a risk that the resultant assessment will fail to achieve its potential usefulness (or offer a false sense of security). Clearly regulators have a useful role in this context as experts at arm's length from the proponents of a particular project. They represent the public interest and are expected to ensure that the process protects the public. The challenge posed by the various questions is to find the most productive role suited to the circumstances.

21.4 Part B: Getting Through

Privacy impact assessment on the model assumed in this chapter is performed not by the regulator but by another person or team typically answering to the organisation whose project is being assessed. So what role, if any, should a regulator play? Is it useful to be in touch with an assessor or does this affect the arm's-length relationship of assessor and regulator? Can contact lead to burdens being thrown onto the regulator who might be asked for ad hoc advice or opinions? Does ad hoc intervention undermine the systematic and scientific aspect of PIA and make it more "political"? If the regulator is entirely uninvolved during an assessment, will that lead to problems being deferred until it is too late for the regulator to influence events? Does close involvement compromise the regulator?

Questions for consideration:

- What roles do regulators currently perform? Are all of these appropriate?
- Are there further roles that should be performed?
- What problems are encountered in these roles?
- Which are the priorities for regulators at this stage?
- What regulatory action most contributes to successful outcomes?
- In the interactions between regulator and assessor, what works well for assessors? For regulators? For organisations? What causes most problems?

The role of the regulator during an assessment is prone to misunderstanding. In some PIA arrangements, the regulator has no relevant role pending production of a PIA report. In some people's view, this fails to make most suitable use of the expertise and resources of the regulator. On the other hand, if the regulator is to become involved during that stage, it is essential that all parties, including the regulator, understand the role to be performed. Whatever approach is adopted, clear understandings and good communication are essential.

21.5 Part C: Getting Results

At some point, any PIA process delivers up a report of the findings and recommendations. Depending upon the local practices, this may come to the regulator, perhaps in draft form with opportunity to comment, perhaps just for information. There may be a range of views as to which approach is most effective from a regulatory perspective.

The reports delivered to regulators may range from projects of major national importance through to systems solely affecting one company and its employees. Regulators will always have limited resources to devote to PIA work. A PIA report may arrive at the same time as several others, and no doubt there will be many other tasks competing for attention. How can under-resourced and busy regulators make the most of this stage of the work? Can classes of PIA be differentiated by their importance or the appropriate regulatory action and responses? Does the practice of receiving PIAs "for information" (but no analysis or action) represent a pragmatic and appropriate response or an abrogation of responsibility? What do organisations expect and want? What does the public and legislature expect? What can regulators do with the reports in an individual or systemic way? How much regulatory resource is sufficient to do a credible job?

Now that PIA has been operating for a number of years, a project manager may have submitted multiple PIA reports on one project, service or system or inter-related systems. Does this complexity over time and between systems pose special challenges for regulators? Can regulators keep track of recommendations and system changes? Does it create special opportunities in getting the "big picture" and, if so, how can these be taken advantage of?

Questions for consideration:

- What roles do regulators currently perform? Are all of these appropriate?
- How actively do regulators perform the role of receiving PIA reports? Do they sit back and wait or chase assessors? Should they chase them?
- If offered an opportunity to critique a report, how is that performed? How resource intensive is the process? How thorough?
- What problems are encountered in these roles?
- What talents are required to perform this kind of work?
- Are there further roles that should be performed?
- Which are the priorities for regulators at this stage?
- What regulatory action most contributes to successful outcomes?
- Are regulators making the most of the PIA reports they receive? If not, why is this and what can be done?
- Are regulators operating transparently? Are the results of PIAs made available by regulators or organisations to affected communities or those working in privacy management?

Most arrangements for PIA that accord a role to regulators involve delivering a PIA report to the regulator either as primary outcome or as a complementary step to submitting the report to another decision-maker. Recognising the expertise of the regulator and the usefulness of review and feedback, assessors often deliver the reports in draft form and seek comment. This point in the process is full of promise and opportunity for assessor, organisation, regulator and other stakeholders but also contains risks for several of these. Making the most of this moment is essential for the success of PIA as a modern means for understanding privacy risk and opportunity and managing processes to deliver good privacy outcomes for individuals whether as citizens, consumers, employees or otherwise. Further exploration of the regulator's role and the way that role might be performed will point the way to improvements in PIA processes.

21.6 Part D: Getting Value

DPAs are multi-faceted regulators with many tools and powers to call on. Are regulators using PIA in the right way and for the right projects? Are other tools sometimes more useful? Do PIAs make a difference in privacy outcomes? How do we know?

In our attempts to systemise privacy management through PIA and similar systems, are we "dumbing down" the process to the point where it is not useful? Some commentators have cautioned that routinisation of procedures may result in fairly mindless procedures and documents.[6] Does the regulator's involvement encourage or discourage that tendency?

Are there lessons to be learned from other fields of regulatory endeavour, both within data protection and elsewhere, that might point the way to better assessing and ensuring value for the community and privacy?

Questions for consideration:

- What do regulators currently do to ensure PIA delivers value?
- How is this measured or tested?
- Are internal or external benchmarks used?
- What more should be done individually or collectively?
- What regulatory action contributes most to successful outcomes?
- Does PIA support other privacy management approaches or does it stand alone?

The potential for PIA to provide and inform an intelligent response to modern privacy challenges is an article of faith for many privacy advocates, compliance managers and regulators who have studied the subject. However, with PIA operating in many jurisdictions for a decade or more, has it delivered on the potential? While it might be too early to say, it is important that, before too many more years have passed, an attempt is made to check on whether PIA has "delivered the goods". The potential is undeniable but it is not unreasonable to ask to see the evidence of PIA's usefulness in practice.

---

[6] Clarke, op. cit.

21.7 Closing Comments

PIA has established itself as one of the most flexible and promising techniques for grappling with ever variable privacy challenges of our complex times. Increasingly, it finds a welcome spot in the processes of corporate risk managers and government officials. Amongst regulators, it is viewed as a useful adjunct to other regulatory and legal responses and as a guide to informed and rational decision-making.

PIA can be an integral or additional feature of virtually any information privacy regime from those based entirely on self-regulation to the most rigidly enforced system of prior approvals. The role of the regulator will differ substantially between and within the various models of PIA. In one model, the regulator might be simply an informed commentator, seeking to influence opinion and drawing upon a PIA report in aid. In another, the regulator may have the last word on every key decision starting by settling the terms of reference for the PIA and selecting the assessor and perhaps ending with the power to approve the PIA recommendations. Wherever a PIA system falls upon this continuum, it is important that the regulator's role be properly understood if the full potential is to be realised.

Detailed examination of success in performance of the regulator's role in particular contexts might result in the regulator's preferring less involvement in some cases and more in others. The nature of the involvement may also be varied to make it more useful. Perhaps the ideal situation will be where the PIA process can operate successfully for the most part with little regulatory involvement but in the cases where involvement in depth is warranted, such involvement should be facilitated in such a way that it is more effective from the perspective of the regulator, the assessor, the organisation and the affected community. Even in relatively mature PIA systems, there may be substantial room for improvement. Addressing the questions in this paper may help to achieve this improvement.

Chapter 22
Findings and Recommendations

David Wright and Paul De Hert

In this final, concluding chapter, we present our key findings and recommendations from the contributors to this book for privacy impact assessment (PIA) policy and practice. They are addressed to those who undertake PIAs and those who set policy with regard to the use of PIAs. Not surprisingly, we do recommend much wider use of PIAs in the public and private sectors. PIA is a potentially important instrument in the privacy toolbox which includes other instruments such as data breach notification, privacy by design, the right to be "forgotten", collective redress mechanisms (i.e., class action lawsuits) and privacy-enhancing technologies such as encryption and access control. A PIA may well recommend the use of one or more of these other instruments.

There are differences in PIA policies and practices, as indicated in Chapter 1 and throughout this book. PIA comes in many different shapes, sizes and flavours, as Nigel Waters says in Chapter 6. This fact reflects the wide range of motives and objectives for undertaking PIA; the identity, status and experience of both the client and the assessor; the stage of the project at which the PIA is undertaken; the involvement of third parties and the development and approval process into which the PIA is inserted.

PIA policies and practices in Australia, Canada, New Zealand, the United Kingdom and the United States have good points, but also shortcomings. By taking the best elements of each, one can construct a PIA policy and practice that realises the "great potential" of which Nigel Waters writes. This chapter reflects what we believe to be the best elements.

This chapter contains three sections. The first addresses PIA policy issues and, as such, is especially aimed at policy-makers who may be developing a PIA policy in their countries or who might be considering how to improve an existing policy. The second offers guidance on how individual PIAs should be undertaken. The third concludes the chapter with remarks on how PIA could be improved.

D. Wright (✉)
Trilateral Research & Consulting, London, W8 5JB, UK
e-mail: david.wright@trilateralresearch.com

D. Wright, P. De Hert (eds.), *Privacy Impact Assessment*, Law, Governance
and Technology Series 6, DOI 10.1007/978-94-007-2543-0_22,
© Springer Science+Business Media B.V. 2012

Our recommendations can be found in the subheadings, with the text following each of those subheadings drawn from the contributors to this book in support.

22.1 PIA Policy Issues: Recommendations for a Better Framework on PIA

22.1.1 PIAs Should Be Conducted by Any Organisation Impacting Privacy

If an organisation undertakes a project, develops a new technology or service or policy which impacts privacy, they should conduct a PIA. If the risks to privacy are negligible, then a limited, small-scale assessment may be all that is necessary. If it seems there might be significant risks, then they should conduct a full-scale assessment. Although government departments and agencies have been the primary users, PIA practice has been spreading to the private sector as indicated by the inclusion of chapters in this book from representatives of three large multinational companies, i.e., Nokia, Siemens and Vodafone.

Robin Bayley and Colin Bennett (Chapter 7) add that private sector PIAs are frequently conducted for information technology projects, and have been conducted by telecommunications companies, those providing back-room services in human resources and payment processing, banks and other financial institutions, international energy companies and major retailers. PIAs are spreading from the public to private sectors through contracting out, public-private partnerships and other joint initiatives, particularly in the health care field with shared information systems. PIAs may also be conducted by those seeking access to publicly held information as a due diligence exercise before information sharing agreements are concluded.

22.1.2 PIA Needs Champions, High Level Support and an Embedded Privacy Culture

If they are not to disappoint, PIA requires championing across organisations and "culture change". David Parker in Chapter 3 notes that the introduction of impact assessment procedures may be treated by politicians and officials as an unwelcome or even "pointless" extra burden on their time and resources. He is convinced that the proper adoption of impact assessment is undoubtedly reliant upon unequivocal and continuing high-level political support within government.

Kenneth Bamberger and Deirdre Mulligan (Chapter 10) attach importance to "the role of internal agency structure, culture, personnel and professional expertise in whether the PIA process can be meaningfully integrated as an element of bureaucratic decision-making". Specifically, they point to the importance of substantive experts combined with internal processes for insinuating privacy into daily practice, and the need for status and structures that respect the different roles privacy professionals play in protecting privacy during policy-making and integrating privacy into the bureaucracy. They say that one of the factors that led to the relatively successful implementation of PIA policy and practice within the US Department of Homeland Security (DHS) was "the existence of a high-status privacy expert within DHS, a CPO [chief privacy officer], specifically charged with advancing privacy among competing agency interests, located in a central position within the agency decision-making structure, able to draw on internal relationships and external sources of power, and operate with relative independence". Privacy professionals in the private sector interviewed by Bamberger and Mulligan also stressed the importance of embedding expertise within business units and establishing specific staff who are personally responsible for privacy.

Nokia's Tobias Bräutigam (Chapter 11) agrees that "privacy assessments only make sense when they are embedded in a governance model that supports the implementation of the results". From Bräutigam, we learn how Nokia has embedded a privacy culture in its organisation. "There are organisational unit specific roles, such as the unit privacy officers and unit privacy managers. These staff interpret Nokia's privacy approach for the specific unit and define a unit-specific privacy strategy, mode of operation, implementation guidelines and related practices. To complement the relatively few resources who deal full-time with privacy, there are literally thousands of employees who take care of privacy implementation in concrete projects."

Privacy requirements, says Bräutigam, must be integrated into each unit's management systems and processes. The units are responsible for compliance with such requirements. They must proactively drive the inclusion of privacy considerations into the design of their products and services. Without the right culture, assessments will not be done consistently. So what is done to foster that culture? Privacy has been included in the code of conduct and the general e-learning that every employee needs to take. Nokia fosters a privacy-sensitive culture through training, awareness campaigns, blogs and the company's intranet.

Stephen Deadman and Amanda Chandler (Chapter 13) say that Vodafone also seeks to embed privacy management deeply within its business, and then go on to say that the company's privacy policy allocates clear governance and accountability for implementing the policy. At a Vodafone Group level, the policy is sponsored by a member of Vodafone's most senior executive committee, and "owned" by the Group Privacy Officer. Vodafone uses the expression "programme maturity" to mean the degree to which accountability and operational controls and processes for privacy risk management are embedded into its business, and managed by competent and trained privacy professionals. Vodafone aims to ensure that privacy risk management is built into the organisational culture and delivers tangible benefits. Experience has shown that this approach is successful in getting the business and commercial teams to participate in, and provide support and resource for, delivering compliance activities. Deadman and Chandler say, "It is essential that these teams are fully engaged because privacy risks arise through and out of their business and commercial activities and projects."

Canada's Privacy Commissioner, Jennifer Stoddart (Chapter 20), says an organisation might wish to consider the implementation of cross-functional authorities for program approval. This might mean mandating the approval of a privacy head for projects involving personal information or instituting a requirement for their sign-off where a program authority believes that a PIA is not required. All in all, and when combined, these components may prove to be effective instruments in identifying projects that require privacy analysis.

22.1.3 A PIA Should Be "Signed Off" by a High-Level Official and Tied to Funding Submissions

In Canada, a PIA must be "signed off" by a deputy minister or other high level official when making a submission for funding by the Treasury Board. This appears to be a good practice for ensuring accountability and responsibility. This is like the impact assessment procedure in the UK, as David Parker (Chapter 3) points out, where all new legislation is accompanied by a final IA signed off by the relevant government minister before introduction to Parliament. If a minister or his deputy or a board member of a company has to sign off (i.e., approve) the PIA, it increases accountability. Senior officials are unlikely to want to affix their signature to a substandard document where there is a risk that they will be criticised subsequently for having agreed to an inadequate, deficient PIA.

While linking PIA conditions to project funding is intended to serve as a critical external control in enforcing privacy analysis for project proposals, Stoddart says the submission process does not provide sufficient coverage over program changes (or the various micro-initiatives often undertaken within larger approved programs). Yet these smaller initiatives or program changes, particularly when combined, might have serious privacy impacts and should therefore have been considered as potential PIA candidates. Thus, when organisations perform a PIA, they should use the opportunity to consider the privacy implications of their activities beyond the immediate project.

22.1.4 Risk Management Should Be a Part of PIA, and PIA Should Be Part of Risk Management

Several authors make the point that risk assessment and management are a key part of a PIA and/or that PIA should be a part of risk management. The Treasury Board of Canada Secretariat's Directive on PIA says "a PIA is a component of risk management that focuses on ensuring compliance with the Privacy Act requirements and assessing the privacy implications of new or substantially modified programs and activities involving personal information".[1]

---

[1] Treasury Board of Canada Secretariat, Directive on Privacy Impact Assessment, Ottawa, 1 April 2010. http://www.tbs-sct.gc.ca/pol/doc-eng.aspx?id=18308&section=text

The first attempt by industry in developing a PIA framework in response to the European Commission's Recommendation on RFID was dismissed by the Article 29 Working Party as unacceptable because, among other things, it avoided any kind of risk identification process. Subsequently, as Sarah Spiekermann informs us in Chapter 15, a European group from a variety of industries and academic backgrounds forced the initial authors to outline a methodology that identified privacy risks and mitigation strategies. This group also insisted that the PIA report provide enough details about an RFID application and its back-end infrastructure to allow for a comprehensible identification and judgement of such risks.

Laurent Beslay and Anne-Christine Lacoste (Chapter 16) report that the first RFID PIA framework produced by industry did not meet the Article 29 Working Party's expectations because, inter alia, it did not include an effective procedure for risk assessment, nor did it give consideration to the risks linked with tags carried by individuals. The Article 29 Working Party considered that, in order to be assured that measures taken by an operator are adequate or proportionate to the risk, it was essential that a procedure be developed that allows an identification and assessment of the risks linked with the processing of RFID data. ENISA made a similarly critical comment. ENISA called for a structured approach in the RFID PIA Framework based on existing risk management methodologies, especially the ISO/IEC 27005 standard. ENISA said that, in order to better encourage the early consideration of privacy risks, there was a need to integrate PIA practices with an organisation's overall approach to risk management.

Jennifer Stoddart says an organisation should create and embed administrative linkages between PIAs and other risk mitigation tools. She envisages the integration of IT threat and risk assessments (TRAs) or other business case documents with a requirement to complete a PIA under certain specified conditions. When one is performed, so is the other.

22.1.5 Privacy Commissioners Should Play a Key Role in PIA

Privacy commissioners, or data protection authorities (DPAs), as they are more narrowly known in Europe, play a key role in promoting PIA. From their survey of DPAs in Europe, reported in Chapter 4, Gwendal Le Grand and Emilie Barrau find that DPAs and data controllers alike are showing increasing interest in PIA. They say that many authorities already perform "PIA-like activities" such as audit or assessment activities in specific cases such as the development of new legislation. A couple of authorities mentioned that they do not have the resources to regularly carry out PIAs or that they do not have a model to use PIA.

In contrast, some authorities have been much more proactive in promoting PIA, as a self-assessment tool, amongst companies who are designing new policies or systems. Two authorities (United Kingdom, Denmark) have developed handbooks that guide data controllers through the process of conducting a PIA. However, while these authorities give advice on how PIAs should be conducted, they do not approve or sign off an organisation's PIA.

Nigel Waters believes privacy regulators need to become more active in following up on PIA reports. They should ask project proponents which recommendations in a PIA they accept and, if they do not accept all, to explain why they do not do so. Where recommendations are accepted, there also needs to be follow-up to ascertain if they have actually been implemented.

Privacy commissioners may not be able to approve or audit all PIAs, says Waters, but they could review at least some PIAs and publicise the outcomes as a way of demonstrating the value of PIA (or alternatively of demonstrating the risks of not addressing privacy implications). He recognises that privacy commissioners will never be given the resources to carry out a "second assessment" (or audit) of every PIA, and are unlikely even to be able to adequately supervise private sector assessors who are engaged directly by project proponents.

This is what the National Audit Office (NAO) in the UK does: it evaluates a sample of regulatory impact assessments each year.

In Canada, privacy commissioners "accept" but do not "approve" PIAs. For its part, the Alberta Information and Privacy Commissioner has been reviewing and commenting on PIAs since proclamation of the Freedom of Information and Privacy (FOIP) Act in 1995.

Blair Stewart poses questions in Chapter 21 regarding the appropriate role to be played by the DPA or privacy commissioner in the PIA process. Does the practice of receiving PIAs "for information" (but no analysis or action) represent a pragmatic and appropriate response or an abrogation of responsibility? What do organisations expect and want? If the regulator is entirely uninvolved during an assessment, will that lead to problems being deferred until it is too late for the regulator to influence events? He fears that the role of the regulator during an assessment is prone to misunderstanding. In some PIA arrangements, the regulator has no relevant role pending production of a PIA report. In some people's view, this fails to make most suitable use of the expertise and resources of the regulator. On the other hand, if the regulator is to become involved during that stage, it is essential that all parties, including the regulator, understand the role to be performed.

Recognising the expertise of the regulator and the usefulness of review and feedback, assessors often deliver the reports in draft form and seek comment. This point in the process is full of promise and opportunity for the assessor, organisation, regulator and other stakeholders but also contains risks for several of these. Making the most of this moment, says Stewart, is essential for the success of PIA as a modern means for understanding privacy risk and opportunity and managing processes to deliver good privacy outcomes for individuals whether as citizens, consumers, employees or otherwise. He encourages further exploration of the regulator's role in PIA processes.

22.1.6 Prior Checking and PIA Should Be Complementary, But Their Mutual Relationship Needs More Study

Gwendal Le Grand and Emilie Barrau made a comparative study of the implementation of prior checking in Europe. Prior checking is the subject of Article

20 of the EU Data Protection Directive 95/46/EC, which provides that Member States shall determine processing operations likely to present specific risks to the rights and freedoms of data subjects and shall check that these processing operations are examined before they start. Le Grand and Barrau's study examines how prior checking has been implemented, how it works in practice and what can be learnt from it as a regulatory instrument in the development and use of PIAs in Europe.

Although most DPAs are satisfied with the current prior checking system and wish to keep this control mechanism, some authorities have pointed out that prior checking is sometimes considered to be burdensome and time-consuming for both data controllers and DPAs alike. It is also said to prevent DPAs from focusing on ex post investigative actions. To remedy the burdensome aspect of prior checking, some DPAs have already adopted simplified processes to make prior checking more efficient. Electronic registration systems, appointment of DPOs and reinforcing the role of PIAs were also highlighted as potential ways forward.

Regarding the interaction between PIAs and prior checking, the vast majority of DPAs believe that PIAs should complement, but not replace, prior checking – as the pros and cons of PIAs are still unknown. The rationale for considering PIAs as complementing prior checking is generally that it will improve data protection and help determine the appropriate security measures which should be implemented in a system. Only one authority believes PIAs represent a serious alternative to prior checking.

Prior checking is at the very heart of the activities of the majority of DPAs: it allows authorities to monitor and assess "risky" developments and to exercise a control ex ante as in the vast majority of countries processing operations cannot start before a decision of the data protection authority is received by the controller. Authorities have been developing specific instruments and procedures for processing operations subject to prior checking. In this context, PIAs are increasingly considered as a complement to prior checking.

Florian Thoma indicates in Chapter 12 that Siemens at least views prior checking in a positive light: "Prior checking... can be seen as a sub-type of privacy impact assessments: such prior checking is a means to ensure compliance of high-risk processing operations with the law, and effectively limit or even exclude such risks to data subjects." He says Siemens is convinced that prior checking provides benefits to both the individuals and the company:

> If conducted early enough, it is an efficient means to protect the privacy of individuals in directing projects onto the right tracks. It offers the company significant advantages because it can ensure its compliant behaviour, foster employees' and customers' trust, achieve a higher degree of quality, transparency and security and avoid incurring additional costs and delay that could result from non-compliant actions, in particular, in the design of IT systems. While reliable data on these effects seems to be rare, we are convinced that this will outweigh the resources consumed for the assessment itself in nearly all cases.

22.1.7 Transparency Contributes to the Success of a PIA

Many of the contributors to this book say that a vital condition for the value and success of a PIA is transparency – of the PIA process itself as well as ensuring that the assessor and stakeholders have all relevant information to assess the privacy impacts of a proposed new project or service. Or, as Paul De Hert puts it, a proper assessment is not possible if all the cards are not on the table. Nigel Waters says the potential for different conclusions to be drawn from the same facts strengthens the case for maximum transparency – if all PIA reports are made public, then interested parties can compare them and form their own judgement about their relative strengths.

Kenneth Bamberger and Deirdre Mulligan point out that bureaucrats can use technical projects to stifle transparency: "Decisions about the design and deployment of technical systems can permit bureaucrats to cloak policy decisions and mask the exercise of discretion behind claims of technical neutrality and complex jargon." On the other hand, Siemens' Florian Thoma has found that

> PIAs can support transparency and trust to a very high degree. We have seen many situations where some project teams' initial reluctance to work with us in documenting and assessing privacy aspects (typical arguments were missing resources, expected delays, additional cost, lack of need) changed completely within a short time. The transparency achieved through documented processes and the broad availability of such documentation both showed that there was nothing to hide but supported an open discussion and helped to make stakeholders understand in more detail what the aims of a project were.

Laurent Beslay and Anne-Christine Lacoste speak of the need to communicate in a transparent and appropriate way with DPAs as well as end users about the identification of residual risk as one of the end products of a risk assessment.

Artemi Rallo (Chapter 18) also touches on transparency, which he says is strengthened by the Madrid Resolution, which sets out in the proposed standard the information to be provided to data subjects, including a special case regarding the need to use particularly clear and plain vocabulary when dealing with minors. The obligation for transparency is especially important when the basis used to legitimise the processing of data is consent, which must be freely given, unambiguous and informed. A failure in the duty to inform could nullify consent and therefore result in unlawful processing.

Jennifer Stoddart says enhancing the transparency of the PIA process is critical to improving the quality of privacy analysis in government. Greater scrutiny generated by public exposure can prompt greater care in the preparation of PIAs and provide Parliament and the public with the necessary information to inform debates concerning privacy protection. Public disclosure may also provide additional assurance that privacy impacts are being appropriately considered in the development of programs, plans and policies – essentially holding each institution to public account for the adequacy of the privacy analysis that was undertaken. Whereas improved public reporting can be a constructive tool for organisational development and the enhancement of internal privacy practices, poor public reporting may have a profoundly damaging effect on the trust of individuals in their government.

Sarah Spiekermann comments that one pitfall involved in the negotiation of PIA reports with industry is the difficulty of establishing consensus on what needs to be reported in the different phases of analysis. Companies often want to avoid a description of data flows, push for the publication of just a summary about the results of a PIA (as is the case in Canada), or both. Europe's PIA Framework for RFID states that the "initial analysis must be documented and made available to data protection authorities upon request" and that this documentation not only describes the RFID application, but contains all information needed to judge the potential privacy impact of the system.

22.1.8 Publish the Results of the PIA and Communicate with Stakeholders, Including the Public

Paul De Hert says PIAs should be made public in order to allow individuals to go to court. A decision-making process should be based on facts and needs to be fair. Elements such as the cost of technology and health implications need to be made public. A principled distrust of impact assessments needs to be the default position; they are always fitting a certain agenda and therefore they will never be undisputed. That is, however, precisely the reason why these documents need to be made public: they allow contestation and public debate. Ideally, there is public consultation when technology is designed (technology can still be redesigned) or planned. A true assessment can only be made when all the details are known. The first concept of the assessment document should subsequently be made public in order to gather reactions.

In the UK, David Parker says that drafts of an impact assessment are prepared and published during the policy-making process, with public consultation taking place (normally a minimum of 12 weeks are allowed for consultation).[2] In the UK, impact assessments are created over a normal policy development time period of six months to two years and are referred to at the first stage of the process as "preliminary", "partial" or "consultation" stage impact assessments, and at the second stage as "final" ones. In this respect, regulatory impact assessments differ from PIAs, which are almost never published.

Robin Bayley and Colin Bennett note that, generally, only PIA summaries are published (by posting on an organisation's website) in Canada, and individuals wanting to see the entire PIA must apply under freedom of information legislation, which is typically the case in the UK too. Commonly, information relating to security controls would be withheld. Other exceptions to release relate to policy advice, legal privilege and executive confidence and harm to intergovernmental relations, international affairs and defence, law enforcement and financial, economic or third-party business interests. Jurisdictions have slightly different wording and precedents regarding the interpretation of these exceptions.

---

[2] The government has published a code of practice on consultation since 2000. The latest version was released in 2008. See http://www.berr.gov.uk/files/file47158.pdf

They go on to say that the timeliness of posting summaries varies as does compliance with the basic requirement to publish and the descriptiveness of the summary. Of the jurisdictions Bayley and Bennett studied, Ontario is the only one with no requirement to publish PIAs or summaries. The most fulsome summaries are provided by government of Canada public institutions but even those can be brief and do not generally confer a full understanding of the privacy issues and mitigation strategies. Most provincial summaries describe the initiative in a paragraph or two and serve only as a notice that a PIA has been completed. Exceptions exist and some organisations post entire PIAs or very detailed summaries. It is, however, more common to find meaningless statements that risks were identified and appropriate mitigations implemented or planned, with no hint to what those might be. In the case of multi-jurisdictional or multi-party initiatives, one can often find out more from one party than another.

In the UK, Adam Warren and Andrew Charlesworth point out that the ICO *Annual Report* published in July 2010 noted that "over 300 Privacy Impact Assessments have been started across central government and their agencies", yet very few UK PIA reports have reached the public domain. Moreover, evidence of private sector activity in this field is almost non-existent.

Sarah Spiekermann encountered the same reluctance to publish on the part of companies in the RFID domain. "The compromise reached for RFID PIAs is that PIA reports will not be public, but must be made available to competent authorities in line with section IX of the Directive 95/46/EC. This requirement means that, in most cases, a company's data protection official or the department responsible for the RFID deployment will prepare the PIA report for authorities."

22.1.9 Guard Against Conflicts of Interest

John Edwards says in Chapter 8 that it should not be surprising that a client, whether a company or a government agency, will seek a PIA that sanctions his project or policy or at least with a few cosmetic changes. It is natural that a client who has invested his psychic energy, if not material resources, into a proposal is not likely to welcome a naysayer, someone who raises alarms about the privacy implications, especially if the naysayer is in the client's employee or is a consultant, perhaps hired with the expectation that the assessor will put an acceptable gloss on the proposal. However, as he so colourfully puts it, it is not the assessor's job to apply lipstick to a pig.

Even so, the client may have decided that he will, no matter what, undertake a project or implement a policy, despite the privacy implications. In such a case, the assessor may need to frame his report based around certain stated givens. The assessor might recommend a robust statutory regime, including penalties for misuse, and tight constraints on permitted uses of the personal information. The assessor might also make recommendations related to internal policies, staff training, public notification and the security of and permitted access to IT systems.

Nigel Waters says the typical model adopted for engaging and funding a PIA is that the proponent of the scheme to be assessed both engages the assessor and pays for the PIA. He expresses surprise that there has been little commentary on or criticism of this model, particularly given the widespread criticism of the same model in the field of environmental assessment. He asks if the pressure to qualify or water down analyses and recommendations could be reduced if a different model were adopted. Because of the pressures on the assessor, PIA reports will often only hint at potential problems. Assessors trying to fully document adverse privacy effects, or to suggest alternatives or safeguards, but constrained in their ability to do so too bluntly, can often nevertheless include clues that can be detected and interpreted by experienced readers.

22.1.10 Ensure Third-Party Review and Audit of PIAs

A third-party review and/or audit of PIAs is necessary, as Nigel Waters points out, because it is all too easy for project proponents to say initially that they accept and will implement suggested changes, only to find reasons later to backslide, and either partially or wholly abandon their initial commitment.

Robin Bayley and Colin Bennett say that reviews are an effective part of PIA in Canada and provide much additional value. Where reviews are not required or recommended, less formal, voluntary consultations may take place. At the national level, public agencies are required to share their PIAs with the Privacy Commissioner of Canada. The government of Canada has developed a PIA Audit Guide, "intended as a reference tool for Internal Auditors in the Government of Canada and may also be of assistance to the privacy community, including PIA Coordinators".[3]

At the provincial level, PIAs are reviewed by central agencies responsible for privacy within government or the privacy commissioner or both. The reviewing agency generally accepts but does not "approve" the PIA or may only note that consultation has taken place. During the review process, there is generally some back and forth communication. PIAs may be sent back to the originating organisation for clarification, further work on the specifics of personal information collection and handling, or for more fundamental program redesign to address privacy risks. However, they say that the extent to which the PIAs are revisited and revised and the promised mitigation measures implemented is unknown. Privacy regulators have reason to believe that PIA plans are not always carried out. The system would benefit from increased accountability for implementation of PIA plans. Currently, there is no reporting mechanism in Canada for the implementation of PIA plans. A requirement to conduct post-implementation reviews would work only if there were sufficient

---

[3] Treasury Board Secretariat of Canada, Privacy Impact Assessment Audit Guide, as archived. http://www.collectionscanada.gc.ca/webarchives/20071211001631/www.tbs-sct.gc.ca/ia-vi/policies-politiques/pia-efvp/pia-efvp_e.asp

resources dedicated for meaningful and ongoing review within a system that entailed mandatory independent review of PIAs and focused on high-risk initiatives.

In her chapter, Jennifer Stoddart describes the extensive audit in 2007 of PIA practice in government departments and agencies, the first of its kind in Canada and probably anywhere. It was an important initiative, not only for its findings, but also for its salutary effects on PIA practices government-wide and its promotion of PIAs as an effective risk management tool. She underscores the importance of internal oversight in the conduct of PIAs. "Absent appropriate and operational management controls, PIA infrastructures are unlikely to operate as intended."

In the US, Kenneth Bamberger and Deirdre Mulligan say their findings "suggest the importance of continued research into the role of alternate methods of external accountability as a means for strengthening the hand of privacy officers internally". They found that implementation of the PIA requirement has been neither swift nor uniform. Government Accountability Office (GAO) reports have documented specific failures to comply with privacy requirements for programs covered by the E-Government Act. These findings suggest that third-party review and/or audit of PIAs is necessary so that recommendations can be made on improving PIA practice.

In Germany, Florian Thoma explains that processor audits are mandatory. Data processors must not only be chosen diligently and bound by detailed written contracts, but also need to be audited on a regular basis throughout the contract term. Siemens requires each of its providers to be audited prior to the commencement of its operations, and then in defined intervals thereafter.

22.1.11 Common Standards and Good Practice Need To Be Better Identified

As mentioned above, PIAs vary considerably as a practice, process and reports. Currently, there are differences in approaches to PIA, not only between countries, but even within governments, as Kenneth Bamberger and Deirdre Mulligan point out in their review of how two US agencies have implemented the PIA requirement in the adoption of RFID technology. "The two different approaches reflect the highly inconsistent adherence to the PIA mandate across agencies, and even between programs within a single agency."

Stephen Deadman and Amanda Chandler say Vodafone encourages privacy standards across the industry wherever possible by working with its partners, competitors and industry and technology standards bodies. On the other hand, they say there is no single model or form of PIA, as PIAs are used in different contexts, including strategic and operational contexts.

Some steps towards standards have been taken. There is the ISO 22307 voluntary standard which is focused on PIA for the financial services industry. According to Marty Ferris (Chapter 14), the development of ISO 22307:2008 recognised that the frameworks for providing privacy protection among the members of the financial services industry as well as within each country may be different. He says the internationalisation and standardisation of PIAs are critical for cross-border financial transactions.

Sarah Spiekermann says that all industries using RFID will need to develop PIA templates and that industry associations will need to set standards for how to go about PIAs in their respective domains. Laurent Beslay and Anne-Christine Lacoste say that the question of harmonisation of criteria for the assessment of PIA reports will also arise. It is not yet completely clear if an assessment (positive or negative) made in one Member State will be recognised by the DPA of another Member State or if the RFID system owner will have to go through the whole process again for each Member State where a decision is required. Mutual recognition of DPAs' decisions on PIA reports will have to be elaborated and clarified. Further reflection is also needed on the desirability or utility of some sort of certification.

In a globalised world, the problems arising from the existence of different protection systems in different geographical regions can only be a cause of constant concern, says Artemi Rallo. And not only due to the differences that arise when guaranteeing a fundamental right, which may be alarming in themselves, but also due to the subsequent difficulties in relation to international exchanges of personal data. Achieving harmonisation between the multitude of existing legal systems while also guaranteeing a high level of protection in data processing is the ambitious challenge that underlies the Madrid Resolution.

In its explanatory note, the Resolution states that recognition of privacy rights requires the adoption of a universal, legally binding instrument establishing, drawing on and complementing the data protection and privacy principles laid down in several existing instruments, and strengthening the international co-operation between data protection authorities.

In its paper on "The Future of Privacy", the Art. 29 WP stated that "global standards regarding data protection are becoming indispensable" and, to that end, affirmed that the Madrid Resolution deserves support.[4] The Resolution is a first step towards a relevant internationally binding agreement guaranteeing an appropriate protection to privacy rights around the world. PIA is part of the set of principles, rights, obligations and procedures that make up the standards proposed in the Madrid Resolution.

22.1.12 Create a Central Registry of PIAs

The Canadian Office of the Privacy Commissioner's audit report recommended creation of a central registry of PIAs. It would help people to find a particular PIA which might otherwise be buried on a website. Jennifer Stoddart says the purpose of a registry would be to provide a single window of access to PIAs across government, regardless of the originating department and program authority. The registry could

---

[4] Article 29 Data Protection Working Party, The Future of Privacy: Joint contribution to the Consultation of the European Commission on the legal framework for the fundamental right to protection of personal data, Document WP 168, Adopted on 1 December 2009, p. 10. http://ec. europa.eu/justice/policies/privacy/workinggroup/wpdocs/2009_en.htm

be used by the public to better understand the substance of government projects and by central agencies such as the Treasury Board Secretariat and the Privacy Commissioner to monitor PIA activities. Such a registry, she says, might enhance the project management capabilities of institutions and facilitate knowledge sharing between government departments. Precedents for a central index exist, such as that in use by federal institutions to help the public find information about environmental assessments conducted by the Canadian government.

The Alberta Information and Privacy Commissioner has already developed such a registry of all PIAs that have been accepted by the OIPC.[5] Its PIA registry contains summaries taken directly from the PIAs submitted. They do not convey OIPC opinions on the programs or projects referenced.

A central registry might help overcome the current situation in the UK to which Adam Warren and Andrew Charlesworth point in Chapter 9, i.e., there appears to be an inefficient use of government resources, with departments apparently unable to draw effectively upon each other's prior experience and PIA outputs. Lack of cross-governmental communication regarding PIAs signally decreases their use as an effective mechanism for strategic review of privacy risks.

An easily accessible central registry could serve several purposes. One is that it would make it easier to find examples of good practice. Wright and Mordini (Chapter 19) say that, in the instance of ethical assessments, a registry could be strategically important from a policy point of view in the sense that the existence of some assessments, as shown in a central registry, might encourage other organisations to undertake similar assessments and provide guidance on how to do so. The value of good practices depends on how well information about such good practices is disseminated and how easy it is for project managers to find them.

22.1.13 Multi-agency and Transnational Projects Should Be Subject to PIA

So far, there are few instances of multi-agency or transnational PIAs. Yet projects or data exchanges between different organisations, including those based in different countries, may also have privacy impacts. Examples abound. US access to European passenger name records (PNRs) is one such. While a trans-national PIA might be problematic on procedural and organisational terms, say Raab and Wright (Chapter 17), the countries involved in an international surveillance operation, for example, could nevertheless conduct their own PIA. Following its recommendations, each country could negotiate with the others involved to ensure that the surveillance operation was proportionate and necessary or subject to the oversight of a parliamentary committee and/or a court of law.

New Zealand's *Privacy Impact Assessment Handbook* foresaw some years ago that

---

[5] The registry can be found at http://www.oipc.ab.ca/pages/PIAs/Registry.aspx

certain projects will have significant privacy implications in more than one jurisdiction. Indeed, some initiatives will have truly global implications. In such cases, comment might be invited from the privacy commissioners of several countries before finalising the privacy impact report. A significant objective of a PIA in such projects may be to ensure that the project meets or exceeds the data protection and information privacy requirements in all the relevant countries and achieves a level of trust amongst consumers and regulators.[6]

The message here is that transnational projects should not escape the scrutiny of a PIA, simply because they are transnational. Mechanisms and procedures can be developed to deal with such projects – even if that has not happened yet.

Raab and Wright note that transnational PIA has attracted some attention in the corporate world. The international consultancy Deloitte & Touche published a guide to cross-border PIA as long ago as 2001. More recently, a PIA has been performed for a transnational medical information project in Europe. Robin Bayley and Colin Bennett refer to a PIA of a biometrics field trial involving the Canadian Citizenship and Immigration department, the US Immigration and Naturalization Service and the US Department of State. Canada's national police force, the RCMP, has also participated in multi-agency PIAs including multilateral information agreements regarding immigrants.

Artemi Rallo (Chapter 18) supports PIA of transnational projects: "PIAs could be extremely useful in the context of international transfers of data, precisely due to the appropriateness of this instrument to generate evidence demonstrating due diligence.... Those assessments could be used, to a certain extent, to provide a clear record that the transfer was intended to be carried out with the necessary care, a relevant factor in order to determine liabilities in case of non-compliance."

22.1.14 Should PIAs Be Mandatory?

A key issue of debate among PIA experts is whether PIAs should be mandatory, for both public and private sector organisations.

Although PIAs are not mandatory in Australia, Roger Clarke reports in Chapter 5 that the Australian PIA guide has been relevant to corporations since it was first published in 2006. Amendments in 2010 were designed to make clearer the guide's applicability to business enterprises. He says that, given the range of organisations whose operations are seriously privacy-invasive, the PIA notion has a long way to go.

In no jurisdiction in Canada are PIAs mandatory in the private sector, with the exception of Alberta where PIAs are to be conducted by "private" health-care organisations and any other health service providers named in the regulations. National government departments and agencies, however, are subject to the PIA policy. Thus, a PIA should be completed for any initiative involving personal information and

---

[6] Stewart, Blair, *Privacy Impact Assessment Handbook*, Office of the Privacy Commissioner, Auckland, June 2007, p. 14. http://privacy.org.nz/privacy-impact-assessment-handbook/

state security, crime prevention or an international project or agreement. However, the exceptions to release under freedom of information (FOI) legislation allow information to be withheld by redaction where it is harmful to federal-provincial affairs, international affairs and defence, law enforcement and investigations, and security.

Robin Bayley and Colin Bennett conclude that the likelihood of PIAs being conducted is a function of the policy compulsion to undertake them. The requirement to conduct a PIA helps ensure that an organisation puts in place proper privacy and security policies and strategies.

Adam Warren and Andrew Charlesworth note that PIAs have no statutory footing in the UK, and thus cannot be made a legally mandated process for either the public or private sector without further legislative enactment. However, as in other jurisdictions, recent developments in the UK have resulted in a requirement being placed on some parts of the public sector to adopt PIAs as a required element of internal project development processes.

Although the introduction of PIAs into the UK was primarily promoted by the production of the ICO-commissioned Handbook, further impetus was added by a number of data handling scandals involving public and private sector organisations. Arguably the highest profile incident, the loss of 25 million child benefit records by HM Revenue and Customs, resulted in a Cabinet Office review. The resulting report, *Data Handling Procedures in Government*, mandated the use of PIAs in central government departments from July 2008.

From the survey of European DPAs in the context of their chapter, Gwendal Le Grand and Emilie Barrau found that PIA practice is not yet widespread amongst companies. It seems that those who do use PIA are multinationals or at least larger companies. Only two countries (Macedonia, Norway) impose PIA on all data processors but experience suggests that many entities do not comply with this obligation. They found that only one country (the United Kingdom) obliges just public entities to develop PIA for all new central government projects involving significant amounts of personal data.

The survey results show that DPAs in Europe are split on the issue of whether PIAs should be mandatory. Some authorities believe that making PIA compulsory will increase administrative and financial burdens. As a consequence, it could lead to a "ticking the box" exercise, instead of being a process with which entities can properly engage, and it would thus be less effective than current audit practices carried out voluntarily. These authorities believe that PIAs should rather be promoted as "best practice".

Other authorities believe compulsory PIAs would be a good way forward, at least in the long run. PIAs could, for instance, be made available to the DPA at the time of an inspection. Some authorities, while backing a compulsory instrument, believe that it should nevertheless depend on the sector (e.g., administration), size (e.g., big companies) and/or risks involved in data processing (e.g., for sensitive data).

At the European level, there seems to be a trend towards mandatory PIA, at least in some cases. In its 4 November 2011 Communication on a comprehensive approach on personal data protection in the European Union, the European

Commission stated that it will consider whether the future EU legal privacy framework should include "an obligation for data controllers to carry out a data protection impact assessment in specific cases, for instance, when sensitive data are being processed, or when the type of processing otherwise involves specific risks, in particular when using specific technologies, mechanisms or procedures, including profiling or video surveillance". Also, the European Parliament, in a recent resolution on Passenger Name Records has considered that "any new legislative instrument must be preceded by a Privacy Impact Assessment and a proportionality test".

The European Data Protection Supervisor (EDPS) says he "fully supports making data protection officers and privacy impact assessments mandatory, under certain threshold conditions".[7]

The European Commission has already taken steps towards a mandatory PIA. Its RFID Recommendation indicates that *all* RFID operators should assess the impact of their operations on privacy and data protection. Sarah Spiekermann says that the bulk of responsibility for conducting a PIA lies with the system vendor or system implementer and not necessarily the customer. The responsibility of system vendors becomes particularly important as small enterprises (e.g., small retailers or kiosks that just check out goods with an RFID scanner) begin to purchase turnkey RFID systems. The authors of the RFID PIA Framework assumed that system vendors that develop standardised RFID applications will conduct PIAs for all system versions they bring to market because they are the ones who determine the purposes and means of those applications. The authors also thought that in cases where RFID systems are tailored to customer needs, then system vendors would have the prime responsibility to inform their customers of the privacy implications of the RFID application and to use (potentially standardised) PIA templates to check for the privacy risks together with them. The PIA Framework therefore specifies that PIAs need to be done only once for a product series.

Laurent Beslay and Anne-Christine Lacoste question what will happen if companies do not comply with the PIA Framework methodology. Will there be any sanctions? This issue has yet to be discussed in any detail, either in the context of the RFID PIA Framework or in the instance of PIA more generally if PIA is made mandatory.

With the recognition of data protection as a fundamental and autonomous right within the EU legal order, Paul De Hert (Chapter 2) sees no obstacle to imposing via law a duty for all to assess in advance the impact of a technology or a processing operation taking into account the provisions of the EU regulations on data protection. He finds support for his view in the contention of the European Court of Human Rights that stakeholder involvement and opposition to given facts and choices need

---

[7] European Data Protection Supervisor, Opinion of the European Data Protection Supervisor on the Communication from the Commission to the European Parliament, the Council, the Economic and Social Committee and the Committee of the Regions – "A comprehensive approach on personal data protection in the European Union", Brussels, 14 January 2011, p. 22, para 105. http://www.edps.europa.eu/EDPSWEB/edps/Consultation/OpinionsC/OC2011

to be possible at the beginning, but also later on throughout the process (e.g., when new facts emerge).

22.2 PIA Practice: Guidance for Individual PIAs

David Parker writes that impact assessment is intended to be both a continuous *process*, to help policy-makers think through and understand the consequences of government intervention, and a *methodology*, to enable an objective assessment of the positive and negative effects of contemplated intervention. One can so describe PIA too. Indeed, all contributors to this book emphasise the importance of seeing PIA as a process.

PIA processes differ, however. Hence, in this section, we put forward our findings of key elements in good PIA practice based on the comments by the contributors to this book. These findings are particularly addressed to project managers who have the responsibility for initiating a PIA. Again, we use the word "project" as a catch-all for any project, service, technology, program, policy or any other scheme that might impact privacy.

22.2.1 When Is a PIA Necessary?

There are at least two ways one could address the question of whether a PIA is necessary. One is to ask whether the project involves the processing of personal data or could impact any type of privacy or whether the project raises ethical issues. If the answer to any of these questions is yes, then a PIA is necessary.

A second way to address the question is to consider some brief "what if" scenarios the aim of which would be to contemplate what could go wrong if the organisation proceeds with the project. If these scenarios show there are some privacy risks, then a PIA should be initiated.

Blair Stewart offers this caution regarding the initiation of a PIA:

> If this stage is not handled well, there are significant risks. If a PIA is required in circumstances that do not justify an assessment, limited privacy policy or compliance resource may be expended needlessly. If the starting processes are incapable of focusing the assessment on the key issues, there is a risk that the resultant assessment will fail to achieve its potential usefulness (or offer a false sense of security).

Bräutigam identifies four main reasons for conducting privacy assessments at Nokia:

1. to measure the implementation of privacy requirements, to get an understanding of the current status (risks, controls, root causes, etc.);
2. to find out if new projects follow privacy requirements;
3. to serve as a repository for information requests from authorities and consumers;
4. to improve general awareness.

Vodafone's Stephen Deadman and Amanda Chandler also identify several reasons for conducting a PIA:

- as an element of accountability, to demonstrate that the PIA process was performed appropriately;
- to provide a basis for post-implementation review;
- to provide a basis for audit, which is an objective and neutral assessment undertaken by a person or team who is *not* part of delivering the PIA;
- to provide "corporate memory", ensuring that the information gained during the project can be shared with future PIA teams and others outside the organisation.

22.2.2 Determine the Objectives, Scale and Scope of the PIA

Next, organisations should consider the objectives, scale and scope of a PIA. Conducting a PIA can be a resource-intensive exercise. Hence, a PIA should be conducted in a manner that is commensurate with the privacy risk identified. If the risks are not significant, then the scale and scope of a PIA could be limited. If the risks are significant, then the PIA should be more detailed. If the initial assessment reveals that there are significant risks, then the project manager should involve stakeholders to help in considering those and any other risks that may become apparent in the course of the PIA. At this stage, the project manager should identify who the PIA is for (e.g., the organisation itself, the privacy regulator, stakeholders…) and the reasons for conducting the PIA.

Marty Ferris lists PIA objectives for the financial services industry, which could equally apply to PIAs more generally:

- ensuring that privacy protection is a core consideration in the initial considerations of a service and in all subsequent activities during the system development life cycle;
- ensuring that accountability for privacy issues is clearly incorporated;
- providing decision-makers with the information necessary to make fully informed policy, system design and procurement decisions for proposed services based on an understanding of the privacy implications and risks and the options available for avoiding and/or mitigating those risks;
- reducing the risk of having to terminate or substantially modify a service after its implementation in order to comply with privacy requirements;
- providing documentation on the business processes and flow of personal information for use and review by staff and to serve as the basis for consultations with clients, privacy officers and other stakeholders.

He further advises that the PIA process requires a plan indicating the scope of the PIA and systematically establishing the steps to be followed, questions to be answered and options to be examined. This plan should guide the PIA process by stating

- the objectives of the project or service to be examined;
- the privacy policy compliance objectives of the PIA, which as a minimum should comply with the privacy principles in the OECD's 1980 guidelines[8];
- the life cycle phase of the project or service.

Prior to the assessment, the PIA practitioner should follow these steps:

- provide a description of the project and a description of the context in which it is to be undertaken;
- identify the competent expertise needed to perform the PIA and develop the PIA report within the defined scope;
- agree how the PIA report should be integrated into decision-making processes;
- identify known and relevant risks to personal information associated with the project.

While PIAs are usually focused on specific projects, the organisation undertaking the PIA should also examine its organisation-wide practices that could have an impact on privacy, as the Office of the Information and Privacy Commissioner of Alberta counsels.[9]

The scale and scope of a PIA might be determined by the use of scenarios. At Nokia, the business unit scopes the assessment based on a privacy scenario, and agrees an organisation of the assessment and a preliminary schedule. A full-scale PIA may be needed if the consumer service is new or if there are fundamental changes to an existing service. At this stage, the project manager needs to consider who should be involved in the assessment and the schedule for interviews, workshops and testing.

Paul De Hert proposes a bundle of at least seven tests as part of an "honest" PIA, to be carried out by private and public actors planning to develop and implement privacy-relevant technologies or to process personal data. He has formulated these tests from criteria applied and identified by the European Court of Human Rights in privacy case law. The seven tests are the following:

1. The technology should be used in accordance with and as provided by the law.
2. The technology or processing should serve a legitimate aim.
3. The technology or processing should not violate human rights.
4. The technology should be necessary in a democratic society.
5. The technology should not have or give unfettered discretion.
6. The technology should be appropriate, least intrusive, proportionate.
7. The technology should not only respect privacy requirements but also be consistent with other human rights.

---

[8] Organisation for Economic Co-operation and Development (OECD), Guidelines Governing the Protection of Privacy and Transborder Flows of Personal Data, OECD, Paris, 23 Sept 1980. http://www.oecd.org/document/18/0,3343,en_2649_34255_1815186_1_1_1_1,00.html

[9] OIPC of Alberta, PIAs webpage. http://www.oipc.ab.ca/pages/PIAs/default.aspx

22.2.3 Initiate a PIA Early, When It Is Possible to Influence Decision-Making

Nigel Waters has found that PIAs of individual projects are typically undertaken well after the main design parameters have been set, an organisational structure committed and significant costs incurred. Organisations are often only persuaded to commission a PIA late in the development process, and the conduct of the PIA often overlaps with the commencement of operations. Privacy experts should be engaged at much earlier stages, when policies are being formulated and key choices are being made about how to meet organisational objectives.

To be effective, a PIA needs to be conducted at a stage where it can genuinely affect the development of a project, as Adam Warren and Andrew Charlesworth say. They add that PIA needs to be seen as a separate process from compliance checks or data protection audits, both of which comprise analyses of systems already in place against a prevailing legal, management or technology standard.

Artemi Rallo agrees that timing is one of the essential characteristics of a PIA, since this is the only way that its ultimate objective can be achieved: to adapt the project in question to the results obtained, improving it from the moment that it is conceived and preventing certain risks from even occurring.

22.2.4 Who Should Initiate and Conduct the PIA?

Robin Bayley and Colin Bennett provide a concise response to this question:

> Typically, the organisation itself undertakes the analysis and produces the final PIA document(s), usually at the program or project level. The locus of responsibility differs by organisation, but often entails a team approach, with privacy, program and systems staff participating.... By the time a PIA is completed, it should have been reviewed and approved throughout the organisation's hierarchy and have drawn on widespread expertise. Sometimes external consultants will also be contracted.

They cite the Ontario PIA user's guide which recommends that a senior project team member lead the PIA team, taking on the role of project privacy manager. The team should have expertise in policy development, operational program and business design, technology and systems, risk and compliance analysis, procedural and legal and access to information and privacy.[10] Where it is determined that public opinion should be measured or consultations undertaken, PIA teams are urged to work with communications professionals.

At Nokia, IT unit privacy managers have a strong role in PIAs. They are responsible for planning and organising the PIAs, interviewing the product team, suggesting corrective actions and following up on those actions.

---

[10] Information and Privacy Office, Management Board Secretariat, Ontario, *Privacy Impact Assessment: A User's Guide*, June 2001, p. 12. http://www.accessandprivacy.gov.on.ca/english/pia/index.html

At Vodafone, Stephen Deadman and Amanda Chandler say the privacy officer plays a central role in the overall management of operational privacy risk, but others are involved too. For example, the data gathering part of the PIA process could be carried out by the business continuity manager or team, provided with the right questions, with the privacy officer subsequently carrying out the privacy risk assessment. The information security team could gather the relevant privacy-related information in regard to new suppliers during their information security review. Information about the privacy implications of new products and services can be collated by properly trained business analysts, with the privacy officer making the required risk assessment.

John Edwards makes the insightful observation that if the independence of in-house staff can be impugned by regulators or opponents of a particular project, "why should a consultant, whose livelihood and reputation depend on delivering work which pleases, rather than annoys those who pay him or her, have any extra credibility?"

22.2.5 Describe the Proposed Project and Map the Information Flows

The PIA should contain a description of the proposed project or service as well as of the organisational privacy management structure and policies. It should also describe the information flows, i.e., the creation, collection, retention, use, disclosure and disposition of personal or personally identifiable information. It should also include an identification of those who handle the information during the administration of a program or an activity.[11]

22.2.6 Identify and Engage Stakeholders

Merely complying with privacy laws will provide organisations with no assurance that their schemes will be acceptable to citizens and consumers, writes Roger Clarke. He describes consultation as central to the PIA process. "The objectives of a PIA cannot be achieved if the process is undertaken behind closed doors. In a complex project applying powerful technologies, there are many segments of the population that are affected. It is intrinsic to the process that members of the public provide input to the assessment, and that the outcomes reflect their concerns."[12]

The lack of engagement and/or consultation with stakeholders is a weakness in most PIA activity. Despite the US E-Government Act's explicit commitment to the

---

[11] Treasury Board of Canada Secretariat, Directive on Privacy Impact Assessment, Ottawa, 1 April 2010. http://www.tbs-sct.gc.ca/pol/doc-eng.aspx?id=18308&section=text

[12] Clarke, Roger, "Privacy Impact Assessment Guidelines", Xamax Consultancy Pty Ltd, February 1998. http://www.xamax.com.au/DV/PIA.html

production of PIAs before developing or purchasing technology systems, and to the publication of PIAs, Kenneth Bamberger and Deirdre Mulligan note that it fails to provide for public consultation.

> The lack of explicit mechanisms for public participation in the PIA process limits the opportunities for outside experts to assist. . . in identifying the privacy implications of often complex technological systems. Absent external direction or internal efforts to engage the public through a comment process or other means, public input is limited to the stage in which proposals and programs are already well developed. Relegated to this late stage, the comments – whether by experts or the general public – are more likely to result in revisions on the margins rather than fundamental switches in technology or architectural design.

Like their American counterparts, Canadian PIAs seldom involve public consultation, opinion polling or other means of gauging the privacy values of the Canadian public. They tend to focus on legal compliance rather than asking larger questions. Although most methodologies include guidance about considering these issues, the end product, and that which gets reviewed, tends to resemble a compliance checklist and does not require documentation of deliberations.

An exception to the prevalent Canadian practice, the Alberta PIA guidance features consultation, because, it says, "focused public discussion conducted early in the process can help program or system designers anticipate public reaction to proposals or help to eliminate options that meet with significant resistance".

Some companies recognise the need to engage external stakeholders. In describing Vodafone's strategic PIA process, Stephen Deadman and Amanda Chandler say engagement of external stakeholders helps to "shape and inform opinion, conduct research or seek to agree standards with other industry players, as well as provide feedback to shape Vodafone's internal policy."

There are many good reasons why organisations should engage stakeholders in a PIA, some of which can be found in the ISO 27005:2008 standard on information security risk management. Engaging stakeholders provides a means to

- provide assurance of the outcome of the organisation's risk management,
- collect risk information,
- share the results from the risk assessment and present the risk treatment plan,
- avoid or reduce both occurrence and consequence of information security breaches due to the lack of mutual understanding among decision-makers and stakeholders,
- support decision-making,
- obtain new information security knowledge,
- co-ordinate with other parties and plan responses to reduce consequences of any incident,
- give decision makers and stakeholders a sense of responsibility about risks,
- improve awareness.[13]

---

[13] International Organization for Standardization (ISO), Information technology—Security techniques—Information security risk management, International Standard, ISO/IEC 27005:2008(E), First edition, 15 June 2008, p. 22.

Wright and Mordini also offer various reasons why project managers should engage stakeholders and undertake a consultation when developing new technologies or projects. For one thing, Article 41 of the Charter of Fundamental Rights of the European Union, entitled the Right to good administration, makes clear that this right includes "the right of every person to be heard, before any individual measure which would affect him or her adversely is taken. . .", which suggests that consultation with stakeholders is not only desirable but necessary. But there are other reasons too. Stakeholders may have some information or ideas or views or values which the project manager had not previously considered. They may be able to suggest alternative courses of actions to achieve the desired objectives and may have some good suggestions for resolving complex issues.[14] They may be able to suggest some safeguards which would minimise the risks that might otherwise explode after a technology or project is launched. By consulting stakeholders before launch, the project manager may be able to lower his liability and avoid some nasty surprises. As a minimum, the policy-maker or project manager will earn some good will by consulting stakeholders who might otherwise be among his chief critics.

Also, technology development is often too complex to be fully understood by a single agent, as Sollie and others have pointed out.[15] Similarly, Palm and Hansson state that "It would be delusive to believe that technology developers are conscious of all the effects of their products. In many cases, negative side effects come as a surprise to technology developers themselves."[16] Furthermore, by engaging stakeholders, project managers may avoid subsequent criticism about a lack of consultation. Engaging stakeholders before the project is implemented may be a useful way of testing the waters, of gauging the public's reaction to the project. In any event, "A central premise of democratic government – the existence of an informed electorate – implies a free flow of information."[17] Even if participation does not increase support for a decision, it may clear up misunderstandings about the nature of a controversy and the views of various participants. And it may contribute generally to building trust in the process, with benefits for dealing with similar issues in the future.[18]

---

[14] Stern, Paul C., and Harvey V. Fineberg (eds.), *Understanding Risk: Informing Decisions in a Democratic Society*, Committee on Risk Characterization, National Research Council, National Academy Press, Washington, DC, 1996.

[15] Sollie, Paul, "Ethics, Technology Development and Uncertainty: an Outline for Any Future Ethics of Technology", *Journal of Information, Communications & Ethics in Society*, Vol. 5, No. 4, 2007, pp. 293–306 [p. 302]. Moor also supports better collaboration among ethicists, scientists, social scientists and technologists. Moor, James H., "Why We Need Better Ethics for Emerging Technologies", *Ethics and Information Technology*, Vol. 7, No. 3, 2005, pp. 111–119 [p. 118].

[16] Palm, Elin, and Sven Ove Hansson, "The Case for Ethical Technology Assessment (eTA)", *Technological Forecasting & Social Change*, Vol. 73, 2006, pp. 543–558 [p. 547].

[17] National Research Council, Committee on Risk Perception and Communications, *Improving Risk Communication*, National Academy Press, Washington, DC, 1989, p. 9. http://www.nap.edu/openbook.php?record_id=1189&page=R1

[18] Stern and Fineberg, op. cit., pp. 23–24.

Paul De Hert argues that the current human rights framework requires States to organise decision-making procedures that involve the persons affected by technologies. Art. 8 does not contain an explicit procedural requirement, but the decision-making process leading to measures of interference must be fair and such as to afford due respect to the interests of the individual as safeguarded by the article.[19] This requirement of fairness implies at least that evidence is gathered and that the impact of technologies are studied in advance, that the public has access to this evidence and that individuals can come up in court against decisions that, they feel, do not take their viewpoint into consideration.

Laurent Beslay and Anne-Christine Lacoste note that one of the reasons why the Art. 29 Working Party did not approve the first draft RFID PIA framework proposed by industry was because it did not include a provision for stakeholder consultation. The revised draft, which was endorsed by the Art. 29 Working Party on 11 February 2011, did include such a provision. As an aside, Beslay and Lacoste say that a difficult issue for the Working Party was just how representative were the industry stakeholders who submitted the draft. According to the European Commission's RFID Recommendation, Member States were supposed to ensure that industry proposed a framework. Implicitly, Member States should have made sure that this group of industries was representative enough; however, throughout the process that led to approval of the Framework, the adequacy of representativeness was never demonstrated clearly to the Art. 29 Working Party.

If the stakeholders engaged in the PIA are not reasonably representative of those concerned about or affected by a new technology or service, there is a risk that the validity of the PIA may not be accepted. A PIA should assess a project against the needs, expectations and concerns of all stakeholders, including but not limited to legal requirements.

Clarke suggests that a preparation stage be undertaken which includes developing a consultation plan. He says that "Any project that is sufficiently complex and potentially privacy-threatening that it requires a full-scale PIA is likely to affect many parties."[20] Further, he recommends embedding PIA consultations into the project stakeholder management strategy.

Engaging stakeholders may be easier said than done, judging by an observation from Adam Warren and Andrew Charlesworth about the difficulties encountered by the Office for National Statistics (ONS) in its PIA in the run-up to the UK's 2011 census. Only two groups attended the ONS consultation event (with another individual contributing via e-mail). This experience suggests the need for a clearer, more consistent process for ensuring wider societal engagement with PIAs, particularly in the early stages of projects. Despite the ONS experience, Warren and Charlesworth

---

[19] ECtHR, *Taskın and Others* v. *Turkey,* Judgment of 10 November 2004, Application no. 46117/99, § 118.

[20] See "Part II – The PIA Process, Chapter IV – Full-scale PIA, 2. Preparation Phase", written by Roger Clarke, in *Privacy Impact Assessment Handbook*, Version 2, Information Commissioner's Office, UK, June 2009. http://www.ico.gov.uk/upload/documents/pia_handbook_html_v2/html/2-Chap4-2.html

say that wider availability of user-friendly PIA reports, combined with innovation in public engagement strategies should, over time, create a greater expectation amongst the public of involvement in policy decisions that affect their privacy.

Project managers can employ various techniques or methodologies aimed at ensuring effective consultation and engagement with stakeholders. The ICO PIA Handbook says some useful ways of ensuring effective consultation include:

- priming discussions by providing some initial information about the project;
- making sure there is ongoing dialogue with consultees throughout the PIA process;
- ensuring the participation of representatives of, and advocates for, stakeholder groups who have appropriate background in the technologies, systems and privacy impacts involved;
- facilitating interactions among the participants;
- making sure that there is sufficient diversity among those groups or individuals being consulted, to ensure that all relevant perspectives are represented, and all relevant information is gathered;
- making sure that each group has the opportunity to provide information and comment, even including multiple rounds of consultation where necessary;
- making sure that the method of consultation suits the consultation group, for example using workshops or focus groups as an alternative to, or even as well as, formal written consultation;
- making sure that the information provided by all parties to the consultation is fed into the subsequent rounds of design and implementation activities; and
- ensuring that the perspectives, concerns and issues raised during the consultation process are seen to be reflected in the outcomes of the PIA process.[21]

It also offers suggestions where there are security concerns. It says that parts of a PIA that have security concerns can be separated into closed or confidential appendices and separate, relatively closed discussion sessions. Where security considerations result in the suppression of information, proxy measures could be devised. For example, the security-sensitive information could be provided to a trusted third party who could then deliver to the PIA consultation group members evaluative comments that avoid exposing the information.

Techniques for engaging stakeholders include interviews, workshops, Delphis, focus groups, forecasting, mediation, participatory assessment, monitoring and evaluation techniques, policy exercises, role-playing, scenario analysis and SWOT analysis.

One of the first things to be done in engaging stakeholders is to explain to them what the process will be, why the consultation is being undertaken, what results are expected and how they might be used. Stakeholders should be invited to suggest other stakeholders who are not represented in the group but should be.

22.2.7 A Compliance Check Is Only Part of a PIA

While a PIA report should include references to relevant laws, codes and guidelines, as well as any internal policies, Paul De Hert says one must consider more

---

[21] Ibid.

qualitative requirements that have to do with legitimacy, participation and, especially, proportionality. References to these requirements are included in data protection regulations, but they share their place with more technical or formal requirements such as the requirement to secure data and have data closed off to third parties. These qualitative principles – accounting for the difference between a compliance check and a true impact assessment – are key considerations in determining whether privacy is respected in the context of the European Convention on Human Rights and the relevant case law of the European Court of Human Rights.

John Edwards agrees: "It is evident that a privacy impact assessment based solely on compliance (in spirit or in law) is hardly going to be a comprehensive review of privacy issues. Data protection or information privacy is just a subset of the innate integrity, autonomy and dignity possessed by all humanity, which is capable of being compromised by the thoughtless actions of others and which we sometimes call 'privacy'".

Siemens' Florian Thoma says a compliance check is only part of the PIA. "PIAs can and should go further: in particular, where other laws and regulations require the collection, processing and use of data, a PIA helps to understand what really is required by such other rules, how they interact with data protection legislation and to what extent they mandate not only the collection of data but are prescriptive or flexible regarding the means." Similarly, say Stephen Deadman and Amanda Chandler, Vodafone views privacy as a core corporate value, beyond simply meeting legal obligations.

Laurent Beslay and Anne-Christine Lacoste note that the data protection framework remains applicable, with or without an endorsed framework for impact assessments. This means notably that the principles of necessity and proportionality must be complied with, as well as the obligation to inform individuals about the processing of their data.

22.2.8 A PIA Should Address All Types of Privacy

One can identify several types of privacy. Informational privacy or data protection is only one type of privacy. Drawing on Clarke, the ICO PIA Handbook refers to four conventional but overlapping types of privacy: privacy of personal information, privacy of the person, privacy of personal behaviour and privacy of personal communications.[22] Vodafone's Stephen Deadman and Amanda Chandler say that Vodafone's most fundamental privacy obligation is to protect the secrecy of communications, but they also speak of other types of privacy, including location-based privacy. They say that Vodafone's approach to privacy provides a principles-based framework, rather than a prescriptive, rules-based approach. The nature of privacy risk is not fixed, nor is it easily defined. While data protection regulation seeks

---

[22] ICO, PIA *Handbook*, p. 14. These four types of privacy draw on Roger Clarke's categorisations. See Clarke, Roger, "What's Privacy?", 2006. http://www.rogerclarke.com/DV/Privacy.html

to provide a framework for the protection of personal data, this only reflects a portion of privacy harms, particularly as new forms of privacy risk emerge with new technologies and services. Vodafone's privacy principles provide a simple but flexible framework to help manage the company's response to a variety of privacy risks across diverse markets, where perceptions of privacy are shaped by social and cultural factors, and where the legal and operational contexts vary widely. At the same time, Vodafone's local teams are required to ensure they address local privacy concerns and are not out of step with best practices or behaviours of its primary peer-group companies in any particular local market.

In addition to privacy's value to the individual and as an individual right, Raab and Wright remind us that privacy has a social value, as Priscilla Regan and others have pointed out. "Whether or not one is particularly concerned about the loss of one's own privacy, the reduction in society's ability to sustain privacy as a general good and a constitutive value has consequences for citizenship and the relation between the individual and the state or other organisations."

22.2.9 ... and Other Values Too

John Edwards alludes to the difficulty of addressing other values – the assessor may bring his or her own values into the process and to assumptions and assertions about what factors are to be taken into account, and how serious they are. The PIA report must ensure that subjective assessments are clearly flagged as such, and be couched in terms of a "sensitivity analysis" to reduce the effect of the subjectivity. In other words, an assessor must recognise the bias and subjectivity that he or she brings to the task, declare that in the report, seek empirical backing for any position taken (e.g., public surveys on attitudes) and present a range of scenarios with different consequences evident for decision-makers.

Raab and Wright are of the view that the scope of PIA in regard to surveillance currently is too limited because it mainly concerns impacts on individual privacy. They argue that the range of impacts or risks to be considered should be extended to other rights and values pertaining to the individual (such as dignity, autonomy and a sense of being a person) as well as its impact on other targets and consequences, intended or not, that may not normally be recognised in the risk analysis that PIA prescribes.

Wright and Mordini strike a similar chord, i.e., that the development and deployment of new information and communications technologies and applications, fuelled by the use of personal information, may raise not only privacy concerns, but also ethical issues. They point to important ethical values, such as human dignity, freedom, democracy, human rights protection, pluralism, non-discrimination, tolerance, justice, solidarity and gender equality. They propose and describe an ethical impact assessment (EIA) framework, which could complement a privacy impact assessment. Like a PIA, an EIA could be used as a way to ensure ethical implications are adequately examined by stakeholders before deployment so that mitigating measures can be taken as necessary. While it may be impossible to foresee all of the ethical and other consequences of an emerging technology, nevertheless, an

EIA, involving different stakeholders from different disciplines and backgrounds, may be a good way of examining its critical implications for individuals, groups, organisations and society.

22.2.10 With Stakeholders, Identify the Risks and Impacts of the Project

Sarah Spiekermann advocates the risk assessment process depicted in Fig. 15.3 in Chapter 15, which was used in development of the RFID PIA Framework. An organisation needs to first understand its *privacy targets*, then analyse how these targets are threatened and then identify options (or controls) for avoiding or mitigating the risks. However, the RFID Framework focuses on only one type of privacy, i.e., informational privacy or data protection, rather than all types of privacy. Its identification of privacy targets is essentially based on the fair information principles, promulgated in the OECD Guidelines and adopted or adapted by data protection legislation and other PIA guides. Spiekermann recognises that taking legislation as the privacy target for PIA also has drawbacks, one of which is that data protection laws may not cover all of the privacy risks.

A PIA must not only identify threats, but also rate them, as ENISA does. The project manager or policy-maker, informed by the principles of proportionality and necessity, should consider the *likelihood* that various privacy threats will occur. Threats can occur from within and outside of a particular system or service and derive from likely uses and possible misuses of the information. A full-scale PIA would typically involve a stakeholder group in identifying threats and determining their likelihood. This group should include technical staff, managers who collect and process personal data, those responsible for data protection and end users of the technology or service. Potentially, additional external stakeholders, such as privacy rights groups, may be consulted.

Agreeing with ENISA, Wright and De Hert in Chapter 1 see the need for PIA to identify vulnerabilities and threats. Risks could arise from vulnerabilities in the scheme under consideration (a lack of security safeguards, for instance, or the fact that sensitive information is processed), as well as from external threats (such as theft or misuse of data). In the view of the authors, the risk assessment should also take into account the impact on the individual and on society.

22.2.11 Questions

Questions feature in virtually all PIA methodologies as a way of stimulating consideration of the issues raised by a new technology, service or policy. Wright and Mordini emphasise the importance of asking questions, which may help in identifying issues and/or risks that might not otherwise be uncovered. John Edwards concludes his chapter with a set of questions for the assessor, while Blair Stewart's chapter has questions for the regulator.

Tobias Bräutigam says that, "in addition to some core privacy issues (e.g., data sharing with third parties, profiling), many questions are common with security issues. This is also the reason why the most common assessment done at Nokia is called a privacy impact and security assessment (PISA)." Nokia has more than 100 privacy and security questions in its PISA, which has free text fields and the possibility to attach information. Bräutigam says it is not advisable to rely only on closed questions, such as yes/no type of questions or questions that let the interviewee choose from a set of given answers. While closed questions are needed, as they are easier to evaluate and help with the scoping, open questions are essential to find hidden privacy problems. "What if" questions, implicit in developing scenarios, are also important.

22.2.12 Identify Options (Controls) for Avoiding or Mitigating Negative Privacy Impacts

PIAs conducted in both the public and private sectors often entail cost-benefit analyses of various mitigation strategies in order to arrive at decisions. Robin Bayley and Colin Bennett report that those conducting large numbers of PIAs have been able to compile privacy risk and control/mitigation matrices to improve the efficiency with which PIAs may be completed as well as the quality of the PIA product. With this approach, knowledge is accumulated and passed on within an entity or from consultant to client in a cost-effective manner.

The crucial step in the privacy risk assessment process is to identify controls that can help to minimise, mitigate or eliminate the identified privacy risks. Controls are either of a technical or non-technical nature, as Sarah Spiekermann explains. Technical controls are incorporated into an application, e.g., access control mechanisms, authentication mechanisms and encryption methods. Non-technical controls, on the other hand, are management and operational controls, e.g., policies or operational procedures. Controls can be categorised as being preventive or detective. Preventive controls inhibit violation attempts, while detective controls warn operators about violations or attempted violations. In the privacy context specifically is a category of "natural" privacy controls created by the environment. Natural privacy controls are physical or social artefacts in the environment that enforce privacy-sensitive behaviour simply through the force of their existence. For example, if RFID readers cannot track items or individuals and are not physically installed (i.e., because there is no business case for it), then "naturally" there is also no (likely) threat to privacy.

22.2.13 Justify the Business Case for the Residual Risk and Maintain a Risk Register

Following the PIA, one or more risks may remain if a new project is to be undertaken. However, the benefits may be such that these risks are regarded as worth taking. These residual risks should be explicitly justified and logged in the organisation's risk register.

Vodafone includes in its PIA report a section that provides the business case justifying privacy intrusion and its implications, where treatment or mitigating action has not been recommended and/or agreed. At Vodafone, the privacy officer is required to log in a risk register all privacy risks and associated management information (such as business owner, description of mitigating action, deadline for implementation, decision to accept risk, etc.).

Capturing information for the risk register is not a one-off exercise, as Stephen Deadman and Amanda Chandler point out. The information captured is only accurate for the date that it was collected. It is, therefore, imperative that not only are the outputs kept under review by the privacy officer, but that the PIA is repeated on a regular basis to capture any new privacy risks that may have arisen due to a re-organisation of the business or commercial teams, or because of a change in commercial or business strategy.

22.2.14 Review and Update the PIA as the Project Progresses

As indicated by the preceding paragraph, the process of identifying, discussing and dealing with issues should be ongoing throughout the project and perhaps even after it has been implemented, if only because new issues may arise that were not evident at the outset of the project development. Moor has made this point: "Because new technology allows us to perform activities in new ways, situations may arise in which we do not have adequate policies in place to guide us." Ethical problems can be generated at any point, says Moor, "but the number of ethical problems will be greater as the revolution progresses".[23]

John Edwards points out that, as the practitioner works with the project team, the PIA report may change over time as the risks are avoided or mitigated, so much so that the final report "is very bland, and contains reassurances about the project without the context of how bad things could have been had the privacy impact assessment not been running alongside the development of IT solutions and business processes". He goes on to say in Chapter 8 that

> If the report is to inform the project staff of privacy issues as they arise and to make recommendations which are then taken up and incorporated into the design, it will look different at the end of the project than a report prepared for a regulator or steering group. . . . It will be a living document, informing decision-makers at all critical points and, at the end, will be largely spent, its purpose fulfilled.

---

[23] Moor, op. cit. In his paper, Moor proposes the following hypothesis, which he calls "Moor's Law: As technological revolutions increase their social impact, ethical problems increase."

22.2.15 Prepare the PIA Report and Implement the Recommendations

As John Edwards suggests above, the assessor should prepare the PIA report (the end to a means) as a "living" document, updated as necessary as a project progresses, and the project manager or his organisation should implement the recommendations, some of which may be implemented before the PIA report is even written. The report should include a description of agreed treatment or mitigating actions together with timelines for implementation.

A PIA report is not an end in itself and will not generally lead unaided to better privacy outcomes, as Nigel Water says. And, adds Tobias Bräutigam, "Even if assessments are conducted, there is a lot of work to do in implementing the findings. It is best to think of privacy governance as an interlinked system which needs to be constructed in a way that information is shared freely, both bottom-up and top-down."

Stephen Deadman and Amanda Chandler say the regularity with which PIA is repeated will depend on the privacy sensitive nature of the personal information involved and/or the privacy intrusive nature of the activity. Thus, for a high privacy risk, the PIA may need to be repeated on a six-monthly basis until the agreed mitigating actions have been implemented and therefore have reduced the likelihood of the privacy risk materialising, while for a low privacy risk activity, the PIA may only need to be repeated every two years unless there is a relevant legislative change or a major re-organisation in the business and commercial arrangements.

The different iterations of the report should be retained for audit and other purposes. The report should have value as corporate memory. In case key personnel leave the project or other stakeholders (including those from the regulator) move on to other matters, the PIA report can be an important resource to explain what has happened with the project.

22.2.16 Training and Raising Awareness

An ongoing employee awareness program is needed to effectively raise the profile of PIAs and regulatory requirements for their performance with program managers and new hires, as Jennifer Stoddart and others have commented.

Tobias Bräutigam says, at Nokia, "It is imperative that all personnel supporting the product or service have been trained on privacy and security. The training should include the communication of the information security policy and data privacy requirements." He adds that "General awareness campaigns should go hand in hand with targeted training. Culture and awareness need time to grow. Privacy assessments are in themselves a step towards changing corporate cultures." Nokia uses innovative ways to raise awareness and provide training on privacy to its employees. Bräutigam mentions desktop e-learning programs, privacy screen savers and a fantasy privacy game called *Privacy Pursuit*.

Siemens' Florian Thoma agrees that training is important:

The need for practical advice and training remains high, but this is a must to familiarise staff with privacy and avoid its being seen as a field that is best left exclusively to the experts. . . . Our training program (comprising both onsite and web-based trainings and other elements) has acquainted major parts of the data protection organisation and, subsequently, the legal, compliance, IT and HR functions with insight into the rights and freedoms and the underlying values. Realistically though, this will be a long-term program requiring significant resources.

22.2.17 PIA Has Value – Get It!

PIA encourages cost-effective solutions, since it is less expensive to build "privacy by design" into projects, policies, technologies and other such initiatives at the design phase than attempt a more costly retrofit after a technology is deployed or a policy promulgated. A PIA creates an opportunity for organisations to anticipate and address the likely impacts of new initiatives, to foresee problems and identify what needs to be done to design in features that minimise any impact on privacy and/or to find less privacy-intrusive alternatives. Some organisations recognise that privacy can give them a strategic advantage. Others conduct PIAs as a risk management process, recognising that business can be affected by privacy incidents such as breaches and complaints.

Robin Bayley and Colin Bennett say that PIAs are useful in two ways: "first, for the analysis they force an organisation to undertake during the development of new programs and services, often resulting in program modifications and privacy improvements; and second, in their use by regulators, including central agencies charged with privacy responsibilities, those who allocate funds and independent privacy commissioners. . . . Further, PIAs can be used in internal and external audits to determine if planned mitigations have been implemented."

Adam Warren and Andrew Charlesworth similarly argue that

The data controller will benefit from engaging in a risk management assessment which reduces the likelihood of negative public reaction, and increases its ability to reduce the need for costly retroactive amendments to systems and processes. The regulator may have access, either as part of the process, or retrospectively, to information detailing the actions and decisions of the data controller based on its assessment, which would then inform its own actions in regard to that data controller. The data subject may have greater access to information about the data controller's processes and the steps that have been taken to ensure the integrity and security of their personal data.

Laurent Beslay and Anne-Christine Lacoste say that "The use of this tool by industry will contribute to a higher level of trust and ultimately will also facilitate the legal procedure by demonstrating the level of risk and the corresponding mitigation measures."

The company representatives who have contributed chapters to this book profess to be convinced of the value of PIA. Tobias Bräutigam says the general opinion in Nokia is that they are a cost-effective way to ensure privacy compliance. In fact, he says, "the costs of corrective actions are a thousand times more costly when a service is in the operational phase compared to the design phase". All experts at Nokia to whom he spoke in preparing his chapter stated that the benefits of PIAs far outweigh the costs. Privacy assessments have helped Nokia to decrease the risk of financial loss caused by compensation and penalties. They are also part of implementing privacy-by-design principles. This is why it is so important to have (self-)assessments at a very early stage, when changes can easily be implemented.

Florian Thoma says at Siemens PIAs are regarded as having value in several ways, including:

- avoiding risks to individuals, to the company's operations and reputation;
- avoiding unnecessary cost to the company;
- protecting the company through an increased level of IT security.

Despite these apparent benefits of PIA, Adam Warren and Andrew Charlesworth comment that "Whilst some private sector companies do engage in PIA-like processes, in general, the private sector has up till now shown little enthusiasm for the ICO's handbook."

Kenneth Bamberger and Deirdre Mulligan have a similar view:

> it is notoriously difficult to make organisations take into account 'secondary mandates' – values at best orthogonal to, and at worst in tension with, the institution's primary mission. This is true when the goal is to force business organisations to prioritise legal goals such as market fairness or consumer safety along with their pursuit of profit. It is equally true when the aim is to force government agencies primarily responsible for security, transportation or the efficient administration of social benefits, to consider secondary goals, such as environmental protection or policy-making transparency.

Blair Stewart asks whether PIA has delivered on its potential. He says the time is arriving when an attempt should be made to check on whether PIA has "delivered the goods". The potential is undeniable but it is not unreasonable to ask to see the evidence of PIA's usefulness in practice. Laurent Beslay and Anne-Christine Lacoste make much the same point: the efficiency of PIA will eventually need to be measured, and the way it will be measured has yet to be defined.

22.3 Room for Improvement and Concluding Remarks

Although the use of PIA is growing in both the public and private sectors, there is room for improvement and a sharing of good practice. Robin Bayley and Colin Bennett find room for improvement in the scope of analysis for complex initiatives, such as those involving new technologies, sensitive personal information or vulnerable groups or where there is coercive collection. In a 2004 speech, a Canadian privacy commissioner official described some of the common deficiencies in PIAs:

- confusing privacy with security and confidentiality, and thereby overlooking broader issues such as consent, excessive collection of personal data and so on;
- attention limited to the disclosure of information outside the organisation, rather than access controls within;
- seeing the PIA process as a legal compliance audit;
- the failure to link identified risks with the specific design elements of a project; and
- the proposed mitigating measures often not appropriate to the risks identified, for instance, using public communications to allay fears instead of directly addressing the risks from which such fears might arise.

As expertise has spread, practitioners and organisations have learned that standard mitigations will be accepted for certain privacy risks. There is a risk that complacency will set in and that a cookie-cutter approach rather than serious analysis of a particular initiative will take place, especially when a large number of similar PIAs are completed for different organisations using a common framework. Such analysis might not take into account peculiar aspects of an individual application such as the physical setting.

Another challenge to quality comes with universality. When a great number of initiatives require a PIA, this necessarily leads to those PIAs being completed by people with little knowledge of privacy or stretching the resources of qualified staff. It can take experience and a good deal of knowledge to recognise a privacy issue. In part, this is addressed by review of draft PIAs by the organisation's specialised privacy officers, but there is a chance that some issues will be missed or understated, as privacy novices will not have knowledge of privacy commissioner decisions, past incidents and all available mitigation options. One way to address this is by providing specialised training. This challenge can further be addressed by classifying PIAs into two types and ensuring that knowledgeable people are assigned to PIAs for initiatives with higher privacy risks.

Although PIAs are mandatory in the US government, they have been performed in a highly variable way. Kenneth Bamberger and Deirdre Mulligan note that one PIA that was less than two pages long: "The Department of State (DOS) proposed a Rule incorporating RFID technology into US passports. Its one and one-half page 'e-Passport' PIA, consisting of seven paragraphs, failed to discuss the technical aspects of the program, alternative technologies, risks or their mitigation. The program was ultimately adopted with significant modifications late in the process of program development, but with criticism as to its security vulnerabilities and privacy risks."

Tobias Bräutigam says that Nokia has learned that having the findings alone is not enough; the key is to have a supporting structure that follows up on the status of those findings. This sounds obvious; however, implementation requires different people with different roles in the company to be aware of the findings. Almost all persons whom he interviewed for his chapter saw implementation of reported findings as one of the core challenges. Nokia has been addressing the problem by involving some management teams in the PIA reporting process.

Siemens intends to implement a more uniform approach to PIA, including further steps towards a harmonised understanding of PIA, to ensure a minimum level of assessments occurs throughout the company. It also sees value in developing some metrics to get a better understanding of the costs and benefits associated with PIA. Ultimately, effective PIA that shows clear results can help to support the role and function of the in-house data protection officer and thereby businesses' self-regulation. Siemens believes in the benefits of a methodical approach towards PIA. In a complex environment, however, the implementation and full development of the concept needs to occur step by step.

Laurent Beslay and Anne-Christine Lacoste note that in the environmental field sector-specific best available techniques (BATs) are commonly defined between the European legislator and the main industry stakeholders. The implementation of these BATs is not an obligation for the industry. However, their implementation, which is technologically neutral, should guarantee a level of pollution emission which will be below the ones authorised. This procedure could be adapted to the RFID field. The European Commission together with representatives from the industry could produce and adopt reference documents on best available techniques. These reference documents could then be used by industry as guidance to implement applications in compliance with the legal framework. DPAs could also use them to facilitate their evaluation of those implementations.

Jennifer Stoddart says that, notwithstanding Canada's policy requirements, PIAs have not always been performed as and when required. As recently as 2007, nearly 70 per cent of federal government departments reported that they did not have a formal management framework in place to support the conduct of PIAs. Despite the government's aim of ensuring that privacy protection is a key consideration in a project's initial framing, PIAs were often completed well after program implementation. In many cases, PIAs were not completed at all. She says, "How an organisation manages the privacy issues arising from its operations is often a function of the administrative infrastructure it has in place to support and guide the production of PIAs. The absence of any such framework is likely to have a direct and measurable influence on the effectiveness and quality of PIAs. Once privacy is understood as a strategic variable for organisations, the need to factor privacy analysis into the management of organisational risk becomes increasingly compelling."

The previous sentence is a fitting one with which to draw the conclusion to this book. In organising this book, the editors had three main objectives, as stated in Chapter 1. We wanted to provide a reasonably comprehensive overview of PIA activity around the world. We wanted to identify open issues in PIA policy and practice. We wanted to identify some of the best elements of existing PIA policy and practice in order to make recommendations on how PIA policy and practice can be improved to achieve "the great potential" of which Nigel Waters speaks. We hope the reader will agree that these objectives have been achieved. With the growing interest in PIA, we also hope this book's findings will be taken into account by policy-makers as they frame new or revised PIA policies and by project-managers as they undertake a PIA, preferably at an early stage when it is still possible to influence the decisions aimed at improving a project, technology, service or other scheme with privacy impacts.

We whole-heartedly agree with Roger Clarke who says that PIAs play a vital role in achieving both privacy protection for individuals and risk management for organisations.[24] Therefore, most of all, we hope that those reading this book will use PIA to avoid or minimise privacy risks. Whether the costs of taking early action to deal with those risks are a thousand times less than later retrofits, as one of our contributors effusively puts it, the cost-benefit ratio seems clearly to favour PIAs, at least in the views of the editors and contributors to this book. Engaging stakeholders in the process will foster trust and confidence that the organisation is doing the right thing and, who knows, help to reinforce privacy as a cornerstone of democracy.

---

[24] Clarke, Roger, "An Evaluation of Privacy Impact Assessment Guidance Documents", *International Data Privacy Law*, Vol. 1, No. 2, May 2011, pp. 111–120 [p. 120]. http://idpl. oxfordjournals.org/content/1/2.toc

About the Authors

Kenneth A. Bamberger is Professor of Law at the University of California, Berkeley, School of Law (Boalt Hall), and an affiliated faculty member with the Center for the Study of Law and Society. He teaches courses on Administrative Law, First Amendment Law, and Technology and Governance. His research focuses on regulatory decision-making; the roles of public and private actors in governance; business regulation and corporate compliance; and related issues of technology in governance, with a particular focus on information privacy and other forms of risk management.

Emilie Barrau holds the position of legal advisor at the CNIL, the French data protection authority. She has been working in the European and International department since May 2010, primarily on the review of the EU privacy framework. Previously (2004–2010), she worked for BEUC, the European consumer organisation in Brussels, as a legal officer and a European project manager. She was leading the BEUC team on consumer rights' in the digital environment, following the issues of unfair commercial practices, advertising, data protection and privacy. She holds a Master's degree in consumer protection and competition law (Université de Montpellier, France) and a LL.M. in International Business Law (Exeter University, UK).

Robin M. Bayley is President of Linden Consulting, Inc., Privacy and Policy Advisors, which she started in 2003 after a career in the British Columbia government. Robin developed policy and legislation and advised ministries on compliance with information and privacy law. She has conducted and reviewed privacy impact assessments and developed personal information sharing agreements. She advises public bodies and private organisations on meeting their legal privacy/data protection obligations while achieving their business goals and has assisted data protection authorities by developing internal processes, public information and complaint tools. Robin has co-authored several articles, chapters and reports on Canadian administration of information and privacy law, video surveillance law, and privacy impact assessments.

Colin J. Bennett is Professor of Political Science at the University of Victoria, BC. He has held Visiting fellowships at Harvard's Kennedy School of Government,

D. Wright, P. De Hert (eds.), *Privacy Impact Assessment*, Law, Governance
and Technology Series 6, DOI 10.1007/978-94-007-2543-0,
© Springer Science+Business Media B.V. 2012

the Center for the Study of Law and Society at University of California, Berkeley, and the Center for Cyberspace Law and Policy at the University of New South Wales. His research has focused on the comparative analysis of surveillance technologies and privacy protection policies at the domestic and international levels. In addition to many scholarly articles and chapters, he has published six books: *Regulating Privacy: Data Protection and Public Policy in Europe and the United States* (Cornell University Press, 1992); *Visions of Privacy: Policy Choices for the Digital Age* (University of Toronto Press, 1999, co-edited with Rebecca Grant); *The Governance of Privacy: Policy Instruments in the Digital Age* (MIT Press, 2006 with Charles Raab); *The Privacy Advocates: Resisting the Spread of Surveillance* (MIT Press, 2008); *Playing the Identity Card: Surveillance, Security Identification in Global Perspective* (Routledge, 2008 co-edited with David Lyon) and *Security Games*: *Surveillance and Control at Mega-Events* (Routledge, 2011, co-edited with Kevin D. Haggerty). He is currently the co-investigator of a large Major Collaborative Research Initiative grant entitled "The New Transparency: Surveillance and Social Sorting."

Laurent Beslay works as Co-ordinator on Security and Technology for the European Data Protection Supervisor based in Brussels, since September 2004. His responsibilities include security and technology co-ordination of prior-checks opinions, policy opinions, complaints, inspections, audits and their follow-up. He previously worked, for six years, for the Joint Research Centre of the European Commission, the IPTS (Institute for Prospective Technological Studies) as a project officer in the field of cyber-security. He holds a post-Master's degree in Global Management of Technological Risks and Crisis (University of Paris, Sorbonne) and a Master's degree in International Relations.

Tobias Bräutigam is Legal Counsel (Privacy) at Nokia Corporation. He works on various aspects of privacy compliance, such as international data transfers, employee privacy and privacy in consumer services. He also plans and executes awareness-raising campaigns and privacy training throughout the company. He holds a Master's degree from the University of Freiburg i. Brsg and a PhD from the University of Helsinki. His research focuses on issues of information access, information privacy and comparative law. Learning new things everyday is his goal. He is an Affiliated Research Fellow at the Erik Castrén Institute of International Law and Human Rights, Helsinki.

Amanda Chandler is Global Privacy Manager at Vodafone. Prior to joining Vodafone in June 2003, she worked as a compliance and policy manager with the UK Information Commissioner and then as European Privacy Manager for a US online ad-serving company. Since joining Vodafone, she has been responsible for the implementation of data protection policy and strategy, and played a key role at an operational level in building data protection compliance into business processes across the company, ranging from new products and services to customer services. She works with operational colleagues across the Vodafone corporate family to help build processes and structures to help Vodafone meet its customers' privacy expectations while at the same enabling its privacy officers to develop as a community of privacy professionals.

Andrew Charlesworth is Reader in IT Law in the School of Law and Department of Computer Science at the University of Bristol, where he is the Director of the cross-disciplinary Centre for IT & Law. His post was initially funded by a range of commercial sponsors, and Andrew continues to work with organisations such as Vodafone, Herbert Smith LLP and HP Labs on a range of legal issues. He has considerable experience in the areas of privacy and data protection, including authoring the Data Protection Code of Practice for Higher Education; working on the methodology for the conduct of effective privacy impact assessments in the UK and the associated handbook on PIAs, for the ICO; and ongoing collaborative work with researchers at HP Labs on issues such as privacy in cloud computing, and developing an automated business decision support methodology for PIAs.

Roger Clarke is a 40-year veteran of the IT industry. For the last 20 years, he has specialised in strategic and policy aspects of e-business, information infrastructure, dataveillance and privacy, as Principal of Xamax Consultancy Pty Ltd, Canberra. He is a Visiting Professor in the Cyberspace Law & Policy Centre at the University of New South Wales, and a Visiting Professor in the Department of Computer Science at the Australian National University. He has been a board member of the Australian Privacy Foundation since its establishment in 1987, and has been its Chair during 2006–12. He has been a member of the Advisory Board of Privacy International since 2000. He was a member of the Victorian Data Protection Advisory Council in 1996, and of the federal Attorney-General's Core Consultative Group in 2000, and has performed consultancies for various organisations. In 2009, he was the second person to be awarded the Australian Privacy Medal, following Justice Michael Kirby.

Stephen Deadman is the Group Privacy Officer and Head of Legal – Privacy, Security & Content Standards at Vodafone Group where he is responsible for leading Vodafone's global privacy policy and strategy, and the development and implementation of Vodafone's global privacy programme. He is also responsible for legal and regulatory guidance to the Group on law enforcement, security, Internet regulation and policy. Since joining Vodafone in 1997, he has managed a number of teams with a particular focus on building the governance mechanisms and processes for addressing the importance of law and regulation in the development of products, services and technologies. In 2002, he founded and chaired Vodafone's international network of privacy and security law experts and in 2005 formulated and succeeded in the adoption of Vodafone's global privacy policy. With more than 14 years in the mobile industry, Stephen has worked on many of the emerging privacy issues for the sector including geo-location, mobile advertising, identity management and human rights. A significant portion of his work involves engaging with regulators, policy-makers, civil society, investors, academia and other industry players.

Paul De Hert is an international human rights expert. The bulk of his work is devoted, but not limited, to criminal law and technology and privacy law. At

Brussels, Paul De Hert holds the chair of Criminal Law and International and European Criminal Law and Historical introduction to eight major constitutional systems. He is Director of the VUB Research group on Fundamental Rights and Constitutionalism (FRC), Director of the Department of Interdisciplinary Studies of Law (Metajuridics) and core member of the research group Law Science Technology & Society (LSTS) (see: www.vub.ac.be/LSTS). He is an associate professor at Tilburg University where he teaches Privacy and Data Protection in the Master's programme at the Tilburg Institute of Law and Technology (TILT). He is a member of the editorial boards of several national and international scientific journals such as the *Inter-American and European Human Rights Journal* (Intersentia), *Criminal Law & Philosophy* (Springer) and *Computer Law & Security Review* (Elsevier). He is co-editor in chief of the Supranational Criminal Law Series (Intersentia) and the *New Journal of European Criminal Law* (Intersentia).

John Edwards is a New Zealand lawyer specialising in information law. From 1990–1993, he worked for New Zealand's parliamentary Ombudsmen, reviewing government decisions to withhold information sought under the Official Information Act (New Zealand's freedom of information statute). In 1993, he assisted the first Privacy Commissioner to set up his office, managing the Wellington office, preparing educational material, and developing complaint investigation processes. Since late 1993, he has been in practice on his own account working for a wide variety of clients in the public and private sector including the Ministry of Justice, the Crown Law Office and the Law Commission. He has been engaged on a temporary basis as solicitor in the State Services Commission, the Department of the Prime Minister and Cabinet, the Inland Revenue Department and the Ministry of Health. He has undertaken many privacy impact assessments and investigations and often provides commentary to the media on information law issues. He has published widely in New Zealand and abroad and has addressed many conferences in New Zealand and elsewhere in the world on privacy matters.

John Martin Ferris is the President of Ferris & Associates, Inc., and has more than 40 years of experience in information security and privacy including the life cycle engineering of information systems. He is a member of ANSI Accredited Standards Committee (ASC) X9 and is currently an ANSI ASC X9 liaison to ISO Technical Committee 68 and an ISO TC 68 liaison to the ISO Privacy Steering Committee. His consulting clients have included US agencies, the American Bankers Association and the Financial Services Technology Consortium. Mr. Ferris is retired from the US Department of Treasury where he was responsible for the US Treasury information security program and policies that directed Treasury's bureaus in compliance with federal security laws, policies and standards. Mr. Ferris holds a BS in mathematics from Drexel University and a MS in computer science from The Johns Hopkins University.

Anne-Christine Lacoste is a legal advisor at the Office of the European Data Protection Supervisor (EDPS). She co-ordinates the activities of the EDPS in relation to the Article 29 Data Protection Working Party, drafts official opinions and follows issues such as transfer of personal data to third countries (transatlantic dialogue on data protection, passenger name records, binding corporate rules) and privacy in the context of new technologies. She has completed a degree in law and a post-graduate degree in International and European law at the Catholic University of Louvain. She worked for a few years as a researcher at the Department of Economic and Social Law of the University, on legal assistance programmes of the European Commission. She joined the EDPS after 10 years at the Belgian Privacy Commission where she was head of the legal service.

Gwendal Le Grand is the head of the IT experts department at the CNIL, the French data protection authority, since April 2007. He contributes to the activities of the Article 29 Working Party (Art. 29 WP) on technology-related issues such as RFID, behavioural advertising, search engines and social networks. He is the liaison officer of the Art. 29 WP to ISO/IEC JTC1/SC27/WG5, which develops privacy standards, and is a member of the ISO Privacy Steering Committee. He represents the CNIL and the Art. 29 WP within several expert groups of the European Commission such as the RFID expert group (2007–2009), the data retention expert group (since 2008) and the Internet of Things expert group (since 2010). Before joining the CNIL, he worked as an associate professor at the École Nationale Supérieure des Télécommunications (ENST), Paris. He received his PhD in computer science from the University of Paris 6 in July 2001.

Gary T. Marx is Professor Emeritus from M.I.T. He has previously taught at the University of California, Harvard University and the University of Colorado and been a visiting professor at many other schools in the U.S. and Europe. In a distinctive voice for almost five decades, he has contributed to the fields of race relations, collective behaviour and social movements, law and society and surveillance studies. His writing has appeared in academic and popular outlets across disciplines and cultures and has been widely recognised with awards, fellowships, many reprints and translations. He is the author of *Protest and Prejudice*; *Undercover: Police Surveillance in America*; *Undercover: Police Surveillance in Comparative Perspective* (with C. Fijnaut); *Collective Behavior and Social Movements* (with D. McAdam), among other books. He has written many articles with his students and 12 introductions to colleagues' books and served on an array of editorial and review boards, panels, committees and commissions. Much of his work in recent decades is at www.garymarx.net.

Emilio Mordini is an MD (University of Rome La Sapienza), specialised in psychiatry and trained as a psychoanalyst. He was a partner of the Psychoanalytic Institute for Social Research (1986–2001), Professor of Bioethics at the University of Rome (1994–2006), Secretary of the Bioethical Commission of the Italian National Research Council (2000–04). In 2002, he founded the Centre for Science, Society and Citizenship (CSSC), an independent, non-partisan, research centre based in Rome, the aim of which is to contribute to a better understanding of the contemporary world by clarifying the social, cultural and ethical factors that shape technological innovation. He is the scientific secretary of the Italian Technology

Platform on Biometric Technology, and serves on the board of a number of international scientific associations. He has published extensively in peer-reviewed journals, and edited nine books.

Deirdre K. Mulligan is Assistant Professor at the University of California Berkeley School of Information and a Faculty Director of the Berkeley Center for Law and Technology. She teaches and writes on law and policy issues related to information and communication technology. Her research focuses on issues of information privacy, information security, surveillance and the interplay between legal rules and technical systems. She is the Policy Lead for the National Science Foundation's TRUST Science and Technology Center, Chair of the board of the Center for Democracy and Technology, and Co-chair of Microsoft's Trustworthy Computing Academic Advisory Board. Her recent publications include "Privacy on the Books and on the Ground", *Stanford Law Review*, Vol. 63, January 2011, and "New Governance, Chief Privacy Officers, and the Corporate Management of Information Privacy in the United States: An Initial Inquiry", *Law & Policy*, Vol. 33, No. 4, October 2011, both with Kenneth A. Bamberger.

David Parker is Emeritus Professor of Economics at the Cranfield School of Management, Cranfield University, UK. Previously he was Research Professor in Privatisation and Regulation at Cranfield. He is a former Member of the UK Competition Commission and currently a Member of the UK Government's Regulatory Policy Committee. David has written extensively on regulation issues and has acted as a consultant on privatisation, regulation and competition in over 20 countries, most recently in the Philippines. He is a member of the Editorial Board of the *Journal of Regulatory Economics* and the Editorial Advisory Board of *Public Money & Management*.

Charles Raab was Professor of Government in the University of Edinburgh, and is Professor Emeritus and Honorary Professorial Fellow. He serves on advisory or editorial boards of many research projects, funding bodies and academic journals, and on governmental expert groups. With the Surveillance Studies Network, he co-authored *A Report on the Surveillance Society* (2006) and an *Update Report* (2010) for the UK Information Commissioner. He has conducted funded research on information policy and regulatory issues, including privacy, data protection, surveillance, police co-operation, identity management, data sharing and e-government, and has written a large number of publications, including (with C. Bennett) *The Governance of Privacy* (2003; 2006). He has co-authored reports for the European Commission, UK and Scottish government agencies, and civil society groups. He was the Specialist Adviser to the House of Lords Select Committee on the Constitution for their Inquiry resulting in *Surveillance: Citizens and the State*, HL Paper 18, Second Report, Session 2008–09. His participation in European research projects includes PRIME (Privacy and Identity Management for Europe) and SIAM (Security Impact Assessment Measure). He is an Academician of the Academy of Social Sciences (AcSS).

Artemi Rallo Lombarte is Chair of Constitutional Law at the Jaume I University of Castellón in Spain. He was also Professor of Constitutional Law and Head of the Constitutional Law Department at the university from 1993 to 1998. Before his return to the university, he was Director of the Spanish Data Protection Agency, in which capacity he wrote his chapter on the Madrid Resolution for this book. He graduated in Law with Extraordinary Prize Honours (1988) and has a Doctorate in Law from the University of Valencia (1990). He has authored numerous monographs, books and scientific articles in specialised national and international magazines. He has participated in national and international research lines and projects on contemporary transformations of the public administration. He was Director General of the Judicial Studies Centre of the Ministry of Justice from 2004 to 2007.

Sarah Spiekermann is a professor for Business Information Systems Engineering at Vienna University of Economics and Business (WU Wien) where she chairs the Institute for Management Information Systems. Before starting her career in Vienna, she completed her "Habilitation" and Ph.D. at the Institute of Information Systems at Humboldt University in Berlin and held Adjunct Professor positions with the Heinz College of Public Policy and Management, Carnegie Mellon University in Pittsburgh and the European Business School (EBS). Her areas of expertise are electronic privacy, RFID, personalisation/CRM, user interaction behaviour in e-commerce and m-commerce environments as well as knowledge management. For more information, see: http://www.wu.ac.at/ec/faculty/spiekermann

Blair Stewart is an Assistant Commissioner with the Office of the Privacy Commissioner, New Zealand. Mr. Stewart worked in legal practice before joining the Office when it was established in 1993. His roles in the Office over the years have included privacy policy, codes of practice, technology and international issues. Mr. Stewart has contributed to international privacy work through the Asia Pacific Privacy Authorities Forum, the International Conference of Data Protection and Privacy Commissioners and as a member of the APEC Data Privacy Subgroup since its inception in 2003. He has placed a special emphasis in his work on developing flexible and effective regulatory and institutional mechanisms for protecting privacy at national and supra-national levels. Since 1996, Blair Stewart has promoted privacy impact assessment as an adaptable tool for decision-makers and regulators dealing with novel and complex technological challenges to privacy. In 2002, Mr. Stewart wrote a Privacy Impact Assessment Handbook which has been influential in New Zealand and elsewhere. He convened international workshops on privacy impact assessment in 2003 and 2007. He holds a B.A. and LL.B.(Hons) from the University of Auckland and has been admitted as a Barrister and Solicitor of the High Court of New Zealand and as a Solicitor of the Supreme Court of England and Wales.

Jennifer Stoddart was appointed Privacy Commissioner of Canada in 2003. Since then, she has overseen a number of important investigations and audits of personal information handling practices in the public and private sectors. She was the first data protection authority in the world to conduct a comprehensive investigation of the privacy policies and practices of the popular social networking site, Facebook. She also investigated with the Alberta Commissioner a massive data breach at US retail giant TJX, which owns Winners and HomeSense stores in Canada. More recently, she found that Google Inc. contravened Canadian privacy law when it collected personal information from unsecured wireless networks for Google StreetView. In 2011, she concluded that an audit by her Office had found that Staples Business Depot stores had failed to fully wipe customer data from returned devices such as laptops and USB hard drives destined for resale – even though the company had previously committed to addressing the long-standing problem. Commissioner Stoddart also led a number of important investigations on the public sector front, and has conducted audits of, for example, the government's personal information disposal practices, its use of wireless technology, the Passenger Protect Program, Passport Canada, the Financial Transactions and Reports Analysis Centre of Canada (FINTRAC), and the Royal Canadian Mounted Police's Exempt Databanks. Throughout her mandate, she has advocated the need to ensure that both PIPEDA and the Privacy Act continue to provide the strongest possible protections for Canadians in an era of constantly evolving risks to privacy. Commissioner Stoddart was previously President of the Commission d'accès à l'information du Québec, an organisation responsible for both access to information and the protection of personal information. She has held several senior positions in public administration for the Governments of Québec and Canada. Commissioner Stoddart holds a Bachelor of Civil Law degree from McGill University, as well as a Master of Arts degree in history from the University of Québec at Montréal and a Bachelor of Arts degree from the University of Toronto's Trinity College.

Florian Thoma is Chief Data Protection Officer of Siemens, a global electronics and electro-technical company with more than 400,000 employees. He is responsible for ensuring the effective protection of personal privacy rights and compliance with data protection laws and internal regulations and for the worldwide coordination of the Siemens data protection organisation. He serves as member of the IAPP Board of Directors and the IAPP European Advisory Board, and chairs the Workgroup on data protection of BITKOM (the German IT and Telecom Industry Association). He is founder and chair of the non-profit Bavarian Society for Data Protection. Prior to his current position, Florian acted as Siemens lead counsel for the CIO organisation, senior counsel to the in-house IT services provider and chaired the e-commerce, telecoms and data protection practice. He graduated from Regensburg University in 1994.

Adam Warren started his career in the financial services sector. He is currently employed as Research Associate and Lecturer at the Department of Geography, Loughborough University, UK. In 2007, he co-ordinated the project work on privacy impact assessments for the UK Information Commissioner's Office. His current work includes research into the impact of UK biometric residence permits on foreign nationals, the use of event-based surveillance technologies to predict emerging infectious diseases and the effectiveness of existing health security practices at UK airports. He has a PhD from the Department of Information Science, Loughborough University.

Nigel Waters is a Board member of the Australian Privacy Foundation (www. privacy.org.au) and represents Privacy International (www.privacyinternational. org) at meetings of the APEC Privacy Subgroup and other international fora. He is Principal of Pacific Privacy Consulting (www.pacificprivacy.org.au) and a researcher and visiting lecturer at the Cyberspace Law and Policy Centre, at the University of New South Wales (www.cyberlawcentre.org/ipp). He was Deputy Australian Federal Privacy Commissioner from 1989–1997, and before that Assistant UK Data Protection Registrar. He holds Masters degrees from the Universities of Cambridge and Pennsylvania and from the University of Technology, Sydney.

David Wright is Managing Partner of Trilateral Research & Consulting, a Limited Liability Partnership based in London (see www.trilateralresearch.com). He is co-editor and co-author of *Safeguards in a World of Ambient Intelligence* (Springer, 2008) and author of "Should privacy impact assessments be mandatory?", which appeared in the August 2011 issue of *Communications of the ACM*. He is a partner in a consortium with Vrije Universiteit Brussel (VUB) and Privacy International, undertaking the PIAF (Privacy Impact Assessment Framework) project for the European Commission's Directorate General Justice, a 20-month project which began in January 2011. He has been a partner in numerous other consortia and European projects dealing with privacy, data protection, security, surveillance, risk, trust, ethics, ambient intelligence and e-inclusion. He has been in four expert groups for the European Network and Information Security Agency (ENISA) dealing with privacy, trust, cloud computing and the Internet of Things. He is a free-lance researcher on the faculty of the Research Group on Law, Science, Technology and Society at the Vrije Universiteit Brussel (VUB), and has published many articles in peer-reviewed journals.

References

80/20 Thinking Ltd., *First Stage (Interim) Privacy Impact Assessment for Phorm Inc*, February 2008. http://blogs.guardian.co.uk/technology/Phorm%20PIA%20interim%20final%20.pdf

Association of Chief Police Officers (ACPO), *Guidance on the Management of Police Information*, Second Edition, 2010. http://www.acpo.police.uk/asp/policies/data/MoPI%202nd%20Ed%20Published%20Version.pdf

Albrechtslund, Anders, "Online Social Networking as Participatory Surveillance", *First Monday*, Vol. 13, No. 3, 3 March 2008. http://firstmonday.org/htbin/cgiwrap/bin/ojs/index.php/fm/article/viewArticle/2142/1949

Allio, Lorenzo, "Better Regulation and Impact Assessment in the European Commission", in Colin Kirkpatrick and David Parker (eds.), *Regulatory Impact Assessment: Towards Better Regulation?*, Edward Elgar, Cheltenham, 2007, pp. 72–105.

Ambler, Tim, Francis Chittenden and Monika Shamutkova, *Do Regulators Play by the Rules? An Audit of Regulatory Impact Assessments*, British Chambers of Commerce, London, January 2003.

Ambler, Tim, Francis Chittenden and Andrea Miccini, *Is Regulation Really Good for Us?*, British Chambers of Commerce, London, April 2010.

American Institute of Certified Public Accountants and Canadian Institute of Chartered Accountants (AICPA/CICA), Privacy Maturity Model, AICPA/CICA, New York and Toronto, October 2010. www.cica.ca/service-and-products/privacy

Anderson, Ken, "You Can Get There from Here: *IPC Tools and Approaches for Privacy Compliance in Ontario*", speech by the Assistant Commissioner of the OIPC of Ontario, 27 April 2006. http://www.ipc.on.ca/images/Resources/up-2006_04_26_PIPA_Presentation.pdf

Arai-Takahashi, Yutaka, *The Margin of Appreciation Doctrine and the Principle of Proportionality in the Jurisprudence of the ECHR*, Intersentia, Antwerp, 2001.

Arbeitskreis Vorratsdatenspeicherung [Working Group on Data Retention], "Serious criminal offences, as defined in sect. 100a StPO, in Germany according to police crime statistics", [German] Federal Crime Agency (BKA), 19 February 2011. http://www.vorratsdatenspeicherung.de/images/data_retention_effectiveness_report_2011-01-26.pdf

Arthur, Charles, "Simon Davies (of Privacy International, and 80/20 Thinking) on Phorm", Technology Blog, *The Guardian*, 20 March 2008. http://www.guardian.co.uk/technology/blog/2008/mar/20/simondaviesofprivacyinter

Article 29 Data Protection Working Party, Transfers of personal data to third countries: Applying Articles 25 and 26 of the EU data protection directive, Working Document WP 12, Brussels, Adopted 24 July 1998. http://ec.europa.eu/justice/policies/privacy/workinggroup/wpdocs/1998_en.htm

Article 29 Data Protection Working Party, Working document on data protection issues related to RFID technologies, WP 105, 19 January 2005. http://ec.europa.eu/justice/policies/privacy/workinggroup/wpdocs/2005_en.htm

Article 29 Data Protection Working Party, Results of the Public Consultation on Article 29 Working Party Document 105 on Data Protection Issues Related to RFID Technologies, WP 111, Adopted on 28 September 2005. http://ec.europa.eu/justice/policies/privacy/workinggroup/wpdocs/2005_en.htm

Article 29 Data Protection Working Party, The Future of Privacy: Joint Contribution to the Consultation of the European Commission on the legal framework for the fundamental right to protection of personal data, Document WP 168, Adopted on 1 December 2009. http://ec.europa.eu/justice/policies/privacy/workinggroup/wpdocs/2009_en.htm

Article 29 Data Protection Working Party, Opinion 3/2010 on the principle of accountability, Adopted on 13 July 2010. http://ec.europa.eu/justice/policies/privacy/workinggroup/wpdocs/2010_en.htm

Article 29 Data Protection Working Party, "European Data Protection Authorities find current implementation of data retention directive unlawful", Press release, Brussels, 14 July 2010. http://ec.europa.eu/justice_home/fsj/privacy/news/index_en.htm

Article 29 Data Protection Working Party, Opinion 9/2011 on the revised Industry Proposal for a Privacy and Data Protection Impact Assessment Framework for RFID Applications, Brussels, Adopted on 11 February 2011. http://ec.europa.eu/justice/policies/privacy/docs/wpdocs/2011/wp180_en.pdf

Assuras, Thalia, and Joie Chen, "House and Senate Committees Will Begin Rare August Hearings", *CBS News Transcripts*, 24 July 2004.

Attorney-General [of Australia], "Privacy Impact Assessment Guide and Layered Privacy Policy Launch", Press release, 26 August 2006.

Attorney-General's Department / Salinger Privacy, "Privacy Impact Assessment – The AusCheck Amendment Bill 2009 and The National Security Background Check", Canberra, 3 March 2009. http://www.ag.gov.au/www/agd/rwpattach.nsf/VAP/(712B446AA84F124A6F0833A09BD304C8)~AusCheck+PIA+-+Final+report.pdf/$file/AusCheck+PIA+-+Final+report.pdf

Australian Law Reform Commission, "For Your Information: Australian Privacy Law and Practice", ALRC Report 108, August 2008. http://www.alrc.gov.au/publications/report-108

Australian Privacy Foundation, "Resources – The Law". August 2010. http://www.privacy.org.au/Resources. See also the website of the Office of the Australian Privacy Commissioner: http://www.privacy.gov.au/government

Australian Privacy Foundation, "The Federal Government Calls It a 'Human Services Access Card'. We Call It for What It Is: A National ID Card System", 2007. http://www.privacy.org.au/Campaigns/ID_cards/HSAC.html

Australian Privacy Foundation, "Submission re Exposure Draft of Australian Privacy Amendment Legislation", August 2010. http://www.privacy.org.au/Papers/Sen-APPs-100818.pdf

Ball, Kirstie, David Lyon, David Murakami Wood, Clive Norris and Charles Raab, *A Report on the Surveillance Society*, for the Information Commissioner by the Surveillance Studies Network (SSN), September 2006. http://ico.crl.uk.com/files/Surveillance%20society%20full%20report%20final.pdf

Bamberger, Kenneth A., "Regulation as Delegation: Private Firms, Decisionmaking and Accountability in the Administrative State", *Duke Law Journal*, Vol. 56, No. 2, November 2006, pp. 377–468.

Bamberger, Kenneth A., and Deirdre K. Mulligan, "Privacy Decisionmaking in Administrative Agencies", *University of Chicago Law Review*, Vol. 75, No. 1, 2008, pp. 75–107.

Bamberger, Kenneth A., and Deirdre K. Mulligan, "New Governance, Chief Privacy Officers, and the Corporate Management of Information Privacy in the United States: An Initial Inquiry", *Law & Policy*, Vol. 33, No. 4, October 2011, pp. 477–508.

Barbaro, Michael, and Tom Zeller Jr, "A Face is Exposed for AOL Searcher No. 4417749", *The New York Times*, 9 August 2006. http://query.nytimes.com/gst/fullpage.html?res=9E0CE3DD1F3FF93AA3575BC0A9609C8B63

Bartels, Cord, Harald Kelter, Rainer Oberweis and Birger Rosenberg, TR 03126 – Technische Richtlinie für den sicheren RFID-Einsatz, Bundesamt für Sicherheit in der Informationstechnik (B.f.S.i.d.), Bonn, 2009.

Bayley, Robin M., "Appendix C, Jurisdictional Report for Canada", in *Privacy Impact Assessments: An International Study of their Application and Effects*, Report to the UK Information Commissioner, December 2007. http://www.rogerclarke.com/DV/ICOStudy-2007-Apps.pdf

BBC News, "Phorm Needs 'Better Protection'", 18 March 2008. http://news.bbc.co.uk/1/hi/technology/7303426.stm

BBC News, "Sites Hit in Massive Web Attack", 2 April 2011. http://www.bbc.co.uk/news/world-us-canada-12944626

Beauchamp, Tom L., and James F. Childress, *Principles of Biomedical Ethics*, 5th ed., Oxford University Press, New York, 2001.

Beekman, Volkert, et al., Ethical Bio-Technology Assessment Tools for Agriculture and Food Production, Final Report of the Ethical Bio-TA Tools project, LEI, The Hague, February 2006. http://www.ethicaltools.info

Bellanova, Rocco, and Paul De Hert, "Le cas S. et Marper et les données personnelles: l'horloge de la stigmatisation stoppée par un arrêt européen", *Cultures & Conflits*, No. 76, 2010, pp. 15–27.

Bennett, Colin J., and Charles Raab, *The Governance of Privacy: Policy Instruments in Global Perspective*, Ashgate Press, Aldershot, UK, 2003. Second and revised edition, MIT Press, Cambridge, MA, 2006.

Bennett, Colin J., Charles D. Raab and Priscilla Regan, "People and Place: Patterns of Individual Identification within Intelligent Transportation Systems", in David Lyon (ed.), *Surveillance as Social Sorting: Privacy, Risk, and Digital Discrimination*, Routledge, London, 2003.

Bennett, Colin J., "In Defence of Privacy", *Surveillance & Society*, Vol. 8, No. 4, 2011, pp. 485–496. Respondents, in the same issue, were Priscilla M. Regan ("A Response to Bennett's 'In Defence of Privacy'", pp. 497–499), John Gilliom ("A Response to Bennett's 'In Defence of Privacy'", pp. 500–504), danah boyd ("Dear Voyeur, Meet Flâneur... Sincerely, Social Media", pp. 505–507) and Felix Stalder ("Autonomy beyond Privacy? A Rejoinder to Colin Bennett", pp. 508–512). The debate can be downloaded as a single file: http://www.surveillance-and-society.org/ojs/index.php/journal/article/downloadSuppFile/privacy_defence/privacy_debate

Berman, Jerry, and Deirdre K. Mulligan, Comments of the Center for Democracy and Technology on the Draft "Options for Promoting Privacy on the National Information Infrastructure", 29 July 1997. http://old.cdt.org/privacy/ntia.html

Better Regulation Executive, *Measuring Administrative Costs: UK Standard Cost Model Manual*, BRE/Cabinet Office, London, September 2005. http://www.berr.gov.uk/files/file44503.pdf

Better Regulation Executive (BRE) and Department for Business, Innovation and Skills (BIS), *Impact Assessment Guidance*, BRE, London, April 2010. http://www.bis.gov.uk/assets/biscore/better-regulation/docs/10-898-impact-assessment-guidance.pdf

Better Regulation Task Force, *Less is More*, BRTF, London, March 2005. http://www.bis.gov.uk/files/file22967.pdf

BeVier, Lillian R., "Information About Individuals in the Hands of Government: Some Reflections on Mechanisms for Privacy Protection", *William & Mary Bill of Rights Journal*, Vol. 4, No. 2, 1995, pp. 455–506.

Bloomfield, Stuart, "The Role of the Privacy Impact Assessment", speech for Managing Government Information, 2nd Annual Forum, OPC of Canada, Ottawa, 10 March 2004. http://www.priv.gc.ca/speech/2004/sp-d_040310_e.cfm

Bowker, Geoffrey C., and Susan L. Star, *Sorting Things Out: Classification and Its Consequences*, MIT Press, Cambridge, MA, 1999.

Brisbane, Arthur S., "Bill Keller Responds to Column on Swift Mea Culpa", *The New York Times*, 6 November 2006. http://publiceditor.blogs.nytimes.com/2006/11/06/bill-keller-responds-to-column-on-swift-mea-culpa/

British Standards Institution, 10012:2009 Data protection. Specification for a personal information management system, London, May 2009. http://shop.bsigroup.com/en/ProductDetail/?pid=000000000030175849

Bryant, Beth C., "NEPA Compliance In Fisheries Management: The Programmatic Supplemental Environmental Impact Statement On Alaskan Groundfish Fisheries And Implications For NEPA Reform", *Harvard Environmental Law Review*, Vol. 30, No. 2, 2006, pp. 441–479.

Cabinet Office, *Data Handling Procedures in Government: Final Report*, Cabinet Office, London, 2008. http://www.cabinetoffice.gov.uk/media/65948/dhr080625.pdf

Cabinet Secretary to the Australian Government, "First Stage Response to the Australian Law Reform Commission Report 108", October 2009. http://www.pmc.gov.au/privacy/alrc_docs/stage1_aus_govt_response.pdf

Calame, Byron, "Banking Data: A Mea Culpa", *The New York Times*, 22 October 2006. http://www.nytimes.com/2006/10/22/opinion/22pubed.html?pagewanted=2

Cameron, Iain, *National Security and the European Convention on Human Rights*, Kluwer Law, The Hague, 2000.

Campbell, Clark A., *The One-Page Project Manager for IT Projects*, Wiley, Hoboken, NJ, 2008.

Canadian Charter of Rights and Freedoms, Part 1 of the Constitution Act, 1982, being Schedule B to the Canada Act 1982 (U.K.), 1982.

Cavoukian, Ann, *Privacy by Design*, Ontario Information & Privacy Commissioner (OIPC), Toronto, 2009. http://www.ipc.on.ca/images/Resources/privacybydesign.pdf

CCTV User Group, *Model Code of Practice and Procedures Manual*, 2002. http://www.cctvusergroup.com/index.php

Center for Democracy and Technology, "Public Interest Groups and Academics Call on Bush Administration to Fill Privacy Position", Press release, Washington, DC, 16 April 2001. http://old.cdt.org/press/010416press.shtml

Center for Democracy and Technology, Statement Before the Senate Government Affairs Committee, Washington, DC, 11 July 2001. http://www.cdt.org/testimony/010711cdt.shtml

Center for Democracy and Technology, Comments of the Center for Democracy and Technology on US-VISIT Program, Increment 1, Privacy Impact Assessment (December 18, 2003), 4 February 2004. http://old.cdt.org/security/usvisit/20040204cdt.pdf

Center for Democracy and Technology, "Letter to Secretary of State Condoleezza Rice Re: State Department Release of Privacy Impact Assessments", Washington, DC, 2007, pp. 1–2. http://www.cdt.org/security/identity/20070502rice.pdf

Charlesworth, Andrew, "Implementing the European Union Data Protection Directive 1995 in UK Law: The Data Protection Act 1998", *Government Information Quarterly,* Vol. 16, No. 3, 1999, pp. 203–240.

Charlesworth, Andrew, "The Future of UK Data Protection Regulation", *Information Security Technical Report*, Vol. 11, No. 1, 2006, pp. 46–54.

Chope, Charles, "Preparation of an Additional Protocol to the European Convention on Human Rights, on the Right to a Healthy Environment", Rapporteur, Opinion presented to the Committee on Legal Affairs and Human Rights, Council of Europe, Doc. 1204329, September 2009. http://assembly.coe.int/Documents/WorkingDocs/Doc09/EDOC12043.pdf

Citizenship and Immigration Canada, Access to Information and Privacy, Privacy Impact Assessment Summaries, webpage. http://www.cic.gc.ca/english//department/atip/pia.asp

Clarke, Jeanne Nienaber, and Daniel C. McCool, *Staking Out the Terrain: Power Differential Among Natural Resource Management Agencies*, second edition, State University of New York Press, New York, 1996.

Clarke, Roger, "Information Technology and Dataveillance", *Communications of the ACM*, Vol. 31, No. 5, May 1988, pp. 498–512.

Clarke, Roger, "Matches Played Under Rafferty's Rules: The Parallel Data Matching Program Is Not Only Privacy-Invasive But Economically Unjustifiable As Well", Xamax Consultancy Pty Ltd, November 1993. http://www.rogerclarke.com/DV/PaperMatchPDMP.html. Versions published in *Privacy Law & Policy Reporter*, Vol. 1, No. 1, February 1994, and in *Policy*, Autumn 1994.

Clarke, Roger, "Privacy Impact Assessments", Xamax Consultancy Pty Ltd, February 1998a. http://www.rogerclarke.com/DV/PIA.html

Clarke, Roger, "Privacy Impact Assessment Guidelines", Xamax Consultancy Pty Ltd, February 1998b. http://www.xamax.com.au/DV/PIA.html

Clarke, Roger, "The Fundamental Inadequacies of Conventional Public Key Infrastructure", *Proceedings of the Ninth European Conference on Information Systems (ECIS 2001)*, Association for Information Systems, Bled, Slovenia, 27–29 June 2001. http://www.rogerclarke.com/II/ECIS2001.html

Clarke, Roger, "What's Privacy?", 2006. http://www.rogerclarke.com/DV/Privacy.html

Clarke, Roger, "Privacy Impact Assessment in Australian Contexts", *Murdoch eLaw Journal*, Vol. 15, No. 1, June 2008. http://www.rogerclarke.com/DV/PIAAust.html

Clarke, Roger, "Privacy Impact Assessment: Its Origins and Development", *Computer Law & Security Review*, Vol. 25, No. 2, April 2009, pp. 123–135. PrePrint at http://www.rogerclarke.com/DV/PIAHist-08.html

Clarke, Roger, "An Evaluation of Privacy Impact Assessment Guidance Documents", *International Data Privacy Law*, Vol. 1, No. 2, May 2011, pp. 111–120. http://idpl.oxfordjournals.org/content/1/2.toc

Clayton Utz, Lawyers, "Proposed Western Australian Government Number: Privacy Impact Assessment", prepared for the Western Australian Department of the Premier and Cabinet: Office of e-Government, 19 June 2007, pp. 84–91. http://www.publicsector.wa.gov.au/SiteCollectionDocuments/FINALWAGNPIA.pdf

Commission d'accès à l'information du Québec, *Biometrics in Québec: Application Principles - Making an Informed Choice*, July 2002. http://www.cai.gouv.qc.ca/home_00_portail/01_pdf/biometrics.pdf

Commission d'accès à l'information du Québec, *Cadre de référence concernant l'Obtention d'un avis de la Commission pour un dossier technologique*, February 2004. http://www.cai.gouv.qc.ca/06_documentation/01_pdf/cadre_reference.pdf

Commissioner for Law Enforcement Data Security (CLEDS), "Review of Victoria Police Major Project Development MOUs Under s11(1)(e) of the Commissioner for Law Enforcement Data Security Act 2005", August 2010. http://www.chiefexaminer.vic.gov.au/retrievemedia.asp?Media_ID=60421

Convergence e-Business Solutions Pty Ltd, "Identity & Access Management Framework", v.2, prepared for the West Australian Government Office of e-Government, Department of the Premier & Cabinet, Perth, 15 September 2005. http://www.publicsector.wa.gov.au/SiteCollectionDocuments/WA_IAM_Framework_rpt_V2.0.pdf

Council on Environmental Quality, *The National Environmental Policy Act: A Study of Its Effectiveness After Twenty-Five Years*, January 1997. http://ceq.hss.doe.gov/nepa/nepa25fn.pdf

Culnan, Mary J., and Cynthia Clark Williams, "How Ethics Can Enhance Organizational Privacy: Lessons from the Choicepoint and TJX Data Breaches", *MIS Quarterly*, Vol. 33 No. 4, December 2009, pp. 673–687.

Cyberspace Law and Policy Centre of the University of New South Wales, "Necessary improvements to the Australian Privacy Principles", August 2010. https://senate.aph.gov.au/submissions/comittees/viewdocument.aspx?id=9b3bffed-935d-4ea7-8a8a-123433c9eaec

Cyberspace Law and Policy Centre of the University of New South Wales, "Communications Privacy Complaints: In Search of the Right Path", A consumer research report supported by the Australian Communications Consumer Action Network (ACCAN), Sydney, September 2010. http://www.cyberlawcentre.org/privacy/ACCAN_Complaints_Report/report.pdf

Dalton, C., D. Plaquin, W. Weidner, D. Kuhlmann, B. Balacheff and R. Brown, "Trusted Virtual Platforms: A Key Enabler for Converged Client Devices", *Operating Systems Review*, Vol. 43, No. 1, 2009, pp. 36–43.

Dearne, Karen, "Reject E-health Identifier Bill, Says Law Professor", *The Australian*, 16 March 2010.

De Beer De Laer, Daniel, Paul De Hert, Gloria González Fuster and Serge Gutwirth, "Nouveaux éclairages de la notion de 'donnée personnelle' et application audacieuse du critère de proportionnalité. Cour européenne des droits de l'homme Grande Chambre S et Marper c. Royaume Uni, 4 décembre 2008", *Revue Trimestrielle des Droits de l'Homme*, 2009, No. 81, pp. 141–161.

De Hert, Paul, "Balancing Security and Liberty Within the European Human Rights Framework: A Critical Reading of the Court's Case Law in the Light of Surveillance and Criminal Law Enforcement Strategies After 9/11", *Utrecht Law Review*, Vol. 1, No. 1, 2005, pp. 68–96. http://www.utrechtlawreview.org/index.php/ulr/issue/view/1

De Hert, Paul, and K. Weis, "La Conservation pour une durée indéterminée d'empreintes digitales, d'échantillons cellulaires et profils A.N.D. de personnes acquittées porte atteinte au respect de leur vie privée", Comment on Marper, *Vigiles. Revue du droit de police*, Vol. 15, No. 2, 2009, pp. 79–83.

De Hert, Paul, and Serge Gutwirth, "Privacy, Data Protection and Law Enforcement: Opacity of the Individual and Transparency of Power" in Erik Claes, Anthony Duff and Serge Gutwirth (eds.), *Privacy and the Criminal Law*, Intersentia, Antwerp, 2006, pp. 61–104.

Delmas-Marty, Mireille, *The European Convention for the Protection of Human Rights: International Protection Versus National Restrictions,* Martinus Nijhoff, Dordrecht, 1992.

Dempsey, James X., Executive Director, Center for Democracy and Technology, "Privacy in the Hands of the Government: The Privacy Officer for the Department of Homeland Security", Testimony before the Subcommittee on Commercial and Administrative Law of the House Committee on the Judiciary, 108th Congress, 2d Session, 2004. http://old.cdt.org/testimony/20040210dempsey.shtml

Department for Business, Innovation and Skills (BIS), "New Rules to Hand Over Powers to Individuals and Companies by Cutting Red Tape and Bureaucracy", Press release, London, 5 August 2010. http://nds.coi.gov.uk/content/detail.aspx?NewsAreaId=2&ReleaseID=414871&SubjectId=15&DepartmentMode=true

Department for Transport, *Impact Assessment on the Use of Security Scanners at UK Airports*, Consultation, March 2010. http://www.dft.gov.uk/consultations/closed/2010-23/ia.pdf

Department of Communities and Local Government, *Making Better Use of Energy Performance Data: Impact Assessment*, consultation, March 2010. http://www.communities.gov.uk/documents/planningandbuilding/pdf/1491281.pdf

Department of Defence (DoD), "Defence Privacy Impact Checklist", Canberra, February 2008. http://www.defence.gov.au/fr/Privacy/defence-piachecklist-Feb08.doc

Department of Finance and Personnel (Northern Ireland), *Review of Domestic Rating Data Sharing Privacy Impact Assessment (PIA)*, Bangor, 2008.

Department of Homeland Security, *Privacy Impact Assessments: The Privacy Office Official Guidance*, Washington, DC, June 2010. http://www.dhs.gov/files/publications/gc_1209396374339.shtm

Department of State, *Abstract of Concept of Operations for the Integration of Contactless Chip in the U.S. Passport*, Abstract of Document Version 2.0, 2004.

DeShazo, J.R., and Jody Freeman, "Public Agencies as Lobbyists", *Columbia Law Review*, Vol. 105, No. 8, December 2005. http://papers.ssrn.com/sol3/papers.cfm?abstract_id=876815

de Vries, Katya, Rocco Bellanova and Paul De Hert, "Proportionality Overrides Unlimited Surveillance: The German Constitutional Court Judgment on Data Retention", in CEPS Liberty and Security in Europe publication series, Brussels, CEPS, 2010a. http://www.ceps.eu/book/proportionality-overrides-unlimited-surveillance

de Vries, Katya, Rocco Bellanova, Paul De Hert and Serge Gutwirth, "The German Constitutional Court Judgment on Data Retention: Proportionality Overrides Unlimited Surveillance (Doesn't it?)", in Serge Gutwirth, Yves Poullet, Paul De Hert and Ronald Leenes (eds.), *Privacy and Data Protection: An Element of Choice*, Springer, Dordrecht, 2011.

Di Iorio, C.T., F. Carinci, J. Azzopardi et al., "Privacy Impact Assessment in the Design of Transnational Public Health Information Systems: The BIRO Project", *Journal of Medical Ethics*, Vol. 35, 2009, pp. 753–761. http://jme.bmj.com/content/35/12/753.abstract

Dixon, Tim, "Communications Law Centre Wants IPPs Revised in Line with Australian Privacy Charter", *Privacy Law and Policy Reporter*, Vol. 3, No. 9, January 1997. http://www.austlii.edu.au/au/journals/PLPR/1997/4.html

Dworkin, Ronald, "It Is Absurd to Calculate Human Rights According to a Cost-Benefit Analysis", *The Guardian*, 24 May 2006. http://www.guardian.co.uk/commentisfree/2006/may/24/comment.politics

Easton, Marleen, Lodewijk Moor, Bob Hoogenboom, Paul Ponsaers and Bas van Stokkom (eds.), *Reflections on Reassurance Policing in the Low Countries*, Boom Juridische Uitgevers, The Hague, 2008.

EEF (The Manufacturers' Organisation), *Reforming Regulation: Improving Competitiveness, Creating Jobs. Report by the EEF Regulation Task Group*, EEF, London, September 2010.

Electronic Privacy Information Center, *Public Opinion on Privacy*, Washington, DC, [undated]. http://www.epic.org/privacy/survey/

Espiner, Tom, "Data Breaches Cost an Average Business £1.4m", ZDNet.co.uk, 25 February 2008. http://news.zdnet.co.uk/security/0,1000000189,39341215,00.htm

ESRC Seminar Series, *Mapping the Public Policy Landscape: Assessing Privacy Impact,* 2009.

European Commission, European Governance: A White Paper, COM (2001) 428 final, Brussels, 2001.

European Commission, Communication: A Sustainable Europe for a Better World: A European Strategy for Sustainable Development, COM (2001) 264, Brussels, 15 May 2001.

European Commission, Communication on European Governance: Better Law-making, COM(2002) 275 final, 5 June 2002.

European Commission, Communication from the Commission on Impact Assessment, Brussels, COM(2002) 276 final, Brussels, 5 June 2002.

European Commission, Better Regulation for Growth and Jobs in the European Union, COM(2005) 97 final, 16 March 2005.

European Commission, Impact Assessment Guidelines, SEC(2005) 791, Brussels, June 2005.

European Commission, Proposal for a Council Framework Decision on the exchange of information under the principle of availability, COM(2005) 490 final, Brussels, 12 October 2005.

European Commission, Radio Frequency Identification (RFID) in Europe: steps towards a policy framework, Communication to the European Parliament, the Council, the European Economic and Social Committee and the Committee of the Regions, COM(2007) 96 final, Brussels, 15 March 2007.

European Commission, The European Research Area: New Perspectives, Green Paper, COM(2007) 161 final, Brussels, 4 April 2007.

European Commission, Ageing well in the Information Society, Action Plan on Information and Communication Technologies and Ageing, An i2010 Initiative, Communication from the Commission to the European Parliament, the Council, the European Economic and Social Committee and the Committee of the Regions, COM(2007) 332 final, Brussels, 14 June 2007.

European Commission, Recommendation on the implementation of privacy and data protection principles in applications supported by radio-frequency identification, C(2009) 3200 final, Brussels, 12 May 2009. http://ec.europa.eu/information_society/policy/rfid/documents/recommendationonrfid2009.pdf

European Commission, *Impact Assessment Guidelines*, SEC(2009) 92, Brussels, 15 January 2009. http://ec.europa.eu/enterprise/policies/sme/files/docs/sba/iag_2009_en.pdf

European Commission, "Commission earmarks €1bn for investment in broadband – Frequently Asked Questions", Press release, MEMO/09/35, Brussels, 28 January 2009. http://europa.eu/rapid/pressReleasesAction.do?reference=MEMO/09/35

European Commission, A comprehensive approach on personal data protection in the European Union, Communication from the Commission to the European Parliament, the Council, the Economic and Social Committee and the Committee of the Regions, COM(2010) 609 final, Brussels, 4 November 2010. http://ec.europa.eu/justice/news/intro/news_intro_en.htm# 20101104

European Council, Resolution of 8 October 2001 on "e-Inclusion" – exploiting the opportunities of the information society for social inclusion, 2001/C 292/02, *Official Journal of the European Communities*, 18 October 2001. http://eur-lex.europa.eu/JOHtml.do?uri=OJ:C:2001: 292:SOM:en:HTML

European Council, Framework Decision 2008/977/JHA of 27 November 2008 on the protection of personal data processed in the framework of police and judicial cooperation in criminal matters.

European Data Protection Supervisor, Opinion on the Communication from the Commission to the European Parliament, the Council, the European Economic and Social Committee and the Committee of the Regions on 'Radio Frequency Identification (RFID) in Europe: steps towards a policy framework', COM(2007) 96, C 101/1, *Official Journal of the European Union*, 23 April 2008. http://www.edps.europa.eu/EDPSWEB/webdav/site/mySite/ shared/Documents/Consultation/Opinions/2007/07-12-20_RFID_EN.pdf

European Economic and Social Committee (EESC), Opinion on Use of Security Scanners at EU airports, 16–17 February 2011. http://www.eesc.europa.eu/?i=portal.en.opinions.15111

European Group on Ethics in Science and New Technologies (EGE), Opinion No. 20 on Ethical Aspects of ICT Implants in the Human Body, Adopted on 16 March 2005.

European Network and Information Security Agency (ENISA), Emerging and Future Risks Framework – Introductory Manual, Heraklion, 2010.

European Network and Information Security Agency (ENISA), Flying 2.0 – Enabling automated air travel by identifying and addressing the challenges of IoT & RFID technology, Heraklion, 2010.

European Network and Information Security Agency, ENISA Opinion on the Industry Proposal for a Privacy and Data Protection Impact Assessment Framework for RFID Applications [of March 31, 2010], Heraklion, July 2010. http://www.enisa.europa.eu/media/news-items/enisa-opinion-on-pia

European Parliament, Resolution of 23 October 2008 on the impact of aviation security measures and body scanners on human rights, privacy, personal dignity and data protection, Strasbourg. http://www.europarl.europa.eu/sides/getDoc.do?pubRef=-//EP//TEXT+TA+ P6-TA-2008-0521+0+DOC+XML+V0//EN

European Parliament, Resolution of 5 May 2010 on the launch of negotiations for Passenger Name Record (PNR) agreements with the United States, Australia and Canada. http://www.europarl. europa.eu/sides/getDoc.do?pubRef=-//EP//TEXT+TA+P7-TA-2010-0144+0+DOC+XML+ V0//EN

European Parliament and the Council, Directive 95/46/EC of 24 October 1995 on the protection of individuals with regard to the processing of personal data and on the free movement of such data [Data Protection Directive], *Official Journal*, L 281, 23/11/1995, pp. 0031–0050.

European Parliament and the Council, Regulation (EC) No 45/2001 of 18 December 2000 on the protection of individuals with regard to the processing of personal data by the Community institutions and bodies and on the free movement of such data.

European Parliament and the Council, Directive 2002/22/EC of 7 March 2002 on universal service and users' rights relating to electronic communications networks and services (Universal Service Directive), *Official Journal*, L 108 of 24 April 2002.

European Parliament and the Council, Directive 2002/58/EC of 12 July 2002 concerning the processing of personal data and the protection of privacy in the electronic communications sector (Directive on privacy and electronic communications), Brussels.

European Parliament and the Council, Directive 2006/24/EC of 15 March 2006 on the retention of data generated or processed in connection with the provision of publicly available electronic communications services or of public communications networks and amending Directive 2002/58/EC.

European Parliament and the Council, Regulation (EC) No 300/2008 of 11 March 2008 on common rules in the field of civil aviation security, *Official Journal*, L 97, 9 April 2008, pp. 72–84.

European Parliament and the Council, Directive 2009/136/EC of 25 November 2009 amending Directive 2002/22/EC on universal service and users' rights relating to electronic communications networks and services; Directive 2002/58/EC concerning the processing of personal data and the protection of privacy in the electronic communications sector and Regulation (EC) No 2006/2004 on cooperation between national authorities responsible for the enforcement of consumer protection laws.

European Parliament and the Council, Directive 2010/75/EU on industrial emissions, 24 November 2010. http://eur-lex.europa.eu/LexUriServ/LexUriServ.do?uri=OJ:L:2010:334:0017:0119:EN:PDF

Evans, Carolyn, and Simon Evans, "Evaluating the Human Rights Performance of Legislatures", *Human Rights Law Review*, Vol. 6, No. 3, 2006, pp. 545–569.

Financial Services Authority, *Data Security in Financial Services*, London, April 2008. http://www.fsa.gov.uk/pubs/other/data_security.pdf

Flaherty, David H., *Protecting Privacy in Surveillance Societies,* University of North Carolina Press, Chapel Hill, NC, 1989.

Flaherty, David H., "Privacy Impact Assessments: An Essential Tool for Data Protection", Presentation at the 22nd Annual Meeting of Privacy and Data Protection Officials, Venice, 27–30 September 2000. http://aspe.hhs.gov/datacncl/flaherty.htm

Flaherty, David, "Privacy Impact Assessments: An Essential Tool for Data Protection", *Privacy Law and Policy Reporter*, Vol. 7, No. 5, November 2000. http://www.austlii.edu.au/au/journals/PLPR/2000/

Flaherty, David, "Criteria for Evaluating the Adequacy of Privacy Impact Assessments in Canada", 29th International Conference of Data Protection and Privacy Commissioners, *Privacy Impact Assessment Issues and Approaches for Regulators*, Workshop Workbook, Montreal, September 2007. http://www.privacyconference2007.gc.ca/workbooks/Terra_Incognita_workbook12_bil.pdf

Flanagan, Mary, Daniel C. Howe and Helen Nissenbaum, "Embodying Values in Technology: Theory and Practice", in Jeroen van den Hoven and John Weckert (eds.), *Information Technology and Moral Philosophy*, Cambridge University Press, Cambridge, 2008, pp. 322–353.

Foundation for Information Policy Research (FIPR), *Children's Databases – Safety and Privacy: A Report for the Information Commissioner*, March/August 2006. http://www.cl.cam.ac.uk/~rja14/Papers/kids.pdf

Fujitsu Research Institute, "Personal data in the cloud: the importance of trust", Tokyo, 2010. http://ts.fujitsu.com/rl/visit2010/downloads/Fujitsu_Consumer_Data_Privacy_Report_part2.pdf

Fusco, Claudia, Presentation at the INEX Roundtable on Body Scanners, Brussels, 27 January 2011. http://www.ceps.eu/event/roundtable-body-scanners.

Gellman, Robert, "A Better Way to Approach Privacy Policy in the United States: Establish a Non-Regulatory Privacy Protection Board", *Hastings Law Journal*, Vol. 54, April 2003, pp. 1183–1226.

German Working Group on Data Retention (AK Vorrat), "Study finds telecommunications data retention ineffective", 27 January 2011. http://www.vorratsdatenspeicherung.de/content/view/426/79/lang,en/

Gerrard, Graeme, Garry Parkins, Ian Cunningham et al., National CCTV Strategy, Home Office and Association of Chief Police Officers, London, October 2007. http://www.bhphousing.co.uk/streetcare2.nsf/Files/LBBA-24/$FILE/Home%20Office%20National%20CCTV%20Strategy.pdf

Gill, Martin, and Angela Spriggs, *Assessing the Impact of CCTV*, Home Office Research, Development and Statistics Directorate, February 2005.

Goffman, Erving, *Behavior in Public Places: Notes on the Social Organization of Gatherings*, The Free Press, New York, 1963.

Goffman, Erving, *Frame Analysis: An Essay on the Organization of Experience*, Harper and Row, London, 1974.

González Fuster, Gloria, "TJCE – Sentencia de 04.12.2008, S. y Marper c. Reino Unido", *Revista de Derecho Comunitario Europeo*, Vol. 33, 2009, pp. 619–633.

González Fuster, Gloria, Serge Gutwirth and Erika Ellyne, "Profiling in the European Union: A High-Risk Practice", INEX Policy Brief, No. 10, 2010.

González Fuster, Gloria, Paul De Hert, E. Ellyne and Serge Gutwirth, "Huber, Marper and Others: Throwing New Light on the Shadows of Suspicion", INEX Policy Brief, No. 11, June 2010. http://www.ceps.eu/book/huber-marper-and-others-throwing-new-light-shadows-suspicion

Goold, Benjamin J., "Surveillance and the Political Value of Privacy", *Amsterdam Law Forum*, Vol. 1, No. 4, August 2009.

Goslett, Miles, "Your Office May Have Been Bugged by BAE, Investigators Told MP", *Daily Mail*, 3 October 2009. http://www.dailymail.co.uk/news/article-1217919/Your-office-bugged-BAE-investigators-told-MP.html

Government Accountability Office (GAO), *Privacy Act: OMB Leadership Needed to Improve Agency Compliance*, GAO-03-304, Washington, DC, June 2003.

Government Accountability Office (GAO), *Data Mining: Agencies Have Taken Key Steps to Protect Privacy in Selected Efforts, but Significant Compliance Issues Remain*, GAO-05-866, August 2005. http://www.gao.gov/new.items/d05866.pdf

Government Accountability Office (GAO), *Border Security: US-VISIT Program Faces Strategic, Operational, and Technological Challenges at Land Ports of Entry*, GAO-07-378T, Washington, DC, 31 January 2007. http://www.gao.gov/new.items/d07378t.pdf

Government Accountability Office, *Homeland Security: Continuing Attention to Privacy Concerns is Needed as Programs Are Developed* ("Homeland Security Report"), GAO-07-630T, Washington, DC, 21 March 2007. http://www.gao.gov/new.items/d07630t.pdf

Government Accountability Office (GAO), *Homeland Security: Prospects for Biometric US-VISIT Exit Capability Remain Unclear*, GAO-07-1044T, Washington, DC, 28 June 2007. http://www.gao.gov/new.items/d071044t.pdf

Greenleaf, Graham, "Hong Kong's 'smart' ID Card: Designed To Be Out of control", Chapter 5 in Colin J. Bennett and David Lyon (eds.), *Playing the Identity Card: Surveillance, Security and Identification in Global Perspective*, Routledge, London, 2008. Chapter available separately at http://www.austlii.edu.au/au/journals/ALRS/2008/10.html

GS1 and Logica CMG, European passive RFID Market Sizing 2007–2022, Report of the BRIDGE Project, February 2007. http://www.bridge-project.eu/data/File/BRIDGE%20WP13%20European%20passive%20RFID%20Market%20Sizing%202007-2022.pdf

Guenther, Oliver, and Sarah Spiekermann, "RFID and the Perception of Control: The Consumer's View", *Communications of the ACM*, Vol. 48, No. 9, 2005, pp. 73–76.

Guild, Elspeth, "Global Data Transfers: The Human Rights Implications", INEX Policy Brief, No. 9, May 2009. http://www.ceps.eu/ceps/download/3400

Harris, David, Michael O'Boyle, Edward Bates and Carla Buckley, *Law of the European Convention on Human Rights*, second edition, Oxford University Press, Oxford, 2009, pp. 385–392.

Heath, Chip, Richard P. Larrick and Joshua Klayman, "Cognitive Repairs: How Organizational Practices Can Compensate for Individual Shortcomings", *Research in Organizational Behavior*, Vol. 20, No. 1, 1998, pp. 1–37.

Heimer, Carol A., "Explaining Variation in the Impact of Law: Organizations, Institutions, and Professions", in Austin Sarat and Susan S. Silbey (eds.), *Studies In Law, Politics, and Society*, Vol. 15, Emerald Publishing, Bingley, UK, 1995, pp. 29–59.

Hildebrand, Stephen G., and Johnnie B. Cannon, *Environmental Analysis: The NEPA Experience*, Lewis Publishers, Boca Raton, FL, 1993.

HM Government, Code of Practice on Consultation, Better Regulation Executive, Department for Business, Enterprise and Regulatory Reform (BERR), London, July 2008. http://www.berr.gov.uk/files/file47158.pdf

HM Government/BERR, *Regulatory Budgets: A Consultation Document*, London, August 2008. http://www.berr.gov.uk/files/file47129.pdf

HM Government, *Summary of Simplification Plans*, London, 2009.

Hofmann, B., "On Value-Judgements and Ethics in Health Technology Assessment", *Poiesis & Praxis*, Vol. 3, No. 4, December 2005.

Hope-Tindall, Peter, "Privacy Impact Assessment – Obligation or Opportunity: The Choice is Ours!", Prepared for CSE ITS Conference, Ottawa, Ontario, 16 May 2002. http://www.home.inter.net/gt/grabbag/Tindall_PIA_Material.pdf

House of Lords, Constitution Committee – Second Report, *Surveillance: Citizens and the State*, London, January 2009. http://www.publications.parliament.uk/pa/ld200809/ldselect/ldconst/18/1808.htm#a56

Humpherson, Ed, "Auditing Regulatory Impact Assessment: UK Experience", in Colin Kirkpatrick and David Parker (eds.), *Regulatory Impact Assessment: Towards Better Regulation?*, Edward Elgar, Cheltenham, 2007, pp. 132–144.

Information and Privacy Office, Management Board Secretariat, Ontario, *Privacy Impact Assessment: A User's Guide*, June 2001. http://www.accessandprivacy.gov.on.ca/english/pia/index.html

Information Commissioner's Office (ICO), "Appendix E: Jurisdictional Report for Australia" in *Privacy Impact Assessments: International Study of their Application and Effects*, Wilmslow, UK, December 2007. http://www.ico.gov.uk/upload/documents/library/corporate/research_and_reports/lbrouni_piastudy_appe_aus_2910071.pdf

Information Commissioner's Office (ICO), *Privacy Impact Assessments: International Study of their Application and Effects*, Appendix I, Wilmslow, UK, December 2007. http://www.ico.gov.uk/upload/documents/library/corporate/research_and_reports/privacy_impact_assessment_international_study.011007.pdf

Information Commissioner's Office (ICO), *Privacy Impact Assessment Handbook*, Wilmslow, Cheshire, UK, December 2007. Version 2.0, June 2009. http://www.ico.gov.uk/for_organisations/topic_specific_guides/pia_handbook.aspx; http://www.ico.gov.uk/upload/documents/pia_handbook_html_v2/index.html

Information Commissioner's Office (ICO), *Information Commissioner's Annual Report 2009/10*, Wilmslow, 2010. http://www.ico.gov.uk/upload/documents/library/corporate/detailed_specialist_guides/annual_report_2010.pdf

Information Security Forum, Standard of Good Practice for Information Security, London. http://www.isfsecuritystandard.com/SOGP07/index.htm

Information Systems Audit and Control Association, *COBIT 4.1*, IT Governance Institute, Rolling Meadows, IL, 2008.

Internal Revenue Service, IRS Privacy Impact Assessment, Version 1.3, Washington, DC, 17 December 1996. http://www.cio.gov/documents/pia_for_it_irs_model.pdf

International Conference of Data Protection and Privacy Commissioners, "The Montreux Declaration – The Protection of Personal Data and Privacy in a Globalised World: A Universal Right Respecting Diversities", adopted by the 27th Conference in Montreux, Switzerland, 16 September 2005.

International Conference of Data Protection and Privacy Commissioners, *Privacy Impact Assessment Issues and Approaches for Regulators*, Workshop Workbook, 29th Conference, Montreal, September 2007. http://www.privacyconference2007.gc.ca/workbooks/Terra_Incognita_workbook12_bil.pdf

International Conference of Data Protection and Privacy Commissioners, "Resolution on the Urgent Need for Protecting Privacy in a Borderless World, and for Reaching a Joint Proposal for Setting International Standards on Privacy and Personal Data Protection", adopted by the 30th Conference in Strasbourg, France, on 17 October 2008.

International Conference of Data Protection and Privacy Commissioners, Resolution on International Standards of Privacy, 31st Conference, Madrid, November 2009. http://www. privacyconference2009.org/dpas_space/space_reserved/documentos_adoptados/common/ 2009_Madrid/estandares_resolucion_madrid_en.pdf

International Organization for Standardization (ISO), *Information Technology — Security techniques — Information Security Risk Management*, International Standard, ISO/IEC 27005:2008(E), First edition, Geneva, 15 June 2008.

International Organization for Standardization, ISO 22307:2008 Financial services – Privacy impact assessment, Geneva, 2008. http://www.iso.org/iso/iso_catalogue/catalogue_tc/ catalogue_detail.htm?csnumber=40897

Jacobs, Colin, "The Evolution and Development of Regulatory Impact Assessment in the UK", in Colin Kirkpatrick and David Parker (eds.), *Regulatory Impact Assessment: Towards Better Regulation?*, Edward Elgar, Cheltenham, 2007, pp. 106–131.

Johnson, Bobbie, "Finland Makes Broadband Access a Legal Right", *The Guardian*, 14 October 2009. http://www.guardian.co.uk/technology/2009/oct/14/finland-broadband

Karkkainen, Bradley C., "Toward a Smarter NEPA: Monitoring and Managing Government's Environmental Performance", *Columbia Law Review*, Vol. 102, No. 4, May 2002, pp. 904–906.

Karol, Thomas J., *A Guide to Cross-Border Privacy Impact Assessments*, Deloitte & Touche, 2001. http://www.isaca.org/Knowledge-Center/Research/ResearchDeliverables/ Pages/A-Guide-To-Cross-Border-Privacy-Impact-Assessments.aspx

Karol, Thomas J., "Cross-Border Privacy Impact Assessments: An Introduction", *ISACA Journal*, Vol. 3, 2001. http://www.isaca.org/Journal/Past-Issues/2001/Volume-3/Pages/Cross-Border-Privacy-Impact-Assessments.aspx

Karygiannis, Tom, Bernard Eydt, Greg Barber, Lynn Bunn and Ted Phillips, *Guidelines for Securing Radio Frequency Identification (RFID) Systems*, NIST Special Publication 800-98, National Institute of Standards and Technology, Gaithersburg, MD, April 2007.

Kelvin, P., "A social-psychological examination of privacy", *British Journal of Social and Clinical Psychology*, Vol. 12, 1973, pp. 248–261.

Kirkpatrick, Colin, and David Parker (eds.), *Regulatory Impact Assessment: Towards Better Regulation?*, Edward Elgar, Cheltenham, 2007.

Kirkpatrick, Colin, David Parker and Yin-Fang Zhang, "Regulatory Impact Assessment and Regulatory Governance in Developing Countries", *Public Administration and Development*, Vol. 24, Issue 4, Oct 2004, pp. 333–344.

Kirkpatrick, Colin, and David Parker, "Regulatory Impact Assessment in Developing and Transition Economies: A Survey of Current Practice", *Public Money and Management*, Vol. 24, No. 5, 2004, pp. 291–296.

Korff, D., and I. Brown, *Different Approaches to New Privacy Challenges in Particular in the Light of Technological Developments*, European Commission, DG Justice, Freedom and Security, Brussels, 2010. http://ec.europa.eu/justice/policies/privacy/docs/studies/new_ privacy_challenges/final_report_en.pdf

Kroes, Neelie, "Smart Tags – Working Together to Protect Privacy", SPEECH/11/236, at the Privacy and Data Protection Impact Assessment Framework Signing Ceremony, Brussels, 6 April 2011. http://europa.eu/rapid/pressReleasesAction.do?reference=SPEECH/11/ 236&format=HTML&aged=0&language=en&guiLanguage=en

Langevoort, Donald C., "Monitoring: The Behavioral Economics of Corporate Compliance with Law", *Columbia Business Law Review*, Vol. 2002, No. 1, pp. 71–118.

LaPerrière, René, "The 'Quebec Model' of Data Protection: A Compromise Between *Laissez-Fair* and Public Control in a Technological Era", in Colin J. Bennett and Rebecca Grant (eds.), *Visions of Privacy: Policy Choices for the Digital Age*, University of Toronto Press, Toronto, 1999.

Leake, Jonathan, "Strip Search: Camera that Sees Through Clothes from 80ft Away", *The Sunday Times*, 9 March 2008. http://www.timesonline.co.uk/tol/news/uk/science/article3512019.ece

Lee, Norman, and Colin Kirkpatrick, "Evidence-Based Policy-Making in Europe: An Evaluation of European Commission Integrated Impact Assessments", *Impact Assessment and Project Appraisal*, Vol. 24, No. 1, 2006, pp. 22–33.

Leenes, Ronald, Bert-Jaap Koops and Paul De Hert (eds.), *Constitutional Rights and New Technologies: A Comparative Study*, T.M.C. Asser Press (Information Technology & Law Series, Vol. 15), The Hague, 2008.

Lessig, Lawrence, *Code and Other Laws of Cyberspace*, Basic Books, New York, 1999.

Lewis, Paul, "Big Brother is Watching: Surveillance Box to Track Drivers is Backed", *The Guardian*, 31 March 2009. http://www.guardian.co.uk/uk/2009/mar/31/surveillance-transport-communication-box

Lichtblau, Eric, and James Risen, "Bank Data Is Sifted by U.S. in Secret to Block Terrorism", *The New York Times*, 23 June 2006.

Linden Consulting, *Privacy Impact Assessments: International Study of their Application and Effects*, prepared for the [UK] Information Commissioner's Office, October 2007. http://www.ico.gov.uk/upload/documents/library/corporate/research_and_reports/privacy_impact_assessment_international_study.011007.pdf

Lipton, Eric, "Bowing to Critics, U.S. to Alter Design of Electronic Passports", *The New York Times*, 27 April 2005. http://www.nytimes.com/2005/04/27/politics/27passport.html?scp=11&sq=biometric+passport&st=nyt

Lupia, Arthur, and Mathew D. McCubbins, *The Democratic Dilemma: Can Citizens Learn What They Need to Know?*, Cambridge University Press, New York, 1998.

Lyon, David (ed.), *Surveillance as Social Sorting: Privacy, Risk, and Digital Discrimination*, Routledge, London, 2003.

MacDonald, Reagan, "EESC Condemns Body Scanners as a Breach of Fundamental rights", *EDRi-gram*, 23 February 2011, Number 9.4, sub 2. www.edri.org.

Maiese, Michelle, "Principles of Justice and Fairness", Beyond Intractability.org, July 2003. http://www.beyondintractability.org/essay/principles_of_justice/

Majone, Giandomenico, "From the Positive to the Regulatory State", *Journal of Public Policy*, Vol. 17, No. 2, May 1997, pp. 139–167.

Management Board Secretariat, Government of Ontario, *Privacy Impact Assessment: A User's Guide*, 1999, revised 2001. http://www.accessandprivacy.gov.on.ca/english/pia/index.html

Marks, Paul, "'Pre-crime' Detector Shows Promise", *New Scientist*, 23 September 2008. http://www.newscientist.com/blogs/shortsharpscience/2008/09/precrime-detector-is-showing-p.html

Marx, Gary T., "Ethics for the New Surveillance", *The Information Society*, Vol. 14, 1998, pp. 171–185.

Marx, Gary T., "Identity and Anonymity: Some Conceptual Distinctions and Issues for Research", in J. Caplan and J. Torpey (eds.), *Documenting Individual Identity*, Princeton University Press, Princeton, NJ, 2001.

Marx, Gary T., "What's New About the 'New Surveillance'? Classifying for Change and Continuity", *Surveillance & Society*, Vol. 1, No. 1, 2002, pp. 9–29. http://www.surveillance-and-society.org/journalv1i1.htm

Marx, Gary T., "Turtles, Firewalls, Scarlet Letters and Vacuum Cleaners: Rules about Personal Information", in W. Aspray and P. Doty (eds.), *Making Privacy*, Scarecrow Press, Lanham, MD, 2011.

Mashaw, Jerry L., "Norms, Practices, and the Paradox of Difference: A Preliminary Inquiry into Agency Statutory Interpretation", *Administrative Law Review*, Vol. 57, No. 2, 2005.

Maurer, Robert, *One Small Step Can Change Your Life: The Kaizen Way*, Workman, New York, 2004.

Medicare Australia, "Privacy Impact Assessment (PIA) – Increased MBS Compliance Audits", Canberra, 28 April 2009. http://www.health.gov.au/internet/main/publishing.nsf/Content/C010759A8FB2E35DCA25759300011241/$File/Privacy%20Impact%20Assessment%20for%20the%20IMCA%20initiative.pdf

Meingast, Marci, Jennifer King and Deirdre K. Mulligan, "Embedded RFID and Everyday Things: A Case Study of the Security and Privacy Risks of the U.S. e-Passport", *Proceedings of IEEE International Conference on RFID*, 2007, pp. 4–5. http://www.truststc.org/pubs/157/Meingast_King_Mulligan_RFID2007_Final.pdf

Meyer, John W., and Brian Rowan, "Institutionalized Organizations: Formal Structure as Myth and Ceremony", *American Journal of Sociology*, Vol. 83, 1977, pp. 340–363.

Ministry of Citizens' Services [British Colombia], *Privacy Impact Assessment Process* webpage. http://www.cio.gov.bc.ca/cio/priv_leg/foippa/pia/pia_index.page

Ministry of Justice, *Undertaking Privacy Impact Assessments: The Data Protection Act 1998*, London, 2010. http://www.justice.gov.uk/guidance/docs/pia-guidance-08-10.pdf

Monaghan, Angela, "EU Laws to Cost UK £184bn by 2010, Think Tank Says", *The Telegraph*, 21 December 2009. http://www.telegraph.co.uk/news/worldnews/europe/6859987/EU-laws-to-cost-UK-184bn-by-2010-think-tank-says.html

Monahan, Torin (ed.), *Surveillance and Security: Technological Politics and Power in Everyday Life*, Routledge, New York, 2006.

Moor, James H., "What is Computer Ethics?", in Terrell Ward Bynum (ed.), *Computers & Ethics*, Blackwell, 1985, pp. 266–275.

Moor, James H., "Why we need better ethics for emerging technologies", *Ethics and Information Technology*, Vol. 7, No. 3, September 2005, pp. 111–119.

Mowbray, Alastair, "The Creativity of the European Court of Human Rights", *Human Rights Law Review*, Vol. 5, No. 1, 2005, pp. 57–79.

Munday, Roderick, "In the Wake of 'Good Governance': Impact Assessments and the Politicisation of Statutory Interpretation", *The Modern Law Review*, Vol. 71, No. 3, 2008, pp. 385–412.

Myslewski, Rik, "Apple Tweaks Privacy Policy to Juice Location Tracking", *The Register*, 22 June 2010. http://www.theregister.co.uk/2010/06/22/apple_location_terms_and_conditions/

Nardell, Gordon, "Levelling up: Data Privacy and the European Court of Human Rights", in Serge Gutwirth, Yves Poullet and Paul De Hert (eds.), *Data Protection in a Profiled World*, Springer, Dordrecht, 2010, pp. 43–52.

National Audit Office, *Better Regulation: Making Good Use of Regulatory Impact Assessments*, HC 329 2001-2, NAO, London, 2001-2.

National Audit Office, *Evaluation of Regulatory Impact Assessments Compendium Report 2003-04*, HC 358 2003-4, NAO, London, 2004.

National Audit Office, *Evaluation of Regulatory Impact Assessments Compendium Report 2004-05*, HC 341 2004-5, NAO, London, 2005.

National Audit Office, *Evaluation of Regulatory Impact Assessments Compendium Report 2005-06*, HC 1305 2005-6, NAO, London, 2006.

National Audit Office, *Assessing the Impact of Proposed New Policies*, Report by the Comptroller and Auditor General, HC 185 Session 1010-11, NAO, London, 1 July 2010. http://www.nao.org.uk/publications/1011/impact_assessments.aspx

National Commission on Terrorist Attacks upon the United States, Tenth Public Hearing: Law Enforcement and the Intelligence Committee, Testimony of Attorney General John Ashcroft, 13 April 2004. http://www.9-11commission.gov/hearings/hearing10/ashcroft_statement.pdf

National Institute for Standards and Technology (NIST), *Risk Management Guide for Information Technology Systems*, Recommendations of the National Institute of Standards and Technology, NIST Special Publication 800-30, July 2002.

National Policing Improvement Agency (NPIA), *Police National Database – Privacy Impact Assessment Report*, National Policing Improvement Agency, London, 2009. http://www.npia.police.uk/en/docs/Privacy_Impact_Assessment.pdf

National Research Council, Committee on Risk Perception and Communications, *Improving Risk Communication*, National Academy Press, Washington, DC, 1989. http://www.nap.edu/openbook.php?record_id=1189&page=R1

New Zealand Privacy Commissioner, "A Compilation of Materials in Relation to Privacy Impact Assessment", NZPC, 1997.

Nissenbaum, Helen, "Values in the Design of Computer Systems", *Computers in Society*, Vol. 28, No. 1, March 1998, pp. 38–39.

Nissenbaum, Helen, "Privacy as Contextual Integrity", *Washington Law Review*, Vol. 79, No. 1, 2004, pp. 101–139. http://www.nyu.edu/projects/nissenbaum/main_cv.html

Nissenbaum, Helen, *Privacy in Context: Technology, Policy, and the Integrity of Social Life*, Stanford University Press, Stanford, CA, 2010.

Northern Territory Information Commissioner, "ALRC Review of Privacy: Submissions on Issues Paper 31", January 2007.

Office for National Statistics (ONS), *Report of a Privacy Impact Assessment Conducted by the Office for National Statistics in Relation to the 2011 Census England and Wales*, London, 2009. http://www.ons.gov.uk/census/2011-census/2011-census-project/commitment-to-confidentiality/privacy-impact-assessment--pia--on-2011-census.pdf

Office of Management and Budget, *Making Sense of Regulation: 2001 Report to Congress on the Costs and Benefits of Regulations and Unfunded Mandates on State, Local and Tribe Entities*, OMB, Washington, DC, 2001.

Office of Management and Budget, Fiscal Year 2009 Report to Congress on Implementation of The Federal Information Security Management Act of 2002. http://www.whitehouse.gov/sites/default/files/omb/assets/egov_docs/FY09_FISMA.pdf

Office of Management and Budget, *OMB Guidance for Implementing the Privacy Provisions of the E-Government Act of 2002*, 26 September 2003. http://www.whitehouse.gov/omb/memoranda/m03-22.html

Office of the Australian Privacy Commissioner, "The Use of Data Matching in Commonwealth Administration – Guidelines", 1992, revised February 1998. http://www.privacy.gov.au/publications/dmcomadmin.pdf

Office of the Australian Privacy Commissioner (OAPC), Privacy and Public Key Infrastructure: Guidelines for Agencies using PKI to Communicate or Transact with Individuals, December 2001. http://www.privacy.gov.au/materials/types/download/8809/6609

Office of the Australian Privacy Commissioner, Submission to the Joint Committee of Public Accounts and Audit (JCPAA) on Management and Integrity of Electronic Information in the Commonwealth, January 2003. http://www.privacy.gov.au/publications/jcpaasubs.doc

Office of the Australian Privacy Commissioner, *Privacy Impact Assessment Guide*, August 2006. http://www.privacy.gov.au/publications/PIA06.pdf

Office of the Australian Privacy Commissioner, "Privacy Impact Assessment Guide", August 2006. http://www.privacy.gov.au/publications/PIA06.pdf. Revised version, May 2010. http://www.privacy.gov.au/materials/types/download/9509/6590

Office of the Information and Privacy Commissioner for British Columbia, Privacy Impact Assessment Template, Victoria, BC, 2008. http://www.oipc.bc.ca/index.php?option=com_content&view=article&catid=16%3Aresources-for-public-bodies&id=80%3Apublic-sector-g-privacy-impact-assessment-pia&Itemid=76

Office of the Information and Privacy Commissioner for British Columbia, *2009–2010 Annual Report*, July 2010.

Office of the Information and Privacy Commissioner (OIPC) of Alberta, PIAs, Registry. http://www.oipc.ab.ca/pages/PIAs/Registry.aspx. Recent PIA summaries are on the *What's New* page. http://www.oipc.ab.ca/pages/PIAs/WhatsNew.aspx

Office of the Information and Privacy Commissioner (OIPC) of Alberta, "Commissioner Accepts Privacy Impact Assessment for the Alberta Security Screening Directive", Press release, 16 January 2003. http://www.oipc.ab.ca/pages/NewsReleases/default.aspx?id=519

Office of the Information and Privacy Commissioner (OIPC) of Alberta, Investigation Report F2003-IR-005, Edmonton Police Service, 6 August 2003. http://www.oipc.ab.ca/downloads/documentloader.ashx?id=2081

Office of the Information and Privacy Commissioner (OIPC) of Alberta, *Privacy Impact Assessment Requirements for Use with the Health Information Act*. http://www.oipc.ab.ca/Content_Files/Files/PIAs/PIA_Requirements_2010.pdf

Office of the Information and Privacy Commissioner (OIPC) of Ontario and the United States Department of Justice, Office of Justice Programs, *Privacy Impact Assessment for Justice Information Systems*, August 2000. http://www.ipc.on.ca/English/Resources/Discussion-Papers/Discussion-Papers-Summary/?id=326

Office of the Privacy Commissioner, *Privacy Impact Assessment Guide*, Sydney, NSW, August 2006, revised May 2010. http://www.privacy.gov.au.

Office of the Privacy Commissioner of Canada (OPC), "A Citizen Profile in All But Name—HRDC's Longitudinal Labour Force File", in *Annual Report to Parliament,* Cat. No. IP 30-1/2000, Minister of Public Works and Government Services Canada, Ottawa, 2000.

Office of the Privacy Commissioner of Canada (OPC), Fact Sheet on Privacy Impact Assessment. http://www.priv.gc.ca/fs-fi/02_05_d_33_e.cfm

Office of the Privacy Commissioner of Canada (OPC), *Assessing the Privacy Impacts of Programs, Plans, and Policies*, Audit Report, Ottawa, 2007. www.privcom.gc.ca

Office of the Privacy Commissioner of Canada (OPC), Annual Report to Parliament 2008–2009, Report on the Privacy Act. http://www.priv.gc.ca/information/ar/200809/200809_pa_e.cfm

Office of the Privacy Commissioner of Canada (OPC), Letter in response to the Privacy Impact Assessment (PIA) completed by the Canadian Air Transport Security Authority (CATSA) in anticipation of the deployment of millimetre wave (MMW) screening technology at selected Canadian airport, October 2009. http://www.priv.gc.ca/pia-efvp/let_20100108_e.cfm

Office of the Privacy Commissioner of Canada (OPC), Audit of the Passenger Protect Program, Transport Canada, November 2009. http://www.priv.gc.ca/information/pub/ar-vr/ar-vr_ppp_200910_e.cfm

Office of the Privacy Commissioner of Canada (OPC), "Message from the Privacy Commissioner of Canada" [regarding 2008-9] Contribution of Priorities to the Strategic Outcome. http://www.tbs-sct.gc.ca/dpr-rmr/2008-2009/inst/nd6/nd601-eng.asp

Office of the Privacy Commissioner of Canada (OPC), *Investigation finds that RCMP handled polling appropriately*, Report of Findings, Complaint under the Privacy Act. http://www.priv.gc.ca/cf-dc/pa/2009-10/pa_20091216_e.cfm

Office of the Victorian Privacy Commissioner (OVPC), "Privacy Impact Assessments – A Guide", August 2004.

Office of the Victorian Privacy Commissioner (OVPC), "Submission to the Commonwealth Senate Legal and Constitutional Committee on its Inquiry into the Privacy Act 1988 (Cth)", March 2005. http://www.privacy.vic.gov.au/dir100/priweb.nsf/download/ED6E90678C836311CA2570110019833A/$FILE/Sen%20Leg%20Con%20Ctte%20sub.pdf

Office of the Victorian Privacy Commissioner (OVPC), *Privacy Impact Assessments – A guide for the Victorian Public Sector*, Edition 2, Melbourne, April 2009. http://www.privacy.vic.gov.au/privacy/web2.nsf/pages/publication-types?opendocument&Subcategory=Guidelines&s=2

Office of the Victorian Privacy Commissioner (OVPC), Accompanying Guide – A guide to completing Parts 3 to 5 of your Privacy Impact Assessment Report, Melbourne, April 2009. http://www.privacy.vic.gov.au/privacy/web2.nsf/pages/publication-types?opendocument&Subcategory=Guidelines&s=2

Office of the Victorian Privacy Commissioner (OVPC), Privacy Impact Assessment Report template, Melbourne, April 2009. http://www.privacy.vic.gov.au/privacy/web2.nsf/files/privacy-impact-assessment-report-template

Ontario Information and Privacy Commissioner (OIPC), *Privacy Guidelines for RFID Information Systems*, June 2006.

Ontario Information and Privacy Commissioner (OIPC), *Privacy by Design*, Toronto, 2009. http://www.ipc.on.ca/images/Resources/privacybydesign.pdf

Oracle, "Oracle Welcomes New EU Policy on e-Inclusion". http://www.oracle.com/us/corporate/european-union/new-e-inclusion-policy-070508.html

Organisation for Economic Co-operation and Development (OECD), Guidelines Governing the Protection of Privacy and Transborder Flows of Personal Data, OECD, Paris, 23 Sept 1980. http://www.oecd.org/document/18/0,3343,en_2649_34255_1815186_1_1_1_1,00.html

Organisation for Economic Co-operation and Development (OECD), *Recommendation on Improving the Quality of Government Regulation*, OECD, Paris, 1995.

Organisation for Economic Co-operation and Development (OECD), *The OECD Report on Regulatory Reform: Synthesis*, OECD, Paris, 1997.

Organisation for Economic Co-operation and Development (OECD), "Regulatory Performance: Ex Post Evaluation of Regulatory Tools and Institutions", Working Party on Regulatory Management and Reform, Draft Report by the Secretariat, OECD, Paris, 2004.

Organisation for Economic Co-operation and Development (OECD), *RFID Guidance and Reports*, OECD Digital Economy Papers, No. 150, OECD Publishing, Paris, 2008.

Organisation for Economic Co-operation and Development (OECD), *Risk and Regulatory Policy: Improving the Governance of Risk*, OECD Directorate for Public Governance and Territorial Development, Paris, April 2010.

Orlikowski, Wanda J., and C. Suzanne Iacono, "Research Commentary: Desperately Seeking the "IT" in IT Research—A Call to Theorizing the IT Artifact", *Information Systems Research*, Vol. 12, No.2, June 2001, pp. 121–134.

Oxford Internet Institute, "Me, My Spouse and the Internet: Meeting, Dating and Marriage in the Digital Age", January 2008. http://www.oii.ox.ac.uk/research/projects/?id=47.

Palm, Elin, and Sven Ove Hansson, "The Case for Ethical Technology Assessment (eTA)", *Technological Forecasting & Social Change*, Vol. 73, 2006, pp. 543–558.

Payment Card Industry Security Standards Council, Payment Card Industry Data Security Standard. https://www.pcisecuritystandards.org/security_standards/pci_dss_download.html

Pearson, S., "Trusted Computing: Strengths, Weaknesses and Further Opportunities for Enhancing Privacy, Trust Management", in Peter Herrmann, Valérie Issarny and Simon Shiu (eds.), *iTrust 2005, Proceedings*, Lecture Notes in Computer Science, 3477/2005, Springer, Dordrecht, 2005, pp. 305–320.

Pearson, S., and A. Charlesworth, "Accountability as a Way Forward for Privacy Protection in the Cloud", in M.G. Jaatun, G. Zhao and C. Rong (eds.), *CloudCom 2009: Proceedings*, Lecture Notes in Computer Science, 5931/2009, Springer, Dordrecht, 2009, pp. 131–144.

Peev, Gerri, "Labour in Retreat as ID Card Plan is Axed", *The Scotsman*, 1 July 2009. http://thescotsman.scotsman.com/uk/Labour-in-retreat-as-.5415982.jp

Pfeffer, Jeffrey, and Gerald Salancik, *The External Control of Organizations: A Resource Dependence Perspective*, Harper and Row, London, 1978.

Phillips, David, and Michael Curry, "Privacy and the Phenetic Urge: Geodemographics and the Changing Spatiality of Local Practice", in David Lyon (ed.), *Surveillance as Social Sorting: Privacy, Risk, and Digital Discrimination,* Routledge, London, 2003.

Privacy and Data Protection Impact Assessment Framework for RFID Applications, 12 January 2011. http://cordis.europa.eu/fp7/ict/enet/policy_en.html

Privacy Commissioner of Canada, *Assessing the Privacy Impacts of Programs, Plans, and Policies*, Audit Report, October 2007. http://www.priv.gc.ca/information/pub/ar-vr/pia_200710_e.cfm

Privacy NSW, "Submission on the Review of the Privacy and Personal Information Protection Act 1998", 24 June 2004. http://www.lawlink.nsw.gov.au/lawlink/privacynsw/ll_pnsw.nsf/vwFiles/sub_ppipareview.pdf/$file/sub_ppipareview.pdf#target=%27_blank%27

Privacy NSW, "Submission in response to the Review of Privacy Issues Paper of the Australian Law Reform Commission" Privacy NSW, February 2007. http://www.lawlink.nsw.gov.au/lawlink/privacynsw/ll_pnsw.nsf/vwFiles/sub_alrc2007.pdf/$file/sub_alrc2007.pdf

Province of BC, "Privacy Impact Assessments: Mitigating Risks – Maximizing Benefits", Presentation for Private Sector Privacy in a Changing World, PIPA Conference 2007, Vancouver, 20–21 September 2006. http://www.verney.ca/pipa2007/presentations/420.pdf

Queensland Government Chief Information Officer (QGCIO), "Information Standard No 42 – Information Privacy", 2001. http://www.qgcio.qld.gov.au/SiteCollectionDocuments/Architecture%20and%20Standards/Information%20Standards/Current/is42.pdf

Queensland Government Chief Information Officer, "Information Standard No 42A – Information Privacy for the Queensland Department of Health", 2001. http://www.qgcio.qld.gov.au/

SiteCollectionDocuments/Architecture%20and%20Standards/Information%20Standards/
Current/is42a.pdf

Queensland Government Chief Information Office, "Queensland Government Information Security Classification Framework", Version 1.0.1, April 2008. http://www.qgcio.qld.gov.au/SiteCollectionDocuments/Architecture%20and%20Standards/QGISCF%20v1.0.1.doc

Queensland Transport and Main Roads, "New Queensland Driver Licence – Privacy Impact Assessment", 30 September 2010. http://www.tmr.qld.gov.au/~/media/7496f017-55bb-4853-8c7b-da9150800707/new_qld_licence_privacy_impact_assess.pdf

Raab, Charles, "Privacy, Social Values, and the Public Interest", *Politische Vierteljahresschrift*, Special Issue 46 (2011) on "Politik und die Regulierung von Information".

Raab, Charles, Kirstie Ball, Steve Graham, David Lyon, David Murakami Wood and Clive Norris, *The Surveillance Society – An Update Report on Developments Since the 2006 Report on the Surveillance Society*, Information Commissioner's Office, Wilmslow, Cheshire, November 2010. http://www.ico.gov.uk/news/current_topics.aspx

Radaelli, Claudio M., "Diffusion Without Convergence: How Political Context Shapes the Adoption of Regulatory Impact Assessment", *Journal of European Public Policy*, Vol. 12, No. 5, 2005, pp. 924–943.

Rallo Lombarte, Artemi, "El derecho al olvido y su protección", Fundación Telefónica, Revista TELOS, No. 85, October–December 2010, pp. 104–108.

Råman, Jari, "European Court of Human Rights: Failure to Take Effective Information Security Measures to Protect Sensitive Personal Data Violates Right to Privacy – *I* v. *Finland*, no. 20511/03, 17 July 2008", *Computer Law & Security Report*, Vol. 24, No. 6, 2008, pp. 562–564.

Randerson, James, "Eye in the Sky: Police Use Drone to Spy on V Festival", *The Guardian*, 21 August 2007. http://www.guardian.co.uk/uk_news/story/0,,2152983,00.html

Reding, Viviane, Vice-President of the European Commission responsible for Justice, Fundamental Rights and Citizenship, "Towards a True Single Market of Data Protection", SPEECH/10/386, Meeting of the Article 29 Working Party re "Review of the Data Protection Legal Framework", Brussels, 14 July 2010. http://europa.eu/rapid/pressReleasesAction.do?reference=SPEECH/10/386

Regan, Priscilla M., *Legislating Privacy: Technology, Social Values, and Public Policy*, University of North Carolina Press, Chapel Hill, NC, 1995.

Regulatory Policy Committee, *Reviewing Regulation: An Independent Report on the Analysis Supporting Regulatory Proposals, December 2009 – May 2010*, RPC, London, July 2010. http://regulatorypolicycommittee.independent.gov.uk/rpc/wp-content/uploads/2010/08/RPC-Report-Final-Version-August-2010.pdf

Reidenberg, Joel R., "Lex Informatica: The Formulation of Information Policy Rules through Technology", *Texas Law Review*, Vol. 76, No. 3, February 1998, pp. 553–584.

Renda, Andrea, *Impact Assessment in the EU: The State of the Art and the Art of the State*, CEPS, Brussels, 1 January 2006.

Renn, Ortwin, *Risk Governance*, Earthscan, London, 2008.

Richards, Jonathan, "Top officials to be held to account for data losses", *The Times*, 22 April 2008. http://technology.timesonline.co.uk/tol/news/tech_and_web/article3797278.ece

Robinson, N., H. Graux, M. Botterman and L. Valeri, *Review of the European Data Protection Directive*, Information Commissioner's Office, Wilmslow, 2009. http://www.ico.gov.uk/upload/documents/library/data_protection/detailed_specialist_guides/review_of_eu_dp_directive.pdf

Rössler, Beate, "Soziale Dimensionen des Privaten", *Politische Vierteljahresschrift*, Special Issue 46 (2011) on "Politik und die Regulierung von Information".

Royal Canadian Mounted Police (RCMP), Privacy Impact Assessment Executive Summaries. http://www.rcmp-grc.gc.ca/pia-efvp/index-eng.htm

Saarenpää, Ahti, "The Importance of Information Security in Safeguarding Human and Fundamental Rights", Stockholm, 18 November 2008.

Salinger & Co, "Privacy Impacts of the Anti-Money Laundering and Counter-Terrorism Financing Bill and Rules, 2006, A Privacy Impact Assessment for the Australian Government Attorney-General's Department", 15 September 2006. http://www.ag.gov.au/www/agd/rwpattach.nsf/VAP/(CFD7369FCAE9B8F32F341DBE097801FF)~88Privacy+impact+assessment+aml-06.pdf/$file/88Privacy+impact+assessment+aml-06.pdf

Sample, Ian, "Security Firms Working on Devices to Spot Would-be Terrorists in Crowd", *The Guardian*, 9 August 2007. http://www.guardian.co.uk/science/2007/aug/09/terrorism

Sample, Ian, "Government Abandons Lie Detector Tests for Catching Benefit Cheats", *The Guardian*, 9 November 2010. http://www.guardian.co.uk/science/2010/nov/09/lie-detector-tests-benefit-cheats

Sax, Joseph L., "The (Unhappy) Truth About NEPA", *Oklahoma Law Review*, Vol. 26, May 1973, pp. 239–278.

Schaar, Peter, "Privacy by Design", *Identity in the Information Society*, Vol. 3, No. 2, April 2010, pp. 267–274.

Scheinin, Martin, Presentation at the INEX Roundtable on Body Scanners, Brussels, 27 January 2011. http://www.ceps.eu/event/roundtable-body-scanners

Schmid, Viola, "Radio Frequency Identification Law Beyond 2007", in Christian Floerkemeier, Marc Langheinrich, Elgar Fleisch, Friedemann Mattern and Sanjay E. Sarma (eds.), *The Internet of Things*, Proceedings of IOT 2008, LNCS 4952, Springer-Verlag, Berlin, 2008.

Schoeman, Ferdinand D. (ed.), *Philosophical Dimensions of Privacy: An Anthology*, Cambridge University Press, Cambridge, UK, 1984.

Schwartz, Paul, "Data Processing and Government Administration: The Failure of the American Legal Response to the Computer", *Hastings Law Journal*, Vol. 43, 1992, pp. 1321–1399.

ScienceDaily, "Intelligent Surveillance System to Detect Aberrant Behavior by Drivers and Pedestrians", 21 September 2009. http://www.sciencedaily.com/releases/2009/09/090918100010.htm

Scott, W. Richard, *Organizations: Rational, Natural and Open Systems*, fourth edition, Prentice Hall, Englewood Cliffs, NJ, 1998.

Senate Committee on Homeland Security and Governmental Affairs, "Government Privacy Protections Fall Short, Lieberman Calls for Leadership, Greater Commitment of Resources", Press release, Washington, DC, 30 July 2003. http://hsgac.senate.gov/public/index.cfm?FuseAction=Press.MajorityNews&ContentRecord_id=96af45f1-8460-4a3b-aea0-7ef37c689403&Region_id=&Issue_id

Senate Committee on Homeland Security and Governmental Affairs, "DHS Violates Privacy Impact Requirements with US Visit Technology", Press release, Washington, DC, 4 December 2003. http://hsgac.senate.gov/public/index.cfm?FuseAction=Press.MajorityNews&ContentRecord_id=8103bcce-8436-4e87-82f4-fe04642e6db2&Region_id=&Issue_id=

Senate Community Affairs Legislation Committee, "Healthcare Identifiers Bill 2010 and Healthcare Identifiers (Consequential Amendments) Bill 2010", Report, March 2010. http://www.aph.gov.au/senate/committee/clac_ctte/healthcare_identifier/report/index.htm

Senate Finance and Public Administration Committee (SFPAC), "Human Services (Enhanced Service Delivery) Bill 2007 [Provisions]", March 2007. http://www.aph.gov.au/senate/committee/fapa_ctte/access_card/report/index.htm

Senate Finance and Public Administration Committee, "Australian Privacy Principles – Exposure Draft", June 2010. http://www.aph.gov.au/Senate/committee/fapa_ctte/priv_exp_drafts/guide/exposure_draft.pdf

Senate Standing Committee on Legal and Constitutional Affairs, "Provisions of the Anti-Money Laundering and Counter-Terrorism Financing Bill 2006, and the Anti-Money Laundering and Counter-Terrorism Financing (Transitional Provisions and Consequential Amendments) Bill 2006", Report, November 2006, Chapter 4. http://www.aph.gov.au/senate/committee/legcon_ctte/completed_inquiries/2004-07/aml_ctf06/report/index.htm

Service Alberta, *FOIP Guidelines and Practices (2009)*, section 9.3 Privacy Impact Assessments. http://www.servicealberta.gov.ab.ca/foip/documents/chapter9.pdf

Simitis, Spiros, "Reviewing Privacy in an Information Society", *University of Pennsylvania Law Review*, Vol. 135, No. 3, 1987, pp. 707–746.

Sollie, Paul, "Ethics, Technology Development and Uncertainty: An Outline for Any Future Ethics of Technology", *Journal of Information, Communications & Ethics in Society*, Vol. 5, No. 4, 2007, pp. 293–306.

Sollie, Paul, and Marcus Düwell, *Evaluating New Technologies: Methodological Problems for the Ethical Assessment of Technology Developments*, Springer, Dordrecht, 2009.

Solove, Daniel J., "A Taxonomy of Privacy", *University of Pennsylvania Law Review*, Vol. 154, No. 3, January 2006, pp. 477–560.

Solove, Daniel, *Understanding Privacy*, Harvard University Press, Cambridge, MA, 2008.

South Australian Department of Health (SADOH), Code of Fair Information Practice, July 2004. http://www.health.sa.gov.au/Portals/0/Health-Code-July04.pdf

South Australian Department of Premier and Cabinet, Cabinet Administrative Instruction No. 1 of 1989: PC012 – Information Privacy Principles Instruction, 1989. http://www.premcab.sa.gov.au/pdf/circulars/Privacy.pdf

Special Committee to Review the Freedom of Information and Protection of Privacy Act, Legislative Assembly of BC, Report, May 2010. http://www.leg.bc.ca/cmt/39thparl/session-2/foi/reports/PDF/Rpt-FOI-39-2-Rpt-2010-MAY-31.pdf

Spiekermann, Sarah, *User Control in Ubiquitous Computing: Design Alternatives and User Acceptance*, Shaker Verlag, Aachen, 2008.

Spiekermann, Sarah, *PIA II – A Proposal for a Privacy Impact Assessment Framework for RFID Applications*, Vienna University of Economics and Business, 2011. http://cordis.europa.eu/fp7/ict/enet/policy_en.html. Published there under the title: German Industry Alternative Proposal on the RFID Privacy and Data Protection Impact Assessment Framework [21 October 2010].

Spiekermann, Sarah, and Lorrie Faith Cranor, "Engineering Privacy", *IEEE Transactions on Software Engineering*, Vol. 35, No. 1, January/February 2009, pp. 67–82.

State of New York Public Service Commission, *Privacy Policy Statement No. 1: A Privacy Impact Statement* in "Statement of Policy on Privacy in Telecommunications", 22 March 1991, reprinted in Longworth Associates, *Telecommunications and Privacy Issues: Report for the Ministry of Commerce*, Wellington, 1992.

Steering Committee for Human Rights (Cddh), Committee of Experts for the Development of Human Rights (DH-DEV), Working Group on the Environment (GT-DEV-ENV), *Decision-making Process in Environmental Matters and Public Participation in Them*, Draft nr. GT-DEV-ENV(2011)_Draft_11_PII-SecA-ChV, Strasbourg, 21 December 2010. http://www.coe.int/t/e/human_rights/cddh/3._committees/07.%20other%20committees%20and%20working%20groups/08.gt-dev-env/working%20docs/GT-DEV-ENV_2011__Draft_11_PII-SecA-ChV.pdf

Stern, Paul C., and Harvey V. Fineberg (eds.), *Understanding Risk: Informing Decisions in a Democratic Society*, Committee on Risk Characterization, National Research Council, National Academy Press, Washington, DC, 1996.

Stewart, Blair, "Privacy impact assessments", *Privacy Law and Policy Reporter*, Vol. 3, No. 4, July 1996. http://www.austlii.edu.au/au/journals/PLPR/1996/39.html

Stewart, Blair, "PIAs – an early warning system", *Privacy Law and Policy Reporter*, Vol. 3, No. 7, October/November 1996. http://www.austlii.edu.au/au/journals/PLPR/1996/65.html

Stewart, Blair, "Privacy Impact Assessment Towards a Better Informed Process for Evaluating Privacy Issues Arising from New Technologies", *Privacy Law and Policy Reporter*, Vol. 5, No. 8, February 1999. http://www.austlii.edu.au/au/journals/PLPR/1999/8.html

Stewart, Blair, "Privacy Impact Assessment: Some Approaches, Issues and Examples", 2002. http://jeb.cerps.org.tw/files/JEB2002-009.pdf

Stewart, Blair, "Privacy Impact Assessment Roundup", *Privacy Law & Policy Reporter*, Vol. 9, No. 5, September 2002. http://www.austlii.edu.au/au/journals/PLPR/2002/index.html

Stewart, Blair, *Privacy Impact Assessment Handbook*, Office of the Privacy Commissioner, Auckland, March 2002, revised June 2007.

Stoneburner, Gary, Alice Goguen and Alexis Feringa, National Institute for Standards and Technology (NIST), Risk Management Guide for Information Technology Systems, Recommendations of the National Institute of Standards and Technology, NIST Special Publication 800-30, July 2002.

Swire, Peter, "The Administration Response to the Challenges of Protecting Privacy", Draft, 8 January 2000. www.peterswire.net/stanford7.doc

Tancock, David, Siani Pearson and Andrew Charlesworth, *The Emergence of Privacy Impact Assessments*, HP Labs Technical Report (HPL-2010-63), 2010. http://www.hpl.hp.com/techreports/2010/HPL-2010-63.html

Tancock, David, Siani Pearson and Andrew Charlesworth, "A Privacy Impact Assessment Tool for Cloud Computing", in *Proceedings of the Second IEEE International Conference on Cloud Computing Technology and Science (CloudCom 2010)*, Indiana University, USA, 30 November–3 December 2010, pp. 667–676. http://ieeexplore.ieee.org/xpl/freeabs_all.jsp?arnumber=5708516

Taylor, Serge, *Making Bureaucracies Think: The Environmental Impact Statement Strategy of Administrative Reform*, Stanford University Press, Stanford, CA, 1984.

Tetlock, Philip E., "Accountability: The Neglected Social Context of Judgment and Choice", in Barry M. Staw and L.L. Cummings (eds.), *Research in Organizational Behavior*, Vol. 7, 1985, pp. 297–332.

The Economist, "Surveillance Technology: If Looks Could Kill", 23 October 2008. http://www.economist.com/science/displaystory.cfm?story_id=12465303

The Inquirer, "Head Taxman Quits After 25 Million Peoples' Data Lost", 20 November 2007. http://www.theinquirer.net/gb/inquirer/news/2007/11/20/head-taxman-quits-million.

The New York Times, "GPS and Privacy Rights", Editorial, 14 May 2009. http://www.nytimes.com/2009/05/15/opinion/15fri3.html

The Washington Post, "Gallery: Anti-deception technologies", 18 July 2010. http://projects.washingtonpost.com/top-secret-america/articles/a-hidden-world-growing-beyond-control/

Thomas, Richard, and Mark Walport, *Data Sharing Review Report*, 11 July 2008. www.justice.gov.uk/docs/data-sharing-review-report.pdf

Treasury Board of Canada Secretariat, "A Guide to Preparing Treasury Board Submissions", Ottawa [n.d.]. http://www.tbs-sct.gc.ca/pubs_pol/opepubs/TBM_162/gptbs-gppct09-eng.asp#d4.

Treasury Board of Canada Secretariat, Archived – Privacy Impact Assessment Policy, 2 May 2002. http://www.tbs-sct.gc.ca/pol/doc-eng.aspx?id=12450&section=text

Treasury Board of Canada Secretariat, Privacy Impact Assessment Guidelines: A Framework to Manage Privacy Risks, Ottawa, 31 August 2002. http://www.tbs-sct.gc.ca/pubs_pol/ciopubs/pia-pefr/paipg-pefrld1-eng.asp

Treasury Board of Canada Secretariat, Communications Policy of the Government of Canada, Policy Statement, November 2004. http://www.tbs-sct.gc.ca/pol/doc-eng.aspx?id=12316&section=text#sec5.10

Treasury Board Secretariat of Canada, Privacy Impact Assessment Audit Guide, as archived. ttp://www.collectionscanada.gc.ca/webarchives/20071211001631/www.tbs-sct.gc.ca/ia-vi/policies-politiques/pia-efvp/pia-efvp_e.asp

Treasury Board of Canada Secretariat, A Guide to Preparing Treasury Board Submissions, Ottawa, December 2007. http://www.tbs-sct.gc.ca/pubs_pol/opepubs/tbm_162/gptbs-gppct-eng.asp

Treasury Board of Canada Secretariat, Policy on Privacy Protection, Ottawa, April 2008.

Treasury Board of Canada Secretariat, Directive on Privacy Impact Assessment, Ottawa, 1 April 2010. http://www.tbs-sct.gc.ca/pol/doc-eng.aspx?id=18308&section=text

Treasury Board of Canada Secretariat, Directive on Privacy Practices, Ottawa, April 2010. http://www.tbs-sct.gc.ca/pol/doc-eng.aspx?section=text&id=18309

Unabhängiges Landeszentrum für Datenschutz Schleswig-Holstein, EuroPrise Criteria, Version 1.0, Kiel, Germany, 2009.

UK Border Agency (UKBA), *Report of a Privacy Impact Assessment Conducted by the UK Border Agency in Relation to the High Value Data Sharing Protocol Amongst the Immigration Authorities of the Five Country Conference*, London, 2009.

UK Cabinet Office, *Better Policy Making: A Guide to Regulatory Impact Assessment*, Regulatory Impact Unit, London, 2003.

UK Cabinet Office, Data Handling Procedures in Government: Final Report, London, June 2008. http://www.cabinetoffice.gov.uk/reports/data_handling.aspx

UPI, "Chertoff: RFID program to be abandoned", 9 February 2007.

US Department of Health, Education and Welfare, Secretary's Advisory Committee on Automated Personal Data Systems, *Records, Computers and the Rights of Citizens*, July 1973. http://epic.org/privacy/hew1973report

US Department of Homeland Security, US-VISIT Program, Increment 1, Privacy Impact Assessment, Washington, DC, 18 December 2003. http://www.dhs.gov/xlibrary/assets/privacy/privacy_pia_usvisit_inc1.pdf

US Department of Homeland Security, Transportation Security Administration (TSA), Airport Access Control Pilot Project Privacy Impact Assessment, 18 June 2004. http://www.dhs.gov/xlibrary/assets/privacy/privacy_pia_aacpp.pdf

US Department of Homeland Security, Privacy Act of 1974; Systems of Records, 1 July 2005. http://www.dhs.gov/xlibrary/assets/privacy/privacy_sorn_usvisit_aidms.pdf

US Department of Homeland Security, "Department of Homeland Security Announces Appointments to Data Privacy and Integrity Advisory Committee", Press release, 23 February 2005. http://www.dhs.gov/xnews/releases/press_release_0625.shtm

US Department of Homeland Security, Privacy Impact Assessment for the Naturalization Redesign Test Pilot, 17 January 2007. http://www.dhs.gov/xlibrary/assets/privacy/privacy_pia_uscis_nrtp.pdf

US Department of Homeland Security, *Privacy Impact Assessments: The Privacy Office Official Guidance*, Washington, DC, June 2010. http://www.dhs.gov/files/publications/gc_1209396374339.shtm

US Government Printing Office, Protection of Privacy in the DHS Intelligence Enterprise, Hearings before the Subcommittee on Intelligence, Information Sharing, and Terrorism Risk Assessment of the House Homeland Security Committee, 109th Cong, 2d Sess (2006), in CQ Congressional Testimony (statement of Maureen Cooney, Acting Chief Privacy Officer, Department of Homeland Security).

van Drooghenbroeck, Sébastien, *La proportionalité dans de le droit de la convention européenne des droits de l'homme*, Bruylant, Brussels, 2001.

Van Gorp, Anke, "Ethics in and During Technological Research: An Addition to IT Ethics and Science Ethics", in Paul Sollie and Marcus Düwell (eds.), *Evaluating New Technologies*, Springer Science, Dordrecht, 2009.

van Lieshout, Marc, Luigi Grossi, Graziella Spinelli et al., *RFID Technologies: Emerging Issues, Challenges and Policy Options*, European Commission, Joint Research Centre, Institute for Prospective Technological Studies, Office for Official Publications of the European Communities, Luxembourg, 2007.

Vedder, Anton, *The Values of Freedom*, Aurelia Domus Artium, Utrecht, 1995.

Vedder, Anton, and Bart Custers, "Whose Responsibility Is It Anyway? Dealing with the Consequences of New Technologies", in Paul Sollie and Marcus Düwell (eds.), *Evaluating New Technologies*, Springer Science, Dordrecht, 2009.

Verbeek, Peter-Paul, "The Moral Relevance of Technological Artifacts", in Paul Sollie and Marcus Düwell (eds.), *Evaluating New Technologies*, Springer Science, Dordrecht, 2009.

Vibert, Frank, *The EU's New System of Regulatory Impact Assessment – A Scorecard*, European Policy Forum, London, 2004.

Victorian Department of Education and Early Childhood Development, "Privacy Impact Assessment Report: The Ultranet", Melbourne, 19 March 2010. http://www.eduweb.vic.gov.au/edulibrary/public/ultranet/ultranet-pia.pdf

von Schomberg, René, "From the Ethics of Technology Towards an Ethics of Knowledge Policy & Knowledge Assessment", Working document from the European Commission Services, January 2007.

Waldron, Jeremy, *Law and Disagreement*, Oxford University Press, Oxford, 1999.

Walsh, James P., "Managerial and Organizational Cognition: Notes from a Trip Down Memory Lane", *Organization Science*, Vol. 6, No. 3, May–June 1995, pp. 280–321.

Warren, Adam, Robin Bayley, Colin Bennett, Andrew Charlesworth, Roger Clarke and Charles Oppenheim, "Privacy Impact Assessments: International Experience as a Basis for UK Guidance", *Computer Law & Security Report,* Vol. 24, No. 3, 2008, pp. 233–242.

Warren, Samuel, and Louis D. Brandeis, "The Right to Privacy", *Harvard Law Review*, Vol. IV, No. 5, 15 December 1890.

Waters Nigel, "Privacy Impact Assessment – Traps for the Unwary", *Privacy Law & Policy Reporter*, Vol. 7, No. 9, February 2001. http://www.austlii.edu.au/au/journals/PLPR/2001/10.html

Waters, Nigel, "'Surveillance-Off': Beyond Privacy Impact Assessment – Design Principles to Minimize Privacy Intrusion", Paper for the 16th Annual Privacy Laws and Business International Conference: *Transforming Risk Assessment into Everyday Compliance with Data Protection Law*, St John's College, Cambridge, England, 7–9 July 2003.

Waters, Nigel, "Getting through Privacy Impact Assessments", 29th International Conference of Data Protection and Privacy Commissioners, *Privacy Impact Assessment Issues and Approaches for Regulators*, Workshop Workbook, Montreal, September 2007. http://www.privacyconference2007.gc.ca/workbooks/Terra_Incognita_workbook12_bil.pdf

Weiser, Marc, "The Computer for the 21st Century", *Scientific American*, Vol. 265, No. 3, September 1991, pp. 94–104.

Welsh, Brandon C., and David P. Farrington, *Crime Prevention Effects of Closed Circuit Television: A Systematic Review*, Home Office Research, Development and Statistics Directorate, August 2002.

Westin, Alan, *Privacy and Freedom*, Atheneum, New York, 1967.

Whitman, James Q., "The Two Western Cultures of Privacy: Dignity Versus Liberty", *The Yale Law Journal*, Vol. 113, 2004, pp. 1151–1221.

Wichelman, Allan F., "Administrative Agency Implementation of the National Environmental Policy Act of 1969: A Conceptual Framework for Explaining Differential Response", *Natural Resources Journal*, Vol. 16, 1976, pp. 296–300.

Wiener, Norbert, *The Human Use of Human Beings: Cybernetics and Society*, Houghton Mifflin, New York, 1950.

Williams, Rachel, "CCTV Cameras to be Given 'Ears'", *The Guardian*, 24 June 2008. http://www.guardian.co.uk/uk/2008/jun/24/ukcrime1

Winner, Langdon, "Do Artifacts Have Politics?", in Donald MacKenzie and Judy Wajcman (eds.), *The Social Shaping of Technology*, second edition, Open University Press, Philadelphia, 1999.

Wray, Richard, "T-Mobile Confirms Biggest Phone Customer Data Breach", *The Guardian*, 17 November 2009. http://www.guardian.co.uk/uk/2009/nov/17/t-mobile-phone-data-privacy

Wright, David, "Should Privacy Impact Assessment Be Mandatory?", *Communications of the ACM*, Vol. 54, No. 8, August 2011, pp. 121–131.

Wright, David, "An Ethical Impact Assessment Framework for Information Technology", *Ethics and Information Technology*, Vol. 13, No. 3, 2011.

Wright, David, Kush Wadhwa, Paul De Hertand Dariusz Kloza (eds.), "A Privacy Impact Assessment Framework (PIAF) Deliverable D1", *A Report of the PIAF Consortium Prepared for the European Commission*, September 2011. www.piafproject.eu

Yost, Nicolas C., and James W. Rubin, "Administrative Implementation of and Judicial Review under the National Environmental Policy Act", in Sheldon M. Novick, Donald W. Stever and Margaret G. Mellon (eds.), *The Law of Environmental Protection*, West Publishing, St. Paul, MN, USA, 2007.

European Cases

BVerfG, 1 BvR 209/83 vom 15.12.1983.

BVerfG, 1 BvR 370/07 und 1 BvR 595/07 vom 30.4.2008, "OnlineDurchsuchung".

BVerfGE 65 E 40, "Volkszählung", Judgment of 15 December 1983.

Court of Justice of the European Union, *Huber* v. *Germany*, Judgment of 16 December 2008, Case C-524/06.

Court of Justice of the European Union, *National Farmers Union*, Judgment of 5 May 1998, Case no. C-157/96.

Court of Justice of the European Union ECJ, *Opinion of Advocate General Poiares Maduro in Case C-524/06 (Heinz Huber* v *Germany)*, delivered on 3 April 2008.

Court of Justice of the European Union, *United Kingdom* v. *Commission*, Judgment of 5 May 1998, Case no. C-180/96.

ECtHR, *A.D. and O.D.* v. *The United Kingdom*, Judgment of 2 April 2010, Application no. 28680/06.

ECtHR, *Airey* v. *Ireland*, Judgment of 9 October 1979, Series A-32, Application no. 6289/73.

ECtHR, *Amann* v. *Switzerland*, Judgment of 16 February 2000, Application no. 27798/95, *ECHR* 2000-II.

ECtHR, *Ashworth and others* v. *The United Kingdom*, Admissibility decision of 20 January 2004, Application no. 39561/98.

ECtHR, *Association for European Integration and Human Rights and Ekimdzhiev* v. *Bulgaria*, Judgment of 28 June 2007, Application no. 62540/00.

ECtHR, *Copland* v. *The United Kingdom*, Judgment of 3 April 2007, Application no. 62617/00.

ECtHR, *Craxi (no. 2)* v. *Italy*, Judgment of 17 July 2003, Application no. 25337/94.

ECtHR, *Dudgeon* v. *The United Kingdom*, Judgment of 22 October 1981, Series A-45, Application no. 7525/76.

ECtHR, *Fägerskiöld* v. *Sweden*, Admissibility Decision of 26 February 2008.

ECtHR, *Giacomelli* v. *Italy*, Judgment of 2 November 2006, Application no. 59909/00.

ECtHR, *Guerra* and others v. *Italy*, Judgment of 19 February 1998, Reports 1998-I, Application no. 14967/89.

ECtHR, *Handyside* v. *The United Kingdom*, Judgment of 7 December 1976, Series A-24, Application no. 5493/72.

ECtHR, *Hatton* v. *The United Kingdom*, Judgment of 2 October 2001, Application no. 36 022/97.

ECtHR, *I.* v. *Finland*, Judgment of 17 July 2008, *European Human Rights Cases (EHRC)*, Vol. 9, No. 9, 10 September 2008, pp. 1136–1140, Application no. 20511/03.

ECtHR, *Iordachi and others* v. *Moldova*, Judgment of 10 February 2009, Application no. 25198/02.

ECtHR, *Klass and others* v. *Germany*, Judgment of 6 September 1978, Series A-28, Application no. 5029/71.

ECtHR, *Kruslin* v. *France*, Judgment of 24 April 1990, Series A-176 A, Application no. 11801/85.

ECtHR, *Lambert* v. *France*, Judgment of 24 August 1998, *Reports*, 1998 V, Application no. 23618/94.

ECtHR, *Leander* v. *Sweden*, Judgment of 26 March 1987, Series A-116, Application no. 9248/81.

ECtHR, *Liberty and others* v. *The United Kingdom*, Judgment of 1 July 2008, Application no. 58243/00.

ECtHR, *Loizidou* v. *Turkey (prel. obj.)*, Judgment of 23 March 1995, Series A-310, Application no. 15318/89.

ECtHR, *Lopez Ostra* v. *Spain*, Judgment of 9 December 1994, Series A-303-C, Application no. 16798/90.

ECtHR, *Malone* v. *The United Kingdom*, 2 August 1984, Series A-82, Application no. 8691/79.

ECtHR, *Marckx* v. *Belgium*, Judgment of 13 June 1979, Series A-31, Application no. 6833/74.

ECtHR, *Messina* v. *Italy (no. 2)*, Judgment of 28 September 2000, ECHR 2000-X, Application no. 25498/94.

ECtHR, *Olsson* v. *Sweden*, Judgment of 24 March 1988, Series A-130, Application no. 10465/83.

ECtHR, *Oluić* v. *Croatia*, Judgment of 20 May 2010, Application no. 61260/08.

ECtHR, *P.G. and J.H.* v. *The United Kingdom,* Judgment of 25 September 2001, Application no. 44787/98.

ECtHR, *Peck* v. *The United Kingdom,* Judgment of 28 January 2003, Application no. 44647/98.

ECtHR, *Perry* v. *The United Kingdom*, Judgment of 17 July 2003, Application no. 63737/00, *ECHR* 2003-IX.

ECtHR, *Powell and Rayner* v. *The United Kingdom,* Judgment of 21 February 1990, Series A-172, Application no. 9310/81.

ECtHR, *Rotaru* v. *Romania*, Judgment of 4 May 2000, Application no. 28341/95, *ECHR* 2000-V.

ECtHR, *Ruano Morcuende* v. *Spain*, Admissibility Decision of 6 September 2005, Application no. 75287/01.

ECtHR, *S. and Marper* v. *The United Kingdom*, Judgment of 4 December 2008, Application nos. 30562/04 and 30566/04.

ECtHR, *Soering* v. *The United Kingdom*, Judgment of 7 July 1989, Series A-310, Application no. 14038/88.

ECtHR, *Stubbings and others* v. *The United Kingdom,* Judgment of 22 October 1996, *Reports*, 1996-IV, Application nos. 22083/93 and 22095/93.

ECtHR, *Surugiu* v. *Romania*, Judgment of 20 April 2004, Application no. 48995/99.

ECtHR, *Taskın and others* v. *Turkey,* Judgment of 10 November 2004, Application no. 46117/99.

ECtHR, *Tatar* v. *Romania*, Judgment of 27 January 2009, Application no. 67021/01.

ECtHR, *Tyrer* v. *The United Kingdom*, Judgment of 25 April 1978, Series A-26, Application no. 5856/72.

ECtHR, *Uzun* v. *Germany*, Judgment of 2 September 2010, Application no. 35623/05.

ECtHR, *von Hannover* v. *Germany,* Judgment of 24 June 2004, Application no. 59320/00.

ECtHR, *Weber and Saravia* v. *Germany*, Admissibility decision of 29 June 2006, Application no. 54934/00, *ECHR* 2006-XI.

ECtHR (Grand Chamber), *Hatton* v. *The United Kingdom*, Judgment of 8 July 2003, Application no. 36022/97.

ECtHR (Third Section), *Hatton* v. *The United Kingdom*, Judgment of 2 October 2001, Application no. 36022/97.

US Cases and Legislation

District Of Columbia District Court, *Electronic Privacy Information Center* v. *U.S. Transportation Security Administration*, Case No. 03-1846, 2006 WL 626925, 2006.

E-Government Act of 2002, Pub L No 107-347, 116 Stat 2899, 44 U.S.C. § 101, 2006. http://www.gpo.gov/fdsys/pkg/PLAW-107publ347/content-detail.html

E-Government Act of 2002, Pub L No 107-347, 116 Stat 2899, 44 U.S.C. § 3501 note (2000 & Supp 2002). http://www.gpo.gov/fdsys/pkg/PLAW-107publ347/content-detail.html

Great Falls Historic District Study Act of 2001, Pub L No 107-59, 115 Stat 407. http://www.gpo.gov/fdsys/pkg/PLAW-107publ59/content-detail.html

Homeland Security Act of 2002, Pub L No 107-296, 116 Stat 2135, 2007. http://www.gpo.gov/fdsys/pkg/PLAW-107publ296/content-detail.html

Homeland Security Act of 2002, Pub L No 107-296, 116 Stat 2135, 6 U.S.C. § 142, 2007.

Homeland Security Act of 2002, Pub L No 107-296, 116 Stat 2135, 6 U.S.C. § 142(a)(6), 2007.

Intelligence Reform and Terrorism Prevention Act of 2004, Pub L No 108-458 § 1061(c)(4), 118 Stat 3638, 3884 (2004), 5 U.S.C. § 601 note (2000 & Supp 2004). http://www.gpo.gov/fdsys/pkg/PLAW-108publ458/content-detail.html

Intelligence Reform and Terrorism Prevention Act of 2004, Pub L No 108-458, 118 Stat 3638, 3819. http://www.gpo.gov/fdsys/pkg/PLAW-108publ458/content-detail.html

National Environmental Policy Act of 1969, Pub L No 91-190, 83 Stat. 852, 42 U.S.C. §§ 4321-4347, 2000.

National Environmental Policy Act of 1969, Pub L No 91-190, 83 Stat. 852, 42 U.S.C. § 4332(2)(C), 2000.

Protection and enhancement of environmental quality, Executive Order No. 11514, 35 Fed. Reg. 4247, 1970. http://www.archives.gov/federal-register/codification/executive-order/11514.html

U.S. Department of Homeland Security, *Privacy Act of 1974; Systems of Records*, 70 Fed. Reg. 38699-38700, 2005. http://frwebgate2.access.gpo.gov/cgi-bin/PDFgate.cgi?WAISdocID=pU4etl/5/2/0&WAISaction=retrieve

U.S. Department of State, *Electronic Passport*, 70 Fed. Reg. 8305, 2005. http://frwebgate3.access.gpo.gov/cgi-bin/PDFgate.cgi?WAISdocID=o4OYOy/22/2/0&WAISaction=retrieve

U.S. Supreme Court, *Kleppe v Sierra Club*, Case No. 75-552, 427 U.S. 390, 1975. http://supreme.justia.com/us/427/390/

Index

Printed by Printforce, the Netherlands